FROM DEPTFORD TO ANTARCTICA

- THE LONG WAY HOME -

An autobiography by Pete Wilkinson

Published by Fledgling Press, 2014
Cover Design: Graeme Clarke
graeme@graemeclarke.co.uk

Printed and bound by:
MBM Print, Glasgow

ISBN: 9781905916764

Paper from responsible sources

MIX
Paper from
responsible sources
FSC
www.fsc.org   FSC® C117931

For

Gaye Wilkinson,
Emily May Wilkinson and
Amy Rose Wilkinson

My loves, my life and my light

Preamble

This book started life when I decided to transcribe the diaries I had kept during each of the Greenpeace Antarctic expeditions in which I was involved between the years of 1985 and 1992. After the death of my mother in 2004 I realised that I had little to hand on to my children, born in 1996 and 2000, to give them a sense of family, lineage, history or continuity. The previously transcribed diaries became the body of work around which the book was built: I decided it would be helpful to preface the diaries with an explanation of how I came to be in the Antarctic. That exercise in itself demanded a fuller explanation of events which occupied the UK branch of the organisation which had sent me to the ends of the earth and how I came to have been selected to lead the expeditions. The incongruity of a former south-London lorry driver leading Antarctic expeditions itself demanded a look even further back into my past: at my family, its working class roots and my own path through childhood, school, adolescence, the 60s and the world of revolutionary events in those momentous years which sowed the seeds from which grew the counter-culture that today is such a familiar and comfortable part of the political furniture.

Then I decided that, having begun at the very beginning, I should at least try to end the book as close as I could to the present. The book soon became a tome which recorded my life from Deptford roots to Antarctica and then back again to the post-Greenpeace world which I now inhabit, and in which I still try to keep alive the flame of environmental activism at which we were passably successful in the 80s. That tome has been edited many times into the book before you now. It was written for my children, but I trust a much wider audience will find in engaging and insightful. If it does nothing else, I hope it gives the reader a smile or two.

It is strange how the years pass like the flickering of a film at the back of your head and how things that were present and immediate recede through the intervention of time between the event and the new 'now'. After a few days, the memories remain vibrant, fresh and vivid; after a few months, they wane a little and eventually merge into the general bank of memories which form the past and which arrive, unbeckoned, or which have to be specially excavated. At least, that's how I imagine things to be, but I still have memories which keep me awake at night, which come to me in three-dimensional, stand-out, in-your-face reality, which sweep away mere trifles such as sleep and which cast me back 30 years. Often, I'm back, having agreed to go on 'one last' Antarctic trip and I wake after various nocturnal escapades involving the crazy, loveable people with whom I worked, full of anxiety, excitement and uncertainty about the 'trip' ahead: can I really go through another three months of ship-based freneticism, sea-sickness and ennui? Will my constitution be able to withstand the onslaught of emotional highs and lows which inevitably accompany such an enterprise which will take us to the other side of the world and then a further 2000 miles across the unpredictable Southern Ocean to what was known for centuries as Terra Incognita – the unknown land? These feelings are as real to me now as they were 30 years ago.

Well, I did those trips in 1985, 1986, 1987, 1988, 1989, 1990 and 1992 and I did them voluntarily while apparently sane. They formed a period of my life which stands out like a beacon of not only successful campaigning – we forced the Antarctic Treaty nations to agree to a mining ban for 50 years and a World Park status for an entire continent – but also of personal satisfaction in that I met and worked with people who remain lifelong friends, despite the fact that they are mostly dotted all over the world and we meet only on rare occasions. It was also, for a working class boy from Deptford, the pinnacle of a life into which I fell years previously, thanks to my old card-playing mentor, travel companion and all-round rock-solid friend John Morton, when I read the Environmental Handbook he casually tossed to me across the room.

The circumstances which led me to the steps of an aircraft on a cold October day in 1985, bound for New Zealand and the Antarctic, were extraordinary enough and as I sat on that plane on the Heathrow tarmac preparing for the next chapter in this roller-coaster ride to unfold, I looked back on a period which saw my rise and fall within an organisation to which I gave my heart and soul only to be sidelined as the new, post-Rainbow-Warrior-sinking organisation emerged from its awkward and ungainly carapace into the gaudy creature of notoriety, celebrity and wealth. Just as Blair's New Labour turned an honourable extension of working class hegemony into a parody of the Tories, so Greenpeace seems to have transformed itself into a troupe of theatrical activists, undertaking heroic demonstrations parading as direct actions which to me appear devoid of imagination and barren of vision and inspiration. This is my interpretation of the organisation as I see it today. It may be a jaundiced, even an erroneous view. But this impression is likely to be the same as that of the average member of the public, who does perhaps register the actions Greenpeace undertakes but has no real yardstick by which to gauge what their policies are, what they are attempting to achieve and, crucially, how successful or otherwise they are at their job. I am left with a sadness that such power and influence as Greenpeace once had pretentions to wield and which it aspired to over the last twenty years can have been frittered away, that the legacy handed on to those who came after the *Warrior* sinking could apparently be so casually thrown to the winds. My mum was a good touchstone of what ordinary people thought of things. Not long before she died, she asked me, 'That Green-whatever-it-was you started years ago with that American (she was referring to McTaggart who was in fact Canadian), has it packed up? You never hear of it any more do you?'

On a rare bus trip to the West End of London to participate in the London Schools Games, circa 1957. . .

We kids crammed against the window of the number 188 bus as it turned into the Strand. There! THERE!! It was true! Allcock and Nobles. There is a shop called Allcock and Nobles! If ever eleven year-olds needed something by which to recall their childhood in later years, it was a shop named after the unmentionables of a boy's undercarriage. Thanks you Messrs Allcock and Nobles for having the wit or the innocence to go into business together.

Introduction

Bulge babies – the generation of lucky gits

The political and social background to the decade which gave rise to the plethora of what might be termed modern pressure and splinter groups began, for most of those involved, in the post-war years of the 50s and 60s. To this day, I find it hard to believe that when I was born in 1946, Europe was still in ruins, Hitler had only been dead for little more than a year and the task of rebuilding Britain, let alone the rest of Europe and the far-flung reaches of the world, had not even begun. The radioactive fall-out from the Hiroshima and Nagasaki bombs was still circling the planet in the jet-stream.

But something else had begun even before minds were turned to regeneration: the arms race. The bomb which has been credited with forcing Japan to capitulate became the prize which transformed one-time allies, embracing each other across the battlefield, into post-war belligerents, hungry for the ability to annihilate each other and the rest of the world in the process.

'Babyboomers' as we're called – reflecting the boom there was in births within a year of the second world war ending and the troops coming home to welcoming wives – have lived, and do live, with war; from Suez to Iraq, from Afghanistan to Libya and we continue to pursue foreign policies which invite an Anglophobia, surely be the most burdensome legacy we leave our children's children. But 'boomers', while rightly envied for living lives in which most never donned a uniform or took up arms in anger, were nonetheless subjected to a form of psychological terror from the belief that WW3 was inevitable.

I can't recall a day between the ages of 12 and 25 that I did not spend at least some time thinking about, talking about or fretting about the prevailing political situation which we had inherited at the end of the war and which had festered over 15 years or so, to a point where we all lived with the possibility of being fried to death at any point of the day or night. Every news bulletin was heavy with threat, every international incident riven with anxiety. This culminated in the Cuban missile crisis of 1962 when the world held its collective breath as Soviet ships laden with missiles headed for Cuba and what seemed to be an unavoidable and cataclysmic confrontation with the USA which would surely trigger Armageddon.

As the radioactive fallout from the two nuclear bombs dropped on Japan in 1945 was still settling over that fated country, project scientist Kenneth Tomkins Bainbridge's words to Robert Oppenheimer, often referred to as the 'father of the bomb', on seeing the El Alamo test a few months before were already prophetic. As he watched the mushroom cloud billow a mile into the sky over the test site in the Nevada desert minutes after the flash of nuclear fusion that was 'brighter than a thousand suns', he reportedly said, 'Now we're all sonsofbitches'. We had opened Pandora's nuclear box and within five years of the bomb dropping, 40% of the Hiroshima population, around 350,000 at the time of the blast – mostly women and children – were dead: either incinerated on the spot to a point where only a dark smudge on the pavement recorded their existence, buried under rubble of the buildings literally blown down in the nuclear blast, asphyxiated by the absence of air the blast created or dying more slowly – some within minutes, some within weeks, months of even years – from the radiation exposure from the bomb.

Not content with these horrific results and eager to 'test' the impact of a plutonium bomb, especially in an area where the effects of reflected blast could be assessed, the American authorities dropped a second nuclear bomb on Nagasaki, nestling in the bowl of a group of hills, with equally devastating effects. Twenty-five percent of the 270,000 people in Nagasaki on that fateful morning were dead within a year. Articles I have read suggest that the Japanese were suing for peace from as early as 1943, two years before the bombs were dropped, yet the justification for dropping these bombs in order to 'hasten the end of the war' and saving the lives of thousands of US and allied troops, remains.

In the decade that followed, the UK, the former Union of Soviet Socialist Republics (USSR) and China all developed the nuclear bomb. In order to test these weapons, the UK, with limited and crowded land space, relied, until the 1991 ban on the US test ranges in the Nevada Desert, having previously detonated more than twenty devices in the atmosphere over Australian territory and Pacific islands, sometimes removing voiceless and helpless indigenous peoples in advance of the tests which have left an uncertain radiological legacy in these areas. The Soviets tested at Novaya Zemlya and soon China joined the nuclear club. It is estimated that something approaching 2,000 nuclear weapons tests have been conducted globally since 1945. Key to the nuclear arms race which dominated and menaced life in the 60s and 70s was a plant with which I was to become intimately familiar in later years – Windscale – which produced the plutonium required for the nuclear weapons, either directly from the original Windscale 'piles' or, subsequently, from the chemical treatment of the waste nuclear fuel from the first generation of nuclear plants the UK built called 'Magnox', a name taken from the fuel which was clad in magnesium oxide.

The nuclear age was with us in all its force and within 20 years of the Hiroshima and Nagasaki bombs, France, India, Pakistan and others, with varying degrees of success, used the 'peaceful development of nuclear technology' umbrella to hide the unseemly race towards nuclear arms. Over 500 nuclear tests were conducted in the atmosphere: we still register the radioactive fallout they created to this day.

This was the political and environmental backdrop which characterised my life and the lives of my contemporaries. As a teenager in the early 60s, the world was an infinitely dangerous and nightmarish place of unworldly contradictions. On the one hand, London was the 'swinging capital city' where all the barriers and stiff attitudes of the 40s and 50s were being dismantled in a sea of liberalism and hedonism. Music was revolutionary, style and fashion outlandish, cultural shackles were enthusiastically thrown aside. At the same time we were four minutes away from violent immolation, a contradiction which was utterly and implausibly bizarre. Perhaps the latter drove the former – perhaps we were so close to the edge that we really did believe, subconsciously or not – that anything went.

This book, then, is an attempt to recall events in my early childhood which capture the mood of the 50s, through adolescence and into the 'never had it so good' times and the 'free love', music and pill-popping days of the Wilson Labour government; my working life and how it was in the 60s and how I 'found' the embryonic environmental movement and began to learn the language of 'ecology'

(US early billboard – 'Ecology? Look it up. You're in it.')

My journey is one that took a working class boy from Deptford, through a series of chance meetings, helping hands and circumstances often beyond his control, to a life of derring-do as one of the first practitioners of peaceful direct action in defence of the natural world, culminating in seven unforgettable voyages to the Antarctic. As if that was not enough, I then found my true love in Gaye Jerrom and started a family, being blessed with two wonderful daughters, Emily May and Amy Rose, at an age when I really thought such joy from a family had passed me by, and I went on to rediscover my campaigning flair and verve as the nuclear industry once again threatened to re-establish itself. And throughout, my desire to bring together commercial viability and environmental sustainability, an aspiration seared into my head through the sheer delight, romanticism and peace I found from being at sea, never left me. Attempts to realise that desire led me into all sorts of adventures. I am still living that life as I attempt to complete my life's journey which has taken me from Deptford to Antarctica, the long, sometimes lonely but never dull, way home.

Chapter 1

Deptford – playground of the poor

The name Deptford is a corruption of 'Deep ford'. At one time, the river Ravensbourne could be forded at the point where the settlement which later became Deptford stands today. Deptford is steeped in history. It was here that Henry VIII built his ships and established his dockyard, here that Samuel Pepys lived, where diarist and town planner John Evelyn lived for a time and here that Sir Walter Raleigh draped his cape across a puddle to save Elizabeth I's dainty feet from getting wet. Technically, I am a Bermondsey boy as the district boundary between Deptford and neighbouring Bermondsey went through our prefab at a point which put the back bedroom, in which I was delivered, in the latter's jurisdiction, but in the territorial disputes which followed between these neighbouring boroughs, I was proud to be a Deptford boy.

We lived at 40 Chilton Grove, a pre-fabricated, square box of a dwelling on one level, made largely of asbestos. It was modest but functional, and thousands were erected as temporary homes for returning soldiers, sailors and airmen. Best of all, it had a garden – just a square of grass, but enough space to kick a ball around, hang out the washing on the line and for Dad to build a small shed. Our 'temporary' residency at 40 Chilton Grove lasted 11 years, but they were very happy and memorable years for me. I lived a free and easy life and from an early age, enjoyed the company of lots of kids like me, immersing ourselves in the freedom of the still-bombed out environment around us and the absence of motor cars which allowed us to play street games uninterrupted until the early evening.

I was born shortly before two am on the 21st November 1946 – on the cusp, as my mother would later inform me. Not a good start. As a 'cusper', I'd more likely than not be 'awkward'; pulled hither and thither by two potentially conflicting star signs, not knowing if I was Arthur or Martha much of the time, in the parlance of the day.

My father, Sidney George Wilkinson, normally a gentle and considerate man, was prevented by a visiting nurse from throwing me – at the age of about three months – through a window, since, apparently, I had spent my entire brief life screaming incessantly. After a year of this purgatory my parents took me to the doctor for the umpteenth time. He advised that I was in perfect health and that my screaming was a result of 'sheer, unadulterated temper'. According to family mythology, I was named Pete as it formed a catchy couplet – Prefab Pete.

Childhood in Chilton Grove was a very happy time. It was a round of days and late nights spent 'scouring out' for anything combustible with which to fuel our fires, building 'camps' from corrugated iron and chasing each other around playing potentially violent 'cowboys and Indians'. We would regularly raid the gardens of our neighbours to dig up spuds, skewer them on any old piece of wire and then poke them into the heart of the fire, dragging them out once thoroughly charred and burnt to break open the blackened skin and gorge on the hot, fluffy potato. As night drew in, the calls of our mothers would drift over the bombed-site. 'Bobbbblllles!' came Nell Killick's yodel to her youngest, Gordon, who for some reason was always known as Bobbles or Bothells. One by one, we would drift off to our homes, promising to be at the dump again the following evening.

Gordon was my age and we would hang out together. He was as hard as nails and on one particular occasion when he had sliced his hand open very badly on a shard of glass, my father dressed it for him since Gordon's parents had left him in our charge for the day. Gordon, only five, didn't flinch as my father poured a liberal dose of antiseptic into the cut and watched as my father pressed the edges of the cut together and bound his hand in swathes of bandage.

We kids led liberal lives and were constantly 'out'; over the bombed site, around the flats across the road, down 'the Georges' as we called it (St George's Wharf), climbing trees or exploring the mysteries of the power station up the road. Knocks and bruises were common. My brother suffered most. He would regularly come home with a gashed foot or hand, black eyes and bruises on various parts of his body. He once had a sparrow fly into his knee cap as he ran around the corner of a building in the opposite direction to the hapless bird. He almost lost his life when he jumped from a tree and a nail which workmen had hammered into the tree to serve as a coat hanger ripped his scrotum.

My collection of injuries ran to cuts and grazes mostly. At Deptford Park primary school however, a kid called Geoffrey Bond decided that it would be a wheeze to set me swinging back and forth on the equipment in the gymnasium and I lost my grip, fell three feet and broke my arm. Mother worked in a bakery at the time, at the Red Lion, the junction which connected Evelyn Street and Lower Road. I was carried into the shop whereupon Mum, on seeing it was me bundled in a blanket, threw the change she was just about to hand to a customer up in the air and rushed to gather me up.

It is strange the things we recollect: of that incident, I distinctly remember the nurse cutting my shirt away from my arm and I also recall, with some embarrassment, that I asked her if I would 'be in the papers'. While I languished in hospital, Geoffrey Bond's mortified father attempted to make amends for his son's stupidity by lavishing presents of Dinky toys on me. In a very short space of time, I had a collection to be proud of. Had I kept them, I would be a wealthy man today.

Mum – Minnie Amy Edith Wilkinson, née Cremore – was a frustrated music hall star. She played piano – left hand 'vamping' and right hand picking out the tune, and sang in a passably good voice. She was a vivacious person, always up for a laugh, quick to make a remark, guarded or not, outspoken and opinionated, with a heart of gold. Mum told us kids stories to make your hair stand on end of her young days in 'the flats' down Adolphus Street in the days when her mum and dad – Minnie Frances Cremore (née Hodge) and George Cremore – would join other couples, after a few bevvies, outside the Cricketers pub in Lower Road to indulge in stand up, drunken fights, often with their spouses.

She told us of the time when Nan – Mum's mum – finally took on the woman who ruled the street like some brooding colossus and intimidated most of the families living there. Nan saw the only pair of bed sheets she possessed flapping on the clothesline of this woman who was leaning on the fence, just daring anyone to challenge her about her ill-gotten gains, surrounded by her equally aggressive brood. Apparently, Nan came into the house, rolled up her sleeves and curled her (then) long hair into a bun at the back of her head and pinned it up. As she strode purposefully towards the door, the kids asked, 'Where are you going, Mum?'

'You'll see.'

She walked down the road followed by her own kids and a growing entourage of neighbours. She walked up to the woman and without so much as a challenge, laid into her. She got her sheets back and never had any trouble from her again. During WWII, Nan would always be the first into bomb-damaged buildings after an air raid. She told us herself how she found a man, trapped by the rubble of a collapsed building, still alive after two days but 'half-eaten alive by rats'.

Most old people died at home in those days, and my Nan would be the 'layer outer' of the dead bodies in the flats, making them presentable; dressing them in a clean shirt and perhaps a threadbare suit or putting a dress on the women. Mum would tell us of the poverty which dogged their lives: Nan would soft-boil an egg, break it in a saucer and scrape yoke and albumen across half a slice of toast on each of the plates for the five kids – Mum's sisters, Emmy, Beatty and Ivy and her only brother, the youngest, George, – with the words, 'There, now you can tell your mates you've 'ad eggs for ya tea.'

Nan would tell us about how it was possible to make a small amount of money go an awfully long way in the 'old days'. She swore that in the 30s and 40s, it was possible to go to the pictures, have a pint, a bag of chips, get the bus home and still have change from half a crown Her stories of childhood hardship were eagerly devoured by us kids, especially the one about the bed bugs and the fleas which infested many of the slum areas in which her mother and 'Granny 'odge', grew up. She would tell us how the walls of the room in which they slept (it could not be dignified with the title of bedroom) literally undulated as bugs moved around under the wallpaper. To stop the bugs crawling into the bed, Gran would stand each bed leg in a saucepan filled with water, across which the bugs would be reluctant to venture, and move the bed into the middle of the room. The bugs would then climb the wall, move across the ceiling and drop onto the bed to feed from the blood of the sleeping kids, packed five to the bed.

Pawn shops were a lifeline to many working class poor in the 30s and 40s and I recall going to get Dad's one and only suit out of the pawnbrokers on a Friday so that he could wear it for a family function on the weekend, only to return it again on Monday morning in exchange for a few bob with which to boost the meagre weekly allowance Mum had to feed us.

Mum's stories of the war were as rare as those from Dad, but she did confide that the war years were times of great bonhomie and closeness with neighbours and strangers alike, punctuated by times of unbearable terror. Community spirit blossomed in the face of a common enemy. But the scares and the close shaves were real. A rogue German fighter plane strafed the houses along the road which follows the avenue through

Greenwich Park up to General Wolfe's statue (the bullet holes and gouges can still be seen on the plinth today), along Creek Road, into Evelyn Street and onto Lower Road and the docks. Aunt Beatty took a bullet in the heel as this maniac fired indiscriminately on fleeing civilians.

Nan was stoical and abrupt; often purposely distracted by way of ensuring she wouldn't be drawn into a conversation in which she would have to offer an opinion that would invariably be at odds with other views. She feigned ignorance but was in fact very astute and sharp. She suffered husband George's presence with studied indifference. It was always rumoured, mentioned in hushed whispers and truncated sentences (so typical of the working class when the last few words of a sensitive sentence are silently mouthed), that granddad George Cremore was not the kindest husband in the world. I remember very little of him. He died when I was still very young and had suffered a stroke which left him virtually incapacitated, unable to speak apart from a few elementary words and paralysed down the left side of his body. Thrombosis set in, requiring both legs to be amputated, one below the knee and the other at the calf.

It was again rumoured, although I saw no direct evidence of it, that Nan used Granddad's incapacity to wreak her revenge for years of being treated unfairly, and would taunt and tease Granddad mercilessly. But whatever her actions were to her husband, she was a fine Nan to me and looked after me well when Mum was at work; scrubbing my face with a cold, wet flannel in the mornings, masking my protestations with a song.

She was coarse on the outside but soft as a pudding on the inside and would do anything for you, especially me, her youngest grandson at the time. But her carefully cultivated lack of social skills was something to behold. She burped every five minutes or so, whether she needed to or not, exaggerating the noise with an artificial continuation of the expelling of air which made it surreal, an apology or an 'excuse me' never entering her head. She would deliberately mispronounce names in a sort of weird homage to Mrs Malaprop: 'sirstifamakit' was her way of saying 'certificate' and 'hospital' sounded suspiciously like 'horse's piddle'.

She was a past mistress at swearing and could out-profane any man, although she would be outraged if you dared accuse her of having a foul mouth. I recall one stiflingly hot summer's day, sitting in her flat with the doors wide open in the vain hope of creating a cooling draught when two six year olds were heard at the bottom of the staircase to Nan's floor, effing and blinding like a couple of argumentative old men. Nan's face was a picture of outraged embarrassment.

'Would you just listen to that language? Where do they get it from? Wait till I . . .' With that, she was up and heading for the door from where she shouted, 'Oi! You little bastards! Stop that fucking disgusting language. Gern! Fuck off!'

I will always regret the fact that I never took the time to write down some of the stories Nan told me about her childhood. She died in the mid 60s at about 75 years of age so she would have been born around 1885, and she had always lived in south London. As a kid she would travel to Downham – in those days that was the countryside and that, to her and her family, was the equivalent of going from Deptford to the Lakes today. It was a journey and an adventure and took two to three days to complete by foot and bus. Although I do have faint recollections of 'Granny Hodge': my mum's grandmother, sitting propped up in bed in Aunt Maud's apartment in Douglas Way, halfway up Deptford High Street, George and 'Frarn' were the furthest back in time my sphere of domesticity took me in real terms, but Dad's mum and dad were another story altogether.

I never knew Dad's parents because both died when Dad himself was a boy. Dad never spoke of them, mainly because his own recollections of them were few and faltering, but also because, in my opinion, he was a shy and retiring boy who had grown into a kindly but reserved man. He was only a lad – 12 or so – when his parents died which perhaps goes some way to explaining his sometimes painful reticence. As legend has it, his father died during WWI and his mother, Flossie, died of a broken heart a year later. I have one treasured picture of Dad as a baby with his parents. His mother was beautiful and purportedly from more well-heeled roots than Dad was driven to after their deaths. But Dad's side of the family was always a mystery to me.

Dad was brought up by Aunt Anne and Uncle Herb, his real aunt and uncle and therefore my great aunt and uncle. Dad's cousin, Lilly , always had a large entourage of people around her, whose relationship to me I never really understood. Chief among them was a couple, Iris and Jack. Jack was always smartly dressed in a dark blazer and slacks with cravat under an open-necked shirt and Iris wore flouncy, full dresses and was always immaculately coiffured. There was a younger sister called Pauline as well, more ungainly and what I considered 'ordinary' and approachable. Jack and Iris were always 'looking down their noses' at us with an air of social superiority, giving credibility to the rumour of Dad's better-off origins. Mum was a good-looking woman and according to family legend, Jack made a pass at her during one Christmas party. Dad fronted him and apparently a fight ensued. The visits to Dad's side of the family for the traditional Christmas gathering abruptly ceased and the families grew apart.

Mum did a variety of jobs to keep the money trickling into the household. One of the most bizarre would entail her bringing home a heavy sack from a company which had set itself up in one of the arches formed by the railway viaduct running from New Cross to the centre of London, known as the 500 Arches. The sack was full of unfinished handles – door knobs – fancy ones that you get on wardrobes and drawers in bedrooms. They emerged from the mould with the cavities still encumbered by defiant pieces of metal and our communal job was to file away the excess metal to leave the handle clear and defined. Mum received a pittance for this work – £1 per hundred handles filed and 'made good'. It was a job which had us all sitting around in the evenings filing away as Mum and Dad sang their favourite songs: I'll be seeing you, Apple Blossom Time, Always and the one that always – even today – has me filling up, The Folks Who Live on the Hill.

The earliest job I recall her having was as a case-maker, a skill she learned during the war when she was employed making ammunition boxes. She could knock a six-inch nail into a piece of wood with four blows: a skill which she employed to great effect at a funfair we visited in Southend where the challenge was six blows of the hammer to sink a four inch nail up to the shaft, an accomplishment which most men failed to achieve. Mum won many prizes from a clearly agitated showman before he paid her off with a giant teddy bear and told her to 'sod off'.

The last job she had was as a cleaner in a police station during which time she seriously injured her arm when it was caught between two swing doors. She never sought nor received compensation and over the years her arm deteriorated to the point where she was increasingly unable to use it. Mum was the ever-present constant in my life and I adored her, although perhaps I never expressed that adoration as fully or as regularly as I should. In fact, in the last few years of her life, she confided to my wife that she never felt as though she knew the real Pete, a statement which fills me with remorse at my inability to redress that view now that she is dead.

My brother Brian, five years my senior, figured large in my life until he left home to marry when I was but a slip of a lad of 14 or so. But in the early days his presence was something of a dominating influence, particularly as we shared a bedroom, an arrangement which neither of us welcomed. I can't say that we were close: we naturally played together when we were very young, but soon the five year gap between us began to show. I can't remember much about it but as I got older, I would, I'm informed, insist on tagging along with Brian's gang of friends, threatening to grass him up to Mum about their illicit visits to the docks 'down town' unless I was either taken along or adequately bribed.

Brian took to sleepwalking when he was around the age of 10 and, as part of his nocturnal repertoire would piddle in the most unlikely of places. His perambulations would sometimes take him unerringly to the foot of Mother and Father's bed where he would stand in silence, sleeping eyes wide open, until usually Mother would wake to see him standing silently before her. At this point, she was known to elbow Dad awake with, 'Sid! Sid! Wake up. It's here again.' Dad would reply as he dragged himself out of bed, 'What do you mean, 'it'. He's your son, for crissake!'

Brian and I slept in the same bedroom. In winter, we used coats of all shapes and sizes as substitutes for extra blankets. Being five years my senior, he would read horror comics avidly while that sort of material scared the life out of me. Worse still, some of the comics he read came with a set of cardboard glasses with one red, cellulose lens in one side and a blue one in the other. Somehow, this brought about a 3-D effect when looking at these particular comics. I remember one day he had been reading a particularly scary comic about the 'Wolf Men' who abducted children and ate them. This particular night, as we were asleep, the Wolf Men came to get Brian. At some ungodly hour of the morning, with a shaft of moonlight falling across Brian's bed, I was woken by him sitting bolt upright in bed, staring eyes widened as he opened his mouth to scream. The hairs on the back of my neck stood up as he let out the most unearthly scream and shouted, 'The Wolf Men are coming to get me!! Aaaaaggggghhhhhh!'

I screamed, the dog went berserk, my father arrived in his y-fronts at our bedroom door, his sparse hair akimbo, minus his false teeth. Mother, convinced that we were all about to be murdered in our beds, was screaming too, as she lay in bed with the covers pulled over her head. The pandemonium was something to behold.

As we grew older, Brian and I argued constantly. Despite the provocation, Dad never hit us and I only ever remember him once losing his temper to the point where he swore, when he just lost it with our constant bickering. Despite the antipathy which existed between us on a daily basis, my brother and I got on well at an academic level and we were drawn closer when I began attending his grammar school and found myself in urgent need of his protection against those in the school who insisted in justifying mindless violence against little ones like me by calling it 'traditional fagging', as though we were still occupying the pages of Tom Brown's School Days. In truth, they were just bullies and cowards and we made them pay for it on one or two spectacular occasions, more of which later.

Chapter 2

Chavvies, glocks and bewers

'Wire in, Nell!' Mum would shout to Nell Killick across the garden
fence as the latter beat shit out of her one carpet with a broom as it hung
over the clothes line in the garden. Nell would shout back something
unintelligible without looking up and without taking the fag from her
mouth. The Killicks next door were rough and ready but no-one messed
with them and, by proximity, nor with us. While the glocks and the bewers
maintained an uneasy truce, the same was not true of the chavvies.

Kids can be cruel to each other and we were no exception to that
generalisation. Our games of cowboys and Indians which we played with
great vigour, and into which we injected as much realism as possible,
(including the rescuing of the token white girl tied to a totem pole) seemed
the more believable as we swooped and 'whooped' over the undulating
terrain of the bombed site which we kids referred to as the 'debris', but
while we happily thus indulged ourselves, petty jealousies and grudges
were ever present. It always seemed important to keep one of the gang on
the 'outside'. We needed a butt for our pettiness, a boy whom we could
ridicule and pillory, the more to make us feel like part of the crowd. That
unfortunate child was David Price.

I think the reason he fell foul of the rest of us was that his mother
and father had a 'nice' prefab and gave the impression of considering
themselves a cut above the rest of the families in Chilton Grove. They were
the first to buy a TV and the first to own a car. Poor David's reward was to
be shunned at every opportunity, to be jibed at and to be excluded, when
we could avoid him, from our games and schemes. This feud developed
into a personal antipathy between us to the point where, one fine Sunday
morning, it was time to have it out with him. He was the identified enemy
of the gang and I was deputised, through the unspoken language of eight
year olds, to front up for the group. Somehow the entire street got to
know of the impending fight. Even my mother came along to witness her
son's first blooding. As I walked towards his house, neighbours hung over
their garden fences offering advice and egging me on.

He emerged with his mother and walked to the fence. We stood face to face and I was a little surprised at his bravado. I mumbled a justification as to why I was about to punch his lights out, when from behind his back he produced a hammer with which he belted me over the head. Fortunately, his mother had had the sense to arm him only with a toffee hammer, so the blow was relatively light and did little damage, except to my self-esteem. I collapsed in a heap of aggrieved, blubbering shock at the thought that he could have been so well prepared and I so naive. The inevitable happened. My mother and his mother had the fight and I was led home to perpetual ignominy. The incident was the talk of the street for a week.

Such occasional run-ins notwithstanding, we had a wonderful time as kids. Street games of British Bulldog, tin-tan-tommy, knock down ginger, cricket, football and bike racing around a chalked track on the tarmac kept us in bruises and trouble for weeks.

Tin-tan-tommy involved the assigning of one person to be 'it' (the process of deciding who would be 'it' was carried out by performing a round of 'scissors, paper, stone'), and that person would be required to retrieve a tin can thrown by another member of the gang, by walking backwards while the rest of the crowd 'scattered out', as we called it. The object was to get from your chosen hiding place back to the base without being spotted, or before the child who was 'it' had the chance to rap the can on the chalked base point and shout, 'Tin-tan-tommy I see Billy Hawkins running towards me!/behind the hedge next to Mrs Jones'!/hiding behind the tree in front of number 6!' Arguments about the accuracy of the call would engage us well into the evening.

The favourite game among the tougher kids was British Bulldog in which one person, out of twenty or so and selected by a complicated round of knock-out 'scissors, paper, stone', would be the sole defender of a chalked line while the other kids would charge him, only being 'safe' when the base line was reached. The sole defender of the line had to stop at least one assailant by dragging down, tripping, tackling or generally clobbering them. Thereupon, there would be two defenders of the line for the next assault. This process would continue until there would be perhaps only two kids left to make an assault on the line, now defended by fifteen or more bruised and thoroughly excited kids. If you were unfortunate enough to be one of the last to be caught, the prospect of running at a line of whooping, mass-hysterical eight to ten year olds was daunting. The effects of the thumping you received would last a week.

On the bombed site next to our prefabs, we built 'ghost camps' and charged the younger kids a penny to be scared, although in truth, our attempts to exploit this market failed when the quality of horror was reduced to the laughable. Billy Hawkins would sit in one corner of the hut we had constructed from sheets of corrugated iron and asbestos and then covered in turf. He would hold a torch under his chin which shone upwards onto his grimacing and, supposedly, horrifically contorted face. Geoffrey Bond would lie in another corner making ghostly sounds and on the way out, the kids were subjected to the horrors of grass suspended from a cross-timber tickling their faces. Most kids emerged from our ghost camp in hysterics of laughter, but we made our penny a head and invariably saved this income for fireworks on November 5th. We would bury penny bangers in the squares of butter we had encouraged one of the lads to steal from his dad's shop and watch as the explosion scattered butter all over the debris as we hid behind convenient mounds of earth.

Gyp, our dog, was a big part of my childhood. He was a mongrel which Mum had brought home one day from a friend's house as her family circumstances would no longer allow her to keep a pet. Gyp landed on his feet and with us lived the life of Riley. No amount of barricading could keep him confined to the house or the garden and after every attempt at fencing him in had failed, my father gave into Gyp's ingenuity and allowed him to roam free. Gyp would wake up in the morning to breakfast, stretch luxuriously as he contemplated another day out on the razz and slip away for the day.

He would return during the late afternoon, more often than not with a few war-wounds, hungry, thirsty and very evidently glad to be home. After slaking his thirst and satisfying his hunger, he would invariably nuzzle his way behind my father's back as he sat in the easy chair while we listened to the radio, and sleep the evening away. Despite his freedom, Gyp would go wild with excitement if anyone of us went within a yard of the cupboard in which his leash was kept as it heralded a 'proper walk', and Gyp would behave himself perfectly on the leash, apparently proud of the fact that we cared enough about him to take him with us on the occasional outing.

His freedom, however, caused us grief. He was notorious around the shops of the Red Lion shopping area. Johnny Best, the butcher, told us quite openly that if he caught Gyp, he would 'put him on the chopping block with no regrets' because Gyp had stolen so much meat from his shop. My grandmother lived in perpetual fear of meeting Gyp on her travels. On one particular occasion, she was trying to cross the road at the busy Red Lion junction and was waiting for the policeman on point duty to hold up the traffic (no traffic lights in those days) when she saw Gyp calmly trotting down Lower Road, right in the middle of the tram lines. Behind him, the tram driver rang his bell furiously but fruitlessly to scare Gyp away and behind the tram was a royal traffic jam of fuming cars and lorries. Gyp espied Granny and broke into a gallop. He leapt at my grandmother, covering her with sloppy licks, his tail going nineteen to the dozen. The irate policeman, trying to control the traffic chaos Gyp had caused, turned to my gran, 'Your dog, madam?'

'Never seen him in my life before officer', said Nan, without missing a beat. 'Gert ya, bust'd dog. Gern. Get away!'

Gyp's eyesight began to fail. He began following me to school, sticking to me like a shadow, never losing sight of me in his myopia. He would look at me with heart-rending pathos as I told him to go home. He was approaching the time for his last walk up the road and I'll never forget watching my brother walking Gyp to the vet's, unaware of his fate and proudly trotting beside Brian on the end of the leash which he had so seldom worn. Brian wore his favourite black and white flecked jacket for the occasion.

Deptford, as in all areas of London at the time, teemed with wildlife. In the summer, we kids would delight in collecting Death's Head hawkmoth caterpillars from the swathes of purple, swaying weeds to be found all over the bombed-site and putting them into a collection of glass jars to watch them pupate. The moth state of these amazing insects was a joy to behold. My favourite, common in the 50s in London, was the Privet Hawk moth which is the most delicate shade of pink and surely the most streamlined and beautiful of all the moths.

The shed at the back of our prefab was home to my collection of insects throughout the summer months and, on occasion, to waif and stray kittens which I persuaded Mum to let me keep. Insects, moths, caterpillars, beetles, butterflies were everywhere in 1950s London which had not yet had its bombed sites concreted over, nor seen high rise blocks of offices and flats puncturing the skyline.

Dad was an amateur entomologist and would collect beetles and bugs, staking them out after a spell in the killing jar, opening wing cases and displaying the wings which I was surprised to find nearly all beetles possess. He had a collection of live stick insects which fascinated him and scared the life out of Mum. His pride and joy was a Goliath Beetle which he bought in a glass case, already 'presented', when he was in the West End for some reason or other. It must have been six inches long and had claws on the end of each three inch long leg which themselves must have been half an inch long. Over the years this amazing specimen was handed around the family and eventually I gave it to my cousin Graham and it has since been lost to the world.

Dad was a skilled engraver, undergoing a long and intensive apprenticeship, whose career was interrupted terminally by the war. On his return he worked on the railways for a time, but then got a break with my uncle's firm, United Glass Bottles (UGB), which used to nestle next to the Millwall football ground, the (old) Den, in Cold Blow Lane, just off the Old Kent Road. He employed his skills engraving the moulds for specialist glass containers.

I remember his proudest day when he brought home the first glass jar of 'Three Bears Honey' produced from the mould he had engraved. He was particularly pleased as his boss had considered the job of engraving metal with the reverse image of three bears impossible. After 28 years of loyal work with United Glass, he was fired at the age of 54. His skills were no longer required as increasing mass production and automation took hold of British industry.

He finished his working days putting vacuum cleaners together for £28 a week in Orpington and then working as a pipe fitter for a west London brewery. Despite the callous way in which he was treated throughout his working life, Dad retained a 'forelock-tugging' attitude to his employers: he was conscientious to a fault and while he was the most quiescent of workers, if he did believe that an injustice had been done, he would ponder long and hard over his position and then, but only rarely, would he throw his full weight behind a particular course of action.

I recall him striking on only one or two occasions and once committed, he would be the most ardent of supporters of the cause. Both Mother and Father were the epitome of working class conscientiousness, never once 'poncing on the state', and fiercely proud of their ability to pay their own way. When Dad came home from work on Friday evening, he would immediately hand Mum her packet of Kensitas cigarettes, put some chocolate on the mantelshelf for the weekend and then go to his money box in his bedroom which had several labelled divisions. Into each he would put the exact amount required to pay for insurance, holiday savings, rent, school clothes for us kids and other requirements, leaving him with his 'spending money' of a couple of quid for the week.

On more than one occasion, before Dad got home on a Friday night, Mum would be seen frantically replacing money she had found it necessary to borrow from Dad's money box to make ends meet during the week. In later years, I would urge them to fight back against a system which shackled them to a life barely rising above the poverty level and which cowed them into reverence for the bosses, the political system which forsook them and for the Royal family whom most of the working classes perversely revered. Surely the most inappropriate and ironic of all working class icons.

It is true, however, that Mum had a healthy disregard for royalty: every time she saw a picture of or a news item referring to the late Queen Mother, she would remark, in her coarsest working class accent, 'Gern you old cow! Seventy years a scrounger and still taking our money!'

I can't honestly recall a bad day in my childhood. Every year, from as early as I can remember, Dad would save up enough money to hire a car and we would set off on holiday at 4 o'clock in the morning, bundling blankets and sleepy kids into the back of the car, along with thermos flasks of tea and a handful of pre-rolled Old Holborn fags for Dad. He would chuck the suitcases in the boot and drive off through the silent London streets, en route for the West Country and Brean Sands. We stayed at the Three Acres Caravan site at Brean, just south of Brean Down. Caravanning was a real adventure for us kids and the lighting of the mantle around the calor-gas lights produced sights and – in particular, smells – which stay with me today.

Dad would allow Brian and me to drive the car on the endless stretches of sand at Brean, and swimming in its gently shelving waters was a delight. Invariably, we kids would end up outside the local pub with a coke and a bag of crisps while the adults imbided, but the annual holiday was a real treat. In those days when health and safety were virtually unheard of, Dad would hire a car with a sun roof and Brian and I would spend most of the time as Dad drove along country roads, standing on the seats with our heads out of the sunroof, singing our hearts out and occasionally spitting out flies which inevitably found their way into our open mouths. In fact, singing was something Mum and Dad did a lot of and it was a pastime which made driving the long distances in slow cars something of a joy rather than a bore. Not that all the cars Dad hired were slow. I recall him hiring an Austin Atlantic convertible one year. So while we were anything but rich, somehow Mum and Dad scraped together enough money to give us a decent week off every year and with it, a wealth of fond memories.

Despite the fact that I object strongly to the way in which we celebrate Christmas since it represents what I can only describe as an orgy of consumerism (in which I happily and hypocritically indulge when it comes to spoiling the children), the festive season in the fifties held nothing but delights for me. Presents, naturally, brought joy to us kids, but Christmas was a time when we would set up camp for three days in my aunt Lil's house in Brixton. She and Uncle Tom lived with Carol and Graham, their daughter and son, in a 'tied' house.

In later years, after the death of Uncle Herb who was 'Dad' to my father, Aunt Annie, Herb's wife, also later lived with Tom and Lil. Tom was a chauffeur to Lord Vesty, the butcher magnate, and lived in a house attached to an enormous garage in which Lord Vesty's collection of cars was housed, on the corner of Mayall Road in Brixton. For years – certainly most of the 50s – we held parties there, to which our extended family came, many of whom I didn't know, many of whom, I'm sure, were no more a part of the family than was the guy who lived next door. But the parties became legendary in the street and in family folklore.

Uncle Tom had a Grundig tape-to-tape recorder which was state of the art in those days and as likely as not came off the 'back of a lorry'. We would let the tape run all Christmas night throughout the party, recording our antics and singing. First to rise the next day would have the job of running the tapes backwards and playing them, the better to encourage us to party again on Boxing Day. Mum and Tom would take turns on the piano to knock out songs which seemed to have the same melody and which could only be distinguished, one from the other, by Mum shouting out the words. Only then did we know that she had changed songs from Roll out the Barrel to Lambeth Walk. Both Mum and Tom would end the evening – morning by the time it was winding down – with plasters taped to blistered fingers as they crashed the keys and kept us dancing and singing.

16

My enduring memory of these years is of thirty or forty people in Aunt Lil's front room singing the 'Okey Cokey at full volume and knees-ing up to the point where the light fixing was swinging and the floorboards were bending beneath the weight of the Wilkinson/Cobdens, collectively lost in the pursuit of a good time. And after lights out, us kids would creep up the stairs to watch the Christmas spectacle of Lil and Tom lying in bed, asleep but engaged in their individual night antics. Tom would hum hymns beneath his breath. Lil would have her hands above her head, hands and fingers agitated in a bizarre dance, the purpose of which only she knew.

There was a dark side to these events and one I mention reluctantly. While our annual family celebrations were anticipated with great joy, they held some fear for me. Rumour has it that Mum and Dad had wanted their second child to be a girl. Instead, they got me. Perhaps – and I'm sorry Mum, if you're reading this from wherever you might be – there was a subconscious desire in Mum to live out her fantasy of having a daughter and to experiment with the idea at Aunt Lil's parties, when she would insist that I dressed as a girl and – particularly galling – as if that wasn't enough embarrassment for an eight year old – 'flutter my eyes', at which all involved would roar with laughter.

'Do your eyes, boy!' Mum would command. And I would duly oblige while cringing with embarrassment which I hid well enough, I hope.

I am sure that this mild form of abuse, this forced and mostly false (on my part) enjoyment in which I had to pretend to engage, gave me a lifelong aversion to staged family activities revolving around alcohol, parties and family gatherings. It is an aversion which my wife has suffered for the duration of our relationship. She comes from a large East End family which lives and dies by the regular family 'get-together' – far too regular for me – at which this form of required enjoyment, 'fun to order', is standard. Don't get me wrong, I love a party, but I like to party on my own terms, to sing when I want to sing, dance when I want to dance and sit quietly when I want to sit quietly. This is not an option at most family gatherings and my antipathy towards them has deep and very long roots.

But by far the best part of Lil and Tom's gatherings, and one which swept away any misgivings about my reluctant and imposed forays into tranvestitism, was the fact that it was in Lord Vesty's cars – Rolls Royces, Bentleys and classics, the company lorries and other vehicles parked in the cavernous building at the side of the house – that exhausted party-goers would crash when their stamina was expended and when the large number of beds had been occupied. For us kids, the garage and its contents were like an Aladdin's cave of fun and adventure as we clambered from one classic car to another, running small hands over the smooth walnut trim, nostrils filled with the smell of expensive leather. By the early 70s, Tom and Lil moved out of their house in Mayall Road on the order of the boss, Lord Vesty. I believe they were not sad to leave since Brixton was becoming, in their opinion, a 'ghetto' for black immigrants. All over London, it seemed, traditional communities were on the move either because they were being re-housed into tower blocks or because many simply would not live next door to black neighbours. It was a time of great change, a watershed in the lives of so many Londoners who were set in their ways, comfortable with their communities and, generally, with their lot in life, although what they had was not a great deal, it must be said. But there was an order and a routine to life: as people say as a cliché these days, people knew their place, and to a large extent, that is true.

I'm sure that Lil and Tom, along with thousands of other families who grew up in the years before, during and immediately after the war, had no inclination to move to the further-flung parts of the south east of England to which they felt compelled to go to avoid what they saw as the upheaval of their comfortable lives and well-worn traditions. Those lives and their routines were challenged not only by the arrival of immigrants from the Caribbean, but also by their own prejudices which simply could not assimilate or accommodate the idea of living in the same area as people who, apart from being different in appearance, were seen as being so utterly different in their customs and the ways in which they conducted themselves. At least, from the shock of those times, Britain has demonstrated its tolerance and adaptability in that there can be only a few areas in the country now – Suffolk being one of them – where the sight of black or Asian people still turns heads, although it is sadly true that racism still stalks most areas of society.

Football was central to the Wilkinson's social life. Brian was near-professional and had trials for a number of professional teams and Uncle George played for Millwall for a few seasons. Weekends revolved around playing, watching or training for football. I adored playing but was not as talented as either Brian or George although I was so eager to play that I would religiously trudge up to Blackheath every Saturday and Sunday morning, fixture or not, and browbeat a team into giving me a game.

I played left wing and compensated for my lack of height by using my pace to dodge past fullbacks. I rose to the great heights of playing a few games for the Isthmian League but I couldn't sustain the high standards they expected. I played for Greenwich Town Social, at 14 I was their youngest player, and scored, in front of a touchline crowd of around a hundred supporters, a memorable goal about which I remember little other than I shut my eyes as the ball came towards me and when I opened them again, the ball was hitting the back of the net.

I was surrounded by players who could not believe the shot I had just produced. I hated to tell them, but neither could I. It was a pure fluke but it ensured me a further six games before 'wonderboy's' luck ran out and I was exposed for the ordinary, slightly tackle-shy player I was. I did however, go on to play senior-level football in later years and, had it not been for cartilage and tendon trouble which required three operations, and a hip replacement in 2004, I would still be playing today, should I be able to find an over-60s team!

But the idyll of living in Chilton Grove among friends with whom I shared the joys of a close community was soon to end. The 'temporary prefabs' which had housed us for more than 10 years were to be demolished and the council offered us a bright, new flat on Trinity Estate, a mile up the road, past Blackhorse Bridge. It was the age of washing machines, fridges and televisions. The brave new world of the post-war era was upon us and in 1957, we waved goodbye to Chilton Grove and settled into our new flat, 27 Keppel House, Trinity Estate, Evelyn Street, Deptford SE8. We even had a phone – Tideway 6176.

I remember going to see the flat before we moved in. It smelled of new paint, drying plaster and had an air of optimism about it. It was on the third floor of the block, with only one floor above us. Its aspect gave out onto Blackhorse Bridge and only a low block of flats obscured the view to the main Evelyn Street A2 trunk road. It had a veranda, compensation for the fact that from now on, gardens would be communal, in the shape of the greens and grassed areas dotted all over the estate. It wasn't Chilton Grove and a detached prefab, but it represented a new way of living: all tubular kitchen chairs and Formica tops. Dad even bought a new stereogram with a sliding record deck, integral radio and record rack all encased in shining 'teak'.

The greatest novelty for us kids was the lift which we used endlessly, whether we wanted to get back to our flat or not. Improbably, each flat had a coal bunker and an open fire place. We were also allocated a lock-up shed in a communal building attached to the block of flats, into which went bikes and all the old junk from the prefab that we didn't have the heart to throw away. We still viewed the future with some trepidation given the still-edgy political situation which saw nuclear armed 'East and West' ranged against each other, but generally, we were optimistic, due to our new circumstances. Dad and Mum had work, Brian was doing ok, if not brilliantly, at school. I had just passed my 11 plus and the music scene was being revolutionised like every other aspect of British life. The gloom of post-war Britain was gradually being discarded, the still-raw memories of stark and crippling austerity were slowly fading and people were cautiously embracing the post-war world.

With typical selflessness, our parents gave the largest bedroom in the flat to Brian and me. He was now 16 years old and grappling with rock and roll, Elvis, Cliff Richard, acne and Brylcreem, not to mention a budding love life and his passion for football. Brian had trials for Millwall and Charlton but, to my utter amazement, he turned down a potential football career in order to take up a position with the Trustee Savings Bank, a job he kept for life, well, until he was 49, at which point he was made redundant. I never quite forgave him for turning down the opportunity of a lifetime in football for the security and – surely – the relative drudgery of a bank.

The move to a brand new flat was at once exciting in the extreme, since we were about to embark on a new way of life in a new environment with new friends, but at the same time it signalled the end of an age of childhood innocence. I had known nothing but life in a prefab and the freedom of car-less roads and the ability to wander more or less wherever I wished (free-range kids) for ten years. Chilton Grove was my entire, if brief, life at that point in time. I knew every alley and back street within miles. I knew every neighbour, every kid and every wheeze there was to know. We were all streetwise in a way which today has come to mean something sinister and malevolent.

It wasn't like that in the 50s. Not once can I ever recall any maliciousness in our antics. We were certainly a rough bunch, but were never violent, rude or impolite to our elders. The police were rarely needed in our neighbourhood. The parents in every family were those who carried out such policing as was required, and the social servicing was likewise carried out by the extended families of the time and by the collective actions of the neighbours.

I often view the 50s as the romantic era in my life, although I am fully aware that, in truth, it was as rough, unfair and as unequal as life is today. Litter was a much rarer sight, wildlife was abundant and every soft drinks bottle (there were no aluminium cans) carried a reward of 3d (1.5p) which gave us kids a steady income and discouraged litter. It would have been impossible to predict the way in which life and society would be so transformed over the course of fifty short years and that transformation began for me with the shock of moving out of my comfort zone in a Deptford which I wore like an old t-shirt into the harsh and often violent world of secondary education.

Chapter 3

Shooters Hill Grammar School – survival of the funniest

I remember my mum sitting with me at primary school, beaming one of her wonderful, crooked smiles and telling me that I had passed my 11 plus. Apparently, I gained high marks in general knowledge and English, but terrible marks in arithmetic. Luckily, the two good subjects outweighed the bad and I was eligible for a grammar school education. The choice was not a choice at all, really. My brother Brian was already attending Shooter's Hill Grammar School – not his first choice, it has to be said – and this became my first choice simply because he was attending what was considered to be a good school.

I went for the interview with the headmaster, a severe-looking, cloaked and mortar-boarded man of middle age called Harry Hanks (who turned out to be a real diamond).

After a general chat, he asked me, 'What are thirteen twelves?'

'A hundred and fifty six', I replied without hesitation.

'And how did you make the calculation?'

'Twelve twelves plus twelve.'

One of his eyebrows rose in mild surprise. 'And this ship on the wall . . .' he indicated a painting of the school's man-o-war emblem behind him. 'How many guns would that ship have?' I counted the gun ports. 'Thirty six, sir,' I replied.

'Hmmm. And what about the guns on the other side of the ship?'

'Well, you can't see those, sir, but if you could, it would be seventy two, assuming there are the same number on each side.'

'Hobbies?'

In an effort to impress him, I had decided before the interview that I wouldn't say making Airfix kits of World War II aircraft or stamp collecting but that I would claim a more upmarket hobby as might befit a grammar school kid.

'Birdwatching, sir.'

'Really. How interesting. And what sort of birds do you regularly see?'

I thought this was a dumb question. I came from Deptford. You saw sparrows and pigeons and not much else, but I knew about 'tits'. 'Bluetits, sir. And swallows,' I lied.

'Ah, swallows! Yes, and what are they doing when they swoop around just feet from the ground in summer?'

'Looking for food, sir.'

'And what do they eat?'

I thought this was an even dumber question than the one about what birds I normally saw in Deptford. All birds eat the same things, right?

'Worms, sir.'

To give him his due, Harry didn't miss a beat and ignored this risible reply. 'Thank you, boy.'

Somehow, I was accepted as a pupil of Shooters' Hill Grammar School and a few months later I joined the throng of eleven year-olds piling off the 89 bus at the top of Red Lion Lane on that September morning in 1957 to wend my way down the hill to the school, dressed in my stiff uniform and with a hat on my head bearing the green and gold roundels of the school. It didn't stay on my head for long. In a portent of what was to follow, my hat was variously knocked off my head, passed from kid to kid and/or kicked around the pavement on that ten minute walk from the bus stop to the school.

As we walked through the gates, the second, third and fourth formers were there to greet us with howls of derision and gales of laughter. The fifth formers were above all this, thankfully. They, including my brother, were allowed the freedom of the school's corridors and rooms in which to while away the pre- and post-school periods. The air of impending unpleasantness increased and soon, the traditions of 'fagging' – a hangover from public school days which the management at Shooter's Hill Grammar School tolerated, due to their warped belief that this somehow reinforced its status as a superior establishment – were revealed to us.

The first year of my secondary education was nothing but a nightmare. I was terrified of many of the kids and almost as many of the teachers. Corporal punishment – caning on the arse with a bamboo cane – was the accepted and legal form of punishment. I found myself on the wrong side of the cane on two occasions whilst at school. Once I was caned for telling the kid sitting in front of me what to say as he struggled to translate a passage of Latin text (that was deemed 'cheating' and thus worthy of a caning), and once for playing football in a restricted area and smashing the newly installed plate glass window in the newly completed physics laboratory.

The worst thing about the canings was not the pain, (the cane itself left two red stripes for every stroke as the blood was pushed to either side of the point of impact due to the force of the blow. I therefore had twelve red stripes on my arse – I checked in the mirror after getting six of the best), but the fact that Harry Hanks the headmaster always allowed the sadistic deputy head to administer the punishment. Bailey seemed to take great delight in inflicting punishment and did not spare the rod.

During the punishment for playing football and smashing the physics lab plate glass window, about ten of us were to be caned and we jostled for position as we waited outside the head's office so as to be the last in the queue, on the grounds that Bailey would be exhausted by the time he had to give the last of his sixty strokes. I remember waiting outside his office and listening to the 'thwack' of each stroke, to discover if anyone blubbed or let out a squeak of pain. No-one did, much to Bailey's undoubted chagrin.

I kept my anguish about the violence at school as concealed as I could but it was difficult to hide from my mother in particular, who seemed to have a sixth sense which sniffed out problems. Apart from a platitude here and there, Dad didn't do much about it on the grounds that my brother had gone through this and had survived, so there was no reason to suspect that I would not follow suit. I suppose, looking back, that while my initiation into secondary school was brutal, much of the brutality was ritualised. There were one or two extremely violent episodes at school which resulted in expulsions, but on the whole, it was usually good-natured and seen – by teachers and the headmaster alike – as part of the rough and tumble of a grammar school tradition, a toughening-up process which gave kids a bit of backbone.

The punishments for daring to be first year students were wide in range and inventiveness. A blocked-off set of stairs to the toilets served as a 'squash box' which saw ten or so 'fags', as we were known, pushed into the iron railing and squashed by a press of bigger boys who squeezed up the stairs and attempted to asphyxiate us. I saw one boy pass out during this treatment which happened pretty regularly and which was not over quickly: sometimes, the older kids would 'squash' us for the entire length of the lunch break – about an hour – by taking it in turns to keep us trapped. Another little wrinkle was to tie our shoe laces to the iron railings while we were incapacitated which would leave us late for the next lesson or without shoes laces as we broke them to be quicker released, or both.

Then there was 'crucifixion'. A ten foot high wall divided the two quadrangles which were built at different levels. Unlucky 'fags', who may have caught the eye of an older kid by saying something to which exception was taken, were hung over this wall for the entire lunch break. But not just 'hung' by the arms: the arms were twisted through 180 degrees so that they stretched out from the back at an awkward angle and then you were hung over the wall for an hour or so. These punishments were in addition to the straightforward beatings we took regularly, not to mention vindictive acts such as taking a ball away from our football game and cutting it in two with flick knives.

We had no choice but to fight back. We organised our own vigilante group, a 'one-for-all and all-for-one' collection of six of us which had its victories against the weaker bullies but which attracted even more attention from the hard-nuts. All-in-all, my initial experience of grammar school, something for which I had qualified with some fanfare, was not something to be recommended.

My brother was at this time in form 5R (fifth year removed to take the GCE 'O' levels again). As such, he was allowed the run of the school during break times. Although I was under a great deal of stress at the time, due to the bullying, I tried not to involve Brian in any retaliatory actions on my behalf, conscious of the fact that he would be leaving school soon and I would be left defenceless if I relied on him to dig me out of a hole. On one occasion, however, I exploited my brother's presence to the full.

I had just bought a chocolate bar from the tuck shop and, as usual, I was being hassled by an older boy who was trying to make me hand it over. Out of the corner of my eye, I saw Brian and some of his fellow 'untouchables' lounging in a corridor. Brian was looking at me and could see what was going on. I saw him tap the arm of his friend, point in my direction and then disappear, obviously to come to my rescue. Fortified with the knowledge that help was on its way, I grabbed my assailant's tie, pushed him with all my strength and told him to 'Piss off, bastard!'

He could not believe my bravado. He walked towards me and grabbed me in an armlock. He pulled me back and was about to push my face into a wall when he was taken out by my brother. I rearranged my jacket and turned to look at the action. Brian lifted him by his lapels a foot up the wall and banged his head against it a few times while asking him what he thought he was doing. My assailant swore by every God that he would never again hassle a first former and as Brian let him go, he delivered a great right cross which sent the boy sprawling. The entire episode had been witnessed by others of the bullying ranks and from that time forward I was never bothered again. Until Brian left school, that is.

It was not only the boys who were violent. There were one or two teachers who were not averse to doling out a bit of corporal. Our second year French teacher, 'Pongo' (can't remember his real name), had a permanently twisted hand, skewed at right angles to his wrist. His story was that a bullet fired by a nationalist in the Spanish civil war, in which he fought on the side of the rebels, had entered his elbow and exited at his wrist. This did not stop him from using his twisted and bony hand as a weapon with which to hit you hard across the arse as he perversely required you to go down on all fours on his teaching plinth at the front of the class while he delivered four, five, six blows with his deformed extremity.

He would bury his head in a book for a while until we were all nattering away amongst ourselves. With a jerk of his head, he would say, 'Stand up all those boys who are talking.' If you stood up to admit your guilt, you'd be certain to receive punishment. However, if you decided to chance it and remain seated, you ran the risk that Pongo had previously identified you as a culprit. His wrath at seeing a boy attempt to 'cheat' him, as he put it, was boundless and the punishment was normally doubled for those thus caught. A more sinister and infinitely more painful method of chastisement was to hit you across the back of the fingers with a steel rule. I bear the scar of that punishment to this day.

As we graduated from the amoebic form of life as first years to the dizzy heights of second formers and beyond, Shooter's Hill Grammar School became the centre of my life. The fagging episodes dropped off entirely and we became more confident and more at ease with the masters and with the pulse of school life. I loved it. I loved the stage it provided for my limited academic talents, but more for the opportunity it provided me to express my humour and burgeoning sporting talents.

My abiding memory of balmy summer afternoons at school is of surreptitiously changing out of my school shoes and into plimsoles during the last ten minutes of the French lesson before lunch, the better to be ready to play the second my feet touched the turf. The smell of the newly-mown grass on the field fuelled by the impossible-to-contain excitement of the anticipation of playing football (using jackets as goalposts, of course) is a memory that still assails me to this day. And we were pretty talented at football. Not that it did us or the school any good because, officially, football was banned as a 'lower class sport': we grammar school types played rugger, don't you know?

Being small and supposedly nimble, I played hooker for Brodies, the 'House' to which I was assigned, but the pummelling I usually received during the game was not to my liking. Rugby was a rough and thoroughly uncivilised version of British Bulldog, in my opinion, and left a lot to be desired in terms of ball control and flair for playing a team game. Regardless of my dislike for the sport, I played for the school on a few occasions but made sure that my performances were sufficiently lacklustre to avoid being picked as a regular.

The same couldn't be said for cricket, which I loved, and at which I was a reasonable bowler for the school and my House side. A batsman I was not, however, and I would play the wrong shot on just about every occasion presented to me. My most memorable innings was hitting a six (I had my eyes shut as the ball clipped the shoulder of the bat and spiralled away for the winning runs) and I was feted by being given a whole shilling to spend in the tuck shop after a whipround among the team.

School was taking a very firm grip on me and it was to my liking. My academic progress was good. I played cricket and swam and dived for the school. I enjoyed the company of good friends and, increasingly, of good teachers. As we moved through the school, the teachers became more familiar and treated us more and more as equals. We joked and played pranks on them, big time, but these were increasingly taken in good spirit. We would rub candles over the blackboard so that it could not be chalked. We would balance the teacher's desk on the very edge of the raised plinth at the front of the class so that the moment he applied pressure to it, down it would come.

On one notable occasion, we made 'fart machines' by stretching thick rubber bands between the arms of a piece of metal bent into a half-circle and in the middle of which was threaded a stout, metal washer. These we would wind up and sit on them. By leaning to one side and releasing the pressure, the metal washer would unwind, spinning around to make a passable 'fart' as it came into contact with the wooden seat of the desk. On discovering these contraptions beneath one unfortunate boy, the teacher asked him in all seriousness what on earth it was. He replied to instant hoots of laughter, 'Please, sir, it's a fart-machine.'

I was good at languages and enjoyed the clipped French of our moustachioed and dapper French teacher, Henderson, as much as I did the guttural German from 'Ollie', our German teacher, whose real name escapes me after all this time. Ollie was a good sort: square, solid, a little in awe of the class and its growing reputation for hi-jinks. He must have pushed his glasses back on his nose at least a hundred times in the course of a lesson. He was dedicated but painfully naive. Our antics drove him to distraction over the years and at the end of each term, it was plain to see that he was less of a man than at the beginning. As awful as it is to admit today, I think we consciously attempted – and largely succeeded – to wreck him, despite the fact that he was a good, honest and thoroughly likeable teacher.

My prowess in languages was impressive and as the time for the GCE examinations approached, I began to concentrate more on having fun than on honing my knowledge of the language. Ollie was quick to spot my potential decline and pulled me aside to advise me to stay away from the clique I had fallen in with if I wanted to pass my German 'O' level. I took his advice and determined to sit a few rows in front of my fellow conspirators for the last term. Despite this, any disruption in the class seemed to be blamed on me, and the teacher, no matter how much I protested my innocence, fingered me for the culprit.

It all came to a head one afternoon. The teacher's resolve snapped. We had finally broken him. A minor disturbance the back of the class caused him to spin round from the blackboard, eyes bulging, face reddening, breathing coming in short gasps.

'That's it. That's it!' he wheezed. 'You have done nothing but make my life hell for the past three years. Wilkinson! Stand up!'

'Please, sir, it was nothing to do with . . .'

He fairly leapt from his raised platform and launched himself at me. He cracked me a decent right-hander to my nose. As my head spun to the left, a line of blood created a splattered arc across the wall. He grabbed me by the shoulders and screamed into my face, demanding that I continue to read from the text book we were in the middle of studying. It was difficult to read with a handkerchief held to my nose, blood dripping onto the page, but I did it. When he told me to stop, I continued. He told me to stop again, but I continued, unable to leave this situation without having the last word, so to speak. He sat down and allowed me to finish the passage. Despite the severity of the incident, Ollie and I developed a mutual respect as the last term slipped by and I am indebted to him for the 'O' level pass I achieved in German.

It was around this time that I met and became friends with Geoff Lee, who lived in Sanderson House, a few hundred yards from Keppel House. We both shared a passion for aircraft and joined the Air Training Corps (ATC) 1198 Squadron whose club house was at the Marquis of Granby, New Cross. My enthusiasm for planes and the RAF stemmed from the fact that my uncle, Bob Cobden, had been a Spitfire pilot during the war and he was a natural hero for an impressionable 12 year old. Only after years of such adoration did he take me aside quietly when I was in my teens and tell me that he only flew two missions during the battle of Britain: on the first occasion he was so terrified that he could barely fly, let alone focus his gunsights and fire, and on the second, his guns jammed and he was forced to leave the dog-fight and scoot for home. Nonetheless, he represented all that was glamorous about the RAF and I harboured quiet ambitions to join the RAF and follow in his footsteps.

1198 Squadron's clubhouse was a terraced house in Florence Road, a wide avenue of grand Victorian houses. A flagpole in the front garden proudly flew the RAF duster along with the Union Jack. We wore smart uniforms and were encouraged to buff our boots to a dazzling shine, but discipline was virtually absent. We paraded on Sunday mornings and marched around various streets in Deptford and New Cross, but the lessons and instructions we received were optional and most of the nights we spent at the clubhouse were spent rough-housing and horsing around. Geoff and I were, however, voracious pupils, and such education as we did receive, we absorbed hungrily and wore our uniforms with pride. We passed all the tests we were set with flying colours.

The highlight of our ATC careers was being sent to Lynton-on-Ouse RAF station in Yorkshire with twenty other uniformed oiks from Deptford for a week's induction course during which time, we were sternly warned, we would be under strict RAF military discipline. Our first outing was to the target range, known as the butts, where we were – amazingly, it seemed to me – given brief instructions on the use of 303 rifles and then allowed to fire live ammunition at targets. The rifle was almost as tall as me and as I lay down to fire it, my excitement was tempered by the realisation that not only was it impossibly unwieldy and had a kick so fierce that the rifle butt would hit me under the chin with every round I fired, but also, being left-handed, I had to eject the spent shell casing from across the breach. As the shell casings came spinning from the breach, they hit my nose and burned me. Undeterred, I prepared to fire my fifth round when the red flag was waved from behind the butts indicating we were to immediately stop firing.

An officer rushed towards us waving his arms frantically. It transpired that one of us was so inept at firing these rifles that he was missing the steep sandbank in front of the targets, missing the 20 foot high concrete wall behind the targets and had narrowly missed hitting a Chipmunk trainer parked beyond the butts. The errant marksman turned out to be me and I was quickly hustled away from the butts.

Some ten 'squadrons' of kids from all over the country were sharing the Lynton experience and rivalries were quick to surface. When we learned that the kids down the hall from us in the same barrack room were from Lewisham, raids were planned. Before long, midnight sorties were taking place regularly and the initial good-natured pillow fights quickly turned into full-blown punch ups. It was finally stamped out, too late, when one of their guys was knifed and suffered a superficial wound.

Our hosts at Lynton also had a character-building exercise in store for us – the initiative test, during which three of us rookies would be sent with an NCO, out into the wilds of Yorkshire with instructions about what to do after we were dropped in the middle of nowhere contained in a sealed envelope which the NCO of each group held. On being dropped off at a particular point, the group were to open their instructions while the lorry went off to deposit another bunch of unfortunates elsewhere. The first map reference at the top of the page of instructions was the point at which we had been dropped and the instructions then gave us six further map references to follow. We also had to answer questions such as 'how many telegraph poles are there in the main street?' The route had been designed to bring us all, in differing circular routes, back to the RAF base. Our strict instructions were that if we were nowhere near the base by 1800 that evening, we were to telephone the duty officer who would arrange for us to be collected.

Our particular day went well. In fact we won the event, arriving back at the base with six correct answers scribbled on the paper which bore the questions before any of our colleagues appeared. By midnight, however, Geoff Lee's little band of heroes were still not back on the base and we sat around speculating on their fate. Eventually we turned in, hoping that everything was well. At 0200, the door to our room burst open and in marched – that's marched – Geoff and his NCO followed by two dishevelled-looking rookies, all backed up by a Military Policeman, peaked cap obscuring his eyes, baton stiffly at right angles beneath his arm.

Stocker, the NCO who had led our group that afternoon, sleepily realised the guys had finally returned and with his hair-lip affected voice shouted, 'Where the n'uck n'ave you bee'h?'

The MP came to a sharp halt, turned in the direction of the voice and shouted, 'That man there, shut the fuck up, or you'll be on a charge as well!'

Geoff and his group stood stiffly to attention before the MP barked 'Fall out! Collect your personal belongings and fall in again, at the double!'

To the accompaniment of 'One, two, one, two, one two!!' they were gone. The story later emerged that Geoff's team had become hopelessly lost during the afternoon. The NCO in charge of his group was reading the map the wrong way and had therefore taken the party to what he thought were the right locations, but which had, in one instance, turned out to be an Army firing range from which they only narrowly escaped serious injury. By 1700, Geoff's troupe had found themselves on the outskirts of Leeds. Hungry and thirsty, they had persuaded the oldest looking of their number to go into an off-licence and purchase a dozen beers which they had proceeded to drink while walking through town. By the time they found a phone box from which to call the base, they were all sufficiently inebriated to decide on a whip round for more beer.

They were picked up by MPs at about 2200, staggering through town singing some of the ruder ditties for which the ATC was renowned and were promptly arrested. They spent the rest of their time at Lynton on guard house duties, ironically making sandwiches for the rest of us for our daily sojourns.

But our time at Lynton-on-Ouse was not all guardhouse and being bellowed at. One night we were taken out to the airfield where a twin-engined, medium bomber stood – a Boston, I believe – engines purring. In true WWII form we donned parachutes which drooped between our legs, climbed on board the darkened aircraft and took to genuine wartime canvas seats. An officer came in last and secured the door behind him. Over the throb of the engines, he told us we were going on a flight out over the North Sea and we would be in the air for some 90 minutes. The engines roared to full power and we were rushing down the runway. I was back in 1942. The rumble of the tyres was silenced as we left the ground. I watched the lights of the airfield below shrink to pinpoints of white as we made height. The officer handed us headsets and we heard the pilot telling us to look out of the port window to see the landmarks he was pointing out to us and which he used as navigational aids. This was my first ever flight and I stupidly yearned for the war years to be replayed to allow me to be part of that great conflagration which tore Europe apart and yet somehow united everyone in a common cause against the horror of fascism.

Our time at the ATC brought Geoff and I into contact with a group of people with whom we became friends and with whom we shared an increasingly active social life. It was also around this time that I had my first serious date with a girl. I had gone through the usual gamut of childhood romances and had formed a brief relationship with another girl on the estate for a while and then with a girl called Sharon with whom I fell briefly and hopelessly in love, but at that age, my passion was more for football and Airfix plane kits than women. The kindling of fiery loins, however, was happening apace and before I knew it, I had plucked up the courage to ask a girl called Iris out on a 'real' date.

We went to the pictures at Greenwich, and I spent a good hour pondering how to get my arm around her shoulders and, glancing down at her legs sheathed in glistening stockings, I remember thinking that here I was sitting beside a girl – no, a woman – who was wearing stockings. Real stocking, for crissakes, with a suspender belt, no doubt! My imagination as to what lay beneath the skirt ran wild, but despite these interludes I held a candle for one girl in particular into whose house we would pile on a Sunday night.

If we were lucky, her mother and father would stroll up to the pub and we could indulge in a game of 'Postman's knock'. I would go weak with desire, embarrassment and overpowering lust if, as on occasion, I was lucky enough to draw Christine's name from the hat and get to spend a blissful two minutes with her in the next room savouring what I knew to be the true taste of heaven. Yet, even as the stirrings of young lust percolated through my veins, I was still a little boy in reality. No taller than 4' 10", I fancifully and only half-heartedly lusted after women, but in truth, and with more overt desire, I longed for a Youngs, drop handle-bar, double 'clanger' racing bike, the like of which I had seen and drooled over in a cycle shop at Lee Green.

My long-suffering Dad gave me a few quid towards the deposit without which I would not have secured the beautiful, shiny, lime green beast, but to pay it off, I took a paper round. I received 17/6d (87.5p in new money) a week and worked morning and evening five days a week. The piles of papers waiting for us kids at 5.30 in the morning as we sleep-walked into the paper shop next to the John Evelyn pub were daunting in their height: I swear that on a Sunday, a shift we were unlucky enough to cop for once every two weeks or so, the stack of Sunday newspapers was far higher than myself. How I managed to get them in the canvas bag slung round my neck, how I managed to walk under such conditions, let alone deliver the papers all over Deptford, is still a mystery to me and an occurrence that my children listen to with disbelief to this day.

I now forsook the bus in favour of cycling to school. It was no mean feat: down Evelyn Street, along Creek Road and into Greenwich Park, up the steep hill of Constitution Walk and out onto the Heath where, after a ten minute slog, I'd begin the long, slow climb along Kidbrooke Park Road and Shooter's Hill, gratefully turning left at Red Lion Lane and free-wheeling down the steep, short hill into school. The return journey was a dream, being mostly downhill once Red Lion Lane had been negotiated – a road so steep that it had to be walked while pushing the bike. I did that bike journey, morning and afternoon for the best part of two years, riding my prized Youngs sports bike.

As my sixteenth birthday appeared on the horizon, I prepared for the inevitability of owning a motor scooter. Believe me, it was inevitable in those days that a sixteen year old would own a scooter. Not owning one was unthinkable. The music scene was exploding with captivating rock and roll music. The Perry Comos and Bing Crosbys of this world were being thrown aside for the thump and twang of guitars and percussion of

Little Richard, Jerry Lee Lewis and Elvis. Scooters and 'mod' gear was de rigeur. Within days of turning 16, I bought an old, beat up Lambretta Li150 and was given permission to park it in the school grounds.

I could now join the junior ranks of the 'scooter boys' and took delight in speeding past the bus stops at which stood the hordes of Kidbrooke Park schoolgirls who had made my life a misery on the bus for so long. Just past the Sun in the Sands pub on Blackheath there was a crossroads, twenty yards beyond which was a bus stop, always crowded with girls waiting for the bus. I would regularly drop down a gear as I approached the crossroads and then gun the throttle as I drew adjacent to the bus stop. Invariably, I would give the girls a wave as the scooter roared past, purposely loosened silencer blatting its combustive roar.

What a dickhead! And soon the dickhead had his comeuppance, in the shape of a car which was turning right across my path and which I failed to see (being too intent on watching the reaction of the girls at the bus stop). I ploughed into the bonnet of the car and was sent flying through the air, landing in a heap ten yards down the road. I was unhurt but for my pride, which was sorely dented as I sat on the curb giving details to the police in earshot of the now-giggling line of girls.

At home, things were pretty good too. Mum and Dad were clearly still very much in love. During the evening, more often than not, they would simply sit in the living room, Dad at Mum's feet, and talk, occasionally breaking out into song as they reminisced. We would visit Uncle Jim and Aunt Emmy from time to time – just a short walk down Evelyn Street to their flat opposite Molins' Machine Company – where they would generally knock off the best part of a bottle of gin for the women and rum for the men or Jim, Dad and I would come back to our flat to play snooker on a mini-sized table Dad had bought. Dad was working now at United Glass Bottles in Cold Blow Lane, right next to the Millwall football ground known as the Den. Mum was working literally across the road in the woodyard as a case maker. Brian had by then eschewed the life of a footballer on the grounds that it was a short and (in those days) a rather poorly paid profession.

He had other reasons: he had met Margaret, a Kidbrooke Girls' School pupil who got on the same 89 bus as Brian and they met when both were very young. They intended to marry and Brian had his sights set on a steady job providing a regular income.

Brian's life-path always fascinated me in that it was diametrically opposite to mine and Brian's outlook and attitudes were likewise largely alien to me. I have no idea how much or how little of his approach to life was due to the influence of Margaret, but there is no doubt in my mind that she wore the trousers in the relationship which developed, very soon after their meeting, into an engagement and then marriage. As our life paths diverged, he quickly became estranged from me and although I saw him regularly during the time I was still hanging on to Mother's apron strings, I felt him slipping away from me in every sense.

Politically we became poles apart and I learned to my horror later in life that he had even taken out private health insurance, something which to me, is close to criminal. Even then, in small ways, he seemed to change and his opting for what seemed to me to be the 'safe' path while eschewing anything you could remotely call dangerous or exciting, seemed a waste. But who am I to talk? Despite what I thought would be a dull life, he was the happiest guy I knew, always laughing and always up for a kick-about or a rough and tumble. I can't honestly remember a time I saw him without a smile on his face.

His tragic death at a relatively early age was another episode which shook me to my boots and showed me how far we had drifted apart, and how his immediate family – Margaret, his boys and his (admittedly still very young) grandchildren – appeared to unintentionally reinforce that distancing between Brian and myself at the time of his illness and in the immediate aftermath. Despite everything, I loved Brian and I recall thinking at his funeral – at which I was not invited to speak – that of all the people in the funeral parlour, I had known him the longest and probably the most intimately, over more than sixty years, longer than anyone else there.

Chapter 4

The 60s and adolescence

They say that if you can remember the 60s, you didn't enjoy them. Admittedly, my memory of the decade is patchy, but I do recall them being a time of great liberation and excitement, of breathless expectation and elation, although also times which were massively tempered with a sort of foreboding which comes with the sudden and frequent realisation that the unthinkable is, in fact, part of your daily reality. The 60s were great if you didn't think about politics or of the increasing likelihood of an intercontinental nuclear weapons exchange. One which would either fry you to death on the spot, asphyxiate you, leave you as an inconsequential smudge on the pavement or expose you to radiation which would kill you in days, weeks, months or years.

I would read the newspapers or watch the news and if Kruschev or Kennedy had made some mildly provocative statement, it would be enough to make the hairs on the back of my neck bristle. Then there was China, of course. What the hell was that country of a billion souls plotting? Who knew? No-one, really. But it was generally agreed that their secret weapon was to get every last one of their billion to simultaneously jump in the air which would cause the world to shift on its axis due to the weight transfer and take us all to hell. The 60s were rapidly turning from a time of free love and liberation into a period of unadulterated fear. It was a decade of total contrasts: barriers in technology, music, art and culture were being torn down while, at the same time, politics and international relationships were heading back to the dark ages.

Light and dark vied for supremacy. Good and evil were never before cast in so stark a contrast and never before was the battle so keenly marked. John F Kennedy, probably the most charismatic and empathetic of all world leaders at the time, was elected. At the same time, the Russians were dividing Berlin with a monstrous wall. The first man ever to escape earth's gravitational pull orbited the earth in 1961 while people were being killed for the crime of wishing to travel from one part of Berlin to another. Silent Spring: Rachel Carson's warning of the impact of pesticides in the future was published and the green movement put down its first recognisable roots.

I remember my mum waking me the morning after the US Presidential elections which brought Kennedy to power to tell me, to my utter relief, that Senator Barry Goldwater, a Republican presidential candidate who had made blood-chilling speeches about what he was going to do with respect to the Cold War between East and West if elected, had been defeated: it was that important.

The Cuban missile crisis in 1962 was an incident which brought the world within hours of a nuclear exchange: to say that the world held its breath on that morning is not an overstatement. As Soviet ships ploughed towards Cuba where they planned to install missiles pointed at the US, Kennedy deployed naval vessels with the intention of turning them back. In a test of mettle between Kruschev and Kennedy, played out from July to October 1962, the United States was put on 'defence alert condition 2' (DEFCON2) and was prepared to force the removal of missiles from Cuban territory. The Soviet ships were finally diverted by Kruschev after he had secured an agreement that the US would not invade Cuba, but only after various compromises had been explored and rejected, the most notable being that the US should remove its missiles from Turkey if the Soviets removed their missiles from Cuba. The entire event summed up the 60s – knife-edge diplomacy, high drama, high adrenalin and momentous incidences which would shape the next 100 years.

The day after my seventeenth birthday on November the 22nd, 1963, the most shocking event of the 60s took place when President Kennedy was assassinated in Dallas, Texas. Those few frames of film which show the third bullet ripping off his scalp as his wife turns towards him are probably the most chilling and arresting anyone will ever witness. For impressionable kids of a certain tender age, it seemed that the world had gone mad. As the US attempted to 'halt the spread of communism' in Vietnam, the superpowers shaped up to one another on a regular basis and we lived on the precipice of the unknown.

It seems perverse to recall, after living through such nightmarish times, that the 60s were not all bad, but in truth, and possibly driven by the 'what-the-hell' attitude foisted upon us by the mad political leaders of the day, life beyond thoughts of the frying pan was, to most, pure joy. It was the time of Harold Wilson, the 'you've-never-had-it-so-good' days of MacMillan and the good times of the 60s – assuming you could ignore the Cuban missile crisis, the fact that a megalomaniac was running for Presidency in the US and that we were still testing nuclear weapons all over the world, some still being detonated, believe it or not, in the atmosphere.

Music was becoming more and more important to me and my peers. After the wild 'rocking' beginnings of new musical experiments, music became more considered, more cerebral and, underpinned by the growing use of drugs and a growing anti-war sentiment, deeper and more engaging. Crosby, Stills, Nash and Young were, perhaps, favourites with us teenagers and Simon and Garfunkel's early albums encouraged me to write and made me feel that my increasing teenage angst was not evidence of the onset of madness. But while music moved me to emotional extremes, even in those early days of stirring awareness about the world, it was much later that music really gripped me to a point where I doubt if I could do without it today.

My GCE 'O' Level results were good. I attained six passes and failed one – geography. Billy Evans and I found the French exam so easy that we'd finished within half the allotted time and through sign language indicated that we'd go and share a fag in the bogs. We were not allowed to go together so Billy returned after his allotted five minutes and palmed the remains of a Player's Weight on my desk as he passed. The stench of a half-smoked cigarette filled the examination room and wafted after me as I headed for the bogs with it tucked into my top pocket.

So here I was, 16 years old and determined to leave school. Brian had already left home, and I looked at life from the vantage point of a flat in a housing estate in Deptford. We had no money, I had few prospects and was determined that, given these circumstances and the fact that all my friends from the estate and the area in which I operated, bar two, were now in paid work, I would forego further education and A-levels and get myself out to work. Stuffed into my back pocket was the sum total of my careers advice session – a sheet of paper which contained the addresses of ten print firms in London, most of which had long ceased trading.

The transition from school to work is a massive leap for anyone: I saw my life as probably being truncated by an exchange of intercontinental ballistic missiles and presumed the steps I took between that point and the inevitability of mass incineration would be rather academic. I therefore adopted an entirely ambivalent attitude to work and where I might be taken by the world of semi-adulthood. If real adults could not do better than to threaten to mutually assure each other's destruction, what I did with my life seemed to be of little consequence. Despite the upsides to all of these goings-on, I fell deeper and deeper into depression, finding solace in writing. I wrote some very depressing poems around this time, but then I assumed every other 16 year-old was doing the same.

I saw an advertisement for a salesperson at a department store – Chiesman's in Lewisham. On the grounds that it was close by, I applied and got the job. I wandered through the job with as little application or enthusiasm as I could muster. I had no appetite at all for selling soft furnishings to couples who, I was convinced, would live to see them disappear in a flash of atom-splitting fire and doom within a year or two. I became obsessed with the political situation and resigned to my fate. I became even more introverted and reclusive, retiring to my room as soon as I could and remaining there, writing and generally emoting for hours on end.

Chapter 5

Work life and love life

At Chiesman's, I struck up a friendship with a senior salesman called Ernie Whittington. Ernie was a delight to work with, happy to help and advise, but always ready to horse around and always on for a pint or two. We lived quite close to each other and he would tempt me from my lair where I wrote tortured poetry about our imminent immolation, for a pint once in a while. We would drink at the Globe, just across the way from the Trinity estate. He was a very nice guy and I owe him my sanity during that year or two which saw me write endless depressing poems and polemics and which, in many ways, set me on the path for my NGO future.

Despite the fact that I came to enjoy the job at Chiesemans, having my own customers who would insist on being served by me and with the management lining me up for better things, I had to move away from the 'Are you being served?' rigidity of the department store life and find an environment in which I could start to live a little closer to the edge. A friend called Keith Hunt had recently secured a position working as a despatch scooter rider for Greatwood Printing on Deptford Bridge and was earning £15 a week – a small fortune in the 60s, especially for humble kids from Deptford. What was more, they had a second scooter driver's job available.

I leapt at it and within a week I was roaring around on a brand new Li 150, all over the West End, delivering jobs for Harry Greatwood, a huge, chain-smoking bear of a man whose reputation of being a hard task master went before him.

Typical of the Victorian attitudes which pervaded the printing business at the time, his skilled workforce and apprentices lived in mortal fear of the man, yet the despatch drivers enjoyed a first name relationship with him. He apparently saw us as separate from the 'trade' as such, and felt as though he could banter with us openly whereas his relationship with his tradespeople was strictly one of master/servant.

Harry and I bantered and ribbed each other, despite the fact that he had an air of superiority about him. He treated me well and was always fairly; I did a good job for him, working late when required and being flexible.

After a few months, he asked me what I wanted to do in the longer term, assuming, rightly, that I didn't want to be a scooter driver forever. I told him that some of my mates had joined the print as apprentices and indeed I had been 'advised' in this direction at school.

He looked me up and down. 'You're too old at 17, but I'll see what I can do.'

A month later, he called me into his office and handed me some paperwork. 'These are your indentures', he said. 'You're an apprentice printer. Congratulations. On Monday, you report to me and I'll explain how our relationship will change. You'll be on £3.10 shillings a week.'

Harry had really pushed the boat out for me. I was an apprentice printer. If I knuckled under and buttoned my lip for six years, I could emerge as a well-paid professional at the top of my trade. But within minutes of me being handed the paperwork, the banter stopped. Harry was now 'Mr. Greatwood'. I had sunk from being the lairy scooter driver to the lowest of the low in the hierarchy of the print world, and I was told regularly that I should be grateful for all that I had. I was sent out to buy the snacks: three soup sandwiches, one soup in a basket and a couple of sky hooks while I was at it.

Harry ruled with a stern and strict regime of hard work and, when time allowed, hard play. He would keep us working until late, particularly on Fridays when we were all anxious to get home and start the weekend. Occasionally, he would loosen up just a fraction which meant that people would actually dare crack a mild joke in his presence. As Friday afternoon wore on, we would start looking out for the 'wobbly head' which Harry would give as he walked through the shop. We would all furtively glance at him as he walked through the room. If he held his head still, it meant that we were to continue working. On the fourth pass, he would, if we were lucky, tilt his head back, half-close his eyes and give an imperceptible nod of his head. The 'wobbly head' meant we could leave. I didn't know how long I could suffer this sort of deference and the next six years stretched away into what seemed like an eternity.

I arrived back at work after the New Year break and walked into the building, squeezing past Harry in the narrow passageway.

'Wilkinson!' he called.

'Yes, Mr Greatwood?'

'It's the second of January, What are you going to wish me?'

'Good morning.'

'Anything else?'

'No, just good morning.'

'You ungrateful little bastard! It's January the second, so don't you think you should wish me a Happy New Year?

I unloaded months of pent-up bile on Harry and walked out. Three jobs down after my first year out of school . . .

Out of work, not for the first or last time in my life, I signed on the dole and drifted around Deptford, hanging out with various friends in the same predicament. I tried all manner of office jobs but could settle to none. After trying my hand at labouring and driving, I ended up working at Greenwich Town Hall as a cost clerk. My boss was a man named Basham and I worked with him and his junior in a rabbit warren of an office in which every move, cough or tap of the pencil caused Mr Basham to look at me over his spectacles in an inquiring and authoritative manner. Every day passed painfully slowly and I realised that while I had landed what my parents classed as a 'good job', one from which I would never be fired and which could, theoretically, lead to great things within local government, my academic qualifications were only useful in qualifying me for office work which I found tedious and untenable. There had to be more to life than this.

A thought struck me like a bolt of lightning – the forces! After all, had that not been in my mind when I joined the ATC and thrilled at the prospect of a flying career? The RAF! Yes, why didn't I join up? I had the qualifications for aircrew. My Uncle Bob flew Spitfires in the war. It would be adventurous and it would surely satisfy my gathering wanderlust, dissatisfaction and ennui. I determined there and then that I would, sooner or later, join the forces. But in the meantime, there was the small matter of women to deal with and an integral part of meeting women was the machine you drove around on. I had to smarten up my old Lambretta.

I took my scooter to Eddie Grinstead's in Leyton and asked for a quote for the 'customisation' of my machine. For £27 – a small fortune in the 60s – I could have chromed side panels, double horn-casting, front and back carriers, a spare wheel mounted inside the aprons, twin-barrelled exhaust and a dark-blue paint re-spray. How I paid for it, I can't recall, but I suspect my father was dragooned into underwriting my extravagant tastes. But the result was sensational and caught the eye of all the right people in Deptford – mostly female as far as I was concerned.

Naturally, we wore no crash helmets, only cheese-cutter hats, the stitches in the peak of which we unpicked to allow the hat to resemble the headgear which was all the rage in Soho at the time – the doughboy. These gave no protection whatsoever, of course, but did allow a forward-facing surface on which to inscribe – normally in brass paper studs – the identity of your bike, Li 150.

I proudly took my blue and chrome pride and joy to the Thursday night dance at Greenwich Town Hall, (after securing the chrome panels which were highly sought after and which would not be on the bike for long without security precautions), and chatted with the other Li owners as we anticipated the best part of the evening. This was to take the bend at the start of Creek Road (around the corner from which a line of girls would be waiting for the 188 bus) in such a way as to 'deck' the silencer, sending out a shower of sparks as we dropped down a gear and let the throaty roar of the silencer add to the spectacle.

Occasionally, when we'd had a bottle of light ale too many, we'd whip out a spanner or two and remove the entire silencer. We'd potter down to the bend at the start of Creek Road in a low gear and then, just as we rounded the bend, open up the throttle at which the engine would suddenly fire into life, blatting out its un-silenced explosions to frighten the hell out of every one around.

Greenwich Town Hall bops were the highlight of the week for us and many bands which came to be well-known a few years later played there. Cathy McGowan, the Tops of the Pops 'dance spotter', would occasionally descend to our humble dance venue to pick out those who could actually gyrate in a passably co-ordinated way and invite them to the BBC studios to be part of the audience for this increasingly popular programme. Geoff Lee and Chris Samuels were thus 'spotted' one week and I remember the fact that they were 'on telly' (only very briefly captured by the roving BBC cameras) was the talk of the estate for a while.

The divisions between Deptford and Bermondsey boys became, inevitably, the spark which turned Thursday nights from what started as just rough and tumbles into quite violent fights involving chains and knuckle-dusters. But before the mayhem, when we were calm and collected, before the music and the dancing, girls crowded round our gleaming bikes outside the town hall and we tried to look as cool as possible and aloof to the attentions of the women. The best of the women appeared unimpressed by our primping and preening and walked by without so much as a glance – all except one, a dark-haired cracker called Geraldine Daley, who glanced my way with the hint of a smile.

I was 17, it was 1964, the Beatles were at number one and we regularly went to the coast on wild weekend trips which invariably ended in disturbances of varying degrees. But for me, all that 60s excitement paled into insignificance at the sight of Geraldine. I was smitten and realised in the blink of an eye what infatuation was: painful, unbearable, exhilarating and totally, totally wonderful.

There was a major hurdle separating me and Geraldine, in the shape of Chrissy Samuels, Geoff Lee's cousin, who was courting her. One night, after returning from the Greenwich Town Hall bop, I drove my scooter slowly and quietly down Geraldine's street. As I turned into the street, I could see a figure walking away from Geraldine's flats at the other end, perhaps 300 yards away. I had to take a gamble. I waited for this figure, who I assumed was Chris, to turn the corner and then drove towards Geraldine's flats. Sweating, and unsure of what reception I would get, I lifted the knocker on her door and let it fall. She opened the door and her eyes widened slightly to see me there.

'Hello, Geraldine. I thought Chris might still be here and I was gonna offer him a lift home,' I lied.

'He left a few minutes ago,' she said with the merest hint of a smile. 'Do you want a cup of tea?'

Do I want a cup of tea?!?! I want to take you in my arms and crush your delicious mouth against mine, that's what I want, I thought.

'I'd love one. Thanks.'

Geraldine and I sat on her doorstep until the early hours of the morning, talking, courting and getting closer and closer. I stood up to leave and held out my arms to her. She fell against me and we kissed a kiss of ecstasy. I literally swooned. I couldn't leave her. When her father came in and broke it up, we agreed that I'd wait for a while and then go to her bedroom window to extend this moment until the morning, until Wednesday next week, forever. I rode my scooter home amongst the clouds.

I saw her every day. I wanted to be with her every minute. I had never believed that I could experience such emotions. I calmly told Chris that Geraldine was my girl now – sorry, mate. We were soon engaged and our families came together in a huge celebration. We set a wedding date for 'a couple of years' time'.

Meanwhile, my mates could not believe the transformation in me. I was not interested in going to the pub, going to watch Millwall ('dahn the Den', as it was referred to), or even playing football. They waved at us from their scooters on a Saturday afternoon as they headed off for the coast while Geraldine and I walked arm in arm down the High Street, window shopping. ("E's only looking at furniture,' Geoff was later reported to have commented with incredulity).

I was just eaten up with this woman and all else paled into obscurity – for a while. After a few months, I thought I should really go off with my mates, at least once in a while. After all, I was missing out on the all the 60s fun. Grudgingly, Geraldine concurred, and late one Friday night we all met at Dorking Road, waiting for 'the word'. 'Hayling Island' came the call and at a little after midnight, 40 scooters left Deptford, four abreast, ignoring traffic lights, and swept out of London.

I was a somewhat reluctant rebel, it must be said. That first ride to Hayling Island marked me out as such, since, much to the amusement of my peers, I was inclined to stop at red traffic lights. That was pretty uncool. Falling in with the crowd, however, I broke the law like everyone else although I did it with bad grace. I felt as though I was running with the pack of 60s rebelliousness while in truth we were just a bunch of kids growing up. At the time, it felt far more important than anything I'd ever done before. I was breaking my own moral code as well as the law and I was determined I would not buckle, but no matter how hard I tried, I don't think I ever convinced my mates – nor myself –that I'd actually fully embraced the 60s ethic.

But I was determined to enjoy myself and as we whined our way down through the Kent countryside, characters like Franny Evans and Peter Jarvis – well known as scooter 'kings', and guys who brooked no nonsense – would overtake us at speeds which I found astonishing for 175cc machines, despite the fact that they had 'bored-out barrels' (whatever that meant) and 'skimmed heads' (ditto).

This was the age of the Who, Small Faces and the Stones, of what I considered as pathetic excuses for bands like Peter Noon and the Seekers, and of the mods and rockers riots on Brighton beach front, none of which we – that's me and my immediate groups of friends – were directly involved in. But it was exciting and adrenalin-pumping stuff, especially if you had a few pills inside you.

My first of only a few experiences with pills, (dope was another matter entirely), came in Brighton, years later when we had graduated from scooters to cars. There we sat, six guys squashed tightly into my 'sit-up-and beg' Ford Poplar, each with five purple hearts in hand and a bottle of light ale between us.

After a few false starts, we did it: pills in mouth, a swig of the beer from a decidedly saliva-rich bottle top, and sit back and wait. And in my case, wait and wait and wait. It must have been hours later, well after my friends had left this particular planet that the impact of the pills kicked in for me. The Who were playing My Generation and all around was a sea of bodies writhing to the music in various states of ecstasy. Suddenly I was with them, high on the pills, on youth, on the music and on the beauty of life; suddenly I couldn't stop talking, to anyone about anything. I smiled and laughed as I danced the dance of the entirely uninhibited – everyone was my friend and I could even sort out potential fights, which was what most people who had popped a few pills were doing as tensions broke out in the dance hall. What a night it turned out to be. Indeed.

Later, as we wandered down Brighton sea front among other groups of people from all over the country, the mood was happy-go-lucky and amiable. The effects of the pills had not entirely worn off and bonhomie was still evident. As a group of guys came towards us, we mingled and talked. They were a bit more 'tight' than us, a bit more aggressive and loud, after all, my lot were mostly comprised of embryonic lawyers, stock-brokers and professionals. In the melee, someone shouted out, 'Does anyone want to buy a starter?'

He was referring to a starting pistol, much sought after in those days by the more dangerous elements of youth culture as a relatively inoffensive weapon. As it happened, the starter motor on my old Ford Poplar was on the blink and I thought that I had had the great good fortune to find, in this unlikely place and at this unlikely time of the night, someone who just happened to have a starter motor for sale. I asked the obvious question, 'Does it fit a Ford Poplar?'

I stunned the crowd into momentary silence before there was an eruption of laughter at my naivety or what I hoped some thought was my innate and spontaneous humour. My mates knew it was the former but I think I got away with it as far as the strangers went.

How we survived those days relatively intact is a miracle, and the juxtaposition of my wild-man incarnations at the weekend with my straight-as-a-die weekday persona was stark. During the week, I would barely say a word to anyone as I sat in my office with Mr Basham and one other older guy, in virtual silence, processing bits of paper and surreptitiously glancing at the clock with astonishment and deflation since the hands seemed never to actually move across the face.

At weekends, although with some trepidation, I would be transformed into a weak and rather pathetic version of a wild thing, running with the crowd and 'enjoying' the 60s as we were told we should be doing. We saw live performances of bands which are now icons of the 60s; we popped a few pills, drank a lot of beer and smoked cigarettes. But my heart was never really in it. Truth to tell, I would rather have been at home watching football. But despite being a somewhat reluctant rebel, I was swept up with the vibe of the time and had some memorable moments, although most of my memories revolve around the unlikely liaisons with women – during the periods that Geraldine and I were temporary parted – that had my heart soaring at the drop of a hat. I was – perhaps I remain to this day – an incurable romantic, and I would have a brief encounter with a woman and swear that I was in love with her and that unless we married within days, we would both end up as tragic, broken figures, forever ruing the missed chance of eternal happiness. There were many such brief encounters which spawned affairs, some of which lasted weeks, some months but never years.

One other trip we made sticks in my mind. As we sped towards Brighton, we found an early morning cafe and poured into the parking area. The first person inside shouted to the proprietor, 'Forty teas, and forty crocodile sandwiches please mate. And make it snappy!' We cleaned the place out, leaving shelves and display cases looking as though a plague of locusts had passed through. We pulled into petrol stations to fill up our machines and, it has to be said, some of our number left without paying.

I faced Geraldine after two years of such a double life and suggested that we finally part for good. She was distraught and I faced the demands of reconciling the two sides of my character: one, the home-loving, deeply caring and regular guy who needed the security of a loving relationship, the warmth of family and the steadiness of life at a pace I could deal with. The other, the eternal rebel who craved excitement, mocked and vilified 'normality' and sought fresh challenges, a different horizon and going against the grain of acceptability. It was time I stepped out of this life of contrasts and uncertainty and into another which would offer even greater uncertainty and contrast. I finally decided it was time to join the RAF.

Joining the RAF, I felt, would force upon me some discipline and would, moreover, have the great advantage of taking decision-making out of my hands. I absented myself from my mind-numbing job at the town hall and went to Biggin Hill for the officer's selection course. I had to pack pyjamas – something I never wore – and as I went to don these cumbersome articles on the first night of my stay, I found a letter Geraldine had written to me tucked into the top pocket of the jacket. It was such a beautiful letter, full of hope, praise and understanding that I cried myself to sleep, wishing I could be home, safe in her arms and for that instant, that's all I wanted to do. The old needs of security and love washed over me like a tidal wave and I cursed whatever it was – or is –that prompted my misgivings about the course of action I had chosen.

I awoke in the austere environment of a working RAF airfield. The second world war had only been over for a mere twenty years or so, and the atmosphere of post-war Britain was alive and well, somewhere on this airfield, and I intended to sniff it up to the max. I steeled myself for the trials and tribulations ahead. The selection course, outlined by the induction officer, promised to be arduous but exhilarating, but the first test was to pass the chest x-ray. One guy from an intake of 60 was immediately hoicked out and sent home, poor bastard, when they found a shadow on his lung.

Should you fail a particular section of the selection course there was no second chance: you were out and on the way home that very day. On the morning of the sixth and final day, I was still there, in a group of kids which had been winnowed from 60 to 10. I stood a chance here. I might well be accepted to join the RAF, I thought. Then what, clever Dick? Is this really what you want?

Then I was found to be partially colour-blind, and the fatalism which I relied on swam into view: another event beyond my control dictating my fate. But I was told that my colour-blindness did not prevent me continuing with the course: I seemed to be excelling in other directions. Doubt and uncertainty swamped me again. Christ! I was going to pass the test and join the RAF. Did I really want to? Sure I did. But maybe I didn't. As it turned out, despite being the only applicant who passed an initiative test within the allotted time, I knew I was not going to be accepted when I emerged from the final and quite brutal interview with three officers.

The letter of rejection came two weeks later. 'The ministry regrets to inform you that you have not been selected to receive a commission as aircrew or ground crew. We are not at liberty to explain the reasons for your unsuccessful application but you are invited to apply again in two years.' I was disappointed but not mortified. It was another decision which had been forced on me and for which I could therefore shed responsibility. I had tried and I had failed, so what followed was not of my doing. A school friend of mine, Terry Bushnell, had been accepted into the RAF a year before I applied. His first task was to attend elocution lessons. He died in a Harrier in which he was about to take off when it exploded on the runway.

I returned to the claustrophobia of the Town Hall with great reluctance. I was carpeted, believe it or not, for having applied for the RAF commission without the permission of the Town Clerk, into whose hands it appeared I had committed my life when I joined local government employ. To my great relief, I was transferred away from the claustrophobia of the tiny office in Greenwich to the wages department within the council. I was therefore relocated to Woolwich, into a much airier and more convivial office where people were quite jocular by comparison. My engagement to Geraldine had irretrievably broken down and I was footloose and fancy free. I still lived at home with my long-suffering parents and decided to throw caution to the wind and get out of stuffy local government for more lucrative pursuits. Lorry driving seemed to be the most easily available job and I had heard that lorry drivers earned good money. Of course, all that was baloney. I earned more than at the Town Hall, for sure, but the hours I put in and the graft I undertook were in a different league.

Before I embarked on a driving 'career', I had one last throw at a job which would give me, at face value, prospects for promotion, a future and a real career. My father told me that his firm, United Glass, was looking for a new breed of professionals peculiar to that time: time and motion personnel. Snoopers, in other words, committed to increasing productivity by getting more from a worker at less cost to the management. He had mentioned me to his boss who was keen to meet me since my 6 'O' level passes at school qualified me for the job. I arrived at Dad's firm one Friday afternoon for the interview, suited and booted accordingly.

I was taken on a tour of the factory by my Dad's boss, an affable and avuncular man in his 50's. What he showed me was my dad's normal working environment. To me, it was a vision of hell itself. The 'shop' in which my dad worked, was full of lathes and turning machines from one end of its 80 foot length to the other; these sculpted metal into the shape of moulds for bottles. The noise was deafening. Worse, the air was full of iron filings: a shaft of sunlight falling through the window illuminated a column of particle-filled air which the guys breathed for eight hours a day. My tour guide shouted a conversation with me over the deafening noise of the machinery. I tried not to think of my dad having to endure this hell every day.

When we had retired, finally and thankfully, to the sanctuary of his office, the manager turned to me with a smile and asked me what I thought of the opportunity he was offering me. 'Well, that's it, Peter. What do you think?'

I composed myself. I had to choose my words carefully. 'Thanks for letting me see my dad's shop which I understand is where I'd be spending much of my time, should I be offered the job. But quite frankly, I wouldn't work in there for a thousand pounds a week. What's more, I think it's a disgrace that in this day and age you subject your workforce to that sort of environment.'

After withdrawing my application, I walked away from the firm, close to tears. I had had no idea that my father was working in such a place and I wished I could do something about it and give him the dignity he deserved. Digging ditches is more honest labour than what my father put up with.

One of the first lorry driving jobs I took was with Atlas Express, the massive parcel delivery service, then based in Rotherhithe. I drove a long-wheel-base, seven ton Ford on what was known as the West End bulk run. It entailed loading your own lorry in the morning with a maximum of seven tons of gear destined for West End department stores and shops, delivering the same – mostly offloading it single-handedly as well – then in the afternoon, if you had managed to finish the delivery round, collecting parcels destined for other locations from various shops, factories and the like around town, and then offloading that little lot back at the base. So, on a bad day we were expected to handle several tons of material a day.

To help the process while at the Rotherhithe base, an army of 'bank staff' were employed to sort the parcels coming in from the 'trunkers' from all over the country, destined for London; to prepare and help stack the loads and help with the unloading from the lorries returning in the afternoon with their collected loads. The 'bankers' were paid according to the number of parcels they handled. Thus, on returning to the depot in the afternoon, a driver was regaled with all manner of shouts, bribes and threats, imploring him to unload at particular banks.

We worked hard. The West End department stores to which I delivered were relatively hassle-free as they had loading bays and were well equipped, but a good proportion of the 'drops' were at small firms in the back alleys of London's labyrinthine layout, often to 'rag trade' outfits around Gower Street. These were not easy. I recall delivering 100 rolls of material to a shop which was situated three flights up, in what can only be described as a sweatshop. I was prone to insisting that the recipient of the goods provided some assistance to me, especially if I was required to drag 100 rolls of material up three flights of stairs. Remarkably, some customers refused this request and would happily see me struggle for hours to deliver their goods without lifting a finger or providing one person to help. These miserabilists usually got short-shrift from me and it was not uncommon for me to return to the depot with 'undeliverable loads'.

Some goods, especially cashmere jumpers for some reason, often destined for the big West End department stores, would mysteriously go missing.

As objectionable as it may seem to us today, thieving – for that is what it was – was tolerated to a far higher degree in those days. I'm not saying it was any more acceptable then, but blind eyes were more readily turned and a level of loss was expected. At every job I took, I was taken aside and told 'the ropes'. It wasn't necessarily advice on what level of thieving was tolerated by the management (although that did happen on one or two occasions), but more about how the management and the workforce interacted and what was the accepted 'norm' of behaviour.

For instance, I worked for a brief period for a company in Slough which hired drivers and vans to the BBC (I once had a Dalek in the back of my van – seriously – much to the envy of my cab-driving father-in-law!) The BBC had a contract with the drivers it employed which guaranteed a maximum speed at which the lorries would be driven, stop-over rates for driving after 5pm and other fringe 'agreements'. A new driver doing a London/Liverpool run in one day (as I did on the first day) was not appreciated by drivers who had negotiated hard and long to gain their perks which allowed them to drive at twice the minimum allowable speed for half the time and then take time off.

The acceptability of pilfering appeared to be the case at the fisheries company I moved to after Atlas Express. We delivered fancy seafood to even fancier West End restaurants. (One thing we had to deliver – something I can barely recall today without shivering in disgust – was live, skinned eels). Usually, we had to begin the day with a dawn trip to Billingsgate market to collect boxes of fish which were needed to complete last minute orders from customers. Even here there were perks: a box on the side into which fish for the drivers would be placed for divvying up later.

I enjoyed the work. Despite the fact that I had driven lorries in and around the West End for some time with Atlas Express, my knowledge of London was still patchy. Associated Fisheries changed all that but I had to learn the geography of London the hard way. The first day at work, after having told the boss that I knew London 'backwards', I took charge of a van loaded with fish, lobsters, prawns and scampi. As I sat in the driving seat, engine running waiting to go, the boss handed me 40 delivery dockets.

'No problem, guv!' I said, false bravado hiding my anxiety at the prospect of finding all these outlets.

I arrived back at the depot at 6pm that evening. I had worked a 12 hour day and somehow managed to find all forty 'drops'. The exercise increased my knowledge of London hugely. Within a week, I really did know London like the back of my hand and it's a familiarity I have never lost.

Delivering wet fish for a living had many disadvantages, but the most objectionable was also the most overpowering – the smell. How my parents tolerated it is beyond me. Here was this bright lad of theirs, with 6 GCE 'O' levels, driving a wet fish van around London for a living and coming home smelling to high heaven. Dad would set his alarm at ungodly hours to ensure I was up at the right time for the unspeakably early starts we were required to make, and I recall his 4am knocks on my door and a toothless, 'Come on, boy. It's time to get going. Here's a cup of tea.' God love him.

On Fridays, when it was time for the weekend to begin and for beer to be drunk with friends and girls to be flattered, I would make extraordinary efforts to rid myself of the smell of stale fish juice. I'd bathe and then shower and then bathe again before covering myself in aftershave, talcum powder and whatever else I could find in the bathroom. The first thing mates would say to me when I met them as the evening began was, 'Christ, Wilkie. You stink of fish!'

On and on the lorry driving jobs went, from one outfit to the next – Air Filter Supply in the East End (all the loads were lightweight which was a decided bonus), British Road Services at the Elephant and Castle, a cowboy outfit in Slough. The latter sent me to Leeds in a three tonne low loader to collect an aeroplane engine from a factory. As it was loaded, the suspension on the lorry sank almost to breaking point and I phoned the company to advise them that I was being required to drive an unsafe load. The boss laughed off my concerns and asked me to get it down to Heathrow as soon as I could. Oh, and by the way, he said, he had a customer he was courting for work and would I go to his address just outside Leeds to pick up a letter and drop it off at the addressee's London location?

It was late afternoon. I had an unsafe load to deliver 250 miles south and he wanted me to act as a postman to a potential client. Irritated, I suggested that his potential customer put a stamp on the letter and stuck it in the post. He made it clear that he expected me to play postman with no ifs or buts. I drove straight back to London. So unsafe was the load that the lorry slewed from side to side the moment my speed went above 40 miles per hour. A hitch-hiker I picked up asked if he could get out after three minutes, that's how bad it was.

I delivered the engine and reported for work the next day. I told the boss that I hadn't collected the letter from his client as it was beyond the call of duty and irresponsible of him to expect that of me. He exploded in a rage and fired me on the spot. I told him I was going to sue him for unfair dismissal. He calmed down at that and said that I could keep my job. I told him to stick it where the sun don't shine.

Chapter 6

Spread your wings

I was now 20 years old. It was 1966. I felt a burning need to experience life beyond the cloying atmosphere of south London. The Ford Poplar in which we had first experienced purple hearts in Brighton years before, had died a death. The compression rings had long since burned out but I still drove it. I fitted a 'breather pipe' which was designed to direct the thick smoke from the burning oil outside the cab so as to allow me to drive without choking. The pipe fell off as I drove one Christmas to Aunt Lil's for the traditional party. As I turned into Mayall Road, someone was looking out of Lil's window.

'There a car on fire at the end of the road. It's still moving. Blimey, I think it's Peter's car!'

It was indeed, and it drove at a maximum of 20 mph due to the lack of compression and looked as though it was on fire. It's not surprising, then, how my head was so easily turned by Mark 1 Ford Zephyr Zodiacs which were the limousines of their day for the working class. I bought one because I liked the colour – mustard – and because it was cheap, being left-hand drive. Naturally, I put a go-faster stripe down the side of it but, typically, I ran out of enthusiasm with the job only half done so couldn't be bothered with painting a strip on the off-side. I did have the patience to white-wall the tyres, however: that was de rigueur. It was a mighty beast of a car with a bench seat at the front and column gear change.

I would have gone to the ends of the earth to find the Ford Zephyr Mk1 I desired – a convertible – and when I saw one advertised in the Exchange and Mart, I forsook everything – the pub, a Saturday night out, Millwall – to get it. I travelled to Hemel Hempstead on my long-suffering Dad's Lambretta Li 150 to buy a pea-green convertible with money I borrowed (about £100, but did repay) from my impoverished father. It had an automatic hood and, unbelievably for its day, a working, integral radio. Despite my age, I still had the appearance of a 15 year old and I was constantly being pulled by the police. I suppose, looking at it from their perspective, it was odd to see a young boy barely able to see over the steering wheel, driving any sort of car, let alone a pea-green convertible Ford Zephyr.

Our days were spent working and on at least three nights a week, we would meet in pubs around Deptford and Greenwich for a few pints and a laugh with friends which often found John Morton, Don Gardner and I bitterly divided on the topics of the day and arguing until the small hours as we wandered home. But our greatest pleasure was found in football – playing it and watching it. We would meet at a pre-arranged location, maybe ten or fifteen of us, two 'tribes' united by common friends and contacts. John and Don, my ever-closer 'soulmates', 'Bootsy' Mann, Alan 'Awabi' Wescott, Geoff Lee, Kenny Halloway, Bobby Baker, Denny Dabin, , Billy Stevenson, Chrissy Samuels, Danny Catchesides were among them. Sometimes we lived and played in an atmosphere of uneasy alliance. There are undercurrents of aggression among testosterone-fuelled young men of any grouping and we were no different. When we'd horse around, Bill Stevenson would noticeably be more truculent and vindictive in his 'play' than others and he confided to me that his older brother had told him that, when 'playing' with your mates, make sure you hurt them just enough to let them know who is boss. Bill took the lesson to heart.

These were heady days. It seemed we genuinely didn't know what was going to happen from one day to the next: jobs were two a penny, music was evolving rapidly and psychedelia was everywhere, reflecting the increasing influence of drugs. The birth control pill was now an everyday part of life, removing the embarrassment of using condoms and further liberating the young from the angst of unwanted pregnancies (as long as the women were prepared to do the pill-popping of course). The Vietnam War dragged on and on, fuelling more and more vocal and belligerent opposition to the domination of a peasant community by a superpower in the name of political ideology and the desire to halt what the USA saw as the spread of communism. The Mi-Li massacre was the final straw, and barely-palatable pictures emerging of the unending suffering of a people who didn't care whether their country was ruled by men from Mars, capitalists, Maoists or Trotskyists tore at everyone's heartstrings.

I began to read those books which would perhaps fan the flames of my emerging, left-leaning political opinions. I read Kafka and Orwell, Huxley and Zola. I was always outspoken, but now I had something to be outspoken about. My emerging politicisation (today, it would be called radicalisation) was largely thanks to American foreign policy and was enhanced by the realisation that politics was a vast and as-yet unknown sphere of life which I had was hitherto left largely unexplored. I became an ill-informed but well-meaning liberal leftie and I used every opportunity to voice my new-found passion.

Apart from the political and social upheaval of the 60s and 70s, our individual lives were in a constant state of flux – a result of our age and the new freedoms we were all experiencing. Just one generation on from that of our parents were new-found attitudes and indulgences at which our grandparents shuddered. I could very easily have fallen in with the wrong crowd during this period and ended up on the wrong side of the law. Any one of us could have done the same. Some, sadly, did go down that route and on more than one occasion, I recall using the phrase, there but for the grace of God go I.

It was 1969 and time, at 23, to visit Europe, a place for which my appetite had been whetted by a series of TV programmes which followed the lives of two French teenagers and I dreamed of experiencing the sort of carefree and 'foreign' life they apparently lived.

Sitting around in my parents' flat one Saturday afternoon my old mate John Morton said, 'Fancy going abroad, Wilk?'

'OK,' I replied, 'Where?'

'Anywhere. Let's get to France and then go south. See where we end up.'

With no more planning than that, John and I piled a sleeping bag each on the back of a £40 scooter bought for the occasion, cadged £30 each from friends and family and found ourselves three hours later in Dover, queuing to board the ferry. We had no tent, no wet weather gear and, normal for those days, no crash helmets. We had the clothes we stood up in, passports and sleeping bags.

It was dark by the time we reached Calais and it was only then that we discovered the scooter headlight produced only a dim arc of light, no better than that from a few candle stubs. As we drove out of the port, I took a short cut and drove straight into a railway sleeper which pitched us and the bike onto a gravel path. We limped out of the port and headed for anywhere out of town. It was midnight by the time we found a suitable 'kipper down', as John called it – somewhere convenient to sleep. Having no tent, we simply searched out a suitable field or hedge and climbed into our thin sleeping bags.

I was woken that night by a sight I had never before seen – the Milky Way. It was so bright that when my eyes succumbed to the nagging light penetrating my eyelids, I gasped. I was totally entranced. City boys don't get to see such sights.

John Morton recalls the trip we made: 'On that first trip, we made it to Paris (quick shuffty at the Tour Eiffel, which was shrouded in low cloud, and then we legged it, pronto and unimpressed). Then down through the Loire Valley area, right the way down to Toulouse (or thereabouts – I remember eating in a village on the way and getting my first experience of a basic French pissoir – a painted black wall in the garden). Then we crossed the Pyrenees somewhere (not too high an area I think, but I do remember having to pay a toll of 8 pesetas – you might recall the intercultural difficulties there, when the guy at the barrier finally got our accents: 'Si, oight pesetas!').

Then down the Costa Blanca to Barcelona, (about which I remember nothing except juddering along cobbled streets). A quick u-turn across the border and up the Rhone Valley, up through Lyon and onwards to the German border somewhere round Mulhouse/Strasbourg way. Then we headed down the Rhine Valley, staying for a night with the Sieg family in Neuss-am-Rhein. (I especially remember being impressed with Germany's industrial might on the Ruhr – much more impressive than all that countryside! The Siegs, by the way, were the family with whom I stayed when I was 16 or so, on a school trip.) Then what? We cut across to go through Belgium and across to Ostend, where we caught the ferry back to Harwich.'

The following year, we did it all again, this time a little better prepared, but still using a decidedly ancient scooter and very little in the way of equipment.

We lived on peanuts and chocolate. We washed in public toilets. We slept in our clothes, in sleeping bags in ditches. As the second trip began to turn into a moving disaster due to an increasingly sick motor scooter, I had the idea of imposing on someone I had met while he was in London and with whom I had corresponded some years previously, who was therefore a 'friend'. His name was Harold Rurlander and all we knew was that he lived in Bad Gestein in Austria, a town which, thankfully, caused us only a mild deviation from our intended route.

On arrival, we parked the bike up and began wandering through town.

People crossed the road to avoid us. We were hairy, unkempt and, no doubt, smelly to strangers. We asked in every shop in town after Harold with no success. Then finally, as we were about to accept defeat, a woman in a newsagent said, 'Rurlander? Ja, ja! Er wöhnt darüber!' She pointed to a block of flats not twenty yards away.

Harold and his family treated us like royalty. We spent a week in their company, during which time he refused to take a penny from us (just as well, really, as we were down to a fiver) and we left with sweet memories of hospitality, saunas (our first ever experience of that particular luxury) and wonderful walks in the woods and through the town while Harold gave us the history of this enchanting area. When we left, Harold and his family were helpfulness personified. They gave us wet gear, food and money (the sooner to be rid of us?) We headed off on an increasingly sick-sounding machine which knocked loudly when the engine was under any load at all. Big end, no doubt. We left Austria and had a choice: left up a steep hill to Lichtenstein or right along a motorway to Germany?

John shouted, 'Left! We haven't done Lichtenstein yet!'

The scooter laboured painfully and noisily up the hill. At the top, the engine gave one final death cry and seized. I whacked it into neutral and coasted down the slope to a village. There was a garage on the left hand side of the road and we turned in. Sadly, it was Sunday and the garage was closed, but a ten-year old lad wandered out onto the forecourt. He opened up the garage and allowed us to hoist the scooter into the air on the jacks so that we could drop the head. Removing the cylinder casing, the problem was evident: the gasket had blown, the scraper rings were shot and the big end about to fall apart. It was a total loss as far as its value to us in getting us further on our journey, or home. After weighing up the options, John and I quickly conferred and then we turned to the boy.

'Dieses motoroller ist kaput, fini, had-it, knackered,' John explained in his best German. 'Wir wollen es ihnen geben, verstehen Sie?'

He obviously didn't verstehen very well, because the boy answered that he had no money.

'Nein, das motoroller ist dein – dein! Wir gehen nach England auf dem bus!' Suddenly, the penny dropped. His eyes lit up and he moved forward to shake us by the hand in a very adult manner. 'Danke. Danke schon.'

John and I hitched to the nearest town, got the train to Paris, then to Calais where we had to ask the police to arrange a transfer of money from our parents to the ferry company and to retroactively pay the debts we had incurred in travelling to Calais We arrived at Dover and while we waited for the bus to London, began kicking a ball around on the grass with a group of kids. As I went to drag the ball back with my left foot, my right knee twisted and collapsed. I had torn a cartilage. I arrived back home after having hobbled from New Cross to Deptford with a knee the size of a melon but having completed a quite incredible and rewarding journey. It was time to resume the normality of life in Deptford.

Sitting in the bedsit of my friend Keith Hunt one night, listening to the Beatles 'White Album', we discussed moving into a flat together. I took the plunge and spent an evening talking over with my folks the idea of moving out – there was no attempt on their behalf to dissuade me and no histrionics, only Mum and Dad's calm 'if that's what you want to do, boy' approach to life.

Keith and I moved into a flat in Blackheath, at number 11 Glenluce Road. The flat, on the first floor, sported a large kitchen and an even larger bed-sitting room. The bathroom, down a flight of stairs, was shared with only two other tenants. The flat was nicely situated close to the heath but its greatest attraction was that it was located only a stone's throw from a nurses' home where Keith's mum worked as a cook.

Keith and I went overboard on the decorating front: the table in the kitchen was painted in orange and white stripes (cups of hot coffee placed on its surface for more than a minute were difficult to remove) and we painted the walls of the bed-sitting room in the brightest colours we could find – violets, purples, yellows and reds. A fireplace dominated the room and the wall above it was crying out for something dynamic to set off the rest of the room. Fortunately, I had kept a file of doodles which I was wont to draw from time to time: one of my favourites vaguely resembled an exploding face with eyes, brains and ears dotted around the picture, all set to a background of a violent explosion depicted in overlapping lines radiating from the centre to the end of the drawing.

I suggested to Keith that I transcribe this doodle onto the wall above the fireplace, an idea to which he readily agreed. Over the next two months, I painstakingly carried out this onerous task. Once drawn, it was up for grabs to 'colour in' and a procession of people took great delight in spending an afternoon making the drawing spring to life with different colours. When it was finished, it rounded off our 60s room in garish style. In retrospect, the room was bizarre in the extreme, but at the time it was the talk of Blackheath and we were never short of visitors who came to view 'Hunty and Wilks' flat'.

Keith met and fell in love with with a woman called Jacky Moody (whom he eventually married). She was a model and worked for the Joanna Lumley agency. Lithe, thin and stunningly attractive, she dragged Keith out of his working class apathy into a world of leather trousers, platform shoes, velvet jackets and make-up. They bought a sports car – a Triumph Spitfire – and later went into the hamburger business. Their foray into the potentially lucrative world of selling hamburgers from a converted van was short-lived: after a few nights selling dogs and burgers outside the Lewisham Odeon, some heavies told him in no uncertain terms that the 'pitch' was taken and if he ever turned up there or anywhere else in South London, he'd have his van burned to the ground. Keith struggled on for a while but the threats continued and he gave it up as a bad job, but one which, as ever, added to the tapestry of richness of life in the suburbs.

Years previously, when we had hung around in a group of 11 year-olds, a gangly seven year old called Frances always tagged along, being the younger sister of one of the 'gang'. Poor Frances was the butt of everyone's amusement, largely due to her prominent teeth and rangy gait. At the age of 19, I walked into the newspaper shop on Evelyn Street one day and my eyes locked onto an apparition of beauty standing behind the counter at the end of the shop. The smile on her face spread as I walked towards her, recognition dawning on me with incredulity.

'Frances?' I asked.

'Hello, Pete. How are you? Haven't seen you for years.'

Frances had metamorphosed into a stunningly attractive 16 year old with huge, round, dreamy eyes and cascading brunette hair, framing a face which would not have been out of place in one of the best modelling agencies. We spoke briefly – I couldn't take my eyes off her – and agreed a date for the following Saturday. My affair with Frances was brief and wild. Her youth, my indecision and the close relationship between our mothers conspired to make our separation the most prudent course of action after only six months.

Three years after our first brief encounter in the newspaper shop, I turned into Deptford High Street one Saturday afternoon to see her standing at the bus stop. She was fuller in the figure now, tanned to perfection, and glowing with the prime of young womanhood. We talked and went for a drink. The story of the last year of her life rolled over me like a surreal dream. She had become associated with a wealthy man who apparently treated her as an occasional 'companion'. For weeks at a time she would stay in a London flat awaiting his call. When it came, she would jet off to some exotic place to spend time with him for a week, a month or longer, returning to London to await his next call.

That night, Frances sat in my Greenwich flat pouring out her heart to me about how she needed to end this relationship, but telling me of her fears about the reaction such a termination would provoke. I told Frances to write to him, tell him it was over, that she was staying with me. She did so with great trepidation, not only for her own safety but for mine as well. For weeks afterwards, I was on constant edge, looking out of windows for characters standing in the shadows, waiting to pounce on me and beat the living shit out of me. It never happened although Frances did indeed get a few phone calls which left her weeping with worry and pain.

We stayed together for some time, our romance being more mature and sensible second time around. She moved into the flat with me and Keith, but within months, the wanderlust which has never left me, began to bite and I suggested we went away somewhere exotic. We saved hard and kept our money under the mattress. A few months later, we had saved enough to buy two 'early bird' tickets to visit a friend of Frances who lived in Antigua. This woman had, like the guy Frances had fallen for years earlier, met a much older man. He was an Austrian and earned his living by chartering his yacht in the South of France. When the market became too crowded he moved his business to the West Indies and an invitation for us to visit was extended. I will never forget the trip to the travel agents to buy the tickets where we handed over £250 in fivers – the most money I had ever seen. We were about to embark on an adventure on a scale neither of us could imagine.

On arrival in Antigua we were met by Frances's friend and her man, who was now her husband. His refusal to accept my handshake set the tone for our time on board his yacht. Frances had warned me that he was a 'right-winger' who did not take kindly to long hair – mine was past my shoulders at the time – and he didn't appreciate my shabby jeans and 'sloppy joe' vest either. On board his boat – a 40 foot sloop called the

Caribia, life was difficult. It was clear that he wanted us off as quickly as possible. I felt inclined to oblige. The 'boat set' filled me with disgust. Rich Europeans and Americans lived in ostentatious luxury aboard their yachts while all around them indigenous islanders scratched a living and lived in corrugated iron lean-tos.

I refused to dress up for the soireés to which we were inevitably invited and usually spent the evenings working the conversation around to politics, much to the annoyance of the assembled guests. Being the right colour and from the right part of the world swept us into the inner circle of social life on Antigua. We were invited to dinner at the Governor's house which had begun its life as the gunpowder store for English colonists. The house had no windows, only shutters, and as we ate and drank, huge moths fluttered through the open shutters and lizards scampered across the table.

Within a few days of our arrival, we met and became friends with a group of American guys who were as out of step with the Antigua set as we were. There were six of them and they seemed determined to cock a snoot at the comfortable world of the rich yachting fraternity. They quietly negotiated the purchase a yacht of their own – one which had been lying, half-submerged, on a mooring in the bay, following a collision with a reef. She was considered to be a write-off and was purchased for a ridiculously small amount of money.

It transpired that the boat was suffering only from two cracked ribs and had shipped water up to where she was slightly holed. They pumped her out, patched up the planking and towed her to an isolated mooring out of sight of the main activity in the harbour. Secretly they prepared her for sea, begging, borrowing or stealing sails, anchors, chain and equipment, and replacing the all-important ribs. After a month, she was ready to sail and the guys invited Frances and I onto the ship for a few beers before they left in the morning. As we climbed into our dinghy to row back to the Caribia, one of them told us to be sure to be on deck at 0900 in the morning to wave them out of the harbour. They had quietly given the same message to the entire English Harbour ex-pat community.

At the appointed time, the yatchies lined the decks of their sleek vessels in the harbour as the nose of the little boat appeared from behind the curve of the bay. As she putt-putted out into the main reach of the harbour, she came into full view of the assembled crowd. Overnight, the guys had given the yacht her final coat of paint – bright pink – and had painted down the side of the hull in big, black letters, 'FUCK YOU, ASSHOLES!'

The six guys lined the rail and silently stood with impenetrable expressions giving the finger as their incongruous little vessel slipped past the multi-million dollar yachts anchored on the glittering water. Only two people waved and cheered their departure – Frances and I. I often wondered if they ever made their Californian landfall. I hope they did.

Life for the claret set in Antigua appeared to be a continuous round of partying and sailing off to the idyllic beaches dotted around the islands. It was a life to which I could have warmed, had I not been confronted daily by the sight of indigenous islanders living in comparative squalor. Tensions between myself and my Austrian host spiralled downwards every time I broached the subject of social inequalities and within a month of our arrival, I had a set-to with him which would, curiously, convolute and give a different dimension to our adventure. After our relationship descended into fisticuffs which saw us rolling about the main deck while the yacht dragged its anchor and approached rocks (my host considered me incapable of operating the windlass), Frances and I were, not unreasonably, ordered us off his boat.

That evening, we dragged our bags into the bar in English Harbour and ordered beers. Cockroaches the size of mice scuttled across the floor. Within minutes, we were approached by a Yugoslavian with whom we were on nodding acquaintance. After hearing our story and learning that we had another two months to wait before our return tickets became valid, he offered us a job on his two yachts; living on one to prepare it for charter while the second was booked out, then transferring to the second and performing the same task.

'Cleaning' the vessel took the form of putting a 'bomb' in the accommodation – this being a cocktail of chemicals which, once tripped, would kill the hundreds of cockroaches which inevitably invaded a vessel in those latitudes, regardless of where the vessel was moored. The task of sweeping up the huge and still kicking carapaces turned my stomach, but it gave us a small and welcome income. Moreover, it gave us somewhere to stay while we waited out our time to return to the UK. Every morning I dived off the side of the boat into the clear waters of the harbour and took a swim, by way of a morning constitutional. In the bar one evening, the talk was of 'the big white-tipped shark they caught this afternoon'. I casually inquired about this incident and was told that the shark had been cruising the harbour for the last month and the locals had finally decided it should be eliminated. I blanched at this news and asked why no-one had bothered to tell me. The answer was that lots of people just ignored the shark issue and got on with enjoying the delights of the Caribbean. I pointed out that I came from Deptford, where the biggest threat was being mugged down the High Street on a Saturday night when the pubs turned out. I stopped swimming in the harbour.

After a week of working the 'bare boats', our Yugoslavian friend came to see us. He put to us a proposal which was to lead us on an another adventure. Would we travel to Florida and help him sail back a new boat he was having built? On the way, he would teach us to sail, we would do some snorkelling in the Florida Keys and he would offer us a job skippering the yacht for his rich customers. The prospect was too good an opportunity to miss and we readily agreed; all previous antipathies about living decadent lifestyles forgotten.

'I'll send you a cable from Florida when the boat's ready,' he told us.

The cable duly arrived, but not from Florida. It read, 'Problems with boat. Must sail instead from New York. Tickets arranged. Pick them up from St Johns and fly soonest. On arrival, take limo to Howard Johnson motel Long Island, South Beach. See you there. Regards.'

We flew, on a virtually empty Boeing 707 (who wants to go to New York from the Caribbean?) from tropical Antigua into a New York gripped by a harsh winter. The airport limousine duly dropped us at the motel where we found our Yugoslavian friend curled up with his girlfriend, a half-consumed bottle of whisky on the sideboard. Our stay was brief. In the morning we motored down to the harbour where his new boat, *Black Fox*, was still supported in a cradle at the water's edge. The water was freezing over as we watched. Engineers worked furiously on the engine and the boat crawled with workmen laying decks and caulking planking. We busied ourselves in the local stores, piling up food on trolleys and ferrying the contents into the bowels of the ship. This was going to be no picnic. No time for stopovers in the Florida Keys, no time for snorkelling: it was a straight push from New York to Antigua, as fast as possible to capitalise on the tourist trade and the lucrative charter market. Time was short.

We set sail on Christmas morning. As we motored down Long Island

Sound, people waved at us from their lofty apartments decked out in Christmas lights and winking good-will messages. This was to be my very first time at sea, apart from a short trip with our Austrian host around the calm waters of Antigua. A ten-foot swell soon caught the boat and, long before we reached open sea, I was honking luxuriously. Frances, while she held out much longer than I, soon succumbed as well. It was a memorable if uncomfortable trip. I was sick for most of it, only managing to take one watch in three. Every time I raised my head, I was overcome with nausea. Only by blind willpower could I force myself to the cockpit from where I would steer the boat, honking over the side regularly while doing so. Once on deck, however, the nausea would ease and after a few days, I began to stand my watches. The other crew members – two hardened American seamen in their early 30s – began to rib me mercilessly about my mal de mer, deliberately blowing cigarette smoke into my face and salaciously eating their bacon butties in my face, slobbering over the flesh and doing their best to unsettle the fragile sealegs I had found. I persevered, however, and gained a modicum of respect one notable night. Lying in my bunk at four in the morning, I looked up to the cockpit hatchway to see the helmsman silhouetted in the frame by great sheets of lightening illuminating the sky. The usual rush of the sea past the hull had been reduced to the slop-slop of the waves as they slapped the hull, now almost still in the water as we lolloped in the eye of a storm.

'Hey, Peter, you'd better rouse the crew to come up here and get this sail in before this storm breaks. Tell them to hurry: I don't think . . .'

His final words were torn away on a shrieking gust of wind. The boat heeled alarmingly as the wind careered down the face of a wave and sent us roaring along at break-neck speed. One gunwale was awash as the boat heeled before the wind. As I staggered on deck, I glanced at the speedometer: it was off the dial which showed a top speed of 15 knots. The boat was close to being out of control. With all sail set, she was at the mercy of the winds and the heel was becoming more pronounced. Hanging on for grim death, the crew scrabbled around the deckhousing undoing ropes and pulling in sail for all they were worth, bundling it up beneath them and dragging it to the hatch covers.

The helmsman, fighting the wheel, screamed instructions above a roaring wind. Waves hit the boat from the beam, then she would buck into a wave on the bow, digging deep as water cascaded over the deck, trying to grab us as we slithered upto the guard rails. Then she would roll and we'd be thrown against deck combings and capstans, cutting and bruising ourselves as we were flung this way and that while all the time hanging on to the sails.

The wind gradually eased, the seas became flatter and comparative calm returned at the passing of a tropical squall of great intensity. The sails were stuffed unceremoniously into the saloon area and we ran before bare poles, the heel now manageable, the boat more navigable. We took turns at the wheel throughout the remainder of the night and the morning, setting a small storm jib to give her headway, keeping the bow as best we could into the weather. I realised that I had long forgotten my sickness.

'Bermuda Radio, Bermuda Radio. This is Black Fox, this is Black Fox. How do you read? Over.'

These words are seared into my memory. Our Yugoslavian skipper, despite his claims to the contrary, did not really know our position and could not raise Bermuda radio through the damp radio set. We were lost. Had I realised it, we were lost in the middle of the Bermuda Triangle to boot. The weather, thankfully, had turned from tropical storms to tropical delight and we rolled along on sparkling seas. I took to sitting as far forward as possible on the bowsprit getting the occasional dunking as the bow dug into a wave. This was a delight: we may have been lost and we may have come close to drowning, not to mention the fact that I had lost a stone in weight, but this was the life!

I spotted something floating towards us.

'Port bow! What is it?' I asked the skipper.

'Ok, we're nearing the Virgin Islands. That's the daily garbage they dump at sea.' As we sailed closer to the drifting island of rubbish, my heart sank at the sight of a million cans, bottles and containers of all descriptions bobbing along in the sparkling waters of the Caribbean.

And so it was that 16 days after we left New York we arrived at the US Virgin Islands. Despite the seeds of fascination for the sea which had been sown by this trip, Frances and I could not conceal our delight in seeing land. We tied up alongside and my first thought was to use a toilet which didn't move around under you.

I looked at myself in the mirror on the wall of the public urinals on the quayside. It was the first glimpse I had of myself for two weeks. A tanned but gaunt face stared back at me. I had lost a stone in weight and my shoulderlength hair was bleached blond in places by the sun. I felt good and in trim, but the discomfort of those days at sea being sick was hard to dispel. Nothing that I had previously experienced came close to being as awful as seasickness. Friends had told me before I left on the trip that if I discovered I was prone to nausea at sea I would contemplate throwing myself overboard, so bad was the effect of the malady. (In a typical statement of clarity, McTaggart told me years later that if you're seasick, you'd throw your mother overboard if someone told you it would bring relief from the symptoms).

We were faced with a decision. My Yugoslavian employer was busily restocking the boat for the next leg of the trip to Antigua. Despite my sickness and that of Frances, he was still keen to go through with his plan to have us skipper the Black Fox on charter work in the West Indies, saying that the malady we suffered was usual and expected for first-timers at sea, and I had to admit that this was a once-in-a-lifetime opportunity. The trouble was that if we stayed, we would lose our return ticket which expired in three days and would be stranded in Antigua with no alternative but to work until we had saved sufficient for our tickets back to London. Or we could go now and make the Antigua – London connection.

We decided that, as much as we would not have missed this adventure for the world, we were poor sailors and to chance a life at sea when our recent experience indicated we would probably be throwing up for a good proportion of it was not the most sensible option. Truth to tell, we were both feeling a little homesick anyway, having been away from home for three months. I buttonholed the Yugoslav in the saloon of the Black Fox. Stripped to the waist and sweating profusely, he was stowing food boxes when I put my head into the hatchway and told him we had decided to fly back to Antigua and catch the flight home.

He looked up and said, 'You guys are crazy. I offer you a life of sun, sea and fun, with a good salary thrown in, and you want to go back to a shithouse like London. Is this the way you repay me for having given you an experience you'll never forget? You want to go home? Here . . .' he pulled $100 from his back pocket, 'take this, get your flight back to Antigua and spend the rest of your life regretting what you're about to do. If you change your mind before the flight leaves, you know where I am.' With that, he bent down to continue lifting and stowing boxes.

I was suitably chagrined and his speech forced Frances and I to examine our decision all over again. But we were resolute. We booked our ticket and the following day went to see our Yugoslav mentor for a final goodbye. His magnanimity was overwhelming and he hugged us both with genuine affection. We turned and climbed into the cab. As it sped away, the masts and topsides of the Black Fox were visible above the jetty and our friend waved at us until we were clear of the marina. What an adventure we had just had! What an adventure we had just denied ourselves!

I always thought that I would regret the decision we had made to the point of perpetual self-loathing. But had we not left the West Indies when we did, the course of our lives would have been changed to the point where I would never have met McTaggart or have been involved in establishing the foremost environmental organisations the world has ever seen. While I was naturally inclined to be environmentally aware, the experiences of the trip – especially seeing the garbage island in the middle of the Caribbean – welded me to the cause of environmental improvement but it was to be a year or two before the opportunity arose to do anything about it.

On returning from the West Indies, I headed at the first opportunity to the Deptford Arms, our local pub in Deptford High Street, to see the collection of mates and acquaintances which were collectively known as 'The Mugs'. I walked in just after noon on the first Saturday after I got home. There they were, sitting in the seats they regularly occupied – Geoff 'Lairy' Lee, Dave 'Soapy' Howe, Ray 'Bootsie' Mann, Bill 'Pretty Boy' Stevenson, Bobby 'Railings' Baker and the rest of the gang. My arrival turned a few heads: I was extremely brown and stood out in the sea of wan and pale faces in the bar.

'Blimey, it's Wilky!' came the choice welcome. 'Where you been?'

I opened my mouth to begin the story of the West Indies, of giant spiders, yachts, cockroaches the size of mice, the Caribbean, islands of rubbish, tropical storms and an offer which nearly changed our lives forever. Instead, I simply replied, "Ello boys! Just been away for a few days. Yeah. Lovely jubbly. Get us a pint in, Denny!'

'Coming down the Den?' Bootsie continued, apparently satisfied with my answer.

'Bet your life I'm going down the Den! Pie and mash first?'

I was back in the real world but I didn't have any proof of my adventures: unlike today when we document everything, particularly when we go on holiday, Frances and I had not one photograph to show of our incredible journey.

We moved into a large flat on Shooter's Hill with my old mate Keith and his model girlfriend Jacky Moody. At first, the arrangement was ideal. The four of us lived together happily and were inseparable. Keith and I drove for British Road Services together and then moved to drive tipper lorries for a mate of Keith's who lived at Dartford.

We would drive from the flat at ungodly times in the morning to pick up the lorries parked outside our employer's house, starting them up with a tremendous din and clouds of exhaust to what must have been great annoyance to the neighbours. These great brutes of vehicles – 'six leggers' as they were known – had short-shift, close ratio gearboxes and, most satisfying of all for impressionable 20-somethings in our pastel jeans, tight T-shirts and shades, hissing hydraulic brakes.

They were difficult to start at 5.30 on cold November mornings, and when they finally did fire after liberal applications of 'easy start', they did so amid clouds of oily smoke and much high revving to keep them from stalling. Once started, I found that, with a 20 tonne load of mud on board, they were just as difficult to stop. I remember going down the steep hill on the A2 just outside Dartford, practically standing up on the brakes to try to avoid running into the back of stationary traffic at the lights. But it was fun and it seemed that life at the flat with Keith was going from good times to better.

Keith and I lived, worked and socialised together constantly. It was a recipe for disaster. Frances and Jacky began to have a few words about the state of the flat. The living room we shared was in constant chaos – not that it bothered me or Keith, particularly – but the two women began to have increasingly heated exchanges about the responsibility for keeping the place tidy. These frictions began to rub off on Keith and I and we began to have words ourselves.

The tension increased over the next few months, fuelled by the fact that Keith took to playing music at an excruciatingly high volume at all times of the day and night. Then we decided to have a party in the hope that it would ease the tension. I told Keith that I had invited neighbours from the left and right of us and had warned others that there was to be considerable noisy revelry until the early hours. I was looking forward to the evening and informed Keith with tongue in cheek that he could turn the volume up as loud as he wanted to that evening. It was time to defuse the situation with a right royal bop. The evening ended in a fight which Keith easily won, largely due to the fact that his mate, Lenny Ives, grabbed me from behind in what appeared to me to be a pre-arranged move.

In the morning, I awoke with a lip the size of a tomato and about the same colour. Keith was sitting sipping coffee with his right hand bandaged.

I tried to get my misshapen lips around, 'Well, I'm glad to see you got hurt as well.'

He forsook the opportunity to reply and from then on, we spoke not a word to each other. We drove to work together in silence, we ate at the same table in silence and we lived our lives in silence until we had found places to live apart from each other. Only then did Keith and I go out together and get roaring drunk as we laughed off the tensions of the past year. My top lip still sports a lump to this day, a constant reminder of Keith whom I haven't seen now for more than 20 years.

Chapter 7

Toil and trouble

Frances and I moved out of the flat we had shared with Keith and Jacky and into what can only be described as digs, a first floor bedsit in a house in Greenwich. Frances found a job across the road in a tyre warehouse and I mooched about looking for work after signing on at the dole office, having given up the tipper driving job out of concern for my health and that of other road users.

My visit to the employment office – a place with which I was fairly familiar – was memorable for the fact that I had a sharp lesson on the boundaries of the welfare state, even then, in the late 60s, when we actually had a functioning one. I was broke and, after queuing for an hour and finally getting in front of a clerk, I asked for a fiver to tide me over as I had 'just got back from a trip abroad and was a bit short of cash.' This had the clerk chuckling before telling me that I should 'sign on' to receive benefit.

The old ruse of saying that you wanted a job as a deckhand on the Woolwich Ferry, (a legitimate request but one unlikely to be granted as there were only four such positions and the waiting list was three years) didn't work and I was sent off to look at a number of deathly jobs for which my GCE passes qualified me. All were office based and all had as much appeal to me as snow in July.

My indolence was threatening to get me into trouble. I was always outspoken – lippy, you might say – and my morose state of mind at not being able to find a job, let alone find a career path which might be construed as fulfilling, was prompting me to take a swipe at the world in general and my mates in particular. I was becoming notorious for bristling at the slightest hint of discourtesy or rudeness and provoking 'an incident'.

I took umbrage at being asked to pay for food in restaurants before we had eaten – this was standard practice in Chinese restaurants – people would often 'do runners', eating and then legging it without paying. This was part of a ritual love/hate relationship between alcohol-fuelled young men with a love of Chinese food and the management of the establishments in which we ate, who were anxious to ensure we paid for the services they provided. I railed against stroppy barmen and lying politicians alike. No-one was safe from my vitriol.

I was becoming schizophrenic in that I revelled in being a Millwall-loving, outspoken working class contrarian while at the same time aspiring to be an intellectual – widely read and considered in my views. This dual personality was reflected in the friends I chose, and I was soon gravitating more than ever to two mates in particular, Don Gardner and John Morton. Of my immediate peers, these were the only two who had aspired to a university education and were both accepted at Sussex University in Brighton.

We organised a visit to Brighton on John's birthday and travelled in a convoy of cars, including Bill Stevenson's Vauxhall which moved along the road sideways due to severe and clearly critical misalignment of the front and back wheels, a potentially fatal mechanical fault which he ignored with a, 'Nah, it's ok. Goes dahn the road, don't it?'

After meeting up with Don and John, we went to a pub and over the next few hours, we moved from pub to pub to savour different bands and music. I noticed a group of miserable-looking geezers following us and glowering at us. When we moved pubs, they arrived a few minutes later. We were being hunted down.

Towards the end of the evening, we moved along the sea front on our way back to the hotel we had booked in an uncharacteristic demonstration of foresight. The gang of ne'er-do-wells were walking towards us. As they reached us, one pointed at John and began to mimic him, clearly attempting to goad him into a reaction by roundly ridiculing his articulate language. His mates laughed that laugh which precedes a clump. From behind me, I heard John.

'Am I to assume you are laughing at what my friends and I are discussing because you find our topic of conversation amusing, or because you are attempting to provoke us into a reaction?' he asked.

Oh, shit, I thought, here we go. He's studying philosophy, I recalled. This was not exactly the right time to test his theories on real, live hooligans, hell bent on smacking someone in the chops. There was no way we were going to talk our way out of this little corner. The ape to whom John had addressed his question replied with a hay-maker of a right hook which miraculously missed John completely.

His attack was the signal to the rest of the louts waiting in the shadows to get stuck in. I was beaten to a pulp by an unknown number of assailants and, to my utter despair I only managed to land one decent punch before being overwhelmed. I lay on the ground as the thugs finally responded to my pleas for mercy. The last one to get off me took a step back and kicked me full in the face. Fortunately, he caught me on the forehead, the force of the blow causing hairline pressure cuts to appear on my eyelids, top and bottom.

As they beat a hasty retreat, I dragged myself to my feet and noticed Keith lying about ten yards away with his sheepskin coat pulled over his head. To my great consternation, he was screaming at the top of his voice. Fearing he had been knifed, I rushed over to him only to find that he was virtually untouched.

'Yes, I'm ok,' he replied to my garbled inquiry after his health. 'If you scream loud enough, they leave you alone,' was his philosophical response. John hadn't fared too badly either. It was me who seemed to have been the target and I was in a right old mess, blood streaming from my eyes and feeling generally as though I'd been run over by a train.

A policeman finally arrived on the scene, ushered in by some concerned by-standers. His only retort was, 'Come down from London and let yourselves get turned over by a bunch of yokels? Should be ashamed of yourselves.'

We walked to the university for the final hour of music but I was refused entry – not surprisingly – due to my grotesque appearance. Not to be denied, I found a back entrance and bunked in over a wall. As I dropped to the ground, I came face to face with a bouncer. He blanched when he saw my blood-covered face. 'Jesus! You frightened the life out of me. For Chrissake get yourself cleaned up.' He led me to the washroom. My reflection in the mirror was not pretty to behold. Even after washing off the congealed blood I looked like a Quasimodo double.

As time passed and as our lives in and around Deptford and Blackheath wove their mysterious patterns, it became clearer and clearer to me that my wandering lifestyle of not being able to settle into a decent job, let alone my inability to form a lasting relationship, would have to change. I could no longer blame my frequent depressions on the anger of a young man growing into adulthood. Everyone else seemed to be able to deal with their burdens although John Morton was indeed going through a particularly rough patch. It seemed as though he was oblivious of anything going on around him. He was withdrawn to a painful degree and carried his cares and woes deep within him. He would sit for hours saying nothing, doing nothing and almost transfixed in one position. We took him to parties and to our social events all to no avail. It took a move to Australia, years later, to finally and totally lift John out of the depression which had beset him.

Keith Hunt threw a 'vicar and call-girl' party. My partner at the time, a lovely Irish woman with long, ginger hair, agreed to swap roles, something I thought most couples would do. It was to be my first and only foray into cross-dressing. But we were the only couple bold enough to do so and I arrived in a short skirt, suspenders, wig and lipstick. None of my mother's shoes would fit so I was forced to wear my work boots. The party was a roaring success and we had a great time, but even at the height of jollification, John sat in the corner, sipping a beer and wrestling with his thoughts in his own private hell.

John, Don, Keith and I were in and out of driving jobs like ferrets in a maze, John and Don taking up these positions to supplement their grants as they strove for their degrees; Keith and I because we had nothing better to do. It was John who was to provide the impetus for the turning point in my life but not before my notorious bad luck gave me an insight into the dark side of the law enforcement business and brought me within a whisker of being sent down.

One particular evening, we were having a drink at the Old King Ludd in Luddgate Circus (now a Pret a Manger outlet, I noticed recently) and planned to attend a pop concert at Hampstead Heath later. Emerging from the pub and bristling with self-induced indignation which some said you could see shimmering around me from the distance of a mile, two guys hovered in the shadows next to Johnny Raggett's car. Upon inquiry, they turned out to be plain-clothes policemen and not too friendly either. I gave both of them a volley about 'skulking around trying to nick ordinary people when the City of London was stuffed full of the real criminals' (at which everyone yawned) before we headed off to the concert in Hampstead.

There was no trouble and everyone we met was friendly and jovial as they listened and danced to some good rock and roll. The smell of dope permeated the air (which probably had a lot to do with the convivial atmosphere). As we wandered through the crowd, I became separated from the rest of my friends but caught a glimpse of them sauntering along towards the exit about ten yards away.

'Hey, Don!' I called, through a group of people. 'Where are you guys going?'

'Come on Wilky. We're heading off. Raggett's got to go to work in the morning.'

'Well, fuck work! Let's stay. I'm enjoying . . .' Crunch! I was hit from behind by what felt like a ton of bricks. Three guys pinned me up against a wall. A knee went into my back and a hand twisted my hair into a ball. Don saw the attack and alerted the others who began barging their way back through the crowd to assist me. As they approached and prepared to knock shit out of my assailants, the three guys flashed their ID.

'Stay there lads! We're police! And you . . .' The knee in my back indicated he meant me, 'are under arrest.' With that I was frog-marched out of the park and towards a squad car into which I was bundled unceremoniously.

Every time I opened my mouth to ask what I had done to deserve being arrested, I was shouted at, 'Shut the fuck up, you, hippy!'

I was addressed in this way for the duration of the trip to the police station, a trip which was interrupted by radio messages to which my charming captors responded in a stream of profanities and racist language. They marched me to a cell on arrival at the station. I was then transferred to another cell which required me being marched through the lobby of the police station where I saw my friends – every one of them – gathered there to demand my release. I shouted at them to get my father on the phone – and get me a lawyer! I was bundled into a cell and two officers stood at the door until the arresting officer arrived. So aggressive were these officers that I honestly thought I was going to be beaten. One of the Neanderthals walked up to me and swung a left hook into my stomach which doubled me up. 'Sleep well. See you in the morning.'

The following morning, the door to my cell opened to admit a policeman carrying a tray. A plate of eggs and bacon was placed before me. A spoon was the only implement I was given with which to eat the food. I laughed as I saw it.

'Is this to make sure I don't cut my wrists to avoid the humiliation of getting stitched up?'

The arresting officer arrived. Gone was the hippy garb he had used as a poor and unconvincing disguise last night, replaced by a smart, three-piece suit. 'Good morning Mr Wilkinson,' he said with clipped politeness.

'Before you are allowed to see your friends and family outside, I'm here to tell you that a lawyer has been summoned for you and that you will be charged this morning before the circuit judge with assaulting a police officer and with abusive language. I strongly advise you to plead guilty to both charges and I can assure you that the maximum penalty will be £40 fine.'

'Go to hell. I'm innocent and you know it.'

'Very well. If you insist on pleading not guilty, you will be risking a much more onerous punishment.'

The trial came up a month later. My father gave me a character reference. My friends, one of whom, John Ragget, was a stockbroker, spoke up for me and told the court what had happened. John Morton did the same. The judge had clearly heard enough and waved a hand to indicate as much. It was time for the verdict.

'On the charge of assaulting a police officer, I find you not guilty on the grounds of insufficient evidence. Do you have anything to say?' he said.

'Yes, your honour. I take your verdict as a euphemism for saying that these officers are liars.'

After warning me about contempt of court regulations, he added, 'On the second count of using abusive language, I find you guilty and fine you £5. Do you have anything to say?'

'If it's wrong to say 'fuck' in public, why wasn't Kenneth Tynan fined when he said it on live TV a year ago? And what's more, I suggest you send the entire Metropolitan Police force to Covent Garden any day of the week because there you'll be able to nick someone every five minutes as the word 'fuck' is used in public as common parlance.'

'Yes, yes, very well. Court dismissed.'

As I walked from the court, I took a detour in the direction of the arresting officer. As I passed him, I bent down so that my face was inches from his. I gave him a softly spoken but vitriolic broadside, just sufficiently loudly to make sure he heard it. I thanked all my friends and family who had so staunchly supported me. But the episode confirmed my deepest fears about the police and changed my attitude to them forever. I shuddered to think what sort of treatment would have been meted out to me if I had been black.

Shaking off the smell of Hampstead police station and the low-life that worked there, I began to cast around for another relationship. Friday nights at the Bali Hi were the highlights of our lives for a time. Often we would go mob-handed, but Bobby Baker and I tended to sneak off regularly on our own since we felt we had a better chance of meeting women, or 'pulling', as it was ungraciously known.

Meeting women at the Bali Hi required nerves of steel and a thick skin. Invariably, the dance floor of the club was populated by women dancing together around handbags parked on the floor at their feet. To 'pull' required the 'walk of terror' – stepping out onto the dance floor, an act which, in itself, drew all eyes towards you as less confident groups of guys watched to see the result of your foray into this bobbing mass of womanhood. Then it was necessary to negotiate several dancing couples to reach the two you were after (Bobby Baker would 'spy' the likely women and I would lead the 'bunny', i.e. do the talking). Once in front of the identified pair of women, the chat would begin while we did our best to demonstrate our dancing prowess.

'Hiya. What's your name, then? Do you fancy a dance?'

'Nah,' would be the invariable reply, whereupon the remaining task was to choose your moment to make the 'walk of shame' back to the periphery of the dance floor, fortify yourself with another bottle of light ale and prepare yourself for another foray. Bobby and I were the recipients of seven consecutive 'blanks' on one evening, but generally, we were successful and mostly left with two women who were, it must be admitted, a little nonplussed when asked to sit in the back of Bobby's A35 van in which we travelled.

We went on holiday together to what Bobby described unflatteringly as the 'centre of the universe for chicks' – Torquay – and we set ourselves a target of taking different women to a particularly nice pub overlooking the bay on every night of the week. We scored five out of six which we felt was a passable success rate.

With the small amount of money I could muster from the various short-term and casual jobs I took, mostly on building sites as a labourer, gambling seemed to be a sensible way of speculating in order to accumulate. Every third Friday or so, we took to playing cards after the pubs had shut. At the outset of the evening, maybe fifteen of us would stand on the corner of Adolphus Street and deliberate for an hour about which pub we would go to: the Apples and Pears at Bermondsey, the King Ludd at Ludgate Circus, the Tiger's Head at Lee Green? After a few bevvies, we would have a meal and then head back to John's dad's flat for cards.

Increasingly, the act of gambling and the challenges it posed conditioned my angst and gave me another focus. But while one undesirable trait diminished, the other, gambling, was becoming more accentuated. The copper we played for soon turned into silver and soon the silver gave way to 'folding'. And news of our card school began to spread. Don Gardner's mate, a lovely man even smaller than me (which is probably why we got on so well), called Paul Ruocco, was a member of the school and he introduced one of his mates, known to me only as Fat Len, to the circle. Len cleaned us out.

His wealth apparently came from the café run by his parents who allegedly sold five hundred cups of tea a day in their Elephant and Castle-based establishment. Wherever it came from, Fat Len had the ability to out-bluff us all: he would simply bet 'a fiver blind' on any three card brag hand and thereby require other members of the school to either go with him at a fiver a time 'blind' or a tenner 'open'. After two or three bets, it would clear most of us out of any money we might have accumulated for the game.

We quickly excluded him from the school although it didn't seem to have a lasting effect on the alarming speed with which the stakes were being raised. It was soon not uncommon to have close to a hundred pounds in the 'pot' and many's the time one of the guys would walk away 'quids in' – as much as a hundred pounds to the good. More often than not, the money we lost would have previously been borrowed from one of our closer friends in the school and these sums, running into multiples of tens, would be classified as 'card debts' to be hawked around, bartered, transferred along with fortunes at the card table and only occasionally repaid over months or even years. I think Johnny Morton still owes me a twenty pound card debt to this day.

The sign of a good night was running to catch the night bus being weighed down by the 'clods' in your pocket. At least it meant you weren't cleaned out. One notable occasion, as everyone settled in for the card school, I went upstairs to take a leak. On my return, the cards for the first hand had been dealt and I took my seat as others were chatting and pouring beers. I casually glanced at the three cards before me and tried to keep a poker face as I saw three aces – the second highest hand possible in three-card brag. I feigned disinterest as the betting went round the table, fussing with my drink, talking to one of the guys to the annoyance of others.

'Come on Wilky! You in or what?'

I bet a modest ten pence, the better to put people off the scent. Two guys stacked their cards and I thought I was about to go the classic route of winning a few pennies on a prile of cards – a hand which is rare. To my delight – which I was careful not to allow my face to betray – Don raised the stakes to ten bob. He clearly had a decent hand. John went with it and so did I after putting in a mild and unconvincing moan which was an attempt to convince them both that I really didn't want to continue gambling on my 'average' hand.

Don raised it to a pound. John stacked. I went. Just Don and I left now and the kitty already stood at close to a week's wages for me. I tossed in another pound note and looked Don in the eyes.

'Well, Wilky, I'm not giving in. I should tell you that I have a very good hand. I don't want to see you do all your wonga on the first hand,' came Don's warning.

'I also have a good hand, Don. I'm in and what's more, I'll raise it to two quid.'

We were now into IOUs, a familiar part of the evening, based on the fact that if you won the kitty you could honour the IOUs, and if you lost, a monumental card debt would result.

It had now become a battle of wills. I had borrowed everything I dared from friends and had immediately gambled it. Don had done the same. The kitty stood piled high with pound notes and fivers on top of a cascade of silver coin. There must have been close to £100 quid in the kitty. I placed my cards face down on the table. We agreed to turn the cards over and end the gambling frenzy which was threatening to ruin us there and then. I turned over one ace after the other, slowly.

'Told you, Don. I had an unbeatable hand.'

A smile flickered across Don's face. He turned his first card over – a three. No, it could not be that he had three threes. He was bluffing. The chances against three threes when three aces were out were astronomical. His second card was a three. I groaned. He took an age to reveal the third card: it must be a king or a 'rag' card and he must have been bluffing all this time. A three!

Three threes! I had lost on a prile of aces. Unthinkable! We all sat stony faced in silence looking at the two hands on the table. My mouth hung open. Then they all erupted with laughter and rolled about on the floor. It was a stitch up. While I was in the loo, the cards had been dealt so as to force this battle of the two priles. Just another aspect of Friday night entertainment.

Chapter 8

From Friends to FoE

Despite living what some would see as a colourful lifestyle, the call for adventure gnawed away at me and I champed at the bit of ennui as I wrote my poems and paced around the environs of south London like a caged beast.

One day, John Morton threw a book in my direction across his bedroom where we were sitting listening to music. The book was The Environmental Handbook, the first production of a newly created group, Friends of the Earth, which had been earlier established in the United States. It was the progeny of the Audubon Society and acted in many respects as the political arm of that worthy organisation, recruiting more active members in defence of the environment.

The book was a collection of essays by various prominent thinkers of the day on population, pollution, resource use and environmental degradation. I read it from cover to cover in one sitting. Every word resonated with me. Scales dropped from my eyes. There were, after all, people who understood my anxiety, who shared it and articulated it in a manner which left me hopeful and excited. I could not wait to join this band of like-minded contrarians. In the back of the book was a tear-off sheet which volunteers were invited to send to the FoE office at 8 King Street, in London's Covent Garden. I didn't want to wait for a response by post, so I went to the office the very next day.

King Street is in the very heart of what was the central bustling fruit and vegetable market of London before it moved to Nine Elms in Vauxhall. At 9 o'clock in the morning as I arrived at the FoE offices for the very first time, trade was dropping off since the market opened at four. I pushed open the door of the office which bore the name of Ballantine Books and climbed two flights of stairs. On a second door was the FoE sign, cellotaped at a wonky angle. Behind it was a tiny room in which three people were stacking boxes of empty bottles.

'Hi. I'm Pete Wilkinson. I just read the handbook and wondered in you could do with some help.'

Thus, with those words, I began my 'career' in the environmental movement. The response I received from the people in the office was cursory and understandably so: they were hard at it, collecting 2,000 non-returnable soft drinks bottles in order to return them to Schweppes as a protest about the waste of resources represented by the increasing use of inappropriate packaging, particularly 'one trip' bottles and containers, introduced largely at the behest of the supermarkets which professed themselves unable to cope with a returnable glass bottle trade.

A tall, bearded man, whom I later learned was Graham Searle, told me that I could help by grabbing a bag and going out to collect as many of the bottles as I could find, in and around Covent Garden. I was happy to oblige and began working five hour days, wandering the streets of Covent Garden and Soho with a plastic bag over my shoulder, picking up Schweppes bottles from the gutter, from rubbish bins and from window ledges where considerate souls had left them.

We worked extremely hard at Friends of The Earth and the rewards did not come in the shape of green folding material. They came in the growing camaraderie of our small band of crusaders and in the occasional features and articles written about us that served as a platform from which to espouse our cause. Graham was asked to do a live interview on a London news programme one evening and we sat in the Essex Serpent (they would open the pub for us on request by this time), discussing what Graham should stress in his interview. By the time he left for the studio, we'd had a few pints and I cycled home furiously to be in time to hear the broadcast.

I switched on the radio with time to spare. The interviewer sounded pompous as he introduced Friends of The Earth as an 'extreme' organisation and I could feel Graham bristle from where I was. He was not the sort of guy you annoy lightly.

'So Mr Searle, what exactly do you do at Friends of The Earth?' came the question eventually.

'Well, I'll tell you what we do', Graham replied in a measured tone, 'We work our bollocks off trying to save the environment for people like you, that's what we do.'

There was a rustling of papers and a few muffled comments off microphone.

'I really must apologise to our listeners for Mr Searle's choice of words there. Now, Mr. Searle, perhaps you'd care to elaborate.'

Astonishingly, Graham repeated his statement about gonadal employment and then, to give him credit, went on without a pause to champion the cause of environmental sustainability with all the eloquence of a statesman, a delivery which left the interviewer speechless.

This episode summed Graham up for me. He was mercurial and could be, and mostly was, withering in his treatment of the opposition yet he had a self-destructive streak a mile wide. His eloquence and largess was unsurpassed, but on occasion, mostly when he suddenly decided he didn't like somebody, he could resort to the most crass language and outrageous antics you could ever wish to imagine. Yet he was a teacher and a mentor whom I admired immensely. He was also a cracking centre-half.

We occupied the King Street office for about six months. During this time, Graham and I became good friends. The fact that I cycled up from Greenwich every day impressed him. We began to socialise and I was invited on several occasions to visit the Isles of Scilly with him and his Scillonian wife, Jenny. And we drank together. My god, did we drink together. The Essex Serpent next to the King Street office was a 'market' pub and was therefore open at times which suited the porters – between 4am and 10 am and then from 12 midday to 2pm. We also played football together, my left-wing to his centre half.

The Schweppes bottle campaign climaxed with the return of 2000 bottles to Schweppes House which was then at the Piccadilly end of Park Lane. Compared to what we got up to later at Greenpeace, it was a tame event but, for its day, it was ground-breaking. The media had seen nothing like it and the arguments we used – resource use, environment, supermarkets holding the environment to ransom etc – were new to the press.

We gained notoriety quickly and the membership grew steadily. I felt as though I had found my niche at last, and revelled in the adrenalin rush from demonstrations, planning them and then actually getting out there and doing it. The point at which, as an activist, you commit to doing something represents the pinnacle of what was probably months of planning. Simply engaging with the public on these issues was – and remains, no doubt – a hurdle in itself. Most people keep themselves to themselves. Most don't want to be bothered, especially by people who, like us, were invariably dressed in strange garb. (I once dressed as a bottle and walked up and down outside a supermarket in the Edgware Road (standardising containers) and once as an ant (opposition to RTZ's plans for a copper mine) in Snowdonia National Park)).

As we grew, we expanded our staff and the number of campaigns we took on. The original band of five (me, Jonathan Holliman, Graham Searle, Angela King and Susi Newborn) were joined by Richard Sandbrook, Walt Patterson, Amory Lovins and Colin Blyth.

We moved to 9, Poland Street, known as Freak House due to the fact that it was a Rowntrees' building which housed a number of 'alternative' organisations, including Social Audit, run by a charming and very agreeable Charles Medawar and his equally affable side-kick, Maurice Frankell.

Social Audit did some amazing work, publishing annual reports which gave the true social and environmental impact of the companies they were investigating and thereby countering the often one-sided, rosy depictions of corporate activity the companies preferred its shareholders to swallow. The issues which increasingly attracted FoE's attention were commercial whaling, RTZ's outrageous plans to mine for gold in the Mawddach Estuary and to open-cast mine for copper in Snowdonia National Park in Wales. Graham convinced a TV company to finance the construction of a model of the proposed gold mine to demonstrate its scale and appearance should it receive the required permission to go ahead. He crossed swords with RTZ executives and reduced their arguments to the tawdry excuses for environmental despoliation for private profit which they were. RTZ abandoned their plans.

We refined the one-trip packaging campaign into a call for standardised packaging – one type of returnable and re-useable container for each product – and held a demonstration in Edgware Road using human-sized replicas of a bottle and a jar which Reg Boorer and I made from papier-mâché plastered over chicken wire frames. I was the bottle and Susi Newborn was the jar. There was only one flaw in our preparations: we had run out of space on the banner Reg and I had made and had to improvise at the last minute. The banner read, 'FRIENDS OF THE EARth', the last two letters squeezed into a tiny space at the end of the banner and therefore virtually unreadable.

Commercial whaling through modern methods using fast catcher boats armed with explosive harpoons had decimated most of the whale stocks all over the world and FoE decided to speak up on the issue. We prepared a basic document on the issue to set out our stall. The task fell to me to draw the pictures of the whales, which I did reasonably well. These were then pasted into the body of the research document to complete an impressive master copy of the Friends of the Earth Whale Manual – everything you needed to know about whaling and why it should stop.

The whale manual was a seminal document and provided indisputable and referenced proof that whale stocks were declining to the point where most would not recover even if commercial whaling ceased. Blue whales, bowhead, right whales (so named because they float when killed and therefore were the 'right' whales to hunt), fin whales, humpbacks and sperm whales had all been decimated to critically low levels.

The political focus in the 70s on the whaling issue was, like today, the International Whaling Commission (IWC). It was holding its annual meeting in Riverside House, next to Vauxhall Bridge. Friends of the Earth were not given to undertaking what was later labelled as 'non-violent direct action' (NVDA). It 'demonstrated' its distaste. There is a world of difference between NVDA and demonstrations, of course. The former is designed to directly intervene and stop an activity at the point of abuse rather than, in the latter's case, demonstrating a general displeasure by banner waving, or occupying someone else's property.

Our planned protest took the form of demonstrating our displeasure at continued commercial whaling by waving banners outside the International Whaling Commission when delegates from all over the world met to 'regulate' whaling by setting 'sustainable' catch quotas which of course they routinely and historically had failed to do. The IWC simply presided over the demise of one species after another. A group of other whale-friendly campaigners offered us the use of an inflatable whale for the occasion and we prepared our first major 'action' which was still, regardless of the excitement with which we approached it, a 'demonstration' and as such, to me at least, a weak response to an unforgivable environmental crime.

While the Friends of the Earth 'knobs', as I increasingly came to see them, were pressing the flesh of the IWC delegates inside Riverside House, I was organising the cabaret outside which involved towing the inflatable whale (dubbed Peter by the press for some unknown reason) behind a borrowed motor boat at the time the delegates were taking their tea break. Media and delegates would be invited to leave the building and witness our river-borne antics while being asked questions by the likes of Graham and Richard on the matter of why the IWC failed to do its job of protecting whales.

We had a large 'Save the Whales' banner on board the boat but had been instructed by the police that it was illegal to undertake 'political' activity within a mile of Westminster on the river. So we had to hope that Peter would be sufficiently photogenic – and buoyant – to make the point without having to spell it out for the media with a banner or two. Nonetheless, we kept the banner on board just in case.

We approached Riverside House and Peter was behaving himself, but there was a wicked tide running and we were finding it difficult to make way. As we came under Vauxhall Bridge at the appointed time, Riverside House swung into view on the port side and we opened up the throttle at the exhortations of the knobs on the bank where a large group of people were assembled, cameras pointing in our direction.

As we moved closer to the bank, we exposed Peter to a greater proportion of the current and in an instant, a seam between two bits of his superstructure parted. He was deflating quickly and we tried desperately to get to the shore and in front of the cameras while Peter retained some semblance of a whale.

From the assembled people outside Riverside House, came Richard Sandbrook's voice, 'Put the bloody banner up! Never mind the law, just put the damn' thing up!'

As Peter finally collapsed into a heap, looking more like a discarded piece of tarpaulin than a whale, we hoisted the banner: 'Save the Whales'.

The sinking of Peter made headlines around the world. Had Peter remained inflated, it may have made page two or three in some newspapers, but a heroic failure seemed to have infinitely more media appeal than a success. It was a lesson well-learned.

As time passed and as out notoriety increased, others joined our ranks: Walt Patterson and, briefly, Amory Lovins, Canadian and American respectively, nuclear savants both. They taught me a huge amount about energy generally and nuclear power specifically and, unknown to any of us then, were responsible for putting me on the path which I tread today. Others arrived: John Burton, still a friend and colleague, came to advise us on wildlife issues and was instrumental in seeing through the Wildlife Bill which became the Endangered Species Act forbidding the importation of pelts of endangered species of animals. Reg Boorer came permanently on board. He was a graphic designer with whom I was to be associated for good and bad over many a decade. Celebrities and the well-connected gravitated to FoE, all seemingly wanting a piece of the action we were creating. One woman, in particular, was memorable and her connections led to the first non-governmental organisation benefit pop concert I can recall in the UK. Her name was Tina Shand. I don't know what her background was, but she was a selfless beneficiary to FoE. In the summer of 1972, she organised for meteorically-rising star David Bowie to play a benefit gig for us. It was a stunning performance. Bowie's incarnation as Ziggy Stardust playing around with his Spiders from Mars made the occasion – and the benchmark it became in FoE's development – highly memorable, apart from the loss of that faculty I suffered in the days which followed as a result of too much whisky on the night.

My primary roles at FoE were to write a column for the Ecologist and develop FoE's local group network. The discovery that a former lorry driver could actually write, encouraged the board to invite me to write The Campaigners' Manual, a step-by-step guide to environmental campaigning at local, regional or national level.

Breathing down my neck at the time was a relatively new import who had made his mark running the very active and successful FoE group in Birmingham, Tom Burke. Despite the fact that Tom was an extremely able and competent campaigner, his manner and voice annoyed the hell out of me. It was clear that Tom was destined for the top: he just had that pushy, self-confident air about him and was later to run the Green Alliance before being appointed as adviser to a series of Environment Ministers during and after the traumatic and thoroughly dispiriting Thatcher years.

The prospect of life at FoE with Tom in charge was too daunting to contemplate, and after a few months, I pulled Graham aside and told him that it was my intention to leave in the next year. To my amazement, Graham confided that he was thinking of doing the same thing.

He said, 'It's like a 1500 metre race, Wilks. In order to beat the record, we have to run like hell for the first 500 and then hand on the baton to someone else. We've both put in five years of hard, honest slog and we deserve a break.'

There was a strong suspicion, echoed by others once they were made aware of this situation, that Graham had made his announcement merely to show solidarity with me, whom he felt had been treated badly, and actually had no intention of leaving at all.

It was 1975. I had stuck with Friends of the Earth for five years. It had certainly been a period of steep learning for me and an education that would stand me in good stead for the future. Friends of the Earth had grown from a small band of four people, working out of a borrowed office in Covent Garden, to a well-established and respected environmental organisation running well-organised campaigns on issues as diverse as nuclear power to land use, working from a well-appointed but modest office in the middle of Soho. It was growing in stature and was attracting a broad range of experts who supported its aims and contributed to the intellectual mass. But it wasn't for me. The fact was that Friends of the Earth was a club for Oxbridge types, for those with clipped accents and/or aspirations of grander things. There was a marked absence of glottlestops around the office and the fact that I was a working class boy from Deptford left me at a disadvantage in that I was given no sustained campaign responsibilities and I felt that any natural talent I had for campaigning would never be given a chance to flourish and grow in this claustrophobic atmosphere. I think working at FoE forced me into a peculiar social niche, one from which I have never really escaped.

While I was in genuine awe of people like Graham Searle, whose erudition and articulation I envied, I was also scathing of what I saw as the Oxbridge approach to the environmental issues we were addressing. Graham could strip the wallpaper with a well-chosen volley in defence of a particular point of view, but he did this in the manner of an Oxford Debating Society evening (or what I imagined one of those was like): it was all very wordy and gentlemanly, even if the venom with which his argument was delivered had to be seen to be believed. At the same time, my ire was turned on the 'working class' society from where I came. I had changed during my time hanging around with the FoE academics. Now I was not at home with my working class peers – too narrow and limited in their horizons, not sympathetic at all to my campaigning zeal - but neither was I happy to identify with my FoE colleagues – too snooty and not grounded in the real world of labouring and lorry driving. It is a cleft stick from which I have never really escaped

In the final few months of my tenure at FoE, I began to cast around for another job. There was an interesting job on offer at the Family Planning Association, an organisation with which we had campaigning links through the issue of population growth and control. Someone was needed to make analyses of the sex education outreach programmes by taking the feedback forms and drawing broad conclusions about the efficacy of the programme and then identifying specific learning points from the exercise. This was, at face value, right up my street, and I began work in an office in which I was the only man among fifteen women, one of whom, Annette Cross, was particularly attractive.

The work quickly became tedious as there was no variation and as repetition was not something I could tolerate. But the compensation came in the shape of Annette and we quickly became lovers and good friends. I was 29 years of age. I had no formal training at anything. I had worked on building sites, as a lorry driver, as a cost clerk, an apprentice printer, scooter driver and general factotum. I had a general understanding of various environmental policy matters, strong views and a more in-depth understanding of the energy sector and nuclear power in particular and I had spent the last thirteen years since I left school going from job to job, living life to the full, laughing a lot, enjoying myself, but hardly advancing my prospects if I was ever to think about getting married, something I had not contemplated seriously since those heady days of youthful aspirations and dreams I entertained with Geraldine. All of my friends at home, bar two, were married. Annette was a beautiful woman and the idea began to germinate that perhaps she and I might marry. A chance meeting with a horse racing journalist made such an event more realistic as my financial outlook improved dramatically – for a while.

Chapter 9

Marriage and a monkey on the nose

It was 1976. I had worked at Friends of the Earth since 1971. I was a founding member. My Deptford friends thought I had lost the plot. I had to wonder too. What drove me to cycle from Deptford to the West End every day to work with these Oxbridge types? (And back most evenings, unless I ended up in a pub with Graham in which case I'd inevitably stay at his Walthamstow, Hoe Street house). It was clear that I was not going to be given the sorts of opportunities I thought I deserved. I didn't have the right accent, or the right education pedigree. Even Richard Sandbrook acknowledged the existence of a classist glass ceiling at FoE and while that admission was depressing, it did not dampen my enthusiasm for environmental campaigning. I just thought it could have been done with more panache and in a manner which appealed to ordinary people more.

The topical anecdote doing the rounds was: question – 'What is an environmentalist?' Answer – 'A bearded man on TV.' Question – 'What is an environmental disaster?' Answer – 'Two bearded men on TV.' I thought that was not very far from the truth. But I enjoyed the banter and the disrespect that people at FoE had for authority and their willingness to articulate it. It was so refreshing to be enveloped in this culture of cynicism on a daily basis as opposed to being engaged in it sparingly when Don Gardner, John Morton and I got together; an increasingly rare event as time progressed.

I felt like a round peg in a square hole at Friends of the Earth and it was clear that my departure would be a relief to the board as well as myself. In five years, I had not been asked to run a campaign, act as a spokesperson or graduate to the board. I was a working class former lorry driver and the class system thrived at FoE: clearly, opposition to classism didn't come within the remit of 'being green'.

As the time of my departure approached, I became friends with a journalist from a London newspaper who, like me, had the occasional dabble on the horses. One day, he suggested that I might want to back a particular horse which won at a canter. I made a couple of pounds profit and when I next saw my contact I thanked him, only to have him offer me another tip, this time in more hushed and conspiratorial tones. I was informed it was a 'stable tip' which meant nothing to me at the time, but I backed the horse, this time a little more generously. It won. I made more money. Over the course of the next few months my contact gave me a further three tips, all of which won. One horse won at very long odds and I was beginning to build up a nice cash balance.

One Saturday afternoon, I was about to leave my mother's flat when the phone rang and a breathless voice said, 'Phantom Freddie, 4 o'clock, Brighton' and hung up. With just a few minutes to go before the 'off', I rushed to the betting shop and put a tenner on the horse against which, I noticed as I studied the betting, odds were not even posted. It romped home, winning by several lengths. I waited for the price. I swooned when I heard, 'The winner of the 4 o'clock Brighton is Phantom Freddie, starting price 50 to 1.' The betting shop erupted. Despite being told to keep these tips secret, I told everyone I could so that they could share in these highly accurate and clearly well informed tips, regardless of their origin. I collected £510, a sum I had never seen before.

Three weeks later, I lost the lot. My tipster and I went to an evening meeting at Windsor, feeling so flush that we hired a chauffeur driven car. I asked my wife-to-be, Annette, to bring a friend to make up a foursome. We walked into the members bar where many of the then Chelsea football team – Peter Osgood and Allan Hudson I remember seeing - were having a drink. The rest of this story you can write yourself. The tipped horse on which I put my shirt – having first borrowed £100 to make my bet up to a monkey (£500) came stone last, bursting my bubble and reducing me, after what was a memorable and exciting few months, to my customary penury.

It was around this time that Dad started to complain of pains in his chest and back. He and Mum had finally arranged a holiday to the Scillies, after I had routinely and regularly told them how much they would love it there among the peace and quiet of the tranquil islands and the tropical gardens of Tresco, washed by the warm Gulf Stream. They went to the Scillies that summer but had to return earlier than planned because Dad was in pain. He found it impossible to walk more than a few hundred yards before back pain stopped him in his tracks and chest pains followed. Mum and Dad came home to find Annette and I planning our wedding.

What on earth could I do to start a 'real' career while at the same time indulging my desire and flair for expressing my outrage at environmental and social skulduggery? After talking it through, Annette and I hit on what seemed like a masterly plan. In retrospect, it is a wonder how we ever agreed it in theory let alone went through with it in practice. In essence, it was this: I would get a 'straight' job and use the stable base that would give me to consider a career in politics. I applied to join the Post Office and was soon inducted into the course for aspiring counter clerks at the Post Office HQ in Chippenham, Wiltshire. We decided that, after we were married, we would live in Somerset, an ideal setting for a romantic rural idyll if ever there was one, although the digs in Bristol we ended up in were the very antithesis of romance.

Our weekly search for houses in Somerset found us looking at a tiny hamstone cottage in a small village called Kingsbury Episcopi. Immediately opposite the cottage, on the village's handkerchief-sized green, was a medieval lock up, a small round building big enough for one noisy drunk. Soon after the wedding which took place in Swanley, Kent, we moved to our house and I found a job as a postal clerk in the Yeovil Central Post Office having qualified after the course in Chippenham. From day one, the relationship between me and the Post Office was rocky, to say the least. I had moved from the relatively liberal atmosphere and philosophy of a non-governmental organisation into an atmosphere and work environment worthy of a Dickensian novel.

By now, Dad was undergoing endless tests at the hospital and had been forced to give up work. It was a time of constant and nagging worry about his health during which we feared the worse but refrained from voicing our views, always 'looking on the bright side' and hoping against hope that the doctors would identify the problem and find a cure. Every time I saw Dad, he seemed worse. The analgesic tablets he was taking gave him scant relief from the pain and he took to aspirin as his favourite pain relief tablet. I didn't know it, but two massive events were about to converge in a period of time which would fundamentally alter the entire course and shape of my life.

As Dad's condition declined, I realised that I would have to move closer to London. Living in Somerset, I was feeling very much geographically and politically isolated from what was going on in London. In addition, the locals in Kingsbury were not exactly gushing in their welcome for us 'incomers' and I had already crossed swords with the hunting fraternity who would regularly hold up traffic on the minor roads between Kingsbury and Yeovil in order to ensure their hounds and horses – not to mention the utterly ridiculously-attired and mounted aristocracy – were allowed unhindered access to the beleaguered quarry.

I recall telling one officious blue-rinsed snob sitting on her jittery charger as she held her arm across the line of traffic, 'You're the sort of person who'd create merry hell if you got to the Post Office and couldn't be served because postal clerks were being held up by the poxy hunt! You don't see the connection, do you?'

Her response said it all: 'Piss orf!'

I was also itching to be politically and environmentally active again but didn't really want to spend too much energy on the pursuit of a political career in the boonies as I saw them. So we began to think about moving closer to London. In the meantime, having attended a few Labour Party meetings in Yeovil, I was courted heavily by the Labour Party officials who began schooling me as their candidate in the upcoming district elections. Somerset in the 70s had barely heard of the Labour Party and as a Labour Party candidate on the hustings, I was given very short shrift, being told in one shop to 'clear off' and take my communist manifesto with me. Choice.

As predicted, I lost the election but the experience was electrifying and I wanted more. Within a year, I had joined the 'B' List of prospective Labour Party candidates and underwent a selection process for the nomination at Taunton which I sadly lost, although I lost to a fine competitor who argued not for worker participation as I had, but for worker's control. The natives, although few in number on the left, were far more revolutionary in attitude than I gave them credit for.

Tony Benn endeared himself to me then (and even more so later when we attended Labour Party compositing meetings together when I was with Greenpeace) by coming to our tiny Labour Party meeting in Yeovil and giving a speech which was as rousing and as impassioned as if he were addressing ten thousand at a rally in Trafalgar Square. Never before or since have I been exposed in such a stirring manner to the links between the Labour movement and those early and often persecuted pioneers as the Levellers and the Tolpuddle Martyrs. It is a heritage which today's Labour movement, to its eternal shame, attempts to hide and rarely mentions as it seeks to emulate and accelerate the move to the right which modern life and the cult of celebrity demands.

Clear of political encumbrances for now, Annette and I looked around at the options we had for moving closer to London and my increasingly sick dad. I would go and see Dad as often as I could and he would do his best to put on a brave face and play down the suffering he was undergoing. He was very ill and yet the doctors would not, or could not, give us a clear diagnosis. We heard about lesions and a shadow on his lung, but what was clear was that Dad secretly felt he had cancer and that he was dying. Often I would walk past his bedroom to find him kneeling on the floor, body bent at the waist, his torso prostrate across the bed, half-sleeping and moaning in pain. It was a sight which broke my heart and, Mum, living with him day after day, was worn down with worry and angst.

After a few false starts, Annette and I managed to sell the cottage in Kingsbury for £10,000 making a clear £2,000 profit which we put as a deposit on a secluded semi-detached cottage at Sussex Cottages, Fir Tree Lane, Haughley Green, just outside Stowmarket in Suffolk. Still clinging to my shaky Post Office job, I sought and was given a transfer to a post office in Halstead, in Essex. I determined to leave the post office at the earliest opportunity. An event at my new place of work made that happen quicker than I had bargained for.

Chapter 10

An ornery son-of-a-bitch

At work in the post office one day, I was astounded to hear the overseer call from her office doorway, 'Phone call for you, Mr Wilkinson.' It was rare for anyone to get a phone call: as I walked towards her office, she said with a raised eyebrow, 'It's someone calling from Canada.' Canada? I knew no-one in Canada. I took the handset.

'Hello.'

'Is that Peter Wilkinson?'

'Yes.'

'Hi. My name is David McTaggart and I'm in the UK to set up Greenpeace here. I wonder if you'd like to come and help us get Greenpeace set up in the UK.'

'Sure.'

'Can we meet?'

'Come to my parent's flat in London next weekend. Do you like football . . . soccer?'

'Sure.'

'Well maybe you'd like to come to the game. My team is playing at home on Saturday.'

In just a few words lives can be utterly and irrevocably altered. My life changed that day so fundamentally that I would never again work at what might be called a regular job.

We finished the conversation with an exchange of contact numbers and I gently put the receiver back in its cradle. I looked into the middle distance and let things sink in. I had just been headhunted by Greenpeace, an organisation I had read about and admired from afar for two years as they carried out imaginative and headline-grabbing peaceful direct actions in North America: protesting about the clubbing to death of tens of thousands of seal pups before their lactating mothers on the ice floes of Newfoundland; sailing ships into exclusion zones around nuclear weapons testing sites and disrupting commercial whaling in the Pacific carried out by the Russian fleet. Wow! That's what I called environmental campaigning. That's what I'd been longing to be involved in. And now the head honcho McTaggart, had called me, had sought me out in an obscure post office in Essex and offered me a job. I drove home that evening on cloud nine.

McTaggart and I met in the Black Horse pub, close to my parents flat the following Saturday. He was short, stocky and balding. His eyes sparkled with a fire I hadn't seen since I met Graham Searle six years previously. McTaggart was overly effusive yet strangely evasive. He dismissed any question relating to himself, his past or to his exploits, yet painted a visionary picture about the embryonic Greenpeace with a few sweeping statements delivered with economy and directness. His face, tanned as a result of his outdoor lifestyle, could crumple like a piece of well-worn leather one minute as he grinned at a remark, only to assume the impression of an impenetrable wall of disinterest if the topic of conversation moved onto issues he felt were too close to home or not on the agenda. He was a rogue, I decided, and in his flitting mannerisms and his deep, fathomless eyes, I knew I had met a man who would do – had already done – great things. I didn't know, as I sat with McTaggart in that pub, but his mind was already planning and scheming events for Greenpeace years hence. While he was bodily in the here-and-now, he was without a shadow of doubt light years ahead of me and anyone else I knew, with respect to his vision and determination.

As an opener, I had to ask the question which had been burning inside me since that fateful phone call.

'Tell me why you decided to track me down in particular, and how you did it,' I demanded.

'Well, I called FoE and asked them if they could tell me who the most 'ornery son-of-a-bitch that ever worked for them was. They told me, straight up – Wilkinson. I need 'ornery sons-of-bitches. How did I track you down? Oh, I just called around. People knew where you were.'

We finally got round to talking money. 'How much do you need?' he asked between sips of beer and drags on his cigarette. 'I have to make £50 a week.' 'I'll guarantee you £25 a week for two and a half days. You'll have to work out the rest. Take a part-time job until we can take you on full time. Shit, it's a shame you're married,' he muttered, as if he didn't really want me to hear it. I downed my pint. 'Let's go and see the game.' I drove back to Suffolk in a state of highly mixed emotions: I was about to embark on an unknown journey with Greenpeace, the prospect of which made my spirits soar and the hairs on the back of my neck to involuntarily stand on end.

My dad was ill – in excruciating pain for much of the time and when I visited him, I could see his face lined with stress and pain. He was thinner than I had ever seen him and I feared that he had cancer. The doctors, however, refused to confirm that fact, giving us hope by telling us they were still carrying out tests. Every time I left, I felt despair welling up inside me. Dad was in and out of hospital like a yo-yo and some of the tests the doctors were carrying out on him, Mother told me later, would cause him to burst into tears of embarrassment when he arrived home. His stoicism was something to behold. I can't recall him ever once complaining. Every time I lamely asked him, 'How is it, Dad?' he would reply with a predictable and dismissive, 'Not too bad, boy.' Yet I knew it was bad. His face was lined and drawn. I wanted to hug him and sob together, to tell him how much I wanted to get next to him, to bare my soul and talk about both our fears for his health. But we never did. We were too stiff and proper to do any of the things that I take for granted with my own children. Our relationship was hands-off and almost cold although he knew that I loved him with an emotion we had silently agreed not to discuss.

Having finally left the Halstead office, I secured a part-time job at a sub post office in Ipswich which, along with the money McTaggart had promised, would bring in just enough to keep us fed and a roof over our heads. I turned up at the Greenpeace office in Whitehall, just down from Trafalgar Square, a few days later. I walked into a sparsely furnished office. A tall guy with lank hair squatted, rather than sat, on a chair, a baseball cap back-to-front on his head, typing fast on a manual typewriter. He nodded a chiselled, handsome face adorned by a moustache briefly in my direction. This was Allan Thornton. He was a vegetarian; passionately defensive of animals and, as he later showed to my own discomfort, politically astute, although I thought him to be more than a little over-confident of his own abilities. Susi Newborn, a colleague from Friends of the Earth days, bounced around the room with her undiminished energy and zeal. Denise Bell – in-your-face, uncompromising and straight-talking – was the third and, later in the day, Charlie Hutchinson arrived.

He was courteous, spectacled and spoke with the clipped, precise accent of the upper echelons of the Home Counties.

Within the hour we were discussing the publication which had been proposed as the first collected, public utterances of Greenpeace in the UK on the range of issues which exercised it. I was asked to write the nuclear section. I was amazed to have been given such a responsibility with so little preparation or questioning. I reflected how this sort of thing would never have happened at FoE but here, within minutes of meeting, these guys gave me the onerous responsibility of articulating Greenpeace's energy policy. I got down to writing my piece for the Greenpeace Chronicles, based solely on the fact that I had worked at FoE for a few years under the unofficial tutelage of Professor Amory Lovins and Dr Walter Patterson.

Of all the things which Greenpeace were in those early days, and for all the reservations I was to eventually harbour about Allan Thornton, it was the total freedom of action everyone was allowed which attracted me to the organisation. You went to the desk, pulled out a blank sheet of paper and designed your own campaign programme. In my first article for Greenpeace, I outlined the case against nuclear power and mapped out a campaign profile. It went straight from my typewriter into the first edition of the Greenpeace Chronicle. No-one had time to vet copy and indeed no-one asked to vet it. A few weeks before I arrived, Greenpeace had been donated £38,000 with which to buy a ship. The grant came from the Dutch branch of the World Wildlife Fund (WWF). The air in the office was electric with expectancy and anticipation. I adored the connection Greenpeace had with indigenous, North American Indian people.

Greenpeace promised excitement and difference. Its imagery exuded challenge, possibility, adventure. It was vibrant, engrossing and international. It united, welded and moulded everyone who came within its influence into a unit of common purpose. Its early merchandise material smacked of mythology and internationalism: the Rainbow Warrior myth of the Red Indian tribe had allegedly been adopted by the early Greenpeace people in America as the embodiment of their belief that, one day, a tribe of people from all walks of life, all backgrounds, creeds and colours would unite to protect the natural world against the avarice and excesses of the modern world. This myth united us in the belief that, unlikely as it was and as implausibly romantic as it sounds, we were its embodiment. This rainbow tribe would be comprised of those from all walks of life, from different creeds and colours and from all parts of the world and would be called Rainbow Warriors.

The links Greenpeace had developed with indigenous peoples on the back of that relationship was vital to the psychology behind the organisation and was to bring the UK office of Greenpeace into sharp and terminal conflict with its international HQ years hence, with devastating consequences for us all and me in particular. However, for the moment, I figured that if Greenpeace would have me, if I could meet the demands of the Rainbow Warrior legend and help realise the dream, then I wanted to stay. And to be in the organisation at such an early and influential stage in its life was an added bonus, although, at the time, the subject of the longevity of Greenpeace, let alone its structure and individual roles within in it, were the furthest things from my mind. David Fraser McTaggart was to change all that.

Chapter 11

Enter McTaggart

I hadn't seen McTaggart since our conversation over a beer in the Black Horse pub, a few months previously. Now he was to arrive at the office in Whitehall and I looked forward to seeing him. I had retained mixed impressions of him from our previous encounter and wanted to reinforce or alter my prejudices with a more considered assessment of this guy.

He'd been in London for a few days and had been busy looking at the ship purchased with the WWF grant. She was laying in King George the Fifth Dock (KGV) and was a former side-trawler, recently retired from service as a fisheries research vessel for the Department of Agriculture, Fisheries and Foods (DAFFS). She was called the *Sir William Harvey* and we decided to rename her *Rainbow Warrior* in honour of the native Indian myth enshrined in a book of the same name (Warriors of the Rainbow). The identity of the person who came up with the name Rainbow Warrior for the first vessel Greenpeace owned in Europe is hotly contested but, on balance, I think the honour has to go to Susi Newborn.

McTaggart was the sort of guy who would exploit this ethnic connection mercilessly if it suited his needs but would, with equal ease, dispel it and its importance as just whimsical tosh if it was clear that by doing so he could gain an advantage. McTaggart was always looking for an angle, always searching for an advantage, constantly seeking out weaknesses and chinks in the armour of the opposition, whether that opposition was a government or people within his own ranks with whom he disagreed. And he was brilliant at it. Well-connected and ruthless, there were many occasions when I found it necessary to thank our lucky stars that he was on our side and not an arms dealer or a nuclear baron. He was magnetic, crass, infuriating, pedantic, brilliant. When he was around, things happened, not always good things either, but something was bound to happen if you were in his company. Many women found him either irresistible or obnoxious, sometimes both. Whatever he was, you could not ignore him.

I settled into a routine at the office and pondered the causes we should address beyond that of commercial whaling. One issue – although I believe it was more of an animal welfare concern than what I considered to be a mainstream environmental concern – simply would not go away, no matter how much we tried to ignore it. Greenpeace were known for their opposition to the Canadian cull of harp seals. In fact, that issue had launched the organisation in the USA, Canada and in the UK, and,, in its drive for membership and funds, it mercilessly exploited the image of a cute, cuddly but manifestly helpless seal pup. Now, it appeared, we were to have our very own seal cull on our door step. The Department of Agriculture and Fisheries for Scotland (DAFFS) had authorised the culling of grey seals in the Orkney Isles. Five thousand eight hundred seals were to be shot every year over a ten year period in an attempt to halve the population since they were, according to DAFFS, responsible for the plummeting fish catches in the area and for the decimation of salmon catches in particular. The cull was to begin in November 1978. To compound the matter, DAFFS had decided to bring in Norwegian marksmen to carry out the kills which would include pups and breeding females.

We started a file on the Orkney Seal Cull.

As I became more deeply embroiled in the world of Greenpeace, the strain on my home life increased. To add to this, my father's health was at its lowest ebb and all talk of recovery had largely ceased. I was all the time conscious of the fact that my dad would surely die within months or even sooner.

One day, I rushed out to make a forgotten call to McTaggart from the phone box. I also called Mum who told me that Dad had gone back into hospital. I drove to Guys in London and saw Dad in his bed from the corridor outside the ward. He was deathly pale and weak. He opened his eyes momentarily and saw me, a smile flickering across his lips. He tried to raise an arm to wave, but the effort was too much and his arm dropped back on the bed as he closed his eyes. Mum arrived. Uncle Tom arrived. I left to drive home with a heavy heart and Dad died during the night. In a fury of self-loathing at my inability to demonstrate my love for my dad over the previous 30 years, and in a slough of self-pity at my own weakness over the years of dad's illness, I sobbed and sobbed for most of a day and wrote the letter to Dad I should have written years previously.

Dad was dead. What would this mean for Mum? How would she live without her soulmate? I could not bear the thought of Mum without Dad in the flat where they had sung together most evenings, danced and spent the years bringing up us kids. Yes, Dad's death was a terrible thing but it had relieved Mum especially of an awesome and heavy burden. Dad was no longer in pain, Mum no longer had to worry about him constantly, look after and minister to him. To that extent, Mum was liberated, as were we all.

Looking at the world through the lens of a still relatively young man (I was 31 when Dad died), through the eyes of a working class boy who had suddenly and unexpectedly been given an insight into what life could offer among a crowd of like-minded, outspoken and care-free people determined to fight for the environment, Dad's death seemed liberating more than sorrowful, seemed to provide a release rather than create a burden. And after I had cried myself to sleep for a few nights, after I had seen Mum, Brian and the rest of the family and gone through the awful ordeal of the funeral, I realised that I had married too young, that I was just setting out on my own life's journey, admittedly a few years later than most, but that I wanted to be free to do what I needed to do. I knew a few days after Dad's death that Annette and I would divorce and, while it was not something I began plotting, it was clear to me that marriage and the style of life I was beginning to live during my Greenpeace hours were incompatible. The next couple of years proved that to be the case.

Chapter 12

Sealing a victory

Back at the ranch, the energetic and animal-loving Allan Thornton was becoming increasingly agitated about the planned government cull of grey seals in the Orkneys. With typical absence of consultation, DAFFS had issued licences to Norwegian sharp-shooters to halve the population of grey seals which haul out around the islands during the breeding season in order, so it argued, to protect the fish stocks from avaricious predation by a growing number of seals which had hitherto benefited from protection.

At face value, the cull seemed to be entirely unjustified since while the females were whelping, they didn't eat at all. Greenpeace asked DAFFS for a copy of the grandly titled 'Grey Seal Management Policy' to which ministers would loftily allude when questioned on the issue. After weeks of ignoring our request, they finally sent us the minutes of a meeting at which the decision to cull the seals was taken. There was no such thing as a management policy: the government was reacting to pressure from the salmon fishermen in Scotland, and the Scottish fishing fraternity at large, in the time-honoured manner of taking the line of least resistance. This time, the seals were to take the hit.

Our early research demonstrated that the figures used by DAFFS to demonstrate the quantity of fish being taken out of human mouths by the seals bore no resemblance to the truth whatsoever and had, in fact, been based on what captive grey seals eat. When it was pointed out to government 'scientists' that captive seals, bored and anxious by their lives of incarceration, would eat and eat and eat for want of something better to do and that wild breeding females actually fasted during gestation, the response was an embarrassed silence. When we pointed out that the real reason for a decline in catches for the Scots was perhaps linked to the lack of a sustainable yield fishing policy which Soviet fishing fleets were exploiting by hoovering up fish by the shoal just north of Orkney, the response was typically pathetic and unconvincing.

We decided to act. The *Warrior* was despatched, fresh from her exploits in Iceland where she had been involved in anti-whaling activities. Our pledge was to physically protect the seals; to prevent the cull until the government had satisfactorily addressed our arguments and demonstrated beyond all doubt that halving the grey seal population would result in the return of the fish stocks around the islands. I was left back in the office Cinderella-like while the action guys – including Allan who had returned for the whaling actions in Iceland – travelled to Orkney.

McTaggart came through the office as the *Warrior* was making her way north to tell me with typical foresight, 'This seal thing will be big. I want you up there to co-ordinate the press. You're a goddam limey. It's your country and I want you – not a Canadian (Thornton) – talking to your press.'

I made the call to Annette and grabbed my bag, a constant companion these days, and set off for the isles of Orkney. I arrived in a wind-swept Kirkwall, the capital, and checked into the deserted Kirkwall Hotel in time for a late tea. Three whiskered locals sipped whisky in the bar. I set up my 'office' in my room and made a call to the ship. She was 24 hours away and had received information that the Norwegian vessel, the *Kvitungen*, carrying the marksmen, was a day behind her. They would arrive in 48 hours. I phoned the office and dictated a press release, giving my number as the contact point. I had a beer and went to bed.

In the morning I was woken by the phone ringing. The BBC wanted more background, questioning me about the likelihood of a confrontation. I hyped it to the point where they decided to send a crew. Their reporter was to be Michael Beurk. Then the Daily Mail rang, then the Daily Mirror, ITN and a stream of others. They were all coming. Christ, I thought, I hope we can deliver.

Over the next 48 hours, Kirkwall became a hive of activity as reporter after reporter arrived and film crew after film crew. I arranged a press conference in the bar and outlined our campaign. I explained that Greenpeace volunteers would be posted on every outlying island known to support a colony of seals and that they would physically protect the seals with their bodies to prevent a kill. I also explained that the *Warrior* would dog every move made by the *Kvitungen*, intending to out-manoeuvre any attempts to land marksmen on the islands. I assumed this was what we were going to do. I was making tactical decisions on the hoof, but it seemed to create the right sort of Gunfight at the O.K. Corral atmosphere and journalists began filing background pieces.

The following morning, the *Kvitungen* sailed into Kirkwall where its skipper had a meeting scheduled with DAFFS' officials. She was followed into port by the *Warrior*. The quayside was lined with local well-wishers who appeared from nowhere, as well as the assembled world's press. McTaggart, having been collected from the *Warrior* by dinghy en route, stepped off the ship in full maritime gear – galoshes, woollen hat and flak jacket, to confer with me. The press moved en masse to the DAFFS office to get a reaction from the officials there and David and I sunk a few beers and discussed tactics. Things were pretty straightforward in actual fact. Dinghies from the *Warrior*, and those borrowed from local people, began ferrying activists carrying tents and provisions to the outlying islands in preparation for the arrival of the marksmen. I pinned a piece of paper to the notice board in the lobby of the hotel announcing a regular Greenpeace briefing every evening at 6.30 and McTaggart made his way back to the ship to await the *Kvitungen's* departure. Night fell before the *Kvitungen* left, shadowed by the *Warrior*. I was left in the hotel, along with the majority of the press who could not be squeezed on board the *Warrior*. In the event, the *Kvitungen* merely steamed around the islands by way of keeping Greenpeace on their toes: no killing took place that first night and we claimed a victory – of sorts.

The next ten days developed into a kind of circus. McTaggart's prediction came true. The longer the campaign went on, the more interested became the media. On the third day, a German and a Japanese TV crew arrived to take up the last remaining rooms in the hotel. Those that followed would have to resort to taking digs with any locals willing to put them up or, in one case, to sleeping in tents in the hotel grounds. The place was awash with press and media. It was my first large scale interaction with the media and I loved it. I was the only conduit for news they had available and I was constantly being sought out, interviewed and grilled by Italian, German, Japanese, Australian and British press and media.

The Guardian's correspondent, the Mail's, Joe Palin of Radio 4, Michael Beurk and I formed a tight little team which pumped out the news on the impending death of 6000 seals daily. The story began to be covered on the front pages of every daily newspaper in the UK and across Europe. Will they kill the seals? Will Greenpeace change government policy? Can Prime Minister Callaghan afford to back down? Why

106

slaughter these innocent creatures just when they are whelping? Why kill them at all? Why isn't the government addressing the central issue of fish management policy?

The RSPCA decided to send an inspector, Frank Milner, to investigate DAFFS' claims that the activities of the Greenpeace protestors was disturbing the seals to the point of panicking the females into leaving their offspring to starve. During a day of truce called by DAFFS to 'prove' this story and thus deflect criticism back onto Greenpeace, the *Warrior* came to collect Frank and cart him off to one of the islands to carry out his inspection. Realising Frank's and the RSPCA's impartiality in the matter, we held our breath as he walked towards the waiting press core at the Kirkwall hotel to deliver his findings at the 6.30 regular press briefing we had established.

I kept pace with him as he strode from the ship and asked him under my breath, 'Well, Frank? Good, bad or ugly?' He replied, without breaking step and with skills a ventriloquist would have envied, 'Disturbance factor negligible. Colony in the peak of health with mortality rates entirely normal.' Frank destroyed DAFFS at the press conference, calling their accusations divisive and a weak attempt to divert attention away from the central issue which was that 6000 seals were about to die for the crime of eating fish – something they were not even doing at this time of year.

On day ten, another 24 hours of endless radio interviews and liaison between the press and the ship stretched ahead. The story had grown out of all proportion to its importance – unless you were a grey seal, of course. Ten-year-old boys were leaving home to hitchhike to the Orkneys to help us. In and around the Kirkwall hotel, a veritable city of tents had been erected. Mums, dads, animal welfare organisations, well-meaning enthusiasts as well as a collection of cranks from all over the UK had gravitated to this spot to save the seals. It had become a cause celebre of unimaginable proportions.

The day wore on and the time for the press conference arrived. DAFFS had asked if they could make the running at this particular briefing and asked me if I would kindly allow them to brief the press without interruptions from me. I sat in the bar sipping a pint. At 6.05, the doors to the conference room burst open and an avalanche of journalists and TV crews spilled out. I was surrounded by a forest of microphones.

'DAFFS have called the cull off, Pete. You've won! What's your reaction?'

I was gobsmacked. I fired off a stream of comments about the ability of ordinary people to call government to heel over environmental abuse, how this was a victory for common sense, for environmentalism everywhere, and made my hasty excuses to leave. I had to phone the ship at once. Of course, every line out of Orkney was jammed by 200 journalists filing their story and it was only an hour later that I managed to get through to the *Warrior*. The crew, of course, knew nothing about the victory and were dutifully dogging the *Kvitungen* out into the North Sea on her way back to Norway. The Norwegians hadn't had the courtesy to call the *Warrior* to save them a wasted journey. It was midnight before the *Warrior's* lights were visible as she steamed into Kirkwall Harbour.

The quayside was lined with TV cameras, floodlights, well-wishers and locals. The atmosphere was carnival and most – including me – had celebrated in the traditional manner. The *Warrior's* lines came snaking ashore. Pete Bouquet, the skipper, long hair trailing in the stiff breeze, one elbow crooked over the lip of the bridge wing window, was calling instructions to the helmsperson as he manoeuvred the vessel against the quay.

A press man asked me, 'What's that man's name?'

'Bouquet,' I replied.

'Captain Bouquet!' he called. 'Can you give us your reaction to the government's decision to call off the cull please?'

Pete looked up with a scowl. 'Would you mind if you stopped asking me questions, please? You might have noticed that I'm trying to park a ship!' A fine and appropriate final statement on a quite extraordinary ten days, delivered with all the panache, directness and conviction of a true warrior.

Media coverage of the victory was knocked off the front pages by news of the Pope's death, but we had won our first campaign in the UK. It took ten days of campaigning and a few thousand pounds. We had set our feet on the path which would, decades later, see Greenpeace employing hundreds of people around the world, having a presence in between 35 to 50 countries, securing incomes of millions of dollars a year and, arguably, presiding over a decline in effectiveness in inverse proportion to their income.

I took stock of the events of the last few months. I had been plucked from the living hell of the Post Office and catapulted into an organisation which had to work hard to qualify for such a label: we were more disorganised than organised. Somehow, the Orkney seal cull had captured the imagination of the press and the public. More importantly, we had won the campaign hands down. Prime Minister Callaghan had apparently received more than 8,000 letters of complaint about its grey seal management policy in just one day's post. 8,000 letters from people who felt moved to write represented a further 800,000 who felt the same but couldn't be bothered to write. That was a lot of votes to risk. The climb down was very significant in Greenpeace's history. To launch on a successful and high profile campaign introduced and endeared the organisation to hundreds of thousands, if not millions of people, through the media. In ten short days it had planted Greenpeace firmly in the political firmament as a force to be reckoned with.

The fact that I had something to do with it was largely incidental but hugely relevant to me as an individual. Apart from being involved in forcing the government to abandon a manifestly ridiculous and unjustified policy, it had given me a lot of air time and had established me as a capable and reasonably articulate campaigner. I had been all over the media, I had dealt with the demands of my Greenpeace role with some aplomb, we'd won a campaign hands down and I had emerged as a half-decent tactician and strategist. How I hoped Friends of the Earth were wringing their hands in frustration. As I made my way back home to Suffolk, I felt that even if my marriage was under pressure, Annette would be pleased with the way the campaign had turned out and the effect of my extended absence would be assuaged by the fact that her husband had been in charge of such a slick and effective campaign. On getting home, I found that was only partially true.

Chapter 13

Nukes, whales and pirates

No sooner had I returned to the office after the Orkney seal victory than I found myself heading north again. The Scottish Campaign to Resist the Atomic Menace (SCRAM) requested that the *Rainbow Warrior* call in at the site of a planned nuclear reactor on the east coast of Scotland to support a mass occupation of the construction area. I called the ship which had just left, headed for Iceland to fulfil its agreement with Netherlands WWF and continue the disruption of Icelandic whaling activities and Allan readily agreed to divert the ship.

As de facto nuclear campaigner, my presence would be required and I hastily made travel arrangements to enable me to meet the ship which would arrive in Torness three days hence. I had to tell Annette that, having just arrived home after an extended absence in Orkney, I'd be away for a while yet again.

The proposed construction site for the nuclear plant was awash with hundreds of people; stalls sporting material propounding all manner of alternative philosophies, flags and banners of every description, hippies, dippies, yippies, anarchists and an assortment of dogs and other animals. It was as though every alternative lifestyler – along with a healthy number of locals – had descended on Torness to register their disapproval of the nuclear age and their determination that Torness would not be built. And standing off to sea, half a mile out, was our proud little ship, riding gently at anchor. A dinghy came into shore to pick me up and for the first time since my adventures in the West Indies I was to step on board a ship at sea.

I grabbed the access ladder and clambered on board to be met by McTaggart in seafaring garb of galoshes, hi-viz jacket, life vest and woolly hat. He grabbed me and together we staggered forward onto the main deck as the ship pitched on the swell.

We ended up at the inevitable encounter group later that evening organised by the Torness Alliance. Encounter groups were a regular and mandatory part of any gathering of protesters in the 70s. They were designed to 'break down the social barriers and put people at their ease with one another.' A lot of old baloney as far as I was concerned. I knew it was a mistake to attend. It was not that I had anything against the anarchistic attitudes of many of the attendees: my philosophy was and is, live and let live so long as no one gets hurt, but the arrogance of some of these people and the distance from the real world at which they lived made me fear that there was no hope at all for change if we had to rely on mobilising the alternative elements. After a series of 'activities' designed to allow us to 'shed our inhibitions', we were encouraged to give our views about how to proceed with the campaign against the planned Torness reactor.

I suggested that we had to organise, streamline, strategise and, more importantly, reach out to the local population. In order to do the latter, I suggested, with some trepidation, we should smarten up, get haircuts and wear appropriate clothing before knocking on the doors of the good people of Berwick, for fear of frightening the bejesus out of them. Unsurprisingly, these proposals were roundly scoffed at and ridiculed and I rose to leave the tent in a pretty foul mood at my inability to argue a case for organised opposition rather than putting our faith in the government changing its mind by the power of thought. My departure ended in an unseemly scuffle with someone who made a remark as I passed him. Reg hustled me out of the meeting before the incident escalated. So much for peace, harmony and unity.

The following day, the Greenpeace inflatable dinghies came ashore bearing McTaggart whose presence was demanded on the stage, set in the middle of the mass of tents and mobile homes which occupied the site. Lithe figures clad in figure-hugging wet suits leapt from the dinghies. McTaggart clambered onto the stage to a roar of approval. Sea-dog, pirate, rogue. He put a cigarette in his mouth.

'Anyone got a light?' were his first words. People applauded. 'Better still, anyone gotta joint?' The crowd roared its approval. 'All I want to say', he said, 'is don't let the bastards grind you down! No nukes!!'

Despite the crowd's obvious affinity with Greenpeace and the respect they had for its brass balls and in-your-face campaigning style, I was a little uncomfortable with what I saw as the immodesty and lack of humility it displayed at the Torness gathering. These concerns gnawed away at me and I quietly determined that I would do my utmost to ensure that Greenpeace would embrace and empower ordinary people wherever and whenever it could. Environmentalism should be something we all participate in as naturally as sleeping and breathing: having it demonstrated to you by a third party has always seemed to me as disingenuous and patronising.

The *Warrior* departed the following morning for Iceland. It, Greenpeace and I had fulfilled our obligations to the anti-nuclear movement and had supported the cause to see the Advanced Gas-cooled Reactor (AGR) at Torness abandoned. It was built and operating within eleven years.

McTaggart was alternately living in Paris and in Amsterdam, setting up Greenpeace organisations in both capitals; often calling on the services of disillusioned FoE people, notably Remi Parmentier, a nervous but thoroughly capable guy with whom I was to be involved in years to come.

McTaggart made one of his rare appearances in London. His arrival marked a notable day for several reasons. We had finally employed the services of an accountant to look at our financial state. I recall him asking Janie and Denise – the two people ostensibly in charge of finances – to direct him to the paperwork. Denise ducked behind her desk and surfaced with four shoe boxes overflowing with receipts, scraps of paper and half-completed lines of figures on graph paper.

'It's all yours,' she said, pushing them towards the open-mouthed accountant. In those boxes was a financial record of the first year of Greenpeace activity.

'Listen' McTaggart whispered to me as we strolled down the corridor, 'we've gotta get going on this thing, you know what I mean, man. We can't sit here whacking off, doing this stuff when we don't have the structure, you know, we've gotta get real, so in order to be in a strong position, when the shit really hits the fan, we must expand the board and sort out the . . . No . . . lemme finish. I suggest seriously (eyes boring into mine now, unblinking) that you accept a directorship of Greenpeace . . . right . . . now.'

I was just a lorry driver with a fiery temper, an inbuilt awe of nature and a hatred of despoilation. I made the big mistake of treating the subject lightly. 'Sure, I'll be a director, but it won't make the slightest bit of difference to me. I'll carry on the same way I have been carrying on.'

His hand slowly came up and gripped my arm, turning me more squarely to face him. 'Let me tell you something, Peter. You bet your sweet ass it'll make a difference to you. Don't ever think that this is just something you'll do for the hell of it. This is damned serious shit, believe me. And if you want to change things as much as I think you do, then you'd better accept your responsibilities and take them very seriously. Welcome aboard the board. Ha! Here, sign this.'

I was a director of Greenpeace UK. I was issued one single ordinary share of the limited company.

McTaggart explained that when Greenpeace had begun its crusading activities in Canada in the late 60s, support groups calling themselves Greenpeace had spontaneously set themselves up all over the world. One, Greenpeace London, existed in the capital and posed a threat to the formal development of the Greenpeace he wanted to see, since the 'other Greenpeace' were avowed anarchists to whom organisation, structure and hierarchy were anathema.

McTaggart had registered the name Greenpeace a year previously and had bought a company 'off the shelf' for £100. The original shares of that company had been transferred to himself and Allan Thornton who were also directors. In McTaggart's mind it was time to expand the organisation and to reinforce our claim to the name of Greenpeace, should there be any argument with the anarchists bearing the same name. Unknown to me then, the issuing of the two original shares, the share issued to me and a fourth which Thorton had apparently issued to himself a few months later, were to be at the centre of a bitter struggle for the soul of Greenpeace in years to come. But for now, thoughts of anything but campaigning rarely entered my head.

The International Whaling Commission (IWC) was to meet in London in 1978 to set the commercial whaling quotas allocated to the nations which continued to whale. I suggested to McTaggart a peaceful invasion of the meeting during the plenary session when the world's press would be present. Over a few beers we discussed the shape of the protest and decided that we should simply walk into the meeting, occupy it and deliver an address which the TV media present would undoubtedly report.

A small matter of security stood in our way. We had to get past the guards who had orders to scrutinise the lapel badges of people entering the conference room. Anyone not wearing an identifiable badge would be turned away and we needed to spirit at least 20 people into the meeting. Reg Boorer came to our aid. With skill worthy of a master forger, Reg designed lapel badges for us based on totally fictitious newspapers and magazines which we hoped would fool the guards.

I suggested to McTaggart that we should keep the demonstration simple and orderly and that we should deliver scrolls to the whaling nations which could be unfurled in front of the cameras, condemning them and the non-whaling nations which supported continued whaling for 'crimes against nature.' To representatives of nations which supported an end to whaling, we would ask the women in our ranks to present them with bouquets of flowers. Yes, I know that is considered sexist today, but I'm talking about the late 70s and I'm talking about ensuring the tactics matched the mood of the day and maximised the coverage.

McTaggart was despatched to the hotel where the meeting was to be held and he booked a room from which he investigated the layout of the building. He discovered that a staircase led from the end of the passage where his room was located to a set of fire doors at the back of the conference room. It was decided that we would enter the hotel individually, using Reg's lapel badges as cover, make our way to the room booked by McTaggart who was an accredited delegate to the International Whaling Commission, and wait for him to give us the word to move. I took the precaution of checking the distance, route and time it took to walk between the room and the conference hall. We would need no more than a minute.

On the appointed day we met at the Greenpeace office, the guys in smart trousers, ties and shirts; the women in make-up, skirts and dresses. We'd never seen each other in this garb before and much merriment was had, taking the piss out of each other. We made our way to the hotel in the West End. Reg's badges worked a treat and soon there were twenty of us crammed into McTaggart's room. We were all nervous; many a surreptitious swing of something stronger than tea was taken and the fog from cigarette smoke was thick. After a tense twenty minutes McTaggart opened the door.

'Ok, you guys. Move!'

We proceeded in an orderly fashion to the fire doors, beyond which the hubbub of conversation and activity could be heard. I only hoped the doors had not been locked as a precaution. I glanced behind to make sure we were all present and pushed open the doors into the conference room. Immediately, the glare of TV lights were on us, thanks to McTaggart's tip-off to the crews present, and we filed into the room as the chattering gradually subsided. I walked past the platform where the IWC honchos sat. Ray Gamboll, the IWC director, looked at me in dismay.

114

Demonstration, Barrow, 1980

Dumping radioactive mud

High pressure hoses used to repel Greenpeace protesters

Greenpeace protest against disposal of radioactive waste, North Atlantic, 1981 © Gleizes Greenpeace

Greenpeace attempts to stop dumping of radioactive waste into the Atlantic, 1981 © Greenpeace Gleizes

Direct hit on a Greenpeace dinghy, radioactive waste action, North Atlantic, 1982 © Greenpeace Gleizes

MV Cedarlea, dubbed Wilkinson's Folly, North Atlantic, 1982

Time to Stop Nuclear Testing, Big Ben protest 1984

Looking for the Windscale pipeline, Irish Sea, 1983

Divers use equipment in a vain attempt to block the Windscale pipeline, 1982
© Gleizes Greenpeace

David Fraser McTaggart, Chairman of Greenpeace International

Above: Grandfather George Cremore, second left, in the Cricketers

Below: Brother Brian and wife Margaret

The Rainbow Warrior after the French attack, Auckland Harbour, 1985

I paused to tell him, 'This is a peaceful Greenpeace protest. We simply want to say a few words.'

Accepting his fate, he shrugged and said, 'The floor is yours.'

We went through our routine which went perfectly. The crowd of delegates, press reporters, aides and embassy officials was gradually drawn into the atmosphere of the event and began applauding the delegations who received the bouquets and booing those condemned by us.

I told the meeting that public opinion, which we represented, was totally opposed to whaling and in the name of the people, I therefore declared commercial whaling over. I thanked the delegates for their time and for coming to this vitally important meeting, closed the meeting and wished delegates a safe and pleasant journey home. As we sat down to observe our two minutes silence, the room erupted into applause. In fact, it went so well and we exercised so much control over the meeting, that when one TV crew who had failed to catch the full speech asked me to repeat it, the request was granted by the IWC secretariat.

The demonstration over, we stood and began to file out of the conference room. We had to pass behind the Japanese delegation and one of the protesters could not resist the opportunity to vent his pent-up anger on the country seen as the biggest obstacle to an end to whaling.

From his jacket, he produced a bottle of red ink and tipped it all over the head of the delegation, shouting, 'You want to see blood? I'll give you blood, you arseholes!'

He was immediately set upon by three sumo-proportioned bodyguards. As I glanced back at the melee, I saw McTaggart wrestling the protester from the grip of the bodyguards and somehow spiriting him away, out into the street. I was impressed by McTaggart's resourcefulness. The result, however, was as predictable as it was disappointing. Our peaceful and stylish protest, which would have explained clearly to the public what the issues were with respect to whaling, was ignored by the news bulletins that day. Instead, they covered the ink-throwing incident and we were cast, not for the last time, as a bunch of unruly, yobbish demonstrators who would go to any lengths to create havoc.

Despite our growing notoriety, we were still poorly financed. So it was with wide eyes that we gazed at the contents of a bulging brown envelope brought to our office one day in the summer of 1979 by a mysterious character who did not want to identify himself. The envelope contained one hundred twenty pound notes – a cool two grand to boost our beleaguered account which struggled regularly to get above a few hundred quid. In return, we were asked to deliver fuel to a ship anchored off Essex just outside UK jurisdiction. She was called the Mi Amigo and housed the pirate radio station, Radio Caroline. It was deemed an illegal operation by UK broadcast laws and therefore aiding or abetting the vessel was technically illegal, but the notes lying across the desk made all that seem petty and of little consequence and, in any case, it was en route to Iceland where we were returning to continue the previous year's anti-whaling activities. We agreed.

Chapter 14

Greenpeace grows/directorship/dumping

McTaggart had been busy. Greenpeace France was up and running, headed by Remi, a self-confessed 'nasty little agitator' and an aspiring opera singer, if Greenpeace folklore is to be believed. Greenpeace Holland followed under the tutelage of a young Hans Guyt, a former seaman. Greenpeace UK, which for the present was the limit of my horizon, was growing steadily and we were rapidly outgrowing our cramped offices in Columbo Street.

My old mate from FoE days, Reg Boorer, was helping us out with publicity material and was around the offices regularly. Tony Marriner was plying between the *Warrior* in KGV Docks and the office. Janie Read, Denise Bell and Susi Newborn, Allan Thornton and I, plus a growing body of volunteers, drawn to Greenpeace's bombastic and extrovert style, were busy researching and plotting campaigns and actions.

Tony Marriner found a bigger office in Crucifix Lane – highly appropriate for us band of martyrs – which we lost because we began carrying out major structural alterations to the office before we had signed the lease, so for a period of three months we were forced to operate out of peoples' flats, from park benches and from public telephone boxes. We finally found an office opposite Charing Cross station, in Chandos Place.

Allan Thornton, who could legitimately lay claim to having been the founder of Greenpeace in the UK since it was his determination which had forced the BBC to show the documentary on the Greenpeace campaigns to stop the killing of 250,000 harp seal pups on the ice floes of Newfoundland, was beginning to flex his muscles in the office a little too much for my liking. I felt he was taking on too much responsibility and saw himself as the 'leader'. He had begun, quietly and unobtrusively to begin with, to require that all decisions were made only with his approval. While he was perfectly affable most of the time, he could quickly turn into a fiery adversary. I agreed with many of his views, but I didn't like having them foisted upon me in what I considered to be a patronising way.

During this time, and over the coming months, I perceived him as becoming increasingly bullish and secretive – not on a major scale – and

I watched him gather a group of confidantes around him, seemingly at my expense, as the contact between us lessened and became more strained. Gradually, I was being squeezed out of his coterie of intimates and I began to feel the chill wind of change – or at least the portents of an impending clash – in my day-to-day work at Greenpeace.

McTaggart had cajoled us into forming Greenpeace Europe, comprised of the UK, France and Holland and each office appointed a representative (later to be dubbed trustee) to this body. Greenpeace Europe met infrequently but was vital in order to commit the different offices to a common campaigning agenda.

I recall Allan going abroad for a period of time, during which I was to become the trustee in his absence. We had increased our number in the office with the addition of Maureen Falloon, a very able, dedicated and enthusiastic woman, who had held an executive position in her profession and who now wished to dedicate her considerable skills to saving the world with Greenpeace. We also acquired the services of Elaine Lawrence whose background was not something I was made privy to. She was entirely affable and became my campaign assistant and did the job admirably. She and Maureen seemed to have fallen into Allan's sphere of influence, perhaps due to the perception of me as sexist and classist – not that I was either – but I think my outspokenness on social issues did not suit the 'new age' image and atmosphere that some in the office were keen to foster.

As Allan was about to leave the office for his sojourn, leaving the fragile creature of Greenpeace in what I can only assume he considered to be the insensitive hands of an ex-lorry driver, he was forced to have his say. In essence, he said that when I took over for the coming few weeks, I would be required to consult those people in whom he had confidence – namely Elaine Lawrence and Maureen Falloon. Denise and Susi had by this time moved on for pastures greener, unsure of the 'organised' direction in which Greenpeace was moving.

The politics of an evolving organisation were already beginning to surface with more regularity than I cared for. Feeling increasingly isolated, I knew that I had to rely more and more on the support of David McTaggart. He and I were growing closer (well, as close as anyone could get to him, outside of being family), and I knew that in me he saw a kindred spirit. At Greenpeace meetings he would generally seek me out, and towards the end of an evening while others talked environment and campaigns, he and I would watch football or snooker on TV and indulge in the talk of ordinary, if far from normal, geezers.

The demands made on me – indeed, on everyone associated with the organisation – were increasing. I was at home less and less. Incredibly, we had no telephone at home in Haughley Green, hardly ideal for the press liaison role I performed. So the more I was in the office, the more I was able to do my job with a semblance of efficiency. While being in the office was good for Greenpeace and me, it was just the opposite for Annette and my increasingly awkward marriage.

Meanwhile, in Iceland, the *Warrior* was inevitably arrested by the coastguard for interfering in a legitimate national activity – killing whales – and was asked to return to Reykjavik after days of harassing the catcher vessels out in the North Atlantic. I must admit I was amazed when David McTaggart willingly turned the boat around and went quietly back to Reykjavik under the ship's own power It didn't seem very rock 'n' roll to me, but I thought perhaps there was something to his actions that I didn't understand. That hunch turned out to be correct and was to lead to the first of many bust-ups between David and me a few months later.

McTaggart negotiated the *Warrior* out of Icelandic incarceration and she was making her way to Spain where plans to continue anti-whaling activities, against whaling vessels operating out of the north west coast of Spain, had been laid. Sitting in the office, I idly plotted her intended route on an old chart that was lying around. The line I traced traversed an area of sea around which a neat box was printed with the words, 'Dumping Zone' written in its boundary. It lay some six hundred miles southwest of Land's End and the *Warrior* would be sailing within a few miles of the spot.

I made a few calls and quickly established that it this zone was a region into which the British, Dutch and Belgians had been dumping radioactive waste since the mid 70s. Typically, the UK would dump 2,000 tonnes of low to intermediate level waste into the ocean at this spot every year. Further digging revealed that the UK, cursed with an insoluble problem, largely generated by its nuclear weapons aspirations, had been dumping radioactive waste in all manner of locations since the 50s.

One location was the Hurd Deep, just north of the Channel Islands, which had also been used for the marine disposal of WWII ordnance, but sailors we talked to would relay tales of cavalier dumping as soon as the ship had cleared port, no matter where the vessel might be. Now, at least, the dump was taking place in a deep trench, according to the charts, but that hardly justified the practice in my mind. As the *Warrior* made her way slowly south, I talked the radioactive waste issue through with friends. It seemed to us that this was the Achilles Heel of the nuclear industry as it was – and remains – the most intractable problem the industry had to deal with. Sweeping waste under the carpet of the Atlantic was not a solution, however, and represented the worst of all attitudes to dealing with this lethal poison. I called the *Warrior*. McTaggart bade me dig deeper and find out when the next dump was taking place, saying that it would be highly serendipitous if a dump was in progress while the *Warrior* was in the area. I did and it was.

Chapter 15

The Battle of the Atlantic

Greenpeace was gradually dragging itself to its feet. Its public appeal was steadily, if a little erratically, growing. In the UK it had a clear cut victory under its belt: it had faced down the government and saved thousands of grey seals in the Orkney Islands. McTaggart worked tirelessly to realise his vision of a truly international, co-ordinated organisation addressing the big issues of the day. He bridled at any hint of nationalism, but grudgingly recognised that a strong international organisation was only as effective as the strength of its constituent parts. The tension between the need for each national office to pander to its domestic 'market' while playing an effective role on international projects surfaced regularly.

Despite these tensions, Greenpeace exuded romanticism and a buccaneering approach to environmental campaigning. Its connection to native North American peoples, McTaggart's seemingly unending fight against French nuclear weapons testing in the South Pacific and the growing interest from and exposure it enjoyed in the media created an irresistible mix for the public. Greenpeace dominated every waking hour of my life. I lived and breathed it, only vaguely registering that the UK office, despite its success, was being eyed by McTaggart as a potential 'problem' office largely because it was to begin courting, with some success, the trades union movement.

In 1977 the *Rainbow Warrior* made her way into that area of international waters marked on the charts as a 'dumping ground'. On arrival, Captain Pete Bouquet began a search pattern in the prescribed area on a relatively calm sea. Within hours, a vessel was spotted on the horizon, some 12 miles distant. It was the *MV Gem*, on charter to the Atomic Energy Authority, and she was carrying close to 2000 tonnes of low and intermediate level radioactive waste. She was hove to.

As the *Warrior* approached, the crew could see splashes of water erupting along the starboard side of the ship: barrels hitting the sea as they were pitched overboard, each weighing around two tonnes. On the VHF radio, Pete announced to the skipper of the *Gem* our belief that disposing of radioactive waste in the international commons of the Atlantic was offensive, potentially dangerous and most definitely unethical, even if it was legal. He asked them to desist.

'No' came the reply.

That first direct action against disposal of packaged, solid radioactive waste into the Atlantic was poorly documented by modern standards, but the crew and the on-board media managed to capture for the first time the dumping of radioactive waste at sea: activities which the UK in particular would rather have kept off the screens. The images – both moving and still – were soon to be reproduced on TV screens and in the newspapers of Europe with repercussions we could only dream of at that time.

Greenpeace had arrived unprepared for taking on radioactive waste disposal rather than anti-whaling activities and many on board saw this as a distraction from the main event of getting to Spain and protecting their beloved whales. Athel von Koetlitz took the Avon inflatable over to the *Gem* from the *Rainbow Warrior*. The *Gem* was lying a-hull, gently rolling on the long swell. Barrels of waste were being lifted by the derricks from the hold, placed on platforms along the gunwale and secured with wooden wedges which were removed as the ship rolled in the direction which would take the barrels into the sea.

Athel calmly placed the nose of the *Avon* directly beneath the tipping platform. The seamen on board the *Gem* ignored him and sent the barrels crashing down around him. One hit the nose of the Avon, another hit the pontoon on the port quarter. It was clear that we would have to up our game if we were to prevent this deliberate pollution of international waters, and as the *Warrior* broke off its engagement with the *Gem* and resumed its actions against commercial whaling, I focused my mind on developing the nuclear campaign, to see what more we could do to prevent the disposal next year, and to think about what the consequences of denying the nuclear industry this disposal route for its nuclear waste might be in the long term.

We had brought to the attention of the public the fact that the UK, along with a few other nations, had been using international waters as a convenient carpet under which to sweep their increasing volumes of embarrassing waste. Now it was time to flesh out our arguments and develop a campaign strategy. The 1978 dump was to take place in July and it was imperative that we capitalised on the success we had had in highlighting the issue a year previously.

122

We wrote to every member nation of the London Dumping Convention (LDC), the body charged with regulating the disposal of waste into international waters. From their replies we produced a statement of concern, reproducing extracts from the replies we received. It appeared that sea dumping of radioactive waste was indeed a hotly contested, and thoroughly disapproved of (by some important nations), method of disposal. It was clear from the letters we received that the UK and its co-dumpers were in a very small minority of nations supporting this method of 'waste management' as it was loftily referred to by ministers. In actual fact, the UK's radioactive waste management policy could be summed up in three words – chuck it away.

The tactic of putting inflatable dinghies beneath the tipping platforms as pioneered by Athel von Koetllitz and other Greenpeace activists the previous year would be repeated. But we needed to build the story up for the media. We visited Sharpness Dockyard, near Bristol, where the *Gem*, the ship chartered by the UK Atomic Energy Authority, was being loaded with her nuclear cargo. Posing as a BBC TV crew, Tony Marriner, camera over his shoulder, and I were afforded access to the ship and filmed away to our heart's content on board. On the quayside were two large, yellow canisters bearing MOD identification stencils.

When asked what they contained, a seaman told us, 'Oh, they're fuel rods from submarine reactors.'

If true, the UKAEA would have been in breach of the restrictions imposed by the LDC which forbade the disposal of high active waste such as submarine fuel rods. Later, the ministry told us the barrels contained 'ion exchange resins', no more dangerous than 'luminous dials from wrist watches.' Yeah, right.

Having developed the strategy for the coming action, it was expected that I would act as on board campaigner. It was my first sea-based action. On board the *Warrior*, McTaggart pulled me to one side.

'Listen, Peter, me boy', he said, putting his arm around my shoulder and guiding me away from the rest of the crew. 'When you stood on the *Warrior* last time, she was at anchor and you were close to throwing up. If you get on this ship and feel sick, I'm telling you, man, you won't give a damn what they're dumping in the briny. They could be throwing your mother over the side and you'll feel so ill that you won't give a damn. Let's see how it goes and if you are sick, I'll take over and we can talk about it later.'

With those words reverberating in my ears, I wandered out on deck and pondered my future with Greenpeace. Every experience to date indicated that I did suffer from the old mal de mer, but I desperately wanted to demonstrate to David that his faith in me was well placed and that I could overcome it.

We set out from Falmouth on a shimmering, glassy-smooth, gently undulating sea. The sun beat down and Sue Lloyd Roberts from ITN, Jack Saltman and his TV crew from Thames TV, together with most of the crew, took the opportunity to work up their tans. Despite the calm sea, a swell took the ship in regular, undulating motions and within an hour, to the amazement of the salty dogs on board, and to my own huge disappointment, I began to feel sick. I ignored it. I ate and convinced myself that I was being stupid. We had a week before reaching the dump site and I busied myself by sending out the all-important press releases which would alert the press to what they had dubbed the 'new battle for the Atlantic.'

Within two days, I was feeling fine and enjoying every minute of my first trip with Greenpeace. In the evenings we would gather in the cramped saloon of the *Warrior*, sink a few beers and someone – usually Athel – would play guitar.

We took watches on the bridge, periods of intense boredom in which we simply watched the sea for two hours, and then indulged in the great privilege of steering the ship for a further two hours – not daring to lift our eyes from the mesmerising compass to keep our course as accurate as possible. During long sea passages in the open ocean, steering would amount to little more than keeping a straight course, the direction of which was given to the helmsperson by the mate on watch.

After a seven day steam we arrived at the dumping area in remarkably persistent good weather. It covered about 900 square miles of ocean and John Castle, our barrel-chested skipper from Guernsey, began a search pattern. On our second day in the dump zone, we found the *Gem*. She had already jettisoned the two large yellow containers – something we had hoped to film – and was engaged in hauling the smaller drums from her hold, two at a time with her derricks, swinging them onto metal tipping platforms which were mounted fore and aft and which stood proud of the gunwale, where the barrels were chocked temporarily before being cast into the depths.

Before any action we always gave the opposition the opportunity to see sense and desist from their activities before things got nasty. I duly climbed to the bridge and lifted the VHF from its cradle.

'*Gem, Gem, Gem.* This is *Rainbow Warrior, Rainbow Warrior.* How do you read?'

'*Rainbow Warrior*, this is Gem's skipper speaking. How can I help you?'

I went through the routine about polluting international waters with nuclear waste, the commons of the oceans, to which the response was a metaphorical yawn.

He would not stop a legitimate, licensed activity and we should leave the area immediately. The representative of the National Union of Seamen on board was equally unmoved by my pleas made by VHF radio. I had no option but to inform them that we would be carrying out peaceful direct action to prevent the dump.

At that point, the *Gem*, which had been steaming slowly into the swell, put on a turn of speed which the *Warrior* could barely match. We hurriedly prepared the inflatables and the large 28 foot semi-rigid boat (RI28) we used as a filming platform, into which climbed Jack Saltman and his team, plus Sue Lloyd Roberts. As agreed the night before, the crews for the inflatables paired off to their individual boats. I walked towards my dinghy with Chris Robinson, a burly, hirsute Australian who had a reputation of being the best driver we had.

As our boat was lowered on the small derrick perched on the boat deck, I glanced over at the *Gem*. She was now making about 13 knots, moving away from us at a sedate pace as the *Warrior* cleaved the water in pursuit. As our inflatable hit the water, the bow rope was made fast to a cleat on the *Warrior's* deck which effectively put the small craft under tow while Chris fired up the engine amid clouds of exhaust smoke. Once running, Chris nodded to me and I climbed over the gunwale and clambered down the short ladder, timing my jump into the inflatable to coincide with its rise on the swell. Chris engaged the gears and the bow rope slackened as we moved under our own power, keeping pace with the *Warrior* until someone on deck released the bow rope and threw it to me. Now we were free of the *Warrior* and sped off over the glassy sea to rendezvous with the other action boats and the RI28.

I asked Jack to station his film crew parallel to the forward tipping platform, about 100 yards off the *Gem*. That would be the tipping area we would be concentrating on, the aft one being used only occasionally. We would position ourselves under the tipping platform so that if a barrel was tipped overboard, it would hit us before hitting the sea. I recalled the picture of the inflatable crushed by a falling barrel last year and quickly pushed the image from my mind. We prayed that they would not be so stupid as to dump a barrel on us, especially as we had the camera crew filming every move. I noticed that the *Gem* now had hoses playing in a criss-cross pattern across the approach to the tipping platform, in readiness for our arrival, and the bow wave she was creating was sizeable.

We careered towards the *Gem*, through the jets of high pressure water as Chris slammed the dinghy up against *Gem*'s hull, directly beneath the tipping platform. As he held her there on full throttle, our heads were at times level with the platform as the dinghy rose on the bow wave and snatched exchanges with the crew were possible. To my amazement, Chris immediately began a running verbal exchange with the seamen, telling them to respect the oceans and to take their 'crap' home.

A white-overalled official arrived on deck to take charge of the situation. He ordered barrels to be delivered to the platform and as they were swung up from the holds he directed two seamen to untie the hoses and direct them at us. The jets of water were very powerful and when they hit your head, they hurt. More critically, the dinghy began to fill up with water. This additional weight would eventually overcome the power of the engine and we would be forced to drop back. The barrels swung ominously onto the platform above us and were chocked with two small wooden wedges.

The UKAEA official leant over the gunwale. 'This barrel is coming over whether you're there or not. So get out of the way NOW! It's your funeral!'

The dinghy was bucking wildly on the bow wave thrown up by the *Gem* as it cleaved the waters at 13 knots, and we were being hit by powerful jets of water. There was a cacophony of noise and the dinghy's engine was screaming at full revs. The metal bar holding a canvas covering across the bow of the dinghy came up and smacked me in the face. To make matters worse, the water filling the dinghy was causing the engine to labour horribly under the strain.

Chris shouted, 'I'll have to pull out, Wilks! Losing power!'

With that, he shut the throttle and we dropped back along the hull of the *Gem*. As the stern passed us, the tops of the propeller blades of the *Gem* thrashed a regular and vicious beat through the water. Without power now, the dinghy was sucked beneath the stern and we watched with relief as the propeller blades passed us with only feet to spare.

Chris was grinning from ear to ear. 'Nice one, Wilks! They didn't dump one barrel!'

The dinghy was draining now and as soon as Chris managed to restart the engine and get under way, the remaining water was quickly discharged. We sped up to the *Gem* again. Beneath the platform was John's dinghy, with Dutchman Tom in the bow, undergoing the baptism which we had just survived.

As soon as John's inflatable was just a fraction off station, the barrel on the platform was sent crashing into the sea, only feet from the bow of his dinghy. A great plume of water rose into the air, taking the dinghy to an almost vertical position as the occupants hung on for dear life. Soon, John was forced to drop back, his engine audibly labouring, and in swept Chris and I again, to undergo another round of soaking, verbal abuse and close shaves. The seamen were getting more confident at timing the barrels to avoid the dinghies and only skilful driving could keep us on station permanently. Once we fell back even a few feet, a barrel would be sent spinning into the ocean, missing us narrowly.

Then it was over. We were exhausted and could do no more. We broke off from the *Gem* and trucked over to the film crew. We shook hands all round and Jack Saltman asked me by way of a filmed interview, 'Why are you doing this, Pete?'

Without missing a beat, I looked straight into the camera and said, 'That's a very good question!' At which point we all roared with laughter.

What an incongruous sight we must have made. Three tiny bits of floating canvas, rubber and metal in the middle of a vast ocean with four bedraggled activists and a camera crew laughing their heads off.

The *Warrior* steamed up to collect us. As we forced boiling coffee between parched lips, someone commented, 'We pushed peaceful direct action to its ultimate limit today. Where do we go from here?'

Fortunately, in the years to come we found a few answers to that particular question. The fact was that, with this action and those that followed, Greenpeace had grasped the tail of the nuclear tiger. Much to the surprise of many, but not, I like to think, to my own surprise, we gradually saw the strategy we had devised in a humble office, just south of Blackfriars Bridge in 1977, unfold to realise the campaign success we all dreamed of: the UK's nuclear waste management policy vacuum would contribute significantly over the coming years to the nuclear industry's undoing.

Back on board, McTaggart was beaming. He had already been in conversation with John Castle and met me with the news that we would right now set a course for the southwest of England. I looked at him incredulously.

'First off, David, I'm in charge of this action and I'll discuss with the skipper and the crew the best course of action to take from here on. And secondly, we've only attempted to stop the dump for two hours and you want to head off home?'

He pursed his lips. 'Ok, ok. So you want to hang around here to go and be a hero again – for what? To feel good about it? To risk other lives? Get some more footage of the same stuff in the can? Lemme tell you something which is a central point to the way I believe we should operate. We are in the business of changing peoples' attitudes.

'You're not gonna change your damn government's mind about sea dumping with this action. It's public opinion that'll swing the government and there's no better way to get the public onside than to get that film screened as quickly as possible. You wait around here, you'll do the same stuff, with the same reaction and all you'll do is waste two, three days. And as for me taking control and telling the skipper to get outta here, well that's the way I work.' I realised from the motion of the ship that we were already underway in a north-easterly direction.

We steamed home in a haze of euphoria. Some of the more hardened crew gave me a hard time about leaving so early and our unseemly haste did leave a bad taste in my mouth. There had to be a balance struck between action which was simply a stunt, a photo-opportunity, and action which commanded respect from your opponent because it had integrity. This dilemma was to become a central issue in Greenpeace circles for a long time and is one which still rages today. But we had done a good job and had built another layer of bricks in the wall of opposition to sea-dumping.

We arrived at Falmouth after three weeks at sea. The film was despatched ahead of our arrival, taken ashore by the super-fast RI28, and by the time we were waiting on the platform for our train to London, the ITN crew had produced a mini-tv and were watching the film on the 6 o'clock news. I walked down the platform from the kiosk towards the five people standing in a group, gently oscillating in unison, all finding their land legs, eyes fixed on the tiny screen of their portable TV.

Chapter 16

Icelandic adventure and a centre-fold scoop

As I left the *Warrior* to take the train home to my long-suffering wife, Chris Robinson, my skilful dinghy driver, gave me a goodbye hug and told me he'd see me sooner than I thought. When I questioned him, he confided that the crew intended to take the ship back to Iceland immediately, since the Icelandic delegation to the International Whaling Commission had voted against a ban on killing sperm whales. Apparently, this was a threat made to the Icelandic whalers on the previous visit and the crew were not about to renege on it. The stark facts about the viability of the sperm whale stocks around Iceland spoke for themselves. The scientific committee of the IWC itself had warned only that year that stocks were in decline, as evidenced by the lowering of the age of maturity of the whales, as they struggled to reproduce earlier and earlier in the face of dwindling numbers and by the ever decreasing 'catch per unit effort' – the number of whales caught per ton of kerosene burned in ships engines. It was taking far longer to kill the same number of whales than it had ten years previously.

Chris told me that the crew had unanimously agreed that they wanted me as the campaigner on board. While I was flattered, a few things stood in the way of this arrangement – like my wife and my sorely ignored home life – and the fact that the funds for this trip had neither been approved by Greenpeace nor were available. Despite these 'trivial' problems, as Chris called them, the crew were determined to go and Chris told me he would call me in a week to arrange to collect me in Lerwick. While this was a chance I wanted to jump at, I was concerned that it would put me on the wrong side of McTaggart and the growing hierarchy of the organisation. But my concern was fleeting: who would not want to go to Iceland to protect whales?

I arrived at home to find Annette in a cool mood. While she agreed with the need to fight for the environment, she would have preferred it if I could do my crusading more from home. My absences were becoming longer and longer and I was failing to meet my half of our marriage bargain. When

I told her that I might have to go to Iceland, she expressed her entirely understandable concern that the temptations on board a Greenpeace ship might cause me to forget my marriage vows. My protestations of innocence, which were true, seemed to cut no ice. Annette still worked for the Soil Association but still had the responsibility of running the home, looking after the animals and trying to keep the garden in some sort of order. I felt so guilty about the burden she was carrying that when I was home, I'd forego the luxury of lazing around with my feet up – which was all I wanted to do since I was exhausted – in favour of rushing around the house, putting up partitions, laying breeze blocks and doing what I could in the garden. It was exhausting both at home and at work.

Even so, came the day, I shouldered my trusty rucksack containing a change of clothes, my passport and my toothbrush and set off to meet the ship in Lerwick after only three days at home, promising Annette that I'd be home in three weeks. I recall optimistically telling Annette, 'One week's sailing there, one week campaigning, one week sailing home.' I actually arrived home three months later, via Japan and only then after delaying my train journey from London to give an interview to the BBC.

I arrived in Lerwick to see the *Warrior* lying at anchor out in the bay. No sooner had I been ferried aboard by a grinning Chris than John Castle was ordering the lifting of the hook and we were off towards Iceland and round two in the battle for the whales. The atmosphere on board was piratical. It's a wonder the crew were not flying the Jolly Roger.

This voyage was totally unofficial and unsanctioned by the Greenpeace hierarchy. I was unaware that the whaling campaigners in Greenpeace offices, around Europe in particular, were of the view that a further heavy-handed response in Iceland was politically and tactically flawed: they were developing another strategy which they had failed to communicate with sufficient clarity to alter the opinions of the crew. So here I was, a director of Greenpeace UK and its anti-nuclear campaigner, heading up a whaling protest on board the *Warrior*; a protest which the rest of the organisation had not approved and which was seen as an almost mutinous action. In fact, when I got on board the ship and went to see the skipper about the financial resources on board, he was decidedly evasive. The truth was that we had no money on board at all, fuel having been taken in Lerwick on credit.

I shared a cabin with an archetypal hippie New Zealander called Mike. The cabin was in the extreme aft of the ship and was accessed by descending a short flight of steps into pitch-blackness. The cabin had no port-holes and received no natural light. Walking from the saloon, down the corridor, down the steps to the cabin and crawling into the bunk was like making a journey back into the womb. Lying there in the total darkness with the world around you rolling and pitching at all angles was surreal. I came to dread the unseen hand shaking me at 0730 every morning and the voice whispering quietly, 'Wilks. Your watch. It's 0730.'

As we approached the Icelandic twelve mile limit, I called a crew meeting and laid down the law about our attitude to the whalers, to the authorities and to the Icelanders themselves – civility and friendliness. Just as a precaution, I told everyone that any dope or girlie magazines would have to be jettisoned there and then. I expected that statement to be laughed at, as in: 'Fancy thinking we have any dope or girlie mags on board'. One of the on-board TV crews looked at me aghast and asked if I was serious. When I confirmed that I was, they reluctantly agreed to meet me on deck in five minutes and I stood there while they tossed overboard a lump of hash which could have kept a rock concert going for a few days.

We steamed up to Halvafjord, at the head of which was the whaling station and out of which steamed the whale catchers after they had offloaded their kill. The whales were transported to the station secured alongside the catchers by wire hawsers. The *Warrior* could make only 11 knots at full speed and with a following sea. The catchers could make around 15 knots. In the case of Hvalur No 9, it could put on a turn of speed topping 17 knots.

The plan was to pick up a departing whaler from a couple of miles off Hvalfjord and predict her course to the point where the *Warrior* could get as close as possible to her as she began hunting. At that point, the inflatables would be launched. By using the *Warrior* to close on the whalers as much as possible, the inflatables would not have to suffer too long a chase across wild seas. Our secret weapon, the RI28, was designed to be capable of operating independently of the *Warrior* for days at a time. While this was a risky venture – and one which was decidedly uncomfortable for the crew – it did allow us to confront a whaler for extended periods of time, and, hopefully, to provoke an incident or send the whaler back to port.

From the bridge, we could see little but we could hear via the VHF that the action was going well.

'Whales blowing, John!'

'Got it.'

'Port, port, port . . . whale blowing!'

'He's on the harpoon. Hard a'starboard. Quickly!'

'Tony, get in position!'

'Christ, he's fired. Missed!'

This went on for three hours as our inflatables and crews roared back to the *Warrior* for more fuel to sustain the action. On and on it went into the long Arctic day which brought only a few hours of darkness in those high latitudes. From time to time, the skirmish came within a hundred yards of the *Warrior* as the whalers chased the whales and the inflatables weaved around the ocean, keeping station on the bow of the whalers. It was exhilarating stuff, but the action by the inflatables could be sustained no longer. The crews were exhausted and buffeted to a pulp. The RI28 which had hitherto acted as a filming platform would now take over the role of whale saver, replacing the smaller inflatables.

Whaler number 7 had caught no whales. Its crew had rained everything imaginable down on the crews, from potatoes to lumps of metal. Unbowed, the crews – two to a boat – returned to the *Warrior*. I helped John Welsh Thomas off with his wet suit: his back was a mass of bruises and cuts sustained from being thrown around the inflatable for seven hours.

John Castel called me to the bridge on the intercom. A grey warship was approaching fast from the south. It was the *Tier*. Her commander informed us he had orders to arrest us and asked me to call off the RI 28. In order to play for time, I went into a long dialogue about the legality of the impending arrest and insisted that before we called off the action, I would need to consult our Icelandic lawyer. But the writing was on the wall and it was clear that the 28 was being taken further and further from the *Warrior* as the whaler sought to separate us by steaming north, ignoring the location of whales.

I reluctantly radioed the 28 and recalled them. As she came within 100 metres of the *Warrior*, an inflatable from the *Tier* arrived to arrest the 28 and there ensued a farcical 20 minute sea chase between the underpowered and heavily burdened Icelandic inflatable carrying six military personnel and the vastly superior 28 which simply kept out of reach by a few feet with a quick flick of the throttle control.

I walked down from the bridge with John who had been on the bridge now for 18 hours. He sat down in the saloon and raised a forkful of well-deserved food to his mouth just as the arresting officers came into the saloon.

'You are under arrest, captain, and so is your vessel.' John chewed on and through the mouthful of food said, 'Ok. I'll just finish my food.'

The officer instructed John to steer for Reykjavik, but the engines, as pre-arranged, had fallen silent. I informed the officer that there was a problem and we had no power. I added that we did not intend to spend supporter's money steaming to a place we had no desire to go and that if he wanted us to go to Reykjavik, he would have to tow us. After due arrangements and equipment were put in place that is what the *Tier* duly did.

Back in port, the legal wrangling began. Icelandic news agencies were buzzing with the story and our TV crew was suddenly in possession of hot property and began feeding stations all round the world with our dramatic footage. Supporters began to risk coming to the ship. Icelanders themselves were warming to Greenpeace. On a more mundane level, the ship was clean out of food and I called McTaggart. After an initial broadside about undemocratic and unsanctioned action (that was rich coming from him), he told me he would be in Reykjavik that evening and I should book two rooms at the hotel for himself and Allan Thornton. The big guns were coming to town. I collected £100 he had wired and took it to Denise on the ship. As I handed it over, she grabbed two crew members and headed off for town. Two hours later, the saloon table was groaning under the weight of 20 bags of rice, fresh vegetables, wine and beer. We had a good knees up that evening and we deserved it.

The following evening, at the hotel, two journalists from a well-known tabloid newspaper arrived and bought me a massive and very expensive dinner. As I savoured my first drop of scotch in weeks, we discussed plans for their occupancy on board the *Warrior* for the next round of action. The reporter told me that back home, indeed all over Europe, Greenpeace were 'box-office.' We negotiated our release after three days of purposely staying in port to argue our case in the Icelandic press. Our release was handled by an Icelandic lawyer acting on our behalf, but since we had actually broken no law we simply left port at our own convenience after informing the authorities. But the tactic of delaying our departure and thereby allowing whaling to continue unmolested was frustrating, a mood which was heightened by a further three days of forced inactivity as we hove-to outside Hvalfjord waiting for a whaler which was not whaler number 9, the fastest and most efficient killer in the fleet. To engage that particular ship was pointless, given the *Warrior's* top speed of ten knots. We had to wait for one of the slower vessels and on the fourth day, number 7 puffed into port with two whales strapped to her hull and emerged two hours later.

The *Warrior* gave chase. Weather and sea conditions were against us and within a few hours the whaler had disappeared from the radar screen and we had been unable to launch our boats due to a steep sea and howling wind. But we were now deep into the whaling grounds and John Castle decided we would stay where we were and carry out a search pattern for the whalers which were doubtless in the area. We searched fruitlessly for a further two days. As John went off watch one evening in a particularly foul mood, I asked him for a course.

'Steer what you like,' he said. 'There's nothing out there. Steer 350 and see what happens.'

After an hour on that course, an iceberg appeared on the horizon. We approached it cautiously. From behind it emerged a whaler – catcher number 7. Pandemonium broke out. Inflatables were despatched, the RI28 was hauled up on the derrick and film crews and ship's crew rushed around in well-practised routines which had the boats away in fifteen minutes.

The practice of taking TV crews and media on board was a double-edged sword. We needed the press – particularly the tabloids – in order to spread our message to the millions who read them but at the same time, we felt rather sniffy about them as they tended to trivialise the important issues we were addressing. One particular occasion was a case in point. I was actually on deck helping to pull people on board after their stint in the boats but according to the caption on the picture which accompanied a double page spread of our actions, I was in the inflatable as the 'daring campaigner'. In another example, one of the crew wiped water from his face as he was swept along in one of the dinghies but the caption told readers that, 'A Greenpeace campaigner wipes tears of remorse from his eyes as the whale is harpooned.' It wasn't hugely significant massaging of the truth but it still rankled with me as I was always held the view –

and I still do – that honesty is always the best policy and manipulation will come back and bite you in the bum eventually. I think this has been demonstrated over the years as uncorroborated stories of rubber dolphins tangled in nets for the cameras, deliberate risking of life and vetting of the news that reporters were allowed to file from the ships became more widespread. As this happened, the trust and confidence the media had in Greenpeace dropped off a cliff, if the views of some of the reporters that I came to know well are to be believed.

But the fact is that these stories gave Greenpeace a huge audience. Millions of people heard about, read about and were moved by what we were doing in the frozen Arctic waters in defence of whales and our fortunes rose accordingly. We had not stopped whaling in Iceland, nor in Spain, but we had put the issue of commercial whaling and the extinction of some species of whales firmly before the public and the IWC – quite apart from the animal welfare issues associated with the cruel method of killing them at sea: whales literally haemorrhage to death over twenty minutes or so. We accused the IWC of presiding over the demise of whale stocks. We lobbied the delegates mercilessly. McTaggart constructed a coalition of the great and good, including the late Sir Peter Scott, to back our campaign and exert political pressure for a commercial whaling ban. The direct actions, as McTaggart always told me, were the five per cent of a campaign which people saw and to which they reacted, but the real skill in winning was to be able to turn the outrage people expressed when an abuse was exposed into policy changes by the politicians. A ban on commercial whaling was eventually achieved.

Chapter 17

Trades unions to the rescue and a Spanish inquisition

Radioactive waste dumping, whaling and seals: this had been my 1978. I had been away from home more than I cared to think. Furthermore, when I was in the UK, I was spending more and more time in the office rather than at home. 1979 and 1980 saw a repeat of these campaigns, a renewed Greenpeace presence on the Newfoundland ice-floes to oppose the killing of seal pups, arrests all over the world of Greenpeace personnel and the early stages of development of the campaign against the gigantic nuclear reprocessing plant at Sellafield. The board of directors of Greenpeace UK was now Elaine Lawrence, Maureen Falloon and myself, with Elaine doubling as my campaign assistant. We were a good team and recruited more and more people as the months stretched into years.

As part of the ongoing campaign against radioactive waste-dumping in the Atlantic, I had made approaches to the National Union of Seamen (NUS). Their General Secretary, Jim Slater, and I became instant friends. Jim, a big, burly but thoroughly gentle man, backed the campaign immediately, but before he could bring the NUS's weight to bear, he was required to convince his national executive of the wisdom of opposing a practice which provided employment for NUS members and indeed for the 'snob's' union, the Union of Masters and Airline Pilots Association, whose skippers commanded the Stephenson Clarke ships chartered by the UKAEA. It was a long, slow process which was to occupy me for two years. While our public profile was still high, we were engaged in a period of research and diplomacy, particularly over Sellafield, which, in terms of allocation of time, overshadowed our more public activities. I viewed it as a necessary period of consolidation. Allan, who had adopted a self-styled ambassadorial role and was thankfully rarely around the office, saw it as a dereliction of duty. His wanderings and long absences undermined his role and influence in the UK office and, to some extent, in the wider Greenpeace world.

After months of wrangling and manoeuvring, McTaggart had managed to head off a potentially crippling court battle between Greenpeace USA and

Greenpeace Canada by disbanding Greenpeace Europe and establishing Greenpeace International. We were now all one big outfit and the annual board meetings which now involved five 'voting' trustees and three or four 'non-voting' trustees, (Australia and New Zealand had also been brought into the fold), were already assuming great significance. It was at these meetings that McTaggart excelled. His ability to steer through his own ideas and plans was largely achieved by ensuring that the people with whom he was dealing had little time to dedicate to the finer points of international development, engaged as they were in the daily grind of trying to improve fundraising performances and campaign profiles in their national offices.

McTaggart, on the other hand, was able to set the agenda and stack up his support, often in the shape of the Canadian trustee, Patrick Moore, long before the meeting took place. Us babes-in-the-wood would turn up to the meetings only to have a motion proposed which, if we dared question it or request time to consider it, would bring a withering attack from McTaggart who would accuse us of holding up the organisation's growth or, more painfully, of not having the support and confidence of our national boards to be able to commit national offices to a proposal. Referring back to our boards was not tolerated. We were trustees for our offices and were required to have the power to make instant and binding decisions.

On more than one occasion, this 'steamroller' attitude was contested by the Dutch office and precipitated a crisis. At one such meeting in Paris, the board of trustees was asked to expel the Dutch trustee because he would not vote on an issue, demanding time to refer it back to his board. The trustees, led by McTaggart, refused this permission and threatened to withdraw the right of the Dutch branch to use the name Greenpeace since it was not living up to the requirements of the constitution. The same ignominious fate befell France on one occasion too. If ever we needed a crash course in the establishment of an international organisation and political shenanigans, we were getting it in spades. The meetings left everyone breathless and at the end of five, six or seven days of such mind-bending deliberations, during which friendships and allegiances were stretched to the limit, we were all exhausted and I could only thank my lucky stars that I could conduct these meetings in English. Poor Remi and others had to do likewise and their heads must have been spinning after trying to decipher the variety of drawls around the table from Canadian, to West Coast American and the stilted accents of our Antipodean friends.

1981 was a tough year. As we consolidated our anti-dumping and anti-Sellafield campaigns, whaling and sealing issues continued to impinge on the short 24 hour days at our disposal. The *Warrior* had been impounded for the second time by the Spanish authorities for interfering with its 'legitimate' whaling operations. Mindful of the fact that the previous arrest had embarrassed the authorities when Greenpeace simply sailed away from port, they were determined that this time there would be no such casual cocking of snoots and the *Warrior* was therefore disabled by the removal of a thrust block – a large, hundredweight block of engineered metal which acted as a guide for the tail shaft between the engine and the propeller. Without such a device, the *Warrior* was going nowhere. To make doubly sure we would not leave port, the authorities put armed guards on the quayside and for good measure, allowed only two crew ashore at a time, minus passports. Remi had been the campaigner on the ship at the time of arrest and was therefore dragooned into heading up the negotiations for the *Warrior's* release with the bureaucracy of the Spanish port authorities. After a month of this debilitating and frustrating work, I was asked to go and spell Remi for a few weeks.

I arrived in El Ferrol – Franco's birthplace – to be met by Remi. As we walked through the town towards the ship, Remi delighted in taking the piss out of the guards and army personnel on duty outside every building by imitating a gun-happy squaddie mowing down a line of imaginary dissidents. His mimicking was all too realistic for some and I noticed with alarm that one or two of them began to un-shoulder arms in the face of Remi's over-realistic parodies. Remi's business card read, 'Nasty little agitator'. I knew what he meant now.

On reaching the ship, we went through the procedures which would become familiar to me over the next few weeks – body searches, passport inspections and scowls of contempt from these macho guys forced to guard a bunch of peace-freaks and whale lovers. Remi eventually left for France, leaving me in charge of negotiations with the authorities for the release of the ship. It was clear from what Remi had told me and what I found out that the Spanish authorities had no intention of letting the vessel go: we were there for the duration as far as the Spaniards were concerned and it was clear that other governments around Europe were quite happy with that state of affairs. If we were to get the ship out, we'd have to steal our own vessel. We needed the thrust block to move the ship.

Back in London, people were poring over the blue prints for the ship and studying how to make a replacement for such a piece of equipment. Tim Mark, a marine engineer, set to work. Within two weeks, the replacement was ready and on its way to El Ferrol, covered by a tarpaulin in the back of a Transit van. In the meantime, we were doing our best to support the 'free the *Warrior*' movement in the town and on one particular evening, we all hopped it from the ship without going through the normal procedures, to plaster every building, statue and billboard with posters. It turned out to be quite an evening and after a few beers, followed by wine at dinner, we were all in a boisterous mood. John Castle made a point of wading across a fountain to plaster a statue of Franco with our protest posters.

Back in El Ferrol the van bearing the thrust block arrived, having negotiated all the borders successfully. We now had to create a suitable diversion to get the guards away from the ship long enough to get this heavy piece of equipment on board. We achieved this by staging a mock fight between some 'drunken' Greenpeacers returning from town and while the guards were sorting out the fight, four guys humped the block on board, somehow manoeuvring it below decks and into the engine room. After a day of fitting and generally fussing over the tolerances here and there, we needed to test it and we obtained permission from the guards to fire up the main engine on the pretext of keeping essential equipment in running order. While the engine was turning, the engineers threw in the clutch and let the ship move forwards slowly on the warps while scrutinising the way in which it performed.

Satisfied that it would do the job, the next task was to plan the escape. Before we actually took the ship itself away, we agreed that we'd test the reactions of the Spanish by getting the RI28 fuelled and provisioned for a daring (and, I thought, foolhardy) dash across the Bay of Biscay and the English Channel to Brighton where the International Whaling Commission was sitting. This, we calculated, would not only be an embarrassment to the Spanish if the 28 turned up at the IWC meeting with Greenpeace escapees on board, but it would also convince the authorities that we were truly unable to depart in the ship itself. Thus, we argued, security might be relaxed a little.

On the appointed morning we doubled the fuel tanks on the 28, stocked her up with water and food and rushed on deck to lift the boat into the water. As the derrick took the strain of the heavily laden boat, it was clear that she was not going to move from her davits. She was simply too heavy. As our guards looked on with apparent unconcern, we took the fuel tanks off the boat, lifted her into the water and then hand-balled the tanks back on board. The be-suited crew then dashed from the accommodation, threw themselves on board and took off at high speed before the guards realised what was happening. To give the crew more time to get away, I told the disbelieving guards that they were simply taking the boat out for a spin to check her engines and they'd be back in an hour.

In actual fact, the three guys on board, Athel von Koetllitz, Chris Robinson and Tony Marriner were making a very perilous journey to which I had only agreed because John Castle had assured me their compass was perfectly accurate. My limited knowledge of the boat told me the compass was constantly being affected by the magnetic field set up by the boat's powerful engines. Once the boat was off and clear, John told me the truth. The compass was affected as I feared, but the crew would stop from time to time, switch off the engines and get a compass reading. While mobile, they would, in John's words, 'Keep the north star just off the port bow and keep the wind on their left cheek.' We waited 48 hours for news of the escape. They didn't make it to Brighton. Fuel starvation which forced the engines to cut out regularly required them to terminate their escape at Ile de France but at least they were safe.

Now came the real test. As we rehearsed the procedures for the escape of the *Warrior*, it was clear that I could do more to publicise the escape from the UK than from Spain and I reluctantly left for home. Tony Marriner, who had returned from his dash to Brighton, agreed to call me at home the moment they were clear of El Ferrol – if they ever made it that far. Just before I left, McTaggart showed up. He clearly smelled a story here and he wanted to be involved. He really was just a kid at heart and although I offered him gold to be allowed to stay on the ship, he quite rightly suggested that I organise the press from the UK as planned, so off I went.

I'd been home for two days when the phone rang. It was Tony. Realising that our conversation was being listened to by every boat, ship and station within a hundred mile radius of where the *Warrior* was at the time, I didn't ask him too much.

'All away ok?'

'Yes, all away.'

'Any followers?

'None that can be identified.'

'ETA home port?'

'Three days.'

'Please call again tomorrow when we can firm up arrangements.'

'Will do. Over and out.'

I can only imagine the mood of the crew that night. They must have been ecstatic. They had simply cut the mooring lines in the early hours of the morning and steamed away on a re-cast thrust block which overheated to the point where they could make no more than seven knots. They weaved their way out of El Ferrol through battleships and Spanish Navy frigates – El Ferrol is the largest NATO port in Spain – and made it to the open sea. The Greenpeace myth was being written before our eyes. Now all I had to do was to parade that myth before the public of the world.

When Tony called the next day, the *Warrior* was out in the open ocean with no following vessels. It looked as though they had made it. We agreed an ETA in Jersey from which I begged Tony not to deviate. I would ensure the world's press were there at the appointed time, not a minute before and not a minute later. No-one was to have an exclusive. He replied, 'All agreed.' After I had called every possible press agency, TV station and radio company this side of Moscow and received assurances that they would be on Jersey to meet the ship at the appointed time, Tony called back to tell me the crew had arbitrarily decided to bring the ETA forward 12 hours. I couldn't believe it. Something had to have gone terribly wrong.

'Nothing's wrong, Wilks,' he replied. 'We're just tired of being at sea and no-one fancies stooging around for 12 hours when we can see land.'

I begged and pleaded with him to stick to the original deadline. No go. In the event, the *Warrior* arrived with only one TV company there to record the event and by the time all the other journalists and reporters had arrived to meet the promised deadline, the crew were scattered around the island in various bars and in no fit state to milk the story. I was devastated and to this day, I still feel that I never got to the bottom of that story, although I did know that there existed a longstanding and ongoing feud between McTaggart and Tony which may have caused some sort of rift.

It certainly used up a hell of a lot of brownie points with the press and it took me a long time to regain their confidence. Belatedly, we heard that the Naval Commander in El Ferrol had been summarily dismissed. Back in the UK office we increased the staff to cover the heavy workload created not only by running the campaigns, but also by the gradually increasing administrative burden.

We had moved offices yet again. 36, Graham Street, Islington, where we moved in 1981, was next door to a timber merchant and directly opposite a block of council flats. The canal ran behind the building and the place was surrounded by pubs. It was a fine location and one which was to witness the flowering and then the death of Greenpeace in the UK in its original guise. Within five incredible years, my personal life and the fortunes of Greenpeace, in the UK and internationally, were to change out of all recognition. A bumpy but thoroughly enjoyable ride was ahead.

As we settled into our new surroundings, we reviewed our situation. We were constantly struggling to attract sufficient income for our campaign and administrative needs, although in relation to our earlier straits, we were quite flush. We had an income of around £200,000 a year, 20,000 supporters, a high public profile and a growing reputation. The money was spread very thinly, however. We operated on a wage equality basis which allowed as small a disparity as possible. Staff members were paid a basic disposable income of £45 a week plus an increment of £5 for every year of service, complemented by income tax and rent paid by the organisation, as were travelling expenses. Since I had been with Greenpeace for four years, I luxuriated in a take home pay of £65 a week.

The hours we worked were dictated by need. Everyone was expected to put their nose to the grindstone and finish the job. Only very rarely did anyone cry off and working a 12 hour day was not uncommon. We sent out our quarterly newsletter – 20,000 envelopes addressed, stuffed, sealed and stamped by hand – in a quarterly frenzy of activity. We involved as many people as possible in every action, every demonstration. We received literally hundreds of letters every day ordering t-shirts, badges, stickers, suggesting campaigning targets, requesting information. The media would not leave us alone. Virtually every day, our presence was required for radio, TV or press interviews.

We worked long and hard on the Graham Street offices, over the course of one memorable weekend turning them from drab work-a-day open spaces into a smart, modern work-station environment: each desk discreetly screened and sporting its own angle-poise lamp, telephone and even potted plant. We organised our library where we housed all the reports, books and press clippings we constantly referred to. On the ground floor of the building we created our 'merchandise department' into which we crammed thousands of t-shirts, posters, badges and other material which was becoming increasingly popular, largely thanks to Reg Boorer's impressive design work. And we reorganised the structure of the board of directors.

Maureen had been asked to run the burgeoning Greenpeace Marine Division and Elaine Lawrence had left, recognising that her strengths and weaknesses, coupled with the fact that her friendship with Allan, who was increasingly hostile to the new-look Greenpeace UK, was putting her in an invidious position. I recruited Reg to the board and asked Tony Marriner who was now setting up and managing the Communications division, to join as well. I then took what I thought was an inspired, if risky step and invited Bryn Jones, my old Friends of the Earth mentor, trade unionist and former industrial correspondent for the Daily Mirror, onto the board. Unknown to me, our development and appointments were being closely scrutinised by the Greenpeace hierarchy and one man in particular – David McTaggart.

Chapter 18

Greenpeace International and the battle
for the soul of Greenpeace

My private life was becoming deeply affected by the demands Greenpeace made on my time. Perhaps, in truth, I allowed and encouraged Greenpeace to intrude on my home life. It made the distancing between Annette and me a little more 'beyond my control'. I was spending more and more time in the office, loath to haul myself to the station and endure the long ride home when there were so many things to do, so many distractions and so much energy to spend in getting back to London the following day. Then my guilt would force me to binge on staying at home for two or even three days at a stretch.

My life became a crazy round of rushing here, there and everywhere, plugging perceived gaps in Greenpeace's profile, board meetings, planning meetings, radio and TV interviews, leaving home for weeks on end to attend international meetings, working up strategies, inspiring people as best as I could and trying to take better stock of where Greenpeace was going and what it could achieve.

Our potential was enormous and the harder we pushed and the more notorious we became, the more the demands on us threatened to sink us. At the peak of all this activity, two things happened that year which were to stretch my nerves to breaking point.

Firstly, the office had to be virtually rebuilt since it was falling apart through rising damp. This happened slap bang in the middle of the London Dumping Convention meeting which was taking place in London that year and had brought the international team of lobbyists from Greenpeace France, Holland, Germany and Scandinavia to the capital to use our office as the administrative base for the meeting. The offices from which our colleagues hailed were typically European and, as in most things, they seemed to be able to organise themselves in a thoroughly European manner, leaving us Brits looking amateurish and slip-shod. Their suspicions and our embarrassment were complete when they were required to operate from an office which was divided down the middle and which required a route march to move from one part of the building to the other, down stairs, out on to the road, down the alley at the side of the building and up the fire escape at the rear of the building. We were the butt of everyone's humour.

Then Allan played his hand. He discovered that he had never actually given up his original shareholding in the company. This gave him powers which he now used ruthlessly. A lawyer's letter informed me that an Extraordinary General Meeting was to be called at which the shareholders would propose five motions, effectively kicking me out and installing Allan as executive director. On paper he had me cold. So little attention had been dedicated to the finer points of the company structure that Allan had been issued with two shares and Denise Bell still possessed her original one. The only other share-holders were McTaggart and I.

If Denise sided with Allan and McTaggart stayed loyal to me, it was three shares to two and it seemed that nothing could prevent Allan's coup succeeding. Our lawyers, however, forced a challenge over the validity of Allan's second share which he did not contest. This meant that parity existed, unless, of course, McTaggart threw in his hand with Thornton which would have seen me sunk.

To his eternal credit, McTaggart backed me and took Allan on and the two belligerents retired to glare at each other pending a resolution of this stalemate. It was then argued – erroneously as it turned out – that a further legal search demonstrated that both my share and that allocated to Denise had also been issued illegally and that the only two legal shares were the ones originally issued to McTaggart and Thornton.

Allan was inconsolable, even when I went to see him to personally try to reason with him. I was, in his words, 'a useless campaigner' who had stacked the board with my old drinking pals and who was unable and unfit to run the Greenpeace office. I concurred on the management side of things: I was totally inexperienced at running an office and had hired a series of office managers who had proved to be equally inept. But on the campaign side his attack raised my hackles. The evidence simply didn't bear out his thesis. I dug in my heels and told him that I would fight. Meanwhile, McTaggart, despite his loyalty to me, was scathing of my inattention to detail and claimed that I had brought about this crisis by ignoring the structural minutiae of the organisation, a claim I could not refute.

In the event, after many people had tried valiantly but unsuccessfully to placate Allan, he agreed to a proposal by Greenpeace International that both shares – his and McTaggart's – should be held in trust by the International Board and that they would only be returned to the UK as and when was deemed appropriate. Even this he would not agree to until he had a telex from McTaggart confirming this arrangement which he intended to lodge with his lawyer. I agreed with him that he could collect the telex from our offices the following day and picked up the phone to the harassed McTaggart who grumpily agreed to send the telex forthwith. I breathed a huge sigh of relief. Just one more meeting with stony-faced Allan before I could legitimately forget about him for good.

The following day I arrived in the office expecting to see the telex from McTaggart on the machine. It wasn't. I called him to tell him we only had an hour left before Thornton would arrive to collect it. He moaned and groaned and renewed his attack on me which caused me to shout, 'Just send the telex!'

Twenty minutes later the telex began chattering. I blanched. It was full of tongue-in-cheek remarks, side-swipes and profanities. I dared not call McTaggart back and ask him to resend it. I selected 'local preparation' mode on the telex and forged a form of words which I trusted would meet Allan's and the lawyer's needs. I had just finished the last sentence when I heard the office door being pushed open. As I ripped the telex from the machine, I looked up to see a grim-faced Allan walking purposefully towards me. Without a word, I handed him the telex which he scrutinised as I held my breath. Then he produced a chilling scowl, his eyes bored right through to my soul, and turned on his heel and left.

The year had one more surprise in store for me. A new entity, Greenpeace International, was to be managed by an international board of five people, cutting it down from the nine it had thus far enjoyed, those being the trustees of the various voting nations comprising International. The rationale for this was that during the Iran-Iraq war, a proposal to send the *Warrior* to the Gulf to help wildlife and to belatedly acknowledge the 'peace' aspect of the organisation's name had been so hotly debated and contested within the organisation that we had not only spent a small fortune on ministering the decision-making process, but we had also lost any enthusiasm for sending the *Warrior* to the Gulf, the debate having taken up the best part of three months.

This inability to arrive at rapid and binding decisions was the driving force behind McTaggart's proposal to establish a board which would operate on a virtual full-time basis and which would be empowered to commit the organisation to courses of action without reference to the old board or the national trustees as they were hitherto known. Should the trustees disagree with the decisions thus made, they had the right to fire the board, providing they could muster a 75% majority of trustees to back such a resolution.

At the AGM that year, after the customary arm-twisting, McTaggart got his way, but only at the expense of Bryn Jones, who McTaggart had ensured was at the meeting in my stead, and who had almost publicly agreed to be the patsy to make up McTaggart's numbers for the vote to go through. The other European trustees, with whom, despite our differences, I had formed a tight voting bloc, never forgave Bryn his role at the meeting. They considered him a Judas who had sold out to McTaggart and who had willingly and unforgivably split the Europeans to give McTaggart his votes. Now it fell to McTaggart to appoint the international board members. Many felt that he already had his ideal board compiled. He needed people with long experience and with some credibility in the organisation. He also needed people who would not give him too much of a hard time at board level.

Pat Moore was obviously appointed before the meeting had even begun. Steve Sawyer, then the trustee for the USA, was likewise a prime candidate and accepted the position. Monica Griefahn, the German trustee, a strong-willed and thoroughly uncompromising woman who later went on to become the Environment Minister for Lower Saxony, agreed to do a two year experimental stint. McTaggart asked me to become the fourth board member, to which I reluctantly agreed. McTaggart became the fifth board member and chairman.

The Greenpeace international board was born, and in effect, in that moment, the trustees of nine nations had been relegated to a talking shop with board-firing powers which could only be exercised if and when they could muster the support of seven of their number. This eventuality was considered so remote that, in effect, five people now ran Greenpeace internationally and David McTaggart ran those five people. I could only sit back and admire the man's extraordinary skill. In the space of one meeting, McTaggart had offered the trustees democracy and then snatched it away from them.

148

So now I was a board member and chairman of the UK office, campaigns director for the UK office, principal nuclear campaigner for the UK and an international board member. I promptly handed over the chair of the UK to Bryn Jones and tried to remind myself that I was also a husband and part bread-winner for a wife and potential family in Suffolk. The two roles were becoming increasingly incompatible and I was to find over the next three years that my life became completely absorbed, eaten up and overridden by this organisation which was now firmly established as the foremost environmental organisation in the world, having outstripped the labouring Friends of the Earth and captured the hearts and minds of the public in a way which left even the mighty World Wildlife Fund in the dust of our ascendency.

I was now working six days a week at full tilt and rarely bothering to go home. I slept in the office, preferring the camaraderie of the staff and pints of bitter in the Prince of Wales to the long haul home and the increasingly acrimonious discussions with Annette about our future, then the slog back into London the following day. My social life was disintegrating fast. Life was Greenpeace, from morning till night, from Sunday to Sunday, from month to month and from year to year.

Chapter 19

Campaign heydays

1982 swam into view. Our year began with further direct actions against the Sellafield plant – more specifically against the transportation of spent nuclear fuel from Japan, in particular, to the ports of Barrow in Furness in Cumbria and Cherbourg in France. We sent the *Warrior* on mission after mission to hinder the passage of vessels to those ports and played cat and mouse games with the ships – the *Pacific Fisher,* the *Pacific Teal* and the *Pacific Swan* – dodging in and out of fog banks, running the gauntlet of navies and coast-guards and being arrested time and time again.

Things regularly got extremely dangerous as we hove-to on the 12 mile limit waiting for the spent fuel carriers to arrive. The cargoes of these vessels – a mere few tons of lethal, highly radioactive and extremely hot fuel rods from the cores of reactors in Japan – have a greater radioactive inventory than the bomb which destroyed Hiroshima and the reports we had commissioned from the Political Ecology Research Group, confirmed that in the event of an accident, whole towns and huge areas of countryside would require evacuation to avoid the radioactive deposition from deadly radioactive fall-out. The fuel rods, destined for chemical treatment or 'reprocessing' in the plants at Sellafield and la Hague, would yield hundreds of cubic metres of radioactive waste and plutonium, the raw material for nuclear bombs.

As we waited off Cherbourg one notable evening, bucking around in a fierce southwester, I hung on to the ship's binnacle while trying to keep my sparse dinner in my stomach. Spotter planes from the shore were taking their last look around the approaches to Cherbourg for our elusive quarry which, we calculated, should arrive within minutes since the steaming time from Barrow, its last port of call, could be accurately calculated. Still it did not arrive. As darkness fell, I could feel my bunk beckoning me. I turned to Remi Parmentier, my French co-campaigner, and told him I was turning in, asking him, stupidly, to call me if anything happened. An hour later, as I luxuriated in the warmth and relatively nausea-free prone position on my bunk, Remi burst into the cabin. In his highly endearing and lilting French-accented English, he said, 'Wilks, they are calling the

Pacific Daisy on the VHF. I realise we are looking for the *Pacific Fisher*, but do you think they are trying to fool us?'

I staggered to the bridge. The wind was whipping the tops off the waves as the *Warrior* pitched and rolled, wallowing to the whimsy of the sea. As I arrived on the bridge, John Castle was taking a call from our collaborators ashore. It seemed that the *Pacific Daisy* was indeed the *Pacific Fisher* and she was at that moment taking a pilot at the entrance to the port. John telegraphed 'full ahead' to the engine room and as the ship began cleaving the waves, he told me, 'We'll probably be about 30 minutes too late, but we'll give it a go, eh? Closer to shore, there's no wind and a heavy fog reducing visibility to almost zero.'

Within fifteen minutes, the *Warrior* was bucking along at 12 knots, a few miles from the harbour entrance in a thick sea fog. The wind had died to a slight breeze and only the swell now took the ship. As we entered further and further into the fog and nearer and nearer to the port, the bridge was crammed full of photographers, journalists and crew all trying to peer through the impenetrable fog. CRASH! The *Warrior* slewed sideways as a thumping grinding noise came from the stern. John shouted, 'Everyone except Wilkinson off the bridge, NOW!' as he hustled people through the bridge wing doors out into the gloom.

I took the opportunity to glance into the radar. We were flat out, doing 12 knots into a wall of fog, but on the radar screen the arms of the Cherbourg breakwater could be seen and the centre of the screen, representing our position, was inching its way closer and closer to the images. John was literally steering the ship blind. Other radar echoes surrounded the ship – French tugs. John issued instructions. 'Wilks, go and see what that crash was and then get the inflatable crews together for launching in 10 minutes.'

I went aft. On the rolling deck the ship's lights threw up an eerie halo which penetrated the fog no more than ten feet. As I watched, the bow of a tug boat came roaring out of the fog and crashed into our port quarter, splintering wood and bending metal. The *Warrior* shuddered and everyone was knocked to the deck. Shit, the mad bastards were ramming us! Then from the starboard quarter came another attack – BANG! – slewing the *Warrior* in her tracks again. At that moment a reporter from The Jersey Times who had been on board for the duration of the action came up to me, notebook in hand.

'So, Peter, can you describe your feelings at a time like this, in the thick of the action, being rammed by French tugs?'

I couldn't believe he had the sangfroid to ask such a question under those conditions. 'Sure, I'll tell you!' I shouted. 'I'm scared shitless and you can quote me!'

Unbelievably, I saw John Castle emerge from the wheelhouse onto the boat deck with John Welsh in tow. John Welsh was dressed in waterproofs and lifejacket and was being instructed by the skipper, now standing outside the bridge and shouting into John's ear, about how to find the harbour in the inflatable, and was – incredibly – about to launch the dinghies.

I said to John, 'For Chrissake, John, who's driving the ship? And you're not telling me you intend to launch the inflatables in this fog and mayhem, surely!'

'I've got Sally on the wheel and yes, I've told John to steer over to the right until he hits the sea wall and then feel his way round to the docking berth.'

'No way, John, no way!' I shouted. 'It's madness to launch in this! He'll die!'

He gave me a withering look of contempt. 'Ok, ok, everybody. Call off the launch. Wilkinson, our illustrious campaigner, has dictated the conditions are too bad! Call it off! You heard the man!'

I walked back on to the bridge with John to try to reason with him. As we entered the bridge he stuck his head immediately into the radar as another crash jolted us all off our feet. He scrambled for the telegraph and yanked it in one movement from full ahead to full astern. The engineers below – who must have thought we were steaming through hell itself – were quick to react to the instruction and slowly the ship lost speed. We watched the rev counter on the deckhead slowly drop and then indicate revs astern. We peered into the gloom as the harbour wall loomed larger and larger. Twenty feet to go. The wall was lined with riot police in full riot gear, dogs baying for our blood. The ship slowed more and more. As the bow reached a point only five feet from the harbour wall, we were still doing a knot or two forwards as the propeller did its best to drag us backwards.

John said quietly, 'Oh, fuck it.'

BANG! The bow hit the wall, scattering riot police in all directions. We could only collapse in howls of laughter such was the release of tension. Within minutes we were all under arrest and the ship was overrun with officials and snarling dogs. Remi was rabbiting on in French, nineteen to the dozen, as the official tried to make his way to the bridge to collar John. We had lost the race for Cherbourg by a good twenty minutes but the furore created by our attempt put us on the front pages the following day and prompted mass protests in the port for days to follow, as the anti-nuclear throng chanted 'Liberez le Warrior, Liberez le Warrior!' We were eventually towed to a mooring outside the harbour and then, rather tamely let go, on pain of further charges should we show our faces in Cherbourg again.

In Barrow we repeated the tactics, this time waiting for seven days before the spent fuel carrier arrived. During that time I was doing my best to curry favour with the inhabitants of Barrow and to garner support for the local action group which we had established a year previously. Mums and dads, aunts and uncles, grandmothers and daughters comprised the Barrow Action Group and after five days of waiting with only myself making the forays ashore from the *Warrior*, anchored beyond the jurisdiction of the grumpy and nervous harbour master, the crew came ashore for a much needed pint or two with the locals. After a rather nervous round of introductions in which the two groups gradually warmed to one another, it was time for us to get back on board for a briefing.

I stayed ashore after agreeing that Bruce Crammond, an experienced, mild-mannered Kiwi mate, would collect me. By the time he arrived, it was growing dark. The *Warrior* was ten miles off at the mouth of the channel. To reach her, we had to hack some pretty serious water as it channelled into Barrow through narrow heads. The wind was picking up as we rounded the headland and hit more exposed seas. Within a few minutes, the inflatable was bucking wildly, being thrown this way and that in the steepening swells. Worse still, the weather had clagged in badly and we couldn't see the *Warrior*. I called John on the VHF and asked him to look out for the light from the torch I was holding in the direction of the ship as Bruce wrestled with the inflatable. John called on the VHF to announce that he was lifting the hook and steaming slowly towards us since the conditions were deteriorating very fast. Bruce and I were being thrown around the dinghy quite seriously now and as we crested a wave, I caught sight of the *Warrior*, searchlight blazing, about a mile off.

'John I see you!' I called into the VHF. 'We're off your port bow! Come to port five degrees and we'll make way towards you!'

'Roger, Roger.'

I was never so glad to see that old tub as I was that evening. As we scrambled aboard in the lee John had created for us with the ship's bulk, I learned that the anchor chain had snapped as the hook was lifted, so violent were the sea conditions out here. We were lucky to have arrived in one piece. Bruce and I grinned at each other as we dragged off wet gear and forced hot, sweet tea between parched lips, but inside I was wondering what the hell I was doing getting myself into these predicaments.

Within a few days that question was answered. The *Pacific Swan* arrived with her deadly cargo and we blocked her path with inflatables. Inside the dock the ship crushed the inflatable Bruce and I were on, forcing it up onto a wooden pontoon and popping one of the dinghy sections. The action lasted all afternoon and resulted in the now-familiar arrests and confiscation of equipment. More than anything else, however, the action resulted in a consolidation of opposition to these shipments which united the townsfolk in a great protest of hundreds of people demanding at the very least that proper facilities to deal with emergency situations be provided. I recall with emotion to this day the mum and dad on the quayside begging us to allow them to take part in the protest by clambering into the dinghy with us as they held their little daughter and called, 'It's for her future! Let us be part of the blockade!'

The times we spent in Barrow are among my fondest memories. But risking losing the *Warrior* in these actions was not something a lot of people in the organisation were prepared to contemplate. She was now used internationally and was not the sole property of the European offices. I therefore decided to look around for another ship – cheap, nasty and on her last legs – which I secretly thought we could scuttle in the Barrow approaches to permanently block the spent fuel shipments. I was very serious about this and dismissed the arguments of others about pollution, the impact on benign shipping into the port and other concerns as merely fatuous.

I finagled £5,000 out of the international coffers with the help of John Frizzel who was acting director-in-charge and set about buying a ship. The cheapest I could find was on sale for £12,000. She lay in Ipswich and was a transom-stern side trawler, much in the vein of the *Warrior* but slightly smaller. She had lovely lines but was simply too expensive. I went to see the harbour master at Ipswich to be told that her owner owed £7,000 in port dues and that the ship's main engine overheated and she had a bent crankshaft. Undeterred, I called the owner and, armed with this knowledge, offered him £5,000. He said he'd think about it. I went back to the harbour master and asked if I could pay off the harbour dues to release the ship, to which he agreed and passed me on to a colleague. I peeled off twenty big, fat £50 notes and laid them on the table, pocketing the rest of the money.

'I've only got £1000 for the port fees,' I told him. 'Can we call it quits?'

I then called the owner again. I told him, 'I have some good news and some bad news. The good news is that you no longer owe Ipswich harbour authorities a penny. The bad news is that my offer of £5000 has just gone down to £4000. Take it or leave it.'

He took it, wise person. We owned a second ship. She was called the *Cedarlea* and was as individual, cantankerous and as idiosyncratic as were the on-spec crew we assembled to take her to London. We left Ipswich with nothing more than a £25 VHF on the bridge – no radar, no UHF radio, no navigational aids other than the compass.

Even before leaving the quayside we had caused £800 worth of damage. When the skipper rang up slow astern on the telegraph it registered 'slow ahead' in the engine room. Dutifully carrying out his orders, the engineer threw her into the desired mode only to hear and feel her crash into the quayside. She sported a dented bow henceforth.

Within a few hours of leaving, we were creeping along in a thick fog. It was so bad that the skipper (who, it transpired, had never captained anything bigger than a three berth dinghy before,) had to position himself on the flat surface above the bridge, the 'monkey island', as it's known, to watch for buoys as we entered the mouth of the Thames. His yelled instructions were inaudible to me on the wheel so the engineer rigged up a 'voice pipe' – a length of rubber hosing – down which the skipper shouted his instructions to me.

Further into the estuary the skipper decided to anchor as we were simply not equipped to negotiate the river in this pea-souper. Just as we were about to drop the hook and wait it out, I suggested we called the ship ahead, whose lights we could barely make out, and ask if he would guide us up to the KGV docks. He obliged and we limped into dock a few hours later, having been 'talked' up the length of the Thames.

The *Cedarlea* was a quirky ship. From the wheel you could not see over the bow. The helmsperson had to stand on a box to gain any sort of view. The wheel itself was a pig to turn and instructions of 'hard a port' or 'hard astern' could only be executed with a huge amount of exertion, leaving the arms aching and the brow sweating profusely. The tail shaft from engine room to propeller went straight through the aft accommodation and to access the bridge, it was necessary to go through the engine room. But she was a fine ship in the early Greenpeace tradition. Despite my desires that she be left in a decidedly rusty and sacrificial condition , the longer she remained in the hands of the marine division and the longer her crew lived on board, the more she became to be seen as an addition to the fleet rather than a potential sea-bed obstacle to the spent fuel ships in Barrow. She acquired a few licks of paint which turned into a full-blown livery of rainbows, leaping dolphins and other badges which identified a crusading Greenpeace vessel. I reluctantly gave in to pressure for us not to scuttle her in Barrow and witnessed her transformation into a beautiful vessel I was proud to sail on.

Chapter 20

Japan, 'death ashes' and a memorable sea disposal action

In the summer of 1982, in order to consolidate international opposition to the spent nuclear fuel cargoes, I accepted an invitation to a lecture tour in Japan, from where we imported spent fuel for reprocessing at Sellafield, dubbed Britain's Nuclear Laundry. Peter Taylor of the Political Ecology Research Group and Chantal Girres of the Comite Contre Pollution a la Hague (CCPAH) accompanied me to Japan, a place I had longed to see for a variety of reasons. Manami Susuki, a tireless anti-nuclear activist who had arranged the tour, together with her two helpers, Watanabe-san and Kumura-san, met us at Tokyo airport. Ironically enough when we arrived a pitched battle was in progress between the protesters against the airport expansion and the authorities which made me feel quite at home. The tour we were about to embark on had been arranged with military precision. As we finished one presentation we were whisked off by train or van to the next destination, wheeled in to a packed press conference or lecture hall where we did our stuff only to be whisked out again after questions, on to our next destination. In three weeks, I made 27 presentations.

We saw little of the Japanese people or the countryside. A professional interpreter accompanied us. She was fluent in French, German, Japanese and English. The tour was as exhausting as it was successful. Peter Taylor dropped out after two weeks. He simply could not go on. Watanabe-san, Kumura-san, Chantal and I, together with the tireless Manami, completed the tour which took us to Hiroshima, Nagasaki and every other port and town which had any connection with the nuclear industry in any of its guises. We were followed everywhere by the security agencies. We addressed strikers at the giant Mitsubishi plant which built the pressure vessels for nuclear reactors and which had, against the instructions of the management, decided to recommence the practice of commemorating the dropping of the Hiroshima bomb. We stayed with novice monks in monasteries and with university lecturers in tiny flats in Tokyo. On our final day, we were asked to take part in a Japanese-style demonstration against a nuclear facility.

At the beginning of the march, we were invited to choose a red or yellow headband. Choosing red, we were told, would require us to be at

157

the tail of the march where the trouble would be deliberately provoked while a camera crew would film the police's inevitably heavy-handed reaction for later use as propaganda. The yellow headbands were for the wimps who wanted to steer clear of trouble and who would form the head of the march. I chose yellow. Chantal, to my chagrin, chose red. As we set off, the march was strictly marshalled by brutish-looking riot police in full battle dress. They wielded truncheons on open display and on their hands they wore plastic covers which projected a viciously sharp plastic edge when a fist was formed. We were allowed to march four abreast and not allowed to sway or in any other way touch the line of riot police marching parallel to us. From the outset, the march was intimidated by the right wing nationalists who were, incredibly, allowed to drive armoured cars up and down our ranks shouting abuse at us without so much as a hair being turned by the riot police. At one point they drove at the march in an attempt to scatter it, the more to provoke the wrath of our riot-gear clad minders.

As we approached the nuclear plant, the 'snake marching' began. This involved the red head-bands beginning to deliberately provoke the riot police by linking arms and swaying from side to side as they walked, banging into the line of police who would then retaliate. Before long, the entire aft end of the march was engaged in a pitched battle with the police, all captured on film by the activists. It was quite an extraordinary spectacle which resulted in bloodied protesters being bundled into police vans.

Our last presentation was as guests at the Hiroshima Day commemorative service. Prior to the event we were introduced to members of the hibukushas – a generation of 'second class citizens' who had either themselves been contaminated by radioactive fall-out from the bomb or who were the progeny of such 'tainted' people. These individuals were sometimes denied jobs, found it difficult to marry and enjoy the trappings of the modern age and had been condemned to a life of hardship and hand-outs thanks to the bomb and its legacy.

We visited the hospitals in which these radiation victims languished and we were taken to the domed ruins of the building, left as it stood after the bomb as a memorial to that awful event, directly above which the bomb exploded. And we were invited to the river upon which people annually sailed their tiny paper boats bearing candles, in an emotional ceremony, as they communicated with the spirits of the dead. At the service itself, held at a few minutes after 8 am on the 8th August, the precise time the bomb was dropped, we held a two minute silence for the dead. It was a hugely moving experience and one which will stay with me for the rest of my life. I was here at the very scene where the most appalling act of mass destruction of a civilian population took place and from which the world has since divided into its belligerent, nuclear-armed super-states.

I left Japan the following morning. As I stood on Tokyo station waiting for the train to the airport, Watanabe-san, who had been my constant companion for three weeks, moved away from me a few feet while appearing to rehearse something. Finally he turned to me with tears in his eyes. He had spoken not one word of English to me previously, but he looked me in the eye and in faltering English which he had clearly learned from our interpreter, said, 'Peter-san. You live a long way away and I will miss you velly much. Thank you for coming to our coun`ty and for fighting nuclear industlee. I solly we send death ashes to your counly. Please lite to me. Goodbye.' He gave me the biggest hug I've ever had and, tears streaming down his face, he turned and was gone.

While in Japan, Hans Guyt had taken over the radioactive waste dumping campaign. He phoned me just before I left Japan to tell me that the direct action campaign against the British dump in the Atlantic had gone extremely well. The activists had occupied the tipping platforms of the *Gem* and had managed to prevent any dumping for three days. Now the combined Dutch, Swiss and Belgian operation was to begin and I would be back from Japan in time to participate in the action which would involve both the *Sirius*, the newly acquired pilot vessel purchased amid some controversy by the Dutch office, and the *Cedarlea*. The two Belgian vessels, the *Rheinbourg* and the *Scheldebourg*, would be carrying a record tonnage of waste for disposal. There was no way I wanted to miss this showdown.

The *Sirius* was built for shallow water work and in open sea was slow and would roll on wet grass, as they say. As a consequence, she left earlier than the *Cedarlea* which first went to Belgium to generate media coverage for the campaign. Being a relatively fast and seaworthy vessel, the *Cedarlea* was to wait off the Channel Lighthouse Vessel in an attempt to pick up the two ships leaving Belgium and shadow them down to the dumping ground. The Belgian ships would have to pass within a few miles of us as they came down the English Channel.

I had the pleasure of working with Ken Ballard, technically a first mate, but promoted to skipper for this campaign. We waited for 48 hours at the Channel Light but failed to spot the ships. I suggested to Ken that we may have missed them during the night and that we should head off for the dumping ground, to which he replied, 'Ok. Let's have dinner first and then we'll move.'

As we emerged on the bridge after dinner, Ken was looking intently through the binoculars at two ships about a mile away. He telegraphed 'full ahead' and we took off in pursuit of what he felt sure were the two dump vessels. Within an hour, we had caught them and confirmed Ken's suspicions. Overnight, the weather worsened considerably to a force eight and we came upon the *Sirius*, labouring in the heavy seas. Due to the conditions, the *Cedarlea* was forced to reduce revs slightly but the dump ships ploughed on at full speed, hoping to out-run us, lying deep in the water with waves crashing over the bows – a spectacular sight. The poor *Sirius* was reduced to almost heaving to and the *Cedarlea* ploughed on past her, bucking and slewing around in the great waves which battered the ship. We arrived at the dump site 36 hours later, and although the dump ships had managed to steal a lead on the *Cedarlea*, we still had them on radar and could direct the *Sirius* to them with ease. Hans set about going through the diplomatic niceties which always preceded direct actions, asking the skippers and crews to please desist from polluting international waters, to which the reply was a euphemistic 'Bollocks!' Battle commenced.

These ships didn't use tipping platforms. Instead, the barrels were lifted from the holds by grabs: two, three or even four at a time, and yanked over the side of the ship in one movement at the end of which the release mechanisms would be triggered and the barrels would crash into the sea in a totally uncontrolled manner. The crews from the *Sirius*'s inflatable dinghies were buzzing around the *Rheinbourg* while our contribution from the *Cedarlea* was to dedicate our one and only inflatable to the *Scheldebourg*. Within an hour, the *Scheldebourg* had wisely parted company from its sister ship, forcing us to break off our action. Our primary task was to support the *Sirius* and its crews in the action and to act as a filming platform; we would therefore have to leave the *Scheldebourg* to dump its cargo in peace, a hundred miles away. As the action intensified, the barrels were getting closer and closer to the inflatables as the crews judged the fall more and more precisely. This had little impact on the dumping crews who simply continued to tip the barrels over the side like shelling so many peas.

This mayhem continued for two days until I became very concerned about the way Hans was pushing his crews to risk themselves more and more. I decided a parley was in order and I clambered into an inflatable to be transferred to the *Sirius*. The swell was enormous as we powered across the 300 yards of open water between the two ships, blocking out any sight of the *Sirius* as we plummeted into a trough between the waves. My driver, a Dutchman called Willem, decided to 'wave hop' by opening the throttle and bouncing from one wave crest to the next; the entire experience of crossing a relatively small area of ocean from one ship to the other was most a uncomfortable and dangerous experience. I sullenly climbed on board the *Sirius*. As soon as I had both feet on the deck, the ship's motion was all too apparent. I threw up and felt so sick for the duration of my time on the *Sirius* that I did little more than to tell Hans that I felt we had pushed this campaign as far as we could. He disagreed. Hans continued to deploy his crews until the inevitable happened. One of the inflatables was badly hit by a falling barrel, causing concussion for the driver, Dutchman Gys Thieme. The tactic of using inflatables was called off. Harold Zindler, the burly German 'action specialist' on board the *Sirius* made a rope ladder which was used to board the *Rheinbourg* during one of the infrequent smokoes the crew enjoyed and occupy the cranes used to discharge the barrels.

After two days, the protesters in the cranes were finally dislodged and incarcerated, under arrest, in the chain locker and held on board the ship, courtesy of the Belgian authorities. When they arrived back in Belgium five days later, Harold and his team were heroes. Only when the courts threatened to fine Greenpeace £20,000 for every day of further disruption did Hans agree to call it off. It was a cracking action which, in hindsight, probably broke the resolve of the dumping nations and led, almost directly, to the eventual ban a year later.

But now it was time to celebrate. The two ships, *Cedarlea* and *Sirius*, hove to that evening and a humdinger of a party was held on both ships throughout the night. Unknown to me at the time, the party led to one of our German crew falling desperately and improbably in love with a female on the *Sirius*, a situation of unrequited love which was to hit us straight in the face on the way home. One Greenpeace ship was to go to Spain to capitalise on the huge public support for Greenpeace there, given that it was a Spanish fishing area into which the waste was being dumped without any notice being given. The other ship was to go to Ireland, the country which suffered from the nuclear waste activities of the UK, and a country vital to the anti-nuclear campaign. The *Cedarlea* drew the short straw and went off to Ireland, the *Sirius* to Vigo in Spain where a football match was delayed to give the population a chance to meet the heroic Greenpeace: 10,000 people lined the quayside.

We went off to Cork where two people awaited our arrival and they were the guys waiting to take our lines. The trip back to Cork, however, was not without its drama. Our lovelorn friend tried to commit suicide, an act which required immediate notification to the authorities and we were plunged into a legal situation which we could have well done without.

The *Cedarlea* stayed in Cork for three days during which we did our best to ginger up support for the campaign before I flew home and the ship made her way back to London, in a voyage which has gone down in the annals of Greenpeace folklore. Ken Ballard was skipper and lived at that time in Falmouth. He jumped ship there and handed over the captaincy to first mate John Sprange. En route, the *Cedarlea* almost collided with a cross channel ferry and fouled fishing nets as it cut a swathe of mayhem along the south coast. More importantly, however, Ken's premature departure from the ship was seen as an act of negligence by the marine division hierarchy and was to have serious repercussions years later.

For me, the battle against the nuclear juggernaut continued unabated. I went to Cherbourg where I worked with our French colleagues to make a further attempt at stopping the arrival of a consignment of spent nuclear fuel. I was ashore, working out of a supporter's flat, monitoring the radio signals of the *Sirius* as she made her way into port, against the order of the harbour master. I could hear some muffled activity in the background and then my eyes popped wide open when I heard skipper Willem Beekman come on the radio screaming, 'Mayday! Mayday! This is the Greenpeace ship, *Sirius*, in Cherbourg harbour. We are under attack! Mayday!'

I thought Willem had finally flipped and as we rushed down to the docks I wondered what on earth we would find. A line of riot police stood on the quayside, no more than ten yards from the *Sirius*. They were literally using the ship as target practice for stun grenades and smoke canisters.

The ship was wreathed in smoke and flames licked up from the bridge superstructure. I couldn't believe it. The French were bombing one of our ships, something they were to do again, with devastating consequences, in New Zealand in 1985.

A month later, we prepared round five against spent nuclear fuel ships arriving in Cherbourg. The *Sirius* was due to collect me from Fecamp on France's east coast where I had been attending a series of meetings with other activists. Tony Marriner met me in the hotel in Fecamp and brought news that the *Sirius* would be in port at around midnight. As we sat in the bar of the hotel, I noticed someone watching us quite closely, but thought little of it at the time. Tony and I were joined by a television crew and we moved into the restaurant to eat. My interested party moved with us. After dinner, I decided to walk to the phone booth up the road to make sure that the harbour authorities had been informed of the *Sirius'* arrival. Tony came with me. I had had one beer and one glass of wine. As we stood squashed in the phone box to avoid the lashing wind and rain, two police cars drew up outside the box and I was dragged into a car, accused of being drunk and whisked off to the gendarmerie.

A stern-faced officer began interrogating me. He effectively accused me of illegal entry into France since I had been 'deported' when I was last in Cherbourg. I told him that was nonsense and that he knew it. He said I would have to take a breathalyser test which was of course positive, although I was never shown the result. I laughed at the comedy of it all. I was thrown in a cell for the night and charged with being drunk.

In the morning, the French Greenpeace office had organised a massive press presence which was designed to embarrass the authorities but which backfired badly. The press headlines the next day were 'Greenpeace director arrested for drunkenness' and no matter how much I protested my innocence, I was considered guilty by the press. It was a much more newsworthy story than 'Greenpeace waits for nuclear shipment'. McTaggart, apparently believing the reports, based on his knowledge of me, went totally ape.

Chapter 21

Victory at Sellafield, disaster at home

Greenpeace was going from strength to strength internationally. Our German friends were well organised and making headlines with imaginative actions and dynamic campaigns, but they were saddled with a structure which allowed active supporters to inflict their will on the organisation through a committee called the Verein. Effectively, the German office had pursued a corporate structure which accommodated something which was largely spurned in Greenpeace – democracy. And the German board of directors were threatened – as were the French – with a takeover by the faction in the Verein which could muster sufficient votes to impose its will. This meant that the management of the French and German offices could change with monotonous regularity to the point where continuity ceased and the organisation was hamstrung: even McTaggart's awesome diplomatic skills were being stretched to the limit.

I was spending more and more time on international board duties and constantly commuted between Suffolk, London and Lewes on the south coast where Greenpeace had established its HQ. In the space of three months, I was seconded to the boards of both the German and the French offices and was exposed to a crash course in boardroom skulduggery of the first order. The German situation was quite straightforward and was helped by the fact that there was no split on the existing board. My task of supporting them in the job of fighting off the Verein faction was quite straightforward.

The French situation, however, was totally different and involved all sorts of passions, rivalries and allegiances. I knew all the French board members very well and had campaigned with them on many occasions. I considered Remi and Louis Trussel, who had been living together for years, as my friends. The other members of the board were Katia Kanas, a young, attractive Parisienne, and Jackie Bonmain, mop-haired with the bluest eyes I've ever seen, who had likewise paired off. The two factions had fallen out big-time. Remi had compounded the situation by splitting up with Louis and heading off to Spain, where he not only set up the Spanish Greenpeace office but also eventually married a Spaniard and assumed Spanish citizenship. Louis dragooned her accountant onto the board, who became Remi's defacto replacement.

The two sides wouldn't even speak to each other, despite the fact that they shared the same office and were attempting to work on the same campaigns. One side – the Louis/accountant faction – felt, with justification, that the need was to consolidate the position of Greenpeace in France by underpinning its campaigns with scientific material and dedicating more time to securing the financial base of the organisation before getting too heavily targeted by the forces of vested interest, particularly in the nuclear field. Katia and Jackie, on the other hand, argued, with equal justification, that Greenpeace was an action organisation and should take the fight against nuclear power into the streets and should refuse to be compromised by this woolly idea of 'consolidation'.

It was a philosophical split which was the precursor of debates which were to tear great chunks from the organisation in later years. But this problem had to be dealt with now and my co-director on the Greenpeace International Board, Monika Griefahn, and myself, were drafted onto the French board and told to go and sort the problem out. The AGM was conducted aboard a barge on the Seine, a venue which would have been ideal under different circumstances. One hundred 'founding members' of Greenpeace, those entitled to vote, were crammed into the huge open saloon. After most of the day was spent listening to carefully prepared speeches, which I tried to keep abreast of using my schoolboy French, it was clear that no resolution was about to present itself. The board were asked to sum up and deliver its opinions. One by one we gave our views and a resolution which Monika and I had prepared before the meeting was put to the assembled members. We proposed that the board of Greenpeace France would be Louis, Katia, Monika and myself for a year and that during that time we would prepare and distribute a development paper which drew on everything we had heard. The meeting broke up in good humour and we headed for the nearest bar.

Katia kept her powder dry until the next morning when she accused us, rightly, of simply papering over the cracks and ended an impressive tirade by banging her fist on the table and calling us all the names under the sun. It was clear that she would have to go and we fired her on the spot, effectively handing over the organisation to Louis and her accountant. I was very unhappy about the situation, but at least for the time being the matter was settled and we could all go back to campaigning, not to mention our wives, boyfriends, husbands and lovers.

Back home for what would be a fleeting visit, I took stock of my life. I had no private or social life at all and simply worked every waking minute. I was afraid to be out of the house with Annette for more than a few hours in case I missed a crucial phone call. I had become a Greenpeace junkie; nothing else mattered in my life – not even, if I was honest, my wife, my house or the pursuit of rural happiness which had originally drawn us to Suffolk. Annette told me that I would have to make a decision – Greenpeace or my marriage. I knew she was right, but I pushed the awful thought to the back of my mind and as usual, contented myself with dealing with the now, the immediate, the imperative. Greenpeace had become an excuse for everything.

Sellafield continued to engross me. I had by now been to Cumbria more times than I could count and had made a lot of friends, and a few enemies, both there and in Barrow-in-Furness, our chief area of activity. We had climbed the clock tower in Barrow, occupied the harbour on many occasions, blocked the railway line between Barrow and Sellafield and had underpinned our actions with increasingly sophisticated research.

Sellafield continued to spew two million gallons of contaminated waste into the Irish Sea every day. In the 50s, when the plant began operating, the authorities had openly admitted that they were conducting an experiment by releasing large quantities of waste to examine how it behaved in the water body of the Irish Sea. Thanks to those experiments, and to the continued discharges, more than a quarter of a tonne of plutonium lay on the seabed around the outfall pipe. Instead of remaining locked to the sediments as scientists had once predicted, it was now being mobilised by the action of currents, winds and sun, to be scattered along the Cumbrian coast. The incidence of childhood leukaemia in Seascale, just half a mile from Sellafield, was twice the national average.

Early in 1983, I met James Cutler of Yorkshire TV. James, an extremely likeable, intense, dedicated and very serious man, had, like me, a passionate dislike of the nuclear industry. The high incidence of leukaemia in the area around Sellafield had largely been uncovered by his research and he was in the process of filming a documentary about the plant called Windscale, The Nuclear Laundry. James' activities and those we were developing at Greenpeace coincided nicely since we had resolved to physically block the outfall pipe later that year. It was a risky business as we would be asking divers to expose themselves to a high dose of radioactivity and even finding the pipe outfall would be a difficult task in itself. The pipe end was two kilometres out to sea and lay on the seabed at a depth of 70 feet. Mindful of these problems and recalling the difficulty – not to mention embarrassment – we had encountered previously when the world's media waited for days while we lamely trawled the sea bed looking for the pipe, I asked our action organiser, Dave Roberts, to spend a few days in Cumbria with a small team of people and an inflatable dinghy to pinpoint precisely the pipe's location. BNFL normally marked the pipe end with a buoy conveniently labelled 'BNFL'.

I hoped that a small team of people could unobtrusively pinpoint the pipe end by taking transits from the shore or from sea to enable us to go directly to the pipe, whether it was buoyed or not. That was the theory anyway. Dave and his team set off and we got on with the task of preparing the material we would need for the action. We knew that the pipe ended in an unusual configuration – a diffuser or secondary pipe welded parallel to the main pipe in which three to four inch diameter holes were drilled. Late at night in our workshop down in the London Docks, we fashioned individual wooden bungs for these holes. Each bung was drilled through and a metal bar passed through the middle, on top of which a padlock could be fastened, attached to a chain to wrap around the pipe. We didn't want to make it easy for the bungs to be removed.

As we all beavered away preparing the ship and equipment for this showdown with BNFL, we received some disturbing news. Dave and his team had been bobbing around off Sellafield in their dinghy when Grace O'Sullivan noticed what she thought at first was an oil slick on the water. She put the Geiger counter to the slick and, to her horror the counter went off-scale. They were in the middle of a gigantic slick of radioactive 'crud' used for washing out the holding tanks at the site. Although we didn't know it then, the 'crud' had been wrongly diverted to sea instead of channelled into holding tanks.

Dave brought his crew back to shore immediately and called me in London. The dinghy and most of the equipment they were using were all giving high readings and they were naturally worried. Our first concern was for their safety and I called the National Radiological Protection

Board in Oxfordshire for advice. They instructed us to send the entire team, plus equipment to their laboratories for a thorough checkout. This contamination incident triggered a series of events which culminated in massive publicity for Greenpeace, fines of thousands of pounds both for us and for BNFL and in my finally walking out on Annette and the life I had tried to build in my 'rural idyll'.

In order to impart some idea of the traumatic events of 1983, a story which predates the Sellafield action must be related. After the double-whammy meted out by Hans to the nuclear waste dumping nations in 1982, I had redoubled our efforts to bring the National Union of Seamen in line with our policy of opposition. Jim Slater, the general secretary, had paraded me before his executive several times in an attempt to convince them of the need to stop handling nuclear waste destined for the Atlantic sea bed. In February 1983, Jim convened a meeting of all the related transport unions – Seamen, Transport and General, Railwaymen and ASLEF, the train drivers' union. He called me later that day to tell me that he had all the unions on board except the Railwaymen who wanted more time to consider it.

It transpired that the unions would back the ban only if and when we could satisfactorily provide answers to a series of questions. These related to the routes taken by the waste, through which nuclear free authority constituencies the waste passed, alternatives to dumping and the employment implications of a ban. We had three short months in which to find this information and we set about producing a dossier which would be the final nail in the coffin of radwaste dumping – we hoped. We worked like fury to meet the deadline which would give the unions sufficient time to put all the necessary motions before the necessary committees in time to stop the 1983 dump going ahead.

In the meantime, the London Dumping Convention was meeting in London and Remi, Hans and the other members of the lobby team had been courting the new socialist Spanish government who arrived armed with a resolution calling for the banning of sea dumping of radwaste. In an unprecedented turn of events the Spanish forced a vote – after the British had used every trick in the book to prevent the motion being introduced – and won it handsomely by 18 votes to seven. Sadly the vote was advisory, not mandatory, and the British dismissed it as a politically motivated manoeuvre by the Spanish who were 'in the pockets of Greenpeace' and argued that they would ignore the ban. But the big majority the vote attracted strengthened our hand with the unions enormously and gave Jim a huge amount of leverage.

We presented the dossier to the unions a month before the dump was to take place. While we waited for their response, news arrived that the nuclear authorities were preparing a different vessel, the Atlantic Fisher, to carry out the disposal and, at a cost of £500,000, had installed a moon pool on the vessel which allowed the waste barrels to be disposed of directly through the hull – out of harm's way for any troublesome Greenpeace activists. Then, incredibly, a brown paper envelope turned up on my desk one day. It contained the minutes of a meeting which had been held between the Ministry of Defence, Department of the Environment, Rolls Royce and others, at which it was mooted that plutonium contaminated waste – outlawed for sea disposal under the convention – could be packaged in such a way as to pass for low level waste – permitted to be dumped – and disposed of at sea. This was absolute dynamite, especially when the minutes revealed that it was only the unavoidable use of large and therefore suspicious-looking packages to contain such waste that had forced the abandonment of the ruse.

We released this news at a packed press conference. The story made most front pages and it was clear that we had the UK authorities completely on the back foot. We had won the vote at the London Dumping Convention, we had exposed skulduggery at the highest level in government and had demonstrated that the UK would lie and cheat – not to mention ignore internationally agreed motions – in order to continue to sweep its embarrassing waste beneath the carpet of the Atlantic. We were ecstatic in the office and revelled in our successes. And then the police turned up.

They turned the place upside down. They took files, letters, address books and all manner of material which they thought was relevant to the leaked minutes. I was hauled off to the Serious Crimes Office in Scotland Yard where it was pointed out by the Deputy Director that under the Official Secrets' Act, it was not only the purloiner of secret information who can be prosecuted, but also those disseminating the purloined material. I told the official that perhaps I should be locked up in the Tower or tried for treason. After refusing to tell them even the gender of the person who dropped the envelope off at the office, I was released after a day in custody.

Jim Slater finally called. The ban was in place. The 'unique alliance' as Jim dubbed it had become a reality. The UK would no longer dump radioactive waste in the Atlantic, only because the unions refused to move the waste, not because of any change of heart by government. We had won a hands-down victory. I was whisked to Barrow by the BBC where, standing beside the now-redundant Atlantic Fisher sporting her £500,000 also-redundant moon pool, I was introduced as the 'man who stopped ocean dumping of radioactive waste'. I was beside myself with pride.

The rare peaks of success in a desert of slog and graft were worth all the heartache and angst which paled into insignificance beside what seemed to be at the time, towering achievements. We had won, but what's more, we had forged a link with a sector of society – the trades unions - which, in the 80s, was still relatively powerful, organised and unmolested by Thatcherism. Little did I realise that while I was feeling like a million dollars, some Greenpeace people were watching me with ill-disguised concern at my 'left-wing' tendencies. Jim asked me to go to the TUC meeting that year since he felt it was necessary to consolidate the transport unions' ban on radwaste dumping into a full TUC-backed policy. That was achieved, but only after Jim had been put under enormous pressure to 'remit' the resolution, a euphemism for dropping it quietly into the rubbish bin. His stoicism in the face of the political shenanigans of the executive was heart-warming. Jim never gave up on his planned objectives and was a constant source of inspiration and hope.

Within a year, the International Transport Workers' Federation had, largely thanks to Jim's unstinting work, unanimously supported a resolution to ban radioactive waste dumping at sea. British Nuclear Fuels finally admitted that they had 'accidentally' released the slick of crud which had contaminated our people as they sat in inflatable dinghies taking transits off the end of the Windscale pipeline, the easier to allow us to locate it when we came to block it. The government ordered the closing of the beaches along a ten mile stretch of Cumbrian coast and, at the height of all this interest over radioactive contamination, the activities at Sellafield and the effect the plant was having on normal everyday life, we began our pipe-blocking attempt.

Despite Dave's previous promises about being able to locate the pipe, at the appointed time we could do no such thing. I was beside myself with frustration as Dave and his crew resorted to trawling for the pipeline while I placated a restless, on-board paparazzi. I had sworn the journalists to secrecy about our intentions and although our plan to block the pipeline was known even to BNFL, there existed no evidence to use in court in support of an injunction against us. I had briefed the journalists carefully and explained to them the reason for secrecy. If BNFL had any grounds for an injunction then the press and Greenpeace would be compromised. A BBC journalist proceeded to give them the very evidence they needed by filing a pre-emptive news story and the courts granted an injunction within the space of 24 hours. Now we were in a fine old mess.

It still behoved BNFL's lawyers to deliver the injunction to us – a difficult task as we were on a ship two miles away from land and not receiving guests. They resorted to sending out their tug boat and reading the text of the injunction to us, filming the event, as evidence of the injunction having been served. We sang our way through the delivery of the injunction, asking them with hands cupped behind ears, 'Watssat? Can't hear mate!'

On a second run to deliver the injunction, we turned our ship's speakers on them and blasted them with a bit of rock and roll, demonstrating that we definitely could not hear them. Finally, and incredibly, they made a pass along the starboard side of the ship and threw the injunction on board tied to a brick. At the crucial moment, Dave announced that they had finally found the pipeline outfall.

I told him, 'When we do want it, you can't locate it and now, when it would have been rather convenient to misplace it for another 24 hours or so, you go and find the thing.'

Dave looked at me with a hurt expression and threw a 'double six' – rolled his eyes up into their sockets while chucking out his chin as if to say, 'I can't do anything right for you, Wilks, can I?'

As the press milled around on the ship waiting for us to act, we were faced with a huge dilemma. It was clear to me that the action we were about to undertake had been put before the British public in a series of unprecedented exposures over the course of a year, to the point where we were at a now-or-never position. If we backed off now, we would never again be in such a strong position to foster widespread opposition to the plant. Intuitively, I felt that we should carry public opinion with us and ignore the injunction.

However, I had three hoops through which to jump before I could press ahead. Firstly, I had to carry that opinion with the crew, without whose co-operation I could not continue the action. Secondly, I had a board of directors back in the UK who had to approve of my desired course of action and lastly, I had to convince the international board, plus the trustees, who were at that very moment locked into the politicking of a Greenpeace AGM in Lewes. It was a daunting prospect and I began the process with the crew. Within a few hours of debate, we had a united position – break the injunction and press ahead with blocking the pipe. Next came the UK office. I had several conversations with Bryn, the last of which I taped using a small recording machine on the bridge held up to the VHF. Bryn didn't take long in delivering the board's opinion. In a voice full of emotion, Bryn told us that the UK board and the staff of the UK office were united in their support of our actions. I now felt I had sufficient mandate and left the negotiations with the international gathering to Bryn. As I learned later, those discussions were acrimonious and the decision to back the UK action was far from unanimous and only agreed to on the understanding that the UK office would bear the brunt of the High Court's wrath alone. Now Bryn and Reg Boorer, as representatives of the UK board, had to scuttle down to the High Court in the Strand to face the judge as he considered the effects of the imposition of the injunction. Bryn and Reg listened with false reverence to his pontifications over the dire consequences of any party which wilfully showed contempt for the authority of the judiciary. Meanwhile, back at the office . . .

I realised that the office and its meagre assets were at risk of sequestration. Fearing the bailiff's arrival, the staff set about preparing for a siege. Mike Marmion, a laconic scouser who was Tony Marriner's right hand man, took charge of turning the office into a fortress. He sent people out to buy provisions, sufficient for a month for twenty people, and on their return he began nailing up every possible point of access. Using huge timbers from the wood yard next door, he stressed and secured every window and door in the building. At the rear, the fire escape stairs led to the back of the office. After stressing the door which was the building's weakest point, Mike hinged upright a series of planks, through the ends of which he drove a wicked array of six inch nails, on the premise that should the rear door be breached, the planks would threaten to fall on any invaders. If they survived the prospect of a rain of nails, the planks would at least provide another temporary barrier. Thus secured, the staff settled down over the next few days to wait for the turn of events.

Reg and Bryn came back from the High Court which had granted them a few hour's grace in which, ostensibly, to convince us on the ship not to go through with our planned action of blocking the pipe. Bryn and Reg, suited and booted, stepped out of the taxi and attempted to enter the office. The door wouldn't budge. Bryn tried the entry-phone which prompted a face to appear at the window on the top floor of the building. Bryn was informed that the office had been made secure and that the only way in was via a rope ladder which he could climb to gain access to the first floor window.

Incredulously, Bryn peered up at the face, 'What do you mean, you stupid boy? Let us in this moment. I have to speak to Pete on the boat. We've got to be back in court in 30 minutes! Now let us in.'

When the situation was explained in more detail to Bryn, he became agitated and dropped his clipped 'chairman's lilt' in favour of more direct language.

'Open this door at once. I can't climb up a rope ladder. I'm the damned chairman! Now open up at once!'

Bryn and Reg eventually accepted the situation and, overlooked by guffawing neighbours from the flats opposite, clambered up the rope ladder to be hauled headfirst over the window sill. They made their way back to the packed court just in time to deliver their decision to the weary judge. We would not abide by the injunction.

On the *Cedarlea* we finally prepared the divers for their task. The three guys we were using had been fully briefed on the hazards involved in this dive and had, during the week they had been on board, become thoroughly inured to the crew and what we were attempting to do. Despite the hazards of the dive they agreed to continue and even waived their fee. We, in return, had done everything we could to minimise the risk to the divers. We were equipped with Geiger-counters with which to monitor the extent and nature of the radioactivity the divers would inevitably pick up and had fresh water hoses ready on deck to wash them down the moment they stepped on deck after the dive.

It was time, and as dusk settled over the choppy waters off Sellafield, Dave Roberts, Jan O'Gorman and the divers slipped away from the side of the ship and moved towards the buoy which Dave had earlier weighted at the end of the pipe. We were about to block the notorious Windscale/ Sellafield pipeline in contravention of a High Court injunction and the atmosphere on board was tense as the press endlessly sought interviews and reactions to this snub to the British judiciary.

The divers descended for a recce as Dave and Jan prepared the bungs we had so laboriously fashioned in London. As I watched from the gently rolling deck of the *Cedarlea*, surrounded by camera crews and journalists, I saw the divers surface and hold a brief conversation with Dave. Instead of taking the weighted bags of bungs and making a second dive, I saw them haul themselves back into the dinghy which slowly headed back to the ship. Something had gone wrong, that much was clear. I told the press I'd brief them after I had been informed of the situation by the divers, and walked over to the divers who were climbing up the short access ladder to the deck.

The first thing was to check them for radioactivity. The Geiger counters revealed only modest contamination on the suits, but when we came to run the machine over the hands of one diver, the needle went off-scale. It appeared that actually touching the diffuser on top of the pipeline had caused concentrated radioactivity to transfer to his hands and we washed him down thoroughly until the readings on the Geiger counter registered close to zero. As we hosed him down he told me the grim news. 'The diffuser has been altered very recently, probably within the last 48 hours. There are newly welded rods across the top of the diffuser which sit right in the holes. There is no way we can fit the bungs. We're knackered.'

I made a statement to the press, explaining what had happened and how we had been outfoxed. It transpired that the alterations to the pipe had indeed been carried out very recently by BNFL divers who had been deployed from the tug which had come to deliver the injunction to us a few evenings previously. We were devastated, although the twist in the tail of the story did give the press something else to report.

Ironically, it appeared that BNFL's actions to prevent us blocking the pipeline might have the effect of getting us off the contempt hook: we had not actually blocked their precious pipeline which was the act prevented by the injunction. As we began ferrying the press back to Whitehaven, I wondered how the courts would deal with us the following day when the hearing took place in London.

Bryn had clearly been considering the same point and at the High court the next day, he, unlike me, had no illusions about how the judge would react. Bryn was a past master at playing to the gallery and as he took his seat in court, he made sure that he was in full view of the ranks of press who had come to witness the manner of the vengeance the court would mete out to Greenpeace. The judge made a short speech in which he expressed his lack of doubt concerning the honourable nature of the people who would seek to prevent pollution of the Irish Sea, but informed Bryn that he had no alternative but to find us in contempt, despite the fact that we had not actually blocked the pipeline. We were fined £50,000.

At that point Bryn, glancing to his left and right furtively to ensure the press were looking at him for a reaction, let his head fall in a dead faint onto the wooden rail in front of him, with a dull 'thonk' which reverberated around the court. At a press conference later, he pointed out that Greenpeace had been fined £50,000 for attempting to prevent contamination while BNFL had been fined a mere £10,000 for releasing a huge slick of radioactive crud which had forced the closure of the Sellafield beaches. The routine contamination of the Irish Sea from every day activities was sanctioned and authorised by the regulators.

The Sellafield pipe blocking incident had huge repercussions throughout the Greenpeace organisation. It virtually crippled the UK office financially. But from a campaigning perspective it demonstrated to our opponents that we would not be cowed by the courts when we knew we were right and when we felt confident of having the public's support. It changed the way in which we were viewed in the field of green activism. We pulled in every possible bit of help we could in an attempt to raise the money for the fine. The *Cedarlea* was put up for 'sale' and we asked all our celebrity friends to buy 'shares' in the vessel at £1000 a throw. The response was magnificent. Bruce Kent of CND, the Monty Python crowd, Pamela Stevenson, Barbara Dickson and many, many others, all kicked in a grand. Appeals in the press, unsolicited donations and a stream of £20 notes in the post raised £38,000 in the space of a month. On the appointed date, our solicitors went to court with the cheque and made a case for the waiving of the remainder which the judge accepted without so much as a second thought. In fact, he told the court that he had no doubt that we were honourable people. 1983 was drawing to a close. It had been a tumultuous year but it was to be one which would fundamentally change my life forever since it had one last act to play out.

Yet not even these events could have prepared me for the twist in the tail of this extraordinary year. As our contribution to a campaign against nuclear weapons testing, the UK office had agreed to scale the Big Ben clock tower in Parliament Square to hang a 'Time to Stop Testing Nuclear Weapons' banner over its face. The original demonstration, planned a year previously, had been abandoned after an infiltrator in the organisation had tipped off the police (we never did identify the person to everyone's satisfaction). We arrived at Big Ben to be greeted by a swarm of police officers.

George Pritchard had been planning the next attempt in closely guarded secrecy ever since and as we wound down the Sellafield pipe-blocking action I called George to speak to him in semi-code about the progress of his plans which were due to culminate in two days. To my horror, George indicated that grave problems faced the planned action and he wished to discuss them with me as soon as possible.

'George, are you going ahead or not?'

'No,' came his gut-wrenching reply.

The Big Ben climb was off.

I rushed back to London on the next train. I walked into the office to see George in deep discussion with Robert Taylor, our toxics campaigner and brother of Peter, whom we had used with great effect to underpin our case against the Sellafield discharges. George saw me coming and his look turned decidedly sheepish.

'Sit down, Wilks. Some things have happened that you should know about,' he began.

'I'm all ears, George.'

The story which was unveiled to me was unbelievable, and not because it revealed further infiltration of the organisation which is what I was expecting. George had fallen totally under the spell of Robert and Peter who believed in and indulged in 'astral travelling'. During one of their 'travels' they had met Sir John Betjeman, the former poet laureate, who had warned them of dire consequences should we go ahead with the planned climb of Big Ben. As George laid out the entire, incredible story before me, I couldn't believe my ears. But there was nothing I could do to revive the plans. George had stood everyone down, and the action would not go ahead. My most immediate worry was McTaggart He called on schedule.

'Let me get this straight,' he began in relatively calm tones, 'you called off the action which you had been planning for months, which was paid for by international and which involved three of the best climbers in Europe and formed a central part of a strategy agreed by international as a vital element of a major campaign (I was getting the point by this time), on the word of a guy who has been dead for a year and who Peter Taylor met while he was moving around the stars one night?'

'Bingo. You got it in one.'

He let fly, telling me that there was something fundamentally wrong with our office, that we needed to weed out the 'whackos' and 'get real'. I could feel his venom snaking down the phone wires. I was not his most popular person at that particular time and the UK office was top of his hit list to sort out.

Full of bonhomie and giddy with the notoriety we had achieved, I went home to face a crisis in my marriage. Annette was inconsolable and I was in no mood to pander to her outburst. The local paper did a two page 'personality' piece on me. Annette's picture appeared on the front page. I had been on every news and current affairs programme on TV and radio and BBC2 were about to screen a major documentary about Greenpeace UK. Despite our fine, or perhaps because of it, Greenpeace were riding the crest of a wave of popularity. Bryn Jones had been grilled on Meet the Press, a popular current affairs programme on ITV in which interviewers pulled no punches, during which he gave a stunning performance. The following Monday, an anonymous millionaire had sanctioned a payment of £100,000 to Greenpeace, swelling our pathetic bank balance and allowing us to make our annual payment to Greenpeace international which was a prerequisite for the UK office retaining its vote at the international meetings, retaining its licence and continuing to be allowed to use the name Greenpeace.

Yet Annette and I were at the nadir of our relationship. After ten years of courtship and marriage, a stark and terrifying choice confronted me. I could either stay, and inevitably forego my stewardship of Greenpeace, or leave Annette and the ruins of my rural idyll. I had for years attempted to allow events to dictate my actions in a most cowardly manner and I was now reaping the bitterest of harvests. My head swam with the enormity of what I now felt I was fated to do. I told Annette I was leaving. In a state of blind automation, I packed a bag containing a few oddments of clothing and, ignoring as best I could Annette's state of incomprehension and utter dejection, I walked out one Saturday morning, took the train to London and joined a Greenpeace demonstration in Trafalgar Square.

I can't quite recall what happened during the rest of that day. I know I drank large amounts of alcohol and I know that on the one hand I felt a huge sense of relief that I had finally had the guts to do something about my intolerable domestic state and on the other, a massive, towering sense of loss. Whatever way I tossed it up, I was free to be myself at last rather than the pretend figure I had become.

Chapter 22

Freedom – of sorts

1983 had been unsurpassed in terms of memorable Greenpeace actions. No-one had expected to be involved in such high profile and potentially career-limiting activities as we had undertaken in the last few years. We were the subject of a Natural World documentary programme which was anchored by Trevor Philpotts, the then veteran documentary maker, and we were living up to our box office billing with interview after interview. Yet while all this exposure was happening, the office's transformation into a hothouse of romantic intrigue caused a succession of in-your-face confrontations between current and ex-partners and there was a discernible air of apocalyptic finality in the office, as though something earth-shattering was about to happen and that we had earned the right to a throw of the romantic dice. I quickly fell under the spell of Hilary Ransom, our merchandise manager and within a month I was living with her in her Newington Green flat.

I felt that if Greenpeace could successfully mobilise trade union support to stop the annual sea disposal of a relatively small amount of radioactivity which had only circumstantial health impacts, then, by contrast, the daily disposal of two million gallons of contaminated liquid from Sellafield into an enclosed, shallow and slow flushing Irish Sea which had calculable health impacts would be a pushover. The campaign proposal was not difficult to write. I took it to Jim Slater. We gave it a notional title: 'Shut it', reflecting the level of confidence we had about our ability to force the closure of the giant nuclear plant in Cumbria. Early in 1984, Jim Slater asked me to help him draft a resolution to the TUC conference to support the 'Shut it' campaign, a task I jumped at.

I was not permitted to participate in the compositing meeting later in the year in advance of the conference itself, but I did sit and thrash things out with Tony Benn MP before he went in to do battle. When Jim emerged from the meeting, at which, I was told, Tony Benn took an uncompromising hard line, it transpired that the discharges element had been separated in a stand-alone resolution which was great news. This divorced the pipeline issue from the mainstream anti-nuclear sentiments and made it more attractive and more reasonable. Jim felt confident he could muster sufficient votes from the necessary unions, particularly from Ron Todd and his mighty Transport and General Workers Union, to support the anti-disposal motion. We looked all set for a victory which, although it would not mean the end of all discharges from Sellafield, would in itself give us a fairly weighty club with which to beat the government, BNFL and the pro-nuclear unions in the future.

Jim promised me a seat in the conference hall by slipping me a visitor's pass. On the morning of the debate, Jim told me he had forgotten the pass, but, no matter, he said, I could use Sam McClusky's pass since he wasn't attending the conference that day. Sam McClusky was then the treasurer of the Labour Party and deputy General Secretary of the National Union of Seamen. Jim palmed me the pass outside the Winter Gardens and I squeezed through the crush of bodies into the seedy opulence of the garish foyer, following Jim to the conference hall. As I went to climb the stairs to the public gallery, Jim called and said I could sit with the NUS delegation.

'You've got Sam's pass. You may as well take his seat as well,' said Jim in his broad Scouse accent.

At the interval, Jim was collared by the Electricians Union and spent an agitated few minutes discussing something clearly of great importance while I watched from afar. Jim came over, face reddened with anger.

'Those bastards have seen you with Sam's pass on your coat, mon, and they're goin' ta make a complaint though the chair about 'strangers' in the conference masquerading as delegates. Shit, mon. We're in a fine auld pickle here, I can tell ya.'

Jim went back to the electricians and smoothed things over, but it was a close call. I could just imagine what would happen to my already rocky reputation should live TV uncover a Greenpeace mole in the ranks of the NUS delegation. I made a discreet exit. Despite a spirited fight and tireless efforts from the indefatigable Jim Slater, the T&GWU was threatening to withdraw its support as a last minute compositing change pushed the resolution 'too far' for them. The air was blue that evening as Jim chewed this over with colleagues in an atmosphere of deflation. The speech I had written for Jim for delivery the following day was changed from one of thanking unions for their support to one of criticism at missed opportunities.

I had huge admiration for this man. He had brooked all manner of attacks, even from within his own ranks, to help our cause and had almost single-handedly forged an alliance between the transport unions which he had then unselfishly delivered to us. As we drank and chatted later in the conference bar, Jim let slip that he had been decorated by the Russians during the war, for his heroism during the Archangel and Murmansk supply runs through the submarine-infested North and Arctic Seas. He grew in my esteem every time I was in his company, but for all Jim's political acumen, he was unable to talk Ron Todd around at breakfast and the vote on trades union opposition to the Sellafield discharges fell.

I had decided that I should punish myself for walking out on Annette by living alone for a while and moved into a flat on my own. I remember that my entire wardrobe and belongings fitted into two plastic carrier bags and a small back pack. I had very little money and moved my meagre possessions from Hilary's flat to a bedsit in my old 60s haunt in Glenluce Road, Blackheath, where, as luck would have it, a pokey room was for rent, bang opposite number 11 where Keith Hunt and I had shared those remarkable days, lifetimes ago. This room was spartan and unwelcoming and more often than not I would chose to survive on a diet of fish and chips and beer, hanging around Islington and then wandering back to the office to crash, rather than face the loneliness and Orwellian atmosphere of my bedsit. Its location, however, had one advantage in that it was close to my mother's flat.

After Dad died, Mum had moved to Corelli Road, Blackheath. So on those evenings when I had the time, I would go round to my mum's for tea and not much sympathy. Despite her undying support for me and the path I had chosen in life, she felt that my separation from Annette was a disgrace. I was the first member of the family to have resorted to a separation and although I argued that it was better to live apart than to go through the perpetual pretence of happiness, she could still not quite come to terms with my marriage breakdown. Those were bleak days. I would go home to my tiny bedsit feeling very sorry for myself and spend the evening listening to the couple next door bonking the night away, the walls being so thin that I could hear every utterance, grunt and groan

But events on the campaigning front were moving along at an ever-quickening pace. The Atomic Energy Authority was still, a year on, looking for somewhere to put the nuclear waste which we had prevented from being dumped at sea in 1983 with trades union help. The Nuclear Industry Radioactive Waste Executive (NIREX) was established. Their job was to find a suitable disposal method and a land-based site for the growing inventory of waste with no rubbish bin in which to put it. No sooner did NIREX announce a potential site than the townspeople of that area joined an organisation which began life as 'Billingham Against Nuclear Waste' (BAND) but which swiftly became 'Britain Against Nuclear Waste'. NIREX was targeted everywhere they set up shop; they were hounded out of towns and villages and booed from every stage where their representatives had the temerity to appear. Billingham Against Nuclear Dumping was run by a collection of ordinary and dedicated townsfolk who ranged in profession from lawyers, teachers, estate agents to professional protesters, such as Paul McGhee who had been involved in the Barrow in Furness actions years previously. The local MP, Labour man Frank Cook, was a vociferous and boisterous supporter of the cause and did a huge amount of campaigning in the House of Commons.

The NIREX waste disposal site lottery continued to the point where an announcement was eventually made based on what the government euphemistically called 'suitability criteria'. This had little to do with soil sub-strata or anything remotely geological, but almost everything to do with the strength of local opposition and the political alignment of a particular area. To our overwhelming joy, Billingham was removed from the list of potential sites and BAND invited myself and David Bellamy, who had been equally active in the campaign, to Billingham for a party to celebrate, at which the entire town seemed to be present. I was also asked to appear in a TV programme ten days hence with the then Secretary of State for the Environment, William Waldergrave.

Tioxide UK discharged titanium waste from its industrial activities into the Humber river. Having the acidity of car-battery acid, this waste stream was linked by some to the destruction of the local inshore fishing industry and had left the Humber devoid of life for a good length of its course towards open sea. Yet it was operating within the limits set by its Department of the Environment licence. During the action, to which I was belatedly invited, we blocked the Tioxide pipe and incurred yet more injunctions and fines. I took the opportunity to fill a jar with the waste, screwed the lid on tightly and tucked it into my pocket. It might be useful on the programme a few days hence.

182

The following Sunday I arrived at Lime Grove studios for the programme. The first half of the programme documented my week's work, including the celebrations at Billingham, and the second half was to be the live debate between myself, William Waldegrave, Harriet Harman, and a few other observers and commentators. As Waldegrave began his defence of the Tioxide discharges to the Humber, I slowly withdrew the jar from my inside pocket and placed it on the table in front of me. The chairman, Jonathan Dimbleby, asked me what it was.

'Mr Waldegrave has just announced that the waste issuing from the Tioxide pipeline into the Humber has the acidity of ordinary vinegar. I would therefore ask him to take a swig of the contents of this bottle, taken directly from the end of that pipeline. I'm sure, in the interests of placating public fears, he would suffer a mouthful of 'vinegar', but before he does, perhaps he would be advised to recall that our scientists refute his claims and instead argue that this waste is actually as acidic as car-battery acid.' I offered the jar to Waledgrave. He declined to have even a sip.

In the wake of the Sellafield 'spill' of Purex crud, the media roasted BNFL. The James Cutler film Laundry was screened to international acclaim and a shocked nation heard that the discharges were the highest in the world, that kids locally were twice as likely to contract leukaemia than kids in other parts of the country, that some scientists believed that the only sensible course of action was to evacuate the entire coastal strip of Cumbria. BNFL, having been shown the film before the national screening, were beside themselves with indignation and demanded the right of reply in a live interview at the conclusion of the film. James Cutler asked me if I would take part in the debate, to which I readily agreed.

Two BNFL spokespeople sat at the end of the table in the company of Professor Edward Radford, an eminent American epidemiologist. Dimbleby had been instructed by the Yorkshire TV hierarchy to give the BNFL spokespeople the bulk of the 15 minutes in which to refute the case made by the film and as they locked horns with Professor Radford, I could feel the debate, which centred on roentgens, parts per million, millisiverts and person/rems, going way over my head and the heads of the audience which had, surely, this far been transfixed by the programme. I squirmed in my seat, trying to catch Dimbleby's eye. He indicated that he had acknowledged my desire to speak but he wasn't going to invite me to do so yet. As time ran out, Dimbleby turned to me and said, 'Mr Wilkinson, I'm sorry to have left you out of the debate so far, but what do you have to say to BNFL?'

I had only thirty seconds or so to bring the debate down to the level at which it might engage lay viewers again and I told them that people were not stupid and were perfectly aware that, despite the nuclear jargon they chose to use, the bald truth was that BNFL discharged large quantities of a known cancer-producing substance into the Irish Sea and that, in the light of recognised uncertainties about the health impacts, the practice must stop. As the dust settled after that Yorkshire TV programme, after the fines and the direct actions, BNFL announced that they were to reduce their discharges of plutonium by a factor of five in response to new medical research which indicated that the 'gut uptake factor' – the rate at which the gut transfers plutonium to the blood steam – was five times greater than had been previously thought.

My next port of call was Oslo. Scandinavian members of the Oslo and Paris Commission, known as OSPAR: the international body which controlled liquid pollutants discharged from land-based sources into European waters. OSPAR had submitted a resolution calling for such discharges to be reduced to a level which was 'as low as technically achievable' (ALATA), a definition which would replace 'as low as reasonably achievable' (ALARA). Before leaving, I wanted absolute confirmation of which way the UK delegation was being instructed to vote. I was promised a reply within the 30 minutes left before I had to leave the office.

The telex began chattering away. It was from Waledgrave's office and informed us that a letter explaining the position would be sent to me by despatch rider at once. As I was about to walk out of the door the bike pulled up and I was handed the letter bearing the DoE stamp. I ripped open the letter as I trotted towards the tube station. Yes! YES!

'The UK delegation has been instructed to vote in favour of the Scandinavian resolution.'

I boarded the plane in fine humour. I sat in Oslo a few hours later with my Scandinavian colleagues, eking out a pint of exorbitantly priced beer as I revealed the letter and we discussed tactics.

The following morning we waited in the lobby of the hotel which was the venue for the Paris Commission meeting. The UK delegation arrived and the head of the delegation came directly over to us and introduced himself. I asked him what he felt about the Scandinavian resolution.

'Oh, we'll look at it and enter into the spirit of things, you know. Ha, ha.'

'But will you vote in favour of the resolution?' I asked.

'Well, I think that would be going too far.'

'Perhaps this letter will enlighten you,' I said. 'It's signed by William Waledegrave and if you are not aware what your instructions are in respect of the resolution, we are. I'm pleased to say that you will be voting in favour.'

His face froze as I detailed the events of the last few hours to him and explained that his instructions were already in the public domain. As he turned on his heel to find the nearest telephone, I called after him, 'No need to call London. Here, I can give you a copy of the letter!'

We issued a press release headed, 'UK delegation to Paris Commission receives its instructions from Greenpeace.'

The Oslo episode set in motion a series of meetings of the Oslo and Paris Commission which resulted, eventually, in the 'OSPAR agreement' which called for discharges into European waters to be reduced to zero by 2020. While this lofty objective is unlikely to be met, for many years it has provided a significant aid in arguing for lower discharges in discussions with government and has been an important consideration in regulatory preferences for policies which 'concentrate and contain' pollutants, rather than those which 'dilute and disperse' them.

The last day of the conference arrived and the vote was called on the Scandinavian resolution which was adopted unanimously.

Chapter 23

A train crash, a costly mistake and Antarctica swims into view

The House of Commons Environment Select Committee asked Greenpeace and others to submit evidence for its consideration concerning the impact of the discharges and it seemed that they were about to endorse the recent Paris Commission resolution by enshrining its terms into law. I hurriedly began compiling evidence, but in truth I was running out of steam on the nuclear issue. I was also under pressure from McTaggart to internationalise the UK board of directors and work increasingly on international issues as well as dedicating more of my time to my international (as opposed to my national) directorship responsibilities. As a result I was handing more and more of the responsibility for the Sellafield campaign over to George Pritchard, our affable Mancunian who had joined us two years previously, having earned his spurs fighting off plans for a nuclear power station development in Cornwall.

George was deputed to be 'in charge' of the press interest which accrued from a spectacular demonstration by the UK Atomic Energy Authority when it sought to placate concerns generated largely by the anti-nuclear lobby, concerning the safety of the flasks used to transport spent nuclear fuel. The lobby contended, with some justification, although we at Greenpeace tried to keep out of the central debate, that the flasks, weighing 60 tonnes a piece, were structurally unsound given that they were only tested by dropping the flasks from a height of 10 metres and by exposing them to fire at 800 degrees Celsius for 30 minutes. In real accident scenarios, it was argued, the flasks would be exposed to stresses which far exceeded these artificial conditions: trains upon which these flasks were carried often travelled at 100 mph and fires frequently raged for longer than 30 minutes at far higher temperatures.

In order to lay such fears to rest once and for all, the UKAEA staged a demonstration at Melton Mowbry in conjunction with British Rail in which a regular diesel locomotive would crash into a static spent fuel flask at 100 mph. The prospect of spectacular pictures and the possibility of the nuclear authorities being forced to eat humble pie as their flask disintegrated pulled hundreds of press and television companies to the site. George and I were guests of Jim Slater and we took a grandstand seat as the locomotive hurtled down the track and slammed into the spent fuel flask with a tremendous 'crump' and pushed it a few hundred yards down the tracks, a huge cloud of dust enveloping the point of impact. George and I looked at each other in awe. It was a serious demonstration and when the experts had crawled all over the wreckage and announced the fact that the flask was perfectly intact, George snorted contemptuously, 'I've been told by an engineer that they stitched that demonstration up from start to finish,' he confided.

'Explain, George,' I asked.

George told me that his informant had cast-iron information that the carriage which the locomotive pulled was 'weighted down' by sleepers in order to (curiously to my simple mind) 'lessen the overall impact on the flask'. Moreover, the bolts holding the locomotive's engine to its chassis had been sheared prior to the test so that it would break free of its position within the locomotive on impact and thereby (and again curiously, to my way of thinking) further lessening the impact on the flask. Despite my scepticism of George's claims, I was prepared to be convinced based on the fact that the information came from an impeccable source, according to George. Thus fortified, we sent out a press release claiming the demonstration was a sham designed to hoodwink the public and the press. The story was covered extensively the following day.

Then George started to get cold feet. His source suddenly disappeared. We were inundated by phone calls from an irate British Rail management demanding a retraction of the allegations and the UKAEA were calling for our blood. George was at a loss to know what to do and finally conceded that he had made a grave error of judgement in putting out the story.

I pulled him to one side and told him, 'We'll just sweat it out George. No comments, no press releases, no responses. For the next two weeks, you are not available. Just let it pass.'

George agreed to this strategy but, being a fundamentally honest man, could not live with the fact that he had made accusations which, after much argument, turned out to be a combination of wishful thinking and innuendo and on the fifth day of his enforced silence George cracked. He sent a telex to the Chairman of British Rail accepting the fact that he had falsely claimed the demonstration was rigged. BR did what we would have done, faced with the same circumstances: they paraded the telex from George at a press conference as evidence of Greenpeace's tacit acceptance of the infallibility of the spent fuel flasks.

We had been hoist by our own petard and George was in the dog house for weeks. He was lucky to retain his position and in fact he offered to resign, a proposition we did not entertain for a second. George had simply made a serious error: could any one of us claim not to have done so?

My uncertain state of mind was not helped by the increasing identity crisis I was facing. Quite apart from my roller-coaster private life, I was alternately seen by the UK board as being an agent of McTaggart and the international board, and by the international board of being a left-leaning nationalist unable to control his board. I couldn't win and began to lose perspective. I turned my attention to completing the evidence to the Select Committee

I sent off our submission and forgot about it for a while. I had other things on my mind which were crowding in on me and threatening my fragile sanity. I had kept in touch with Annette and possible reconciliation was something we kept alive. Every month I met her in Ipswich where we would go for a drink and rake over old ground, analysing and dissecting our marriage, exploring the avenues open to us. Annette always believed I would come back home, but as time went on I knew it was not an option for me. Had I succumbed to the temptations of home, wife, dog and all the trappings of normality, I knew that we would have gone through the pain and anguish of a second separation as the same pressures resurfaced. I had not yet – by a wide margin – managed to get Greenpeace out of my system.

I recognised this thought pattern as yet another example of allowing events to dictate the path I chose. I had the gumption neither to end our marriage once and for all or to go back and make a fist of it. I mentioned to Annette, disingenuously, as it hadn't been formally put to me at this point, that I had been asked to go to the Antarctic but that I had turned down such a preposterous suggestion. She told me that if I went then any hopes of our reconciliation would be over. I recognised this ultimatum as an opportunity I could use as an excuse to abdicate responsibility for a decision I did not want to make. I was surprised at the degree of cowardliness to which I seemed prepared to stoop in order to avoid making a decision I found unpalatable .

At work, a crisis was approaching with McTaggart on my back every few days about bringing Greenpeace UK into the 21st Century and doing away with a board of directors he saw as introverted, stale and myopic. The UK board demanded that I stood up to McTaggart and the overbearing international office demands. Bryn Jones was creating huge rifts in the office with his attitude of intolerance of 'incompetence' and had arbitrarily decided to fire all the staff, a move which took us a week to resist and left the office staff openly seething about mismanagement. We were, despite our profile, constantly on the verge of bankruptcy.

Although I had resigned my international board position in 1983, I still continued to oversee the embryonic Antarctic campaign from the Lewes office. The campaign was assuming an energetic life of its own. On the occasions when I would slope off with McTaggart for a few beers in the local bar, he would, between kicking my ass at pool, wax lyrical about a ship which had been offered to Greenpeace as a tax write-off from the Maryland Pilot's Association in the USA. Technically, the vessel – an ocean-going tug called the Maryland – was on offer to Greenpeace at no cost which meant that the Maryland Pilot's Association, a charity in the USA, could claim back large amounts of tax from the US authorities to swell its diminished coffers. In fact, the 'sale' would cost Greenpeace $500,000 in 'finder's fees', but still McTaggart argued the vessel was a bargain and we should buy it. He planned we would send it to the Antarctic and establish a permanent base camp there, to challenge the notion of territoriality exercised – albeit tacitly – by seven of the twenty or so Antarctic treaty nations.

His vision of carrying out such a risky and impish campaign inspired me and we began to plot and plan the ship's acquisition. Although it had already been mooted that I should lead the expedition, I shrugged off such speculation as being so much wishful thinking. By mid-1984 the expedition phase of the campaign was being openly discussed within the organisation and forced many passions to the surface. The German office was bitterly opposed to any Greenpeace occupation of Antarctic territory on the grounds that we were simply adding to the very disturbance the expedition was designed to oppose. The rows raged back and forth for months while McTaggart kept his head down and ploughed on with the planning and carrying out the necessary politicking required to fund the venture.

I was introduced to Andy Hill, an ex-British Antarctic Survey logistics planner who was put in charge of beginning preparation for the expedition. I was appointed his overseer, answerable to the international board. Andy had by this time been working away for a month or so and my first task was to go through the books with him to discover what he was spending, on what, and where the money came from. The reality was that he had no budget and there were no checks and balances on what he was spending.

Andy was a smooth sort of guy, slim and lithe, always smartly dressed, dedicated to his job and highly competent at matters Antarctic. We got on well and formed a tight team which was augmented by a real firebrand of a Falkland Islander by the name of Gerry Johnson, a tough, stocky, no-nonsense 22-year-old who wore his heart, and his antipathy towards Argentinians, on his sleeve. I liked Gerry a lot. He was scathing about anything he saw as smacking of bureaucracy and often opened his mouth before his brain was in gear – something I was prone to do as well.

The budget I had arrived at for the expedition amounted to $1 million, a figure then unheard of in Greenpeace in connection with a campaign budget. Having asked for comments from the international board and received none, I sent the budget to the national trustees, seeking approval, which caused McTaggart to cut the budget in half, re-write the proposal and re-send to the trustees with a note of apology. His argument was that a budget of $1m was politically unacceptable whereas $500,000 would probably get nodded through, given the size and scale of the undertaking. He was correct, of course, but the $500,000 approved budget naturally over-ran by the same amount and it was me who got the blame. Another lesson in politics from the master.

McTaggart had convinced his friend Ted Turner, who was married to Jane Fonda and who owned CNN, to put up a sizeable amount of money towards the expedition costs. He had likewise secured the support and matching financial investment from a German TV company, headed up by Axel Engsfeld, who would film the upcoming expedition. These financial commitments reduced McTaggart's politically acceptable budget considerably and was duly approved by the trustees a few weeks later after the sceptical Germans had been outvoted.

We had the money, we had the ship. Now we needed an expedition leader. McTaggart asked me to compile a shortlist of potential candidates for the job and a few days later I sat with the international board in McTaggart's office reviewing the list. One by one we scratched off the names. Either they were considered unsuitable for the arduous task ahead or they were too fully occupied on other issues. We arrived at the last name and scratched that off the list too. We had no-one available. People leaned back in their chairs and drummed fingers on desks.

McTaggart, 'Well, now what the hell?'

We all shrugged.

McTaggart again: 'Well, there is one guy who could go.'

'Who?' asked Steve Sawyer innocently as if he didn't know what McTaggart was about to suggest.

He pointed his pencil slowly and deliberately at me. 'You, Peter me boy, have the experience and you have the ability to mould crews around you. And, you have the time.'

I began to protest vigorously. I had to sort the UK office out and drag it into line; the UK office was at its nadir and was about to re-group and re-launch with added dynamism and vigour. I also had my life to sort out. But I knew it was all in vain. I had known this was coming. Deep in my heart I welcomed it because it once again allowed the pressure of events to push me in a direction over which I pretended I had no control. This was it: if I went it would remove the need to make a decision about my marriage and I could hear myself saying to Annette, 'There's nothing I can do about it. I must go as there are no other people available. What do you want me to do, tell Greenpeace the expedition can't go ahead because I can't get involved?' God, what a pathetic wimp I was.

I hurried back to the London office to discuss the suggestion with my board. The office was seething with ill-concealed anger and communications between the board and the staff were almost non-existent. I sat for days, talking things through with the board and with the staff and we eventually called a meeting at which I proposed a steering group of people from the staff who would attend board meetings and act as a buffer between the two. It helped a little, but the reality was that Bryn was acting as head cook and bottle washer, claiming that he was surrounded by a sea of incompetence, rushing around the office biting peoples' heads off while puffing out clouds of smoke from his infernal cigars.

There were, fortunately, plenty of distractions. Mark Glover, our laconic wildlife campaigner, had developed a campaign designed to make the incarceration of dolphins and killer whales in aquaria for the amusement of the paying public an unacceptable activity. After compiling an impressive document which demonstrated quite clearly that such animals, ruthlessly plucked from their natural habitat in a vile trade which centred on Iceland, lived miserable and shortened lives of boredom and angst for the titillation of families coming to witness the 'happy' animals cavorting around in pools, we planned demonstrations. We split up into two teams and descended on the dolphinaria in Windsor and Brighton and staged protests which interrupted the shows. The reaction from irate parents was swift and hostile. At Windsor, Reg Boorer was almost thrown into a pool in which swam a killer whale and we in Brighton were attacked by a howling mob of parents and only saved from a beating by the security guards.

But our central activity focused on the plight of a killer whale, languishing its life away on the pier of the Essex seaside resort of Clacton. Nemo was owned by an international conglomerate which had paid £250,000 for him and had a leasing arrangement with the owners of Clacton pier, a well-known family from London's East End. We had to deal with these people in our negotiations over the plight of poor Nemo. Out of the holiday season, he no longer performed and now swam round and round his pool 24 hours a day, obviously lonely and bored witless. We had, a year previously, set up a fund for Nemo in an attempt to buy the whale and release it back into the wild. This fund now stood at £60,000, clearly insufficient for us to make a realistic offer. I was despatched to Clacton to attempt to buy off the security people with the £60,000, which would give us enough time to steal the whale using a helicopter.

The £60k I offered the owners didn't cut much ice, sadly, although the plan for the release of Nemo did seem to impress them with its novelty. We had at least tried and, although Nemo lived out his days in Windsor after being transferred from Clacton and died shortly afterwards, the campaign overall was a success in that, as whales and dolphins died in their prisons, they were not replaced. Mark Glover fought every single application for the importation of whales and dolphins and every licence issued to move the animals around the UK or to export them. He single-handedly brought the trade in dolphins to an end in the UK and has gone on in his post-Greenpeace life, to fight tirelessly and successfully for animals through his own organisation, Respect for Animals.

Ironically enough, Mark's tireless enthusiasm for campaigns on wildlife brought us into direct conflict with Greenpeace International. We needed a home-based animal campaign to get our teeth into. Our high profile on nuclear issues was all very well and good, but it didn't translate easily into hard cash whereas wildlife issues generally tugged at the heartstrings of the animal-loving public, a fact well known and exploited by organisations old and new. We pondered hard and long before deciding to plump for an attack on the trade in furs.

Mark informed us that the global fur trade was responsible for the death of 40 million animals a year, many of those which were wild-caught as opposed to farmed, being discarded as 'trash' simply because the coat was damaged in the kill or the fur colour was not a 'match'. The fur campaign was not long in the planning. As we approached contacts, friends and our jealously guarded 'celebrity names', the campaign fell naturally into place. We would run a high profile public awareness campaign based on videos, films, ads and direct actions to shock people into acknowledging the bloody price of a fur coat in terms of suffering and cruelty. But first, it was necessary to have the campaign rubber-stamped by the Greenpeace trustees. This was done in a rather underhanded manner by using the same sort of tactics McTaggart had taught me over the years. I allowed the AGM of 1984 to conclude its business at the end of an exhausting week before I called the meeting to order again to introduce the fur campaign almost as an afterthought, begging the indulgence of the trustees. I trusted that their tiredness and their anxiety to get to the bar would result in a swift and cursory approval of the campaign. It did.

David Bailey agreed to take the photographs for the posters we would plaster on hoardings all over London. He would hire the models who would work free of charge. Bailey charged us nothing. Celebrity after celebrity came forward to support us.

The video Reg and the artistic team around him came up with is, still to this day, a classic shocker of campaigning material. The usual self-indulgent fashion show pomp of the catwalk is transformed into one of self-disgust when the fur coat being trailed by a model suddenly begins to leave a swathe of blood in its wake. Blood is splattered over the painted faces and bloated visages of the fawning audience as the model swings the fur coat across her shoulders. The end caption is 'It takes 40 dumb animals to make a fur coat, but only one to wear it', which was designed to be deliberately antagonistic to feminists who did not disappoint in making the campaign even more scandalous with their outraged criticism of its 'sexist' overtones.

The video was screened in cinemas all over the country and the support it generated was staggering. We had touched a raw nerve in the British public and the fur industry was caught on the back foot. Ultimately, the campaign succeeded in outlawing all fur farms in the UK and undermining the UK fur industry to the point where it effectively no longer exists in the UK. Ironically, the campaign's success was to precipitate our demise.

1984 was a rollercoaster of office lows and campaign highs. Pursuing the Sellafield issue with the last vestige of collective energy, we agreed to build on the earlier action when 500 people came down from Cumbria to London to dump a small amount of radioactive mud at the entrance of Downing Street. On that occasion Whitehall had been sealed off in the panic and the fire brigade was left to clean up the small but highly embarrassing mess. This time I suggested we brought five tons of the contaminated mud from the Ravenglass Estuary, close to Sellafield and, in Europe, the most heavily contaminated with radioactive effluent, to the Department of the Environment, to see how they liked having this filth on their doorstep.

Les Parris, an asphalter and one of our most active and helpful supporters, was asked to organise the collecting of the mud and hired a skip lorry for the job, telling the hire company he needed it for a week for 'local work'. Les and his team donned fake Cumbria Water Authority jackets while they used a hired JCB to scoop up the estuarine mud and dollop it in the skip on the back of the lorry. The mud was then thoroughly doused with water to prevent the top layer from drying out and releasing plutonium particles before being covered with a tarpaulin for the journey back to London.

After a few scares and a false start or two, we finally managed to back Les's lorry onto the steps of the Department of the Environment just before London's rush hour began to make the roads impassable. I finally pulled the correct lever to set the skip tipping its load. Five tons of radioactive mud began to slide from the skip onto the steps at the DoE right in front of the national press. Bingo!

The action forced the closure of Marsham Street and streets close by and the fire brigade were called to deal with the waste. The waste was subsequently shunted around the country and eventually taken back to Ravenglass as there was no sea dumping route for it to take. We protesters were taken into custody, fined £5 each for disturbing the peace and released. The police complemented us on a slick and respectful action.

As 1984 drew to a close, it was time to revisit the Big Ben action. This time it must not fail. And this time we had an easier task since the tower itself was festooned in scaffolding to facilitate a much overdue scrubdown to remove the grime which had accumulated over the years.

We bought a redundant double-decker bus and cut a hole in the roof from where a ladder would be extended to reach the scaffolding. The protesters would scramble across the ladder onto the scaffolding, climb to the clock face and hang a banner – 'Time to stop nuclear weapons testing'.

In truth, we planned and carried out this protest largely to demonstrate our international credentials to the Greenpeace governing body. While the issue was important and while the UK was still, incredibly, testing nuclear weapons, it was a distraction we could have done without. Our climbers planned to suspend themselves in hammocks from the ropes holding the banner to the clock face in order to put themselves in a position where to be cut down from their perch would mean plummeting to their deaths. That was the plan.

We were all a little apprehensive since the IRA were very active around this time and we feared that our action would prompt a rapid and possibly violent reaction from the security forces. I was personally convinced that we would be arrested before we had even had time to get the climbers away from the bus, but we were committed and it was time to get on with it. We collected the bus from the yard adjacent to the Communications Division in the Docklands area of London and we approached Westminster at around 5.30am. As I turned onto the bridge, I received the thumbs up from the climbing crew standing around trying to look as inconspicuous as possible. With sweaty palms slipping on the steering wheel, I pulled up at the Westminster Bridge bus stop and waited with bated breath as the grating sounds of metal on metal, interspersed with curses and grunts indicated a problem or two with the deploying of the ladder through the hole in the roof. Then I heard it: the wailing of a police siren. Across the road, a cafe was opening up and the proprietor stood open-mouthed as he saw the ladder emerging from the top of the bus and climbing-gear clad figures clambering across to the scaffolding.

The police car came hurtling round Parliament Square and continued straight across the bridge past us, obviously after more dastardly villains than us. Dave Roberts shouted, 'Go! Go! Go!' I was so resigned to the fact that we were about to be arrested that I fumbled the gears, crunched it into first and lurched away from the bus stop, sending people sprawling down the passageway of the bus. We had made it! I couldn't believe it. The people in the bus were singing and dancing with delight and as we sedately drove around the four sides of the square and back across the bridge, we cheered the tiny figures now halfway up the scaffolding.

We had to secure the bus as a priority and drove back to the support team waiting at Vauxhall. By the time we had made our way back to Westminster, it was 7.30 and the sight which greeted us as we walked down the Embankment was one of crowds of people, police everywhere, TV crews and general mayhem. The banner obscured the face of Big Ben and told the world that it was time for the UK to stop nuclear weapons testing. I called the climbers on the VHF. They were comfortable and could see for themselves the chaos their escapade had created. During the course of the next few hours, the chaos was to increase to the point where Westminster Bridge became a melee of snarling traffic and the number of people transfixed by the demonstration rose to hundreds.

I approached the chief police officer and announced that we were from Greenpeace. He asked me to call the climbers down at once which I refused to do. He took out his notebook and began asking me questions about how we had delivered the climbers to the scaffolding. When I explained how we did it, he told me the driver of the bus would be prosecuted. I explained to him that we had used a professional driver to whom we had paid a fee and who was now probably having breakfast somewhere in the West End.

'What was his name?' he asked.

'Billy.'

'Surname?'

'Bunter.'

By mid-afternoon, police efforts to forcefully remove the climbers having failed, the climbers agreed to descend their lofty nest voluntarily and were greeted with cheers and applause as they walked into the arms of the police.

Despite the problems in the office and my own insecurity and uncertainty about my position, we were still making the news and pulling off some good actions in support of national and international campaigns. The office still buzzed with ideas, all the staff shouldered huge workloads and laughter and tears in equal amounts were evident on most days. Celebrities frequented our cramped, over-worked offices regularly.

Barbara Dickson turned up one day with a single she had cut with Labi Sifre called Dangerous Cargo lamenting the death of the oceans through nuclear waste disposal. Suggs and Karl, front men for Madness, regularly popped in for a pint and held a concert for us at the Lyceum, along with Ian Drury and his band the Blockheads and Nigel Planer of the Young Ones in support. Yet despite all this goodwill we could never quite make it financially and although we now had a membership of 25,000, we needed to reach a 100,000 figure to secure a regular, guaranteed income from membership fees sufficient to support the office, meet our salary and expenses bill and satisfy our international obligation to commit 24% of our income, known euphemistically as our 'licensing fee', the price we were required to pay for the privilege of using the name Greenpeace.

In our constant search for money, we left no stone unturned. The Greater London Council was being dismantled by the Tory government and Ken Livingstone had indicated quite unequivocally that large amounts of money were to be had from the coffers of the dying organisation to those who demonstrated innovation in terms of campaign and project proposals. The only problem was that any projects submitted had to be linked in some way or another to London. We put together a proposal to look at spent nuclear fuel shipments through the capital and were delighted when we received notification that two officials from the GLC would visit us to discuss the proposal.

Chapter 24

The final flourish/the *Warrior* sunk/off to New Zealand

I was now living alternately in my hovel of a bedsit in Blackheath, at Hilary's place in Sutton, where she now lived, on the floor of the office in Islington or in a cheap hotel in Lewes when events dictated. I rarely, if ever, saw my old friends from Deptford. Events of momentous importance were looming on my horizon. I was being dragged inexorably into the position of expedition leader on the first ever attempt at establishing a permanent non-governmental base camp in Antarctica which would require my absence from the UK for six months and I was unsure of how I should feel about this de facto appointment.

1984 merged into 1985 in a seamless scroll of work, meetings, discussions, planning and controversy. The fur campaign which had been swept through the Greenpeace Council meeting on the nod was beginning to make a significant impact on the fur industry. The Bailey posters were being displayed all over London. Our local groups, which Bryn was promoting tirelessly, against my counsel, were raising money to display the anti-fur industry billboards all over the UK. The fur campaign video was feted, won awards and was being screened up and down the country. Groups in Scandinavia, South Africa and in Canada were clamouring for anti-fur trade material. The 'national' campaign we had launched in London was now assuming international dimensions and some in Greenpeace were not at all pleased about its success. A row of seismic proportions was brewing which would have cataclysmic impact a year later.

In the summer of 1985, McTaggart asked me to accompany himself and Monika Griefhan to the International Whaling Commission meeting in Bournemouth and use the opportunity to discuss Antarctica. As we opened folders on the table of his hotel room the telephone rang and I leaned over to lift the receiver. It was a long-distance collect call from New Zealand for McTaggart. Knowing that a major meeting was taking place on the *Warrior* in Auckland to plan the upcoming tour of the Pacific, I accepted the charge and handed the receiver to McTaggart. I took little notice of what he said, but as he replaced the receiver in the cradle and turned to look at Monika and I, his face was ashen and his words are seared into my memory.

'The *Warrior* has been sunk. There were two explosions. One guy's missing.'

I looked at him open-mouthed. 'An engine room explosion?'

'We don't know at the moment, but it seems there were two separate explosions which could have been mines. Ok, now listen. The news will be out on the wires already. Peter, I want you back in Lewes to field the press enquiries there. Keep it low-key for the time being until we get more details. Send out a message to all offices to refer all enquiries to you in Lewes. I'll call you later tonight.'

The bombing of the *Warrior* by French secret agents was the single most critical turning point in Greenpeace's development. The consequences of that event are still being felt today, both for good and bad. Of course, the enduring tragedy was the death of Fernando Pereira, the Portuguese photographer who died while trying to retrieve his equipment and nothing will surpass the suffering his loss created among his loved ones and friends.

The news of the *Warrior's* sinking was on the front page of every newspaper the following day. Greenpeace's constituency grew from mainly western nations to become global overnight. The facts associated with this outrage are hard to accept to this day: a sovereign government sent a team of at least ten people, probably more, to deliberately carry out the sinking of a ship – a ship belonging to an organisation promoting environmentalism and international peace, no less – in the first ever act of international terrorism in New Zealand's history.

Using two limpet mines, the *Warrior* was sunk in the shallow waters of Marsden Wharf within minutes. During the panic on board, the crew, many of whom were asleep, were ushered out onto the quay as the second and most devastating blast ripped a six foot diameter hole in her port side, exposing her engine room. As water gushed into the stricken ship she began to list and to settle on the mud a few metres beneath her keel. Fernando Pereira, a Portuguese photographer took the fateful decision to attempt to rescue his valuable camera gear from his cabin. He drowned.

As the crew stood around their vessel, water now lapping the portholes through which, only hours previously, people could be seen celebrating a birthday on board, the world was waking up to the news of a British registered vessel being sabotaged by a French government in a Commonwealth country. Yet British condemnation of the action was conspicuously absent. Mrs Thatcher, then Prime Minister, uttered not one word of rebuke, even at a time when she was crusading against terrorism. Had the Russians been responsible for the sinking, wild horses would not have kept the Iron Lady away from Auckland where she would have encouraged the world's media to capture her nodding in that hollow manner of hers as she listened to eye-witness accounts before delivering a withering attack on the perpetrators. But the perpetrators were French and the French were allies and therefore beyond reproach.

For Greenpeace and its personnel, however, the consequences were catastrophic and life-changing in many ways. Schedules were torn up, holidays cancelled, personnel diverted and the lights in every Greenpeace office burned late into the night. The phones rang hot, the press were beating a path to our door and the sympathy of millions of people throughout the world manifested itself in notes and coins in the Greenpeace coffers. In Auckland the *Warrior* fund reached $250,000, a sum unheard of in the annals of Greenpeace history in that sparsely populated and relatively poor country. Ads run in the press profited enormously. The money literally poured in. And as the money came in, so the shutters went up. In every office security measures were quickly stepped up. Open doors were no longer the order of the day and the laissez-faire attitude which had characterised Greenpeace for so long disappeared. People who had joined Greenpeace out of a sense of well-intentioned duty towards environmental campaigning now suddenly felt exposed and vulnerable. Political reality intruded into the hitherto make-believe world of Greenpeace. We had touched a raw nerve and had been bitten back for our troubles – hard.

It was against this backdrop that I prepared to leave for New Zealand in the late summer of 1985. Although I had been rushing around along with everyone else, covering news interest in the sinking and its aftermath, the newly acquired 'Antarctic' ship which we unimaginatively called the *Greenpeace* (my suggestion of *Antarctic Warrior* was dismissed as too anglophobic) was being dragooned, along with her crew, to continue the *Warrior's* rudely interrupted itinerary.

That the *Warrior* was sunk to prevent her continuing her voyage to Muroroa, the French nuclear weapons testing atoll in the Pacific, was not in doubt. The *Greenpeace* was despatched to this tiny speck of coral in the middle of the Pacific along with her sullen, angry and ultimately Antarctic-bound crew. The vessel was loaded in Hamburg and I went there to familiarise myself with the ship and its crew. I found a team of people labouring hard to fit oblong boxes into square spaces on the ship's deck and in the small hold. The skipper, my long-time friend and veteran campaigner, John Castle, was not pleased with the task. The vessel had been bought with almost no consultation of the seamen in our ranks, and opinion was that we 'landlubbers' were seemingly oblivious to the fact that the crew were now reaping the bitter fruits of our ill-determined decision.

The ship was simply not suited to being used as a cargo vessel and was certainly not built for Antarctic work, despite the fact that extra plating had been added to her bow and ice-fins now protected her rudder. A sweating, grumpy crew worked tirelessly to cram all the Antarctic paraphernalia on board then fretted over the stability of the ship carrying so much deck cargo. The omens for this first ever voyage into Antarctica by an environmental pressure group to establish an NGO base were not good, and as I boarded the plane back to London I prayed that the trip south would be a success. In fact it was probably the most angst-ridden voyage Greenpeace had ever undertaken. Back in Lewes McTaggart engineered a meeting at which my leadership of the upcoming expedition was confirmed and sanctioned. Despite my coy refusal, I was flattered that I was seen as the ideal candidate, although I was not impervious to the view that getting me out of the way for six months on the other side of the world suited some agendas. McTaggart amazed me by telling me, confidentially, that the objective, as far as he was concerned, was to demonstrate to the world that Antarctica belongs to no-one and everyone. The best way of showing millions of people that the USA had other ideas and that it considered the Antarctic legitimate American 'territory', was to provoke an incident which would force their Antarctic personnel to react in an aggressive and territorial manner. To my utter amazement, he told me,

'The base, the wintering team, the science – that all means nothing. All that's important is for you to get the head of the US base to take a swing at you and for you to get that on camera. And you do that by setting up camp right in the middle of the goddamn US base, right there on the roadway, on the airstrip or in the commander's HQ for all I care. The issue is ownership. You have as much right to sit on any piece of land that takes your fancy as they do. They don't own the Antarctic. Neither do the Brits or anyone else. It belongs to all of us and you can do as you goddamn please. Once he's told you to leave, we'll take it to the UN and have the place declared a World Park. That's what you're going to the Antarctic for.'

Simple as that. We buy a base for $100,000, we scour the planet for a base wintering team who are capable of carrying out a carefully prepared programme of monitoring and science, we buy a ship, crew it and spend a further $600,000 getting ourselves to the Antarctic when all we really need to do is to send me and a camera crew down there so that some jerk can take a swipe at me. I felt weak at McTaggart's naivety, innocence and enthusiasm and at his ability to reduce a huge international effort to two words – 'get punched'! While this may have been the secret agenda between McTaggart and I, it really didn't bear any relationship to the reality I faced as the expedition leader. I was fully aware that the dispirited crew harboured feelings of antipathy towards the Greenpeace hierarchy (epitomised by me) for having asked them to do a difficult and dangerous job in an unsuitable vessel; a crew who were seething with anger at the French attack on the *Warrior* and who were ill-prepared for the Antarctic voyage, were being asked to stand in for the *Warrior* and carry out a major campaign at Muroroa before pressing on to the Antarctic.

Had they been given any hint of McTaggart's instructions to me, there would have been a mutiny. Instead, the crew set sail from Hamburg for a tiny coral outcrop in the South Pacific which had been used since the 70s as a test bed for nuclear weapons, the French force de frappe, in a ship crammed with Antarctic paraphernalia. What they would do there would be the decision of a German colleague, Gerd Leipold, appointed campaign co-ordinator on board the ship. I did not envy his task.

The news we received from the ship as the crew arrived at Muroroa was sparse. They had arrived on the 12 mile limit and their presence had prompted the usual over-reaction from the French who sent a flotilla of warships and naval tugs to monitor Greenpeace's activities. The only high point I can recall in this period is McTaggart's outrage when Gerd was manoeuvred into accepting a bottle of champagne from the naval commander, but at least we had demonstrated that we were prepared to throw the necessary resources into honouring our commitments to campaigns, even in the face of bombs and secret agents. But all too soon, the *Greenpeace* was heading for New Zealand and it was time for me to fly from the UK to a country which Graham Searle had once told me would change my life if ever I had the opportunity to visit it.

I arrived at Heathrow and was immediately paged to go to information. Assuming it was McTaggart with last minute instructions, I opened the folded sheet of paper containing the message, only to read: 'Phone Annette urgently.' My heart leapt. I called her at home. She was distraught and through her tears told me that one of the cats was dying and that I was the only one in the world who knew the significance of this tragedy. I didn't know what to say. I simply sobbed at the news and I cried for all the pain and heartache I had caused her over the years and for the mess in which I had left our shattered marriage.

As I said my goodbyes to her, she asked me to realise the implications of my going to New Zealand and the Antarctic. It meant that any thoughts of reconciliation were over. I said yes and replaced the receiver. I never saw or heard from Annette again. The divorce was organised by my lawyer while I was away. I signed everything over to Annette and faced the world with little more than the clothes I stood up in, a meagre income from Greenpeace and two hundred pounds in the bank. I was 39 years old.

In the final few months of my Greenpeace UK tenancy, the international board had turned up the heat considerably regarding the need for us to expand the national board. The fur campaign had begun to attract so much attention in countries like South Africa, Sweden and Canada that the international Greenpeace board was directly asking the UK office to tone the campaign down on the grounds that the organisation could not afford to upset the indigenous peoples with whom it had traditional links. All in all, the UK office was under enormous pressure and I had traditionally been the go-between who took the sting out of the increasing bitterness between the UK board and that of International. Now I was removed, the task of wielding the knife on the UK office would be that much easier. I put these thoughts out of my mind and stared at the purple and orange hues of the sky as our tiny tube of metal winged its way to the Antipodes, the aircraft chasing the sun as it sank beneath the western horizon. Stuff it, I thought, I had enough on my plate as it was.

I arrived in Auckland to be met by Carol Stewart and the late Elaine Shaw, two stalwarts of the New Zealand Greenpeace office whom I had met at previous trustee meetings in Europe. By the time we had driven into town, dusk was falling and the late spring weather was blustery and cold. I asked if we could call in at the harbour to see the *Warrior* and as we drove up to Western Viaduct where the *Warrior*, now re-floated, was moored, her familiar outline looming out of the gathering darkness.

I walked alone towards the ship. She was gently tugging at her mooring lines, mournfully groaning, like some eyeless, tethered hulk unwillingly ensnared. I clambered on board carrying a torch. Her decks were bare. Already, souvenir hunters had stripped anything moveable from her. I walked around the aft deck and entered the starboard side access door, the very door I had reached for when I first stood on the *Warrior* as it rode at anchor off Torness, a lifetime ago. Turning left, I found the top of the short stairway which led to the cabin I normally used and went below to stand in utter dejection, staring at the bleakness and emptiness of the bare cabin in which I had had so many excitements and adventures. Tears rolled down my face.

The main deck was a tumbled confusion of broken washstands, buckled bulkheads and piles of flotsam and jetsam on the floor. I poked my head into the saloon which had reverberated to the singing, music and laughter of young ideological activists over the years and now echoed emptily at my intrusion. At the top of the engine room stairs I shone the torch into the abyss. The sight was one of total confusion. Piping, ducting and metal lay strewn around the floor in haphazard heaps: the stench of mud which had lain there for six weeks was overpowering. The ship had become a tomb. I breathed deeply as I emerged into Auckland's night air, glad to be off the ship.

The MV Greenpeace was due to arrive in three days and I spent the few days overcoming jet-lag and acquainting myself with the town, staying at Carol Stewart's house. I quickly warmed to Auckland with its busy streets, its pretty women and its lively night-life.

The ship arrived on schedule to much media hullaballoo and rejoicing, but the faces of the crew were ingrained with the strain they had endured from three months at sea. Sullen faces glowered at us as we lined the quayside to welcome the ship and our friends on board. The *Warrior* had been warped down the quay a few metres to allow the *Greenpeace* to come alongside and was then brought to lie on its seaward side. Once Customs had been cleared, there was much hugging and tears on the quayside and the *Greenpeace* crew, many of whom had, like me, sailed on the *Warrior*, began a wake which was to last for weeks.

Inevitably, every press briefing we called to promote the Antarctic expedition turned into an inquest about the sinking of the *Warrior*. It was understandable but frustrating for all that. Crew members began drifting off to the *Warrior* rather than working at loading supplies for the trip. They would not bother to turn up at briefings, preferring instead to mooch around the *Warrior* with old friends, plotting and planning some sort of revenge. I was inevitably drawn into this nether world of remembrance and we hatched a plan, immediately dismissed by Greenpeace International, to fit a large outboard engine on the *Warrior* and power her back to Muroroa, confronting the French with the ghost of the ship they had so brutally butchered. Instead, the plan was to sink her in Matauri Bay, a few miles north of Auckland, where she would act as a reef for marine life. This did not go down well with many of the veterans on board and was greeted with contempt within the organisation at large. In the light of the organisation's vociferous and ultimately successful opposition years later to the sinking of a Shell oil rig in the North Sea, the Brent Spar, the second sinking of the *Warrior* at our own hands came back to haunt us.

I had other problems on board. John Castle, the skipper, was in a perpetual foul mood and seemed to have allowed the world's ills to fall on his shoulders. He was scathing of the new, Antarctic-experienced crew members who appeared and made life on board pretty miserable for me. It was becoming increasingly evident that John was simply not in the right frame of mind to skipper the ship on the Antarctic voyage and I broached the subject of finding a replacement for him with John himself and with McTaggart. Reluctantly, but with a grace and humility for which John was renowned, he slowly came to agree that he was not in good shape and agreed to stand aside.

We asked Pete Bouquet to stand in for John. I hadn't sailed with Pete as skipper in all my years with Greenpeace and jumped at the chance of working with him since we had remained friends since the early days. There were problems associated with asking Pete to come to New Zealand, however. He insisted that his wife and four children be brought to New Zealand while the ship was in the Antarctic. This was granted but their eventual arrival caused major disruption to the preparatory stage for the voyage.

Pete duly arrived with his family and took up residence in the skipper's quarters with his wife and four children. Thus began Pete's valiant and onerous attempts to be a father, a skipper and a husband all at once. Pete was fearful of the voyage from the start. The ship was not ice-classed and thus was inadequate for the task as it would not allow us to push through anything but the lightest of brash ice. We would be required to stick strictly to clear water, and be forced to negotiate the outer pack ice we knew we would encounter with great caution and some trepidation.

Pete was obsessed – quite rightly – with the ship's trim and stability. We were carrying so much deck cargo that the addition of the 250 barrels of fuel for the base which would have to be carried on deck, way above the water line, and which would be taken on in Auckland, raised concerns about the ability of the ship to stay upright in the heavy Southern swells we would encounter. The weeks of preparation became one round after another of nail-biting uncertainty. This mood of creeping anxiety was heightened by the arrival of the film crew, a German team comprising of Axel Engsfeld and his sound and cameramen who had put up a sizeable amount of money towards the expedition for the privilege of filming the voyage. Naturally, they were concerned about the increasing criticism levelled at us by the Australian and New Zealand Antarctic Divisions, not to mention that of the USA, for our 'folly' in attempting to venture into the unforgiving Antarctic environment.

At one press conference we held on board, the New Zealand Antarctic Research Programme (ANZARP) dug up from somewhere a Scottish ship builder who apparently knew more about the ship than we did.

'And how thick is the hull, man?' asked the Scotsman of a distinctly uncertain Pete Bouquet.

'About 20mm thick,' came Pete's hesitant reply.

The Scotsman savoured his moment and leaned towards Pete for greater effect, 'Nine millimetres only! Nine! Not twenty!'

We had to concede that we were planning a voyage to treacherous waters in a ship which was built of steel plating only 9mm in thickness.

Pete's mood of uncertainty was gradually and unwittingly increased by his wife, Jane, who begged us to be cautious. Visits from various Antarctic cognoscenti added to our fears as one after the other, they warned us of impending doom. We did our best to ignore such pessimism, pointing out that even small yachts had circumvented the Antarctic and that we would not for one moment enter into seas which promised danger from ice. Then McTaggart put the tin hat on things when he arrived and took

206

Pete out for a few beers and told him, it was later alleged, to 'Go down, have a look and if it's too bad, then turn right around and come back.'

So we now had a campaigner on board – me – who was told to get himself punched by the US officials at McMurdo and a skipper who had been told to take a swing by the continent and have a look. To make things worse, Andy Hill, the logistics officer for the trip and one of only a few Antarctic-experienced people on board, decided to quit. Officially, he told us that sickness had stricken members of his family, but I privately harboured the uncharitable opinion that he was about to see his failings in preparing the equipment for the expedition laid bare for all to see.

Whatever the truth of the matter, his departure put Jerry Johnson, our base leader, in a complete spin. He demanded a logistics replacement in whom he had confidence and we scoured the globe looking for a suitable person. Doug Allen, a Brit with whom Gerry had worked previously, finally agreed to drop his life and hotfoot it to Auckland to come on the voyage.

The voyage was beginning to look amateurish and when we eventually set sail for Australia, we were physically prepared but an indisputably ill-disciplined crew. I had not stamped any sort of authority on the crew simply because the circumstances were so peculiar. I had neither the time, nor, in many cases, the crew availability to work with. Added to which, many of the crew were new and had many different impressions about how Greenpeace operated. The film crew, for instance, firmly believed that Greenpeace worked on a democratic basis. Boy! Did I have news for them! The trip across the Tasman to Sydney was uneventful apart from the sudden departure of McTaggart who decided to jump ship as we rounded North Cape, for reasons known only to himself. We arrived in Sydney to collect the fuel barrels for the base and to top up the ship's tanks with Antarctic blend fuel. This in itself was a source of endless acrimony on board. Pete decided that he would not take the fuel barrels on board in New Zealand as the ship was light on bunkers which would have made her top heavy and he was worried about the stability of the ship. We could only find the correct Antarctic blend fuel for the sh   ustralia, a fact which I found hard to believe but which I was force

The delays caused by the diversion to Australia bega our Antarctic schedule. In order to see for myself what the fuel was, I went to a meeting with the Shell represer seemed that our reluctance to accept what was considered the incorrect blend of fuel in Sydney was misplaced and, in the opinion of Shell, was exactly the same blend as the fuel we were now planning, incredulously, to take from Mobil in Melbourne. The extra expense incurred, not to mention the additional delay we would face in having to call into Melbourne, convinced me that I had an obligation to confront Pete Bouquet with this news. I sat in his cabin and told him this further diversion was entirely unnecessary. His drawn face looked at me blankly. He called chief engineer Pieter to his cabin as I left, not wishing to incur Pieter's wrath as being identified as the harbinger of such gloomy tidings to Pete. But Pete told him anyway that I had told him of this cock-up and Pieter never spoke another word to me – not a 'good morning', not a 'hi' – for the rest of the voyage. I could have done without making so powerful an enemy.

Regardless of the rights and wrongs of this confusion over the fuel, we were Melbourne-bound with light bunkers and no base camp fuel. It was time to get out of Sydney but the inevitable open day had to be organised first. The crew spent the day ushering hordes of people around the ship before the party started. Just as we were getting the beer opened, one of the engineers came up from the engine room to inform Pete and I that one of the generators had been tampered with. Oil had been drained from the sump and wires which would warn of an oil-shortage had been disconnected. Had we sailed without noticing the problem, the generator would have seized up completely without the engineers being warned and we would have had no choice but to turn back: going to the Antarctic in a non-ice-class vessel with two operating generators is bad enough: going with one generator and no back-up would have been reckless.

We did not need another controversy to fuel the fires of dissent and opposition to this trip. At a hastily convened meeting the crew agreed to ignore the incident, the better to keep the news from concerned loved ones at home, but inevitably, at 0200 I was woken by the watchman who told me the quay was lined with journalists who had heard the ship had been sabotaged. I spent the rest of the night being interviewed and doing my best to play down the story, but the headlines in the morning called for the 'incident-prone' voyage to be abandoned. Pete was in an inconsolable mood as we finally left for Melbourne and I felt in my bones this was a trip I should never have agreed to.

Last minute pleas by Australian ministers to abandon the voyage continued even after our departure. Yet, out of Sydney we sailed, the aft deck piled high with base camp sections covered by blue tarpaulins. Our tiny Hughes 300 helicopter – the flying lawnmower as pilot Dave Walley called it – was now safely encased, apart from the tail assembly which stuck out five feet, in a wooden box which our innovative carpenter Hugh had made in the space of a day and which in later years became a mobile home for itinerants in the back yard of Henk Haazen's house in Auckland. In Melbourne, as the fuel was pumped into the ship's bunkers and she began to settle more deeply in the water, the barrels of base camp fuel were loaded on board. They were loaded in the 'tween deck until it was full to overflowing. Those that remained were lashed to the rails on both sides of the ship or stuffed into the deep pilot accesses around the waist of the ship.

Our vulnerabilities and frailties were starkly brought home to us by the rounds of criticism levelled at us routinely from officialdom, criticisms we did our best to shrug off and ignore. But we could not deny that we were an inexperienced crew in Antarctic travel and ice navigation and one which was still vengeful and moody at the sinking of the *Warrior* and the death of Fernando. Neither was the crew best pleased with the job it was being asked to do in a hopelessly inadequate vessel.

The hasty and unavoidably chaotic preparations nearly caused a fatality during barrel loading when I was driving the ship's crane (after only minimal formal operating instructions from first mate Ken Ballard). I began to lower two 250kg barrels of base fuel into the port side pilot access in which Ken was standing, in order to guide them into a space only inches wider than the barrels themselves. As I dropped them slowly on the wire towards the access, the rim of one barrel caught the metal edge and released the tension on the barrel hooks and the barrel fell into the access. The thing that saved Ken – at least, saved him from a cracked skull if not saved his life – was that the barrel jammed diagonally across the narrow access and he was able to scramble out from beneath it. Without a word, he re-hooked the barrel and indicated that I should lift it and try again.

Finally, after a few more scares, we were leaving for the Antarctic at last. All the doubts and uncertainties were now so many shrugs of the shoulder. We slipped the moorings and I took the wheel. The pilot came on the bridge preceded by an overpowering smell of scotch and our fears were confirmed when he was seen sauntering out to the bridge wing with impolite frequency to take another swig from a hip-flask. The green flashing buoys were almost scraping the ship's side before the pilot shouted from the bridge wing, 'Hard a'starboard!' I kept her on hard a'starboard as per the protocol until the starboard channel buoys were hard on our bow when the pilot reappeared and ordered, 'Hard a'port!' In this way we zig-zagged our way out of Melbourne, the final ignominy to set us on our way being that they sent us a pilot who appeared to be as high as a kite.

Dumping the pilot off for his ride home at the turning buoy, we were finally alone and the lights of Melbourne were already low on the horizon. Just the Southern ocean and the mighty Antarctic, about which I had read avidly since I was a kid, lay ahead. Scott, Shackleton, Amundsen, Ross, Mawson, even Cook – all had gone before us in ships made of wood and many in ships which had no mechanical power. And our destination was the very spot upon which Scott had stood before he left for his fateful race against time, against Amundsen and against the fearful Antarctic weather for the Pole. He lost. I was painfully aware that we might 'lose' insofar as we might not even make landfall and that the reputation of Greenpeace was, in part, dependent on this expedition and the achieving of the campaign objectives.

We met none of our objectives. The voyage was a disaster in that we did not achieve our goal. It was a disaster in terms of the fact that relationships between many crew members were strained to the point of physical violence. It was a disaster in terms of the fact that we spent close to $1 million simply stooging around the Ross Sea getting more and more frustrated. The ice was the most severe it had been in twenty years. We couldn't get within 30 miles of our goal and many on board, after one or two attempts, were not willing to try further. Many wanted simply to go home, to get out of that 'awful place', to accept defeat and to return to the comforts of Auckland. Conversely, others, including myself, found the place so enchanting, so mind-bogglingly beautiful that we could have stayed there indefinitely. I hand over the narrative, interspersed with a few asides, recollections and anecdotes, to my diary of that trip: I hope it tells the story more dramatically yet in a more matter-of-fact way than any narrative I could write.

I have tried, above, to set the scene in terms of the background to the voyage and to the atmosphere and circumstances which prevailed before we set sail. It is also necessary to say a few general words about the crew, the people they were and how they came to be on the ship.

People who gravitated to Greenpeace – myself included – were generally, and for obvious reasons, attracted to a different kind of life than was considered normal. The crew selection process required that we appointed qualified people to the roles of running the ship and performing professional tasks associated with the expedition. In order to fulfil the prophesy of the 'Warriors of the Rainbow', we tried to recruit from as wide a range of nationalities as possible, but more importantly, given the need for generating media interest, we had to ensure that we could throw a wide net in terms of the nations in which we generated that interest. In the same way as we needed to recruit four winterers from different national backgrounds, but with the required skills to keep the base operating effectively for a year, so we needed a diversity of nationals possessing the required skills – radio operators, able seamen and seawomen, mates, engineers, small boat operators, outboard mechanics, cooks and helicopter pilots. The task of accumulating such a crew was no mean feat and inevitably some square pegs were required to do their best to sit in round holes. Over all though, the crews and, more particularly, the over-winter teams we appointed over six years, were exceptional and dedicated people with whom it was a privilege and an honour to sail, without exception.

The winter-over team was required to occupy the base for a year before being relieved by the re-supply team and a new group of winter-over people the following year. We made great demands of the potential team: not only would they be left to their own resources for an entire year in the most inhospitable environments on earth, but they would also be required to undertake work – experiments and research in the case of the scientists, medicine and health in the case of the doctor/nurse, maintenance in the case of the engineers, radio communications in the case of the sparks and field trips lead by the base 'commander' in the case of the appointed 'leader'. Thus we needed a scientist, a field expert, someone skilled in radio/electronics and a qualified medic/doctor. The optimum gender balance of such a group was a constant and sometimes insoluble problem.

First Antarctic trip diary

December 1985 to February 1986

26 December 1985

See our first iceberg spotted at 0400. John Welsh (my cabin mate) wins sweepstake.

28 December 1985

Reach pack ice at 1000 and spend three days following edge, looking for a lead south. Find one which takes us 60 miles south then forced east and eventually north until a further promising lead appears on the 31st. We follow and promisingly still find open water ahead after 2 hours steaming, but Pete orders a northerly course due to deteriorating visibility and northerly wind and fog, fearing that ice will close in behind us.

Much consternation and dismay among the crew at Pete's refusal to take the vessel into anything but large expanses of open water. Gerry (Johnson, base leader) states that we'll never get there unless we commit ourselves to ice. Mood on board is worsening. I call a meeting for New Year's Eve where Pete states he wants an 'autobahn' of clear water before heading south to McMurdo (660 miles away!) We continue travelling north to clear the ice pack where we heave to. Laurie Greenfield (scientist colleague at Christchurch University) telexes depressing news: eight to ten tenths pack ice reported in Ross Sea between 73 and 77 south (normally ice-free at this time of year).

2 January 1986

Decide to visit Scott Island (a phallic-looking rock outcrop) to relieve boredom. This will at least take us a further 35 miles further south. Alternatives to landfall at McMurdo now openly being discussed on board. John Sprange (mate) proposes – in writing – that we set up the base on King George Island, some 2000 miles away in the Peninsula. Axel (film producer) anxious to commit us to this course of action as he feels reports on conditions in Ross Sea and Pete's reluctance to push south obviate McMurdo as a possible site.

I insist at a crew meeting that we must wait, be patient, as even if we don't get to McMurdo until the beginning of February, we still have a chance of establishing the base camp. I state this position clearly and forcefully but there are already small committees meeting around the ship and proposals supported by various factions keep popping up. It's my job to keep it together while we wait, but I only have the support of a few committed people and while they may be influential, I am faced with antipathy from many quarters, particularly those with a financial interest in the expedition.

4 January 1986
We move away from Scott Island for a rendezvous with Southern Quest (the vessel used by the Footsteps of Scott expedition supporting their land-based team, which was at that very moment walking in the 'Footsteps of Scott' to the South Pole). Dumont D'Urville (the French base 200 miles north of McMurdo) reported ice-free conditions in the sound which complicates the situation on board as Pete is now faced with more factors. Ice reports indicate an improvement and the wind is backing to the south which looks hopeful as Pete fears a northerly blocking our escape route.

5 January 1986
Forced east and north by the pack. Southern Quest (SQ) tells us, on the regular radio schedule we have now established, that she has just pushed through ice and is now 12 hours south of us, en route to Cape Hallet and that ice conditions are good. Pete agrees to go to the point where the SQ went through to check it out and hopes on board rise.

6 January 1986
At 1600 we are stopped due to zero visibility. Press calls ask for confirmation of reports (origin unknown) that we are beset and asking SQ for assistance. We quell these rumours in a press release but Pete moves around the ship in an aggressive and tetchy mood. Now Gerry and Axel are entering into a telex war against each other, both sending unauthorised tomes to McTaggart, one demanding the trip be cancelled (Axel), the other (Gerry) demanding we be allowed to continue.

11 January 1986
The most frustrating five days of the trip so far: fog-bound, stationary, tempers flaring and Pete continually curt and grumpy. We finally begin to make a southing on the 10th, but only after having retraced our steps to

the north yet again. After lumping through ice-strewn waters to the north and east for 15 hours we come upon clear, open, ice-free water to the south. Whales (three minkes) surface close to the vessel and we follow them for 30 wonderful minutes with crew lining the rails. Stupendous!

Then the complaints begin again. Pieter complains that the fuel is waxing, people complain about the food and petty squabbles break out over the use of the television for watching videos. Gerry is ready to throw in the towel on 'shambolic Greenpeace'. But when the course is between 150 and 190, the mood on board immediately improves. Spirits rise, tempers cool. At 2200 we're still heading south and position is 71.15 South.

Then a disaster occurs. The SQ doesn't come up for her schedule tonight. We call McMurdo control to learn that she sank earlier in the day, crushed between two large floes between which she was attempting to squeeze . All the crew are safe, having evacuated the ship to one of the floes. This news drains Pete of any remaining confidence, yet he doggedly continues to push south in the open water.

14 January 1986

Joy of joys! We're at 77 South! 60 miles east of Beaufort Island. We can see Mounts Erebus and Terror shimmering magnificently on the horizon. Visibility is incredible – 120 miles! The ice reports cool our ardour: eight to ten tenths fast ice surrounding the northern edge of Ross Island, exposing only the far northerly tip of the island. Pete immediately wants to turn around and steam two days to the north to clear the outer pack ice at 69 South – 480 miles away from our destination. He fears that the pack behind us will shift and block our route out of the Ross Sea. His decision causes uproar on board and precipitates the worst period of time on board thus far. Most of the crew are deflated and angry. We are so near yet so far.

The SQ sinking has clearly been the deciding factor in Pete's decision which forced his flagging confidence to collapse. Then the Australian science minister piles on the agony by faxing the ship with an appeal for us to abandon the expedition. Pete is short-tempered and grumpy, but the burden he bears is almost intolerable. The only bright spot today as we turned the ship around was seeing 30 fin and minke whales gambol around the ship for the best part of an hour. I steel myself to speak to Pete about his decision to steam north and he finally agrees to reduce speed although he refuses to change his decision and flatly refuses to stay close to Beaufort Island when the northern pack ice is still heavy and threatening.

15 January 1986
Killer whales all around the ship today. Launched inflatables for filming. Tried to get the ship into Cape Hallet but turned around as soon as a belt of ice appeared off the coast. The Admiralty Range of mountains is simply magnificent and seems to mock our pathetic attempts to get close.

16 January 1986
Steamed a further 100 miles north and stopped. We tested the drift and discover it is north east at one knot. Pete, Gerry, Ken and mates have first open and frank discussion with Pete today and he decides that we can risk going back to the coast as he finally seems to be convinced by the argument that the northern pack ice will not present a threat until at least the middle of February.

17 January 1986
Following the pack south, at last. Spirits soar with the southerly compass heading. Pete seems to have reversed all his earlier decisions. I secretly harbour the belief that he has spoken to McTaggart who has repeated his 'take a look and then get out' instructions to Pete, but whatever the reason Pete now wants to follow the pack ice edge, use the helicopter to fly the winterers to the Footsteps of Scott hut at Cape Evans to check it out as a potential over-wintering base for our team since it is now almost impossible to envisage us being able to erect our base in the limited time available to us, even if we somehow got into Cape Evans today.

Pete's unpredictability is worrying. He announces without any reference to anyone that there will be changes on the watches and he removes me from the 8-12, replacing me with Klaus (the engineer!) I'm most worried by the fact that Pete's change of heart is prompted by the belief that we need to spend only a few days off Ross Island before we call it a day and head back to Auckland. He wants to dash in, dash out and go home. That's not on as far as I'm concerned and I determine to call Roger (Wilson, my campaign superior) and get him to instruct us to stay as long as possible.

Crew meeting was the most aggressive yet. Doug (Allen) and Edwin (Mickleburgh) are vociferous and negative about the use of the helicopter and Edwin shouts at me, telling me to abandon this effort before storming out of the meeting. Thanks Edwin. This outburst and the general negativity on board depresses the over-wintering team who have prepared for a year to winter in Antarctica. Just to add to the misery, Pieter (chief engineer) turns off the water, an act which had John Welsh reduced to melting ice cubes in the micro-wave to produce sufficient water to swallow asprins for a hangover! Then the final straw: Edwin writes a draft telex telling McTaggart that he and the over-wintering team (whom I'm sure he has not consulted) feel the campaign should be terminated.

A blazing row between Edwin and I ensues and I tell Edwin that just at the point when we're doing what the majority on board want to do – head south, check out the ice, visit the Cape Evans site and salvage something from the expedition – he wants to send this garbage to torpedo the effort and to scuttle any vestiges of unity we have belatedly found. I'm beside myself with indignation. I tell him that he's now barred from entering into any discussions with anyone about tactics, that he should henceforth accept his passenger role and keep his nose out of anything but his responsibility to document the trip for his book, which I tell him to shove where the sun doesn't shine. That's it! I'm finished with Edwin and his book and I'm finished with this trip!

18 January 1986
Like me, Pete is in a black mood. He calls me at 0400 and shows me a telex from Roger which instructs us (at my prompting) to stay at least until the 20 February. He is furious and clearly had his heart set on going home within days. The prospect of staying in this place, which he clearly hates, for another month, is simply too much for him to bear. He finally calms down and contributes to the press release and update I send out later. We are still south-bound. The water is back on. Shower. Luxury.

19 January 1986
The Footsteps of Scott expedition people can't allow us to use their hut as a winter-over point as their own team plan to winter there this year. Even the Foreign Office back home has advised Footsteps to have nothing to do with us. Access to Ross Island is clearly impossible – heavy pack ice is still surrounding McMurdo Sound as far out as Beaufort Island. We steam along the Ross Ice Shelf by way of a distraction. The shelf is about 70 feet high and quite breathtaking. A 40 knot wind and a minus five temperature

216

create real Antarctic atmosphere. It is a spectacular place and the mood is enhanced by the presence of hundreds of penguins 'porpoising' through the sea. But depression grips my heart as the realisation of the impossibility of our task dawns on me. All we can do is get the helicopter airborne, fly into Cape Evans and carry out an inspection, then back to New Zealand.

The situation is made worse by the fact that we are only 30 miles from Cape Evans by air. Steamed 25 miles NE and waited in force eight gale for better weather. Agreed to put the helicopter up to survey the coast. Dave Walley really is an excellent pilot. We have no helideck on board and are forced to launch the chopper by lifting it from its box on the starboard side aft with the crane and setting it down on a plywood surface we have constructed on top of the cargo on the aft deck. Dave takes off from here and lands back on this tiny wooden platform, hovering in the chopper with the tips of the blades almost clipping the superstructure. I take my hat off to his flying skills. Yet even the distractions of the chopper flying, and the sense of getting at least something done, does not quell arguments and I'm assailed with criticism from people about the value of the surveys we're carrying out.

20 January 1986
A telex arrives from GP HQ in Lewes: 'Please stay in the Ross Sea for as long as you can and carry out as much useful work as possible. The date you leave is a decision for you to make on board, based on safety and on the work you identify as being supportive of our Antarctic programme. The offloading of the fuel in readiness for next year at a suitable site would be a valuable contribution.' Well, that threw the ball back to us quite quickly! Pete and I agree to mull over the telex for a day or two. We steam back past Beaufort Island to Ross Island, 35 miles east of Cape Bird with pack ice receding, but still very heavy where it concentrates along the coast and across the mouth of McMurdo Sound. The US Coast Guard ship, Polar Star, moves steadily along in the middle of the ice, cutting her way to McMurdo. The temptation to ask Pete to steam down the channel she cuts is overwhelming, but I resist.

21 January 1986
Sleep most of the day. Hilary phones and I suddenly realise how much I miss her and how homesick I am. At the crew meeting Pete relays the information that the US authorities at McMurdo informed him today that

they would be removing their aircraft from the area by the 5th February and their shipping by the 12th February, in advance of the winter and the colder temperatures. I incur his scorn when I voice my opinion that this information is bullshit and designed to pressure us into leaving earlier. Criticism comes about the impending attempt to offload the fuel as it will commit us to a site which may not be found suitable next year.

Some other bright spark argues that the base could be damaged and that offloading would not allow an inspection back in Auckland. I point out that it's a bit late for those fears to be raised now and I dismiss the criticism as a ruse to negate the necessity for staying. I note that they all come from the 'get out of here now' contingent. Axel loses it and walks out of the crew meeting shouting 'No more waiting!' Asshole. Then Bernt threatens to 'tell the world he's being held hostage.'

I can't believe what I'm hearing and I can't stop myself from laughing which infuriates him. Later in the day Pete hears that the second US ice-breaker, Polar Buck, reports 14 miles of ice pack to the north. Pete flips and tells me we're pulling out as soon as the helo flight is over. I notify South Pole (can't raise McMurdo) of our intentions to operate the helicopter – times, positions, type, safety frequencies etc – which is acknowledged with a promise to pass to McMurdo flight control.

Helo ready to lift at midnight with Doug on board for pictures and Gerry to go to Cape Evans. At least Gerry will get to see the place where he was to winter. Agree with Pete that we'll stay until the 5th February unless he feels we should leave earlier due to safety reasons. Bed at 0330.

22 January 1986
Up at 0730 for press calls. Dave Walley reports from last night's helo flight that clear water is to be found to the north of Ross Island, down to Cape Royds, with large slabs of pack ice off the coast. We could get in but should the pack move while we're in the Sound, we'd be trapped. Indeed, the pack moved to the north of us in the night forcing Pete to steam 20 miles north to keep our escape route open. We watch the video Gerry shot on the helo flight and the clear water in the Sound is so, so tempting. We could definitely get into Cape Bird, but the danger from the shifting pack precludes my even mentioning this to Pete. I reluctantly prepare a 'time running out' press release.

23 January 1986

Four hours sleep again last night, but it is a day for decision-making. Dave Woolan misses the radio schedule with Gerry who was airlifted back to Cape Evans in the night. Great start to the day. The mates, Pete, me, Doug and Edwin (the last two uninvited) agree to leave after we have

1. Completed the assessment of Cape Evans.

2. Detailed the access to the beach there, for next year's effort.

3. Carried out filming for ITN who have contracted Axel to shoot a few cans of film for them, and

4. Allowed Axel to film as much of the area as he needs to.

February 1st has been designated by Greenpeace International as 'World Park Antarctica Day' and we further agree that on that day, we will ensure all the crew have a chance to set foot on Antarctica, probably at the Bay of Whales from where Amundsen made his successful bid for the Pole in 1911. Pete began the meeting in a perfectly foul mood until he realised that an end to his agony was in sight, at which point he visibly changed his whole demeanour and attitude, becoming almost jovial. Edwin and Doug, however, are aggressive and negative again and I wish they'd keep their noses out of campaign business.

Sleep from 1500-1800 and awake to learn that Pete is still not prepared to go into the Sound. Ralph John, the wintering scientist, is flown to Cape Evans, but later Gerry's trip is cancelled due to bad communications. Dave performs his amazing helicopter landing feat again while I steer the ship into the wind to give him maximum lift. Dave's a really nice guy, always ready to smile and have a joke amid this sea of bitterness and bad humour. A few beers with Ken in the evening, talking over life's problems and ironies. Bed at 0300.

24 January 1986

Up at 10.15 and luxuriate in an absence of phone calls. Lazy day doing nothing and avoiding the cliques and little knots of people who have lately taken to muttering to each other in corridors. Axel away filming at Cape Bird and we get his ITN film out via the Kiwis at Scott Base. Steak for dinner, courtesy of Gerry. Much to-ing and fro-ing and flying around until 0300 which I blithely ignore.

25 January 1986

We steam away from the ice every day after having completed our business at the ice edge. I have given up all hope of doing anything remotely useful in terms of setting up the base, offloading fuel etc. It's simply a political non-starter and I'm now staring at the reality of leaving this incredible, enigmatic place within a matter of days.

26 January 1986
Last helicopter flights today. We simply need to collect Gerry from Cape Evans and we can then carry out our World Park Day activities and go home. Another acrimonious crew meeting at which Doug in particular is so aggressive. Then we turn east for the Bay of Whales. It's seems like the beginning of the end for this trip and a great weight lifts from my shoulders after having accepted the inevitable.

27 January 1986
Press calls stream in, relating to a statement the New Zealand government put out claiming that the short visit to Scott Base by Gerry was 'very disruptive' to their scientific programme. I reply that dumping waste and old vehicles into the sensitive McMurdo Sound is quite disruptive to the fragile Antarctic ecosystem.

28 January 1986
Arrive at the Bay of Whales around 1700. It's blowing hard with a grey, steely, overcast sky. The wind blowing off the shelf is bitter, but the scene before us is archetypal Antarctic. Seals and penguins lie or stand, coated in wind-driven snow, oblivious to our presence. Leopard seals, crab-eater seals, Adelie and Emperor penguins dot the low ice sheet which occupies the Bay itself, perhaps ten miles long. The ice slope rises gradually to a series of ice-falls and hummocks, a mile inland, before the Antarctic land mass abuts it in the shape of a well-defined step. It is argued that the presence of Roosevelt Island some miles inland causes the ice to part when it flows past the island, weakening the ice front and giving rise to the conditions which form the Bay of Whales.

It was named by Sir James Clark Ross in 1840. When he arrived here the sea was literally full of whales, but today we have seen only the occasional orca – maybe one or two minkes. We secure the ship bow-on to the ice, initially using 'deadmen' sunk into the ice. Then Pete brings the ship alongside the ice and we secure her again port side to. We take great care to ensure she is well fastened to the ice: if the ship was to drift off into the Ross Sea here, when we are all ashore, we would be well and truly kyboshed.

My personal feeling that we are intruding in this 'cathedral' grows: it is stunningly beautiful, but I'll be glad when we leave. We simply don't deserve to see such a staggering place. We are too crass, noisy and intrusive. I eventually find space to go ashore on my own – most of the crew have wandered off into the further reaches of the ice shelf and I spend my time taking photos of the wildlife and sketching an Emperor penguin. Pete has cause to sound the recall signal – two blasts on the klaxon – since many people are cavorting under the ice falls, something we were specifically warned against doing since it is a highly dangerous pastime. Bed at 0130 when the party on the ice begins. I'm not best pleased at the antics of some crew members which I find irreverent. Thank God we don't have a news journalist on board. Can't sleep tonight at the prospect of organising the World Park Day celebrations tomorrow.

29 January 1986
Crew arranged in a choreographed manifestation of united celebration, down the gang-plank and spilling onto the ice for the photo of our Antarctic day celebrations. It's a hollow gesture and one which is thankfully soon over. News of Scott Base personnel being fired for talking to the media reaches us. I'm asked to do a bridge watch from 1000-1200, at which point we let go the ropes and head off to the east to explore what lies beyond the Bay of Whales and then no doubt we'll head for Auckland.

30 January 1986
Hilary phones to tell me she's going to India with some guy who is gay. She tells me she misses me very much, words which at this distance, and under these circumstances, mean a lot to me. Then we get a call from a friend at Scott Base who tells us that McMurdo Sound is finally and totally ice-free. I slump on my bunk in a state of utter dejection.

31 January 1986
We arrive at Ross Island to see our westerly approach to McMurdo still blocked by an ice barrier although it is quite possible that clear water exists on the western side. Maddeningly, the weather is too bad to operate the helicopter so we head north to round the ice barrier. I call a crew meeting to explain the situation and am criticised for keeping people in

the dark about activities and plans, and for 'politicking'. Then Warren (helicopter mechanic) tells the meeting that he's had it playing batman to Dave Walley who 'thinks he's still flying biplanes in the Great War' and promptly 'resigns'. After the cathartic crew meeting, things seem to have calmed down and we agree to heave to for the night.

I can't quite believe that, after all this time and all the arguments and frustrations, we're here in the desired place and that we can now access McMurdo if only we can negotiate this band of ice which blocks our path. I pace around the ship for most of the night, consulting people on their feelings about having one last go at getting to Cape Evans, but for all my persuading the overwhelming attitude is a desire to get the hell out of here to stop any further carping. If I'm honest with myself, I know I'm fighting a lost cause but I can't believe we're just going to sail out of here when there's still a full month of the summer left.

I wander into the saloon around midnight to find Davey Edward in an unusually foul mood. He lays into Dermot the electrician, accusing him of being lazy and work-shy. He throws two punches before he's restrained. He then turns his attention to Klaus (third engineer) and berates him for taking hard-earned Greenpeace money to 'sit on board for a tour of the Antarctic' and squares up to him too. The aftermath is a nightmare. Davey is inconsolable and begins smashing things up. I grab him and he sobs on my shoulder. Ken is called and before long we steer Davey back to his cabin. Warren approaches me and tells me that he apologises for his earlier outburst and that he's now back 'working'. I can't stand much more of this.

1 February 1986

I call a crew meeting at 1300 to clear the air and Pete announces that in future, the crew will run the ship and others are to act as passengers and stop offering him advice. Then he announces in sombre, fateful words, 'I've altered course to the north. We're going back to New Zealand', at which the 'get out of here' contingent – Axel and his film crew, Doug, Edwin and a few of the crew – raise a cheer. It's all over then. The bubble has finally burst. Just a few miles to the east lies Pete's 'autobahn' to McMurdo which we have finally found a month too late. Ironically, Hilary phones to congratulate us on 'finally landing at Cape Evans', another distorted press story. And so we head for New Zealand.

2 February 1986
Heading north. Southerly wind. Following sea. Heavy roll. Bored, worried, fed up and sick of it all.

3 February 1986
Table tennis championship lightens mood, prompted by Bernt finding a long-lost ping pong ball in his pocket, and accommodated by the engineers who make a net and rubber-faced bats in record time. You can't help but laugh when the ball you're just about to smash across the table is suddenly stuck to the bulkhead above you due to the ship dropping through a trough and you're swiping at thin air. I'm the beaten finalist. Then Bernt steps on the ping-pong ball. Very symbolic.

4 February 1986
65, 42 south at 22.00. Invited to Campbell Island. Press report indicates that NZ Premier Lange has promised a review of Antarctic policy. Long. slow swell, pitching easily.

I finished my diary for the trip at this point, although there was still a surprise in store for us. Pete and the base leader on Campbell Island had a minor set-to and we left the island under a cloud of acrimony. Pete decided not to speak to me for the rest of the trip after I told him I thought he acted inappropriately on Campbell in his capacity as skipper. The island itself, however, was a wonderland of wildlife: penguins, sea-lions and elephant seals abounded on this rocky upthrust in the middle of the Southern Ocean and we spent an enchanted time wandering over the island for the best part of the day, before the party that evening.

And so, we eventually approached the southern tip of New Zealand's south island and took a spin around the Snares, an outcrop of rock which acts as a sanctuary for birds. The weather was wild and my abiding memory of that visit is standing on deck in brilliant sunshine, hanging on for grim death as the ship bucketed and plummeted in wild seas around the island. For the first time in months we could walk around on deck in summer clothes. The effect was liberating and the mood of the crew began to mellow. People began talking to each other and to patch up old wounds. As the prospect of reaching port loomed larger and larger, it was as though the crew once more became a cohesive and self-protective unit.

Chapter 25

A second chance and a final blow
1986 – 1987 trip

We headed for Wellington since, I argued to Pete who responded in no more than grunts, it was the capital and thus the place where our presence would have the greatest impact on Antarctic policy, especially given Lange's recent statement. We arrived on the 10th February to see the quayside at the International terminal lined with people bearing all manner of banners. As the pilot on board the *Greenpeace* cut engines to drift towards the quay, there was a physical movement of crew away from the railings and away from contact with those who had not shared this experience with us. The last ten metres of water we travelled towards the quay were the most anxious and awkward I have ever travelled at sea. The silence was palpable and the microphones in the hands of the journalists jockeying for position among the crowd were like fingers pointing at me in accusation. I knew that within minutes, I would be talking into those microphones and that the words I spoke – good, bad or indifferent – would be used on news bulletins all over the world. I can't remember what I said.

All I know is that I went into automatic pilot and abided by the golden rule which is never to acknowledge defeat. 'People don't support losers' were McTaggart's words which swam into my mind every time I spoke in public or for the media. The photographs of me that day speak volumes. My face was etched with the strain of our first voyage to Antarctica; a trip which we had neither prepared for correctly nor had sufficient time to assemble the right tools in order to complete the job. We were due to stay in Wellington for 24 hours before making our way to Auckland, our 'home' port, and the official end of the expedition. The crew went ashore that night and let loose. The following morning, some had already made plans to go home from Wellington rather than prolong the agony by sailing to Auckland.

At midday as I lazed around the saloon, two people came down the staircase and approached me. One was a tall, blond woman, the other a blond man both in their 20s. They were volunteer workers with Greenpeace in Wellington and were off on holiday to Auckland. Naturally enough, they felt that a short trip on the *Greenpeace* would be a novel and cheap way of beginning their holiday. Pete grunted his approval when I asked if they could join the ship for the voyage to Auckland. I soon realised that Fiona would be on the receiving end of a lot of attention on the trip, especially as it transpired that the blond guy was not her partner. As the day wore on towards an evening departure time, the beers began to flow and by the time we slipped our moorings a full-blown party was under way on the monkey island – the area above the bridge. As I finished my stint on the wheel, I made my way up to the party. The ship was now out to sea and rolling along with an easy motion beneath a brilliant sky studded with a million stars. I made a move towards Fiona and slipped my arm around her waist. As the short journey to Auckland reached its end, I realised I was in deep trouble on the female front. I was still married to Annette, although it was inevitable that our separation would now result in divorce. I had belatedly learned that Hilary was en route to New Zealand via Australia to meet me and I knew that Debbie would be waiting for me in Auckland. Now, Fiona and I had struck up a closeness which I hoped would result in a relationship.

In my defence, it must be said that my emotions were in complete and utter turmoil. I had, over the past year in fact, lost or abandoned all my emotional reference points. I was bereft of the ability to focus my short, medium or long-term plans on anything: all my decisions and actions seemed to be taken or made in a vacuum.

As we docked in Auckland, Debbie was waiting. I learned from a Greenpeacer ashore that Hilary was on her way to meet the ship. I had assumed that, despite my affection for Hilary and indeed for Debbie, both relationships were over. I had told Hilary before I left the UK that I felt our relationship should end and as far as Debbie was concerned, I had taken her indiscretions shortly after I had left for the south as a clear indication that our relationship was over and had no future. As soon as we cleared Customs, I took the bull by the horns. Telling Debbie to wait a while, I took Hilary to the pub and explained the situation to her as sensitively as I possibly could under the circumstances. I then went through the same procedure with Debbie. It was probably the most awkward and distasteful hour I had ever spent in my life and although I felt entirely vindicated and justified in my actions, leaving two beautiful and intelligent women hurt was as painful for me as it was for them.

I walked back to the ship where Fiona was sitting reading quietly. Despite the fact that Fiona and I had grown close during the trip from Wellington to Auckland, we had not formally committed ourselves to each other and I was still a little hesitant to let the rest of the crew know that I had fallen for her in anything more than a casual way.

The following day, Fiona and I wandered into town. It was raining hard and as we sheltered in the doorway of a church. I reached awkwardly for her hand and asked if we could assume that we were officially a couple. She concurred and we began a relationship which was to see us eventually set up home together in Wellington and then in London a year later.

A week later, I flew to Wellington with Fiona and spent a week discovering the staggering beauty of this port which is the largest natural harbour in New Zealand (and one which Cook blithely sailed past in the 1700s without investigating what lay beyond the rocky promontories which guard the small entrance). Fiona was at college studying political history and we regularly visited the campus and met her young friends and colleagues. But most of the time we spent discovering the dramatic coastline and deserted beaches. It was a quite magical time and as the week drew to a close my heart sank at the prospect of flying home to a winter-enveloped England and the controversies which still dogged the UK office. I dragged myself to Wellington airport and waved goodbye to Fiona as I boarded the flight to Auckland to make the connection to Heathrow. I had a day to spare before the flight and took the opportunity to visit the ship.

As I stepped off the shuttle bus at the Auckland terminal, I could see the masts of the *Greenpeace* as she lay at Western Viaduct. I climbed the gangplank onto the intimately familiar vessel and was assailed by the instantly recognisable cacophony of voices wafting from the mess. It was like walking back in time and into the bosom of my family. All the tensions had been exorcised and the now mostly deserted ship echoed to the crash and bang of the last of the equipment being lifted out of the holds for warehouse storage close by. Ken Ballard and John Welsh, my old cabin mate, were due to fly on the same flight as me. The next day, we waited for the taxi on the quayside with our bags by our side. The sun beat down unmercifully as two guys approached and extended their hands in greeting. They were both Americans who had just arrived back from McMurdo and after some small talk, one took off his sun glasses and shielded his eyes with his hand and said, 'You guys did a great job raising awareness about the Antarctic, but there's one question I've been longing to ask. Why did you leave so goddamn early? It's still summer down there and the Sound is wide open.'

I looked down to the tarmac and shuffled my feet. The taxi arrived and we three clambered in with mumbled apologies. As we sped out of the Auckland dock complex, it was as though I was leaving behind part of my soul. I was leaving the ghost of the *Rainbow Warrior* and the echoing emptiness of the MV Greenpeace. I was leaving behind an unfinished job and a woman I was in love with. Through the tears which flowed freely down my cheeks, I made John and Ken swear to come back with me to complete what we had started. They nodded in silence

The flight home from Auckland was notable only for John's remarkable ability to sleep for the entire journey while Ken and I took the best possible advantage of Qantas' policy of plying free drinks on their customers. By the time we arrived in London at 0700 two days later, Ken and I had gone through two hangovers and had gotten drunk all over again. John and I hugged Ken goodbye as he boarded the bus for Oxford where he spent time with his folks. As we watched the bus depart, John and I realised we only had each other to remind ourselves that our recent ordeal was a real event in our lives rather than some incredible, surreal dream. We took the bus back to London and walked into the office on Graham Street to find a muted and disorganised staff.

I couldn't deal with the welter of issues which needed attention and soon John and I were propping up the bar in the Earl of Essex trying to ignore the rest of the world. John stayed with me for a week and we were clearly reluctant to part. We lived in a world in which people could not begin to understand the depths of the emotions we were going through. The previous months of working and living in New Zealand, the experience of the *Rainbow Warrior*, the trip itself and all its upheavals and the surreal, distanced feeling we were experiencing made us pensive and withdrawn. It was all too much to handle and John and I sat cosily behind the barrier erected by alcohol, hardly needing to speak. Eventually, John decided it was time to leave. We stepped out onto the street from the office and he ambled off to the train after a short and cheerless embrace.

As he turned, I pulled him back, 'John. We'll do it again and we'll do it right. Ok?'

He shook my hand and winked. 'Deal.'

We embraced, he shook himself free, turned on his heel and walked off. I had the most overpowering sense of eventual, final but total detachment from the emotional roller coaster we had been riding for the last few months. As John's hand had slipped from mine, I felt I was totally and finally alone again. I had never before felt so unutterably isolated and miserable.

I went to see McTaggart. We chewed over all the angles of the expedition and I railed at him for telling Pete to 'have a look and then get out.' His pained, mortally wounded expression of disbelief that I could ever have accused him of such a monstrous thing cracked me up and before I knew what was happening, we were both roaring with laughter. Mine came from a release of tension: this was the first time I'd laughed heartily in months. I told him I wanted to go back to New Zealand as soon as possible and I asked him if he would reappoint me as expedition leader.

He didn't hesitate for a moment. 'Sure, Peter. You go and do it. Stay on pay and get your ass down there as soon as you want. I'll handle the budget approval. But there's one thing you've got to do before you go and that is sort out your board. You must agree to expand it, bring in some fresh blood. I tell you, man, the trustees are not happy.'

'You know we're happy to expand the board, David,' I replied. 'We have the new members identified and approved by you. We have a board meeting planned on the 14th April at which the new board members will be appointed. But you've got to do one thing for me too. Keep the Marine Division off my back for this Antarctic trip. I will appoint the people I want and need. I don't want to be saddled with strangers. I need the crew to be people I can trust and who trust me to do the job.'

We shook hands and I returned to London. I was not to see him again for a year and when I did clap eyes on him again, I would have the mother and father of all rows with him, a row which almost cost us our friendship. The anti-fur trade campaign was a roaring success. Greenpeace was feted in all quarters and the campaign was attracting huge media attention and notoriety. Yet the international Greenpeace community had demanded that the campaign be cancelled as it was having what was described as a deleterious impact on relationships between the Greenpeace organisations in Canada, Denmark and Sweden, whose traditional fur-trapping communities were suffering as a result of the anti-fur climate our UK campaign was generating.

My agenda in the few days I had left in the UK office before heading south again was clear. I had to tee up what I thought would be the final push on Sellafield, oversee the introduction of new board members into the organisation and then prepare for my departure. I flew to Dublin to see a few politicians to help George Pritchard (who had now taken over the campaign on Sellafield entirely) and spent St Patrick's Day in the midst of the day and night-long celebrations.

Sitting in my hotel room waiting for normal service to be resumed, I wrote a long and heartfelt letter to Bryn, pointing out to him that he had taken over the reins of an organisation which I cherished and for which I had sacrificed a great deal. I told him that his attitude and bullish operating methods were not helping to heal wounds and that he was, in my opinion, responsible for much of the grief and bitterness which characterised not only the UK office but also the antipathy which existed towards the UK office within the international Greenpeace community.

In hindsight, sending the letter was not a sensible thing to do. It took Bryn's breath away with its vitriol, but I was about to leave the UK for the best part of a year and I felt the need to affect the survival of the office as much as possible before leaving. I hoped, vainly, to instil some of my authority on the UK office situation by stinging Bryn into a more even handed approach. It backfired badly in that instead of cowing him, it prompted a response of bravado and outrage at the fact that I had the gall to send such a missive. What my letter did, however, was demonstrate to Bryn how deeply and passionately I felt about what I considered to be his mishandling of the UK office and it eventually put Bryn in a more quiescent mood. This fact alone had a major impact on the drama which even then was unfolding and which would see the entire board ousted within a matter of weeks.

I sat with him and mapped out what I touchingly thought would be the final stages of the Sellafield campaign. Our goal throughout ten years of campaigning had been to reduce the discharges of radioactive waste from the plant to zero, knowing full well that such a policy would effectively shut down the plant since the costs of installing the readily available equipment in a plant which was built 30 years previously would financially cripple the operation. Sellafield could only operate under conditions which allowed it to discharge large quantities of liquid effluent to sea.

British Nuclear Fuels had been 'tried' in the public arena and, by our criteria, had been found guilty. The discharges were significantly reduced and the Paris Commission had required BNFL to accept the principle of reducing discharges to 'as low as technically achievable' which meant, in our interpretation, zero discharges. We continued to develop and refine the 'Shut it' campaign and enshrined the strategy and the tactics in a document which was approved by the UK board. The path for a final and successful push on the poisonous carbuncle on the northwest coast of the UK only had to be put into action, I naively told myself. I had now only to oversee the expansion of the board and then I could leave for New Zealand with a clear conscience and the peace of mind I needed to climb the mountain represented by another Antarctic expedition.

Bryn had been engaged in a running battle with international over and increasingly strident call by the other trustees for the UK office to terminate the anti-fur campaign, a demand Bryn resisted with every sinew. I supported him in this struggle as did the rest of the board and the entire UK staff. In this, at least, we were united. But in the far north, indigenous people who relied on fur trapping for a living, despite the fact that genuine trapping communities such as Eskimo or North American Indian were in a tiny minority, were suffering as a result of the downturn in demand for furs which our campaign had created. To us, these people were unfortunate victims of a campaign which had at its heart the desire to end the killing of 40 million wild animals a year by the fur industry, of which the true Inuit trappers were not a part. Nonetheless, the representations came thick and fast, particularly from an organisation called Indigenous Survival International. Their vitriolic attacks forced the request from Greenpeace International for us to end the campaign into a demand and, finally, an instruction. Bryn in particular took the brunt of the reciprocated indignation felt by our UK supporters who had funded and worked hard to make the campaign the success it was proving to be. We announced the withdrawal of the campaign but Bryn was in belligerent mood and wrote an editorial in the Spring UK newsletter vowing that the campaign would be revived once the 'problems' had been ironed out. He commissioned cartoonist Richard Wilson to depict the dilemma in a memorable and fateful drawing which showed well-heeled 'Inuits' sporting high velocity rifles dispatching a fox immobilised in a leg-hold trap, smart skidoos and modern equipment scattered around, the better to dispel the myth of hard-pressed trappers as they had been characterised by the opponents of the campaign. The editorial and the cartoon had the international board in apoplectic mood.

I was to leave for New Zealand on the 20th April. On the preceding Monday, the 14th, we held a board meeting at which the 'new-blood' board members would be inducted. In an effort to placate their wrath, Bryn and I had written a grovelling 'apology' to the international Greenpeace community for having the temerity to run a successful environmental campaign to protect wildlife. Once the UK board had agreed the wording, I called McTaggart to read the text to him.

He listened and then replied: 'That's not enough, Peter. The trustees want your blood and they want you to tender your resignations. It's only a gesture. You'll be invited back on the board immediately but the trustees want to see you take that move as a measure of the seriousness of the situation.'

I told him I'd call him back. I turned to Reg, Bryn, Mark, Tony. 'Well, there it is. We either have it on with these guys or do as they ask. I'm for believing McTaggart. We should tender our resignations. What d'you think?'

The board was divided as to whether or not to accept my advice. McTaggart was viewed with deep suspicion by Tony in particular and Reg in general. Bryn was in quiescent mood and Mark was resigned to quitting anyway, in the face of the international edict to terminate his campaign. Tony told me point blank that if we tendered our resignations, we'd be shafted. Reg concurred. I had a split decision on my hands and I knew that in order to resolve it, I'd have to talk fast and convincingly. After an hour of debate, I managed to convince a reluctant board to go along with my recommendation. We would attend the board meeting on Monday, tender our resignations and trust McTaggart's word that we would be invited back on the board. My naivety was breathtaking – or blind, possibly both. Monday arrived. I was packed and ready to go back to New Zealand. I merely wanted to usher in the new board members, confirm our reinstatement, sign off on the programme of campaigns for the next year and head out for the sun of New Zealand.

At 10 am, Peter Melchett, Sidney Holt and Cornelia Durrant, the three new board members, arrived. They were all recommended additions to the board agreed between the existing board and McTaggart. It had, in fairness, taken two years to arrive at this momentous occasion – the expansion of the UK board beyond what were uncharitably described as 'Wilkinson's drinking pals'. Despite our resignation to the fact that the UK office had to be 'internationalised' and purged of what the rest of the Greenpeace world saw as an introspective and leftist enclave, there was a distinct awkwardness in the air which arrived with the 'new wave' trio. This very moment in time was, in retrospect, the point at which Greenpeace moved, perhaps necessarily, to becoming a career for some rather than a crusade for the majority, as Paul Brown, Environment Correspondent for the Guardian was to put it years later. The hitherto open, accessible and unruly band of environmentalists which had, somehow, operated, overseen and won a clutch of campaign victories over the previous decade were handing over the operation to a Lord of the Realm.

Bryn gave up the chair to Sidney Holt. Sidney looked at the agenda and promptly moved agenda item 7, 'resignation of the existing board' to item number 2, agenda item 1 being the induction of the incoming members. The new board was formally constituted. At that point, for a matter of minutes, we had a legitimately constituted board of eight members. Sidney moved on to item 2 – 'resignation of the existing board'. Trusting to McTaggart's words, I asked for the minutes to record that, in the interests of the furtherance of the UK office's goals and in response to the desire of the international trustees, the existing board, being Pete Wilkinson, Bryn Jones, Reg Boorer, Tony Marriner and Mark Glover, tendered their resignations. The motion was accepted, seconded and voted on. All were in favour. We were out as of that moment. All it needed now was for Sidney to invite one of the new board members to invite us back onto the board. No-one moved, no-one spoke.

Sidney said, 'I think I can therefore move to adjourn the meeting.'

They stood up and left. Simple as that. They went out onto Graham Street and climbed into a taxi and went to see McTaggart who was holed up in a hotel in town. They carried with them their pound of flesh, the price McTaggart had extracted from them as the cost of controlling the UK office which dripped with the sweat and blood of years of sacrifice and denial. We were out. We had been shafted. We had been set up and sold down the river. A lord of the realm was now in charge of our organisation which had forged the first ever environmental link with trades unions. In the silence which followed the departure of the new and now legitimate board of directors of the UK office, I could hardly bring myself to speak.

I croaked, 'I guess we've been had, guys.'

Someone replied quietly, 'And how.'

I sat in the pub staring at a pint. My head spun as I tried to grapple with the whirlwind events of the past couple of hours. The immutable fact was that I was no longer a director of Greenpeace UK and the people I had worked with so hard and long to keep the organisation afloat were under new management. Greenpeace UK, our baby to which we had given birth, had been snatched from us and was now in the control of people who could not, in a million years, begin to understand what we had gone through over the past decade. But the reality of the situation stared me in the face and I knew I would have to walk back into the office and deal with the situation.

Melchett had stayed behind and was addressing the staff. I blundered into the boardroom as he held forth in a monotone voice. He advised the staff that Alan Thornton would be returning to the office to act as executive director but even this news, this final ignominy marking the end of the Wilkinson regime, washed over me like so much additional water thrown onto a drowned man. I was inured to the slaps in the face I had been dealt that day. Melchett told the staff that there would be a new and entirely different administration at the office henceforth and if they didn't like it, there was the door.

Most of the staff walked away from Greenpeace within a matter of weeks. Some – Nick Gallie, Andy Ottaway, Andy Booth and a few others – stayed and made their way under the new regime with varying degrees of success. But within a few months of our departure, the office had been swept clean of any vestige of the infrastructure we had built up over the years. Suppliers, clients and contacts – including our trades union links –had all been dropped as the bright new Greenpeace was built.

As I mulled over the events of the day, two things alternately revolved in my head: after years of scrimping and scraping, surviving financially by the skin of our teeth, Greenpeace was at last, thanks largely to the sinking of the *Rainbow Warrior*, a household name and the money had been pouring into the office over the last few months to a level which would ensure freedom from penury for the foreseeable future. That, plus the years of work we had put into building up the integrity and credibility of the organisation, would bring rewards which the new regime, not the ones who had put in the work, would reap. But even that depressing prospect paled into insignificance at the news that Bryn Jones was to stay on at Greenpeace 'for a while' to facilitate the transfer of power to the Melchett team.

I sought Jones out that evening and castigated him for what I saw as disloyalty of the most despicable kind. I accused him of engineering this coup, of conniving with McTaggart, of complicity in the demise of what we had jointly struggled for over such a long and protracted period. It was Jones, more than any other individual, in my opinion at least, who had hastened the move by McTaggart to oust us and now he was 'sleeping with the enemy' in the most scurrilous manner. That's how I saw it at the time, I was furious with Bryn and massively disappointed in myself for allowing this situation to have arisen. .

The next few days became a blur of acrimony and accusation. I spent most of my time pacing around in the flat in Rheidol Terrace and could barely wait for Sunday to roll around. I was finally heading for the airport, albeit in a kind of mesmeric state, and I tried to ignore the pain of loss, the indignation of being so easily out-foxed by McTaggart and the irony of seeing Thornton sweep back into an office he had done nothing to support for years. I set my sights on New Zealand and Antarctica once again and this time, I'd do it right.

Chapter 26

New Zealand, new life

As the Qantas 747 clawed its way into the air above Heathrow, I could feel the angst leaving me. It was all down there on the ground behind me, not up here where I could do nothing about the events of the past few days. Within 30 hours I would be back in the most wonderful country in the world. I had an approved budget from which to work, a modest Greenpeace consultancy fee to sustain me and a campaign to organise and execute over which I could exert maximum influence in the company of people that I appointed. The challenge was as thrilling as it was daunting.

I had agreed to start work in September which gave me three months of absence in Wellington, a period of leave I had never before contemplated. Fiona and I spent the days wandering on beaches and mooching around the campus at Wellington University at which she was a student. As the New Zealand winter turned to glorious spring and early summer, I began to steel myself for the coming weeks of preparation and the long voyage to Antarctica.

Arriving in Auckland, I was greeted by the caucus of people who between them would be responsible for the success or failure of the second million dollar attempt to set up a permanent non-governmental base in what hitherto had been viewed as the preserve of an elite of national governments. We had two and a half months in which to prepare the trip and I had made it clear to McTaggart that I did not want any interference from the Marine division 24,000 kilometres away in London in terms of personnel recruitment: we would do everything from Auckland and only ask for help when it was absolutely necessary to do so. I walked onto the ship to be greeted by the 'gang of four' who, with me and the skipper (yet to be appointed), would made up the New Zealand ship-based Antarctic Division. They were Ken Ballard, first mate, Kevin Conaglen, base over-wintering leader whom I had already interviewed and appointed during my sabbatical, Martini Gotje, the NZ marine division representative, and Davey Edward, chief engineer. The appointment of the base over-wintering team was largely a matter of choosing those people whom I had identified the previous year but who had then been unavailable for one reason or another.

I had visited Kevin in New Plymouth a month previously and appointed him on the spot. He had wintered in Antarctica with the New Zealanders at Scott Base and was a dog-handler and field expert, having climbed just about every difficult peak there is to climb in the world. Kevin was very brusque in his manner but totally dedicated to the cause. Standing about 5' 9", he was stocky and lithe. He had an easy manner and was quick to joke and laugh at others and himself. I could not have found a more competent or qualified leader. Between us, we sifted through the piles of other applicants before agreeing on a three man/one woman team. The woman, German scientist Gudrun Gaudian, was a strong blond woman of around 27 years. Justin Farrelly, a Kiwi radio technician, joined the team early on and Cornelius Van Dorp, another Kiwi of Dutch extraction, became the base team's doctor. But we needed back-ups for the team to cover the eventuality of one or more dropping out of the team. In the event, we settled for appointing only an understudy base leader who would accompany us on the trip and, at Kevin's recommendation, I called an American called Keith Swenson, with whom Kevin had worked.

I spoke to Keith for no more than three minutes before asking him to fly to New Zealand.

'What d'you mean, Peter?' he asked me.

'I mean I want you to come here and meet me, dummy.'

'Yeah, but I don't want to come all that way to have you tell me I'm not suitable,' came his reply.

'Hey, Keith. I'm employing you as of now, ok? Now get down here.'

It was as simple as that. I felt so comfortable with Keith on the phone that, together with Kevin's recommendation, I knew he was the guy. Keith and I became good friends and hung out together a lot during the preparations for the trip, during subsequent years in New Zealand and indeed in the Antarctic where we managed to get into all sorts of trouble together. Happily, after recent long years in which I have not heard from Keith, we are now in touch with each other.

The problem of the skipper arose very early on. Pete Bouquet would not sail with us again and to be honest, although we are now good friends, I didn't at the time want to sail with him. Ken's suggestion for skipper was Willem Beekman, a very experienced Dutchman with whom we had both sailed previously although he had never sailed in ice before. I liked Willem and he was a highly respected member of the organisation. What was more, he was keen to do the job. We called him and asked him to come to Auckland.

Work on board began to hot up. Graham Woodhead, another Kiwi, had a long history of involvement in Antarctica and when I appointed him as logistics co-ordinator, I felt I had made a significant breakthrough. Graham was very experienced and knew the New Zealand Antarctic division personnel so well that eyebrows in official circles were raised at his association with us, but he brought much-needed credibility to the project. The sniping from official sources was muted this year and that was largely due to the fact that we were trawling their own ranks. Then Willem arrived. I moved out of the skipper's cabin to facilitate Willem for the duration of his stay. Being busy on deck for much of the time, I had to insist that Willem and I made appointments to meet: I couldn't simply drop everything to accommodate him and this he interpreted as a snub. When we did eventually sit down to discuss matters, I was astounded by his arrogance. He told me that he would come as skipper on one condition: his girlfriend would come too as my campaign assistant.

I looked at Willem with ill-disguised astonishment. After explaining to him how unreasonable that request was, he turned it into an ultimatum. I told him, 'There's a plane back to London in two hours. You can catch it if you hurry.'

I walked out of the cabin. Willem left the following day but my brush with him was to have the most serious of consequences a month later. Martini had heard of a master mariner called Jim Cottier, living in the Bay of Islands to the north, who had previously offered his services to Greenpeace. The thing which attracted us to Jim was that he was totally untainted by the politics of Greenpeace and ground no axe whatsoever. We invited him to come down to the ship. He was in his early 50s and was an archetypal mariner with long white beard and a sailor's gait which evidenced years at sea. His eyes sparkled with enthusiasm and he soon became enamoured with the ship and the task in hand. We asked Jim to skipper the ship and to shoulder the burden which only last year had so nearly broken Pete Bouquet. He accepted.

A bombshell arrived a few days later to shatter our buoyant mood. I picked up a telegram from the central Post Office addressed to Ken Ballard. It was from Maureen Falloon, the London-based head of the Marine Division and on the way back to the ship, I opened it as it was clearly related to campaign matters. I could barely believe the words I read. The letter told Ken that as he and I formed a 'potentially disruptive partnership', he should leave the ship. It seemed that, since Maureen couldn't fire me, someone outside her jurisdiction, she chose to fire the person over whom she did have authority – Ken. To add insult to injury, she asked Ken to 'leave the ship without any fuss.' This was pure vindictiveness, in my opinion, and represented payback for the mutual support Ken and I had demonstrated during the previous trip for staying in the Antarctic and doing our damnedest to succeed in our task against the wishes of some powerful media people on board. I was sure that the dismissal of Willem over his unacceptable demands also had some sort of impact on Maureen's incredible and outrageous instructions to Ken.

I walked onto the ship and into the saloon where most crew members were exchanging banter and taking a breather.

Davey Edward looked at me and said, 'What's up, cocker? Seen a ghost?'

I handed the telegram to Ken who read it and handed it to Davey without a word. Others crowded round Davey to read over his shoulder. Davey spoke first. 'Well, fook it, mate. Let's have the bastards on. What do y'say Wilks?'

'It's Ken's decision, I reckon. If he wants to comply with the 'instructions' in the telex, then he must do so and we must all act according to how we individually feel. I'll tell you all right now that if Ken goes, I go. But if he wants to fight it, then I'll help him fight it. That's my reaction. Ken?'

'I just can't believe it,' said Ken. 'It's so full of shit. They're accusing me and you of being fifth-columnists. All I can think of us ever doing is to work our bollocks off for Greenpeace. Christ, apart from last year, the only time we ever sailed together was on the radwaste dumping campaign on the *Cedarlea* in '82. That's four years ago! I'm for having them on.'

There was a general murmur of agreement and I walked off to the radio room to draft a reply from the crew: Ken would send his own response. We went on strike and refused to lift a finger towards preparing the expedition until Ken was reinstated and until a full apology was forthcoming from Maureen. It took a week to resolve the issue in Ken's favour but left a stink which wafted around the ship for months to come and gave strength to the feeling that the organisation was divided in that the Marine Division itself

– the division within the organisation upon which we relied in a case of emergency or any difficulty – was fundamentally hoping that we would fail or, at best, succeed without its two most committed crew members.

More crew arrived. Hugh Sterling, builder of last year's helicopter box, took charge of erecting and renovating the base camp. Gary Dukes, a cool and measured Kiwi helicopter pilot of unsurpassed skill was in charge of helicopter operations and clucked around the Hughes 500D which we had bought for the next attempt. On the aft deck, a brand new helideck glinted in the sun and as the sections of the base camp were returned from the warehouse after inspection, they were packaged and stowed in the 'tween deck aft. Ironically enough, Hugh Sterling and the construction team reported that if we had had the good fortune to make a landfall the previous year and attempt to erect the base, it would probably have proved impossible as parts were missing, warped beyond use or broken. We dispensed with the outer shell of the base camp, designed as a secondary wind-break, and saved ourselves a great deal of space and four tons in weight at a stroke.

We trawled the world for the best people to join us. The bridge crew were: Jim Cottier, skipper, Ken Ballard, first mate, Bob Graham, a dour and thoroughly likeable Kiwi as second mate, Lennard Erhard, a burly Swede, third mate. The engine room was headed up by the irrepressible Davey Edward as chief, Nolan Loveridge, a thoroughly good-natured Kiwi, Brit Bob Wallace, second engineer and Dane Hanne Sorensen as third engineer. The deckies were myself (part-time), Welshman John Welsh-Thomas, Chris Robinson, our redoubtable Aussie sailor into whose hands I had committed my life in the Atlantic during the radioactive waste dumping actions years previously and Spaniard Xavier Pastor, a veteran of Greenpeace even then. Henk Haazen, our big hearted, big-boned and thoroughly likeable Dutch colleague was convinced to join us for his all-round skills and small boat handling qualifications along with Grace O'Sullivan, a veteran Irish activist. Kiwi Phil Durham was employed as the electrician. Austrian Werner Stachl, even then approaching his late forties, was another tireless and invaluable addition to the deck crew. Graham Woodhead was logistics co-ordinator and worked closely together with Hugh Sterling on the base camp construction side and with Ken Ballard on the ship side of events. Keith Swenson acted as base leader understudy, but also put in some grunt on deck.

The helicopter team, led by Gary Dukes, included Justin Farralley who acted as base team radio and communications technician while doubling as the second helicopter pilot, and Alex Geddes, another Kiwi who serviced the helicopter and acted as mechanic. Soon, the base team itself – Kevin Conaglen, Gudrun Gaudian, Justin Farralley and Cornelius van Dorp – was finalised, signed up and in training. Dave Woolan, another chirpy and happy-go-lucky Brit, took care of the ship's electronics and worked with Justin on base communications as well. Ian Balmer, an Aussie, was the ship's radio technician with specific responsibilities for establishing, along with Justin, the base communications. Our indefatigable cooks – the most important people on board – were Irmi Mussak, a German and Natalie Maestre, a Swiss. We reviewed the requests from film crews to join us and settled on a two person Kiwi team, headed by cameraman John Philpotts. Bruce Adams, the sound recordist, proved to be such a hit with the crew that he sailed time and time again with Greenpeace and eventually married Maj De Poorter whom I had asked to come as my campaign assistant. No doubt she and Bruce, not to mention myself, were glad that she accepted the invitation. A Kiwi journalist called Stephen Knight also joined us to file written stories and German Jochen Vorfelder came to cover the European press. We appointed our own photographer, Swede Andi Loor, a gentle and thoroughly personable man.

So there we were. Thirty five souls from ten different countries all squeezed together on a small lump of metal which had no right to be going into treacherous pack ice. We worked hard and partied harder. We played football against teams from other ships in port, and drank beer in the Glue Pot at Ponsonby and the Bird Cage on the other side of the market. We lived a life under the microscope as newspapers and radio stations and TV companies created a caravan of correspondents to the ship. It was a wonderful life and the knowledge that we were off to the most amazing place in the world brightened our days of hard labour.

There was one last rite to perform before we headed off south. The *Rainbow Warrior*, war wounds patched up and refloated, still redolent of the early, care-free days in Iceland and now far from her traditional cold-water haunts of the Arctic and the North Sea, had to be laid to rest. Some of us argued that to sink her in the clear waters of Matauri Bay, while creating a valuable underwater reef for marine life, represented a sad and unfitting end to a warrior of her pedigree. Alternative plans to somehow power her back to Muroroa were dismissed by the international board as implausible. We sunk her as planned.

With anchors fore and aft laid out to keep her steady, hundreds of small boats and a few helicopters buzzed around the manacled ship. Hoses from attending boats played across her decks to settle her lower into the water to the point where access ports cut into her superstructure would then swamp her and she would sink into 70 feet of water. But she didn't go quietly or as planned. As she settled more deeply in the water, the bow dipped and she began to slide beneath the surface before her bow dug into the bottom and she shuddered from stem to stern. Now only the boat deck was visible – the deck from which we had launched the inflatables in seas far less hospitable than those around the New Zealand islands. Soon, this too slipped beneath the waves and she was gone. Old and grizzled campaigners hugged each other and cried tears for a lost innocence, for the loss of Fernando and for the loss of the ship which had for eight years acted as the symbol of hope and faith for a generation. 'You can't sink a rainbow' read the slogan on hundreds of badges and banners sported by the thousands who had turned up to see the *Warrior's* last hours. I wasn't so sure that sinking a rainbow wasn't possible.

The Antarctic preparations were finally over. The equipment was stowed and the gangway was lifted from the quayside as friends and family waved us good bye from the packed jetty at Western Viaduct. It was time to lay the ghost of the previous year and demonstrate that we could accomplish what we had set out to do. It was Cape Evans or bust this time. I wanted to make it this year for myself, of course, but also for the organisation, for its supporters who had paid for the expedition and for McTaggart. Without his help, support and confidence in me, I would not even have dreamt of being here, en route again through the Southern Ocean to Antarctica. For a boy from Deptford, I knew I was blessed. These are my diary entries for that trip.

29 December 1986

Called this morning at 0700 after only 3 hours sleep. Hectic from then on with press on the quayside and lots of well-wishers to see us off. I steer from the quayside to the Rangitoto beacon. Beautiful day with flat calm seas. Tiny swell off Coramandel but the sun is hot and 'long white clouds' – the English translation of the Maori name for New Zealand, Aoteoroa – hang just beneath the horizon. All on board in fine spirits and relieved to be at sea. Fire drill at 1300. Making 10.5 knots, northerly 10 knot breeze. First stop Wellington where we'll stoke the story, then to Lyttelton before we finally head for the Southern Ocean. After five months of preparation, we are finally away and this time, we've been able to concentrate entirely on the task in hand: diversions about the *Warrior* and nuclear weapons testing have been thankfully few. We've stuck to our guns and demanded that the people at the expedition end – me, Ken, Martini and others – have been allowed to make the decisions relating to the voyage and more importantly, on the crew. Now let's hope to Christ we can establish the base and complete our task.

30 December 1986

Called at 0745 after good sleep. Gentle swell causes the ship to roll easily. Sparkling day until it clouds over in the pm. Northerly 10 knots backing southerly. As we switched from one main engine to the other last night, the ship wallowed a little and 30 gallons of sea water slopped into the mess through an open port hole. Ken had us swabbing the decks on watch and even wire-brushing the jack-staff. Weather worsened gradually until we were pitching heavily. The 8-12 watch this evening became an ordeal for me as my weak stomach went through the old familiar routine of contracting. I lasted until 2130 when Ken told me to stand down.

31 December 1986

Fine day and I awake feeling 100%. Good watch and we approach Wellington heads at 1700. Pilot on board at 1745 and we arrive at the quayside to find only one radio station awaiting us – it's a public holiday! Great forward planning! But Fiona is there and is a sight for my sore eyes. Party ensues in the evening which gets quite wild and Stephen Knight cracks his head and requires stitches.

242

MV Greenpeace in a spot of bother, Ross Sea, Antarctica, 1986 © Loor Greenpeace

Antarctic Expedition Crew, 1986-87

MV Greenpeace off New Zealand, 1987

Mt. Cook glacier, 1987

Cape Evans, 1987

Scrap iron, US base, Antarctica, 1987

Bringing supplies ashore, 1987

Mt Minto ascent team 1988

Crew for 1988-89 voyage

Penguins menaced by French digger, Antarctica, 1989

Crater, Ross Island, 1989

French airstrip construction continues, 1989

Celebration at end of occupation of French airstrip, 1989

Tracking Japanese whaling factory vessel 1989

Separating the whale catcher from the factory ship, 1989

Above: Intervening to protect hunted whales, 1989
Top Right: Anti-whaling activities
Bottom Right :Ken Ballard keeps station in front of a Japanese whaler, Southern Ocean, 1989

MV Gondwana, Campaign ship 1988-9 Antarctic copyright GP

MV Gondwana harasses the Nishin Maru Japanese whale factory

Off Ross Island, Antarctica

Parhallion, Ross Ice Shelf, Summer 1989

Barne Glacier, Antarctica

Scott's hut, Cape Evans, Ross Island, Antarctica

unning repairs to the survival hut as the French build their airstrip, Dumont D'Urville, Antarctica 1989

Above: Rubbish outside Scott's hu[...]

Left: Henk Haazen

1 January 1987

To ship by 1100 then off to the beach at Paraparaumu with Fiona, Ken, John, Martini, Lennard. Great day and much swimming and frolicking on the beach. Back to ship at 2000.

2 January 1987

Steer ship to bunker berth. Load remainder of fuel. Finish by 1630.

4 January 1987

Leave Wellington quietly in the mid-morning for the short trip to Lyttelton. Arrive off the heads at 8am on the 5th. Much to-ing and fro-ing as we wait for Dave Walley to arrive with the Hughes 500 which he has flown down from Auckland. Pilot on board finally at 1630 and we're alongside by 1730. Just the one night here and then it is a final goodbye for a few months as we head into the vastness of the Southern Ocean.

6 January 1987

What a day! Hectic is not the word. Live radio at 0745 and it was all uphill from there. Trying to finalise our departure paperwork is almost impossible. People flying about in all directions. Crew photograph at 0900 has Andi Loor close to tears as people go missing and then refuse to stand still. Everyone wants to be a joker and although it demonstrates fine spirit, it is delaying our departure. Into town with Maj, Fiona, Kevin and Andi to see the DSIR people (Department of Scientific and Industrial Research) at 1045. Arrive at the ship by 1300 after last-minute shopping spree (chocolate is a must!) when all hell breaks loose. As 1700 approached and people are still in the pub, lashing down the cargo or partying on board, I go on a search to various haunts to round people up and we finally single up around 1730 and the final ropes are let go at 1745. This is it. Goodbye Fiona for a few weeks. Goodbye all our good friends on the quayside. We're now on our own. Just the sea and the ice to come. God: will we make it? A few beers with a relaxed and contented crew as the ship rolls and pitches gently along the east coast of New Zealand's South Island, the inky blackness studded with pinpoints of light from houses.

7 January 1987

Called at 0700 and breakfasted with the 8-12 watch (me, Ken, Chris Robinson and John Welsh) on orange juice, tea, eggs, bacon and toast.

…tful watch and only Cape pigeons and a few albatrosses
… ship. The picture wire machine screwed up last night and Dave
… e he can't fix it until he can get a spare part probably not until we
…ve at Scott Base! What a great start! Steering 180 and position about
46 south, slight sea with following swell. No land at all in sight by the
end of watch.

8 January 1987

Slept too well last night and did not want to turn to this morning. Finally
made it to the mess where Ken, John and Chris were breakfasting with
my meal sitting there awaiting my attention. Send telex to Roger asking
him interalia to check on rumour Stephen Knight heard about CIA
backing for a drilling project in Antarctica possibly connected with South
African nuclear testing there. It's a hot story but we only have Kevin's
suspicions and a few off-the-cuff remarks as the source. BBC World
Service interview this evening. Gradually settling into a routine but I'm
still very conscious of the ship's movement and my appetite has largely
disappeared but I'm still eating what small amounts of food I put on my
plate. Crew seem to be ok and walk around with smiles on their faces and
a kind word for each other. I resolve to spend as much time as I can with
the crew to ensure that any clique-iness is headed off. Gudrun looks ill
most of the time: she's mostly asleep or in a prostrate position although
she claims she's fine. In two or three days' time, I'll institute regular
meeting with the winterers, with the skipper and mates and with the base
construction team then distil the information for the regular weekly crew
meeting. How I want to succeed this time! I couldn't face going back to
NZ after a second failure.

Light, northeast winds, following sea but the swell is increasing.
Entered the furious fifties today. Three days to the screaming sixties.
Still warm although the temperature is noticeably dropping. Weather
turns to fog with rain and swells are now around 12 feet in height. Vessel
rolling heavily and southwesterlies forecast. Gudrun still very sick which
concerns me a lot. Suggested she takes 48 hours off from the constant
radio interviews but she insists on continuing. Reading The Last Place on
Earth which gives me a sense of history of the place we are heading for.
Two beers after watch and chat to Davey Edward. Sleep like a log but the
vivid dreams – a feature of being at sea – have begun already.

244

9 January 1987

BBC World Service again last night – getting to be a regular contributor! This morning is spectacular. Gone is yesterday's fog and rain and the day is bright and crisp with not a cloud in the sky. The sun is creeping higher and higher every day and soon we'll have virtually no night-time at all. Stiffening breeze makes us roll heavily by lunchtime. Saw our first southern skua this morning. It's just so beautiful to be in the open ocean with what Ken calls this 'open air zoo' all around us. As Jim gives his navigation lesson to the crew, I reply to a few telexes but there will be nothing of import to report until we're in the pack ice. We're at 54 south by 1030 and making a steady southing at 10 knots. Davey reduces revs to counter a clutch-slip. Sleep from 1400-1800 then dinner. Weather worsening until by 2000 it's blowing about a 7 and we're rolling heavily. Fridge in galley goes flying and Hugh Sterling's cabin is a mess of tools, nails and screws after a particularly heavy roll. Eventually, Jim turns us into the weather to take it on the bow and we pitch mightily. Feeling queasy but hanging on in there.

10 January 1987

What a night! Ship rolling and pitching heavily all night long. Most cabins are a mess of clothing, boots and Antarctic paraphernalia. Did not want to get up this morning, believe me. I had to wedge myself in the bunk last night by stuffing life jackets under the mattress to force me up against the bulk-head to stop me rolling about. I stagger into the saloon for breakfast but couldn't face the fried breakfast Chris had prepared. Steered between 0800 and 0900 when the swells were level with the bridge windows – 20 feet at least. The wind is backing a bit and the barometer is rising slowly but the seas are totally confused and we roll and pitch along at 85 rpm. Position 57 south 174 east, course comes round from 185 to 175. Slept from 1200-1500 missing lunch. Still have very little appetite but I get seized by cravings for exotic dishes from time to time. Big seas still running with swells from the west causing us to roll heavily. A spectacular display of aerobatics from a squadron of sooty albatrosses livens up watch and a group of hour-glass dolphins briefly visit us. Will cross 60 south at 0800 then three days to the Ross Sea. Seas still massive as I turn in. Course 157.

11 January 1987

Awoke to find vessel still rolling heavily. Almost tipped out of bed earlier as the ship rolled more violently than normal. It takes courage, timing and blind faith to make it from the prone to the vertical. Haven't showered for four days now and feeling pretty grubby. We crossed 60 south at 0700 this morning. Skies are grey and overcast and the swells are bigger than ever. Iceberg look out duties came to nought. Slept immediately after lunch till 1700 when I had my much-needed shower only to find that the water was cold, damn it! Decided it was time to get into my warm Antarctic clothing so out come the thermals, sweaters and boots, not to mention the down jacket. Temperature now only 3 degrees C. Now in the northern reaches of the Ross Sea.

At dinner I'm told that Justin has contacted McMurdo on the radio and despite my annoyance at this unscheduled call which could have serious political ramifications for the trip, I manage to sort it out with Justin in a calm manner and we agree that contact will be made officially at 1245 every day to give position, weather and ice and that we will film and tape the response for the record. Weather thankfully calmer for the first time in days when we spot six elegant fin whales off the starboard bow. We follow and then shut engines down to tempt them closer but they remain about 100 yards away. The old chestnut of video viewing in the saloon reared its ugly head today when Jochen innocently put The Killing Fields on the machine and closed all the deadlights for a better picture. There's nothing worse than walking into the saloon for a beer or a chat to find it in darkness with everyone gawping at the screen and he agreed, after a sensible discussion, to desist until the issue comes up at the next crew meeting. We're now at 62 south and still haven't seen an iceberg. Steering 169 degrees and heading for Scott Island, that phallic lump of barren rock with juts out of the Southern Ocean in such a bleak and lonely position. Air temperature only 1 degree C now. Then, finally, at 2305 we see on the radar and then confirm visually a half-mile long spectacular tabloid iceberg which we circle for 30 minutes while the crew breathes in its majesty in the waning daylight of our southerly position.

12 January 1987

Awoke full of a heavy cold. My head feels like it weighs a ton and my throat feels like a rasp. Surprisingly, I eat breakfast and make it to watch on time where I take the wheel and notice that the sea is far calmer now under lowering grey skies. Another berg on the radar at 19 miles. I call Andi Loor and after getting permission from Jim get him in a boat with Jonathan driving to shoot the ship and the iceberg for the press release I'm preparing. We steam to within 300 yards of the berg and it is a magical moment. It's not white, but indigo, blue, turquoise and other colours which do not feature on the artist's palette. Its immovability and stoicism in the face of the battering it takes from the sea is truly awesome. Finally underway again at 1130. Crew in very good humour and Andi and I work through the afternoon to get the pictures out on the now-fixed machine. I write the press release and captions for the pictures and fire them off. Watch was enjoyable but very cold as we stand on the bridge wing looking for growlers. The wind is 25 knots and the temperature is minus 1 degree C. Flat calm sea, 10 knots and Scott Island only 40 miles off now.

13 January 1987

It was a red letter day today. I was excused watch today but at 0830, Ken sent a message to say we were approaching the pack ice (evidenced by 'ice blink', a sort of reflected white sheen in the sky) and I got up and rushed to the bridge. The swell from the south was big and we pitched through the brash ice which fringed the pack a few miles ahead. This is the beginnings of the outer pack ice through which we must find a way (Pete's autobahn of last year) to enter the Ross Sea proper. Last year we spent a week getting through this ice and this year we were through in 4 hours. By early afternoon we're heading 180 in clear water with a big southerly swell running. We're pitching heavily again and my nausea returns. We agree to reach 70 south and then head on a 210 course for Franklin Island and follow the pack edge. The mood on board is buoyant and Jim is a great skipper – a pleasure to work with. He does not intimidate the mates and is a diplomat of the first order, always ready with a joke and always affable. Position 69, 15 south, 179 west.

14 January 1987

Permanently light now and the value of the heavy curtain across my porthole comes into its own. Good sleep last night after a Chris special – rum, honey, cloves, lemon and hot water. Flat calm at last and a true Antarctic day – minus 2 C, strong sun and flat, deep blue sea. After sleeping through lunch again, I'm up and shower. Despite feeling better, I look haggard. Deep rings under my eyes and beard sprouting all manner of tufts here and there. 72 south, 176 west. We hear 90 Degree South expedition talking to South Pole and Christchurch Radio. They're ok but only at 84 south leaving them 360 miles to go to the pole (they are retracing Amundsen's footsteps) but this means that they'll surely not make it back to the Bay of Whales by the 28th February. A radio report today indicates that they will have to be flown out and will be forced to kill their dogs at the pole, the bastards.

15 January 1987

Flat calm and after watch we prepare the helicopter for its first recce flight. Although we're still 50 miles from Ross Island, we determine to fly in as much gear as possible. We can see Coulman Island 60 miles away and all morning, whales have been blowing around the ship. It's clear weather and flat calm. We are in an area which was ice-covered last week and we are pleased at all the good omens. The ship is a hive of activity as we prepare for a big day tomorrow. Noon position 74 15 south, 173 03 west. Mts Erebus and Terror visible at 1700 hours, 100 miles away! Spectacular! Stupendous! Shimmering above the horizon like some welcome home beacon. Everyone on board is buzzing with anticipation. As we get closer, Franklin Island appears low and flat before us and Beaufort Island stands out stark against the mass of Erebus. Steering at 2000 and the pack appears ahead. Steer off to the east at 2100 and then back west again for Franklin. First penguins seen on ice floes and people begin to wave and shout hello: stupid but understandable I guess. There is great excitement on board as people see their first view of Antarctica proper. It is truly spectacular and despite the ice which is heavily present, we are still making a southing at 2330 towards Ross Island.

16 January 1987

Forced east by the ice on arrival off Franklin and found to our consternation that the ice was much further to the east than last year and seemed much more heavily concentrated. When I steered at 0800, we were heading north and swung in a large arc to head south again to allow Jonathan to give us a report from the crow's nest. His report was bleak and we consoled each other by shrugging and saying, 'Well, this is what we expected. And it's early in the season yet.' Chopper prepared and after a few crossed wires about who's going where, Gary did a test flight then

took Jim up after lunch. His report changed our perspect
our spirits enormously. There is open water further south
Ross Island is only barred by a narrow strip of 6/10 ice whicl
in a few days. Headed further south in the afternoon with
of carrying out press flights but the wind picked up to fore
sheltered in the lee of the barrier and cancelled flying.

Slept from 1630 to 2030. Crew meeting this morning was incredibly dominated by the issue of videos – a perennial and potentially explosive problem involving morals and personal preferences. I find the incongruity of being in the middle of such stunning Antarctic scenery and watching films about death and mayhem in darkened rooms a bit hard to take, personally. On watch this evening, the lenticular clouds over Erebus were quite breath-taking. The ice barrier is just as stunning the second time around as it is the first. There is a noticeable lack of whales and in general icebergs and wildlife are sparse.

17 January 1987
Eleven days since we left Lyttelton but it seems like 11 years. How can I describe today? There are insufficient superlatives in the English language to describe this place. I can show people the photos and talk to them about the majesty of this place but unless they are here to see it they will never in a million years have any appreciation of it. Awoke at 0815 and on reaching the bridge, saw Erebus and Terror about half a mile way (actually 8 miles away!). The sea was mirror calm and the sun hurt the eyes if it came within even peripheral vision. The temperature was plus eight! We had circumvented the ice tongue and come hard up against the land. Penguins frolicked on the floes and it was a pleasure to steer the old tub around the floes. Ken asked me to keep as close to the ice as possible and we eventually came to a stop at the end of the lead a few miles from Cape Byrd. The ice off to the north formed a lunar panorama stretching and shimmering into the distance, interspersed with large bergs. Position 77 33 S and 163 15 W.

The lack of whales was rectified this afternoon by the appearance of 15 orcas all around us. Two came right beneath the bows. It was a scene out of a travel brochure and it was too hot to stand in the sun without protection. Lunch was served on the boat deck and a holiday atmosphere prevailed. On the radio we heard hat Europe was gripped by a minus 17

ees cold snap! Recce flights revealed much open water beyond Byrd
and deep into the Sound upto Cape Royds. Jim surprised us all by saying,
'We'll get to within 20 miles on what I've seen.' Everyone walking
around with big grins on their faces and even Davey Edward ventured
on deck (surely the first daylight he's been exposed to for weeks) to mess
around and make a few jokes.

18 January 1987

Hot shower! Luxury! New sheets on my bunk. Cleaned my cabin. Andi
reported that he had managed to get pictures of the McMurdo dump when
he went ashore yesterday and we set about sending them plus press release
to keep the story going. They are quite impressive pictures showing a
pile of discarded junk casually stashed on the ice in McMurdo Sound
awaiting the thaw. There are now estimated to be 'a few thousand tons
of rubbish' at the bottom of Winterquarter's Bay where Scott anchored
Discovery and the Bay itself is thought to be biologically dead. Three
flights today: ice spotting, Graham, Hugh and Ian to Cape Evans to begin
preparation of the site and a further trip to the McMurdo dump involving
Kevin (for sea ice safety) and Gudrun (for the taking of scientific samples
for later analysis). On their return, I began the laborious task of putting
out pictures with captions and the press release to accompany them.
Finally finished at 2250. Andi makes many demands on the helicopter
and I've had to tell him that we're limited in the fuel availability which
will restrict his freedom to shoot when he feels like it. I've also had to
have a few words with him about his use of our precious water supply:
we're down to 100 tons now and we use it at the rate of 2-3 tons a day.
The water maker doesn't operate when we're stopped which we are most
of the time. But we've got through a lot of work today and everyone is
co-operative and the atmosphere is genial.

The weather is still fine – light winds and thin cloud cover for a few
hours a day. The ice conditions improve daily and Jim is confident that we
can pick our way through the ice to McMurdo Sound and Cape Evans in a
few days. He inspires great confidence although Ken raised his eyebrows
at one or two manoeuvres Jim has made going astern which sucks in ice
towards the propeller rather than pushing it away as it does when we go
ahead. We experimented in pushing a floe out of the way today: after
the initial bump, there was no problem. Tried to catch up on my sleep

250

today but a constant procession of people to my cabin for discussions and decisions forced me to give up. Chatted with Xavier, Chris, John and Grace before turning in. Knackered but contented.

19 January 1987

Slept till 1000 when Chris woke me with news that we were making an attempt to get through to the clear water off Cape Byrd. On reaching the bridge, I find we're already underway. Ken and Bob Graham are up the mast, John's on the wheel and Chris is aft in VHF radio contact with Jim who struts around the bridge and the bridge wings purposefully. Jim is aiming for a channel of only about 4/10 ice concentration although the rest of the ice field is considerably denser. As we proceed, the engine room commands – dead slow ahead, stop, dead slow astern, dead slow ahead – increase rapidly and the ice begins to move into our path alarmingly. Very large floes – thousands of tons of ice a piece – lie in our path, roll down the side of the ship and swing in towards the stern. The area of open water we were heading for begins to recede and we're suddenly surrounded by 9/10 pack ice pressing from all sides.

I relay messages from Jim to the helmsperson and watch the engine rev counter like a hawk as the engineers respond to the commands. Jim shouts, 'Stop engines!' I work the telegraph to the engine room and then call out to Jim, 'Engine stopped!' as the rev counter hits zero a few seconds later. 'Dead slow ahead!' comes Jim's command and after repeating his command and working the telegraph, I then watch the rev counter until it begins to respond and I shout out 'Going ahead!' It's a very laborious process but the ship, not having direct bridge control of the engines, requires such antiquated but very traditional antics.

Jim told me earlier as we entered the ice, 'We'll be in Cape Evans by lunchtime!' At lunchtime, we're in the soup good and proper and I gently chide Jim to which he responds sharply with 'Piss off, Wilks!'. Davey emerges from the engine room to ask, 'What the fook's going on? We've made so many engine manoeuvres we're running out of compressed air in the bottles.' He took one look around at the unbroken vista of ice around the ship and disappeared below again, muttering, 'Fookin' hellfire.'

Helo away with Andi Loor, Ken and the film guys for filming and recce at 1310 and I go below for a breather and to read the abandon ship notices in the allies just in case. We're in a tight spot and as I write, I can

251

feel the ship bouncing off one floe after the next. My concern increases as I look out of the ports on the starboard side to see the situation worsening if anything. Then Ken came into the saloon looking very purposeful and told me we were putting the abandon ship procedure into operation. Survival suits are being broken out on the monkey island, rope ladders going over the side, the helo is being prepared and Jim has drawn up a priority evacuation list. I still thought this was precautionary on Jim's part but then I hear the chopper taking off with the journalists and Maj. Jesus! We're evacuating the ship!

I'm detailed to sit on the bow of the ship calling out distances to the next floe to Jim on the bridge after gathering all the important stuff from my cabin into a back-pack, collecting emergency rations and sleeping bag, clothing etc. I also check all bunks for sleeping crew and ensure all the deadlights are secured. This is getting too real! Then at 1730, we finally nosed into clear water and the relief all round was very evident. Much back slapping and banter going on and then someone broke out the beers and people began unpacking their emergency gear. PHEW! That was a close one. We're now all stopped (1850) directly opposite Mt Erebus where we can clearly see the scar left by the Air New Zealand tourist plane which ploughed into the mountain a few years ago, metallic scraps glinting in the sunshine. Poor bastards. As we lie hove to in still water watching orcas gambol in the sunlight, we are in self-congratulatory mood in that we performed without panic and in an exemplary manner. The journalists file mildly exaggerated stories but what the hell?

22 January 1987
Boredom setting in as we find another grey day awaiting us with low cloud making flying impossible, restricted visibility and nothing much in prospect today. Steam to the end of the lead towards Byrd at 0800 and Ken reports from the crow's nest that yesterday's blow has merely served to confuse the situation. The ice is more concentrated and has rafted, becoming more solid around Byrd. Cleaned the bridge and after lunch I slept like a baby until dinner. Ken's off watch tonight and tells me ominously that he 'feels like getting outrageous'. God help us – and him! Hear that an ice-breaker is to move through to McMurdo tonight and we briefly discuss the wisdom of following in the channel she cuts but wisely decide against it. Time is on our side still but it's getting tighter. After the

late watch the weather cleared marginally and the ice spotting crew report improving conditions. Maybe we'll have a go tomorrow.

23 January 1987
Woken at 0700 but didn't make it to the bridge until 0815. Steamed through loose pack for an hours and a half but had to stop at 1145 as the lead disappeared. The 8-12 watch is excruciatingly boring as we lay drifting a few miles from the pack ice edge. Only Ken and I on the bridge most of the time and he's reading a Dutch book out loud to improve his diction while I sketch the scenery. Two beers after watch, bed at 0100.

24th January 1987
Woken by Chris who brought hard boiled eggs to me in bed the better to encourage me to get up. Jim already aloft by 0700 and reports excellent ice conditions. But before we could get underway, the wind picked up and began blowing 50 knots, reducing the sea to a boiling cauldron with white tops being creamed off the tops of the swells. We could see the line of the squall across the water and as we steamed into it, the wind speed indicator went from 25 knots to 50 knots in seconds. It was a spectacular show and whirlwinds and whirlpools skitted across the sea. The ship was heeled over 5 degrees purely by the force of the wind.

By 2200 the wind dropped enough for us to put the helo up again and Jim's report is positive. We get underway by 2300 and nosed into the clear water ahead of us hoping we can find the 'autobahn' to McMurdo. By 2400 we were off Cape Byrd and penguins were evident in their thousands dotted along the coast. It's strange to see Ross Island from a different angle and looking back at Beaufort is a novelty. But the ice just moved out of our path and we steamed slowly but with gathering confidence into McMurdo Sound. We've made it! Despite all the setbacks, the hurdles and the negativity from everyone, we've got through the ice to Cape Evans which is now only an hour's steam away!! Kevin and I do a mad jig of elation around the saloon. The mood is buoyant and carefree as people swarm all over the deck to drink in the new scenery presented to us. Finally fall into bed at 0300 knowing that when I wake up, we'll be off Cape Evans!

Irmi cooks breakfast for everyone this morning by way of celebration and after a hasty meal I rush to the bridge to get my first sight of this place which has haunted me all my life. We've anchored 200 metres from the Cape Evans beach and I gaze at this historic site open-mouthed, not just because of its stark beauty but as much for the history in which this place is steeped. John is all toothy smiles and Ken is as inscrutable as ever, wandering around the bridge with the binoculars glued to his eyes. We had planned for helicopter operations from a distance of 20 miles if necessary, but here we are now within a stone's throw of the beach and all our fuel problems have dissolved. Scott's hut is a low-lying, almost insignificant grey building melting into the scenery and our brightly coloured tents set up by the advanced shore party make a vivid contrast to the bleak back-drop.

Having read The Last Place on Earth, the hut assumes a menacing and foreboding aspect and the 'Scott mentality', which was a criticism levelled at us particularly by Maureen in a negative way, seems to be written all over this beach. It was from here that Scott planned his fateful journey and I am fascinated by the vista before me. The beach is covered with other items which distract my eye, not the least of which is the Footsteps of Scott expedition hut and all their gear – including a Cessna airplane. We can see Inaccessible Island and the stunning coast of South Victorialand in the distance with its glaciers and peaks shrouded in mist one moment, now bathed in the most intense sunshine the next.

The weather is hazy sunshine, cold with snow showers and 30 knots of wind. Ian, Graham, Hugh, Kevin, Chris, Werner and Henk go ashore in the dinghy. Me, Ken, Xavier, Grace and Keith begin the preparation of helo loads on deck, swathed in our Antarctic clothing. To my consternation, Ken authorises Justin to begin sling-loading and while he is a competent pilot, he is a little rusty and his approaches are decidedly unsteady. Xavier, ever the droll one, begins the scary job of hooking loads onto Justin's hovering machine and makes dry comments about his survival after every load.

We shifted 15 loads today. The store shed is now erected and much positive work was accomplished. As Gary was lifting the tractor off the deck during one run, the tractor slipped sideways and put an awkward strain on the helo. As Gary climbed away, the weight of the tractor took the helicopter downwards a good 10 feet and we held our breath as the tractor wheels skimmed the surface of the sea. We expected Gary to ditch the tractor but somehow he managed to turn into the wind on full power and gain the extra lift he needed. But it was close.

The day ended on a rather sour note between Graham and I since I didn't want there to be any contact with the authorities ashore until our official visits and Graham insisted there should be another mail run. We compromised: he got his mail run on the understanding that it was simply a dropping off procedure with minimum contact with the Scott Base personnel. I'm still angry with myself for giving in but it's all in the interests of harmony on board. Ken is harbouring serious misgivings about Graham but I told Ken to keep his opinions to himself until the job is over. Graham can be a pain at times but he does his job well which is all that matters at present. No-one said it would be easy. Pictures out plus press releases. Bed by 10.45 completely bushed.

26 January 1987
24 loads away today. Whales 10 yards from the ship of which I had a grandstand view as I was on the crane most of the morning. I holed one of the inflatables as I put one onto the other with the crane. It's repairable but I felt such a jerk. Graham even more insufferable today and I know it's getting under Ken's skin. Mail drop tomorrow has been agreed. I'm so tired and dirty – no shower for a week now in the interests of water conservation and when the others relax after work, my non-deckie work begins, dealing with Roger who phones every night, dealing with the journalists and the camera crew etc, not to mention press releases and picture captions. The key is to keep the story running and to plan the peaks in the expedition to feed to the press to keep the interest going. OK so far and the reports are that there's a lot of coverage out there.

27 January 1987
17 loads away today. Weather good but a whiteout at Scott Base forced us to cancel the mail run for the umpteenth time.

28 January 1987
Beautiful day today after heavy snow during the 'night'. Bright sunshine, crystal clear, unrestricted visibility and breathtaking scenery. We can see every detail of Mt Erebus and I can't stop taking pictures of this two-mile

high peak, it's so awesome, majestic and imposing. Another 17 loads away today and the work is going very well. Swenson was a great find, easy going and good natured. Graham then sent Ken into near apoplexy by saying that he'd decided to spend a day on board today to 'oversee the discharging', a reasonable suggestion as he is the logistics co-ordinator. Ken's face contorted to the point where I thought he was going to explode but I stared at him hard until he assumed his more familiar inscrutable look. He's champion, is Ken. He works so hard and we rush around him like worker bees.

Gary had another near miss today when he picked up the trailer (450kgs) and it dipped towards the sea. It was only two feet from the sea at one point. If we're all not totally grey by the time we get back, it will be a miracle.

29 January 1987
Dog-tired today. Record 25 loads away today which was another glorious one – shirtsleeve weather. The shell of the main building is finished, generator shed roof completed. John and I took the piss out of Ken all day on deck. We had a good giggle at his expense but he takes it in his stride as long as we do the work. Big party being planned for a few days' time. Lots of people went shore side today to see the erection of the 70 foot high radio mast. Very impressive but of course the guy wires will be a hazard to skuas. Press release and pictures out tonight to keep the story bubbling. Crashed into bed fully clothed at 2200 utterly exhausted.

30 January 1987
So tired I couldn't sleep. Finally drifted off around 0230 and blissfully allowed to lie in until 0800. I was still heavy with sleep as I ate a huge breakfast and was a little grumpy with one or two jokers. Every morning, without fail, I say to Ken as I slurp the first cup of tea, making suitable pig-like noises, 'There's nothing like a nice cup of Rosy Lee in the mornings, that's what I always say, Ken, eh?' There follows a silence during which I look at Ken expectantly, John looks away to hide his laughter, Chris doesn't know what's going on and Ken looks into the middle distance pretending he hasn't heard me. Then he may deign to give me a scathing glance and lift one eyebrow to show distain at which point John and I crack up and Chris sits there grinning since he knows something funny has happened although he doesn't know quite what. And the next morning,

John and I can't keep straight faces as I pour the tea and lift the cup to my lips. It's all very childish and stupid but it lightens the mood and Ken even smiled briefly this morning.

We wind Ken up on deck as well, calling him Banzai Ballard as he's always impatient and will move something by brute force with boot, hammer or axe rather than with science. He works at a furious pace and has normally moved an immovable object on his own before John and I can find the slings or blocks. Xavier is probably the slowest of us all on deck and he is hindered by his imperfect English, but he's a good guy and we love working with him.

Began lifting the fuel out of the holds today – 64 barrels on deck but the guys ashore are not ready for it yet so we closed down for the day on board. Great plans for catching up on sleep were dashed when I decided I had to do my washing and change my bedding and then Stephen Knight asked me to help him with his article. Then the trouble started. As the helo was not employed this afternoon, I decided to get the film guys to the McMurdo dump to get more footage. Kevin told me earlier that he didn't want any more runs to the dump as the sea ice was too iffy. Keith disagreed with this opinion and, suspecting Kevin was acting out of self-interest as he wants all the effort directed at the base camp construction, I overrode him and asked Keith to oversee the trip. I called Kevin ashore to advise him and he went ape-shit. He didn't want his decision overturned and he cited his contract whereby I appointed him as chief field safety adviser etc etc.

Graham and I had a chat during which he expressed his concerns about Kevin's volatile nature and his leadership qualifications, or lack of them. So we'll meet tonight in what promises to be a tough meeting. In the event, Kevin walked into the meeting and promptly resigned! That's helpful! He was red with rage for a while before he calmed down and withdrew his resignation but is clearly far from happy at having his authority usurped. It's my fault, of course, for not making the distinction between responsibilities clearly defined. If Kevin and Keith disagree about ice conditions, I'm left with a recipe for disaster. But it's all over now and Kevin had the grace to apologise for his over-reaction. I'm just wiping my brow at a narrow escape. What with Andi Loor, the press guys, Maj and Roger all making demands on me almost hourly, I'm feeling the pressure, but it's a dream compared to last year.

31 January 1987

Another glorious day in prospect. Not a cloud in the sky, brilliant, almost painful sunshine and quite warm in the sun with no wind to speak of. Mooched around after breakfast and then I was recalled to the wheel as we got a few hundred yards closer to the beach to avoid drift ice coming in astern of us. More barrels lifted and stacked on deck and I then discuss the logistics of the McMurdo and Scott Base visits with Maj. Got a fax off to McMurdo asking them why they refuse to give us local weather. Some rumours suggest that it was the involvement of the McMurdo authorities in the offering of weather advice to the doomed Air NZ plane which crashed into Erebus which has prompted this policy; others say that it's just pure cussedness and their antipathy towards private expeditions.

1 February 1987

Hectic day after the lull in work recently. Sling-loading barrels all day, moving about 90 in the process. It's very tiring and repetitive work and Justin's flying doesn't make it a pleasant experience. He came in once this afternoon to find the ship travelling downwind to get out of the way of ice and decided that in order to keep the helicopter flying into the wind to maintain lift, he'd approach us backwards! I watched all this from the bridge as I was taking a press call and saw Keith, Ken and John dive for cover as the exhaust from the helo fanned across the deck.

We're hoping to clear all the barrels within two days which will leave only the food and personal effects to be discharged. We may even be able to leave sufficiently early to take in Terra Nova and even Dumont D'Urville, but that's all speculation. I told Jim that as long as we're back in Wellington by mid-March or earlier, I'd be happy. The 'campaigning' side of the expedition is assuming less and less importance for me now, although once the work of discharging and erecting the base is over, I'll probably revive. We're working long hours on deck and the additional campaigning work is a real burden after a long day.

2 February 1987

Very tired tonight after working from 0800 to 2130. Offloaded the majority of the remaining barrels – just 63 left and progress ashore and on board is visible. The base is erected and the internal work is going ahead furiously. People are more strung out now and a little edginess is creeping in. A music tape disappeared from my cabin tonight and no-one admits taking it. Nolan, who asked if he could borrow it, feels incriminated since his request preceded its disappearance. Phil Durham is walking around the ship with the hump since someone has taken his shampoo and Kevin is on a very short fuse. Gudrun is still solid but spends a lot of time staring at the wall, lost in her own thoughts at the prospect of a year in this place with her three male companions. Despite these little niggles, the mood is still buoyant and it would have been too much to expect a totally smooth ride.

The weather broke today. Minus 5 and bitterly cold stuck up on the crane with the wind-chill factor taking the temperature down to minus 20. Snow tonight and wind picked up to 25 knots. Dave Woolan calmly told us that the satcom probably won't work as there's not enough elevation to access the satellite above the horizon as we're at such high latitudes. Getting more and more tired with every day. Decreed Wednesday a day of rest.

3 February 1987

Skip lunch and spend time in my cabin alone with music. The ship is swinging around in 40 knots of wind with both anchors deployed. Gone are the halcyon days of last week. It's now bitterly cold in the wind and the air temperature is minus five and dropping daily. The helo broke down this morning and we've had a few false starts. The pressure is on and we only have another ten days or so before we must make our way out of Ross Island. The sun will dip beneath the horizon in four or five days' time and the temperature will begin dropping rapidly after that. God! I just want to be out of here now, heading 360 for New Zealand as fast as we can. After a very positive crew meeting, Jonathan and I work on deck filling the extra barrels we have decided to leave here as insurance for the winterers and we don't finish until 2315. But it was good to spend time with Jonathan who told me that when asked by Stephen Knight what was the most satisfying aspect of the trip for Jonathan, he replied that he was pleased for me as I deserved this success. I was really touched.

After work, it was all downhill. Ken was halfway through a bottle of rum (the dreaded Bundaberg) and I proceeded to help him finish it off. Then Hugh, Chris and Jonathan arrived and I finally got to bed at about 0400, blearily conscious of the fact that it's a day off tomorrow.

4 February 1987

Oh shit! The mother and father of all hangovers today. Staggered into the saloon at 1230 but couldn't hack it. Back to bed with a thumping head until 1830. Hallucinated in my half sleep and kept being disturbed by an infuriatingly healthy and lively Justin who must have come in at least 20 times. Did nothing much else in the evening except prepare the work schedule for tomorrow and a telex for Roger to ask him about my air ticket.

5 February 1987

Winterers off for a 'social' at Scott Base and return with much awaited mail for the ship. Fiona sent me a pile of press clippings from NZ newspapers which I pinned to the notice board. It's great to know that our efforts are being reported and I hope a lot of people are choking on their cornflakes at our success. Ken was being interviewed by Stephen Knight in the saloon tonight and I overheard him call Maureen a 'two faced bastard'. Can't wait to see that in print!

Most of the food discharged today and by 1800 we were all blasted. The winterers are ferried on board at 1900 and Kevin told me that the Officer in Charge at Scott Base does not want us to go there for our official visit on Monday, is firmly against our 'intrusion' here at Cape Evans and refused to give us the key to Scott's Hut (which the New Zealand wintering team is in charge of) and said that no sampling of waste water, snow or ice would take place on 'his' base. Scott was British, I remind Kevin, and we'll go ahead with the sampling programme despite objections. He has no jurisdiction here at all. And if he wants to tell us differently, then perhaps McTaggart's wishes will come true.

A good day today, however. The weather's brightened up and only Kevin's touchiness casts any sort of shadow over our activities.

6 February 1987

Got the official response today from the OIC at Scott to my letter informing him of our planned activities. It's a three-page tirade telling us that we're 'banned' from doing anything remotely connected with Scott Base – we can't go there, can't fly the choppers there and can't take any samples. This puts our planned visit on Monday in very interesting light. What will he do when we turn up? Will he arrest us? For what and with what authority? He has put himself in a very difficult position and must be kicking himself for his knee-jerk reaction. I'm now looking forward to Monday and can feel the old campaigning juices rising again. Press releases out and a lot of information to Roger tonight with Maj's invaluable help and still managed a full day on deck.

The shore party are now making forays into the hinterland around the base to see seals, penguins and to drink in the grandeur of the ice sheet. I'd like to do the same before we leave: I've only been ashore once. Only a few days before we leave. Snow showers and 35 knot winds from the south tonight but a good day's work with food and the remaining radio gear offloaded. Then the satcom phone on the bridge rang and Ken calmly handed me the receiver saying, 'It's for you.' Ian Balmer was on the other end of the phone and after we'd chatted for a few seconds, it finally dawned on me that the only place he could possibly be phoning from was the base. THE SATCOM WORKS FROM THE BASE!! Thank God! He phoned me from 200 yards away via Singapore! The guys had set the cameras up to record my reactions. Jim's birthday party rounded off a great day and I fell into bed completely wiped out.

7 February 1987

Jonathan and I spent the day going backwards and forwards to the shore with bundles of timber strapped to the dinghy. We then worked on deck shifting and re-stowing barrels of helo-fuel. Crew meeting started to get a little hairy when the old stagers started to come on about their reactions to the Scott Base politicking, an issue about which everyone has an opinion. It was all relatively mild, however, compared to last year, and only Jochen raised any substantial criticism when he proffered that we had 'picked on' Scott Base by transmitting a picture of a NZ truck being dropped through the ice on the dump and had thus provoked a retaliatory response. Xavier was great and came to my defence in his faltering English in a nonetheless marvellous delivery. Graham is still proving to be a bit of a pest laying the moral guilt trip on people saying that he couldn't condone this, that or the other as an ex-OIC himself which gets peoples' backs up, especially Kevin's. Unlike Ken who buggered off halfway through, I had to stay the course and felt drained empty at the end. The fact that it was filmed added to the tension and the energy level required to get through it.

Weather minus 8, blustery with 25 knot variable winds. Finished up by arranging the delivery of the notification of our visit to McMurdo and for the reply to Guy's letter to be delivered. McMurdo refused us permission to land on their helipad (nice guys, eh?) and so Gary had to land off-limits. Despite everything, the work is moving ahead quickly and we're now entering our last week before departure.

8 February 1987

Nolan has now gotten into the habit of bringing me tea in bed at 0700. Woke to a beautiful day, but it's harder and harder for me to get moving lately as I'm so tired. Jonathan off today with flu symptoms and as Keith is ashore, it was left to me and Ken to cover the deck work. All the Footsteps gear came aboard today (apart from the aircraft) and we work hard stowing and lashing it. I told Andi to get his arse out of bed at 1130 and I also found it necessary to drop gentle hints to Maj about her habit of sleeping in until 1030, although I think she may have a condition which makes her tired. Shifted 10 loads ashore and received 10 on board and stowed it all before 1400. Then we steamed north for 5 miles to meet the tour ship *World Discoverer* to take part in their visit to Cape Royds to see the penguin rookery there and Shackleton's hut. I decided not to go to the hut: I didn't fancy sharing such an experience with a bunch of tourists although I would jump at the chance to go with just Ken, Jonathan and Chris or at least just a small group from our own ship. So Ken, Irmi, Jim, Davey and I stayed on board while the rest went off to Cape Royds. Graham, who organised the event with 'old friends' on the tour ship, came back eulogising about how 'wonderful' it all was and Ken's face was a picture of contempt.

Our expected itinerary is:

Leave Cape Evans 18th Feb Arrive Terra Nova 20th Feb
Leave Terra Nova 21st Feb Arrive Dumont D'Urville 25th Feb
Leave Dumont D'Urville 26th Feb Arrive Macquarie Island 1st March
Leave Macquarie Island 1st March Arrive Auckland Islands 2nd March
Arrive Wellington 11th March.

9 February 1987

Up at 0400 to check plans and schedules for the trip ashore and the visit to Scott Base. Leave ship in Helicopter at 0600 and arrive at the site on the sea ice (known as Little Greenpeace 3 or LGP3) in four waves of flights. Assemble with camera crew, photographer, Andi Loor, winterers, Maj and Swenson. This flight gave me my first ever sight of the Antarctic interior and it took my breath away. The ice sheet reaches the horizon in a flat and desert-like expanse of uninterrupted ice hundreds of miles wide and deep. I imagined the tiny dots of Scott and his party marching their way in hopeless heroism towards the pole. What a place this is!

We walked into Scott Base past a huge, vertical ice sheet to our right, along a dirt track which quickly gave way to the fast ice across which we had to trudge up the slope to the base. We walked into Scott base expecting the grand confrontation but they had locked up shop – it was deserted. We did our sampling and then trudged over the hill to McMurdo. The route took us up a steep incline for about a mile which gave us spectacular views of White Island and Black Island, the tips of submarine mountain ranges poking through the flat ice-scape to the south. As we walked into McMurdo, we entered a small town with all the charm of a mid-west redneck outpost.

Observation Hill, from which Scott had looked for his relief vessel, stood impressively on our left but its grandeur was tempered by the knowledge that at its base had once stood in the recent past a nuclear reactor (known childishly as Nukey Poo) and which now sported the remains of the 30,000 tons of contaminated soil which had to be removed from the Antarctic after the reactor sprung a leak. Everywhere, including the slopes of Observation Hill, had been bulldozed and the entire base was a haphazard mess of oil spills, piles of junk and an air of total environmental contempt. We did our sampling and photo documentation, receiving a lot of support from the ordinary military grunts on the base. But no-one in authority, except Ron Le Count of the National Science Foundation (NSF) dared show his or her face. All other personnel, according to Le Count, were 'unavailable'.

The US authorities had asked us not to come on this particular day as there was to be 'operation of heavy machinery' which our visit would have disrupted, but there was no evidence of any heavy activity going on. We had exercised our right to the freedom of access to the Antarctic but the confrontation we were hoping for never materialised. A moral victory was declared.

We returned past the spectacular scenery of Scott's last resting place and regrouped at LGP3 for our flights back to the ship. At 2145, we were invited to the *World Discoverer* to have drinks with the skipper and I was asked if I'd like to lecture the tourists to which I readily agreed.

My speech went down well with the well-heeled tourists but it was plain that my message was not welcomed by the Swedish tour leader, nor, to my annoyance, by Graham, both of whom stood up and made a plea for non-confrontation in the Antarctic, both saying or implying at least, that seeing the beauty of the Antarctic from the comfort of a tour ship was the best way of preserving the Antarctic. I was so angry that Xavier had to physically restrain me from interrupting their tirade of rebuttal.

The weather has been absolutely fantastic all day and a quite magical day was only spoiled when one of the tourist ship expedition personnel, slightly worse for drink, I fear, fell into the water when trying to get into one of our inflatables. No harm done though.

10 February 1987

Press releases and pictures out first thing to cover the visits yesterday and finally got on deck to help Ken at 1400. Spent all afternoon stowing rubbish sacks in the hold and emerged covered in dust and filth. I spoke to the NZ Greenpeace office today to hear that the Germans were coming to the next AGM in a week's time with a demand that we pull the base camp out next year. I'm stunned at this news and can't believe they can be so out of touch with what we've achieved here. I can't confide this news to the crew as it would kill the spirit and would crush people who have worked so hard to set up the base. Bed at 2250 but can't recall actually lying down as I was asleep before I fell into bed.

11 February 1987

Woken at 0600 by the anchor chains rattling in the hawse pipes. We're dragging anchors in a 50 knot wind. Visibility down to a few yards, minus 12 and the sea is very choppy. No work today! Ken woke us nonetheless and we had an enormous breakfast at 0730. Tidied up and looked out of the bridge onto a bleak, Antarctic scene. We can just about make out the hut ashore through the driving snow. Ice reports are pretty grim and it looks as though we'll have as much difficulty getting out as we had getting in. Only a few more helo-loads to get away from the ship, the final few days' work on the base, the party and then it's get the hell out.

12 February 1987

I hear that the international organisation is planning an 'assessment' of the trip on our return. In other words, a lot of Greenpeace administrators will spend huge amounts of money coming to NZ to 'assess' the voyage, something which we on board can do quite well in the form of a report which I'm required to write anyway. However, that bit of annoying news aside, it turned out to be a notable day.

Called at 0545 for an early start to make up for yesterday's loss and promptly walked into a metal upright on deck and gashed my shin badly. Later, the wings from the Cessna came on board via Grace's inflatable and Ken and Jonathan grabbed the wide edge of one while I was designated the job of picking up the more manageable wing-tip. We were lifting it into the recess for stowage. The hatch cover was off as it had been all day, but I completely forgot about it and, not seeing the open space due to the wing I was carrying, stepped into thin air. I fell ten feet onto a pile of folded cardboard. I was so sure that I had broken something that I laid still, a little stunned, and heard Ken tell Jonathan to call immediately for Cornelius before I could tell him I was ok bar from a sprained wrist.

Then Justin called the ship and ranted on at me about how dangerous it was to allow Graham to marshal the helicopter since he was 'unqualified' to do so. He sort of 'court-marshalled' Graham and demanded that Jim and I hold an 'inquest'. Graham and Justin came into Jim's cabin where Justin lit into Graham unmercifully and then had to eat his words and make a humble apology when it was pointed out to him that Graham had 10 years' NZRAF experience in marshalling. Ken came up to me and said that if he (Ken) gets out of order at the 'hut warming' party tomorrow night, he's likely to tell Graham just what an arsehole Ken thinks he is. I must say, despite the fact that I told Ken to keep his opinions to himself, I don't know how Ken has kept his mouth shut. Graham struts around in his trendy, unsoiled Antarctic gear, his hair just so, shades on, and talks down to Ken – filthy dirty, sweaty and covered in shit, often literally – from a position of superiority, a superiority I bestowed on him. However, that's all for tomorrow. For now, it's the penultimate day of work on the base and we'll soon be on our way north, thank God.

13 February 1987

Friday the 13th is not a good day on which to finish the base and I was a little apprehensive that after such a relatively accident-free time, we'd come a cropper on the last day. The last few sling-loads were prepared, another 12 barrels of fuel and the freezers sent ashore. Due to my injuries, I was stuck on the crane which I can still drive, fortunately. We worked hard and long to finish today and even after much-heralded 'end' of the work, loads of Footsteps rubbish continued to arrive. It's bitterly cold (minus 10) and the wind is strong. To lift the Cessna fuselage means that Gary cannot turn downwind to get more lift from the chopper blades and we therefore steamed to the other side of the hummock beyond Cape Evans so that he could take off into the wind and continue thus onto the helipad on the ship without having to turn down-wind. It was quite an occasion and everyone turned out to see the fuselage's arrival. Gary positioned it perfectly on the ship's deck and we lifted it with the crane to the port side where it was secured for the journey home.

By 2200 we were finished and I marshalled everyone ashore for the crew photo outside the base. It was the first time I had really seen the base and it was mightily impressive with a very homely atmosphere. Kevin was busy brewing punch, music was blasting out of the stereo and the passageways were littered with boxes and equipment. John Phillpotts had to go back to the ship to get a camera part he's forgotten and when he came back, Jim was with him. As we all crowded round for the delayed picture shoot, I suddenly realised that the ship was riding at anchor with no-one at all on board. Jim said with incredible sang-froid, 'If the ship drags anchor now and makes deep water, we'll all be wintering!'

The picture shoot was its normal chaos and Andi had a hard time trying to control 35 people, all wanting to fool around, using his gentle and almost inaudible voice. When it was all over, we went inside, people taking turns to keep an eye on our precious ship 300 yards away, while the party began. Boots came off and punch was sipped with beer chasers. Then Andi asked us all to go outside again for colour shots! Jonathan refused to go and Hugh got quite angry and no amount of pleading from me or anyone could calm them down.

Finally the party got underway. Ken had been strangely curt towards me all day and I had retorted with a few cutting remarks of my own, but now he came over, gave me a huge hug and apologies. Only now that it's over do we realise what enormous pressures we've all been under and I'm amazed that we've remained so cordial towards each other. There was a pause in the proceedings for the presentation of presents to the winterers and a few speeches at which I found myself welling up with emotion. Then we got stuck into the booze and before long everyone was dancing and singing at the top of their voices.

Gary Dukes christened the toilet with a technicolour yawn (he's now known as Gary Pukes) and at around 0300 Swenson came over and said, 'Hey, Wilks. Wanna take a walk?' We walked for miles along the coast, avoiding crevasses here and there, sitting within yards of penguins and seals, standing on a huge ice-floe listening to the creaking of the ice as it rose gently on the swell and watched the seals either sleeping, yawning, scratching or letting off clapperboard farts. We returned via Scott's Hut and I stood glowing with booze, achievement, with the beauty of the Antarctic coursing through my veins for the first time in front of the Mecca of Antarcticians. I was standing on the very spot where Scott had stood. Behind the hut were piles of his expedition junk. In front of the hut, the mummified remains of his dogs, still chained up, testified to our eternal callous exploitation of faithful and undemanding dogs.

Back at the base, some die-hards were still going as Keith and I crawled into sleeping bags and crashed out. What a day. What a wonderful, glorious and thoroughly satisfying day.

14 February 1987

Ferried back to the ship in various states of distress from hangovers. Most take the day recovering and lying around the mess and saloon: reading, sleeping or listening to music. I have to drag myself to the radio room to pump out yet more pictures and a press release. The winterers arrive in the afternoon for their 'last supper' on board as this is the last day we will be with them. We leave later today and the meal is an emotional affair. We are about to abandon our friends to the rigours of an Antarctic winter and to what might befall them in the coming year. I admire their pluck: although the prospect of experiencing an Antarctic winter is incredibly romantic, it's not something I would choose to do. The winterers eventually make their way onto the helideck at around 1900 and amid much and prolonged hugging and tears, they say their goodbyes.

I found it impossible to stay on deck since my emotions got the better of me. I was briefed to achieve this goal back in the summer of 1985 and the task has finally been completed. We got underway at 2100 and Jim decided to take a final sweep past the base and the four winterers had all climbed onto the roof and were waving their goodbyes. I felt so proud yet so inconsolably sad. They looked so insignificant a group – mere grains of sand dwarfed by Erebus and the majesty of the awesome Antarctic they had come to protect. As they gradually slipped from view, the crew began drifting in from the helideck wiping eyes and there was much staring at walls later as people wrestled with their own thoughts and emotions.

Ken insisted we toast the occasion and I gave up trying to round up Jonathan and Chris (the former is always in his cabin when not working and the latter is reportedly in love with Hanna) so Ken and I downed a few beers then crashed just after midnight, toasting a job well done. The greatest benefit for me resulting from the departure of the winterers is that I have the cabin all to myself and, despite the fact that Justin is a fine cabin-mate, the luxury of a 'single' cabin is indescribable. It's the first time in eight years of sailing with Greenpeace that I have benefited from such unashamed luxury.

15 February 1987

Back on regular watches today. Slept like a baby last night and did not want to rise this morning. Jonathan cooked breakfast – huge piles of fried potatoes, two eggs, bacon, beans and toast – then staggered around the lurching bridge until I awoke fully around 1000. Ken, Garry and Graham flew off to Vanda to lay in Kevin's fuel depot as we steamed towards the Victoria Land coast, an area we have only admired from a distance thus far. Garry returns to tell Jim that since the weather is so good and since we have a little time in hand, he'd be happy to take a few people sightseeing into Vanda Lake. Jim tells me that it has been ordained that I go along.

Jonathan, Natalie, Davey and I squeezed into the chopper and we headed off towards the coast over the huge and spectacular Wilson Piedmont Glacier. The experience was one which stays with you forever. We landed at Lake Vanda and walked along the shoreline. This place is an enigma even in the enigmatic Antarctic. The mountains which flank the valley are enormous and the silence is all-pervading. It is a stunning place which my pictures will not do justice to. We are in the dry-valley region – not a bit of snow or ice to be seen apart from the 'hanging glaciers' which peep over the tops of the colls between the mountains and then mysteriously stop. The river running into Lake Vanda reportedly runs from the sea to the lake. We check out the small weather station here operated by the New Zealanders and find a mummified seal at the doorstep. It is like being in a wonderland where things don't quite make sense but where the sheer size and beauty of the place knock any other thoughts into insignificance. The trip back was equally spectacular. The surface of the glacier is riven with small streams of melting ice as the gigantic glacier inches its way to the sea.

Lunch on the ship and then crashed only to be woken firstly by Graham who tells me (erroneously) that I'm on dishes, then secondly by Stephen Knight who asks me to preside over a meeting called to plan getting the journalists back to McMurdo tomorrow. The complicated logistics of moving even a small number of people around in the Antarctic is daunting. Personally, I'm anxious to go north now the work is over, but I realise that whatever we do now is icing on the cake and I swallow my anxiety about heading north in the interests of extracting as much as possible from this incredible trip. I'm not looking forward to going to Dumont D'Urville as it takes us west, not north. But getting the journalists to McMurdo allows us to carry out one last post run to Scott Base. But the best laid plans, etc . . .

The wind picked up significantly grounding the helicopter and it wasn't until 2300 that we could finally get it airborne as the ship now went back south towards Cape Evans to facilitate the flight. Incredibly, the winterers asked us to drop off one final sling-load of gear which they had forgotten and before we knew it we were in sight of the base again. The helicopter flew off and Justin flew the Hughes 300 back to the ship (we had toyed with the idea of leaving it for the winterers to use, but had decided against it) and as we made our final sweep of the Bay for the second time, Jim blasted a few notes on the ship's klaxon but only Kevin appeared, didn't even wave.

16th February 1987

This was supposed to be an easy day: waiting for the journalists to return to the ship at 1700, getting Justin back ashore and then heading off. But Ken had other ideas. He got us preparing for the open sea and we were all working on deck from 0800. Jim told us that his ice-spotting trip indicated a clear route out providing we kept away from the coast and as we finally set off north with urgency, us deckies were lashing down deck cargo, moving barrels of fuel and covering equipment with tarpaulins in a gathering swell. By 1600 the weather looked too ominous to collect the journalists and get Justin back ashore so we turned south yet again, and sheltered in Lewis Bay before steaming on to Cape Crozier and the ice barrier for sight-seeing and to ride out the weather. It finally passed and we steamed back amid another round of goodbyes – this time for Justin alone – and as he left he gave me a big hug. Then Garry reported that the weather at the base was bad and we had to wait for snow squalls to pass before his return. Technically, we start north tomorrow but who can predict what the Antarctic will decide for us?

17 February 1987

Garry arrived in the wee hours and I awake for watch as we're underway, northbound at last. We steamed past Beaufort Island and took time out to do some sounding around the area that the *Southern Quest* was sunk last year – 2-300 fathoms. We're constantly frustrated in our journey by long, drifting bands of sea ice which force us west. Strange weather: we're surrounded by storm clouds, black and threatening and the glass has dropped to 970 mb. Yet the wind never came and we're bobbing along on a gentle swell, happy to be back in a regular routine. Long telex off to Roger. I hope GP can cough up for another ticket to get Fiona back to the UK with me but I doubt it. I realise it's a bit of a cheeky request, but after all the work I've put in, plus the fact that they seem to find no obstacles to flying unnecessary personnel here for the 'evaluation', I feel it's a reasonable proposition.

18 February 1987

Late for breakfast (my turn to cook as well!) which puts Ken in a bad mood. Now we need to go west, the ice dictates a northerly direction and the day is spent picking our way through bands of ice attempting to close Terra Nova. Slept like a log until 1800 and as I take the wheel at 2000, we're 15 miles from the Italian base heading directly into a 40 knot wind, taking seas over the bow, water immediately freezing on deck superstructure and port holes. The entire forward end of the ship is wreathed in 3 inches of ice. Finally took sanctuary in the bay from where we can see the aerials of the base. Felt the old nausea this afternoon as we were pitching heavily but OK now. Temperature minus 8. Go ashore tomorrow.

19 February 1987

The wind had thankfully dropped this morning and we all went ashore in the dinghies to 'make an inspection' of the Italian base. It's quite a tidy affair: thirty modules in one unit on stilts. A big roadway runs from one bay over the hummock into a bay at the rear of the promontory. Lots of skuas around with a chick or two and it's evident that they have come to rely on scraps from the base to supplement their diet. After being shown around by the OIC, a nice guy called Mario, we finally get back to the ship around 1600. Maj has taken charge of the inspection monitoring and has thankfully made copious notes for the report we'll be required to write for GP.

I confide in Jim once back on board that I am tired and drained from this trip and want to head back with all reasonable speed. Finally get underway for Cape Hallet at 1700 when Ken suggests we stop at Cape Adare as well. I'm getting a bit ratty with people and had to steel myself for a conversation I had with Graham when he insisted on sending a telex to his friends on the *World Discoverer*. He finally agreed to make it an official telex from the ship but our strained relations were not helped when I called his Swedish friend, on the *World Discoverer*, a wanker for sending the NZ authorities a telex demanding a public apology from us over the key to Scott's Hut incident. En route to Hallet now and the swell is increasing, tossing the ship around like a play thing. It's actually almost dark on watch tonight.

20 February 1987

It gets harder every day to keep my motivation and positivity. I only wish we were setting course for Wellington but Cape Adare is ahead of us on the 'corner' of the Antarctic and in all probability, we will head west in the morning towards Dumont. But first it's Cape Hallet where an abandoned NZ/US base exists which is reportedly being re-colonised by the penguins who were dislodged to build the base in the 70s. The ice was thick in the bay and we had to pick our way carefully through heavy concentrations. We hit one bit which sent me flying across the saloon. Maj, Phillpotts, Andi and Keith go ashore in the chopper promising to land well away from the penguins and they return a few hours later smelling as if they'd been rolling in vats of penguin shit.

Underway by 1600 which means that with deck duties I miss the chance of catching up on sleep again. Only a moderate swell running thankfully but the weather's still overcast and miserable. Roger called to tell me that there's no money for Fiona's ticket and nor for me to change my ticket and I lit into him about the unfairness of dealing with practical problems such as getting me to London when it suits me while finding thousands of dollars to bring a bunch of people to NZ for what will be little more than a jolly. All to no avail, I'm afraid, Then he disarmed me by asking me if I'd sign up for next year's Antarctic voyage: apparently, the winterers have been lobbying for my presence which is very nice to know.

21 February 1987

The ice reports we get from NOAA indicate open water at Dumont and the weather forecast is for easterlies – much rolling and following seas – and so Jim, amid much moaning from the lower decks, decides Dumont is on. The morning watch is uneventful with grey skies with not a break in the cloud cover – all quite depressing. The boredom factor seems to be flipping a few people out. Ian stands around on the bridge mumbling to himself and then asking inane questions which beggar a decent response. The watchkeepers simply ignore him and continue staring into the mesmeric grey wall before them. Slept a straight four hours after lunch then called a crew meeting after dinner to brief the crew about the outcomes of Terra Nova and Cape Hallet, let Jim outline weather and ice information and to lay the plans for Dumont.

The question of visiting Leningradskaya inevitably came up and thankfully Jim vetoed it on the grounds of the notoriously bad ice situation which surrounds the approaches. It's simply unsafe in our vessel. Pushing through 30 miles of ice might be possible but the advent of an onshore wind could pile up the ice behind us. A few people expressed regret at this decision, but that's how it is. We're en route for Dumont and will not be stopping to see if we can access Leningradskaya. On watch tonight, the ship began corkscrewing badly and I found myself fighting off nausea yet again. But I hack the watch until Ken takes pity on me and sends me below to my bunk into which I fall with deep gratitude. The trip, I decide, has become tedious and boring and I can't wait to feel the NZ late-summer sun on my face.

22 February 1987

Slept an incredible 14 hours! Ken let me sleep rather than rouse me for watch and I finally rose shortly before noon after Jonathan had kindly plied me with several cups of tea and oranges with instructions to 'take it easy.' Feeling so much better, I rose, had a light meal and lay on my bunk reading whereupon I amazingly slept again until 1800. Weather dull and miserable. Heading 317, changing to 275 tonight. Deep depressions ahead, we're informed. A boring day and a boring evening watch, only enlivened by the need to use the searchlight after 2200 to spot growlers and bergy bits in the deepening evening gloom.

24 February 1987
The ship was rolling heavily in the night with big northerly swells crashing over the bow which caused the cupboard in the saloon housing the TV and video to crash thunderously across the saloon. Excruciatingly boring watch staring into grey seas, grey skies, zero visibility and snow showers. Temperature plus 1 but as we're turning south in the morning, it should drop to minus 4 or so again. Ship still rolling moderately, the pitching having thankfully ceased with a wind direction change. The mood on board is still remarkably buoyant but people are now openly saying they want to get this visit to Dumont over with and head back to white, fluffy clouds, sunshine and more clement weather. Agreed at the crew meeting that our tactics at Dumont where the airstrip is being built across a penguin colony must be decided as a result of what we see.

25 February 1987
As I write this at the end of the day, I can say with finality, it is over. One more crew meeting, one more press release, tying up odds and ends and we're through. Same as usual on watch this morning – staring into greys, fog and snow squalls. Rolled along 40 miles from Dumont in an area literally stuffed full of icebergs of all sizes and descriptions. Picked up Dumont on the VHF talking about our visit and then spoke to them directly. They were very accommodating and gave us local weather and ice reports before asking about the size and draft of the ship and recommending a good anchorage. As we approached, the scenery assumed a very spectacular aspect and we nudged between very large floes into a tiny bay from where we could see the sprawling base dotted with hundreds of penguins. Two boats ashore creeping through thick brash ice to the landing point where the OIC was waiting to receive us. We walked through squawking penguin colonies (no way to avoid them) to the reception at the base where we set up cameras and proceeded with the formalities.

The OIC is a scientist, as are the remaining people here at the base (the construction team having left a week ago) and he proceeded to protest their innocence in responsibility for the airstrip stating that he was a humble scientist and their work was in no way connected with the strip. I believed him and argued with the crew that any direct action was out – the uproar there would be if we uprooted scientific equipment would have been rightly clamorous. Furthermore, our scientist friend dismissed the 'law' which his Parisian bosses had insisted should be invoked to prevent us from going anywhere 'sensitive'. He even pointed out the best access sites to the strip and was happy to show us around.

We left in an amicable mood and went to the strip and held up a few banners for the press. Any action against the strip in a more direct way would have amounted to sabotage and I ruled it out, much to the annoyance of some of the crew. Either the OIC was a smooth-talking lying bastard or he was genuinely between a rock and a hard place: I believed the latter and that was that.

The subsequent crew meeting went ok although Jonathan was quite hostile later, arguing that these guys had been just stringing us along. The press release I wrote seemed to quieten things down a bit as did the question I put to the dissenters: 'Well, what do you want to do? Go and rip out the scientific gear and get pilloried for it?' This visit is icing on the cake and the quicker people realise that we achieved the objectives of this trip when we pulled out of Cape Evans the better. It's as though each visit assumes a life of its own and some people (especially Hanna) want to fight the world at each landfall.

26 February 1987
Aurora Australis brought everyone out on deck at 0200. One of the breath-taking and unique wonders of the world – shimmering, vertical sheets of particles bombarding this fragile planet.

28 February 1987
In the night, all hell broke loose. We rolled and pitched with a violence I haven't experienced before and just about everything not lashed down in my cabin flew across the room. Negative gravity literally lifts your head off the pillow and it is impossible to sleep unless you wedge yourself into the bunk. When I finally cast an eye over the cabin this morning, it was a riot of papers, cassettes, clothes and equipment. Every cabin was the same.

At breakfast we had a good laugh at Stephen Knight's expense. He came into the saloon from the mess and put a plate of toast and jam down on the table while he went back to get his tea. Sure enough, the plate went flying just as he returned – jam side down, of course. He laboriously went through the entire procedure again and did exactly the same thing with the same result. Then tonight after dinner, poor Stephen was sitting on the floor opposite the bench in the saloon when an empty cup left there carelessly by one of the crew flew off the bench, bounced once on the floor and made a direct hit on a full cup of tea Stephen was sitting there nestling between his legs for safety. His face was a picture and it took about 15 minutes before we had stopped laughing at his misfortune.

The weather has been bad for two days now. Force 9 gales with huge swells which toss the empty ship around like a cork. After morning watch I tried to tidy my cabin but it was pointless as cups, books, telexes and all the campaigning dross I've accumulated over the weeks just fly across the cabin at every heave of the ship. People hanging on for dear life at dinner as chairs slide across the room as people sit with raised and charged forks to their mouths. Still rolling very heavily this evening and Jim reduced revs and turns the ship more to the west to ease the motion, but turned NE again just before evening watch so spent it riding the bridge like a cowboy. ETA Mcquarie Island is the 2nd March.

The wind turns southeast at last and we're taking big, big swells on the port quarter before watch end, threatening to poop us. But it's quite exhilarating and I find the motion comforting after two days of pitching into big seas with the ship slamming and jarring from stem to stern. But the trip is nearly over, thank God, and we have done what we set out to do. It's strange on board. People just biding their time, speculating about what they'll do on landfall.

Ken paces the bridge like a caged tiger muttering to himself almost constantly. Jonathan drums out a musical beat on the binnacle and I pick it up and sing along. Ian's almost gone now and I thank God he didn't winter as was the possibility for a time. Dave Woolan has taken to speaking in a high-pitched voice for some reason and Lennard talks on the phone to a Swedish journalist in his native tongue. The bridge is a cacophonic mix of weird noises and weird people. Christ! We're all going round the bend as the vessel rolls along through a big swell, a ship of fools indeed! Watch off in the morning. The prospect of a lie-in is sublime.

1 March 1987

Blissfully lie in until 1130. We're still rolling and pitching crazily and I make it to the saloon and slurp a wonderful, life-saving cup of tea. Staggered back to my bunk, gave lunch a miss and slept again until 1430. Sat and read in the saloon during the afternoon and watched the floor show of people trying to move about the ship as it rolled at crazy angles sending the furniture skidding across the floor crashing into bulkheads. Dinner was very unappetising but watch made up for it.

Pretty spectacular on the bridge this evening. Hove-to heading 330, just riding out the storm. From the bridge, the swells were absolutely magnificent, bows buried deep in the troughs to rise like an express lift out of the following crest. The wind increased again and it was hard to credit the size of some of the swells – at least 40 feet some of them, towering over the bridge, as the ship's bows rose until nothing could be seen forward except the sky and then only to plummet – free falling – into the troughs when you'd think she'd just keep going down. A thump as she hits the bottom of the trough, a shudder through the ship as she jars from stem to stern, then the procedure is repeated again. Incredible!

In the middle of all this, we'd get side-swiped by a cross swell and we'd roll in the middle of this crazy motion. We've lost about half the crockery so far, I'm told, and even the most trivial of events – like pulling on a pair of socks – can become a major drama. Changed course yet again to 050 which eased the motion a bit and as the swell went aft, thankfully, Jim increased the revs and we went surfing at about 10 knots.

2 March 1987

Morning watch was a delight. The ship moves more easily today although we're still rolling heavily. Sunshine at last! Crisp and sunny weather lifts everyone's spirits. Steak and chips for dinner after an afternoon of finishing off paperwork and I hearten myself even more by listening to some loud music in my cabin which I share with no-one. Crestfallen, miserable and worried after trying to call Fiona to no avail. Being confined on a ship like this, contact with loved ones and any reference to the real world out there assumes proportions of gigantic importance. Now all I have to look forward to is a crew meeting and watch this evening. Crew meeting was brief and positive and then I'm called to the bridge to see Macquarie off the port beam. Paralleled the eastern shore and I stood on the bridge wing watching the surf cream along the ship's length from the stern and lift the bows as it raced beneath us.

The stars were brilliant in a cloudless sky and the Aurora Australis promised another show but then faded. I could smell the faintest aroma rising from vegetation on the land, carried on the breeze, and people came on deck just to fill their lungs with the scent of land. Anchored at 2330 just opposite the weather station. Ashore in the morning. The mayhem of the sea passage over the last few days instantly forgotten.

3 March 1987

Roused by Ken at 0815. The ship is a hive of activity as people prepare to go ashore: dinghies buzzing around and Ken shouting and ordering people about on deck. Laughter and joking wafting in from the deck and I get myself together for a day of tourism. Jim clears quarantine with the doctor ashore and the first boat gets away by 0900. While we await our turn we are fascinated at the number of King penguins around the ship. There are at least fifty of the buggers and they swim around and around, clearly curious and unafraid, perhaps waiting to be fed like ducks in the park. I get away at 0930 and arrived on a gently shoaling beach, carpeted with thick kelp. King penguins all over the beach and we all spent the first ten minutes photographing these amazing creatures which will approach to within a few feet once you're on their eyeline, which for me is easy.

We got taken for a tour by one of the guys at the station. It was a magical walk through lush vegetation which we all wanted to roll in. Elephant seals everywhere in wallows: farting, belching and snorting at our approach. The four-ton bulls are engaged in bloody fights at this time of year and they are given a very wide berth. Our guide gives us a highly informative lecture about the island and tells us that a guy called Hooker in the 19th century knocked off 120,000 fur seals in one year here and used to drive penguins into the vats alive in their droves. It must be ignominious to be named after the guy who tried his damnedest to wipe out your species. We make it to the northern shore where the object of Hooker's attentions (fur seals and penguins) thankfully have outlived the bastard.

Back to the base for 1230 for lunch after which I give a talk about GP before we head out to the southern beach to see King, Royal, Gentoo and Rock Hoppers, elephant seals and skuas. It was a grand day – cold, blustery but sunny. The weather station team come on board for dinner and leave us to our own devices at 2130. Underway by 2300 and soon leave the comforting lee of the island back to the familiar rock and roll.

4 March 1987

Late again for my breakfast cooking stint and find Ken frying eggs with a grim face. On watch at 0800 to steer and Ken gradually loses his early morning reticence and we talk about the next expedition. He's very keen and I know it will work well with Ken and Keith involved. I'm constantly tired now and feel that the delayed reaction to the exertions of the trip are catching up with me. Lunch then slept blissfully all afternoon. Nothing much else to report. Routine evening watch during which the base camp calls to tell us that the genny fuel is waxing at only minus 16 (it was guaranteed for at least minus 30). Informed Roger about this problem but there's nothing we can do about it, obviously. Chatted with Keith and identified him as potential base leader for next year. Bruce turned up at my cabin door with a Clapton tape he had copied for me. Good ol' Bruce. Drifted off to sleep to the strains of Layla.

5 March 1987

As the Auckland Islands hove into view, I was looking at them from the porthole of the galley as I cooked breakfast. On the bridge, I had the pleasure of steering the ship into the wide Courtney Sound and upto Figure of Eight Island. It was beautiful – calm, green and untouched. The islands were only discovered in 1806 and since then only a handful of sealers and castaways have been here apart from a vain attempt to settle the island which lasted only 2 years. The day became a GP Tours Inc event as we swanned in and out of fiords to see the sights – no landing permitted on this uninhabited island – Hooker seals, cormorants, beautiful waterfalls and lush greenery. The atmosphere is heady and we all had a great time. Failing light dragged us reluctantly away and we headed north for the Snares. Cleaned cabin as we swept along in fine weather. Jochen insisted on an interview and Ken on drinking a couple of beers with me. Saw 11 Russian fishing boats tonight. Welcome back to the real world.

6 March 1987

Huge breakfast after 6 hours sleep and told that the Snares are on the horizon. Steering 011 on watch to approach as the wind backs and the swell increases. By 1100 we're off the Snares and bucking around in a storm-tossed sea in brilliant sunshine. The mandatory pictures are taken of these jagged outcrops of rocks as we steam past them and then it's off to Stewart Island only 65 miles away. Ken cracks the whip as we clean the bulkheads and generally prepare the ship for landfall. By dinner, we're off Stewart Island and the weather is absolutely stunning. Much late-evening pro-tanning going on as the temperature is in the high teens now. I was about to turn in after watch when Ken burst in holding a six pack moaning that no-one wanted to party. We sat and drank and Ken poured out his heart to me about the future, his emotional involvement with the expedition, Maureen and the 'assessment' meeting coming up. He finally left and I sank into my bunk and slept for a straight nine hours.

7 March 1987
Awoke to eggs on toast à la Ballard. Sunshine, moderate swell, the coast of New Zealand's South Island on the port beam! Still on ship-cleaning duties so no watch. Luxury to sit there supping tea at 0830 without having to worry about rushing up to the bridge. Off Dunedin at 1100 and I find it hard to contain my excitement at the prospect of getting back to New Zealand, to Fiona and to some semblance of normality.

8 March 1987
I've been unable to eat for the last 24 hours and I'm doing my level best not to burst with excitement at the prospect of sailing into Wellington tomorrow. We've been away for 64 days and have travelled 7000 miles. And, what's more, we've given one in the eye to all those governments who had the temerity to assume that Antarctica was their exclusive reserve. We've put an NGO toe-hold on the continent and can look forward to years of cut and thrust towards achieving the goal – World Park status for the continent.

We finally sailed into Wellington during the afternoon of Tuesday the 9th of March 1987. There to meet us were a lot of familiar faces holding their banners of welcome. The newspapers ran a picture the following day of Fiona and I hugging, but the rest of the day was lost in a welter of beer, partying and revelry. We arrived in Auckland a week later to another round of welcomes and parties. The 'international' mob of Greenpeace personnel turned up to 'analyse' the voyage and the coolness between those of us who had actually carried out the job and those who had – certainly in Maureen's case – done their best, in our opinion, to hinder our efforts from the security of their offices – was tangible. The analysis had few benefits for us: it merely confirmed what we had decided on board months previously. I was asked to lead the expedition again and I made it clear that I wanted a clear mandate to operate exactly as I had before – in collusion with a tight group of people who knew what was needed and with minimum interference from the honchos who presumed to organise us and control events.

Chapter 27

Back to London and to the Antarctic again
A close shave in East Germany

Fiona and I went back to the UK via Fiji and Vancouver, arriving in late April 1987. We stayed at 19 Rheidol Terrace for a few days before finding a flat in Stamford Hill. I collected my motorbike from the storage depot and spent weeks driving aimlessly around while Fiona looked for work and came on mini-holidays with me. I bought a car from a friend of my mother's whose husband had died and we set off for the 'grand-tour' of Europe, loosely following a route defined by the towns and regions in which Van Gough had lived and worked but starting in the fiord region of Norway.

Even this far away from McTaggart, I received a summons to travel back to Lewes for an important planning meeting. While such an interruption was inconvenient, in truth, I couldn't wait to get home, get back in the thick of things and begin planning the next trip. Holidays for me were an unnecessary diversion. I was surprised to find that the increasing familiarity between Fiona and I in the drabness of London as opposed to the splendour and exotica of the New Zealand beaches began to distance us.

The tour of Europe had a notable interlude. Fiona's mother was German and her place of birth was a small village which had the misfortune to be within half a kilometre of the dividing line agreed by the occupying forces at the end of the war. For Fiona's mother, the village was condemned to the 'wrong' side, just over the border in what was then Soviet territory. She had illegally absconded from the village shortly after the war and had married – amazingly for the time – an English serviceman whom she had met during the latter stages of the conflict. She had never been back to her village of birth and every attempt to secure the necessary permits and visas had been denied her in the intervening years. Fiona and I told her that we would try to get there, although we felt certain we would have as little success as she had.

We arrived in Berlin and stayed in West Berlin with Jochen Vorfelder, our German journalist friend from the last trip. We crossed into East Berlin after having cleared our bags, on Jochen's advice, of everything which was 'western', and as we were filing through the checkpoint barrier being scrutinised in a very intimidating manner by bullish guards, one of them pointed to me and crooked his finger in an unmistakeable 'come hither' motion. Jokingly, I looked around and mouthed 'Who? Me?' He nodded. I was swept behind a one-way door and ordered to sit on a wooden seat while the guard rummaged through my bag. I offered a silent thanks to Jochen. The bag contained nothing except a map of East Berlin and my note book . . . and a rusting Greenpeace badge which the guard extracted between thumb and forefinger with a look of mixed curiosity and triumph on his face as he held it aloft and viewed it through half-closed eyes. With that, he left. So here I was in East Germany under the control of its Soviet overlords, alone in what amounted to a cell with no obvious way out. Visions of extracted fingernails, salt mines and gulags swam before my eyes. All my deepest fears about communism, into which I had been indoctrinated over 30 years, surfaced. An hour later, the guard returned. They had confiscated the badge and had, no doubt, photocopied my note book in which every Greenpeace activists' number was listed. I was free to leave. Fiona was waiting for me along with twenty other people fretting for their partners and friends who had likewise been detained. One woman had been waiting for eight hours for her friend.

We headed for the Reiseburo where, after an hour's wait, we asked innocently for a permit to visit Fiona's mother's birthplace. To our utter amazement, we were asked nothing more but received the stamp in our passports along with a request for 20 ostmarks each. I pointed out to the woman, this time more forcefully, exactly where the town was.

'There,' I pointed, 'Just half a kilometre from the border. It's possible? Kein probleme?'

Kein probleme. We spent the rest of the day not believing our luck as we tried to wring an ounce of humour from the dour cafes and bars of East Berlin. We still had to get yet another visa when we left the sanctuary of the autobahn running from West Berlin through East Germany to the West but things looked promising. The following day, we came off the autobahn at the designated patrol point and were ushered into a fair replica of the booth I had been held in the previous day. But a very affable guard in full uniform merrily stamped our passports again as I went through the 'do-you-realise-it's-so-close-to-the-border?' routine. It seemed as though we had made it as he waved away our enquiries and gave us directions in half-German and half-English. There was only one requirement: we had to book into a hotel in Magdeburg. Arrangements had already been made and we were expected.

As we left the autobahn, we stepped into the English countryside of the 1950s. The air hummed and buzzed with clouds of insects and every mile or so, we had to clean the windscreen of their squashed bodies. Every village was approached by narrow, unsealed roads on which no traffic was seen. Chickens clucked and pecked in the road and the locals stared at us as though we were from another planet. It was stifling hot and the clouds of midges and gnats were enormous: no Common Agricultural Policy subsidised pesticides here. We saw a sign to our destination announcing that it was one kilometre distant. As we turned a bend, we saw the border up ahead: an endless wire mesh fence standing 20 feet high, observation posts dotted along its length. More disconcerting was the presence of a road block in the form of a single bar painted red and white, weighted at one end at which stood a sentry box. It was empty and the arm of the barrier was up. Our way was unbarred. Feeling slightly uncomfortable, I stopped the car and sounded the horn. Nothing. I did it again. Still no reaction. We had the necessary visas. We drove on.

We entered the village in the late afternoon. Fiona, after she had explained who she was to ageing locals, was greeted like a long lost daughter which, I suppose, in many ways she was. Aunts, uncles and family friends came in their droves to question Fiona about Marga whom they had not seen in forty years and the afternoon was spent embracing and crying on shoulders and wandering around this enchanting village which had not changed in centuries. I walked around with a permanent smile on my face, a lump in my throat and tears in my eyes. The only dark moment came when the local civilian security man questioned us about our visit and insisted – the downcast eyes of the locals told me I should not object – that I went to his house where he would phone the border patrols to get 'clearance', an invitation I refused politely. Big mistake.

Within ten minutes of saying tearful farewells, a motorbike roared alongside the car, a soldier pointing a sten gun at us with one hand while driving with the other. We were under arrest. He covered us with his gun as he plugged a telephone lead into a post in the hedge and spoke to his superior. Within a few minutes, two jeeps and a staff car came careering up the road and half a dozen stony-faced and rather large soldiers piled out of the jeeps, some taking over the task of threatening us with guns. An officer emerged from the staff car.

Dismissing the visas I showed him in our passports, he said in passable English, 'You,' pointing to me, 'drive the car and follow us. She comes in the staff car with me.'

That order went beyond my particular threshold and I flatly refused. 'We stay together. End of story.'

After ten minutes of this test of wills, he relented and Fiona climbed into our car with me at the wheel. Two soldiers climbed in the back amongst the holiday debris of dirty clothes and towels spread out to dry, sten gun muzzles like flag poles sticking out of the windows. We followed the jeep ahead of us to an army camp some miles away. We were escorted into a barrack-like building along the corridor of which silent and stony-faced guards were posted at every door. We were ushered into a small room, bare but for a table and two chairs. We were locked in. Fiona sat on a chair, laid her head on the table and slept while I paced the room wondering if the pain of having fingernails drawn passed after the first one or two. By late evening, I began to fear that we would be held overnight and the thought of being charged as spies even occurred to me. The door was eventually unlocked and in walked a senior officer. He held our passports in his hand, an encouraging sign.

In perfect English he explained, 'Mr Wilkinson, Miss Weightman, I must apologise for the manner in which you have been treated today. Your visas are of course in order to allow you to travel as far as the sentry post a mile from the village at which point you are required to obtain a third and final visa which allows you access to the village itself.'

As I opened my mouth to protest, he held up his hand. 'I know that the post was unmanned and the soldier who was meant to be at his post will be dealt with accordingly. You are entirely innocent of any wrong doing and I hope you will accept my apologies for this inconvenience. But I must ask you now to travel back immediately to your hotel in Magdeburg from where I will be informed of your arrival. Then tomorrow morning, I must ask you to travel directly on the access road into West Germany.'

I said, 'You need have no fear that we will travel directly into West Germany tomorrow morning – at first light.'

With that, he shook our hands and Fiona and I were free. By 10 in the morning we were back in the West and thankful to be there. Our grand tour over, we arrived back in the UK and went through the same procedure as before – staying briefly in the old stand-by, 19 Rheidol Terrace, before finding a flat, this time in Lavender Hill in Battersea.

I went to see McTaggart to mull over the next Antarctic trip and found him as unhappy with the new UK office regime as he had professed to be with the one he had ousted the previous year. Despite his gregarious nature, I had never held out much hope that he would hit it off with an English lord. David knew I was broke. He also knew that people like Ken, Athel, John Castle and others were in a similar position. He told me that he felt it reasonable and fair, especially given the immense wealth Greenpeace had accumulated since the *Warrior* sinking, that us 'veterans' should be given an allowance equal to $1,500 for every year of work for Greenpeace. This would mean a nice $15,000 for me and I shook hands with David and turned my attention to the task of selecting the next wintering team.

Keith Swenson was to be the leader – that was already decided and agreed. I went to Washington where Greenpeace's redoubtable Nancy Foote and red-headed rising star of Greenpeace, Kelly Rigg, oversaw the US side of the Antarctic campaign while thinking they ran the entire show. Between interviewing potential over-winterers, I met a guy called Paul Bogart who was to feature large in the Antarctic campaign in future years and who was to become a good friend. He was having a hard time with his love life at the time, a bind he seemed to get into with incredible regularity over the years, and the fact that I took time to talk to him about it seemed to be appreciated.

The Washington trip had not produced people of the necessary calibre although one guy we saw came very close to being selected. When asked the normal round of questions about drugs, women and living in close proximity to a small group of people for extended periods of time, this guy didn't trot out the normal measured responses of most candidates: instead, he enthused, 'Drugs? Man I've tried them all! And liked them all too! Women? I try to get laid as often as I can, man. Shit! Don't we all?'

He had us in fits of laughter and I damn near appointed him since he would have been such lively and amusing company. I convinced

Greenpeace that I needed to hire a car to travel around Europe to interview the short-listed candidates. My journey would take me to Norway, Germany, France and Italy and I took Fiona along for a second sweep around Europe. In the event, not one of the people I met actually became a wintering team member, although I did select two of the people I saw. They either pulled out at the last moment or events later down the line precluded them.

I now faced a peculiar situation: I was about to go back to New Zealand and leave Fiona in the UK. It was September 1987. I was 40 years old and had worked for Greenpeace for ten years. I had no house, only an uncertain and minimal income from Greenpeace which had admittedly risen substantially in the last few years but was still only running at $15,000 a year pro-rata, and a relationship which was waning in its intensity.

Although I was genuinely upset at the prospect of leaving Fiona for my third trip to the Antarctic, I couldn't wait to get back to the old familiar atmosphere of the ship, the exhilaration of working in Auckland knowing that I would be travelling across the Southern Ocean in the company of good people to see the last truly isolated wilderness on the planet. I was joining what was fast becoming a well-oiled machine: the process of preparing and executing an Antarctic expedition was beginning to be relatively easy to carry out. It was still very hard work but we knew how to pursue our task with something approaching confidence, professionalism and efficiency.

The 1987-88 expedition was to be memorable for many reasons. In terms of the activities we carried out, the trip was quite straightforward: we did nothing of great import apart from establishing our credentials and underpinning our growing maturity in Antarctic circles. But my third expedition was to prove so emotionally traumatic for me that I resigned and refused to go on the first ever 'second leg' trip to the Peninsular region after re-supplying our base and an enforced stop-over in Lyttelton due to engine breakdown pushed the entire crew into a nether-world of parties and hedonism for a three week period which we hoped would never end. As a portent of what was to come, I heard with a heavy heart that the incumbent wintering team of Kevin, Gudrun, Justin and Cornelius was irrevocably split and on a constant war-footing.

Chapter 28

Into the madhouse: 1987-88 trip

I had achieved my goal and met the Greenpeace objective – an Antarctic expedition which established the first ever NGO semi-permanent base on Antarctica, albeit after an initial failure. The opportunity to return yet again was, however, irresistible.

As I packed my battered suitcase in preparation for my third trip, I thought about the visit I had made to Mum's place, a few days before, when we drank a whisky in toast to a successful trip, and I had cried on her shoulder. She told me that she was glad my father had not been around to witness the break-up of my marriage. Her desperate hope, I knew, was that I would marry and have children before I was too old and, more to the point, before she died. I knew she would have been happy to see me abandon this globe-trotting for a life of domesticity and fatherhood.

But whatever the future held, I was here, at Heathrow yet again, waiting for the boarding announcement. I was then, and still am today, a nervous flyer. While I was excited about the flight, Jumbo jets seemed very reluctant to leave the ground and I always had the feeling that we should have been airborne long ago while still stubbornly stuck to the runway. And in any case, a Jumbo weighs 500-odd tons on take-off. How is that possible? I had also realised that even the faintest glimmer of hope I harboured for an eventual return to Greenpeace UK was fast disappearing. I was, quite simply, not wanted and so long as I kept my distance and did not darken their door, it seemed that International was quite prepared to tolerate my involvement in the Antarctic campaign. It suited me for the time being, and I very rarely thought much beyond the next voyage. Never, for instance, did I think about what I would do when and if the Antarctic bubble burst and how I would earn an income without Greenpeace.

This left me in a peculiar position. I was increasingly critical of the organisation which paid me. The UK office had quite literally nosedived in terms of its profile since we had been ousted and while they were clearly benefiting financially from the post-*Warrior* sinking, in terms of campaigns and visibility, the organisation had almost disappeared. But for now, I buried these thoughts as deeply as I could, the better to concentrate on the task in hand.

Arriving in Auckland, Ken, Keith and Martini met me in the ship's van and we drove to the nearest pub for a welcoming pint of ice-cold and almost unpalatable Kiwi beer. Keith, who had been in touch with the wintering team throughout the winter, gave me bleak news indeed. I already knew that things were not exactly going smoothly on the base, but apparently the cohesion had broken down completely and the team had divided into two factions which were virtually at war.

The genesis of this situation were unclear then and remained so even after dissection on board later, but in essence, it seemed that Gudrun had some kind of medical problem during the latter months which required Cornelius to examine her and administer treatment. Gudrun, through the now highly vociferous and table-thumping Kevin, had accused Cornelius of medical malpractice based on what amounted to an assault, a charge he vehemently denied.

The news from Keith got worse. He then calmly told me that the American female doctor we had belatedly appointed, a woman called Lynn Horton, was not, in his view, suited to the task in hand. She was very competent, highly motivated and keen to be part of the wintering team but did not appear to possess the mentality and attitude to the rigours of what would be, we knew, an emotionally harrowing trip.

This was to be the first time we would have to face a retiring wintering team, to collect them and cosset their fragile emotional states when we ourselves were in all likelihood to be in pretty tender conditions ourselves. We not only had the normal run-of-the-mill problems to contend with – the re-supply run itself and planning what were destined to be two very tiring 'legs' to the trip – but we were constantly assailed by the need to form an in-going team of winterers who were strong emotionally, physically and psychologically. As the days passed, the tensions, as usual, began to show and we vented those emotions on Sunday mornings by kicking a football around in a park at the back of Martini's house in Grey Lynn. These games became essential for many of us and were looked forward to and participated in by many of the people from the office or those peripheral to the expedition and the ship. Our photographer for the trip was James Perez, a very likeable, loud and thoroughly engaging American who previously shot official match pictures for the San Francisco 49ers, so his shots of our football games were always eagerly awaited: we were rarely disappointed with the quality.

A month before departure, we learned that Lynn had a boyfriend back in the States. The relationship was only three months old. Despite her protestations to the contrary, we felt that she would not be able to maintain stability over the course of a year in Antarctic isolation without ministering to such a new and fragile relationship. A phone call from McFarlane, the officer in charge of Scott Base via his Christchurch office, alerted us to a worsening situation at the base camp. He advised us that Kevin and Gudrun had been away from Cape Evans for a week without making the necessary radio links with Justin to confirm their safety. They had been seen by a field party from Scott Base, way over in the dry valleys a few days previously, but no word had been received from them since. Keith and I conferred and agreed that the situation demanded a search and rescue request from the authorities. We were not inclined to ask for one at that precise moment since another twenty four hours would not significantly lessen their chances of being found and any search and rescue would confirm our amateur status in the eyes of our detractors, particularly the Americans who were just waiting for just such an opportunity to label all 'amateur' expeditions as liabilities and drains on their own facilities and resources.

Kevin was well aware of the need to demonstrate our self-sufficiency. Earlier in the year he had refused to call on the New Zealanders for help, even when he was lying in a tent only yards from their base with broken ribs sustained from a crash when his skidoo overturned. He had chosen instead to spend three days chewing pain-killers rather than succumb to the Antarctic emergency code of mutual help in dangerous situations. But this situation we now faced was potentially one of life and death and we decided to act.

McFarlane, a thoroughly decent bloke, accepted our call with the request to begin a search and rescue mission in subdued and slightly conspiratorial tones since he knew its seriousness, not only for Kevin and Gudrun's safety but for the credibility of the Greenpeace expedition. Thankfully, they were both found alive and well and in no difficulties before the full-blown operation could get underway but Kevin's attitude to the episode was one of complete contempt for what he considered our over-reaction. We henceforth initiated a 48 hours no-contact-alert programme which was never abused again.

Ken planned an ice/snow-familiarisation trip for some of the crew who would be most in need of it. He planned to take a party to Mount Cook in the South Island and, despite my protestations, he insisted that, as campaigner and expedition 'leader', I should go. We flew from Ardmore airport just outside Auckland in a tiny aircraft crammed full of equipment and vulnerable flesh. Once airborne, our young pilot breezily announced with a grin that he was in fact an aircraft mechanic and was trying for his pilot's licence. And, oh yes, once we had refuelled in Christchurch, the turbulence we were already experiencing would be severe as we crossed the mountains, so be prepared. I looked at Ken with a startled expression: he was lost in reading a book and returned my gaze with a quizzical look. Over Cook Strait, the aircraft moved around so much that Henk Haazen actually threw up but we arrived safely at the airstrip close to the Mount Cook glacier after a gruelling but spectacularly scenic flight.

After ensconcing ourselves in one of the base huts on the valley floor (provided for idiots such as us by the authorities), we prepared our activities for the following few days. En route to the glacier, we practiced abseiling and after an hour or so of this, we began the march along the track which paralleled the glacier 600 feet below. Between the glacier and the path was a scree slope which had been cut by the glacier over the years and down this near vertical scree we slid and slithered to the glacier surface, followed by a few tons of rock and rubble.

We buckled crampons over our stiff walking boots. Ken had provided me with the cheapest pair he could find and within a few paces on the ice, I was limping and blisters were already forming on my feet. Somehow, I made it to the survival hut, but not before I had literally collapsed with exhaustion once or twice, a spectacle which had us all – including me – helpless with laughter. Despite the pain I was in, I was mesmerised by the glacier. It was spectacular in its scale and implacability, but it was also a mess of rocks and dirty ice pushed every which way by the inexorable pressure of the ice descending from the mountain. At the hut, we luxuriated in the absence of heavy backpacks and, in my case, of crippling boots as we drank tea and soaked up the scenery. I spotted two bright green birds flying up the glacier towards our position. To my amazement, they continued in our direction and landed no more than twenty feet from us as we sprawled on the ground. They were Keas, native New Zealand parrots, reportedly the most fearless and inquisitive of all the native bird species. One simply walked towards me, hopped onto my legs, down the other side and began pecking my wind jacket, as if to say, 'Is this good to eat?' I was told that on a previous trip here, Keas were seen to hang upside down from the guttering around the hut to see what was going on inside.

We were now above the snowline on the mountain and began practicing breaking someone's fall into a crevasse by using the rope which attached us one to another. Then we made snow caves which would protect us from exposure should we be caught out in sub-zero, nil visibility conditions. They were surprisingly comfortable and warm, so long as the cold air sink built into them was deep enough. After four days of virtual rest, my feet were recovering somewhat but the thought of going climbing – our next activity – did not bode well for their continued healing. Nonetheless, I tied the tortuous boots lightly and off we set to climb Aguille Rouge which Keith told me as casually as possible, was a five hour climb, at the end of which we would build an ice cave and sleep there that evening.

As the gentle slope of the snow face steepened we began climbing, line astern and using the footholds of the preceding person to gain purchase. All was going well for a while, although my feet were beginning to chafe quite badly again. Then the wind picked up quite strongly. We continued and I noticed that we were now climbing at a 60 degree angle to the horizontal; it had also begun to snow quite heavily. We had now climbed most of the distance and were in a very exposed position on the mountain face. Guys were being knocked flat by the wind which was driving stinging snow into our faces as well as into every crevice of our clothing.

Keith indicated that it was time to leave, but not upwards, thankfully. He told us all to follow him one at a time and to do exactly as he did. He sat on his arse, facing down the vertiginous slope, kicked himself forwards and let gravity do the rest. The only input each of us had into the descent was to use our ice-axes as rudders to steer with and as an emergency anchor if we were about to die or lose control of the descent. Initial terror at the steepness of the incline quickly turned into pure delight. After a minute of descent, we had cleared the bad weather and emerged into sunlight. The mountain was spectacular and we whooped and shouted like a bunch of schoolkids at the pure thrill of sliding down a mountain at twenty miles an hour. Weight and mass soon overcame gravitational pull and we gathered in a grinning, happy group and made our way back to the hut. What had taken us three hours to climb, we had descended in what felt like as many minutes.

It was time to leave Mount Cook and face the possibly more dangerous task of flying back to Auckland. I told Keith that I could not, under any circumstances, contemplate walking out wearing the boots which crippled me so brutally. Even Werner, who manfully agreed to temporarily swap boots with me, agreed that they were excruciating to wear for more than a few minutes. I had an idea: I asked if anyone had had the foresight to bring a pair of trainers with them. Peter Malcolm had and I asked if I could use them. Keith snorted his contempt at this idea, saying that while trainers would be ok on the descent to the glacier as it was a mainly grass and rubble surface, I would need crampons to walk out of the icy glacier. No-one, he said, had ever used crampons with trainers. Well, I did, and I walked out on them, much to the amusement of most and to Keith's chagrin, although to his credit, he asked me to pose for his camera as proof of the event.

We now had to climb up the 600 foot scree slope to the roadway which led back to our base camp, showers and relative comfort. We were told to 'tread on the rocks as though they were eggshells'. Rock falls were regular occurrences. It took us maybe two hours to reach the pathway at the top of the moraine. Only one minor rock fall occurred but at the top we were all exhausted and grateful to be only an hour's march away from our base camp, showers, hot meals and beer. We drove back to Christchurch and I flew from there to Auckland, the sooner to continue the preparation of the expedition while the others drove back, arriving the following day.

With Lynn out as an overwinterer due to fears of her emotional strength over the course of a year, we decided that she should make the trip and act as an understudy but it meant that Keith had to do some fast footwork to line up his team. Two last minute appointments brought his team up to full strength. He decided, with our blessing, not to take a doctor at all. He would act as paramedic, a position which he was qualified to fulfil. He beefed up the science programme by appointing a Polish marine biologist, rotund and jovial Wojtek Moskal, and dragooned Dutchman Sjoerd Jongens in as the electronics/communications expert. With only days to go before we left, we were set and everything finally clicked into place. We had many of the old salts from previous trips on board: Ken was to be my 8-12 watch mentor again and we were skippered once more by the redoubtable Jim Cottier. Bruce Adams was with us again, directing an American camera crew, Ray and Frank. Two journalists accompanied us: an Italian called Massimo and an American called Lesley Roberts. Maj De Poorter came again as the campaign assistant/environmental impact assessor.

Christmas 1987 came and we celebrated it in port before leaving a few days later on the third trip to Antarctica. It was to end, quite literally, in tears.

28 December 1987

Left the quayside in Auckland at 1410 bound for Wellington with sixty people cheering us off. NZ TV and four other media crews present. Hectic morning spent lashing down cargo and preparing for sea, sending off messages and generally trying to survive the chaos of well-wishing friends and supporters clambering all over the ship as we try to get ready for a long sea passage. Mixed feelings as always as we leave good friends and friendly Auckland but it's good to be finally on our way in good weather as we pass Rangitoto, sipping well-earned beers on the foredeck. Swell increases during the evening watch and I take a pill – here we go again. Starboard poop deck barrels come loose within ten minutes of rolling and the fuel pump was found to be unlashed.

30 December 1987

As we're early for our planned arrival in Wellington, we anchor at Castle Point. We rescue people in a small dinghy seen to be in trouble off the coast and hear later that we made it to the front page of the local rag. Leave Castle Point at 2130.

31st December 1987

I proudly steer the *Black Pig*, as she's now affectionately known, into the harbour capital. Only a few press here to greet us.

3 January 1988

Had the Antarctic Association on board this morning who complain that our base is 'too close to the historic site' of Scott's Hut at Cape Evans. They deliver a letter of complaint to me and I asked them if I could see a copy of the letter they (presumably) must have sent to the US authorities making a similar complaint that the huge, polluting and totally unsightly McMurdo base is too close to Scott's Discovery Base at Hut Point, to which there is an embarrassed and awkward silence. I hand them the letter back saying that I'll accept it when they can show me a similar letter to the US. They leave red-faced and so they should. Finally depart port for Lyttelton at 1545. Sit in my cabin with Sjoerd (Dutch base radio operator and electrician), Peter Malcolm , Maj, Henk and Martini and drink far too many beers.

4 January 1988
Jim became a grandfather today and he's roundly congratulated. Arrive Lyttelton at 1030 to a very good reception and a lot of local press on the quayside. Press finally away by noon only to be followed by hoards of people who swarm all over the ship. It's great to see such interest and there's a lot of goodwill here in Lyttelton. To the British Hotel tonight with Jim in fine fettle. The pub is a biker hangout and these Mongrel Mob Maoris – six feet wide, tattooed and clad in ripped leather – turn out to be a great bunch. Peter Malcolm has them in stitches with his fluorescent socks and multi-coloured jumpers, not to mention his very British accent. Great night all round.

5 January 1988
On deck until lunch with Ken. Afternoon spent on the computer until I go for inflatable driving test with Ken which I apparently pass. Lots of messages from all over the Greenpeace empire today, most of them garbage and most of which I commit to the bin without responding. It seems as though people in the 'new' organisation have to justify their existence by sending out hundreds of facile, lengthy messages which generally contain only one pertinent piece of information – if that – hidden in its midst. Wojtek and Keith into Christchurch to outfit Wojtek. He's now officially a winterer.

6 January 1988
Much activity on the ship today. Bob Thompson (NZARP) arrives during the afternoon with an MP in tow and we have a good discussion centring on mining. Attitudes seem to have mellowed but I still feel that Thompson presents one face to us and another to the Antarctic Division about us.

British Hotel in the evening after a visit to see an Irish band at Warners in Christchurch. God, they were bad!

7th January 1988
Routine day for the most part, working on deck and receiving a constant stream of visitors and well-wishers. Presents, gifts of food, wine and beer arrive regularly and the people here, renowned for their hospitality, have taken us to their hearts and vice versa. The British Hotel staff and clients insist on throwing a party for us tonight (we didn't need much persuading) and the party continues back on board the ship until 0430, a very traditional way to mark our last night in port.

The local Mongrel Mob showed up on the quayside and we were warned by the locals that they should not be allowed on board as they would start trouble, at which point Jim ordered us all up on deck to stand there looking as tough as we could while he told them to leave. I'm impressed by Jim's firmness and refusal to be intimidated as just one of these heavy dudes could surely have taken Jim, me and about three of the others out single-handedly.

Later, one of the Mongrel gang waltzed into the saloon as calm as you like and asked to use the loo. As I was escorting him to the forward head, Jim came down the alleyway and asked me what was going on. I told him this guy needed the loo at which point Jim exploded, 'Jesus Christ, Wilks! I've just spent ten minutes telling these guys they can't come on board and now you're taking one of them to the bloody loo! Off! Off! Get off the ship!'

I fall into bed at 0300 and let the party continue. As I drift off to sleep, I wonder how the winterers feel at this moment, their last few hours ashore for 12 months.

8 January 1988
Departure day and I take the opportunity, caused by the last minute delay in the arrival of parts for the satellite communications, to sign an affidavit in support of the court case currently being heard in the UK between the Dutch branch of GP and BNFL for the pipe-blocking action by Hans and his crew. It looks ominous for Hans and I fully expect him to get banged up. Back on board by midday when there's a lot of rushing around on deck preparing to get underway. Then off to Christchurch airport to see the Deep Freeze US outfit where Bob Harler of the National Science

Foundation meets us. He and other officials are very cool towards us but do indicate that the practice of dumping metallic waste through the ice at McMurdo (tide-cracking) has been abandoned (that's one little victory for our presence there) and that the policy towards non-governmental organisations has changed due to a NSF directive. We can now expect to receive local weather and ice information.

We finally slip our moorings at 1915 before a good-sized crowd. By 2100, I've got the press release and photo away and I go on watch for the first of over 100 four-hour stints on the bridge. Moderate swell running which picks up by 2400 as we come off watch and there's a lot of sickness on board as people feel the pitch and roll of the vessel in deep water for the first time. One particular roll devastated the cabin. By 0500 the ship is heading back to Lyttelton as the engine room reports that the rings on some of the pistons on the starboard main engine have disintegrated. We're anchored in Pigeon Bay, just 12 miles from Lyttelton by 0600.

From the 10th of January 1988 to the 23rd January 1988, the *Black Pig* was immobilised in the port of Lyttelton while repairs were made to the ship's starboard engine. The engineers occasionally required our assistance in cleaning up oil or hauling parts through the hatch cover, but in the main, the engineers worked round the clock without needing our unskilled labour, leaving the majority of us free to enjoy an unexpected windfall of thirteen days ashore.

As we cruised into Lyttelton on the port engine, Annie, the landlady of the British Hotel, called us on the VHF at 0700 to tell us that she was opening up the pub! While the enforced stay started out in a reasonably subdued manner, within a few days, we newly adopted sons and daughters of Lyttelton were being endlessly feted by the hospitable townsfolk. We went to countless parties and sojourns into Christchurch and we spent our time as though every day was our last. We organised a half-decent football team which played a quite brutal game against the crew of a Russian stern trawler, leaving us bruised and battered but victorious. People began to compete to invite us to dinner and on just about every evening we'd find ourselves entertained by different folks in town after which we'd invariably end up in the British where Annie would prepare us gigantic late-night snacks of hot-dogs and chips for which she refused to accept payment.

While all this hedonism was in progress, I tried to keep sane by attending to the administrative demands of the expedition and spent most of my days at the computer or driving the crane for the engineers as they pulled out massive pieces of metal from the engine room and lowered replacement parts into the bowels of the ship.

One of the most important decisions we had to make in the light of the ship breakdown was whether or not to cancel the second leg of the voyage to the Peninsular. Based on my experience of previous trips, together with the enforced delay we were experiencing and the fact that the crew would be wasted after even the first leg, I argued with Kelly Rigg that we should abandon the second leg, a view to which she reluctantly and, as it turned out, only temporarily agreed. All this discussion was swept aside on the 22nd when the engineers announced that we could leave whenever we felt ready. In order to get us out of Lyttelton, to which many of the crew were becoming very attached, Jim and I decided we should leave the very next day.

Our final day and night in Lyttelton will remain with me for a long time. It was traditional 'birdman' day in the port when all manner of weird costumes and designs were worn by an endless line of townsfolk as they propelled themselves off the jetty in attempts to 'fly'. The party atmosphere on board was infectious and soon the ship was jammed with literally hundreds of people taking advantage of its close proximity to the action. By mid-afternoon, Ken had rigged up a stereo system on deck which was belting out Talk Talk across the harbour and the mother of all parties was in full swing on board.

I had dinner with some well-wishers that evening and in the early hours of the morning we sat in the long grass at the side of a charming little house on the steep slopes, overlooking the harbour and our little ship beneath a sky studded with a million stars. As we sat there, looking down on the ship and discussing our imminent voyage, I was startled by the arrival of three sheep, kept by the owner of the plot of land, which came and nuzzled us like so many cats. On the 23rd we finally steamed out of the famous harbour from where so many expeditions had set off in the past. Our departure was attended by all the good people and friends we had met who showered us with gifts and presents of food and hooch – as if we hadn't had enough over the previous two weeks. Lyttelton will always have a place in my heart and I will never forget those two weeks or the warm hospitality shown to us.

23 January 1988

Leave Lyttleton at 0900 and I steer out of port (always a bummer as you miss out on all the farewells, but it does mean that you avoid the arduous job of securing the mooring lines in the lockers) and don't get off the wheel until 1030. The sea is flat calm and the engine noise has changed totally – none of the familiar chuff-chuff which so characterised the ship hitherto. Pull into Port Levy Bay to allow the engineers and the helo guys to finish their last minute work away from the slight swell which has developed and finally away by 1330 as we hug the coast to allow a few hours of acclimatisation. Keith a little pensive tonight. Albatrosses all around the ship and three or four big sharks seen. Two beers with Ken then bed by 0100.

24 January 1988

Dog-tired when called at 0700 but make it to breakfast at 0740. Seals, albatrosses and another shark seen during watch. The NZ Royal Navy cutter *Taupo* steams around us during the watch and then shows us her turn of speed as she careers off to the starboard and for the coast. Bruce interviews me in the afternoon and I then prepare a long telex to the base to outline re-supply practicalities. Laze in the beautiful late afternoon sun as I doze on the foredeck. We leave the NZ coast today and head for the 180 meridian on a slightly west of south course (188). Swell increases in the afternoon but still very calm and hot in a gentle southeaster. Talk to the base at 1915. Tensions evident in their voices. Beautiful evening on watch and when it grows dark, the sky is studded with millions of glittering stars. Two beers with Ken and Egon. Bed at 0040.

25 January 1988

Still calm but swell picks up mid-morning. Overcast and foggy after a bright start. Crew meeting planned for tonight to discuss Cape Evans ops and ice safety. Seas still remarkably calm as we pass 52 south at noon. No response from the base to my long telex. Sun disappears as the weather claggs in. Temperature plus 11. Surprise fire drill has us all up and jumping and the muster on the poop deck is in good time.

26 January 1988

Dull, grey weather. Noon position 54 30 south, 176 30 east. Prepare an update for the Greenpeace offices after lunch. In the afternoon, I pack my emergency gear for abandon to ice. This backpack will stand sentinel by the doorway for the rest of the trip in case we are forced into any sort of emergency evacuation. Do the campaign accounts and then ask Dave Woolan for any response from the base to the telex – still none. Still calm but a northwesterly swell is now gathering which corkscrews us along form the starboard quarter. Uneventful watch during which the highlight is making contact with the yacht bearing the ridiculous name of the *Alan and Vi Thistlethwaite* in honour of the couple who bought it on behalf of the Australian Bicentenary expedition, whose five-strong crew is to climb Mt Minto as a celebration – quite what they're celebrating is lost on me. They're off Cape Adare. The temperature at the Greenpeace base is reported to be PLUS 8! There's also apparently more snow around than last year and the store shed is still buried beneath a drift. Strange familiar routine descends on the ship. Not much going on in the saloon at night but the atmosphere is buoyant.

27 January 1988
Weather still overcast, drizzling and generally miserable although wind is still 10 knots from NNE and the resultant gentle following swell makes life bearable. Antarctic Convergence in the small hours of tomorrow and we reach 60 south in the morning. Two beers and a rum with Ken and bed at 0100 after sending a hopefully comforting reply to Kevin.

28 January 1988
Comet day today. Up at 0745, grab some tea after a wash down at the sink and take the wheel at 0800. Grey, lumpy seas from the port quarter, light winds from the NE. The *Greenwave* (US supply ship) reports she's reduced to 4 knots in heavy weather to the east of us and southerlies are predicted for us which thankfully don't materialise. Felt achy all day and I resign myself to the fact that I'm coming down with my seasonal bout of the flu. Feel very tired again and after a long talk with Kevin, (he's marginally more conciliatory) I fall asleep in the saloon and arrive late for watch. 62 south now but still no bergs. Twilight all night for the first time. Should be in the pack ice on Saturday and arrive Ross Island on Monday.

29 January 1988
Saw our first berg at 64 south at 0935 and a school of whales come and feed around the ship a little later on, confirming that we are in the

Antarctic proper now. It's so good to be back. Weather still good to us and more predicted southerlies only blew for an hour or so before backing. Crew meeting today at which I bring the crew up to speed with campaign news and Peter Malcolm goes into re-supply details; Maj talks about environmental constraints on our activities. We then get a tour around a spectacular 'becaved' berg, courtesy of Jim and in lighthearted mood we descend to the daylit saloon at 2400 for a party to celebrate the fact that Ken has engineered a day off watch for the 8-12 tomorrow.

30 January 1988

What bliss and luxury to lie in bed until 1230! Brief messages off to Kelly and others and we enter the pack at 2000. Jim takes his first ice-spotting flight and reports loose pack all around the ship. Ken sends me up the crow's nest and I see the same scenery from this lofty vantage point. We are forced to head NE and even N once or twice to access the southerly leads. First contact with McMurdo at 2200. They kindly give us a 24 hour weather prognosis 'at our own risk' in their peculiar, drawling tone which has the pitch of Mickey Mouse, over the UHF. But the fact that they have agreed to give us weather information is a moral victory of sorts; they now at least recognise us as a legitimate, if unwelcome expedition. Keith and I on the helo deck for fire and marshalling duties and then bed by 0200.

31 January 1988

Clear of pack by 1000. Heading 180, overcast, light NW winds, gentle swell. Confronted by strips of brash ice and pack throughout the day, but in clear water by 2100. Tidy cabin and do my dobying and then Lynn comes to my cabin asking if she can be treated as press which I find laughable. Her justification is that some obscure US magazine has apparently asked her to write an article on her 'US female doctor in Antarctica on Greenpeace ship full of gung-ho males' experience. I tell her 'no' and deny her any special privileges reserved for the press. Can't sleep tonight as I contemplate the coming events of the next few days and my cabin-mate Swenson's snoring does nothing for my ability to drift off into a much needed sleep. Large pod of orcas around the ship this afternoon and the light was quite extraordinary as it was reflected from a huge iceberg which sat implacably on the horizon this evening.

1 February 1988

My restless night left me tired and grumpy and I awoke with a feeling of foreboding at the prospect of the reunion with the winterers. Although it will be a memorable occasion – the first time we've seen them in 12 months – it will, I know, be a traumatic affair as all the pent-up emotions and grudges of the last year come tumbling out. Another flat calm day with snow showers – some heavy enough to encourage a brief snowball fight between me and Ken. Watch was mundane and no wildlife chose to grace us with its presence. Work on deck with Ken in the afternoon shifting the gangway and filling fuel tanks on the inflatables. Interviews with Bruce and Lesley. Strategy meeting with Jim and then retire to my cabin to sketch and listen to music. Re-supply planning meeting in the evening which involves the helo teams, Ken, Jim, Keith and the logistics guys more than me but the sense of impending activity – the first ever re-supply and relieving of our wintering team – is strong.

2 February 1988

Wind too strong at 0600 to permit flying so we're stood down for an hour. At 0800 we're off Cape Royds and the wind is dropping all the time. We're back in this very special place which has grown so familiar to us over the years. During the night, we steamed from brilliant midnight sunshine into a depression visible off the ice-shelf and now that depression is giving us snow squalls. Gary fires up the helo and as planned, he flies me alone to the base at 0830. It's quite a sight from the air and memories come flooding back as we fly the short distance from the ship to Cape Evans. There they are, all of them outside the hut, jumping and waving.

Gary drops me off with a quick wave before he lifts off again and heads back to the ship and then I'm engulfed in arms and bodies clad in bulky down jackets as people greet me with hugs, slaps on the back and the odd tear or two. Justin is a bit subdued. Gudrun's hair is long and golden, Corny's beard has grown long and his hair is tied back in a ponytail. I hand them a sack full of mail and tell them we'll meet in an hour after they've had time to skim the precious news from friends and loved-ones. I take off for a wander round the base. As I walk, I ponder what their reaction will be to the decision Kelly and I have already taken that these guys should not come on the ship for the second leg of this expedition. There is no way they can stand the added stress of such a long sea passage.

We finally sit together and talk and the first thing they do is agree that our decision is wise, although Justin expresses his reluctance in accepting it. Then I bring up the hoary subject of Kevin and Gudrun's trek which took them out of contact for a week and which almost prompted a full scale search and rescue. This immediately brings out the latent hostility, especially between Justin and Kevin, and Justin walks out of the meeting almost beside himself with inexpressible bile and angst. I follow him to his room where he is in a fit of sobbing. He hugs me and completely breaks down telling me I have no idea what hell he has been through in the last six months. I feel so responsible for these guys, especially Justin, who has been so unselfish during the whole episode of the expedition organisation from the very first day I met him. We gather as a unit again after Justin has been consoled and it is clear that my intention of lancing the boil before the team are back in the bosom of the crew is not going to work – there's just too much anger which needs to be purged and I can't do it in a few hours.

The ship appears in the bay at midday and the helo lifts off with the press on board. As they step out of the helo on the Cape Evans beach, tensions are relieved somewhat as they are greeted by a hail of snowballs. The next flight brings in Keith, Sabine, Wojtek and Sjoerd, the in-coming wintering team, and there's another round of hugging and tears. The press fuss around the two teams for a while, getting their shots, and I leave them to it, getting back to the ship around 1400. I now have work of a different kind to do and spend the next few hours with Maj getting a press release out together with James' pictures of the reunion. We're finished by 1700 and I go to my cabin to collect my thoughts and muster my emotions.

By 2000 after dinner, everyone's back on board for a 'homecoming' party which doesn't actually get going with any sort of oomph until 2200. I enjoy it for an hour, watching people renew old acquaintances and letting their hair down after an arduous voyage, but I'm so tired I have to hit the hay at 0030. Quite a day. Many problems still to resolve and I'm sure it is not going to be an easy passage from here on in. But at least they are all alive and in one piece, at least physically: what more could we ask?

3 February 1988
Up at 0730 raring to go. No-one else seems to be in a hurry to begin the re-supply and Ken finally wanders into the saloon at 0830, coffee in one

hand, roll-up in the other, jeans tucked into Wellington boots, pile jacket unzipped, exposing the electronic equipment with which he'll keep in radio contact with the bridge and the helo on the air band, headphones slung around his neck and a balaclava hanging down the front of his chest. Hardly the sort of get-up you'd expect to see an Antarctic expeditioner in, but then Ken knows from experience that within the hour, he'll be sweating buckets and heavier gear would be uncomfortable and impractical. We finally begin sling-loading at 1000. 15 loads away including the satcom tower base sections and the wind generator tower. 30 barrels discharged this afternoon plus the incoming genny and the Apple survival hut which will be used to sleep some of the shore-side people during the re-supply.

Bruce wants to do another interview with me outside the hut so I'm excused deck duties for a couple of hours. Back by 1600 and continue on deck until 1800 when dinner is a welcome excuse to break. Five more loads away after dinner, after which I call Jim, Ken, Keith, Peter Malcolm, Maj and Gary together to plan the next few days. Watch Bruce's video which he shot today and by 2300 we're all sat down relaxing with a beer. Bed by 2400 after a good day. Lots accomplished and took a good bite into the cargo. Weather perfect and I can't resist taking half an hour to sketch Erebus before I turn in.

4 February 1988

After a Ken breakfast, we're on deck at 0845. Wind gusting to 30 knots and a slight swell and more marked chop are evident. Only five loads away before lunch and then I'm required to work on the computer on 'campaign' work until 1400: I send an update to the offices, a message to Kelly and to the OIC at Scott Base informing him of our intended activities and asking for the keys to Scott's Hut since we'd like to look around. Jim lifts the hook and steams around as a result of ice being blown in from the north and we get a spectacular view of the Erebus ice-tongue and the Barn Glacier – absolutely superb.

Kevin, Gudrun, Keith and I spend a couple of hours chatting and I begin to get a fuller picture of the harrowing year they've experienced. Kevin is remarkably forthcoming and accommodating which I hope bodes well for his attitude to this drama. Bed at 2300.

Well. Those last few lines were premature – and how. Wandered onto the bridge just before I turned in to find Cornelius talking on Ch 6 VHF to a woman he's been fraternising with at McMurdo – Vicky Getz. She has apparently been fired for associating with Greenpeace personnel. She is prepared to fight the National Science Foundation to expose their petty attitude and I discuss with Corny and Jim what we should do. I favour the idea of bringing her to the ship and releasing a story that we have offered sanctuary to a victimised and perfectly innocent employee – or better still as a defector – but it's clear that Vicky has been the cause (or one of them) of the tensions between Corny and Kevin during the year and that her presence on board would complicate the situation considerably.

We finally agree to ask Vicky to accept her fate, go home to the States and then to fly to Washington from where the US Greenpeace office can handle the story. This will distance her from the ship and the conflicts brewing and get one problem off my back. The group dynamics are just too complicated on board to handle this from the ship.

Finally get to bed at 0200 and agree to finalise decision at 0700. I'm tired and wrung out by the constant emotionally charged meetings, deck work, desk work, planning and press interviews, all of which are complicated by the need to keep the crew informed of what's going on to avoid the charge of being secretive or elitist.

5 February 1988

0700 meeting agrees that I should meet Vicky today to put our plan to her. Light morning on deck before Keith, Corny, Maj and I go to LGP3 (our little outpost comprising of a wooden shack and tent just outside Scott Base) to get film away to NZ via contacts at Scott Base. The flight over the hummock is stunning – literally breathtaking as we soar over the base, the ice and on into the interior for a few miles. Beyond stretches the plateau across which I could almost see Scott and his party trudging ant-like on their fateful journey to the pole a mere eighty years ago.

Vicki arrives – a small, determined and very vocal woman – and we agree that she should get to Washington after she's been shipped out by the NSF where she will spill the beans on the incredibly aggressive attitude they adopt to anyone fraternising with scum like us. We arrive back at the ship at 1800 whereupon Kevin berates me for leaving Cornelius alone at LGP3 as he fears Corny will be a target for the NSF corruptors. This sounds like paranoia gone berserk and reminds me that these guys – Kevin in particular – are not in the real world at the moment.

Cornelius is very accommodating when I explain why I want him back on board and he arrives full of good cheer at 2330, only to run into Kevin's antagonism again. Kevin and I sit drinking beer for two hours as he details the year from his perspective. It is a grim story indeed if even ten per cent of it is true. I pass on the warnings their experience has thrown up to Sabine in the most gentle terms I can find. Jim cracks the rum to celebrate his birthday and I crash at 0130, leaving some of the more hardy souls to continue. Christ! What a job! Psychologist, mediator, sounding board, shoulder to cry on, decision maker, crane driver, deckie, adviser – you name it!

6 February 1988
Busy day. Due to the increasingly cold weather, we start later than usual to avoid the biting early morning wind, but work later to compensate. Got a reply from Scott base regarding the keys to Scott's Hut – no way. It's almost become a point of honour now and I'm determined to get these guys to back down. Scott was English, after all and there's no way we should be denied access to one of our historical monuments. Work like hell to get the port locker cleared of the walkway sections and then more heavy labouring bringing the food up from the forecastle store room. Finish at 1830 but then have to get messages away to Kelly. Things are starting to move quickly now and I hope I'm keeping abreast of all the developments.

Ashore, the satcom tower is 75% finished and the Footsteps Hut we inherited is installed against the side of our base. Only the food and the fuel are left on board. Latest ice reports indicate only a narrow gap in the outer ice through which we can travel. Jim seems unperturbed. Kevin bends my ear for hours about how we have not sufficiently discussed the policy on approaching the US at McMurdo. He's beginning to really piss me off. He uses the discussion to give vent to his pent-up emotions and I feel obliged to indulge him as long as possible. Weather perfect all day except that a northerly wind has conspired to block the beach with drift ice. Jim's continuing birthday party is still going on ashore and I reach it to find that only six stalwarts are still in revelry mode. Back to the ship by 0130 and gratefully to bed, totally drained emotionally.

7 February 1988
Steam off at 1600 to check out the fuel depots at Butter Point and elsewhere

to check for leakages – none found. Back to Cape Evans by 0115 and find that our anchorage is not suitable for satellite connection. Ken and I have to lift the hook again and Jim repositions the ship in a better place. We earn a beer from Jim for our troubles. Bed by 0300, exhausted.

8 February 1988

Work on deck until 1330 when Keith, Kevin and I prepare for our trips to Scott and McMurdo. We land at LGP3 after circling Scott Base and not being able to pick them up on HF or VHF for landing permission. McMurdo came on air with a strange transmission advising us that we land at our own risk. Meeting with Ayers at Scott Base was predictably formal tinged with a little humanity. No mail runs for us, he tells us, keys to the huts possibly before we leave and happy to have our winterers visit for an informal chat. But they all seem pretty reasonable guys and accept the fact that we are here to stay so they might as well accept us.

Ron Le Count is altogether different. He reminds me of a New York cab driver in his appearance and approach but he's an affable old sod beneath his gruff exterior, even if he is a CIA agent as Kevin would have us believe. I tell him he's dealing with semantics rather than issues when he complains about what we were quoted as saying last year about NSF's operation and he quietly seems to accept that. He sticks to the party line that nothing except science is going on at McMurdo and offers us to inspect his files except those which 'contain information about salary levels' – oh, come on Ron! Oil spillages? Sure they occur, he concedes, but they're doing their best to clean them up. He invites me to meet him in Washington and refuses to believe that I'm an ex-lorry driver.

Ron arranges for a truck to take us back to LGP3 from where we try in vain to call the ship to arrange the helicopter to come and collect us. Finally, Swenson bangs the VHF in frustration and it works. We get picked up at 1930 and I send off a flurry of messages from the ship and fall into bed at 0200. My energy level is nearing zero.

9 February 1988

Heard today that the international board is trying to move Maureen Falloon sideways for some reason we can only guess at: perhaps she has become too powerful in her present position. Hard, hard day on deck. We worked 15 hours solid today with only brief breaks for tea and food. Messages off to Scott and McMurdo to set up the informal visits by the winterers for the 11th, messages off to Kelly debriefing her on the meetings yesterday, press release, pictures out, working on deck, talking to Justin about his problems with Kevin and Gudrun, writing captions for the pictures, meeting the crew to run through the remaining work programme and working like a Trojan on deck bringing food up from the bowels of the ship and then sling-loading it away to shore. I should have demanded double the money I asked for! I don't see much of Swenson these days as he's working ashore most of the time and I miss the miserable little bastard. Peter Malcolm estimates a further three working days to finish off the base re-supply and additional construction. Message from McMurdo confirming the 11th. Stagger to bed half asleep at 0200.

10 February 1988
Left to sleep until 1000. Greeted on the bridge with an ice chart which shows the outer ice pack closing in all the time. Jim is still philosophical but Ken privately expresses his concern to me. Paperwork is a light load today and I spend almost all day on deck – me, Ken and Roger, the helo engineer – known as the A team. Roger is a real character: quiet to the point of being almost invisible and droll as they come. He was helping us drag the frozen meat up out of the forecastle peak the other day and he emerged from the gloom staggering up an almost vertical flight of stairs pushing a 50kg box before him, sweating and quietly cursing with long lines of snot dangling from his nose. He's a hero, is our Roger.

Ayers finally agrees to accept our winterers on the same day as they visit McMurdo which simplifies our logistical arrangements considerably. Thank Christ! That's all the meetings arranged and done with. He even agrees to open up the Scott and Royds huts for us on the 12th. Two crew briefings today – one ashore and one on board at 2200 and 0030. Wind genny is up and running. Sprawl on my bunk at 0100 and pile on the music in some sort of weak celebration about seeing the light at the end of the tunnel. Asleep before the first track is finished.

11 February 1988
Supposed to be up at 0530 to help prepare and steer the ship down McMurdo Sound to the US base but finally fell out of bed at 0645 as we were entering the channel. They had no idea we would accept their invitation so literally – taking the ship to their ice wharf was definitely not expected and as we nudge alongside, Ron is there puffing on his pipe

and turning his back to the wind as we drop the gangway. Tied up at 0845 which prompts Ron to say, as I extend my hand in greeting, 'You're fifteen minutes late, ass'ole.' He turns his back to the wind again and says, 'And you can get that piece of shit outta here as well!' nodding past my shoulder to the ship.

I grin and tell him as I sweep my arm to embrace McMurdo base, 'And you can get this piece of shit outta here as soon as you like, ass'ole.' We both laugh. He's ok is Ron. He comes on board and together with Commander Fisher, they walk calm as you like into the lion's den – the saloon on the ship – and seem totally unconcerned that the cameras are present. They stay for more than an hour, fielding questions from me, Maj and other crew members. Bruce Adams tries to provoke Ron for the cameras but he is rounded on by a perfectly eloquent and capable Ron who minces Bruce into little pieces. I have to hand it to him – he's got some balls. I agree to meet Ron ashore at 1500 and he leaves with Fisher.

Crew are now free to go ashore and Keith, Ken and I go to Discovery Hut which Scott used in his 1908 expedition and which is now surrounded by huge oil tanks, oil spills and the dross of human habitation in this outpost of civilisation. The bay which abuts the hut is contaminated to the point of biological death by the heavy metals and run-off of contaminants from McMurdo. I guess Scott regularly turns in his grave.

Keith and I wander into Mactown and set up a meeting for him with Fisher at 1330. Back to the ship at 1200 to find it seething with people: the merchandise is selling like hotcakes to the McMurdo personnel. Crew meeting at 1400 to brief the crew on the demonstration we're planning at the open rubbish tip above Mactown and then I go to see Ron with Keith and Maj, thus missing out on seeing the inside of Discovery Hut which the Kiwis finally open for us. On the way back to the ship at 1700 we meet several groups of crew members heading into Mactown despite the briefing I gave them earlier about the demo.

Back on board, nothing is ready – no-one has been assigned to watches, no banners are ready and it seems as though my powers of delegation have reached rock-bottom. I finally assemble what can be loosely described as a group of protesters and we struggle through town to the dump, a straggling line of cold, unwilling and windswept protesters and we finally get the shot completed outside the dump which really is a mess. It's an open tip in which the waste is regularly burned sending wind-blown rubbish into the air.

On the way back, Keith and I find a lorry battery casually tossed on the roadside and struggle back to the ship with it to deliver to the NSF in Christchurch as a further focus of some future protest. I had hoped that with the ship docked in McMurdo, we would have been able to drag one of the lorry chassis which have been dumped along the waterline onto the ship with the crane, but Ken tells me it's impractical so that wheeze is out, regrettably. The evening turns into quite a party. The ship is heaving with people and Ron turns up with a bottle of rum. After an hour or so, Ron is surrounded by quite hostile crew and James Perez tells Ron aggressively that he's 'full of shit' and I hustle Ron off to Ken's cabin to make my apologies to him and have a quiet and pleasant drink with him. Thirty one samples of snow and water taken by Sabine today for later analysis for contamination. We finally pull the ship out at 2200 and arrive back at Cape Evans at 0115. Quite a day, but I'm glad to see the back of it.

12 February 1988
Minus 8 and blowing hard today – 25 knots. It improves by 1000 and Gary flies off to collect Ayers and Colin McFarlane from Scott Base for their visit to the ship. They arrive with the keys to Scott's and Shackleton's Cape Royd's Huts. Lunch on board with Ayers, McFarlane and Jim – all very amicable. Continue with paperwork in the pm and watch the helo take off with crew for Cape Royds. As the waves of crew return in the late afternoon, I notice that Lynn has not logged back on board and it transpires that she's gone back to Scott Base with Ayers et al with Jim's blessing. I'm not happy at all with this and tell Jim I think he's made a mistake. Lynn on the loose in Scott Base is not a good idea and Jim reluctantly agrees that he made an error of judgement. Keith gets to hear about it and arrives back on board at 2200 purple with rage and demands to see me and Jim. I've never seen Keith so out of control.

We call Lynn back from Scott Base and as she sets foot on board, Keith 'bans' her from ever leaving the ship again during the expedition. She demands to see me to get a second opinion and I have to back Keith. It's my opinion that Lynne is in danger of becoming a loose cannon. Then Frank the cameraman wants to see me to complain about Bruce who, he feels, is not directing the film shoot correctly. An already hard day turns into a psychotherapy session and many people are left feeling hurt and bruised by the reaction of others. Ship of fools is a phrase which springs to mind. I feel that treading this diplomatic tightrope will crack me up. Bed at 0100 and I don't even bother to undress. The cabin is a mess of papers, clothes and equipment and I lay on it all and sleep the sleep of the dead.

13 February 1988

Technically our last re-supply day. Work on deck from 0830 to 2330 almost solid, frantically slinging load after load of food ashore and receiving backloads of rubbish from the base. We do our best to stow the backloads before the helo arrives with another sling and the frenetic activity pushes us to the limit at times. I just pray that we don't have an accident through tiredness and impatience. The last load from shore arrives at 2300 thank God. Then it's a blissful hot shower and ashore for the party. Exchange of gifts, speeches and much hugging precedes a few drinks only interrupted by the need to take a decidedly drunken Bob Graham back to the ship which I do with Ken, largely to ensure Ken doesn't deck him or push him over the side on the way back, so low has the relationship between these guys become.

We sit talking until about 0300 when the party breaks up and Sabine kindly allows me to use her room. Tomorrow we will say goodbye to these guys and it will mark the end of the job we've spent months preparing for. I lie on the bunk and through the window of the hut I watch the morning sun catching the ship in the bay and a kind of magic descends on me. I wonder how much emotional energy I've invested in this place over three years. Too much probably, but I love it deeply and I hope I can hack what remains of this trip without going completely ga-ga.

14 February 1988

Up at 1000 and straight back to the ship to plan departure. I can foresee chaos unless I nail people down to specific tasks. People on board the ship say their farewells to the winterers at 1400 and then both sets of winterers, incoming and outgoing, come ashore with me with the press for the farewell shots ashore. It's a complete nightmare as the demands of the cameramen clash with the carefree attitude and emotional nature of the occasion.

Wojtek is clowning constantly and Kevin simply refuses to co-operate. After 25 shots, James is losing his patience and begins screaming at them to stay still. All this mayhem is being filmed by Bruce and his crew and

310

I can feel my hair turning grey. I quietly say my goodbyes to Sjoerd who tells me selflessly that I've been a good, strong leader and then to Sabine and Wojtek. I avoid Keith for a long time, not trusting myself to stay dry-eyed when I say goodbye to this character. Eventually we face each other and hug mightily. I won't see this guy for a long time and over the years he has become like a brother to me. I can't hold back and have to wander off to hide my tears.

To regain my composure, I start organising the boats back to the ship and the people who will occupy them, in what order. After the first boat has left I clamber into the second one and sit next to Gudrun, Kevin and Bruce. As we run towards the ship, the winterers look so lost and forlorn on the beach, four tiny figures in front of the hut, itself dwarfed by Erebus and I feel drained and empty as I see Keith give a final wave and then turn his back. Gudrun is openly sobbing and can't take her eyes off the base. It must be so much harder for her to leave this place which she loves and which holds so many strong memories for her, both good and bad.

Back on board, the anchor is weighed and Jim gives five long blasts on the horn which signals the end of the re-supply and seems to turn my legs to jelly. Then James remembers he's left some camera lenses at the base so we have to prolong the agony by putting a boat down again and taking a big sweep past the hut with the ship as we retrieve the dinghy. All the winterers are sitting outside the hut side by side on the settee in the sun – the idiots. Then we head north and gradually the hut becomes a smudge of green and the Cape recedes into the distance. Goodbye, my good friends. Will I be here next year to pick you up? Goodbye Keith, you stupid ass'ole. Who loves ya?

My reveries are cut short by a call from Ken to help on deck and as we steam through the beautiful and tranquil waters of the south Ross Sea, Werner and I work hard for a punishing two hours before watch at 2000. Steer the ship for three hours as others are engaged in deck and helo work and then I start the process of sending out the pictures and press releases with Maj and James. Everything finally away by 0100 and then asked for an interview by Leslie and Mossy as we head for Terra Nova. Finally crash at 0300 totally exhausted. Again, I don't even bother to undress.

15 February 1988
Allowed the campaigner's rare luxury of a long lie in and someone finally

wakes me at 1200 otherwise I'm sure I would have slept all day. Stagger around for an hour and then begin preparing the messages for the Italians at Terra Nova, our next port of call. Before I get too deeply involved in that, however, I look at the cabin and realise it is in a disgraceful mess and that I must do something. I start by doing my dobying and change the sheets on the bunk. I then confront the chair which is piled three feet high in working clothes, all of which smell of diesel and rubbish, a fetid smell which reminds me of the butcher's shop I worked in as a kid. Finally get the room tidy and sweep the carpet for the first time since we've been at sea. It feels so good! 1800 and time for dinner. Expect to anchor at 0400 and I rush off the messages to announce our arrival before going on watch at 2000. Watch is quite exciting as we close the coast and negotiate ice – I'm up and down the nest like the proverbial Tower Bridge. Bed at 0100.

16 February 1988

Confused morning. We steam into Terra Nova at 0820 after hanging around for three hours due to bad ice conditions and I contact the OIC on VHF. We get ashore on the first boat to see a quite dramatic landscape. It's snowing heavily and the sea is icing up by the hour. Visibility is very limited and it's approaching minus 10. As we get ashore, we're greeted by eight people including the OIC, a guy called Mario, who seems to be nice enough but who doesn't stop talking in broken but perfectly understandable English. James drops his camera as he steps from the boat and I retrieve it instinctively by plunging my arm into the water up to my shoulder. The second boat arrives with Maj for whom we wait before walking to the base itself. It's a summer-only base at present and was only built three years ago. Good environmental principles have been applied – catalytic converters on the genny exhausts, sewage treatment systems, etc. We sit in the mess and state our positions: the OIC wants no 'polemic' and reminds us we are a private expedition enjoying the hospitality of a national programme. We express our concerns about future expansion of the base and the possibility of an airstrip which he mentioned. After lunch, I'm anxious to get back to the ship and leave Maj to conduct the formal 'inspection' as we like to call it, since she'll be writing the report for GP.

My plans for a sleep are interrupted by the need to work on deck with Ken and by the Italian journalists who follow me back from the base for interviews. I call for the shore-siders to be back on board by 1400 to ensure minimum disruption to the Italians' work schedule and am then confronted by an irate Kevin who berates me for a poor briefing for the crew prior to arrival which has meant that many crew are wandering off ashore on their own. The party we're invited to ashore is cancelled due to the weather so I invite the OIC to the ship. He arrives on our boat with Mossy (who will stay with them and hitch a ride back to Italy with them) and the chief scientist of the base.

After dinner, a live interview with RAI is set up for me on the bridge but I can't hear a bloody thing from the interviewer and the exercise proves abortive. After an exchange of gifts, the Italians leave amid much bonhomie and back-slapping. Snowball fight breaks out on deck during which I slip and crack my hip a heavy blow on the deck. What with that and my aching back, I feel 100 years old. Decide that as the weather is improving, we can get Maj and Gudrun off to *Gondwana* (the German base) tonight to take scientific samples and they get airborne at 2400 as we steam up and down past spectacular scenery – glaciers, bleak, snow-dusted mountains and fast-ice shelves. What a place! Maj and Gudrun back at 0200 with lichen samples and we get away for Hallet at 0300. Bed at 0330 after helping put the helos to bed.

17 February 1988
Clear the ice by 0900 and our northerly course is interrupted by bands of drift ice which block our path, pushing us east. Eventually, we make a north-easterly course as the ice clears and we head 010 and hit quite big swells driven by strong northerlies. Gudrun gets seasick and I take the wheel but by 1100 I'm feeling queasy too although manage to see my watch out. I hit the sack until 1800. The sea moderates later and we continue on 010 with deviations for ice until the end of the evening watch. Pass Coulman Island at 2300. One beer after watch then bed by 0030.

18 February 1988
On watch at 0800 as we steam into Cape Hallet. The crew meeting to plan the day's events is a bit redundant as it's blowing 70 knots and whipping up a very steep sea. By 1300 it has moderated and a boat is despatched with shore-siders. The abandoned base looks tidier than last year but fewer penguins are here. The masts of the *Alan and Vi Thistlethwaite* can be seen sticking up like matchsticks above the ice of the bay in which the tiny ship nestles. At 1500, the AVT's crew come on board to discuss what

to do about their climbers who are now on the descent from Mt Minto – previously unclimbed, I believe – after a successful ascent. They are not overdue but skipper Don Richards is concerned about the lateness of the season and wants to hasten their departure since they don't want to be the last vessel in the Antarctic and fear that they will be unable to push their way out of the increasingly thickening ice with their crook main engine.

By evening, they formally request that we help to retrieve their climbers with the helicopters and I prepare an agreement absolving Greenpeace of any liability in the event of accident or unsuccessful attempts to retrieve them. The weather is deteriorating but Gary agrees to take an investigatory flight up the glacier to where we believe their base camp has been established. He takes Kevin with him but is back soon having been forced to abandon the flight five miles from his destination by bad weather, high turbulence and low visibility. Gary checks out the ice before he lands and Jim decides to get seaward of the pack for the night. It turns out to be a hairy few hours. The ice has crept up on us during the day and we dump and scrape, turn and dodge, push and nudge until we are clear and after I've been up the nest more times than I can recall. We're finally safe at 0100 and we sit and sink a beer in the saloon. Before I turn in, I take a stroll on deck to see a truly magical landscape. The colours at sunset are breath-taking: golds, pinks, browns and a whole range of pastel shades I've never seen before.

19 February 1988

A day of tension, boredom and cursing the weather. Now that we're committed to helping these people we are hamstrung. We can't leave without knowing they are safe and we must therefore wait until the weather clears. At the 0845 radio schedule, they don't come up and we spend the rest of the day chewing over the options. The weather has clagged in with a low cloud ceiling, low viz and a stiff southerly which causes us to hump around in a steep chop. We shelter in the lee of an iceberg for most of the day and I find that I sleep wherever I sit for more than five minutes and the dreams I have are surreal and almost tangible – so very un-dreamlike. At 2045, the climbers come up on the sked, very weakly, but clear. They agree to the pick up and we plan for a flight tomorrow, weather permitting. Roger's birthday is celebrated with a few beers and a bottle of rum. It is positively dark now at 2300 and we all pray for fine weather tomorrow; it is very late in the season and we must get out of here within a day or two.

20 February 1988
Jim wakes me to tell me the climbers have radioed to say they have perfect weather but here it is still grey and miserable with 10/10 cloud and low ceiling, no higher than 1000 feet. We steam back into the bay but the weather is no better after a few hours. Even at the end of the spectacular Tucker glacier the weather persists in being of the 'no flying' variety. Press release out, in which I stress that we are not 'rescuing' these guys but merely helping them to make an earlier exit from the Antarctic. Fall asleep for two hours after lunch and then sit about anxiously looking at the weather, hoping for a change.

The AVT crew call us and Jim asks them if they want to revise the arrangement with us since we now know their party is safe and that the weather seems to be lifting from the south. This would leave us free to leave in the morning but I suggest to Jim that it's a very abrupt about-face in our position and that I'd prefer to give it another 24 hours at least to complete our agreement. Having committed ourselves, I feel we should finish the job. Without our help, these guys won't be back on board their vessel until the 26th which is far too late and will leave them without any support from other vessels and they may still have trouble getting out of the bay, let alone the Ross Sea.

If we can advance their departure date by 4 days, we will have done the job we have just told the world we are prepared to do. Leaving would be perceived as weird or even irresponsible. Jim agrees and we tell the AVT that the original agreement stands. Bed at 0100 after crib with Ken and a luscious fry up of eggs and chips.

21 February 1988
The weather is the same, dammit! Low clouds, zero viz, lifting occasionally to give us a tantalising glimpse of the glacier and the saddle and the mountains beyond. The morning radio schedule reveals that the climbers are at 1200 metres and they can see cloud below them at 300 metres. Jim and I go to see Don on the AVT, not before Maggie McCaw chews my ear at the crew meeting asking me, not unreasonably, 'Who is making the decisions around here?'

Shades of 1985 loom over me momentarily before I tell her, 'I am, along with Jim with respect to ship and crew safety.'

The AVT is a thoroughly cramped and miserable vessel although the skipper, first mate and cook – the only woman on board – are amazingly cheerful and resilient. The conditions they are living under – have lived under for months – are spartan to put it mildly. The climbers spent a month on this vessel on the way down, sleeping side by side on a shelf constructed in the forward part of the boat. Then they climbed this mountain, and have to look forward to a similarly excruciatingly uncomfortable journey home, sleeping in a dark and cramped 'hole' as they sail across the unpredictable Southern Ocean.

I am deeply impressed and full of admiration for these amazing people. The skipper releases us from our agreement but hints that he would deeply appreciate it if we'd see it through with him, which we agree to do. While ashore, I take my first look at Cape Hallet. The number of dead chick carcasses is staggering – they are buried in guano and the skeletons of these tiny penguins are several layers thick and in the case of the more recently dead, the bodies half-pecked by skuas. Christ, what a hard, short life these birds lead. Back on board it's nothing but cards, music and bed at 0100.

22 February 1988

The wind picks up during the night and the tossing of the ship, coupled with my insomnia makes for a thoroughly uncomfortable night. By 0600 we're pitching like hell in a force 10. On the bridge at 0800 to take the wheel from Gudrun who is looking as green as I feel. We try to shelter in the lee of an iceberg but get little protection. Even trying to shelter behind the massive Tucker glacier doesn't work as we can't penetrate the ice. We're pitching very heavily and I just about manage to keep my breakfast down while on watch. A lot of people lie prone in the saloon. Steering at dead slow ahead is a nightmare – full port and starboard rudder just to keep any sort of course. Finally at 1045, we turn and head back towards the bay. Ah! The bliss of a following sea. Immediately I feel ok and the ship miraculously becomes a hive of activity again. The weather finally moderates and we spend the rest of the day hove-to. Jim optimistically schedules helo ops for 0600 in the morning.

23 February 1988

Woken at 0630 to be told that the first flight has already landed on the glacier! Between then and noon five flights take place, retrieving all the climbers and their gear. They arrive on the ship – five of them, rugged, hairy, tanned and tired – to hot showers and pancakes cooked by Marc. What a great bunch they are! They are naturally beside themselves with delight at their success and at the reception we put on for them. Apparently they planted a flag on top of the mountain calling for 'World Park Antarctica' and will be peddling the pictures in the press when they get back to Oz. Great bunch and a great finale to the trip for us.

We transfer their gear to the AVT by dinghy after steaming to meet the yacht in the mouth of the bay. How eleven people will spend a month in that tiny craft, lumping its way across the Southern Ocean, is beyond me. We say our goodbyes after a helo flight confirms to Don the reasonably good ice conditions he'll be facing as he leaves the immediate area of the Ross Sea and we finally part company at 1500, promising that we'll keep in radio contact for as long as possible.

I now have to face the task of informing the world of recent events and the next few hours are taken up in sending out messages, press releases and pictures. Despite the fact that I took great care to avoid the word rescue in the press releases, the press calls we receive all want to talk about how we rescued the guys from the mountain.

Off we set into the Ross Sea through a few strips of brash ice. The wind quickly picks up and a big swell begins to run. Soon we're rolling like hell in a force 9 and my thoughts go out to the AVT. We alter course and now the swells are coming from the stern and we're picked up arse-first and forced to surf down the face of the swells. The height of the swells must be at least 30 feet – they're level with the bridge windows and we hear from the AVT that she has already been knocked down and has lost some of her radar equipment. Poor bastards! Turn in after a beer with Ken but despite wedging myself into my bunk firmly, I'm thrown around all night and get no sleep at all. Books, clothes and papers fly across the cabin and I simply don't have the energy nor the inclination, to get up and secure things. Christ! What a life on the ocean waves!

24 February 1988

The weather has worsened if anything and on the bridge lines of great, steaming grey-bearded swells, topped by wind-lashed spume, can be seen bearing down on the ship from the starboard quarter in serried ranks, all the way to the horizon. The ship lifts from the stern as the wave passes, corkscrews on the top of the swell and sinks into the trough stern first, the passing wave steaming and hissing past us, level with the bridge windows. It is the Southern Ocean in its full awesome glory and my remark to Ken that I am inspired by this display brings his quip, 'It'll be interesting if this develops into an eleven or 12.'

The weather requires that we forget the plans to visit Leningradskaya and instead we plough on towards the Bellany Islands on a due northerly course turning to 330. At 1100 this morning on watch, Henk Haazen phoned on the satcom to let us know that he and Bunny had a little baby daughter that morning at 0300 – Ruby. Spend the afternoon trying to catch up on my sleep but I feel periodically queasy as we lurch along. I manage to stagger up to the bridge for my evening watch which consists of 80 minutes on the wheel, 80 minutes on lookout and 80 minutes on stand-by which normally means that you crash out in the saloon although you should, technically, be sitting alert and ready to spring into action. Low viz, grey skies and a lumpy grey sea which is now moderating a bit. Kevin is on my case about going straight back to Lyttelton as Gudrun is getting sicker and sicker and it's not just the motion of the ship. Lynn puts her medical skills to work and gives Gudrun a physical. She reports that, medically, Gudrun is ok, but needs 48 hours to determine if she'll be ok on medication or if we should go directly back to Lyttelton. I discuss the matter with Kevin, Gudrun, Jim and Lynn and agree to review the situation in 24 hours. Gratefully to bed at 0130.

25 February 1988

I feel as if I've been away from home and what passes for normality for years and we aren't even halfway through the trip yet. We still have two weeks at sea on this leg then it'll be in port for a few days and off again on a three week sea-voyage to do what? Photograph and document the peninsular bases with no chance of any action at all. The future time away from home stretches interminably into the distance. This negative feeling prompts a negative message to Kelly asking her to review the need for, and the wisdom of, the second leg of the trip. Twenty miles northeast of the Bellanys at 2000. Six days to NZ from here, eleven if we

318

go via DuDu. Slight swell from astern, force four, feeling fine. During watch Kevin comes and stands on the bridge and spends the next two hours dodging off to see Gudrun and I know he's telling me with his body language and his actions that he wants me to take the decision to go straight home. After a series of meetings, consultations and phone calls, I finally agree with Jim that we should do just that – ETA Lyttelton 2nd March. Around comes the wheel and we steer 018 for home as I pass the word among the crew before they all start asking questions about why the ship feels different under its new course. So that's it. NZ here we come.

26 February 1988
Nancy Foote calls me from Washington at 0730 this morning, spoiling my rare lie-in. I talk to her for 15 minutes but what she or I said, I have no idea. As I stagger back to my bunk from the radio room, Jim collars me and tells me Justin wants to talk about the second leg. I give in to circumstances and get dressed. Justin doesn't want to go – that's the top and bottom of it, and I tell him that's fine, he should get home to his family, as should I. I get messages off to GP advising them of the change in plans and then sleep overcomes me and I crash until 1430. Later, talking to Kevin, it's clear that he's eaten up with personally motivated emotional attitudes towards Corny over the incident with Gudrun on the base and our conversation reaches stalemate at 2200. He basically wants me to side with him on his opinions of Cornelius which I can't do and which I wouldn't do anyway. I turn in shortly after midnight to get away from Kevin's constant nagging and leave him to Maj.

27 February 1988
Force 4 from the SW, long moderate swells, overcast with occasional sunshine, plus one degree C. Position 61 south. Morning watch is the usual bore: not even a bird until 1100 when a sooty and a black-browed deign to grace us with their presence. Nancy calls again and I still can't make out what she's on about. On stand-by, I prepare messages and get an update on the Kevin and Gudrun situation to Kelly. I also intimate to her that the second leg is looking less and less attractive to me. Sleep after a sparrow-like lunch until 1700, then to the saloon for a very unappetising dinner. Music, writing and change the bunk before evening watch. After an hour of lying in bed reading, the ship begins to move around dramatically as the wind picks up and large westerly swells take a grip

of the ship. I actually shielded my face against objects which went flying across the cabin, the motion was so bad. I wedge myself in using the old trick of lifejackets under the mattress but I still roll around, flopping from one side to the other like a beached fish.

28 February 1988

Stagger to the bridge at 0750 clutching a life-saving cuppa. Uneventful watch with big swells still running, making accurate steering nearly impossible. She yaws up to 10 degrees either side of the course between the troughs and the peaks of the swells. As the day progresses, Kevin's attitude towards Cornelius hardens and he finds it more and more difficult to keep his trap shut. At 1830, just after dinner, there's a set-to in the saloon between the two of them. Kevin and Gudrun want the forms back from Cornelius on which they monitored their mental attitude throughout the year (known as psych forms) on the grounds that they are useless and don't reflect the real state of their minds at the time. Cornelius refuses to hand them back since they are 'medical records' and of great value to the expedition, and asks me to mediate. I intervene and suggest that, under the circumstances, the psych forms should be scrapped otherwise we'll never send another wintering team south. Then Kevin demands my presence in Gudrun's cabin where he finally makes his ultimatum – fire Cornelius or he resigns. I tell him to shove it and that we'll talk it over again in the morning when we've all had a chance to sleep on the situation. I fire off a message to Kelly getting her to cancel the lecture tours for all the winterers unless I can sort this problem out in the morning, which I doubt.

29 February 1988

Kevin has pulled out of the 8-12 watch so it's just me and Ken now until Peter Malcolm comes on at 1030. During this time alone, he tells me of another problem which has surfaced on board – thankfully it's a crew problem and therefore in Jim's domain rather than mine – but it appears that one of the male members of the crew has been bothering the women for weeks now and was discovered in his bunk with an – I can't believe this but it's true – inflatable doll. I naturally find harassing women a keel-hauling offence, but I have a good laugh about the blow-up woman. I asked Ken if he thought I could borrow it – only joking! Still a fresh westerly blowing and big swells which roll the ship quite alarmingly at times. But a beautiful clear sky and brilliant sunshine at last. Watch is tolerable thanks to the lovely weather and Justin comes and steers for the last third of the watch. I go below on stand-by and immediately fall into a deep sleep.

Peter M wakes me for lunch after which we conduct the 'last ditch' meeting in an attempt to settle the dispute between Kevin and Cornelius. The fight is actually between Gudrun and Cornelius – something that seems to have escaped Kevin – and I insist that the meeting is between those people, me and Jim only. Kevin refuses to accept that as he's the 'only independent witness'. What followed is not reasonable to commit to a diary – very personal and intimate descriptions of what Corny was alleged to have done to Gudrun as he treated her in the last few months of the year. Kevin sees the whole sordid event as a trial of Cornelius, trying to 'prove' his guilt in order to justify his demands that I fire Cornelius.

At the end of 90 gruelling minutes, we're back at square one. Gudrun accuses, Cornelius exonerates himself and refutes the allegations. Me, Maj and Jim continue to talk as the meeting breaks up, looking at the dearth of options.

Perhaps I should resign as a demonstration of the fact that I am in a totally invidious position. I don't have the authority to fire anyone since the winterers are employed by International, not by me, and anyway, how can I sit in judgement of someone when the only evidence I have to hand is contested and when the only 'witness' – Kevin – can hardly be described as independent and when Justin, the other potential witness, wants nothing to do with the matter?

I feel I can only resort to distancing the need to make a decision by putting the onus on the international office, where it should be, rather than on me, here and now, in the middle of the southern Ocean when the events are so fresh and vivid in peoples' minds. But this would mean that Kevin would feel I have not met his demands and would presumably therefore resign himself, (not a bad option under the circumstances but he would doubtless feel obliged to make as much trouble for Cornelius and for GP as possible), and also I feel it is wrong of me to offload a situation somewhat of my making (I chose the wintering team) onto someone else. I'm just so tired and fed up with this entire situation.

The ship's rolling violently as we pass Campbell Island – no stops there this year for the ship of fools – and it's impossible to sit at a table in a free-standing seat as it just skids across the room taking the occupant with it. Write, listen to music until watch at 2000. Three beers after watch and then I lie in my bunk being thrown from one side to the other all night. Great life on a Greenpeace ship, eh?

1 March 1988

Can't get up for watch and finally stagger on the bridge at 0820 and take the wheel from Ken, very sheepishly. Still a big swell coming in from the west, overcast skies and squalls gusting 60 knots of wind. Telexes and phone calls galore while I'm on watch, which adds to the confusion. The biggest laugh I've had all trip arrives when I hear that the video Bruce Adams sent out from Scott Base detailing the appalling squalor of McMurdo base has been screened in every Communist country in the world, including Cuba. I couldn't stop laughing all day and we've dubbed Bruce 'Adamski'. Kevin is on my case again from early morning asking me if I've decided to fire Corny yet and I can't believe the guy's persistence. I agree to a final pre-arrival crew meeting at 1900 and significantly, just before the meeting, Kevin asks me yet again if I intend to fire Corny to which I reply for the umpteenth time, 'No, since I don't wear a wig and I refuse to be the arbiter of someone's morals, especially based on contested evidence. The decision as to whether there has been medical misconduct,' I tell him, 'is that of a medical assessment board, not a Greenpeace campaigner in the middle of the ocean.'

When I arrive at the crew meeting, Bruce has rigged up his camera and sound gear. Unbelievably, in front of the entire crew, and knowing that the meeting is being filmed, Kevin begins to explain in the grossest detail what Corny purportedly did to Gudrun. He also, I learn later, asked Leslie to write about it in a story she was filing for her newspaper. I can't believe what is going on here: Kevin is talking about intimate, personal events between two people – one of whom was not even him – to 30 people, many of whom are total strangers to him. I begin yelling at Kevin to stop this bullshit and when he continues, I almost go for him, but decide instead to leave. He would have murdered me anyway if I had lit into him since he's as strong as an ox.

Jim calls me back after 15 minutes and says that a settlement has been agreed – to put everything on hold until the winterers get to Washington, exactly what I suggested yesterday, and which was rejected. So we go about our business again in a strained atmosphere and Kevin avoids me noticeably. I'm in a foul mood and have a set-to with Bruce when I ask him to hand me the film he shot of the crew meeting. He refuses, since it's 'human interest' stuff that will be valuable to his filmic record. I have a stand-up row with him and threaten to throw every roll of film overboard if he doesn't give me an assurance that the film of Kevin's outburst will never see the light of day. He thus assures me and I storm off. Having a beer after watch, Bob walks into the saloon and hands me a quadruple whisky. Good old Bob. He's a diamond.

2 March 1988
Off watch today and attempt a lie-in which is not to be. Ken calls me to take part in the traditional pre-arrival spring clean but before 0900, Kevin asks to see me again. Gudrun is in tow. He goes over the same ground again and again to the point where I begin to lose my temper quickly. Voices are raised which brings Ted Addicott into the saloon to try to cool things down and I tell him to leave. Then Jim comes in and I storm out of the saloon. After an hour, I go back and Kevin is still there with the same monotonous question on his lips.
I look him in the face and tell him, 'I resign from the position of expedition leader as of now. Take your pathetic demands to someone else'.

He doesn't quite believe me, so I go and type out my resignation, send it to Kelly and hand him the message. It's that simple. I'm out. Relieved, sad, confused, angry and happy that an enormous weight has been lifted from my shoulders. I sleep until 1700. I haven't eaten all day and I feel like shit. I shower, tidy the cabin and have a beer with Ken, James and Justin. I go on evening watch feeling very odd indeed. It's calm now, almost flat with a gentle northerly swell and brilliant sunset which puts on a spectacular show for us, almost reflecting my mood and the events of the day. We're 60 miles south of Banks Peninsular. Gudrun stands on the bridge during my watch and tries to distance herself from Kevin, saying that he's 'gone over the top'. I grunt my responses.

My diary ends at this point. I didn't have the energy or enthusiasm to log our eventual arrival the following day, but it was a brief and sad separation I took from the crew in Lyttelton. Within two days, the ship was pulling out of the port yet again, heading for the Peninsular. Maj took over from me as campaigner. Egon, the chief engineer, handed me a package as he clambered on board, hugging me fiercely. 'Zese are for you, Wilx. It haz been a great honour to sail wiz you. I like you. One day we make strong Greenpeaze action togezer. Aufwiedersehen.'

Inside the package were three beautifully hand-crafted deck knives of different sizes in hand-sewn sheaths. He had made them in his spare time from pieces of 'scrap' metal lying around in the engine room, although the ship was forever short of paint scrapers after Egon had been on board. I was deeply touched.

Then Jim came towards me with most of the crew who had disembarked for one final round of bonding with me. Under his arm, he carried a limited edition painting of the Barn Glacier and Mount Erebus by Shackelton, grandson of the famous Ernest. The crew had signed the picture and Jim handed it to me with the hint of a tear in his eye. I burst into tears and hugged him.

Then they were gone. I watched the ship from the vantage point of the hills around Lyttelton. I watched her until she was no more than a speck on the horizon. I watched even after she had disappeared from view. There went my life, my friends, my world. I felt as though I had let everybody down. Sure, we had done the job and we had arrived safely home with a full crew and everyone healthy – at least physically. But I should have pushed myself harder perhaps. I should have been stronger, perhaps. But then again, bollocks to it. I'd done my stint and I had, I decided, nothing to feel ashamed of. It was time to get home and to get my life back in order.

Chapter 29

The gloves come off at last

I flew home. England was dull and cold. I was approached by Greg Butcher, MD of a company called Montagne Jeunesse, marketing similar products to the Body Shop, who wanted me as their green adviser. I was paid a decent monthly retainer which paid the rent and other constants and still left me money to spare. It was a wonderful arrangement and one which gave me a great deal of freedom since some months I was not required to do any work whatsoever. I wrote articles on the Antarctic for a number of journals and was invited to lecture on the subject frequently. My time was occupied and I was enjoying the freedom of independent consultancy work, yet I could not keep my mind off the Antarctic and what was happening to the *Greenpeace* crew in the Peninsular. Within three months I could think of nothing other than getting back to the Antarctic. The truth was that I wanted to put the icing on the cake and round off my Antarctic interlude with a memorable expedition which went beyond merely re-supplying the base and documenting the impact of the bases we visited. I wanted to put into practice the things McTaggart and I had spoken about in 1985: in short, to carry out direct actions in defence of the Antarctic environment rather than just 'bearing witness'.

As I carried out my consultancy tasks in the summer of 1988, I constantly tossed ideas for Antarctic activities around in my mind and fired them off to Kelly Rigg if I thought they had merit. She asked me if I was up for going again to Antarctica and as usual I moaned loudly but privately I was thrilled at the prospect. I told Kelly I would only consider it if I was given an open brief on how to operate the expedition in its entirety. I wanted Greenpeace to flex its muscles in a region and on an issue it had earned its spurs. She told me that if I went I would have a free run at the tactics we employed, so long as the final plan was agreed by her and the other desk-bound bosses we were required to doff our caps to. It sounded a good deal to me but I had one other demand. If Maj was not available as campaign assistant as she had indicated earlier, then I wanted Bogart, my US friend who was, after all, working on the campaign in Washington. She agreed that he could come on the voyage. Now I was really excited. We were going to finally kick ass in the Antarctic and undertake the first ever direct actions there to make the world sit up and take notice about what was happening to a back yard which belonged to us all.

Friends and colleagues could not believe that I was volunteering to do another trip to Antarctica. Every time I went away, the work I was gradually building up for myself in the UK took a nosedive and clients were never really sure if I could be relied on to be around to see the end of a job.

I plunged myself into finding the next wintering team with every ounce of energy I could muster, after telling my long-suffering benefactors at Montagne Jeunnesse that I had succumbed yet again. I had to find a base team leader who was experienced and who would, through his or her nationality, attract interest in a country hitherto largely unaffected by the gathering exposure of Antarctic matters. One person stood out from the lists of potential leaders like a beacon. Bruno Klausbruckner was something of a celebrity in his native Austria. He had led many expeditions to the Antarctic before and was celebrated for his larger-than-life status in Vienna where he worked for the City Council as a tourism promoter and guide.

Bruno came to see me in the UK. He was very definitely a man's man. While he recognised the need for a wintering crew of mixed nationalities, gender and skills, he was not enthusiastic about sharing a winter in difficult – and potentially dangerous – situations with women. Despite this, he readily accepted that, should he be appointed, he would be required to lead a team which would include women. As I pored over the applicants, an ideal team was there in theory at least: Bruno to lead it, an Italian nurse called Liliana whose nationality alone qualified her since we needed to boost the interest in that country, an American (to ensure interest from the country which had the largest potential for change in Antarctic matters) whom I identified as a female scientist Liz Carr, and a Kiwi, to keep local Antipodean interest alive, technician Phil Doughety. That was my ideal team on paper and I set out to piece it together. I had met Liz in the USA when I attended the inevitable and, to my mind, pointless, 'Expedition Review Meeting' in Washington and liked her. She was small, energetic and thoroughly likeable woman with a great sense of humour, a prerequisite for the expedition in my mind.

I interviewed Liliana in Rome along with three or four other Italians who had applied.

Liliana walked into the room. She was beautiful. She explained her belief in the wilderness values of the Antarctic in fiery, faltering English which I found endearing. I told her I'd let her know as quickly as possible if she had been successful in her application. Three days later, I was waiting on Vienna train station with Bruno Klausbruckner for Liliana's train to arrive from Rome as I wanted them to meet to see if there was a measure of compatibility, or at least, acceptance.

As the passengers disembarked, I saw her casually and languidly stepping out of the carriage, the last person to alight. She walked slowly up the platform, a shoulder bag casually slung over her shoulder. I muttered to Bruno that this was she and his eyebrows rose to the point where I thought they would leave his forehead. Bruno asked, 'Are you sure she is the right one, Wilks?' It was the opening gambit in a war which was to be openly fought between Bruno and Liliana for months to come.

We had, as usual, room on board for only a couple of selected journalists, plus a film team, and I set about snaring the best journalist in the UK, the Guardian's Paul Brown. Paul had become a close friend and colleague over the years, had covered many of the Greenpeace stories and was himself a campaigner. He knew the organisation, he was sympathetic to our goals, was a good friend and knew many of the crew with whom he would sail. The Guardian syndicated to over 200 newspapers around the world, giving us significant added value in taking Paul.

For the second journalist, I needed someone who would cover the USA directly and I asked the Washington Greenpeace office to recommend someone. They eventually suggested Mary-Ann Bendell who was freelancing for USA Today, the only truly national US newspaper. The film team consisted of two guys, Sean Leslie and Tim Fraser, who had been appointed by the Communications Division. The stills photographer was to be an old contact of mine who had covered previous actions in which I had been involved, Steve Morgan. The crew were identified, the campaign assistant, the press, film and photographers too. We were all set – on paper, at least. I now had to put it all together in reality.

It seemed that no sooner had I completed the work in Europe, choosing the wintering team, than I was packing to leave for New Zealand once again. This was to be my fourth consecutive Antarctic expedition as leader.

Paul 'Doglips' Bogart arrived in Auckland. I was delighted to see him and despite his jet lag, we decided to celebrate our reunion and the coming trip. We headed off to the local bar and soon found ourselves in the 'Floating Restaurant' moored alongside the fishing dock, only a short walk away from the ship.

The ship was, as usual, a constant hive of activity, both in the work and social sense. Henk Haazen would be coming with us on this trip and he was appointed the head of logistics. We had a new ship arriving for this expedition which I had previously seen in Amsterdam where she was undergoing her refit. She was an ocean-going tug, quite modern, a fact which did not endear her to many of the crew, and she had been renamed the *Gondwana*. But for the time being, we worked on the old stalwart of many a Greenpeace voyage, the Black Pig of a ship named *Greenpeace*. Henk immediately tacked a picture of Munch's 'The Scream' on the door to the small space we used as an office and dubbed it the Nervous Centre.

Since this was to be a special trip – and definitely my last – I lobbied Ken early on for a single cabin on the new ship which was soon to arrive in Auckland. He pondered it long and hard while I pointed out that if he accepted, as did we all, that the mates and the chief and second engineers all deservedly expected their own cabins, then surely the campaigner and expedition leader, given that his job was just as exacting, if not more so, than the key members of the crew, I deserved – no, damn it – I demanded my own cabin. Ken rubbed the sparse stubble on his chin while he pored over the cabin lay-out on the new ship. 'Ok. You take this one . . .' he jabbed at the lay-out with his pencil. 'It's strictly for two people but with the new accommodation block aft, I think we can stretch a point.' At last! After eleven years of sailing on Greenpeace ships I was to experience the unadulterated luxury of occupying my own cabin.

A few weeks later, the *Gondwana* arrived in Auckland and we all clambered into dinghies to roar off into the bay to greet her. She had been sailed across from Europe by a skeleton crew including Davey Edward who had found her and overseen the refit. He was standing by the rail on the bridge wing, pointing to the ship with one hand while holding his nose with the other – a self-deprecating gesture since he was very conscious that the ship would come under critical review by all the Greenpeace salts waiting to occupy her.

She looked 'all up front' to me: the bridge was almost on top of the foredeck and what had once been a long and empty aft deck now sported a hangar and a helideck on the stern, rather than the hawsers used in her tugging days. A new accommodation block had been extended from the wheelhouse aft, capable of sleeping twenty people. We noted wryly that she was shedding paint from her hull quite liberally as she cut her way – bulldozed her way, more correctly – across Manakau Harbour.

The *Gondwana* had to undergo a serious and lengthy period of further alteration in Auckland to rectify the failings of the original refit which her sea passage had brought to light. She had one overwhelming advantage over another other ship we could have used for the Antarctic runs: she was fully ice-strengthened.

While we carried on working on the *Greenpeace*, the *Gondwana* resembled a building site as welding and painting went on night and day to prepare her for the voyage, now only a scant few weeks away. We literally had to watch out for falling lumps of burning metal as we made our way around the ship and so much building and welding litter was scattered around the ship that I put a sizeable nail through my foot one morning which had me limping around for days and put a temporary halt to footballing activities. But as the work neared completion, it was time to transfer personal belongings and campaign material on to the *Gondwana* – the *Greenpeace* had other campaign fish to fry and we watched with affection as she steamed out of Auckland and out of our lives.

Meanwhile, the unlikely wintering team of Bruno, Liliana, Liz and Phil had taken off for the mountains to carry out their survival training. The reports which came back were at once hilarious and disconcerting. Apparently, Liliana and Bruno had been at each other's throats the entire time. Liliana had reportedly told Bruno to 'Fuck off!' more times than they'd had hot dinners and their relationship was at rock bottom when they arrived back on the ship. It was clear that Liliana was not going to make it in the team. We agreed that she would be replaced. She was genuinely upset by this decision but finally accepted the inevitable. She would stay on the ship to help us prepare but she would not travel with us.

I went to the local hospital to give a lecture to the nurses one evening and as a throwaway line at the end of my talk, I asked if anyone wanted to spend a year in Antarctica as part of the winter-over team. No-one responded, but the following morning a phone call came from a Danish nurse who had not been at the lecture but who had been told of my appeal. She was interested and available. Her name was Lilian Hansen and I met her in a restaurant in town where she was having a meal with her parents. She was a bright, energetic and thoroughly charming woman and she immediately became the first choice in our short-list of alternatives to Liliana.

Despite yet more misgivings from Bruno, to the point where one of his old Austrian climbing mates was flown in to Auckland for an interview – and dismissed from our thoughts on the grounds that he would form too tight a bond with Bruno – we finally appointed Lilian Hansen, much to Liz's delight as she had grown close to her in a very short space of time.

I instituted a regular Friday evening gathering of anyone who wanted to attend, to discuss direct action tactics on the upcoming voyage. Dumont D'Urville was relatively simple to address. We would simply block, with tents, the survival hut (known as an Apple) and ourselves, the hard rock runway the French were constructing in the middle of a 75,000-strong penguin colony , to prevent the French from gaining access to it and continuing their work. The whaling fleet which would be operating in the Southern Ocean at the time of our transit was a different matter. Traditional tactics would be employed, of course, but if we were to sustain the action – assuming there was an opportunity for action since we would first have to find the fleet in 160,000 square miles of ocean – then we needed to be able to build the story day by day and employ a range of actions to sustain interest. We discussed clamping banners across the stern ramp of the factory vessel, throwing nets over the harpoon, dousing the harpoonist with water and molasses and using the helicopter to dangle a banner in front of the harpoonist in order to obstruct his field of fire.

The final direct action would involve the giant US base at McMurdo. We agreed very quickly that we would block the outfall pipe which carries cadmium waste into Winter Quarters' Bay which was now biologically dead from heavy metal contamination run-off and direct discharges from McMurdo. Having agreed in broad terms our tactics, I set about ordering the eighteen banners we would need as visual support for the actions.

We were almost ready. The final days were a frantic round of goods arriving at the ship to be hoisted on board and stowed below in a cacophony of shouting and milling around of sweating bodies. We checked off list after list: equipment, stores, deadlines, campaign material, personnel. I constantly tried to catch Henk out on his ability to remember everything, rounding on him to shout out the name of an item, but he had everything covered down to the finest detail. I could fault no-one. We were all raring to go and all we needed now was to agree on the picture to accompany the press release about our departure. I decided to let the picture reflect our mood and hired a third helicopter from which Sean and Steve Morgan shot their stills and footage. The *Gondwana* steamed out of Auckland escorted by the two Hughes 500 Ds flying close to the ship on either side of her bridge and preceded in a V formation by all the inflatables. The caption read: 'The Greenpeace navy and airforce sets off to protect the Antarctic'. Our intentions could not have been made much clearer.

Our first port of call was Hobart, Tasmania, where we would wave the Greenpeace flag to drum up support in that Antarctic-important country and to collect our final passenger – Mary-Ann Bendell, our second journalist.

Crossing the Tasman, the weather was spectacular and I wrote in an early diary entry: 'The sun is just setting as I come off watch. Cloud banks on the horizon some twenty miles away provide a dramatic foreground to the sun's final curtsey and it leaves a dazzling pink etch to the extremities of the cloud formations which are so evocative and surreal it almost makes you believe in heaven. Maggie (McCaw) comments, 'We must have done something good to be privileged to see such a beautiful sight.' How right she is.'

30 December 1988

As we took on fuel, an airlock in the system caused an estimated 50 litres of fuel to 'blow back' and spill onto the deck from where it quickly ran into the water. Despite our efforts to disperse what is after all a minor slick, the water around the ship is a patchwork of rainbow colours reflected through the oil. We can't contain the news and Arne called me from the bridge to tell me that we are the lead item on the evening news. The ship was crawling with journalists by the early evening and I just had to tough it through.

By 1830 we're underway and passing the Harbour Bridge. Outside the heads, we heave-to in a slight swell to allow Davey to tie up the tail shaft on one engine to prevent it turning in sympathy with the one we intend to use on the way down, but incredibly he reports that 'the spanner doesn't fit' and we're forced to continue on two engines until he can make a suitable tool. Now Henk reports that the inflatable engines are running rough as well. Maybe we should start the entire day over again. Watch is tolerable. Two beers with Ken and Maggie. Bed at 0100.

31 December 1988
Weather picks up a bit today but it's still remarkably calm. Nothing much to report apart from the occasional feeling of nausea and a half-hearted attempt at a party after watch to celebrate New Year which had Ken pouring very generous measures of rum for people. Bed and out of it at 0200. Happy New Year.

1 January 1989
Felt rough on watch with cold symptoms and heartburn and hoped Ken would tell me to crash, but no such luck. Then the giro packed up. At 1230, I caved in and went to bed and didn't rouse myself until 1800. The luxury of my own cabin cannot be overstated. I can go in, close the door and listen to what I like, read, sleep, doze all without having to worry about a cabin mate and disturbance. It is situated as far forward as you can get on the port side main deck, directly opposite the mess, so it's a natural stopping off point for the crew and I delight in entertaining in my bolt hole which is wired up to a terrific sound system and looks very homely.

Two downsides though: it's right on the knuckle of the ship so I'll be getting a severe battering from the ice in this cabin and if I don't want visitors then I have to close the door and put a sign up to that effect otherwise people just assume it's a neat place to hang out for a chat and a beer. But all that pales into insignificance compared to the luxury it affords me. It's noticeably colder now – only plus 6 – and the sea is treating us gently thus far.

2 January 1989
Werner calls me gently: 'Your watch Wilks.'
I mumble 'Thanks, mate,' and immediately go back to sleep, only making watch at 0910. Meeting at 1630 with Bruno, Mark, Ken, Paul to discuss DuDu timing. I interview Bruno for Sean. Bruno did a good job – very succinct and passionate. Evening watch was spectacular with a cloudless sky and the beginnings of a weak aurora. Read for a while, sleep at 0030.

3 January 1989

Busy all day doing interviews to camera and interviewing the winterers for the benefit of the cameras and realise that while others sleep when off watch, I'm flat tack. But that's pretty usual I guess and I knew all this before I accepted the position. Ate the last of my chocolate this afternoon! Position is now 58 South and the weather is still remarkably calm. We still roll heavily but I'm off the pills now and feel ok, despite the usual feeling of being not quite 100%. Carried out a trawl at the convergence twice today, looking for marine litter, at which Davey caustically remarks, 'Aye. Anything to keep the boys and girls amused.'

4 January 1989

The crew meeting at 1100, to discuss DuDu tactics, was filmed and during it the reply from DuDu arrived saying that a peaceful demonstration would be in order provided it was planned and executed in accordance with French law (en metropole), confirming the view that they consider their base as part of their French territory. I transmitted the text to Remi in the Madrid office for his comments. Dinner and then dishes again with Pierrette and I get to the bridge for watch with seconds to spare. At 2130, the visibility is reduced to about 200 metres and we reduce revolutions, peering into the gloom from the bridge wing. Ken spots the first iceberg on radar and we go to port to see it. By 2330, we can see it clearly and the bridge is crowded with people. Ken's like a kid at Christmas and Dog, a little the worse for a few bourbons, is close to tears as he stares at the berg, drinking in its majesty. It is castellated and becaved and looms awesomely out of the grey. We celebrate after watch and my bottle of rum goes quickly between five of us. Bed at 0200.

5 January 1989

Low viz again and we're making 7 knots, 80 miles from DuDu. More bergs around but mostly hidden by mist. 65 South now but it's still plus 2 until a sou'easter takes it to minus 1. Ken revels in the cold and in his glee opens both bridge wing doors and tried to freeze us all. After lunch I'm occupied sending messages and meeting the journalists to go over times and places and story lines. Mary-Ann has been sick for the entire trip, poor love, and Dog has taken her under his wing a little to protect her from the increasingly barbed jibes she attracts. She just has a very unfortunate manner about her which is abrupt and naive to a fault. She'll come to dinner and poke the food around, commenting to the general assembly, 'What is this? Is this good to eat? Wouldn't eat this in California.'

In the pm, I tidy my cabin, discuss things in detail with Paul and then send out another update/press release. Ken comes around before watch handing out our one-piece Mustang survival suits – very flash! Arrive DuDu 1830. Lots of bergs crowd us as we nudge closer to the station and anchor. Ken takes a sweep around the bay in the inflatable as a recce for tomorrow. Bed at midnight.

6 January 1989

Up at 0930 and Tim immediately wires me up for the meeting with the OIC at DuDu, planned for 1100. We get ashore to be met by Houssein, the youngish and spiky-haired OIC who apparently speaks no English. We converse as well as we can in French, using Pierrette as interpreter where necessary. We amble along to his office at which a guy called Engler, a few of their scientists and the base doctor all sit in on the meeting.

Engler is a big guy, pretty brusque and is head of the construction team. He's been here since the airstrip project began five years ago and clearly dislikes a bunch of greenies telling him it is an unacceptable development, built as it is in the middle of breeding colonies of penguins which the French originally and ironically came here to study. His arguments are predictable: no alternative site for the runway, minimal damage created, penguins in fact 'benefit' from the airstrip as it makes access to the rookery easier(!) The discussion predictably broke no new ground and as it progressed I got more and more agitated, using Bogart as the voice of moderation as he weighed in with his scientifically-based arguments.

As we sat in the office we could see the impact of the construction work for ourselves: penguins running and scrambling everywhere before bulldozers and heavy machines and the helicopter overhead was low enough to scare us, let alone the penguins. Back to the ship at 1325 by which time Henk, Bruno, Ken and Marc have recced the site to establish where best to erect the hut for the most impact. Meeting at 1400 where I debrief the crew. Crew are given shore leave for the afternoon and I retire to my cabin to play the mournful Tracy Chapman whose song Sorry brings tears to my eyes.

7 January 1989

By 1030, the airstrip site is heaving with tractors, diggers and heavy machinery moving rocks from the quarries they are creating by blasting with dynamite and dumping them in 12 ton loads into the sea. This work proceeds at both the northern and southern ends of the strip, extending it into the sea in both directions. At noon, we land a party of people who stand at the neck of the strip stretching off to the south holding placards and the banner we prepared in Auckland – amazingly it is exactly the right length!

The workers stop work and sit around watching us with open contempt and Henk sidles up to me to suggest that we allow work to resume and then stretch the banner out again to trap as many of their vehicles in our cul-de-sac as possible. I agree and after a few minutes of truck movements, three of their huge dumpers are at the southern end of the strip and we quickly stretch out the banner again. This results in another period of idleness during which Ken and Henk begin lugging the sections of the Apple hut ashore and furiously begin constructing it.

At first, the workers simply look on with curiosity but as it begins to assume a recognisable shape, they become agitated and Engler rushes up and orders his drivers to start up their vehicles to extricate them from our little trap. A huge digger noses up to our picket line. Bruno and Dog stand firm. Thankfully, the driver stops and switches off the engine, giving us precious time to finish the construction of the hut.

By 1300, the hut is completed and the workers seem to have accepted defeat and have left the site and their three dump trucks blocked in by our picket line. The hut is secured by driving pegs into the permafrost and it is wide enough to leave only a few feet of space between its sides and the steep incline at the edge of the airstrip. We spend a quiet afternoon lazing in the sun and revelling in our victory –work has stopped all over the strip.

I contemplate sending out a press release but something tells me I should wait. At 1900 my intuition is rewarded. A clanking of machinery and the sound of engines heralds the arrival of a huge digger surrounded by a menacing crowd of scruffy workmen. Engler is at the head of it, looking bigger and angrier than before. Houssein calls me on the VHF and asks me to allow the removal of their trucks. I reply in the negative to which he replies, 'C'est un dommage.'

Engler waves forward the digger which lowers a wicked-looking scoop on the front of the machine and ploughs into our line of defence. All hell breaks loose. Werner jumps into the scoop and people clamber all over the machine. Meanwhile, behind us, drivers are firing up the engines on the immobilised trucks and they move towards us from the rear. Our people are throwing themselves under wheels and being unceremoniously dragged away and dumped on the ground and sat on by the workers. This mayhem goes on for twenty minutes. We're hauled out of the way and thrown bodily to the floor. All the time, the digger is attempting to move the hut to one side, using the scoop, to make more roadway available for the lorries. Having bundled us up and sat on us, the dumper trucks squeeze past our blockade, narrowly missing flailing arms and legs.

The lorries force their way past and, to the cheers of the French, make their escape. Our hut, however, if a little battered and askew, is still more or less in place and still guards the access to the southern end of the airstrip. As we regroup and survey the cuts and bruises we have sustained, I call Houssein on the VHF and, as best as my limited French will allow, I complain about the aggression shown by his men. He immediately invites me to his office. He says he will come to the ship later to view the video our reporters shot. This he does, but by then I'm busy sending our pictures and press releases. In the saloon, he views the videos and admits to Dog that he has 'uncontrollable elements' in his workforce, that it was a violent reaction and he accepts responsibility. He agrees to stop work on the strip immediately and to ask Paris for instructions. Bed at 0300 after pix and press release out.

8 January 1989

Crew meeting at 0900. Telex arrives from Houssein at 0930 containing the wording of a telex from the French Antarctic Territory chief which says that we are not abiding by the 'code of conduct' required by French law and that we are therefore 'intruders' who should be 'dealt with accordingly'. I reply that the 'code of conduct' is not binding as this is not French territory and that we'll continue our action: the hut is still occupied and is still preventing work on the southern end of the strip. Now it is time to concentrate on the activity at the northern end of the strip.

At 1800, I inform Houssein that we are to carry out a direct action there by positioning our people directly in the path of the rocks which are being dumped over the eight foot scree slope. We cross to the site in inflatables and climb onto the rocks. Our presence forces the workers to desist from dumping over the edge of the scree, but they begin dumping their 12 ton loads on rocks and huge boulders on the flat, to be pushed over the edge later when we have left. We decamp and climb up onto the flat area ourselves and stand directly behind the trucks as they dump. They ignore us and just keep on dumping on the assumption that we're not going to kill ourselves by standing in the path of 12 tons of falling rocks. Henk seems to have nerves of steel. He simply won't move out of the way. He leaves it to the last split second before moving and I scream at him to get out of the way. Dog has to physically bundle Henk to the side. The French guys seem completely unmoved by our actions – apart from one guy who genuinely pleads with me to stop this madness – and we are very lucky that we have sustained no injuries.

The party is broken up by a long blast on the ship's klaxon – the recall signal –Ken has heard on the VHF that while we've been engaged at this end of the strip, the French have taken advantage of our preoccupation to make another attempt at removing the hut on the southern end of the strip. Ken, waiting in the dingy off-shore, roars in to collect us. I throw myself on board, falling in among arms and legs as Ken opens the throttle and roars off to the southern end of the strip. As we round the headland at full speed, we can see the digger dragging the hut up the runway. We stream ashore as Ken drives the inflatable nose-first onto the scree slope. We climb the scree in two bounds and run towards the melee of hut and bodies half obscured by a cloud of dust.

The French are unnerved and within a matter of thirty seconds, we have dumped most of their guys to the floor in a less-than-non-violent direct action. I am held by two guys preventing me from getting involved in the central melee and then Ken, who by now has secured the inflatable, takes them both out in one flying tackle. As we get to our feet, Ken propels me with a mighty shove towards the hut where Henk is throwing French guys aside like so much confetti. Suddenly, the resistance melts away and we gain the hut entrance. A few more shoves and the French guys are dislodged and we pile inside the battered hut. We collapse in a heap of laughing, sweating bodies on the floor of the hut before pushing it back down the 'piste' and putting it back in position.

Still shaking with anger, I call Hussein on the VHF and scream at him. He simply accuses us of 'violence'. Someone on board suggests we remove the Greenpeace signs from the banners and just have it on with the French. While it's a wild and ridiculous idea which we discard immediately, it is true that there are no laws which govern Antarctic territory. The French have earned a particularly bad reputation with us since the *Rainbow Warrior* sinking and the murder of Fernando, so hackles are already up, but we agree to continue in a responsible and – as far as is possible – non-violent manner.

Up till 0330 firing off the press release and pictures and finally fall into bed, resigned to finding a way to extricate ourselves from this increasingly violent situation with grace. Paul Brown apparently interviewed Engler today who said that if Greenpeace wanted to commit suicide that was fine by him: the work will continue.

9 January 1989
No work on the site today as Hussein declares it a day of 'maintenance' for the vehicles and machinery. I go ashore early and secure an agreement from the shore party that we should desist from any further direct action on the northern end of the site and concentrate our efforts on the continuing blockade at the southern end of the strip, thereby hopefully removing the cause of further 'provocation' and retaliation from the French.

At 1430, Dog and I meet Houssein to tell him we will forego further direct actions in return for a guarantee of no further violence and an agreement to let us stay on the southern end of the strip unmolested, as is our right. He says it is a decision which will have to come from Paris and will depend on how long we intend to stay, the inference being that if we announce we are staying longer than the French want, they'll physically remove us. I agree to let him know our preferred quit-by date by midnight tonight and spend the rest of the day discussing it with the crew on board the ship and those ashore occupying the hut.

The area around the hut has returned to its pre-French-airstrip-project tranquillity. Penguins wander around and bask in the sun and have an altogether different attitude in the peace and quiet we have created. It is a pleasure to sit around the hut, chat, smoke and drink tea while penguins waddle up to us and eye us with curiosity. A more romantic person than I would hope that they were saying thanks.

We agree, after a lot of talking among the crew, to stick to our original ten day occupancy plan, which, means leaving on the 15th. This seemed to me to be a neat way to keep the crew happy (by sticking to our original plan) while fortuitously being able to make what seemed to be a small concession to the French. I communicate this decision by telex to Houssein at 2350. Drinks and bed by 0200 after sorting out a system for alerting the shore party and vice versa of any nocturnal activities spotted ashore.

10 January 1989
Up at 0645 for interview with CNN. Houssein calls at 0930 to advise there's still no official response from Paris but unofficial indications are that they are 'unhappy' with our proposed departure date of the 15th. Finally, at 2330, the message arrives from Paris and it's basically, 'get out by the 13th and we'll offer you a meeting with the scientists for an exchange of information and a tour of inspection'. This causes a mixed reaction from the crew. Fall into bed hoping we can come to a satisfactory and peaceful conclusion to this campaign, but we are sitting pretty; we can't lose!

11 January 1989
Up early for a crew meeting on the bridge, at which I manage to steer the decision towards accepting the French requirement to remove the base by the 13th, on the assurance that conditions are met concerning the tour of the site. Send off our conditions of acceptance but not until I've had a further meeting with the shore party about the wisdom (or lack of it) of this decision. I argue that it's time to focus attention on the real issues at stake here rather than on continued French violence, and that we can't afford to miss the opportunity to get some hard information for once. I get an agreement from all concerned, much to my relief, although not until Henk has soundly trashed the 'long-winded scientific bullshit' and has made a pitch for hanging out until the 15th. This upsets Dog considerably and while I'm preparing the telex back on the ship, he's really down at Henk's attitude and resolves to have it out with him. Reuters, AFP and AP all call wanting pictures of the 'return to work' at the base and Steve duly obliges. Then Ken decides to turn his small cabin into a disco and by 2300 there are at least twelve people in his room, singing their heads off and trying to dance. The party moves to the saloon where it really gets going and people quite rightly let off a lot of steam. Bed by 0030.

12 January 1989

Up at 0630 for interviews with Reuters, AAP, Christchurch Press, German agencies and ABC. A reply arrives from Houssein about 1000. He comes very close to meeting our demands on the conditions of the tour, but curiously talks of unspecified 'sites' which we can go 'around' but not 'on top of' and he also mysteriously calls for a meeting on the 13th not the 14th as agreed. I send off a further telex asking for clarification by midday and then sit around with Dog until Henk calls from the shore telling us they're landing equipment behind the hut from a landing craft. I call Houssein to ask what's going on and the rest of the day degenerates into a sort of Brian Rix farce with workers on shore goading us into a reaction and Houssein and I arguing over yards of territory.

At one time I even allow Houssein to move 'only two' boxes from the equipment they've offloaded and 'no more' as they contained sensitive equipment. The most curious aspect of this is that he agreed! Engler is on the airstrip twice during the afternoon and he must be the most chagrined of all, having to bow to the demands of a bunch of peace freaks. Paul, Dave and Albert are sent ashore to boost numbers in case Engler tries any independent action. All quietens down eventually and the evening passes calmly after I send out yet another update to offices. Another party inevitably erupts around 2200.

13 January 1989

Our last day at DuDu. We all go ashore and dismantle our brave little hut, but before doing so Steve insists that we have a celebration picture taken. We all decide to give the finger in the unofficial version and even Paul Brown, our 'independent journalist' is to be seen grinning from ear to ear with his middle digit held aloft. Houssein and his scientific entourage come over and escort our team off on the inspection tour, including Dog, Pierrette, Liz and Lilian, crowded round by our press contingency and official French observers.

We continue with the hut dismantling and load the sections back onto the inflatables and ferry them back to the ship. On the last of these trips we go the long way back to the ship to take in the paradise of the as-yet untouched but condemned islands which stand in the path of the airstrip . It is just so beautiful to see penguins swimming and squabbling in the sun and when we switch off the engines the tranquillity of the place, away from the construction site, is quite overpowering.

The science party returns at 1900 after a long and hard day. Paul Brown writes a piece which declares this is the first time the French has actually acknowledged Greenpeace as a bona fide outfit whose interests and concerns are genuine. Late night party in Pat's cabin at which a bleary Henk hugs me and breathes rum all over me as he declares, 'You're an asshole, Wilks, but you're the best.' As I wander off to bed, a guy from Paris Match turns up from shore and wants to interview me. I finally get to bed at 0300 but God knows what I told the guy from Paris Match. I still have the presence of mind to put a big sign on the door of my cabin – 'Definitely no calls at all! Any press or campaign work – see Doglips!'

14 January 1989
Luxuriate in bed until 1120. The prospect of a lazy day has me pottering about the ship until 1400 when I can't resist another spin around the glaciers with Maggie, Pat, Merriann, Dave and Phil. It's quite a magical time and we're all dumbstruck by the majesty of the ice, the caves, the colours and the cascading icicles which hang down from the overhangs in sparkling arrays of tumbling ice, gently dripping in the sun. On a sloping ice ledge, we find an empty box of explosives and later, I send the manufacturers name and details from the box to Greenpeace in Sydney and they make another story out of exposing Australia's complicity in the ruination of Antarctica. We return to the small cove we visited a few days ago and watch the penguins squabbling, swimming and preening, and having all sorts of fun in the water. Adelies captivate me – so cute, cheeky and with a constantly surprised look on their faces.

Back on the ship at 1600 and I feel moved to take my sketch pad on deck and draw the scene from deck. Prepare emails while Dog sleeps off his night shift, covering for me. Crew meeting at 1930 after the French chopper pilot and his oppo have the temerity to come on board when he spent a good part of his day 'buzzing' the penguin rookeries just for the hell of it. He gets a full broadside from me and his smile turns to an embarrassed scowl as he slinks off muttering indecipherable French curses. My bile is intensified by Liz telling me that as she carried out sampling work on the strip today, she was followed by a bunch of French jerks who hassled her and made constant rude and sexist comments to her.

Back on bridge watches tonight as we finally leave DuDu and the penguins to the mercy of the French. Ken tells us watchkeepers to go below tonight as there are so many people on the bridge that the 'official' watchkeepers can take a blow. A few drinks with the crew as we head towards Commonwealth Bay. It's good to sit and chat with people I haven't had a great deal of time to see over the last few days and the stories all come out as people crack beers and begin to relax after an intense but highly profitable ten days. Perhaps we didn't stop the airstrip, but we interrupted their work considerably and we put the issue before the public in a major way. We cost them money and we gathered valuable scientific information to use as lobby material in the future.

15 January 1989

Awake to find us stooging around off Commonwealth Bay. Forty knots of katabatic wind whip up long, steep seas from the shore, the tops are snatched into sheets of spray which reflect rainbows in the air against an intense sun. The coast is totally ice-covered apart from a half-mile stretch which marks the entrance to Commonwealth Bay. It was here that probably the greatest Antarctic explorer of all time – Douglas Mawson – suffered such dire privations. During the 1920s, he and two colleagues, Ninnis and Mertz, were left here to complete a scientific and geographical exploration of the interior. Their hut still stands and I was anxious to get to see it.

The three set off with dogs and provisions but Ninnis died after falling into a crevasse, taking with him most of the food and one sledge and dogs. Mertz and Mawson turned around and began the long journey back to camp but Mertz fell ill and died, leaving Mawson alone with hardly any food and only six dogs. He cut the remaining sledge in half and began his tortuous walk home. His dogs were starving and he was forced to feed them on scraps of leather cut from his equipment. Then he began eating his dogs in order to survive. They were so frail and devoid of muscle that he found the livers to be the most nutritional parts available and ate them mostly raw. Eventually his last dog had to be killed and he was alone. As he struggled on, he suffered impaired vision, headaches, blackouts and from hard skin forming the soles of his feet which began literally peeling away like a false sole.

He was suffering from Vitamin A poisoning, although this was not to be established until well after his eventual death. The vitamin was stored in the dogs' livers and is lethal to humans in concentrated doses. Mawson was so weak that he was forced to begin crawling the final thirty miles or so back to his base, knowing all the time that the ship bringing his relief party would depart by an agreed date if there was no sign of his party. Mawson dragged himself over the lip of a hill which we could see from the bridge of the *Gondwana* and looked down onto his hut and the bay, only to see the ship leaving. He had literally missed the boat by a matter of hours.

Two men had been left behind, however, and Mawson was forced to spend a further winter convalescing in Commonwealth Bay until the relief ship, unable to be recalled the previous year due to the absence of radio, returned to take Mawson back to a hero's welcome in Australia. Mawson went on to lead further expeditions to Antarctica before succumbing to the poisoning he had unwittingly administered to himself during that gruelling trip in 1912.

We can't use the boats in this wind so we heave-to and wait. Davey comes up from the engine room and asks Arne to move the ship under power to keep a flow of water through the engines. Then he reappears to ask us to put on more speed to stop the props from cavitating. . The crew are getting anxious to move on to look for the whalers but I insist that it's important politically (for the Australian connection) for us to get into the bay and send back reports to the Australian press about our visit. We agree to wait until 2400 to seek an improvement in the weather and by 1430 we put the boats in the water.

Dog, Bruno, Liz and I go in the first boat. It's a choppy, wet ride but as we enter Boat Harbour the sea flattens and we see before us a wonderland of basking seals and colonies of squawking penguins which seem oblivious to our presence. We radio for the next boat to be sent and wait for 30 minutes, sitting in the sun watching the penguins. There are amazing rock formations everywhere and the entire area has a magical quality about it. Once we're all assembled, we head off towards Mawson's hut, some half a mile inland, which we access across a glassy ice sheet resembling a miniature glacier. The rocks which protrude through the ice are crammed full of dead penguin chicks around their base and I ponder the awful death these poor creatures must have suffered as they lay helplessly trapped by rocks and steep-sided gullies between the ice and the base of the rocks.

The hut itself is like new, the wood having been scoured to a shining white by the wind-blown grit. Around the hut lies the usual tip of discarded equipment – boots, wire, fuel drums, wooden poles, empty containers – all of which have, of course, like Scott's rubbish at Cape Evans, assumed monument status. Amongst the ancient dross I'm horrified to see the litter of those who came here with the express purpose of restoring the hut – modern cans, containers and rubbish left by Project Blizzard. These will form a nice little sting in the tail of the press releases we'll be sending to the Australian press.

All back on the ship by 2130 after a special boat is sent to take the trepidacious Mary-Ann Bendell ashore – her first such venture. Get underway immediately and set to work on the press releases and picture captions and hit the sack at 0200, not before Paul Brown tells me that Naoko has broached the subject of anti-Japanese attitudes on board, evidenced by racist comments. I promise Paul that I'll deal with it tomorrow.

16 January 1989

Only six press calls interrupted my day. After watch, despite my promise to Paul about Naoko, I crash out and sleep from 1230 to 1730 – sheer luxury and unadulterated self-indulgence. The discussion about the attempt to get into Leningradskaya is inconclusive and we agree to wait until we get closer to see what the ice conditions are like. On watch we are missing out on Bruno and Liz's birthdays, but Ken dispatches me to the saloon at 2350 to tell the gathering party to look out of the starboard port holes – Liz and Bruno's birthday presents have arrived – pack ice! The bridge is immediately crowded with people photographing the amazing expanses of sea ice stretching away to our starboard. Bed at 0130.

17 January 1989

We're at 64 South and the weather is very mild and the sea amazingly flat. I decide to confront the issue of racism raised by Naoko. I get Paul and Naoko together with Dog to thrash it out. I promise that I'll have a quiet word with offending crew members whom Naoko names but she's more concerned with the banners we have prepared which read 'Stop the Bloody Whaling' which, in Japanese, translate to 'stop the barbaric whaling'. Since there is no distinction in Japan between killing cows and killing whales, she feels that a display on TV of banners reading thus will put Greenpeace in a bad light. She also points out, disingenuously, that it's the Japanese who consider westerners like us as 'barbarians'.

344

I promise to discuss it with Duncan Campbell, the international whale campaigner in Washington, and change the banners if that is felt to be the right course of action. On watch at 2000 to see a falling barometer, heavy snow and zero visibility. The wind picks up quickly and the ship begins to roll and pitch heavily. Ken alters course to 170 towards the Bellaneys. Bed at 0130 after two beers with Ken, Steve, Liz, Maggie and Merriann.

18 January 1989
The scraping and bumping of the ship negotiating five tenths ice interrupts my sleep. Arne steers us through large ice floes in a flat calm sea under grey, lowering skies and then hands over to Ken. We have decided now to make for Leningradskaya and contact the Soviets to make arrangements. They seem delighted that we'll be making an attempt at a visit. But this slow progress, despite the *Gondwana's* ability to shoulder large floes out of her path with ease, means we're behind schedule. The Soviets don't come up on the 1100 radio schedule. At the 2000 crew meeting to discuss Leningradskaya we agree to continue with the plan to visit since it will be the first time a Soviet base has been inspected. On watch after the meeting to see seven tenths ice now and much reduced progress. We're making only 2-3 knots and hitting ice every few seconds.

19 January 1989
We're supposed to fly to Leningradskaya today but we're still 165 miles off at noon – too far for the choppers. By evening watch we're still over two degrees away (120 miles) and a flight is still out of the question. The ice is getting worse and Arne stayed at the controls for the entire 8-12 watch today. We get deeper and deeper into the ice and the floes get larger and larger – ice-free water is now a thing of rarity. The crashing and banging of ice on metal is severe and sleep is impossible. Finally pass 68 South in fine weather – minus 2 and zero wind.

20 January 1989
We passed the 80 miles from Leningradskya marker today and Bob reports that on the 4-8 he encountered a lot of free water and the log indicates we made 8 knots during the night. I get the helo guys fired up and checking the machines and tell the journalists and film crew to be on ten minutes stand-by. Sean asks, 'Are you really intending to fly from here?' Position at 1130 is 68, 31 South, 161, 14 East and we arrive at a more or less solid sheet of sea ice.

The 0800 schedule with the Soviets indicated 2 miles of visibility at their base and we wait until the 1400 schedule for a more favourable report. Both helos are tested and it appears that they each have faults, most notably a 'dodgy' compass in TN (call sign). The 1400 schedule indicates 11 miles visibility followed by another report almost immediately of an unexpected and severe weather change at Leningradskaya, forcing us to stand down again. By 2000, the ship is basking in brilliant sunshine and visibility is unlimited, but Ian can't raise the Soviets to check the weather their end and Dave Walley, sensibly, will not fly until a weather report is received.

There is a brief diversion for a while as we spend most of our evening watch dislodging a giant rock which has become wedged in the anchor, collected at Commonwealth Bay. Sean does some interviewing with me and Lilian. It is quite an incredible feeling being stuck here in almost ten tenths ice with nothing on any side but endless sheets of ice. We feel a little vulnerable and there is muttered talk in the saloon of being beset. Bed at 0200 after doing my long-overdue dobying.

21 January 1989

It's 0140 and I'm finally in bed after a particularly memorable day. At 0800 this morning the schedule with the Soviets indicated 27 miles visibility, 24 knot winds, minus 5 degrees and a 'go' situation. With ill-concealed excitement, I rounded up those due to fly and told them to be on the helideck at 0945 sharp, having previously allocated seating arrangements with Dave and Pierrette. By 1015, people are still not on station and with rising anger I am forced, yet again, to go and round people up. Paul Brown is eating cornflakes in the mess, if you please! I give him such a broadside that he chokes on his breakfast and promises to be there in five minutes. Then I see Naoko strolling around the foredeck with a cup of tea and I bawl at her, 'Naoko, you're supposed to have been on the helideck half an hour ago!' She seems unmoved. Christ what a bunch!

Then Sean comes to me to announce that he's not coming with us. He's unhappy to fly 65 miles over ice and possibly water and he's unhappy about stories which are doing the rounds concerning 'incorrect maintenance' on the aircraft. (It also transpired later that friends of Sean's had recently died in a helo crash.) I can't believe that he would leave it this long to tell me his fears. We've struggled all this way only to be told that we will not be able to have a filmic documentation of the Soviet base. Mary Ann hears this and bottles out too, although her absence will not be a huge loss to world journalism. So now we're down to seven people and as we're just about to board the helos, Leningradskya comes on again to tell us the weather has crapped out again. I'm just about to call off the entire venture but Arne convinces me to wait until the noon schedule. Sit drumming my fingers until 1200 when Dave appears on the bridge and says, 'Let's go! Weather's fine now!'

Even our reduced numbers of seven can't make it on time and the 1215 departure becomes a 1320 departure. We lift off with a back-bearing to the ship our only guide across this icy wasteland until Dave picks up the Leningradskaya beacon. It is quite an incredible feeling to be blasting off into the unknown like this and within a matter of five minutes we are flying over ice-free water to the south of the ship's position. We fly in tandem and make stupid faces at each other through the windows of the helicopters. After 45 minutes, we can see the coast rising before us, just a hump in the all-pervading whiteness. Bruno picks out the glacier and Dave announces to everyone's relief that he has locked onto the Soviet beacon. Then we can see it – a cluster of buildings perched precariously on top of a thousand foot high nunatak. I am speechless at the view: spectacular is not the word. We make a circuit to come in upwind and watch the figures below rushing about excitedly waving and slapping backs. These guys have not seen another person outside their own number for 14 months; they haven't seen a woman in that time either and we have two with us! We touch down and Dave shuts off the engine.

As the rotors slow, the helicopter is surrounded by excited personnel. The OIC greets me with a formal handshake and we spend fifteen minutes just standing there, talking in a mixture of German, English and Russian, trying to decide what to do first. Through translations, it goes something like, 'Beer first then walk around, or walk around first then beer. Or vodka? While we are deciding, let's go and have a beer anyway.' We're plied with beer as we walk towards one of the larger huts and are ushered into a room set for a meal. Vodka is served to the men, champagne to the women, who have already attracted great interest from the base crew. Much exchanging of gifts and much toasting to nebulous things. A picture of Gorbachev adorns the wall, minus the prominent birthmark on his forehead. I swap my baseball cap with the base commander for a decidedly Russian woolly cap with a cardboard peak. The conversation goes from English to German to Russian, back to German and then finally the answer arrives in English. To a question such as 'What do you do with your rubbish?' the answer arrives five minutes later, 'Two fish' at which everyone roars with laughter.

It's difficult to concentrate on the job of criticising cavalier attitudes to the fragile Antarctic environment in the company of such hospitable people and when your belly's half full of vodka. After the meal, we go walkabout and discover that the base, as predicted, is a complete mess of discarded machines, lorries and containers of all descriptions. All the junk, we are assured, is 'waiting to be retrograded.' Yeah, sure. We do our job of logging the answers and the state of the base but it's hard to be testy with these smiling and happy people. We gather enough information for our report and notice that a recent snowfall has had the grace to cover up most of the junk which undoubtedly lies beneath the snow.

Sanitation is a series of oil drums positioned directly beneath the toilet block which has holes cut in its floor. There is no doubt that once full, they are tossed over the edge of the nunatak onto the ice 1000 feet below: it is littered with thousands of barrels which we mistook for seals on our flight in. Their claims of a recent change for the good in retrograding policies is hard to believe since the base is like Steptoe's junk yard – but worse. Much to their horror, we announce that we must leave. Beds have been prepared for us to stay overnight, but amid much hugging and exchanging of yet more articles of clothing, we prepare to leave. Our hosts are still waving as we lift off and immediately drop down to the ice to inspect the 'seals'.

The flight back to the ship has a dreamlike quality, helped by the vodka, no doubt, but the light and the ice formations are simply majestic and breathtaking. We pick up the ship's beacon with no problem and home in on our tiny speck of metal sitting in the endless sea of ice below. I'm excused watch as the ship does an about turn with some difficulty and after a few drinks with Dave, Bruno, Dog and others to relate our experiences, I crash at 0030, falling into an exhausted but satisfied sleep to the scrape and thunder of ice being beaten into surrender.

22 January 1989
On watch at 0800 to see we're surrounded by ten tenths ice. The temperature

is minus 8 and the sea is freezing. As the bow dislodges a newly-frozen layer of gossamer ice, it skates across the top of the neighbouring sheet with zero friction, to be dashed against the larger and older sea ice some twenty yards away. Fascinating. The sun shines, there's no wind and I'm captivated by it all. Dog remarks that it's like witnessing creation all over again. I can't drag myself away from the bridge wing all morning. I simply stand and watch the seals and penguins and the stunning scenery.

The need to get press releases out brings me back to reality and not until 1600 am I free of such boring work. Onto the bridge to see the helos up ice-spotting and returning with reports that free water is a mere 20 miles ahead. At 3-4 knots in a zigzag line, that could mean another 12 hours. Debrief the crew about Leningradskaya at 1300, after which Henk asks me to stand in for him in helo operations and I agree, not finishing until 1900. Arne pushes the bow between floes, increasing the revs to force them apart, all the time trying to make a course for Sturge Island. Any progress is a struggle. Davey walks around with a disgruntled attitude because the film guys didn't go to Leningradskaya after all the hard work done in the engine room and on deck to get us within flying distance. Davey feels rightly that they had more of a duty to the expedition. But he won't bring it out in the open. Bed at 0230 after waiting for Ken to come off an extended watch.

23 January 1989
Mother's birthday today. Will call her tonight. On watch to see the ice thinning at last and Sturge Island only 12 miles off. The floes are still close together but smaller and curled at the edges, indicating recent origin. We plough through at an increased speed in our red, floating bulldozer. Arne asks Ken to do an ice recce and I'm therefore promoted to organising 'helicopter operations' which is strictly Ken's reserve. So there I am out on the helideck wearing the airband radio and headset, taking and giving instructions between the bridge and the helicopter. Real Boy's Own stuff. Sean is up filming Sturge Island in HOQ as well, so it gets pretty hectic on the flight control deck, but I love every moment of it. Here I am, an ex-lorry driver from Deptford controlling two helicopters from the deck of a ship deep in the Antarctic. Sturge Island is so dramatic: 3000 foot sheer cliffs topped by huge ice-caps waiting to crash into the sea below.

Weather still calm, little wind but dark lowering clouds ahead which portend heavy snow. Bruno asks me at lunch to illustrate a fairy story he has written for his children. I'm touched at the request and also at the tenderness of the story, so incompatible with the Bruno I am used to. Finally clear the pack ice and only a few growlers and bergy bits remain. The wind and sea pick up considerably and we're soon moving around in a steep swell. By 2200 I'm feeling queasy after days of working in ice. As I hang on grimly at my watch post the fire alarm sounds, just to add a bit of spice to the day, and we all rush to our positions. Turns out that a small fire in one of the engine room switchboards has taken out the old accommodation lights, so half the ship is without illumination. After dealing with this little emergency we all get back on watch, but by 2230 still feeling seasick so Ken tells me to go below which I gratefully do. I crash onto my bunk which brings almost instant relief from the nausea and wonder why, after all this time at sea, I still can't finally and comprehensively beat this curse.

24 January 1989

Despite only a slight improvement in the weather, I stand my watch and find Ken in a very strange mood. He's very hyped this morning and mutters constantly 'Saturday night at the base camp.' He doesn't stop laughing and joking and this is very un-Ken-like. Watch over, lunch is a sad affair with only six of us eating. I'm surprised that so many of the crew are in a worse condition than I was yesterday when the weather has actually improved slightly. Perhaps I am getting my sea legs after all and there is no better feeling than the absence of sea-sickness at sea.

After lunch, I have a campaign/ship meeting, with Dog and I representing the campaign and Davey (as chief) and Arne representing the ship. It's a 'cards on the table' discussion and I ask Davey to spill all his bile. He's angry that neither the film crew nor Mary Ann went to Leningradskaya, and feels that the considerable fuel, energy and time we spent getting there was wasted, due to their lack of enthusiasm. In addition, he's furious with Dave and Pierrette for allegedly drinking on the night previous to flying to Leningradskaya and he finally adds that he's sick and tired of all the criticism he's had to brook in the past about his choice of the *Gondwana* as the Antarctic vessel. We all allow Davey to vent his spleen to his heart's content since I in particular recall what happened on the 1985-86 trip when he exploded after bottling up all his

350

emotions for months. Davey has his say, and I give my justifications. All depart apparently happy.

After the meeting, I prepare updates for the offices, Dog gets on with his report and Steve works in the darkroom. I wander into the saloon at 1600 with a cup of tea and a few minutes later Albert sneaks up behind me and whispers, 'There's a ship on the horizon, Wilks. Could be a whaler.'

I'm almost tempted not even to respond to such a wind-up but instead mutter, 'Get outta here Albert.'

He replies, to my growing incredulity, 'I'm serious, Wilks. Come and see for yourself.'

'I'll be up in a few minutes Albert.'

The likelihood of us finding the Japanese whaling fleet in 160,000 square miles of ocean even if we were deliberately looking for them is remote. To literally 'bump into them' would be a million to one shot. But Albert's words get the better of my curiosity and I wander up to the bridge. I can't believe what I see: all the mates and Arne are on the starboard bridge wing, training binoculars on a distant speck. The radar sweep shows three echoes – one a very large ship. Arne passes me the glasses and as the ship briefly appears between the swells, the distinctive shape of a whaler – stubby but very high bow, low freeboard and a crow's nest atop the mainmast, confirms our wildest dreams. We have run slap bang into the Japanese whaling fleet!

Ian Balmer rushes in from the radio room, his face beaming as he announces, 'Wilks! Wilks! We've picked them up on the HF! Naoko and I scanned the frequencies and stopped at the first Japanese language we could hear, and it's the whaling fleet! They're saying to the scout boat to investigate and if it's Greenpeace, they'll try to outrun us and to watch our boarding tactics. Holy shit, I can't believe this!'

The catcher 'scout' ship came within half a mile of us and then headed back to the factory ship, the 40,000 ton *Nishin Maru*, which now loomed large just two miles away. She lumbers up to us, her guardrails lined with aproned workers from the bowels of the ship. I call the ship on the VHF and their chief scientist comes on the line. He's more interested in what we are doing than giving any information away, but he tells us that they are conducting approved scientific whaling and that they have caught 40 whales thus far. I tell him that their actions are condemned universally and that we will be taking peaceful direct action to prevent any further whaling if they resume. Ian, now monitoring the radio constantly with Naoko, reports that the skipper of the *NM* is contacting Tokyo for instructions and has informed his catchers not to kill any whales while we are around. A victory without a shot being fired! Arne asks me if we should tell them how long we'll be monitoring their activities. No way, Arne. We'll keep them guessing as long as possible. Two beers after watch as we all lie a-hull in a peculiar and improbable fleet of two whale catchers, a factory ship and a Greenpeace protest vessel, a thousand miles away from the nearest land.

25 January 1989

The *NM* took off in the night at 10 knots in a NE direction and as I reach the bridge at 0800 she's stopped again, the catchers nowhere in sight. We've decided to stick to the factory ship because we can just about match her for speed and the catchers must rendezvous with her at some point. We realise this is leaving whales at the mercy of the catchers, but to chase a catcher would mean being outrun and losing the factory ship. We send up the helos for some stock shots of the *NM* for possible use later. Out goes the press release: 'GP intercepts the Japanese whaling fleet in the Southern Ocean' – a bit of literary licence, but never let the truth stand in the way of a good story, as my old mate Bryn Jones would say.

Further contact with the *NM*, during which the skipper asks us to ensure that we stay a safe distance from their vessel. The helos are up for a full hour, using up valuable and limited amounts of fuel. A shot of two ships at sea has cost us a barrel of precious fuel which we'll need for the re-supply. This concern prompts a meeting at which I allocate only a further 4 hours of flying time to the helos during this action. At 1600, the *NM* advises us that she is altering course to 090 and she takes off at full speed for eight hours, leaving us eight miles behind her at 2350 when we increase speed to keep station at that distance where she can be monitored on the radar. At 0100, Arne has 'cut the corner' to leave us only 4 miles off her port beam.

As I take to my bunk, I ask that we simply monitor the *NM*'s movements overnight. The weather is a 10 knot northerly wind, slight sea, overcast with snow showers and minus 2. We saw only one whale during the entire chase.

26 January 1989

Staggered onto the bridge at 0800 to see a furious sea in 30 knots of wind, driving snow and visibility down to half a mile. We're thrown around all over the place and the crash of plates and equipment drifts up from below as we plunge through huge seas. The *NM* is clearly taking us through the worst weather she can find in an attempt to shake us off: her course is the most uncomfortable for us – pitching into huge seas – and into squalls as they appear. I take six press calls on the bridge and it's no mean feat to maintain a modicum of composure and some semblance of eloquence when you're being thrown around in a rogue express lift.

The *NM* heads first NE and then N, taking us further and further from where we want to be. Watchkeepers are required to don Antarctic clothing and stay out on the bridge wing looking for growlers through the murk: freezing cold, wet from the spray, going up and down like a yo-yo. What a life! Sleep immediately after watch until 1530 and decide that we're too busy to send out messages. Phil downloads the comets anyway to reveal 27 messages. He hands them to me and I look him in the eyes as I put them straight into the rubbish bin without so much as a glance. He laughs and I smile. On evening watch, the *NM* finally turns SW at 2300 and then stops after 30 minutes. The final chase had the ship slamming, rolling and shuddering every few seconds – absolute hell. The ship's a complete mess below and many have resorted to their bunks in the face of sea-sickness. I haven't seen half the crew in 24 hours! As we finally heave-to, we slap each other on the back. The *NM* tried to out run us and failed. No whaling today!

27 January 1989

The *NM* is still stopped when I go on watch at 0800. The weather has abated a little, although we still roll heavily in a big swell as we lay hove-to, a mile from the *NM*. At 1100, she moves off to the SW but then stops again after 30 minutes. The phone doesn't stop ringing and both Dog and I are busy all day, giving interviews to the media. At 1530, the *NM* moves off to the west with us in tow. By 1930, the *NM* is moving WSW and we're all mystified as to her intentions. At 2230, she turns south and heads for some isolated snow showers, for what reason, no-one knows. Does she think we don't have radar? Crew meeting tonight agrees that we'll wait until the *NM* forms her 'research hunting' pattern with the catchers before we engage her. By 1400 tomorrow on this heading, we'll be back where we started. Bed by 0200. Weather calmer but squalls all around.

28 January 1989

Up at 0530 when Mark tells me the fleet is assembling. Blearly-eyed on the bridge to see two catchers to the port side of the *NM*, the third presumably to the starboard over the horizon. Ian reports that radio traffic indicates a start time for hunting at 0700. I call Ken, Henk and Dog. Ken is as grumpy as hell and refuses to get out of bed until Dog tells him we're unlashing the inflatables. That gets him up in a jiffy! By 0720, we're full ahead with one catcher on either side of us four miles astern. They are gaining on us very quickly, and I've asked Arne to make sure we do not run the risk of losing the *NM*. If she gets too far away, we'll break off any direct action and keep to the factory ship, otherwise we'll be left in mid-ocean being outrun by the catchers and over the horizon from the *NM*.

At 0900, a catcher turns across our bows and ducks into an area littered with spectacular icebergs. We slow to launch the inflatables at 2 miles range as whales begin blowing all around us. I drive the crane to lift the inflatables from the main deck but the roll of the ship makes the operation very hazardous. Ken and Ian get away in the 5.2 metre boat, Henk, Mark and Steve in the aluminium work boat. They hare off across a flattening sea towards the catcher as we get under full power to catch up as best we can. The helicopter is airborne with Sean leaning out of the fuselage like James Bond.

We watch through the glasses as Ken gets in position in front of the catcher and the two vessels disappear behind an iceberg. As they reappear, Ken is directly in front of the catcher which is plying high-pressure hoses over the inflatable. Henk in the work boat is also in position and they're giving the catcher hell. He can't fire at whales with Ken and Henk there but suddenly Henk falls back: the work boat has broken down – shit! We have to abandon after three hours of confrontation: Ken's out of fuel and has to return to refuel.

We're keeping an eye on the *NM*'s position while attempting to stop the catchers from killing whales. Arne is manoeuvring the *Gondwana* into a position which blocks off the catcher's approach to a pod of whales and claxons echo mournfully over the empty ocean. Albert steers the ship by using the extension control, enabling him to steer from the bridge wing. A catcher comes careening along our port side in a chase for a whale which sounds three hundred yards ahead of us. Albert keeps his course and the whaler, making 17 knots and kicking up a huge beam and bow wave, creams alongside us, inching ever closer until only feet separate us.

Albert looks the skipper of the whaler in the eye and shouts, 'Piss off, you asshole. Leave the whales alone. I'm not altering course for you! I have the right of way!'

The bridge is packed with crew, shouting and waving clenched fists at the whalers. The catcher clears our bow and turns sharply to starboard and a loud 'boom!' momentarily deafens us as the whaler fires a harpoon. Dave Walley on the foredeck shouts, 'Missed!' and we cheer.

A second shot is fired and this time, the whaler doesn't miss. The catcher and the *Gondwana* stop dead in the water. As silence spreads across the scene, the incongruity of the situation is palpable. It is lovely and sunny, with no wind to speak of but the sea is already stained with crimson blood. The whale sounds and the hawser goes taut. The whale is hauled to the surface, quivering and pouring blood from its mouth and from the wound in its back.

In stark contrast to the chaos which reigned a few minutes ago, we now watch in silence as the whale contorts and thrashes in its death throes. I comfort Maggie as she cries at the sight. Two electrodes are passed down to the quivering whale from the high bow of the whaler. An electric shock, designed to finish the whale off quickly, merely prompts another quiver and thrash from the whale. Finally, it is dead. It is hauled alongside the catcher and secured by the tail, head beneath the waterline. We follow it back to the catcher where the whale is hauled up the slipway, mouth agape, spilling the last of the seawater which once sustained and nourished it. It looks tiny on the slipway which was built to accommodate the huge blue whales, but the few that are left are hard to find and are afforded some notional protection.

There's nothing quite as dead as a dead whale. Dog looks quite stunned and the ship assumes a sombre mood. We give chase to another catcher but he doesn't have his harpoon manned – he's only sighting. The hunt is over for the day. Only two whales killed. Some sort of victory for us since we've restricted the killing substantially while we've been on station. Two releases out in the evening accompanied by three pictures, one of Ken's action which makes the front page of the Guardian. The other catchers return with three more whales and then the *NM* heads for Scott Island.

The press calls are coming thick and fast. Dog and I run between the phone and the radio room, writing captions, helping Steve to send out no less than 12 pictures to various media all over the world. Fall into bed at 0230. Just before I crashed I had the presence of mind to get Dave to overfly the *NM* tonight to get shots of the flensing of the whale on the *NM*'s deck.

29 January 1989

On watch at 0800 to see the *NM* still steaming west. She then comes to port and then hard a-starboard with us in pursuit. Ken allows me the honour of steering the ship. Call Dog, Steve, Sean, Arne, Dave and Ken together to plan the action for the day. We decide to use our ship to block the loading ramp at the stern of the *NM* as a first tactic and then launch the inflatables to get the shots and to be ready for direct action should an opportunity arise. We agree also to get a 'banker' shot of the helicopter overflying a catcher, with a banner dangling across the harpoon, just in case the weather changes tomorrow and we have nothing for the press. The rule is: one story a day, one tactic a day.

At last a catcher arrives to offload a whale but we're too slow off the mark and can't get in position quickly enough. We have to wait until 1700 before another catcher arrives. This time, Arne times his approach to perfection. We're stuck on the stern of the *NM* and he can't transfer lines to his catchers to transfer the kill. There are now two catchers standing off waiting to discharge. The *NM* tries to give them sea-room by steaming ahead but Arne sticks to him like a leech, just twenty metres off at most. The *NM*'s skipper comes on the VHF asking would we please give him at least 2 miles of sea-room to take his catch. We all fall about laughing at that one. Arne sticks to his task doggedly but is clearly unhappy with this tactic since it goes against all his instincts as a seaman, if not the actual letter of sea law.

After an hour, Arne reluctantly breaks off the engagement. I tell him it's his decision, although I hope he'll stick at it longer. Many of the crew are not happy with Arne's decision and rumblings of dissent begin. We get the necessary shots from the chopper and of the helicopter 'buzzing' the catcher's foredeck: all in the can ready for despatch if nothing better turns up tomorrow. But we have our story for today and at 2100 we give the *NM* a bit of sea-room as the light begins to fail. Ken moans about 'cliques' who insist that we adopt a more gung-ho approach without realising the risks and dangers involved. Henk, Steve and I wallop the rum until 0230.

30 January 1989

The wind has increased and we're rolling and pitching heavily as we chase the *NM*. Press interest is increasing: the Guardian, Daily Mail and NZ Herald, Today Programme and lots of other interest, particularly in Australia. The catchers can't operate in this sort of sea so we're looking forward to a 'down' day. Nothing of note on watch and I sleep and doze the afternoon away in the company of Hendrix and Dylan. After dinner, we're all called to the bridge to see a massive sperm whale lazily swimming off the port bow before showing us his flukes as he sounds – magic! One catcher obviously overcame the inclement conditions and returned with a minke whale along the gunwale but we were too far behind the *NM* to block the transfer. Lots of press all day long and Dog and I are so whacked at the end of the day we agree not to send any pictures or stories out tonight. Just bed at midnight.

31 January 1989

During my four hour watch I deal with ten press calls this morning. A helo recce tells us that all four catchers are on their way back to the *NM* and we prepare to continue with the blockading tactics. By 1300 the catchers are approaching and Ken takes us tight on the *NM*'s stern. The catchers are laying off as they wait for us to move, but Albert, who takes over from Ken, refuses to budge. The usual VHF call comes asking us this time to lay off 300 metres as we are in an 'unsafe position' to which we reply that our position is entirely safe and only the actions of the catchers present a threat. The catcher on our starboard side comes closer and closer as we steam at five knots keeping station on the *NM*.

At one point the *NM*'s warps were trailing over her rear guardrail lying on the surface of the water and the knot in the end of one of the lines was configured in the shape of a pineapple (known in maritime parlance as a 'monkey's fist'). Albert mentions this to Mary-Ann who retorts, 'Monkey's fist? Christ, is there any animal these guys won't kill?' Eventually, the guardrails of the catcher collide with our hull. Paul Brown writes in his notebook, 'Collision at 1346'. It's nothing serious at all but within an hour, the press are calling us about the collision. One UK tabloid calls to ask about the 'sinking', to which I reply that we would have a hard job communicating if we had been sunk.

We stay in position for two hours before the catchers finally give up and scatter, their whales still an encumbrance along their rails. As they appear to be assuming a hunting pattern and as whales are all around, I take the gamble of despatching the boats again. As soon as we slow down to create a lee, the catcher turns and offloads his whale.

We're caught with our pants down and I rue my stupid decision. But we're committed now and after the terrifying task of launching the one ton work boat which swings around like a demented fish on the end of a hook and line, Henk takes off for the factory ship to try to harass the transferring of the whale. He gets in position while we're still launching Ken's boat and we see to our consternation that the Japanese are using grappling hooks on Henk's boat and hosing it down with high-pressure hoses. As we watch, his boat is almost up-ended.

Both Ken and Henk are eventually repelled by the hoses and hooks and the transfer takes place. Now we have the boats launched they both pursue the catcher to engage in 'human shield' activities, but the work boat is simply not fast enough and has to turn back. Henk and Pat the cook are both bruised and shocked by the treatment they received; Pat has a gash across her nose from contact with the bow-dodger bar. Ken manages to get in front of the whaler and stays on station for an hour and we manage to get the helicopter airborne for some more pictures of the 'classic' Greenpeace action. What we don't get, of course, is the picture we wanted: of Henk in front of the catcher in the work boat, displaying his solid banner designed to block the harpoonist's line of vision, something we worked on for weeks in Auckland.

The work boat returns after having overheated and recovery is just as hairy as launching. We set off after the *NM* again and collect Ken on the way. The press calls are almost incessant now and I'm on the phone constantly from 2100 – 0230, five and a half hours! Just before I crash, Naoko tells me that they monitored the skipper of catcher Number

1 telling his fleet commander that he was 'losing his nerve' and wanted to end this dangerous activity of fighting Greenpeace. Naoko also overhears that the fleet commander suggests that hunting should cease 'for a few days' while the more innocuous 'sighting' work takes place. Seems we've got them on the ropes.

1 February 1989
Call a crew meeting at 1300 at which we agree to continue the whaling action for another 24 hours and if no whaling takes place in that time, we'll abandon. I ask the crew for ideas about how we can terminate the campaign in style and Ton suggests that we deliver to the whaling fleet the text of a resolution which the British have just proposed to the International Whaling Commission, along with seven other nations, condemning the Japanese hunt and demanding that it be abandoned. This is a great idea and we agree to his suggestion.

Although we agree in principle to end the action tomorrow, we put a helicopter on standby just as a precaution against resumption in whaling. I leave Naoko translating the wording of the resolution into Japanese and crash out. On waking, I'm told that the helicopter was despatched this afternoon to monitor the activities of the catchers when twelve whales began sounding all around them, and not one harpoon was fired. That is a huge victory for us. Follow the *NM* all day and the press calls are coming just as thick and fast as ever, now also about the *Bahia Paraiso* which went aground today at the US Palmer station, about which we are inundated with a fresh wave of press calls. Beautiful evening watch with feeding orcas all around us. The press calls finally tail off at 0230, then thankfully to bed.

2 February 1989
Called at 0520, 0615 and 0730 for press calls and stayed up after the last to ensure getting on watch in time. This is our last day of activity on the whaling front and already I'm thinking about the re-supply and the visits we plan to make to the Italians and the Germans. As I stand on watch, waiting for Naoko to finish the translation of the UK resolution, I'm anxiously scanning the activities of the catchers since if they do start whaling again there will be an unstoppable imperative for us to continue direct actions against it. The fleet thankfully sails on without a shot fired and we have undoubtedly achieved a moral, psychological and

operational victory. We have reduced the catch of whales from 40 in the ten days before we arrived to just 14 whales since we've been on station over a similar period of time.

The plan to drop off the translated text of the resolution condemning the 'scientific' whaling by the Japanese went hopelessly wrong during the course of the day. As a humanitarian gesture to the whalers we agreed that, along with the translated text, we would also send the whalers some whale-shaped cookies with a note saying, 'If you want to eat whales, try these!' But when the helicopters return from their exercise where every catcher as well as the *NM* were airlifted a basket of goodies in which, I thought, the text was also placed, it transpired long after we had left the scene that the copies of the resolution were still sitting on top of the HF radio. We had forgotten to put them in the baskets.

The whalers must have thought us an even odder bunch than originally when they received – via helicopter drop – a consignment of whale-shaped cookies. I rush to the bridge and explain to Arne and after everyone has stopped laughing, he agrees to retrace our course and find the whaling fleet again, now some three hours away to the north.

Finally Dave takes off again and delivers the text to bemused crews on the whaling vessels and I try to blot out this embarrassing cock-up from my mind. Finally peep away from the whaling fleet and steer 180 at 1830. Press release and update out, interspersed with a steady stream of radio calls which Dog and I share. On watch at 2000 and I'm feeling completely shagged. What a day, but what a victory too. No whaling occurred at all in six of the ten days we have been here. The ship's rolling all over the place as I walk into the cabin and I'm thrown across the cabin and crack my shin a purler. Bed and sleep blissfully through to 1300 the next day.

3 February 1989

Snow showers greet my arrival on watch, low visibility, minus 1, NNE force 4 with the barometer falling rapidly. Dog comes to my cabin at 1330 to tell me that the National Science Foundation (NSF) are back-peddling furiously on the reports they gave us yesterday about the consequences of the grounding of the *Bahia Pariso*. They are now accusing us of 'sensationalising' the event. The press calls are tailing off and, thankfully, the weather is improving. Force 7 during the evening abates into a gentle long swell. Evening watch is all peace and light. It's still quite dark between 2200 and 0300 as we're still only 66S but a further three days southerly steam will see us in 24 hour daylight. Before turning in I hear that Japan formally complained today about 'harassment' of a legitimate whaling operation to the Dutch authorities (*Gondwana* is registered in Holland). Notified Terra Nova and Gondwana (the German base) of our imminent arrival.

4 February 1989

On watch to see visibility down to 400 yards and heavy snowfall which prompts Ken and I into a snowball fight around the bridge wings. During dinner and evening watch I find I'm particularly lethargic and pensive, not to say miserable. This is what is known as 'post action blues' and it affects a lot of people on board. Paul Brown shows me his 2500 word article he intends to file tonight which is good although I can't resist the temptation to correct his grammar. A pod of seven orcas appears and the bridge moodiness and calm is shattered by swarms of people sporting cameras. We saw Cape Adare tonight and the low evening sun burning gold beneath heavy clouds was spell-binding.

5 February 1989

Note with pleasure that despite a falling barometer last night, the sea is still flat calm. On the bridge to see pack ice ahead, lots of it. Call 1500 meeting – me, Dog, Mark, Ken, Arne and Liz – to go over arrival plans at Terra Nova tomorrow. Crew meeting at 1900 to outline the plans and arrangements. This will be a well-earned shore break for everyone. Drew a few more pictures for Bruno's fairy story book in the afternoon, including one I particularly liked of a penguin and her chick, beaks touching. I call Terra Nova during the evening watch and they're happy to receive us tomorrow at 0900. We spend the watch skirting the pack ice and trying to make some westerly progress which we manage at around 2200. The weather is still incredibly calm although overcast and snowing. Bed at 0130.

6 February 1989

Werner wakes me with a cup of tea at 0730, bless his kind heart, and informs me that we're at Terra Nova Bay. Ken already has the boats in the water and it is snowing heavily. Film crew ashore first in order to capture the meeting and I go in Ken's boat with Dog and Mary-Ann.

Mario, the base OIC, is there, and we greet each other warmly. He begins talking before we even reach the jetty and I swear he didn't stop all day. He invites the entire crew to lunch and then we go walkabout, specifically to see the seismographic equipment they have installed in a rock face above the base and which caused Greenpeace to protest about the blasting of rock its installation required. It was obviously done with a great deal of forethought and sensitivity and we praise the skill of the work – unobtrusive and clean. Inside the cavern, it's like a fairy grotto with ice crystals forming all over the walls. We eventually get back to the ship to round up merchandise and the usual piles of gifts and exchange items and already I'm beginning to feel drained. I haven't been able to move all morning without a camera being trained on me or a microphone shoved in my face. Every word I utter is being taped by someone or other. Get back to the Italian base by early afternoon to find some of the crew have partaken too liberally in our hosts' hospitality.

Another trip around the base follows and microphones appear at every turn. Then we go to the science labs and finally to the office again for a last discussion and an impromptu press conference. It's snowing like hell outside and the wind is increasing all the time. Mario accepts an invitation to come to the ship with Roberto and Cristina (journalists from ANSA) and orders the helicopter to be fired up. The last shore party arrives by helicopter and we're all finally back on board. After dinner the Italians decide to leave and it's still quite early in the evening. The thought strikes me that we could make our visit to the Germans this evening, enabling us to go straight to our base tomorrow which we agree to do.

Dog calls Gondwana base at 1800 and they're happy for us to visit tonight, weather permitting. We prepare HTN and begin the reasonably hairy process of shuttling people over to the small base, a little to the north of Terra Nova. All the time the weather is crapping out, the wind increasing and the snow thickening, but we all make it ashore without problem. We're greeted by Jurgen and Michael, two wonderful, bearded geologists who live in tents while storing their equipment in the hut and who clearly love the Antarctic and the wide variety of rocks found around them. In fact, they can't walk past a rock without stopping to explain its age and its origin. They are part of the larger German operation currently in North Victoria Land, trying to determine where Tasmania fitted into the original supercontinent of Gondwanaland.

They show us around the new and incomplete base, designed to house ten people, which will be completed in March. We spend an absolutely delightful hour in the base discussing their fascinating work, drinking cups of steaming hot chocolate. Then Ken comes on the VHF to tell us that the weather is seriously crapping out and that we should get back at once. It's time to go and Dave fires up the helo and we take off into a swirling snowstorm and very low visibility. As we clear what we assume is the coast, Dave asks disconcertingly, 'Anyone see the ship?'

Very comforting to hear that from the pilot. But soon the indistinct outline of the ship looms out of the snowstorm and we land safe and sound. Call the Italian office, lash the inflatables, stow the helos, do what's left of my watch (2230 – 2400), send out pictures and press releases and fall into bed, exhausted, at 0200.

7 February 1989

On watch to see that we've been pushed in circles through the night and are only 20 miles east of Terra Nova as the ice has been thick to the south and east. We head east through band after band of ice, gradually making as much southing as possible and at the end of our watch, we're heading 140, better than the 090 when we came on watch. It puts a 1700 ETA at Cape Evans beyond us and we agree to postpone our arrival until 1500 tomorrow afternoon, using the time to sight-see the ice shelf and Cape Crozier. This will also give us time to prepare the ship for discharging as we steam in flat calm seas deadened by the ice shelf and the sea ice to the north. It will also allow us time for a decent reunion with the base camp personnel and a discharge start the following morning.

In open sea by 1930, passing close to the spectacular Franklin Island. Ken has me scraping the ice off the bridge windows while perched precariously on the tiny ledge which runs the length of the bridge. The ship has a good coating of ice all over her now. It's minus 6 and Beaufort Island is off to starboard. The sky clears to reveal Mt Terror at 10,000 feet. What must Ross have felt when he saw this incredible place 140 years ago? Two beers after watch, bed at 0100.

8 February 1989

Get to see Swenson and other good friends today after 13 months. Deck work is the priority though, and we stow the work boat, unlash palettes, move barrels on the starboard walkway and clear accumulated snow.

Walk over to the port side from time to time to gaze at the ice shelf, Mt Terror and then Erebus as it comes into view, all bathed in beautiful sunshine and looking quite spectacular. Lunch as we round Cape Bird – no ice at all here. Clean toilets and stairs as off duty crew crowd the rails and soak in the amazing scenery. The winterers in particular are seeing what will be their home for a year for the first time and are jubilant. Then Lilian and Bruno have a row during which Lilian calls Bruno a liar. I keep my head down: there's nothing I can do now – they've got to resolve things on their own.

At 1445, we enter McMurdo Sound and get the TV crew, Steve and the journalists away to capture the meeting of the incumbent winterers with the relief team and I take the hour or so before we anchor to retreat to my cabin for some introspection. I muse about meeting Swenson again and how one phone call three years ago changed his life – and mine – so dramatically. Dog arrives at my cabin to tell me the US office have been on the phone to advise us that a US Federal Marshall has been drafted to McMurdo to oversee our activities there and the implications of this are left to sink in. We finally put the boats in the water at 1630 and I put a witch's mask on which Ken has had lying around his cabin for months. As we clamber out of the dinghy, Sabine looks at me in my mask and says, 'You look a little older than you did last year!' and soon we're all embracing and Wojtek is beside himself with delight.

A banner adorns the hut bearing a picture of a graceful minke whale and the words, 'Thanks, Greenpeace. From the whales.' It's very touching and I'm overcome with emotion at being here, at what we've done so far and at the uncertainty I feel for the future. Then we're in the hut chatting away about everything and nothing, touching, hugging and trying to come to terms with the fact that we are in each other's company again. The winterers seem fine and the beer comes out, the music goes on and soon the party is in full swing. I can't get over the length of beards and hair sported by the guys. By 0230, there are only a few hardy partygoers left and I finally crash at 0300 on the floor of Swenson's room.

9 February 1989
Finally start work on the ship at 1000. We make up five helicopter loads and Pierrette is the first to test us out on the familiar but somewhat daunting task of 'hooking on' – attaching the chain between the load

and the helicopter while the aircraft hovers a few feet above your head. Pierette's first approach leaves me running for cover after hooking on as the helo bucks and weaves and nearly takes my head off, but she improves as the morning progresses. By noon, it's minus 10 and blowing 30 knots, but it is glorious weather and a wonderful feeling working in the open with Erebus and Terror as a backdrop. Learn this evening that the Japanese are taking us to court for 'terrorism on the high seas' which brings an avalanche of inquiries from lawyer at the sniff of some international notoriety. We receive a deposition which these lawyers have prepared without any reference to us and which is full of inaccuracies: they seem to have taken their 'facts' about what happened straight from press reports. Chess after dinner where I beat Mark but Tim wipes me out. Reply to Martini's message about the Peninsular trip and then talk to the winterers until midnight.

10 February 1989

It's freezing working on the crane since you're up in the wind with ears and nose getting frostbite while the guys on deck are sweating buckets, sheltered from the wind while humping barrels and equipment all over the place. It's minus nine this morning and the wind-chill factor takes it to minus 20 or so. Port hold equipment finished and we begin on the starboard hold timber. Sling-loading is still a bit hairy and Dave and Pierrette will have to improve to meet Gary's standards of last year. I have a small meeting with Dog after lunch at which we agree that he is the primary campaigner from here on in. I'm very tired after the expedition so far and feel that in order for him to gain experience, he should take charge of the campaign, make the decisions and involve me as and when he feels it necessary: in other words, we reverse our roles, to which he agrees.

Finish deck work at 1745 at which a further small meeting is called (by me, not Dog, which I moan about to him) to discuss Paul Brown's desire to see Scott's Hut tomorrow. It's incredible how complicated such trivial things become as we must invite the NZ official who holds the key to the ship in order for him to open up the hut and that involves using one of the helicopters to pick him up, which in turn denies its use on discharging the ship.

11 February 1989

We are all getting a little tired and ratty with each other. Tonight I stormed out of the lounge after videos were screened for the second night in succession. So much for appreciating the Antarctic environment: they'd rather be inside, in the dark, watching death and mayhem Holywood-style. On top of all that, Paul Brown infuriates me by announcing calmly that since he was 'peeved' at not getting permission to visit Scott Base tonight, he felt justified in having Pierrette take him to the gates of the base for 'a look' and then 'buzzing' McMurdo Base a couple of times just for the hell of it. I got him and Pierrette together and let them know that this is not a private jolly for adventurous journalists and pilots and that their actions would be thrown in my face when we met the National Science Foundation in a few days' time. Apart from anything else, the fuel they used is precious. They must, absolutely must, co-ordinate things through me (technically through Dog) otherwise anarchy will ensue. I storm out of the room after laying down the law and determine that I want this trip to finish as quickly as possible and get the hell out of here.

We lost a package of Bruno's skis today when it was caught in the downwash of the helicopter blades and blown overboard. That's the first bit of equipment we've lost in three years and the accident added to my depression. To add to the misery of today, Werner cornered me after dinner and told me that he was convinced the winterers would have 'major problems in the coming year'. That really cheered me up. It's taken him half way through the re-supply to tell me his fears. I gave in to depression and listened to Tom Waits after sending notifications to Scott and McMurdo of our desire to visit. Bed by 0015 after what can only be described as a bad day.

12 February 1989
Minus 12, snowing with low visibility. Arne wants all the message traffic about the impending court case with the Japanese and that takes me an hour to get together. On deck at 0900 with Henk and Ken to accept the human waste barrels from ashore in an attempt to clean up the base a little before the threatened visit by the Italians. So, as an appetiser to lunch, we unchain a constant stream of barrels from ashore in all manner of states but all of them smelling rank, despite the frozen nature of the contents.

At lunch, Paul Brown tells me that he, Mary-Ann Bendell and the film crew have had a disagreement over the interviews with La Count tomorrow as she wants an 'exclusive', but thankfully, after an hour of

366

discussion, the disagreement evaporates and we decide to send two flights. Barrel back-loading continues during the afternoon but the weather craps out and the Italians cancel their planned trip as a result. Bed at 0030.

13 February 1989
All the arrangements for visits to bases, official visits and meetings between the in-going winterers and officials at the bases are becoming a nightmare to arrange. Paul Brown and Mary Ann Bendell get away for their interview with Ron at 0945 and Dave Walley returns to pick up the film crew for dropping off at McMurdo as agreed. The arrangement is that they will be collected outside the NSF chalet at 1700. Deck work continues as we offload fuel barrels all day which are difficult to discharge; the hangar prevents us lifting them cleanly from the main deck and full boom-up is required to clear it.

At 1530, Dave collects Mark and I assume that Mark is simply required ashore. To my surprise, I see the helicopter overflying the base en route to McMurdo – too early to pick up the journalists. Then Dave arbitrarily decided that he'd use the 90 minutes or so he had 'spare' before the pick-up to go walk-about in Mactown and on to Scott base. Since neither he nor Mark had been there before, they have to knock on doors in Mactown to ask directions to Scott Base and this brings Ron La Count out of his hut to berate them for violating our agreement of not entering the US buildings. This really puts us in a bad position and Ron calls me to ask why I can't control my personnel.

Dave eventually returns with Mary-Ann Bendell on board and she nearly dies at the thought of having to clamber down from the top of the hangar. Henk calls me to admit that the new loo he's trying to install in the base is too big, as I predicted, and he pays up his bottle of rum as agreed. Bed at 0100 after the bottle is demolished by seven crew members during the 8-12 drinking club meeting.

14 February 1989
Beautiful, still day, zero cloud and warm in the sun. Lift hatch covers and discharge barrels in the forward cement tanks. It was the tomming up in these tanks which concussed Werner back in Auckland so many weeks ago; he was in a confined space whacking a wedge into the space behind a barrel with another piece of wood when it rebounded and hit him on the head. His immediate reaction was to move his head out of the

way violently which caused him to hit his head again on the bulkhead. Despite the fact that it almost knocked him out, I was unable to control my laughter at this Tom and Jerry accident.

All the barrels are finally away by 1230 and Dave's flying is excellent: he averages 90 seconds for one run to shore and back. At 1345, Keith, Dog and I leave for Scott Base and have a pleasant if nondescript meeting with Hugh Logan, after which Dave collects us at precisely 1700. We drop down to LGP3 where a guy known simply as 'Dave' meets us and agrees to spirit out 8 rolls of film via the US transport he's about to catch back to NZ.

Back to the ship by 1730 and a crew meeting precedes the lifting of the hook and the short journey to Marble Point where we plan to install a survival hut (Apple) for Bruno's future use, slap bang in the middle of the flagged airstrip the Americans 'do not plan to construct'. The helicopter flights are quite incredible and it's impossible to describe the sheer beauty of this place. Use the evening to finish filing my paperwork as we bump and bore through heavy ice on our way to Marble Point. Hit the sack at 2300 in a very tired state but happy that we are only days away from completing our task.

15 February 1989

Up bright and early to find Ken already on deck bustling about. We two prepare five sling-loads for the lifts to Marble Point and as Pierrette comes in with the helicopter to pick up, I get an almighty shock from the chain which discharges static from the helicopter to my hand. I tell Ken and he calmly tells me he saw one guy get thrown 20 feet through a static charge once on a ship. I take to whacking the chain with a lump of wood from then on before handling it. It seems to help a little although I still get the odd shock.

Marble Point is quite uninspiring; just a low, flat coastline peppered with snow. The Piedmont glacier which runs from left to right across our anchorage is, however, beautiful. Spend the rest of the day on board stowing the human waste barrels, sacks of rubbish and remaining odds and ends. We're through at 1530 and after chatting the afternoon away, the helicopter returns at 1900 when I hear from Tim that Dave took them to the top of a nearby mountain for a ride. I'm furious at this news and immediately go and find him. I tell him that if he had had an accident, no-one on board would have known where he was or where to look for him.

Sort out flying hours with Henk and re-do the allocations. Dog phones La Count to confirm the meeting tomorrow and he informs us that a guy called Stovich is in town. He tells us that he's a US Marshall and has powers of arrest over US nationals. Now this is a poser for us and confirms our earlier information. Coming directly from La Count puts more weight to it. Pictures of the Marble Point installation out with press release, a beer with Phil Durham to celebrate his birthday and bed at 0100.

16 February 1989

No boats in the water today as it's bitterly cold and the sea is too choppy. At 1330, after a briefing chat, we leave by chopper for McM to be greeted by Ron at the chalet. He claims that the US policy on retrograding waste has changed and the practice of 'tide cracking' – letting the summer thaw take waste to the bottom of Winterquarters' Bay – has ceased. We mention direct action and this Stovich character positively bristles and asks how many US nationals we have on board and if they are aware of US law in Antarctica. He also issues a veiled threat at pursuing a court case if we should use any film in which his image appears in a public manner. I tell him that we'll use whatever film we damned well want and that we're not in the habit of bowing to blackmail.

After the meeting we take a look at the pipe we intend to block and arrive back at the ship at 1700. Dog and I snatch a brief chat over our meal in my cabin and agree to simply put the facts before the crew, leaving a final decision about what form of action we should take, given Stovich's presence, until later when we have more information, especially from the US where the lawyers are looking at the implications of blocking a pipe which is polluting a stretch of water subject to no international law. It's a long and constructive meeting but we arrive at no final conclusion. Drink a quick beer with Ken and bed at 0030.

17 February 1989

Woken by Ken at 0400 who tells me to dress in my warmest gear and help him on a particularly difficult job. Bleary-eyed, I arrive on deck to see Ken sitting in the inflatable, beckoning me to hurry up: the Footsteps of Scott raft, the aptly named *Spirit of Incompetence*, has broken her moorings and Ken and I have to retrieve her. She's drifting about a mile away and we battle through a steep chop and 30 knot winds to reach her. By the time we do, we're covered in frozen spray and our clothing is stiff with ice. We get her in tow and make it back to the ship where Bob and Albert take the lines.

I fall back into bed at 0600 and immediately dream of queuing for a giant ice cream. Just as I get to the head of the queue, Bob wakes me and tells me it's time to get up. It's now blowing 35 knots and the snow is driving horizontally across the sea. No flying in this. I'm scheduled to go ashore to brief the shore party but I don't fancy another drenching in ice, so decide to speak to Kelly (Rigg) about the dilemma of the action. She reiterates her view that we should not go ahead with the pipe blocking.

By 1100, we commence flying and accept 12 loads of all manner of rubbish from shore. The helos drop the loads directly onto the top of the hangar and we lift directly from there with the crane. It's fast and the holds begin to fill up quickly. Decide to go ashore at 1900 to brief people about the legal complications of the planned action. Back on board at 2200 after no real resolution of the dilemma and use the evening to sort out the return journey schedule with Arne. We agree on a March 11th return to Lyttelton. Bed at 0100.

18 February 1989
Day off today and I thankfully sleep in until 1015, get a cup of tea and slump back into my pit to read and doze until 1200 when Swenson arrives at my cabin door asking if I want to take a walk to the Barne Glacier. We're all ready at 1300 – me, Ken, Swenson, Sabine, Henk and a few others – but the weather doesn't improve: minus 14 with 30 knots of wind and the sea is too choppy to launch the boats. I veto the use of helicopters for fuel economy reasons and at 1500 we have to call it off. Reluctantly drag myself to the office to work on updates and email messages until 1800 when dinner interrupts my work. Later, I work on the report on the Dumont D'Urville action with Dog and Liz and then bed at 0000.

19 February 1989
Having brought all my paperwork up to date yesterday, I can look forward to doing nothing but working on deck all day. Twenty days left until we're back in New Zealand and today and tomorrow are straight deck work days designed to break the back of the re-supply and retrograde work – 48 hours of bliss at having to do nothing but what I'm told to do by Ken. The tractor and trailer arrive from the shore and we also stow the *Spirit of Incompetence* after chipping her free of ice to enable us to

Spectacular tabular iceberg, Southern Ocean

MV Greenpeace and Mt. Erebus, Ross Island

The Benjamin Bowring

Last Antarctic trip

Grace Base and MV Gondwana Antarctic Expedition 1991-92

Greenpeace Antarctic Crew 1991-92

Me, Jerry Johnson and Dave Woolan, 1986

Keith Swenson, me and Bruno Klausbruckner, Grace Base, Antarctica 1988

Me, Reg Boorer and the late Ivan Taylor 1992

ding Day 2000, Gaye's parents, Sylvie and Jerry, me, Gaye, my mum Minnie

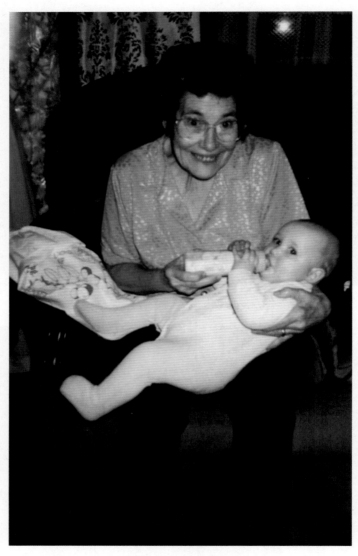

Mum and Amy, 1997

Me and Mum, 2002

Amy, Emily and Sasha the dog, 2005

Pete in pain, 2005

Sunset over Antarctica

lift the deadweight of two tons. The sea smoke is spectacular today. The cold air meeting the warmer seas results in drifts of condensation which shroud the ship. More tired than usual today and gratefully to bed by 0000. Minus 14 today and bitterly cold in the wind.

20 February 1989
Spend the day tidying the ship, lashing barrels, covering deck gear with tarpaulins, getting the ropes out and cleaning the mess, lower toilets and the laundry. Go to the base at 1700 (minus 15 today and the sea smoke is very dramatic) and get covered in freezing spray during the short trip. It's colder than I've known it in Antarctica and I marvel at the blasé attitude of the skuas which are afraid of nothing. They even attack the helicopter if they're feeling particularly grumpy. Two interviews for the cameras with Keith and Sabine and back for dinner at 1830. Over a few beers in the evening, with a decidedly laid-back attitude prevalent on board, Keith, Dog and I rehearse a few numbers from the forthcoming album we intend to release under the band name of The Outlets. Bed at 2345 after having, I hope, finally laid to rest the plans for the action which has been demoted to more of a demonstration, much to some peoples' annoyance.

21 February 1989
A very bad day started at 0830 when Werner moaned about me lashing a banner along the hangar side when he felt it was his job to do it. Werner has been on my case most of the week for one reason or another and the incident put me in a bad mood. The rest of the day went downhill from there. No-one except me was willing or apparently able to paint the letters on the barrels we intend to use tomorrow, so I spent hours in the workshop doing that myself. Then I had to put a press release together and arrange pictures to be sent out and needed Dog's comments but of course he wasn't around as he had gone with Keith and Henk to Crater Lake. Then at 1800, as arranged, the Scott Base team arrived for our social and of course I was the only one available for them to talk to, the other members of the campaign team either deciding not to show or being lost somewhere in the hinterland: their return from Crater Lake was well overdue by now and we were increasingly worried for their welfare. The helo lifted off from LGP3 at 2015 and Dave finally spotted the three of them walking back to their rendezvous point, hours late. We all screwed up badly today and I hope tomorrow's ok. Keith spent a long

time apologising to me but I still didn't get to the bottom of what had caused their delay. Thank God they're all safe and that today is over and done with. Thank God also that this is my last year.

22 February 1989
As I write at 1700, the day doesn't look too bad, although there is no denying that our direct action finale to this expedition was reduced to little more than a stunt due to our fear of retribution from the US authorities in the form of arrests of the US citizens involved, arraignments and future arrests of the non-American nationals should they ever have future cause to visit the USA. We simply judged that blocking an outfall pipe in the Antarctic, thousands of miles away from 'civilisation', a blocking which could have been reversed within a matter of minutes, created a risk of retribution that was too great a price to pay. Yes, we bottled it, and the crew are not feeling too good about it, but I've tried to point out that we have done more on this trip than could have been expected of us and in any case, we do have a mandate from our campaign superiors not to break any laws.

All that justification sounds hollow now, but we did carry out an equally photogenic demonstration and had a lot of fun in the process. By the time I roused myself at 0700, we were tying up at the McMurdo ice-wharf. There was not a soul around ashore. Not one of the 1000+ personnel was to be seen. We mustered on the aft deck as planned at 1000. The plan was to transport 16 barrels, partially filled with cadmium waste from the outfall pipe, on a trailer pulled by the Kubota tractor up to the NSF hut where we would demand they dealt with the waste responsibly rather than discharge it into the Antarctic environment where it contributed to the gross contamination of Winterquarters' Bay.

Despite the liberal use of a can of 'Easy Start' spray, the tractor simply would not fire. After a set-to between five-foot Davey and six-foot two Albert on the techniques of starting the temperamental machine which had us all trying to stifle a fit of the giggles, we decide to man-haul the trailer up the steep slope to the hut. By the time the filling is completed and the barrels are on the trailer, it weighs at least a ton and even fifteen of us pushing and pulling can barely get the trailer moving. After an hour of hard toil, we get the barrels arranged in front of the Chalet and they make a nice centre piece for the cameras: DANGER! CADMIUM!

As Henk and his team climb on top of the Chalet and drop a banner reading 'Clean up or shut up!' Dog begins his speech to Ron Le Count who is, we later learn, watching proceedings from another building. Dog's speech is fine but as he delivers it to the cameras, his lips are visibly freezing and his balaclava is slipping down over his eyes and he eventually assumes a cartoonesque appearance which has me in stitches. Then it's all over, our last activity in Antarctica this year, and we pack everything up and load it back on the trailer, only to see Paul Landrigan hurtle round the corner on the tractor which he has finally got started. We hook up the trailer and all clamber aboard with Wojtek at the wheel of the tractor for a tour of McMurdo.

After a very welcome lunch, we heave all the equipment on board, including the partially filled barrels which we'll deliver to the US Embassy in Wellington, carry out some dredging work from the ship for Sabine's science project and then steam back to Cape Evans, leaving the winterers behind to go to Scott Base for dinner.

Press release and pictures out which occupies me for another few hours before Dog tells me that Ron Le Count has called him to wish us goodbye and safe journey. He apparently told Dog, 'I always knew you were a crazy, but why did you push the trailer up the hill and use the tractor to bring it down?' Dog told him it was in the interests of energy conservation. Agree to sail for NZ in 48 hours. To bed, almost asleep before my head hits the pillow at 0000.

23 February 1989

Last day of the re-supply. We sail tomorrow. Work furiously between 0800 and 1300 before the wind, now gusting to 35 knots, terminates activity. By 1600, we stow the tractor and trailer, coal, rubbish, timber and all manner of equipment and odds and ends and then it's time for the end of re-supply ceremony at the base, where I'll make a speech and Keith will officially hand the base over to Bruno. The helo ride ashore is short but decidedly blustery as the gusts are now reaching 45 knots, beyond the safe speed for helo flights.

The speeches over, Keith hands Bruno the tool used to open the fuel barrels – the official key to the hut – and the party begins. Before long, a full-blown hooly is in full swing, people in rugby scrums on the floor, bodies everywhere, laughing and screaming: all great fun and highly therapeutic, but it leaves Liz needing 4 stitches in her lip. Finally we all begin crashing out wherever we can find somewhere to rest our heads.

24 February 1989

The wind is still gusting to 35 knots but we have to risk it and get back to the ship. Dave ferries us back in twos and threes and we muster the crew at 1100 and set a departure time for the winterers back to shore at 1130. It's goodbye time again and I feel the familiar lump of nostalgia and emotion in my throat which I try to conceal by rushing around getting people organised. As the helicopter warms up, people are hugging and kissing and crying on shoulders and then they're all on board and Dave lifts off to much waving and blowing of kisses. This is always a sad time and the ship's horn is a forlorn farewell as the anchor is raised and our stubby little ship turns her head towards the north. The four winterers become dots on the beach and then the majestic Erebus is our only reminder of our location.

We had decided to visit Capes Barne or Royds on the way out but the wind denies us that opportunity and instead we go to Butter Point where Keith goes ashore for an hour to change the location of the fuel and food depot there. Then after dinner, I go with Mark and Sjoerd to Marble Point to erect the solar panel for the survival hut we have erected there. It's an amazing place – very isolated and very 'Antarctic' but our visit is cut short by falling visibility and increasing winds. Back on board at 2000, stow gear and generally tidy up the deck before watch at 2100. Straight to bed after watch, totally shattered.

25 February 1989

The first thing I did this morning was to transfer all the logistics of planning and executing boat launches, helo operations and personnel mustering to Henk. I told him that as far as I was concerned, the official trip was over and that everything else from here on in was pleasure and that he, as logistics co-ordinator, had just been deputised and would he please sort it out with Ken. Apart from doing my watches, I was a passenger from here to New Zealand.

On watch, I can hardly keep my eyes open, I'm so tired. Bob says to Ken as we take over the watch, 'Everywhere, the sea is freezing.'

Visibility is low, the sea is glassy and the swell is gentle. Ice in the water is forming before our very eyes and we have to slow down due to dramatically worsening visibility and the presence of bergy bits and growlers all around us. But it is a huge relief to be finally back at sea

374

again and although I dread the seasickness which will inevitably seize me at some time, I delight in the movement of the ship and the feeling of freedom and space being at sea gives.

Heading mostly 030 then 065 putting our ETA at Cape Hallet at 2000 tomorrow. Sparse lunch after sending out the final update and then sleep the sleep of the dead until 1940. On watch at 2000 to find that we're down to one engine (fuel pump has crapped out on the port engine) and Davey reports that the head will have to come off the engine, forcing us to stay on one engine all the way home, although this will not apparently affect our ETA. The darkness tonight heralds the end of the summer and our more northerly position. Bed at midnight.

26 February 1989

On watch to see a very mixed and dramatic weather pattern. Deep black clouds off to starboard down to the horizon, with clear blue skies and intense sun off to port. Horizontal snow lashes the ship in a stiff breeze. Minus 2 and Cape Wheatsheaf glints in the sunshine, 40 miles off. The morning gets progressively more beautiful – sun peeping though light clouds and the Capes off to port wreathed in mists which are gradually lifting. Crew meeting at 1400 to organise shore parties which, despite my declaration to Henk, I end up organising.

The first flight is away at 1520 taking people to Cape Hallet as Arne ploughs the ship through thick ice. Cape Hallet is bathed in glorious sunshine against a deep metallic blue sky with incredible ice formations contorted along the coast and icebergs galore. Final flight away by 1650, all complicated by the needs of the photo/film people. Davey throws another minor wobbly about 'joy riding' and all shore personnel return by 1845, all oohing and aahing about the spectacular nature of this particularly beautiful part of Antarctica. It is a very special place – magnificent – and I take a whole reel of film in a pathetic attempt to capture its majesty. While waiting for the helo flights to return, Ken and I sit in the helo safety nets and soak up the amazing scenery in contented silence, both lost in our own thoughts about what we have achieved and what the future holds for us. The scenery is quite awesome, seductive, enigmatic, imponderable and simply breathtakingly beautiful.

Ton's birthday meal is an Indian – the closest I've had to a Lavender Hill Indian meal in months. Music and diary till 1950, then on watch. We steam past the magnificent Possession Islands at 6 knots and adjust our speed to arrive at Cape Adare at 0800 tomorrow. Chat after watch with Keith, Steve, Maggie and Merriann. Ton fixed my glasses today which I sat on earlier, bending one arm and snapping the other off completely. He did a fine job (they actually lasted another two years before they fell to pieces).

27 February 1989

On the bridge to see Cape Adare, ice and snow-covered, towering out of a flat calm sea. It seems as though the Antarctic is laying on its best show for us, knowing that many of us will not be returning. Orcas cavort around the ship as we anchor in the lee of the Cape under grey skies. Borchgrevink's hut can be seen on the flat spit of land snaking out to sea. Ken, Keith, Mark, Wojtek and I take an inflatable to search for a landing but all along the coast the swell is too great and the beach too steep. We have a great time though and skylark about, taking group pictures and generally enjoying ourselves as we quietly meander through the seas dotted with leopard seals while penguins squawk their alarm from the shore.

Since we can't land, we agree to take the crew on boat trips around the bay while the deckies make the deck secure and rig a life-line fore and aft along the main deck – a stark reminder that we are about to face the rigours of the Southern Ocean. Agree to sail at 1400. Six days to Campbell Island, a further three to Lyttelton, putting us home on the 9th, too early for the press arrangements which I'll have to clarify with Arne. Interviewed by Paul Brown for an article on my pending retirement and the establishment of a new organisation Ken and I have been discussing – Greenwave.

To my cabin for a doze, read and music as the sea picks up the moment we're out of the lee of the Cape. We begin pitching heavily and I feel queasy as I dole out food onto my plate at dinner. The conditions worsen and I'm sent round the ship to ensure all deadlights are secure and screwed down. On watch at 2000. Wojtek is on our watch now and calmly walks off the bridge and honks noisily in the loo at the bottom of the short flight of bridge stairs before returning to his post only to honk again ten minutes later. Ken tells the both of us to go and take some rest as Maggie and he can see out the watch. I throw myself on my bunk just in time to quell the nausea and immediately sleep.

28 February 1989

Sea thankfully much calmer today and the sunshine makes it almost a pleasure to be on watch. Antarctic fulmars and petrels around the ship in their droves. The foredeck is coated in thick ice from the seas we are still taking over the bow which freeze quickly. At 68 south at the end of the watch, ten degrees or 600 miles from Cape Evans.

Radio reports of another ship in trouble in Antarctica reach us: a Peruvian vessel which has struck the rocks at Marion Bay in King George Island. The ship is still rolling heavily and some crew are enduring mal-de-mer. On watch at 2000 to see a most beautiful sunset but by 2100 it's dark and Ken turns on the powerful spotlight on the bridge front to help us look-outs spot growlers.

1 March 1989

Just three weeks to go until I get home and only 10 days to Lyttelton. Weather is grey and the sea lumpy with a freshening wind. We spot a spectacular arched iceberg and despite telling myself that I have enough iceberg pictures for a lifetime, I expend half a roll on it. Ken, the eternal prophet of doom, predicts a 'storm of the century' which he claims is brewing up ahead and the barometer is, I must agree, dropping like a stone. 65 South at the end of the watch. After lunch, I call a meeting in Arne's cabin to discuss arrival procedures. As we chat, the ship begins to move more violently and the wind picks up to 30 knots.

Repair to my cabin where I decide to take Ken's storm warning seriously and check the deadlight (which needs packing with a rubber surround to prevent water penetration). By 1500, we're rolling heavily and a peek out of the access door to the saloon reveals quite mountainous swells. The weather deteriorates further throughout the day and I lash down objects in my cabin which might go flying as the ship moves ever more violently. A westerly wind causes a very heavy rolling motion – far better than pitching at least – and by 2130, we're staring into the beam of the search light watching huge troughs appear ahead of us into which we roll and pitch headlong.

Two icebergs loom out of the murk, large, impassive and foreboding in the darkness. Ken mutters from the darkness of the bridge – 'Big depression on its way, guys,' as if what we're currently experiencing is something to be dismissed as trivial. The crawl across the 60s is slow indeed: we're still at 64 south as our progress has been impeded by the weather: we go up and down rather than along. A quick shower after watch then bed by 0045.

2 March 1989

Plus 4 degrees today, but the crawl continues at a snail's pace. Watch is the normal boredom but Wojtek keeps us amused. Every hour we carry out a deck and fire watch which involves Wojtek and I, in tandem while on deck, due to the weather, checking the lashings, ensuring that the helicopters haven't shifted from their moorings in the hangar and making sure no fires are smouldering, especially in the engine room. It's creepy down there, despite the crash and thump of the engine; the ghost of a Swedish engineer who was decapitated by the whiplash of a snapped cable is said to stalk the engine room. Going through the engine room into the aft tween deck is just as creepy and you go from noise into semi-silence and a pitch black space in which lashed-down material groans against its restraints.

Back on the bridge, Ken points out the monumental low ahead of us on the weather chart. Wind speed is force 7 and we're rolling heavily when at 2200, the Jimmy Young programme calls to interview me live about Paul Brown's piece in the Guardian announcing the establishment of Greenwave! Then a call comes through from Amsterdam to tell us that Maureen Fallon resigned today and we celebrate with a glass of whisky which Henk 'found' in his locker. Bed at 0100.

3 March 1989

We rolled around so much in the night I swear I was nearly vertical at times. Almost impossible to sleep as your head is literally pushed into the pillow when the ship comes up on a wave and then is in negative gravity as the ship plummets down into a trough – your head is literally and involuntarily lifted from the pillow. On watch to see a spectacular and awesome sea in the full glory of a force 10. Serried ranks of combers line up to the horizon, marching forward inexorably, their tops whipped into spray by the wind, to batter the ship.

We alter course to 320 to ease the motion and at 0900 we finally cross the 60th parallel taking us technically out of the Antarctic. We recorded a maximum wind gust of 66 knots on the morning watch, sea temperature plus 4 and the same for the air temperature. NW winds and lots of squalls which whip up the sea locally into even greater frenzy and rain lashes the bridge windows in torrents. It gets worse during evening watch and as I do my rounds, the saloon is littered with prostrate bodies trying to avoid the motion which by 1800 is very violent indeed. Wind speeds are up to 77 knots – hurricane force and for the first time ever on a Greenpeace ship I feel the first flutterings of fear.

On watch at 2000 to see an awesome sight: the bows of the ship rise to meet a vertical wall of water 40 feet high and as darkness falls, the searchlight reveals a chaotic scene of confused seas which rear up and crash over the bridge as the ship freefalls into the chasm created by their passing. Barrels break free of their lashings on deck, one of the banners is in shreds and the light on the hangar front has been torn away by the wind. We twice have to brave the conditions to re-lash barrels and the boats on the boat deck and I call out to Wojtek to hang on as a particularly vicious wave towers above us.

Wojtek and I were halted in our tracks as we rounded the hangar onto the windward side of the ship to see a mighty wave teetering 30 feet above us only yards from the ship. I honestly thought we would be swept overboard if it broke, but miraculously the ship's stern rose as though on an express lift and the monstrous wave hissed its path beneath the hull. It's as though the Southern ocean wants to give me a display of what it can really be like as I won't be seeing it again. It's an awesome, humbling, exhilarating and a quite unforgettable experience.

We run diagonally across the swell on 290 and are hove-to, just about, making 2 knots. Bed at 0030 and step into a tilting, crashing and thoroughly jumbled cabin which is reminiscent of being in a barrel at sea.

4 March 1989

After a perfectly awful night of being thrown around the cabin and after being pitched out of my bunk twice – despite the use of lifejackets under the mattress to force me up against the bulkhead – I awake to a sense of greater stability on board. Still a big swell runs, however, and the winds are still gusting to 35 knots, but a mere breeze compared to yesterday. At 0500 this morning, we resumed a northerly course on 355, passing 58 south. Luxuriate in a shower which, despite the improved conditions, is still a feat of balance and dexterity. As I go on evening watch, we pass 57 south = 4.5 degrees to Campbell Island = 270 miles = one and a half days.

The weather fax indicates we're heading for another low pressure region and as I come off watch the ship is already bucketing around in familiar fashion. Ken procures a 'lost' bottle of scotch and pressgangs us into his cabin for a 'pre arrival' drink. Bed at 0130.

5 March 1989

Pass 54 south which puts our ETA Campbell Island tomorrow morning. Lunch then a meeting with Henk, Dog and Ken to discuss next year's strategy and personnel at which I'm rather reticent as it's all out of my hands since I won't be involved and my enthusiasm is at a very low ebb. Sleep in my cabin from 1600, through dinner, and get called for my evening watch to see a weak aurora in the sky. Call a brief crew meeting to discuss the Campbell Island visit tomorrow and then speak to the Campbell Island personnel on HF. They all sound pissed, thanks to the home brew they're reduced to drinking. Picked up Radio Windy tonight from Wellington which made me so very homesick for NZ and England. Dog and Steve rustle up a huge pile of chips after watch which lifts my spirits temporarily. Bed at 0100.

6 March 1989

I squint out of the porthole to see the green hills of Campbell Island to the accompaniment of the clank and clatter of the anchor being dropped. It is a riot of vegetation, the first such lush greenness seen for 14 months for the winterers and for 3 months for the rest of us. The pungent odour of vegetation is overpowering. It's blowing 35 knots, overcast and squally.

Ashore at 1245 when Ken, Dog, Ton and I take off on a tour of the island, past drowsy but aggressive and smelly elephant seals, take the wrong turn and end up on a very isolated but spectacular part of the island overlooking the coast and in the middle of an albatross colony. We lie quietly and watch these incredible birds go through their courting routine and watch in awe as they waddle awkwardly towards the cliff edge, spread their 12 foot wings and soar effortlessly into the sky. Superb! Wander back to the small weather station at 1630 where we indulge in drinks and snacks until 1800.

Back to the ship for dinner. Dog approaches me to tell me that Ken is pissed off at me because I 'withdraw' sometimes and because I no longer seem interested in when the boats are running or whose going where. I tell Dog that this is true. I consider the expedition to be over days ago and that the Campbell Island stopover is nothing more than a 'jolly' which does not need a campaigner's co-ordination. I tell Dog that I've already had a conversation with Henk about him taking over such co-ordination and now Henk is apparently upset for involving him in the argument as he can't remember us discussing the arrangement.

I retire to my cabin in a foul mood and refuse to go to the party ashore. Instead I take an anchor watch with Ken who makes no effort to broach the subject. In an effort to lift my flagging spirits, I call Fiona who doesn't answer. I go to bed, thoroughly miserable, at 0030.

7 March 1989

Ken wakes me at 0740 but for what reason I can't fathom. Wander onto the bridge at 0800 and spend two hours sitting there in total silence with Ken. Launch the inflatable to take Arne ashore (this must be the first time in three months that he's left the ship). Lunch and away to my cabin to sleep after checking with Henk that the deck is secured and that Ken is not expecting me to do anything on deck. At 1400, the anchors are weighed and we steam out of the bay. I hope that someone other than me has taken on the responsibility of representing Greenpeace to the guys ashore, but, to be honest, this unofficial visit needs no formal representation.

Within seconds of hitting the open sea we're being thrown around again. 40 knot winds and big seas force us to reduce speed to five knots and head into the weather. It's a miserable few hours and the ship is deserted as crew take solace in their bunks. At dinner Swenson staggers down the alleyway looking wild-eyed, bearded and dishevelled. His face is a picture of controlled determination not to chuck. Lots of people just play with their food as we hump along in very big swells and then someone foolishly opens the fridge door on the wrong aspect of the roll and the saloon is full of runaway cans of coke and lemonade. Paul Brown appears at the end of the alleyway from where we can see him. His steps towards the lounge are tentative and more in reverse than forward as the ship pitches and gyrates. His face is ghostly white and he is dubbed the 'Grey Ghost'. God, being at sea is a real trial for many people, myself included. Straight to bed after an awful watch and finally fall into a fitful sleep after being tossed around for hours. What an existence!

And to think, people are queuing up to get on Greenpeace ships, the idiots! (Paul later relates a story in which Albert, the mate who was in charge of Paul's watch, asked for a piece of chocolate cake which Paul reluctantly went to fetch from the galley. He managed to find the cake, cut a slice (between honking up) and finally began making his way back to the bridge with his prize for Albert. The ship was now pitching so heavily that as Paul climbed the stairs to the bridge, holding the plate and cake before him, the cake would literally be suspended in mid-air as the ship plunged into a trough).

8 March 1989

Weather has improved a bit but the swells are still huge. It's plus 11, 25 knots of wind and the sun shines which makes it a joy to be on the bridge. ETA Auckland Islands is 1400. Ken still avoids me and I guess apart form a cursory 'good morning', I've said no more than ten words to him on watch over three days. Lunch with Keith, Dog, Steve and Ken then prepare for landfall, 14 miles away.

On arrival, the Aucklands are shrouded in low cloud; it's wet and unspectacular. The depth finder is not working so we can't explore the smaller coves and inlets. We simply lie a-hull, surrounded by steep, lush hills until, after dinner when we steam out into deep water again. To Paul Brown's incredulity, I suggest to him a final 'wrap' story on the Antarctic. When he hears that I'd like to send a telegram to Thatcher demanding from the crew of the *Gondwana* that she sign the minerals moratorium proposal, he has the decency to humour me and duly files the story, more, I'm later convinced, out of friendship rather than professionalism.

Shower, Sabine trims my hair and beard, do my dobying, change bunk linen and prepare for watch. I calculate: Snares by 2000 tomorrow, lee of Stewart Island by 0500 on the 10th, then 330 miles to Lyttelton at 7 knots – 47 hours – 0400 on the 12th! I hope I'm wrong as this will put us behind schedule to meet our press deadlines. Will check in the morning. Spot a fleet of fishing boats just north of the Aucklands. The swell picks up as predicted as we leave the lee of the islands.

I prepare and send an email message to Kelly in response to her outburst in defence of Lena Hagalin who has been quoted as saying that she refuses to release the footage of the DuDu action on the grounds that it is 'unfair' to the French. I can't believe it. We've just been beaten up to bring this story to the attention of the world and now we're being told that it's too sensitive to release. Dare not tell the crew.

9 March 1989

My fears are confirmed. On watch I surreptitiously squared off the distances we have to cover and found that even at 8 knots we would not make Lyttelton until the 12th and I, casually as possible, mention this to Ken – not easy under the prevailing atmosphere. He confirms my opinion and then called for Bob who came puffing up the stairs and agreed that an error had been made. Then Arne's called and the three of them are slightly chagrined by the fact that a mere deckie/campaigner had the temerity to spot such an error. Davey Edward is beside himself with delight and says the only thing that could top it was if I had told him we would not have sufficient fuel to make it to port.

We alter course away from the Snares and head directly for Lyttelton. We have to make 9.5 knots to make it back by the agreed time of 1000 on the 11th and Davey informs us that the second engine is ready for use when we need it. Watch is a bore and I pass it by watching a huge wandering albatross who displays aerial skills of magical dimensions. Lunch, telex off to the UK to Thatcher and then clean the lounge. At 1700, Ken comes to my cabin and we resolve the misunderstanding which has clouded our relationship for the past few days and end up in a bear hug. It's good to be back on an even keel with the old bastard. Screaming along on one engine, still at 9.2 knots in fine weather and a low swell. An echo appears on the radar at 2330 and Ken allows me to plot its course – the first time I've ever touched the radar. This is the last night at sea before we reach NZ. An epic voyage and I sleep deeply in the knowledge and satisfaction of a job well done.

10 March 1989
Ken wakes me at 0630 to come and see the 'sunrise and the cavorting dolphins'. I turn over and go back to sleep. Then he tempts me with bacon and eggs and I can't resist. On watch there are dolphins indeed, and the coast of the South Island is 10 miles off to port. We are home at last. Gentle swell, cloudy with rain. Wash down the bulkheads with Wojtek and Keith and then crash till 1600 when I get a phone call. It's from *Time Out* telling me that the name Greenwave is already being used as the National Front's 'green' arm which mortifies me. Just our luck to use a name which has already been coined by a bunch of Fascists!

Shower and hang about reading and listening to loud music until watch. Off Tairoa Heads now and both engines throbbing through the ship as we cream along at 10.5 knots.

Meeting at 1830 where the 'heads of departments' (me, Dog, Arne, Ken, Henk, Keith, Pat, Ian and Davey) mull over the expedition and have a celebratory drink from yet another 'lost' bottle of hootch. Watch is uneventful. We're off Timaru as we leave our last evening watch before landfall. The 8-12 drains the remains of a rum bottle after watch in a toast to a great trip. Bed at 0030 after receiving my bar bill of $NZ365 – the fourth largest. Ken proudly displays his bill of close to $NZ1000.

11 March 1989
Eighty days at sea are over today. On watch to see the familiar hills of Lyttelton all around – we're more or less hove-to as we peer at the entrance to the port at 0800, waiting for the pilot, scheduled to arrive at 0845. As we get underway to meet the pilot, we drag the ropes out of the holds. As we approach the wharf, Ken ceremoniously hands me the heaving line to throw to the wharfies, something I've never done on a Greenpeace ship before. I'm nervous about making a cock-up in front of a hundred waving and cheering people lined on the quayside, but my aim is perfect and is greeted by cheers from the people behind me and pats on the back.

After clearing Customs, the local schoolkids perform a Hukka in our honour and I'm so overcome with emotion, I can hardly respond as I stand on the quayside, swaying in an attempt to get my land-legs and fighting off a million memories and emotions which crowd my head.

So it was over at last. Wellington next, to deliver the barrels and carry out our final protest against US contamination of Winterquarters' Bay and then a three day steam to our home port. Lyttelton in March was still blooming in late summer finery and we made the most of our brief stay to renew acquaintances with friends and invade the British Hotel. The short hop across Cook Strait took us into Wellington on the 14th March where the barrels we had partly filled with cadmium waste from the McMurdo pipeline were ceremoniously loaded onto the trailer and this time paraded through the streets to the US Embassy, propelled along by an army of willing volunteers.

At the Embassy, the reporters were gathered in number and the familiar round of interviews took place. Since Dog was in charge of the actual 'delivery' of the barrels to Embassy staff, I had to bear the brunt of press interest which was not what I had in mind.

Dog was finally admitted into the Embassy alone and he emerged after a few moments to tell the crowd through the megaphone, 'Well, we gave the US a final opportunity to dispose of this dangerous waste in a responsible manner and they have yet again refused to honour their obligations. They refuse to acknowledge ownership of the waste so we have no option but to leave the barrels outside their gates in the hope that they will do the right thing.'

Greenpeace were fined a nominal sum for 'litter', surely the final and ignominious insult to an organisation which had just spent 80 days drawing the attention of the world to the cavalier way in which we litter by the thousands of tonnes and treat so disgracefully the most vulnerable of environments.

The trip back to Auckland was a pleasure – gentle seas, easy watches and late nights sitting up under a star-studded sky yarning about the trip, laying old arguments and disagreements to rest and renewing friendships which had been put under the most intense strain during the trip. Auckland was a riot of activity and fun, interspersed with hours of work on deck, discharging the cargo which remained after our stops in Lyttelton and Wellington destined for the warehouse where we stored all the essential Antarctic equipment which would be used for the following season's expedition. Our first night ashore in Auckland, however, was to end in acrimony between myself and a few of the new boys on the block.

Chapter 30

A shock, a share and a showhouse

Greenpeace was now a rich organisation. Since the *Warrior* bombing in 1985, it had achieved international notoriety, a new respectability and a bank balance fit to burst. Not only did it wallow in the sympathy money people showered on it, but the French government settled Greenpeace's claim against it to the tune of many millions of dollars. Over a relatively short period, Greenpeace found that it could – and did – expand its campaign base dramatically and was able for the first time in its brief history, to hire all the lawyers, accountants and campaigners it wished. It now assumed a rather attractive aspect to those who had previously considered the organisation too radical or poor to join.

My state of mind as we sweated and swore our way through the discharging of the *Gondwana* in Auckland was not the most sanguine it has ever been, that is true. It was further unbalanced by a rumour I had heard a few days previously that Colin Hines – someone whose skills I so valued that I asked him in vain on several occasions to join us in our formative years – had joined the Greenpeace UK staff. Imagine my astonishment when the truth of the rumour was confirmed when Hines turned up on the ship along with Lord Melchett, hand extended in greeting as we took a breather. I learned that Hines had his wife and child in tow as well and that the Melchett-Hines combo was on a 'fact-finding' tour of Australia and New Zealand. What facts they were after and whether they ever found them is unknown to me, but whichever way I looked at it, I saw unfairness and insult. I did my best to be polite, but I was resentful and my resentment showed. The raw nerve of it all forced me to leave the ship and wander the streets, mulling over the crushing reality of the fact that some people are destined to do all the work whisking the milk while others are destined to lap up the cream.

I met the rest of the crew and a few of the New Zealand office staff for a meal. Sitting at the table, chatting with a few of the staff was another former colleague of mine, Andy Kerr, who had at one time run Friends of the Earth in Scotland. Meeting him here after at least ten years could not be coincidence. As I shook his hand, the penny dropped. He too was now working for Greenpeace. He looked smart in his leather jacket and creased trousers. He had a smart briefcase. His fresh-faced smile contrasted with my worn-out, grimacing face which was still recovering from eighty days at sea. After a few beers, I rounded on him and gave him a verbal savaging for which I was immediately sorry. He quickly left the restaurant.

The following morning, I wrote my resignation to McTaggart. I proposed that he should immediately put a ceiling on the number of campaigns being operated until they were demonstrably 'won' and set a ceiling on salaries of $20,000 a year and see who stayed. This was finally the end of the road for me and Greenpeace. I had formally committed my resignation to paper. The carefully and deliberately inserted dot after my signature represented the final full stop in my Greenpeace involvement.

I sat for a while in my cabin with Jimmi Hendrix's 'All Along the Watchtower' at full volume pulsating through my body, staring at my resignation. I had worked since 1971 – eighteen years – for the green movement, the last twelve, since 1977, for Greenpeace. I had travelled widely, met interesting people and made some life-long friends. I had, moreover, been involved in campaigns which had ended the practice of disposing of radioactive waste at sea, forced the dramatic reduction of liquid radioactive waste discharges to the Irish Sea from the Sellafield pipeline, closed down fur farms – largely through the efforts of the tireless Mark Glover – and which had ended the cruel business of forcing captive cetacean from cavorting in swimming pools for our titillation. We had also closed down the European market for seal pelts from Canada, saved a few thousand seals in Orkney and drawn attention to a number of other environmentally damaging practices such as estuarine pollution and the demise of inshore fisheries. We took on the governments of the world and forced them to protect the entire continent of Antarctica. But the most important job we did was to legitimise environmental issues; we brought them in from the cold and put them centre-stage. The Rio Earth Summit to be held a year later would be testament to that.

I had been on every major TV news and current affairs programme in the UK, had written articles for hundreds of newspapers and magazines and had spoken in public more times than I could recall. I had been involved in every major direct action Greenpeace had conducted. And now it was all over. I pressed the button on the computer which would send my resignation email through the ether to McTaggart, 12,000 miles away in Europe. Goodbye, David. Goodbye, Greenpeace.

*

On my return to the UK, the thanks extended to me for leading an expedition which gave Greenpeace unprecedented profile amounted to having my email facility taken away from me within a matter of days and to receive a bill of $US2000 for the 'purchase price' of the computer which came with the job and which I had indicated to Greenpeace I'd like to keep. I paid this and my bar bill which amounted to $US300, a third of Ken's bill and very modest by some yardsticks, from the fee I received for leading the expedition and was left with a few hundred dollars which lasted all of a couple of weeks.

Paul 'Doglips' Bogart assumed overall charge of the Antarctic campaign on his return to the USA after the 1988-89 trip. I was grudgingly invited to the planning meeting for the 1990-91 Antarctic expedition meeting in Amsterdam where my proposal to spend three months at the French base to totally and finally disrupt the construction of the airstrip was met with incredulity by Lena Hagelin, the blond Scandinavian who had somehow found her way into the Antarctic campaign hierarchy under Kelly Rigg's tutelage while acting, I was told, as a paid nanny for Kelly and Steve's children. She told me that I must be 'mad' to propose such a thing when the French were finally expressing support for the proposal to ban mining in the Antarctic. I asked her how long she had been 'campaigning' and if she really thought that Greenpeace should sacrifice the second most important archipelago in Antarctica based on the overblown premise that opposition from an environmental pressure group would cause the French to reverse their support for the mining ban.

In self-imposed exclusion, I retired to the UK to watch with only mild interest how the 1989-90 expedition fared. The direct action at Dumont D'Urville amounted to placing a bunch of cardboard penguins on the rocks amid the chaos of blasting an archipelago to smithereens, and taking some pictures. The crew reportedly threatened mutiny. The pictures which emerged from the trip were the usual documentation of localised environmental degradation – particularly at bases in the Peninsular – plus those of the expedition team shaking hands and sharing social occasions with the base teams. In terms of the information gathering value of the trip it was a success: in terms of direct action impact, it was not.

Montagne Jeunesse asked me to resume work as their green adviser, something I did eagerly as I liked the work, the people and the income.

388

I wrote articles for magazines and newspapers and a chapter on the Antarctic environment for a book published by the Ecologist team headed up by Teddy Goldsmith. Greenpeace asked me to write a definitive piece on Sellafield. I helped Clem Shaw, a film producer who ran Prometheus Productions, to script and edit the film of the 1989 voyage which was screened in early 1990 under the title *Antarctic Warriors*. Penny Ephson, a director of Wide Open Communications, asked me to write the brochure which was to accompany the display of an 'Ideal Green Home' at the Olympia Exhibition and to advise and front the project. John Burton, a colleague from the 70s, asked me to become the London representative of his new and innovative project, Programme for Belize, which successfully sought to purchase 250,000 acres of threatened forest in that country for development of sustainable forestry and tourism projects. Things were looking up and I decided that there was indeed life after Greenpeace.

Nonetheless, I could not quite erase the organisation from my mind and was constantly, either by misfortune or design, running into people from the organisation, hearing things about them or being pestered by the press about my theories as to their low profile. I was in a curious situation: I used Greenpeace as an organisation to bolster my own credibility but was cast, not unwillingly, in the role of critic. But I was at least busy and earning an income, something about which I had worried deeply as I pondered life without the safety net, however threadbare, of Greenpeace around me.

Speculation about Greenpeace's financial arrangements were rife at this time: the media were aware that the French had compensated Greenpeace handsomely – and quite rightly – for the bombing of the *Rainbow Warrior* and the millions of dollars handed over in reparation were salted away in various bank accounts in order to ensure their safety from the law, and in the event of Greenpeace being in contempt of court and having its assets seized. Two of its staff – one an American fundraiser and the other a failed CEO who lasted barely six months – were paid off with what the media claimed were six figure sums. I witnessed first hand a $10,000 pay-off to someone who had been hired by the Lewes office and to whom McTaggart took an instant dislike. After ten minutes on the phone, McTaggart told his staff to pay him off, to tell him there had been a mistake and to send him on his way. Rumour had it that the unfortunate person who had the distinction of having the shortest ever Greenpeace career had once worked for the CIA.

My mother and family rarely saw me. Mum was now living in a small flat in Kidbrooke, near Blackheath, south east London, and despite the brave face she put on things, her life was dull. My father had been dead for fourteen years and Mother had suffered her loneliness with amazing stoicism although it must be said that my brother – now risen to the status of bank manager for the Trustee Savings Bank – was a constant source of support to her. I tried to see her once a week although I frequently cried off. She saw family from time to time, but essentially, her life revolved around her one bedroom flat, her books and the television. Never once in all my life could I recall her or father, when he was alive, putting any pressure on me whatsoever and that situation remained. Mother would never, ever complain.

My brother and his three kids – Martin, Phillip and Neil – I would see briefly for Christmas and on my return one year from the Antarctic, a family party was dedicated to celebrating my return from a place of which some of my family, I'm sure, had not the slightest knowledge, least of all its location. Despite the fact that Fiona and I were still close, I knew soon after my return that we would part. She knew it too and suggested that to give me more space for a while, she would accept a job offered to her by Mark Glover who had taken over the anti-fur campaign we had pioneered at Greenpeace and who had set up shop in Nottingham with a new organisation called Respect for Animals. I quietly revelled in the thought of freedom from a close relationship: I had been with a partner since my early teens and decided that a year without a partner would do me good.

During the last few weeks of our relationship, before her departure to Nottingham, we lived a pained and saddened life. I went with her to the station and we cried in each other's arms before she disentangled herself and stepped on the train to Nottingham. As I wandered off the platform to the sound of the train's clanking departure, images of sun-filled days in Karori, carefree days on deserted New Zealand beaches and watching the sunset over Castle Rock filled my mind and I sat down and sobbed my heart out.

The experience of bachelorhood was novel and I was determined to steer clear of long-term commitments. The Ideal Home Exhibition was taking place in March 1990 and Penny Ephson and her Chelsea Football

Club-supporting boyfriend, Keith Peck, were running the show. Penny asked me to write the 'Ideal Green Home' brochure to accompany a mocked-up end-of-terrace house at the Olympia exhibition hall into which we had crammed every eco-gadget on the market. Professor David Bellamy was involved and soon we were setting up our 'house' under the regime of the cheeky-chappie persona of Keith.

The three week's activities at Olympia were an absolute riot and we all had a thoroughly good time. Across the way from the ideal green home stand was a crèche operated by the World of Children and the supervisor was a pretty woman whose eye I had caught on a few occasions. As the end of show party got under way, the staff from the crèche arrived and I found myself standing next to the pretty supervisor and asked if we could meet for a drink. Her name was Gaye.

I liked Gaye from the very start. I liked her humility and her grounded nature. I learned to my disappointment that Gaye was already in a relationship, but eventually she called me. I didn't press for information about her relationship but merely agreed to meet at platform seven at Victoria Station on the following Saturday. It took me all of –oh, at least an hour – to realise that I liked this woman a great deal. She is an Eastender in the true tradition – big family, close ties, lots of relations who regularly meet for parties (at which performances are encouraged) and she is eighteen years my junior, a fact which has never seemed to bother either one of us more than momentarily over the years.

We became very close, very quickly, and I found myself careering off down the M4 on my motorbike at every opportunity to her job-tied house which she shared with four other women in High Wycombe. Within weeks, Gaye came to live in my Lavender Hill flat, and I noted ruefully that I had only managed a paltry three months out of the year I'd promised myself a bachelor existence.

A month later, we took the bike to Paris for a weekend and there, over a candlelit dinner in Montmatre, we became engaged to be married. When we came back to London, we moved from 128 Lavender Hill to 144 Lavender Hill. I had been living in the famous South London street for a few months by now and my life seemed quite well organised.

I still kept in touch with McTaggart. As I had come to expect, he was working on all manner of projects in his own quiet way. Whenever he came to town it was good practice to batten down the hatches. His social skills were lacking much of the time, but he was exciting to be around and despite the fact that we fought like a cat and dog we held each other in mutual respect. He had recently moved to Italy and was growing olives. He had well-developed plans to move into the olive oil business, a venture in which I was marginally involved a few years later.

The 1990-91 expedition was being prepared in Auckland. Doglips Bogart had sought a long-term expedition co-ordinator to replace me and had found and appointed a short, bustling American woman called Dana Harmon. She was the new kid on the block and Dog decided she needed some help. He asked me if I would go to New Zealand to help Dana on the preparation phase of the expedition. I asked Gaye if she fancied a trip to New Zealand and a stay on the Greenpeace ship while I did my advisory work with the expedition. I didn't have to ask twice.

In retrospect, accepting that position was probably a mistake. Dumping Gaye into the highly incestuous and closeted environment of a Greenpeace ship was unfair. Despite her gregarious nature and ability to deal with almost any situation, it was insensitive of me to expect her to feel at ease. I felt torn between assuming my usual role of expedition leader, albeit a surrogate role, and paying Gaye the attention she needed. Gaye was out of her normal world and had been thrust ignominiously into the one I habitually inhabited. On top of everything, we were trying to sleep together in a three-quarters-size bunk on a ship which was, as usual, full of noise, even in the small hours.

Dana didn't really want to hear my suggestions. She appeared to take delight in rebuffing any attempt I made at proffering advice. I let her get on with it and restricted myself to helping Ken on deck and ensuring that I spent as much time as possible with Gaye to help her come to terms with this most peculiar of experiences. Soon the vessel was ready. Swenson and Sabine were to winter again, accompanied this time by Wojtek and a Turkish Australian radio operator selected at the very last minute by Swenson after his original choice – an American – had crapped out. The planning seemed very loose to me, but I kept my feelings to myself, happy to at least be here, my ticket paid for and on a decent consultancy fee into the bargain.

Jim Cottier, our old salty sea-dog of a skipper on previous trips, invited some of us to the island which he looked after for his millionaire absentee boss and we all trotted off to Roberton Island in the Bay of Islands, near Russell, to the north. It was, and will remain, one of the most wonderful weekends I can remember. Bas Beentjes and Liz Carr went as did Ken and his wife-to-be Michelle, Swenson and Sabine, Gaye and I plus Wojtek.

Jim's lifestyle on Roberton was one of Robinson Crusoe without the austerity. He lived alone on a beautiful island perhaps a mile long which at high tide was divided in two. He had every facility at his disposal – yacht, speed boat, surfing, wind-surfing and fishing equipment, pool table and an environment which took your breath away. And it was all ours for the weekend. Dolphins regularly visited the island. I attempted windsurfing and failed miserably. But the pace of life on the island was magical and we did whatever took our fancy. On the last day, Jim took us sailing and insisted we went onto the windward side of the island in a stiff breeze. It was exhilarating and on arrival at the small jetty, we moored and sat on the wooden jetty, still soaked through and a-buzz with excitement, and drank Jim's health and the success of the forthcoming trip with a tot of rum.

Departure day arrived and this time I was one of the shore-siders waving the vessel away on its long journey to the place I loved. Ken strutted around the foredeck, hauling in the ropes and glancing up from time to time with a white flash of a smile and a brief wave. The *Gondwana* reversed out into the harbour, went ahead and took a long turn out into the gulf. Soon it was gone and we repaired to the nearest bar. Not even a belly full of cold Kiwi beer could fill the void the ship's departure left in my stomach. This was the first Antarctic trip which I had not been in charge of and on which I had not sailed. I felt as though a usurper – Dana – had stolen my clothes, my campaign, my dreams. It was a very familiar feeling and one which had permeated my being for years after Melchett had moved into the Graham Street office after the coup in 1986.

Gaye and I hired a car and set off to explore New Zealand. We restricted our travels to the North Island as we did not have sufficient time to take in both: we intended to meet ex-pat friends in Australia and had decided to see Tasmania as well. As we waved goodbye to friends in Auckland, the Gulf war was about to break and the same sort of sabre-rattling and jingoism which accompanied the Falklands war winged its way 12,000 miles across the ocean and made me shudder.

Of the entire trip, our tour of the East Cape in New Zealand was, to me, the most restful and enjoyable. We visited beaches which had seen no footprint for months. We stayed in motels overlooking the sea and slept to the sound of crashing surf. We lazed on beaches and became deeply tanned. We had everything going for us yet, after a week or two at best, my old restlessness surfaced and I became anxious, unable to sit in one place for more than a few minutes and conscious of the days and weeks left until we were home again. I felt as though I was missing so much by not being in the loop. I was yet again technically out of work and had succumbed to the lure of another Greenpeace offer of work. But this would be a short-term cure for my problem, like a junkie going cold turkey for a day knowing full well that tomorrow the old craving would return and that a long-term cure was what was needed, despite the pain and anguish which would accompany the treatment.

I had to secure a post-Greenpeace occupation and sitting around in the Antipodes for weeks was not exactly helping me in that task. We flew to Tasmania and spent Christmas at a motel which was alternately lashed by rain and shrouded in mist. We visited the penal colonies at Port Arthur and on the Gordon River. We enjoyed ourselves as much as my preoccupation would allow and my greatest pleasure came from seeing Gaye so happy at being in such a distant land: I wish now I had swallowed my impatience and added more to her enjoyment. But it was to get better.

Melbourne was our next port of call where we would meet my old mate from Deptford days, John Morton, now lecturing anthropology at the Australian National University and then later, Don Gardner, the guy from the Elephant and Castle who became a much revered social anthropologist. John's girlfriend, Narida, was waiting for us at his place in St Kilda, a cosmopolitan suburb of Melbourne, and on the following day, she drove us to Canberra where John was housesitting for a friend and where his mother and father were visiting him. It was a long drive and we arrived as evening was falling. There was Morton, totally unchanged from the last time I had seen him a few years previously – long hair, white strides and speaking as though he'd never left Deptford, so broad was his Cockney twang.

After a wonderful few days in which we celebrated New Year, it was time for Gaye and I to leave. We were booked through to Singapore and then on to Bali before the home run. But Bali for me was a bridge too far. By now I was itching to get home and while I desperately wanted Gaye to have her full bite of the cherry on this trip, I began to worry, probably irrationally, about the war which was about to start in the Gulf. In Singapore, Gaye and I analysed, deliberated and argued over whether we should go to Bali or just get the hell out of it to the UK. I feared being a national of a belligerent nation abroad and felt that if my country was at war, even if I did scorn the justification for it and deplore our participation, there was only one place for me to be – at home.

Much to Gaye's intense displeasure and to my rueful uncertainty, we finally boarded a plane for England. I promised Gaye that we would visit Bali one day, a promise I have yet to make good. Fourteen hours later, we were back in the dankness and chill of a British winter. The adventure was finally over and I looked forward to my non-Greenpeace future with uncertainty and trepidation.

The English winter was cold and harsh. Having no flat to move into, Gaye and I prevailed upon her parents for a roof over our heads for a month while we looked for work and a place to live. In deep February snow we moved into one of those houses which are thrown up in what seems like a matter of weeks on a new estate in Tooting, southwest London. We were extremely miserable in the house and decided that we would move out at the earliest opportunity. The letting agent advised us of a 'lovely flat' up for rent at 69 Parkgate Road, very close to Albert Bridge and bang opposite the gates of Battersea Park, as the road name suggests. We viewed it as soon as our six month's renting period at the Tooting house was up and fell in love with it at once.

While I was still looking around for work and picking up the odd contract here and there, Gaye applied for a position at Violet Melchett Day nursery in Flood Street, just across the river, for which she was instantly accepted, given her qualifications and experience. The flat's convenient location meant that anyone passing through town would come and stay with us and we had a veritable procession of friends, acquaintances and ex-Greenpeace foragers constantly passing through – Pete Bouquet, McTaggart, Doglips Bogart and a host of others regularly graced our humble couch in the living room.

I knew that there was to be one more Antarctic trip to pull the base out. The political work being done by the Greenpeace International team with McTaggart's unseen and unheralded work was beginning to pay dividends. The summer drew on and as the next Antarctic expedition was being planned by those still prepared to hack the arduous task, a remarkable event occurred. The Antarctic Treaty Consultative Parties (ATCPs) finally agreed to observe a 50 year moratorium on mining in the Antarctic. First France and Australia had mooted the plan, to be joined by others. After a time, only the UK, the USA and Japan were holding out for retention of the Minerals Regime and at the 1991 meeting of the ATCPs, Japan capitulated, at which point the UK and the USA had no choice but to agree. Antarctica was safe from mining at least until 2041.

Greenpeace, along with many other campaigning organisations, had saved a continent and there was no question in my mind where the lion's share of the credit lay – with David McTaggart, and I wrote to him to tell him so. I was now anxious to know what Greenpeace intended to do with the base. Would they continue to monitor events, or would they decide to pull the base out and save the organisation close to a million dollars a year? The inevitable happened: Dog called me.

'We're pulling out, Wilks. I want you to be on the team – lot of old guys going back this year. Sort of nostalgia trip. I can't offer you the expedition leader's role – that's Dana's and I must honour the contract – but I can get you in as the leader of the remote team which will hang out at McMurdo for a month, just to give them a hard time and to carry out a full and final investigative programme to monitor their so-called clean-up operation. Waddya say?'

I told him I'd let him know and as it turned out, his offer and another potentially momentous event seemed destined to be intertwined. For the time being, however, armed with this information, I restricted myself to making some suggestions to the Antarctic expedition team (from which I had been dropped the previous year) about what they could achieve on the forthcoming trip. I suggested that the trip should be simply and purely one of celebration: that we should send a team of climbers, including Chris Bonnington, to scale a hitherto-unclimbed peak and that we should erect some form of modest monument on the site of the base camp and round off the stay at Cape Evans by sending a party ashore to walk to Scott's last known resting place, all of which would be documented on film to bring to people in the outside world a sense of the wonder, scale and beauty of this place that we, with their invaluable help, had managed to save for the time being.

I also suggested that Greenpeace held a series of Antarctic lectures in all the signatory nations to the Treaty and had people sign a petition to future generations to extend the mining ban indefinitely. The petitions could then be microfiched and put in a capsule to be buried at the South Pole by a Greenpeace team sent there to specifically challenge the Americans' presence by delivering and burying a 'time capsule'. This would also have the effect of linking millions of supporters around the world in a more direct way with the Antarctic and the Greenpeace efforts to protect it. I sent off my ideas with great enthusiasm and waited for the meeting in Washington to conclude. Eventually, a week after it had ended, Dog deigned to call me. After twenty minutes of conversation, I anxiously asked him how my ideas went down.

'What ideas? Oh, yeah, I know. No, they didn't fly Wilks. Sorry, mate.'

I privately speculated that they were never even broached. At about the same time as Dog invited me to join the upcoming expedition, promising to send me a contract to review within days, I was contacted by Sarah Burton, Greenpeace UK's legal adviser. She invited me to lunch to discuss administrative issues about the organisation which had been thrown up during a company restructuring exercise she had asked a team of corporate lawyers to undertake. Despite letters and phone conversations I had had the previous year with Melchett, confirming that I was no longer a shareholder, Sarah told me, as calm as you like, that it appeared I did indeed hold one of the original shares and that we should talk it over at lunch.

We met in a pub in Islington and over a bowl of salad and a pint of warm beer Sarah explained the situation. The delving by the team of lawyers employed to restructure Greenpeace's empire had uncovered the fact that the shares issued to Denise Bell and I in 1979 which had been sidelined during the Thornton onslaught in 1983 – and which I had put out of my mind in the wake of Melchett's assurances that I was no longer a shareholder – were in fact legally issued and therefore Denise and I would be required to sign two pieces of paper each – one, a retroactive resolution absolving the Greenpeace board from any wrongdoing in the past as a result of monetary and constitutional impropriety and two, a share transfer form giving the shares back to the ownership of Greenpeace.

And if we didn't sign? There was no reason why we should not, explained Sarah; it was all straightforward and merely a matter of 'rationalising' the company structures. She even had the pieces of paper I was to sign with her. The paperwork was pressed between two hard covers of an imposing looking document which she opened for me to read. Was there a copy of the resolution I could take away and study? No. I told her I'd think about it. I called my lawyer as soon as I walked into the flat. Then I called Denise. The Antarctic contract didn't arrive. Matti Wuorri, the then Chairman of Greenpeace International, did. Incredibly, he had flown from Finland with the express purpose of discussing with me the 'UK shares issue' and at dinner that night he told me in no uncertain terms that my signatures and those of Denise were urgently needed on the 'absolution' resolution and on the share transfer form.

When I asked him to explain exactly what the resolution meant, he simply told me, 'It is a very serious issue. The personal wealth of the UK board members is at stake. They may be required to pay a lot of money if the resolution is not signed. Furthermore, unless the signatures are appended, the UK office will be unable to send their considerable contribution of over $1 million to International for the financing of approved campaigns. Many campaigns are in jeopardy if you do not sign, the Antarctic campaign not excluded.'

I told him I would not sign until I knew exactly what had happened to bring about such a dire state of affairs. I also told him that I didn't take kindly to having someone who had been in Greenpeace for a matter of months putting the squeeze on me over the Antarctic campaign. I asked Matti what he thought I might expect in return for this magnanimous gesture of saving the personal wealth of the entire UK board and ensuring that Greenpeace might survive this one-person assault. He spread his hands expansively with a shrug of his shoulders, indicating that I should make a suggestion.

'Well, how about this, Matti? I'll accept a $200,000 pay-off – cheap at half the price, I'm sure you'll agree, on the agreement that I'll run a campaign against Sellafield called Campaign Against Thorp and that I'll be answerable to the UK office.'

Matti was unmoved. I mooted an electoral college idea I had as a rather limp alternative, but argued that it was surely something which was in the interests of everyone concerned, if they had the interests of the organisation at heart. Matti said he'd pass on my comments.

McTaggart breezed through town. He was on his way to Scotland to check out his old family haunts just outside Glasgow. He asked if I'd drive up with him and perhaps go and see Denise who was now running a health farm close to Aberdeen. I was commissioned to go to Ireland that week and agreed that I would fly from Dublin to Glasgow to meet him. We spent a few hours looking over what he claimed was once his ancestral family land before his folks travelled to the 'new world' in the late 1700s. We then headed north for Aberdeen to see Denise.

On arrival, late in the afternoon of a Saturday in September, David was not in the mood to discuss the best place to stay. He simply stopped the car in the High Street and jumped from behind the wheel. He stopped the first person on the street – a woman, naturally – and within ten seconds he was guiding her back to the car with a grin a mile wide on his face.

'She'll show us the cheapo part of town down by the docks,' he said by way of explanation and introduction as he slid back behind the wheel.

After a short drive, we were in what was decidedly the cheapo part of town and as the woman extricated herself from the rear seat, she indicated a bar where she would be partaking of a small port and lemon and we followed. After a refreshing pint or two, we said our goodbyes and walked to the nearest 'hotel' to book a bed for the night before setting off to meet Denise and another old friend from the past, who had likewise gravitated to the far north of Scotland, Janie Read. The hotel was the cheapest McTaggart could find – £9 a night – and we retired to our 'rooms' for a brief snooze before setting off to re-acquaint ourselves with Denise and Janie. I could hear McTaggart snoring within seconds of his door being slammed shut.

The search for Janie's place had us driving into many obscure parts of Aberdeen and we eventually called her, told her we were partially lost and she agreed to meet us in the pub we could see from our position and that she would bring Denise with her. Within half an hour, in they walked looking as if Old Father Time had ignored them. It was wonderful to see them and Janie and I laughed about times gone by when we travelled to work together from our cottages in Suffolk and when I and my trusty dog Blackie had attempted to rescue her from the clutches of a gang of rapists which turned out to be her drunken boyfriend.

Denise was in good spirits too and we discussed the shares issue. She would take my lead. If I told her I thought we had a deal of any description, she would sign, so long as the deal suited her. She waxed lyrical about the possibility of raising the *Warrior* from her watery grave and refitting her back in Aberdeen, her original home port. More realistically, I suggested that the best we might be able to get was the appointment of some electoral college which might have some powers over the complexion of the board of directors while holding it to account for its actions and the wise use of supporters' money. The fact was that while the 1986 board had ostensibly been thrown out for being a self-appointed oligarchy of friends, the incumbent board had done nothing to reverse that situation and were, possibly, even more unaccountable than we had been. We could change that, I argued, by refusing to sign the resolution until such time as a properly constituted electoral college had been installed. Denise concurred.

When we finally left the pub and accepted Janie's invitation to drinks at her place, we all wandered off in good spirits and I engaged Janie in polite conversation about her daughter who was being looked after by a friend for the evening. As we stood waiting for the babysitter to open the door to Janie's flat, I was in the middle of telling Denise and Janie about McTaggart's encounter that afternoon with the woman who took us down to the docks to seek out cheap accommodation when the door opened and there, to our utter and complete astonishment, was the very lady in question. We had stopped and asked for help from the very woman who was not only a friend of Janie's but who had been engaged to babysit that evening. The chances of that happening were at least a million to one, but those sorts of things seemed to happen when McTaggart was around.

Back in London, I discussed the impending Antarctic trip with Gaye. It would mean six months apart and the all-too-familiar strain on a relationship. Gaye looked into my eyes and told me, 'It's your decision and if you decide to go, I'll understand and I'll be here waiting for you when you return. You have worked hard and long to help achieve this campaign victory and you'll always hate yourself if you don't go and finish what you began in 1985. You decide and I'll stand by you.'

I took her head in my hands and kissed her. My love for her overflowed. I picked up the phone and called Dog.

'OK. I'm in. I'm telling my clients that I'll be away between October and March so I need the Antarctic contract within a day or two to confirm I have income for that period of time.'

400

Despite my agreement the contract still did not arrive. I called Dog. 'Where is this contract, Dog? I need it now. I'm going to the other side of the world in two weeks for six months, dammit, and I don't have anything official from you.'

His voice came back, hushed and conspiratorial. 'Listen, Wilks. I'm risking my job telling you this, but I'm being told by a superior not to send you the Antarctic contract until you've signed the UK resolution. That's all I can tell you. You're being squeezed big time, mate.'

I sat back and stared hard at the wall as I replaced the receiver. Almost at once the phone rang. Steve Sawyer, Executive Director of Greenpeace International, was on the line. I didn't have to think twice as to the reason for his call. He mumbled on amiably as he usually did on the rare occasions we spoke, about the respect he had for my campaigning skills and about the old times. Yeah, yeah, Steve. Get on with it.

'Now, about these shares that seem to be causing a problem. Matti tells me that you've suggested an electoral college be set up in the UK. That's a great idea and one which has been doing the rounds at the Council meetings lately. All offices are committed to setting up some form of college and I think we can work out a deal here. Why don't you and I liaise on this for a while, then I'll come over and finalise the agreement.' Sure thing, Steve.

Over the course of the next week, I drafted the agreement and Steve added his touches to it. There was a small matter of compensation for my time, not to mention my lawyer's fees, to be addressed. My lawyer's bill came to £4700 and I calculated my time at 27 working days at £150 a day, totalling as near as damn it, £4000. Steve was advised that when he came to the UK to settle this arrangement, he needed signing authority on a cheque for £8700. I presented Steve with a plan which would see the appointment of a 20 to 30 strong electoral college, one third being appointed from the international Greenpeace personnel, one third from the UK office staff and one third from the 'old timers' list I had prepared.

Steve advised me that appointments from the UK staff would not fly with the UK board, so I dropped any reference to where the other two thirds would come from, an overt indication in my view that I was not hoping to stuff the electoral committee with 'Wilkinson's mob' and that under this arrangement, the one third of old timers could easily be outvoted when it came to board appointments by the other two thirds who could be appointed from Mars for all I cared. I simply wanted to see to it that the people who had worked so hard establishing Greenpeace in the early days, who had worked for nothing most of the time and upon whose shoulders the organisation had weighed so heavily, had a voice in dictating where the organisation should go and who should be running it. Even if they were out-voted, it did at least give deference to these people without whose unstinting work the Melchetts and the Hines of the organisation would not be sitting back in their comfortable offices enjoying even more comfortable salaries while people like me, Ken, Carol, Athel, Martini, Henk and others were all scratching around for an income.

We finalised the agreement and Steve arrived at my lawyer's office a mere week before I was due to leave for the Antarctic. He had the letter of agreement with him, typed on Greenpeace International letterhead. In the presence of Jonathan Hart, my lawyer, Steve signed the letter and handed over a cheque to Jonathan. I signed the forms and I recall thinking at the time that a squiggly line of ink was all that stood between Greenpeace and bankruptcy for the board and the transfer of a million pounds to International. Greenpeace had its pound of flesh and only time would tell if a similar payment would even up the balance sheet. I had no reason to doubt that this historic agreement would not be put in place.

I shook hands with Jonathan and headed off for the nearest pub with Steve where he downed two pints in quick succession and then headed off, presumably to Greenpeace UK's office and then back to Amsterdam. He was gone and I was alone in the deserted bar except for one or two other lonely, early morning drinkers. I sipped my beer and thought of the events of the last few months. It seemed as though my path and that of Greenpeace were destined to cross at regular intervals and, no matter how hard I tried to steer clear of it, I seemed fated to come up against their impressive and resilient might on a regular basis. Now I was off yet again to the Antarctic, still waving the banner of an organisation which had in the past, and would again in the future, work me over good and proper.

Chapter 31

The final hurrah in Terra Incognita

The Antarctic contract arrived in the next post, signed by Steve Sawyer. There was a space for my signature: I decided not to sign it – I'd signed enough pieces of paper lately. I had a few days to go before I left and I spent them in Gaye's company as much as I could. I was going to miss her terribly. I took time out to send Matti Wuorri an email, copied to the international board and to McTaggart, telling him that whoever had tried to put the squeeze on me by attempting to blackmail me into signing the resolution by not sending the Antarctic contract should be rooted out of the organisation and publicly vilified since that person was like a cancer in the organisation which would eventually destroy it. I received no reply.

I did the rounds of visiting family and friends in the final few days before I left and Gaye drove me to the airport in good time to make the flight. It was October 1991 and I was off to see my friends in New Zealand and to relieve the base team for the last time. The base we had sweated over installing in 1986/87 had done its job, as had the hastily cobbled together wintering teams who had so valiantly kept the green flag flying during the cruel winter months in Antarctica.

Swenson, Sabine, Wojtek and the Turkish/Australian Oz were enduring their final three months at World Park Base and we were coming to pick them up, return them to 'civilisation' and pull out the base. Dana Harman was lead campaigner on board but I was at least going on the trip and would see that beautiful place again. Gaye and I hugged each other for a long time at the airport.

'I love you, Pete,' she said.

Tears streamed down my face as I held her head in my hands and kissed her. 'I love you too, Gaye Jerrom, and I'll be back to seal our love in six months' time. Wait for me, darling.'

I turned and walked into the departure lounge. I was alone again, heading off on another adventure and the flag I flew, ironically after all that had happened since we got back from our previous trip, was that of an organisation which had sucked me dry over the last fourteen years and had then tried to spit me out on the pavement.

November passed quickly in the usual round of hard work on deck and evenings spent in various bars around Auckland. Football was again the preoccupation of a hardcore group of ten people every Sunday morning and I took time to catch up with friends from previous stays in this wonderful city. A large Dutch guy was part of the crew – Bastian Beentjes – and we quickly struck up a strong friendship. He was a wonderful guitarist and we were both into blues. Shaun Naylor, an old mate with whom I had sailed years previously, was on board too. It was shaping up to be a good trip, but Dana's presence irked me. There was something about her which I did not like at all. She clearly felt the same about me.

Dana didn't do things the way I would have done them. That didn't make her approach wrong, of course, but her attitude was so alien to me that I simply could not relate to her and it was clear that my 'advisory' role was not going to be put to any sort of use. Her lack of attention to detail and her apparent disinterest in the things which generate a campaign atmosphere – such as banners around the ship, a decent departure media strategy – irked me, but apparently only me, and I resolved early on to be as unobtrusive on this trip as I possibly could; to see it as a payback for four previous trips, as a chance to witness the closure of an important chapter in my life and to drink in, for one final time, the beauty and majesty of the place to which I had become addicted. I realised I was being self-indulgent and selfish, but after years of 'no-such-thing-as-society' Thatcherism at home and bandwagon-jumping by those who would not have touched Greenpeace with a bargepole until the money began rolling in, I didn't see why I should deny myself this luxury, if lumping around in the Southern Ocean for eighty days can ever be seen as such.

We left Auckland for Wellington on the 11th December, 1991. The press representatives on board seemed confused about the immediate plans which were, I heard on the grapevine, to support a demonstration in Wellington; the cause was lost to me then and still is now. I saw out the event which involved letting off firecrackers and lowering lifeboats into the water from the relative tranquility of the saloon of the ship, such was my level of interest. Three days later we left Wellington and turned the bow of the ship towards Antarctica and ran directly into a brutal southerly blow, causing steep seas which threw the ship around like a toy.

The ice charts we received revealed heavy pack – about 300 miles of 9 to 10 tenths ice in the outer reaches of the Ross Sea, but by the time we were approaching Ross Island on the 27th December, it was relatively ice-free.

27 December 1991
Awake to the familiar sound of ice against metal and jump up to see Mt Erebus looming through the porthole. Such a sight! Ice is thickish but gradually peters out as we weave towards Cape Byrd. Work on deck before being called to help Arne with bridge duty. By now we're close to Cape Royds, the sun is brilliant and the view is just as staggering as I recall. The afternoon is taken up with renewing old acquaintances, swapping stories with some very good and old friends. It's great to see Swenson, Sabine and Wojtek again – they lift the atmosphere on board and brighten my day immeasurably. Bed at 0115, secure in the knowledge that I have accomplished at least one pledge I made. Last year, Swenson had told me as he climbed on board the ship while I stood immobile on the quay, 'Come and get us, Wilkinson. You got me into this, I expect you to be there to get me out of it.'

Well, I've done that and in many ways that's what I'm here for. I'll do whatever else I have to do, but I feel that in many ways, my work has already been completed. The scenery, the wildlife and the very air of this place are quite indescribably magical. No words can describe it and no pictures can capture it.

28 December 1991
Work on deck with Shaun, Ken and Cornelius, and the scenery, whales, sunshine and sheer beauty of this place beg our constant attention. The sea ice stretches from the Cape Evans shore line to the ship's position, maybe ten miles from shore. Arne has the ship's bow gently tucked into the ice and keeps the engines turning over at dead slow ahead to keep the bow dug in. Groups of 30 Adelies keep us amused with their antics as they confer on the ice edge, now at ease with our presence, killer whales in large pods, skuas and minke whales against a backdrop of Mt Erebus, lenticular clouds and brilliant sunshine . . .

29 December 1991
Ken insists, amid much scepticism, that every bit of equipment created by the striking of the base will fit on the ship and therefore we used the slogan for this trip – 'One trip, one ship'. Pod of 20 orcas came cruising

by the ice edge causing panic among the poor Adelies, and fearless skuas inspect the helicopters as they approach the ship, almost touching the rotors in their overpowering curiosity. The penguins constantly amuse us as they squabble, sleep, feed and then panic as killer whales approach.

30 December 1991
On deck at 0840 and the day passes in the drudge of barrel crushing, unhooking loads and driving the crane. Arne continues to nibble away at the ice edge with the ship's bow, exploiting leads and using the ship to chip off large chunks of ice. We're now only 6 miles from the base. Fewer whales today but the sun still shines and the wind is a constant 30 knots. 80 barrels processed now. At lunch, Dana arbitrarily changes arrangements Swenson and I had agreed on for discussing the TRAMP work at McMurdo.

31 December 1991
Freshening wind and deteriorating conditions. Full windproof gear required today. Dave and I, plus photographer, take off on a bumpy helicopter ride over McMurdo to get photographic conformation of reports of a large fire which is thought to be burning toxic waste. No bonfire exists. Back on board the weather craps out big time and we sit in the lounge while the wind whistles around us at 40 knots and white-out conditions prevail. The penguins hunker down in the snow and are quickly covered from windward, like little mounds of snow in the flat plain of ice. Real Antarctic weather.

The weather improves around 1800 and we start shuttling people over to the base for the New Year party. It gets going quite well and then, after midnight, I plot my cunning plan. Scott's hut is being worked on by NZ officials who have been invited to the party. Thus, the hut is open and is, more importantly, devoid of other visitors. In all my visits here I have never seen inside Scott's hut and I'm determined that I will only experience it on my own. Here is my once-in-a-lifetime opportunity to realise that ambition.

After a short walk I push open the door and at last I'm all alone in this magical Aladdin's cave of boyhood dreams. I wander around the dark interior and allow the atmosphere to seep into my bones. I sit at the desk Scott once sat at and inspect every corner of this time capsule. My imagination runs wild and I stupidly call out to Scott's ghost to tell me what really happened in these four wooden walls.

I can't believe I'm here, where all those dramas I began reading about as a kid were enacted. I spend an hour alone with my thoughts and with the ghosts of that age of imperialism which shaped so many kids' futures. I am mesmerised. It is worth all the pain and sickness I have suffered to be here. I wander back to our base in the stillness of the Antarctic morning, our ship immobile on a now placid and silent sea.

1 January 1992
Everyone is asleep on board and I take the time to write a long email message to Dog about my misgivings about this trip. A lone Emperor penguin has taken up residency ten yards from the ship on the sea ice.

2 January 1992
We're off Cape Barne now, only 4.5 miles from Cape Evans and the base. The sea ice is visibly thinning: it melts from below through contact with the warmer sea water and the sea seeps into it, making it appear darker than the more solid ice. Barrels all day and Ken reports there are 213 in the locker, 160 of which were pumped free of fuel into the ship's tanks before crushing and stowing – quite a feat.

The work is cold and tiring and by mid-afternoon, we're all flagging a bit. A big pod of orcas cruises by and a couple of minkes sound close to the ship. The Adelies keep us amused as they squabble and wander up and down the ice edge, alternately sleeping and panicking at the latest threat from killer whales, helicopter operations or bangs from the ship as Arne chops off yet more ice with the ship's bow. Meeting at 1900 at which Swenson and I plan the tramp expedition. It is clear that all of us involved – Swenson in particular – find this an exercise in futility: Swenson has been monitoring McMurdo all year and knows what is going on without having to formalise it in this manner.

3 January 1992
40 knots of wind and whiteout conditions – no work yet. I changed my bed linen this morning – the first time since Wellington! Weather brightens up a bit in the afternoon and we resume barrels between 1900 and 2200 – 60 backloaded.

4 January 1992
Up at 0800 to Ken's prognosis – 'You're going nowhere today, Wilks.' The weather has yet again crapped out – half mile visibility, strong winds

driving horizontal snow showers. The weather and Shaun's incapacitation from a strained back, sustained on deck this morning, are becoming real problems. We've had three down days out of seven. Richard films me in my cabin at 1300 for Central TV, after which I minister to Shaun (I owe him a debt of gratitude after he looked after me on the way down), who is rumoured to have a slipped disc. If that's true then it presents us with problems on deck and I counsel Ken about making the suggestion to Dana that she goes and leads the tramp expedition and I stay on board and replace Shaun.

Ken is leery of making such a sensible suggestion, but I argue that if it came directly from me, Dana would probably veto it at once. Weather improves by 1330 and the prospect of more barrels looms; by 1500 we're flying again. We work through to 2200, clearing 70 barrels and the end of the fuel retrograding. Richard continues his interviews with me and we agree on a further filming schedule over the coming weeks. The weather craps out again overnight – Ken reckons it's the effects of El Niño and we're now experiencing 35 knots of wind again. The wildlife around the ship keeps many of us riveted.

5 January 1992

Away to World Park (Grace) base at 1000 and forced to hang around there while Andy and Ian take off to install the VHF repeater on a lofty hummock somewhere, to facilitate communication between us and the ship. Take the opportunity to look around the base and crawl close to some basking seals. The sun is causing rapid melting of the ice around the base and the wet soil is steaming where it is in direct sunshine.

Three of us clamber into Dave's helo which sports external luggage racks piled high with ski, personal gear and equipment, and we arrive at Little Greenpeace Three (LGP3) in absolutely still air and brilliant sunshine – a perfectly glorious day. Two sling-loads of gear arrive, the helos finally depart and we're alone at last on the spectacular sea ice, some ten metres thick, floating on a bottomless sea. The flagged route out to Williams' Field (the ice runway at McMurdo) has lots of vehicular and foot traffic and before long visitors begin to arrive at LGP3. The visitors continue to stream into our little encampment all night as we erect our tents and arrange our gear.

We finally get the food on at 1900 when a further group of people arrive from McMurdo. One guy who is the spitting image of Fonzie, plus his giggling girlfriend, stay for two hours before we have to kick them out. Swenson picked up my camera tonight and immediately broke off the lens quick-release. We have a drop of Glenfiddich and Wojtek and I sit up till 0230 talking politics. I love Wojtek dearly and I am so pleased he's here to share this time with me. Andy can't find my sleeping bag which he brought from the ship so I stay in the Apple hut tonight which is fine by me: it beats tents hands down.

6 January 1992

Walked to Scott Base and participated in the tedious but very convivial meeting with the OIC Geddes and two of his oppos, called Brett and Phil. Lunch followed and we talked generally about GP, its current problems and its philosophy (or the absence of one). Left at 1310 to walk to Mactown after Geddes promises to invite us for drinks on Friday. It takes an hour to walk to Mactown, over the hill and along the roadway which gives a panoramic view of the hinterland of Antarctica over which Scott travelled.

Endured an amicable if guarded chat with Art Brown and Dave Bresnahan who tell us that 800 orphan barrels were discovered in the last 18 months and of those, some 650 had been identified, categorised and were ready to be sent back to the States for disposal. Stupidly, I forgot to ask what had happened to the other 150 and later learned that there had been a detonation on the ice between Williams' Field and Pegasus runway of 'toxic chemicals' involving the use of 400 lbs of explosive.

Planned for an early night but visitors arrived after dinner and we wound up having a few Jack Daniels, supplied by our guests. One of the guys, Lee, is such an engaging and hilarious character that he had us all in fits of laughter for hours and they finally left, after buying t-shirts, at 0230. Absolute silence descends with their leaving, only interrupted by the mournful sound of a passing vehicle making for Mactown from the airstrip.

I'm still sleeping in the Apple and as I lie down, the small construction is littered with clothing, notepads, hats, and all manner of equipment. The most time-consuming activity here is that of trying to keep all your gear in one place: people are constantly asking for clothing, sunglasses and odds and sods to be found and then passed to them. I feel so isolated here at the bottom of the world, sleeping on my own. Sunlight streams in the small windows of the Apple and I look out at the flat ice sheet over which Scott and his party walked to their deaths.

7 January 1992

Another bright, still day and I feel good. Andy decides we should spend some time stowing gear in case of a change in the weather and it's not until 1215 that we finally get away to Mactown, using our bicycles for the first time. Swenson goes earlier to film the radioactive barrel which has been revealed by receding snow fields in an area just outside Mactown; apparently it stands isolated and lonely behind a strip of tape warning people not to approach. I team up with Wojtek: Sabine and Andy go off to investigate area 1 while we head for area 2.

Wojtek, like me, feels that this tramp exercise is redundant but we go through the motions and determine that we'll enjoy ourselves as much as possible in the course of conducting it. We begin looking for leaks in the fuel tanks at Hut Point. The tanks are covered in graffiti and Wojtek picks up a piece of chalk from the ground and with an impish grin on his face, scrawls 'SOLIDARNOSC' on the tank.

We are immediately surrounded by navy personnel who inform us that this is a restricted site. We tell them okay, but continue anyway until a jeep arrives and we are questioned by more senior personnel. Then Swenson, Sabine and Andy arrive and another jeep pulls up and a high ranker slides out surrounded by grunts and reads the riot act about messing around US property. I explain that we've already informed Art Brown of our plans and have had them cleared by him. The officer is reasonably good-humoured but sticks to his official 'get lost' line. We agree to inform Art Brown of our whereabouts and intentions every morning, at which Wojtek and I leave our bicycles at Mactown (they're simply too much of an encumbrance) and walk back to LGP3.

Swenson and the others arrive much later and tell us that their delay was caused by the appearance of Art Brown and Farrell, the naval commander, plus a video team who make a big deal out of the 'defacement' of US property by persons assumed to be me and Wojtek. Swenson immediately denies any involvement of our team, telling Art that 'no Greenpeace people would do such a thing'. The meeting broke up with Swenson reiterating his oath that none of us would chalk slogans

410

on fuel tanks, with Art telling Swenson that we are not to go near the fuel tanks without permission and with Swenson telling Art that we will go where we please in Antarctica where we own the land as much – or as little – as anyone else.

Immediately, Wojtek owns up to having been the guilty party and Swenson storms out of the hut in total disgust. The atmosphere is tense and my intervention on Wojtek's behalf, accepting responsibility since I should have stopped Wojtek from scrawling the slogan, doesn't help at all. I tell Swenson that we are operating in one huge rubbish tip at Mactown where the air, the sea and the land are contaminated and where the fuel tanks themselves are already covered in slogans from 'Black Power' to 'US Rules' and that our little misdemeanour is of little consequence in the overall scheme of things. Swenson won't wear it and remains in a foul mood.

I call up the chopper to film the crater caused by the toxic waste detonation and eventually Dana, Richard and Tim all arrive in the helo and the entire entourage troop out to the crater, reported to be 35 feet in diameter and fifteen feet deep. Then Laurie Greenfield (a scientist friend from Canterbury University in Christchurch) shows up from Scott Base and we have a long chat during which he agrees to take out the film of the crater when he leaves for Christchurch tomorrow and to hand it on to TV NZ. He finally leaves LGP3 at 0400.

Yet another late, late, night and by the time we're all thinking about turning in, the air is electric. Everyone is on a short fuse and I decide to broach it with Swenson. I tell him that as I'm clearly not needed to deal with crises like Wojtek's misdemeanour (Swenson insisted it was his responsibility), nor with issues like the detonation of toxic waste (Dana moved in fast on that one), I feel redundant here, reduced to mooching around Mactown looking at barrels and fuel tanks.

Dana jokingly said to me tonight, 'Your notebook must be full to overflowing with information being passed on by all these visitors.' I replied that I hadn't taken one note as I felt that most of the information is trivial, at which she became very touchy and defensive. Ken called this evening to ask me to go back to the ship soon for two days to help out on deck and that'll do nicely for me.

We set off for Mactown at 1100, Andy remaining at LGP3 to fix solar panels to the green box we use as a store. We restrict our monitoring to the hazardous storage site for two hours, check out the old rubbish tip up on the hill and then head back for the meeting with Laurie at 1600 to arrange the collection of the film. Laurie doesn't turn up and we eventually get a handwritten message from him to explain that a friend of his at Mactown has been taken ill and that, quite naturally, Laurie has re-arranged his priorities. We send a letter back offering our sympathy.

9th January 1992

Off to William's Field. It's my first chance to drive the skidoo – great fun – and I tow Swenson, Sabine and Wojtek on skis. The airfield is a bleak place but the atmosphere is far more relaxed than at Mactown which I'm already getting sick of. Spoke to a few of the guys in charge here but there's really nothing to inspect and we know the plans for the area from the official documentation. We left at 1600 and travelled back across the sea ice that Scott and his party had traversed 80 years previously, laboriously dragging their sledges by manpower. I stared long and hard at the route they took, just southeast of White Island, and lost myself for a while looking at the unending sheet of ice disappearing into the horizon.

We are just about to set off for a look at Castle Rock when Dana calls to tell me that she expects a big reaction to the detonation story so wants to cancel my return to the ship. Her logic puzzles me, but I accept it, despite the fact that I was looking forward to a shower. I'm scruffy, smelly and a little peeved at hanging out in spartan conditions doing a job which really doesn't need doing.

We eventually get away to Castle Rock which is a delight. The snow field rises more and more steeply to the base of the rock which explodes from the ice vertically to a height of some eighty feet or so. We leave the skidoo and go on foot to the rocky outcrop and Swenson takes us to a route up the face which, he claims, is like 'walking up a flight of stairs'. My dislike of heights is put to the test as the route becomes more and more precipitous: at one point, the track is only six inches wide and to the right is a drop of 500 feet to the sea-ice, at the edge of which sits our little ship, a mere smudge of red in the distance.

A few feet from the top I tell Swenson that I'm not moving any further and that I'd appreciate it if he would collect me on the way down. The rest of them continue and within seconds, I can hear their shouts of delight at reaching the top. I'm tempted to follow, but resist. I have an incredible view from my perch – Cape Byrd, Cape Barne, the ice-tongue, Razor Back Island, Inaccessible Island and the whole panorama of the land Scott traversed. Breathtaking. Amazing. I drive the skidoo home, pulling the rest on skis, to find yet more visitors waiting for our return. Finally turn in at 0130.

10 January 1992
Set off at 1115 for Mactown with Wojtek, again spurning the use of the bicycles. We get a lift at Scott Base and are dropped off at the chalet to see Art. Wojtek and I complete our work by 1530 and run into Andy and Sabine down by the foreshore. It's a glorious day and we wander over to Hut Point where we're told yet again that we're in a restricted zone. Arrive back at 1730 to find the hut surrounded by visitors. During the evening I question Swenson and Andy about their apparent overpowering desire – which they talk about regularly – to carry out direct actions at Mactown and ask if they simply want to annoy the NSF or are they interested in addressing real issues.

My feeling is that the NSF is doing what it can, under difficult circumstances, to address the thirty year legacy of environmental abuse at the site. Of course much of it is cosmetic, but they have made significant advances and are, in my opinion, open and frank with us in examining the problem. We finally agree that the most important issue is to demonstrate and exercise the right to freedom of movement in Antarctica and we thus agree to shift our encampment, lock, stock and barrel, to the middle of Mactown. Erling gets the camera out and insists that he films me telling old Greenpeace stories, and I happily oblige . . .

11 January 1992
It's cold today with a biting wind, and the struggle up the hill to Mactown makes you sweat which then half-freezes on you. Wojtek and I go off to look at the refuelling operation after checking in with Art Brown who tells me to stop by at 1500 to find out more on the detonation of nuclear barrels confusion. We go to the foreshore to check area 8 but there's very little to see – it's very tidy and obviously has been recently cleaned up. Art invites me for a tour of the base on Monday to which I agree. This

413

means that I can't return to the ship as planned on Sunday so on the evening call to the ship, I agree with Ken to go back on Monday evening. After dinner I go to the pyramid 'ablutions' tent and strip off for a full washdown – absolute luxury as it's the first time my body has seen water in over a week. A change of clothes and I feel like a new man (to which Keith responds that he'll see if he can find me one.)

12 January 1992

Lazy day agreed. At 1500, Swenson gave me my first cross-country skiing lesson which was very hard work! While he and Sabine took off for Castle Rock, I practiced on the gentler slopes by the hut. Andy sat reading and listening to music and I joined him after an exhausting hour on the skis. Erling was off to see Art Brown and the atmosphere was relaxed and amicable. Dozed the afternoon away until someone knocked on the door of the hut to deliver lobster tails for our supper.

13 January 1992

Up at 0930 and go through the usual and increasingly tedious round of getting ready – evaluate weather and decide on clothing to wear, search for gloves, glasses, windproofs, etc, make tea for thermos, gather food – then we set out for Mactown at 1100. Get to the chalet at 1200 and Art tells me we should meet at 1430 to begin our tour of the base. Wander around aimlessly until we meet up with Swenson, Sabine and Andy and we eat our pathetic lunch of cheese and chocolate, sheltered behind crates of equipment, and then wander off to view the incinerator which is an absolute tip – rubbish spilling everywhere and 50 skuas hanging around, squabbling for scraps. The tour of the base with Art is preceded by a twenty minute question and answer session and I am overwhelmed by the feeling that these guys are doing their best to remedy the appalling situation at Mactown. I begin to quietly question the validity of our more boisterous direct actions which are still being discussed and planned for next week by Swenson and Andy, despite our agreement. After the inspection tour we walk back to LGP3 and await the helo for the flight to the Italica (Italian re-supply vessel) to collect Jussi who has gone on board for some reason. We arrive back at the *Gondwana* at 2010 after an exhilarating flight.

14 January 1992

Ken tells me that today has been designated a half-day break for the crew to visit Cape Royds and I decide to use the tranquillity of the empty ship to luxuriate in a bit of solitude. I call Gaye: how I hate the telephone! She seems so distant and matter of fact and I finish our conversation in an atmosphere of doubt and confusion. I convince myself I'm just being paranoid and force myself to get on with things. Ken appears with beers and we spend a couple of hours catching up on events and swapping stories. He tells me people are starting to crap out.

15 January 1992

We work damned hard stowing timber, heavy bags of contaminated soil from the site and metal tubing. By lunch, we're all exhausted and I'm nursing a bruised head, shoulder and shin. Jussi brings me back to reality, telling me that Gaye is on the phone. She tells me she loves me and that she's sorry she wasn't on the ball last night – I woke her, apparently. We speak for 15 minutes and I'm lost in her love and warmth. Back on deck, I'm light-hearted and in fine mood. I enjoy working with Ken and we horse around and try to wind Shaun up as much as possible. His back is now improved, thankfully. It's good to have him back on deck. We finish on deck and I prepare to fly back to LGP3. It has been such a beautiful day and the evening is mellow.

The flight back across the ice and the hummocks and finally, the saddle at Castle Rock, is quite magical and I take a whole roll of photos which I know, even as I take them, will not reflect the beauty of this place. Have a meeting with the other trampers and agree we'll go back to the ship on Saturday to finalise plans for next week's Mactown events. We play – and lose – another game of softball with the Scott Base guys and then sit and talk until 0130. It's nice to be back here with these itinerants although being back on the ship would suit me better. London and Gaye would be best.

16 January 1992

Erling has me booked for the day and we film the new science lab, the incinerator, the dump, the foreshore and the outfall pipes and he interviews me at each site. We meet the other trampers – who have been checking fuel lines for leaks – and have our modest repast with them. It's a great day – zero degrees, no wind and bright sunshine. Erling, who is still filming the incinerator, suddenly rushes up to me and Sabine and tells us to come quickly. A skua is trapped in a length of plastic and he wants to film us rescuing it. I grab the bird and hold it while Sabine unwraps its legs and we finally free the poor creature. Despite Erling's slovenliness, my earlier antipathy towards him is waning and I'm getting to like him more and more. In fact, I feel a little sorry for him. He has been led to expect more from this trip than he's getting. We sit and chat over dinner and the weather craps out badly. It's snowing like hell, with 30 knots of wind, and we have to rush outside and cover all the equipment. Finally to bed after a long chat with Swenson, during which I try – unsuccessfully – to clear the air, at 0200.

17 January 1992
Lying in the tent with Wojtek who is equally unenthusiastic to rise; he says to me, 'Wilks. Let's agree to make a serious attempt to get up at 1400.' Rose at 1230 and sat around while the rest of the team prepared for their trip by skidoo to Pegasus while I stay at the hut to complete the voice-overs for the broadcasting we plan to do next week. They leave at 1445 and I use the space and time alone to do some chores. I change the human waste bag in the pyramid tent, wash the dishes, tidy the hut and even wash the floor. It looks sparkling and thoughts of Cinderella drift through my mind.

I sit down to concentrate on the voice-overs. The microphone Jussi gave me is not adequate for the job so I switch to the one Paula gave me. But I can't get a sentence out without making some glitch or the other, and after fifteen takes I'm furious with myself. In two hours I only manage to get half of one commentary completed out of six I have to do. The radio crackles and Swenson tells me they're on their way back to the hut as the weather is about to crap out again. I've wasted all this time and still have no tapes completed. Damn!

They arrive at 1730 and immediately fall asleep where they sit. Mike Zulu , over for a brief respite for the engine room on board, falls asleep propped up against the work surface, the rest in various contortions on the benches. The air seems to knock people out after the most unenergetic of exercise. Ken calls at 1830 to tell me that the choppers are grounded due to weather. At 1930 he calls again to advise that the weather is flyable. Paula arrives and takes Zulu, Swenson and Erling back while Sabine,

Wojtek and I settle down to read, eat and chat. Weather craps out again at 2030 and it's snowing hard as I write. Bed at 0000. Read, can't sleep and at 0400 I'm making tea before finally dropping off into an exhausted sleep.

18 January 1992

Sabine wakes me from a deep and much needed sleep at 0745 with the elixir of tea. Ken informs me the choppers are on their way to collect us remaining trampers but warns us that it is still very windy. Mad Dog Maloche arrives and tells us to clamber in quickly. He says, 'It'll be a rough one, guys. The wind over the saddle is gusting to 40 knots.' It was, in the event, one of two flights I will always remember – the other being when I flew from New Plymouth to Wellington in a small plane in similar wind conditions.

The frail helicopter bucked, dropped and soared with a mind of its own as Mad Dog wrestled with the controls. As we reached altitude to pass the Castle Rock saddle the wind played with us as though we were a mere feather. Back on board, I am immediately called for deck work duty for a couple of hours and then take a wonderful hot shower, listen to music and then steel myself to do the voice-overs. I actually get them all finished by 1645 and then crash until the helicopters are ready to ferry us ashore for Liz and Ricardo's party (they share the same birthday). It's the first time for weeks that I've seen the base and its gradual dismemberment is a sad sight. The wall which we covered in graffiti in 1986 still stands and memories flood back to me and Ken as we drink beer and get lost in our thoughts.

19 January 1992

Tomorrow we 'invade' Mactown with our various huts, tents and equipment. We'll set it all down right in the middle of Mactown as a final gesture of 'freedom of movement' and that will be the end of our 'actions' at Mactown. Today is preparation and rejuvenation day so I sleep like a log until 1150 and wake feeling much-rested. Swenson is convinced there will be a determined and rapid response to our presence, but I feel we'll get away with it. We have complied with all the petty restrictions they have put in our path: we won't overfly any of their buildings, we'll stay clear of the fuel tanks and Hut Point and we're accepting, albeit in a rather over-the-top manner, their 'open invitation' to inspect Mactown. We'll see.

417

20 January 1992

We scurry around between 0300 and 0400 and I call Ken to check that he has the list of things we need to have flown over in the first flight. Both helos arrive at 0515. Keith is still not ready. I set off for McMurdo with Tim and Richard carrying the latter's tripod head, which not only weighs 20 kilos but is also impossible to carry comfortably due to its awkward shape. At the top of the hill I'm drenched in sweat and the rest of the party are strung out behind me in a straggling line. I call them to bunch up as we want to arrive at our Mactown site together – dubbed Flat Point (which is in fact a compacted rubbish tip). Sabine arrives on her bike and mercifully puts the tripod head in her backpack.

We arrive at Flat Point and Swenson arrives ten minutes later. I radio LGP3 and Andy tells me the helicopters are not airborne yet. It transpires that the attempts to strop and lift the Apple hut and the 'green store box' have degenerated into farce with strops being blown off by the downdraught, loads too heavy to lift, helos swapping loads, bad comms between ground and air and general mayhem ensuing. Meanwhile, we wait patiently at the Flat, nervously scanning the roadways for the arrival of the Navy.

Eventually, after a lot of radio traffic, the helos appear around the point, flying in tandem. The green box beneath HTN is spinning wildly and it looks both impressive and highly dangerous. As they approach, I marshal the choppers one at a time and they set down their loads with absolute precision. Back they go for the slingloads and we're feeling easier now that the buildings are in position and there has still been no reaction. The helos return and we clear the nets, pack them into the helos and they take off. Paula nearly does a victory roll as she departs!

At 0730, Chang and Bresnahan drive by slowly and we wave to them cheerily. Incredibly, two Mactown personnel stop and ask for t-shirts. At 0830, Chang stops by and asks for a meeting with 'your officer in charge' to which I gratefully reply, 'You mean Dana Harmon, our expedition leader.'

I call Dana and arrange for her to come to the Flat this afternoon for the meeting. By 0930, Bresnahan is back with a letter which he hands me, requesting the immediate removal of our facilities for infringing flight safety, not informing them of our 'visit' and for interfering with their re-supply work – all of which is pretty standard fare, all of which is bullshit and to which we have strong counters on every point.

The meeting with Bresnahan – me, Swenson and Dana – is perfunctory and predictable. By the time we've dealt with the politics of it all, it'll be Saturday anyway and we'll have left. It's time to pitch our tents and we realise that there's nowhere else but on top of the rubbish tip with its light sprinkling of topsoil. We are to sleep in the middle of a garbage patch and by the time we've got the tents up, we're covered in dust and grit and smelling like polecats.

Wojtek can't keep a grin off his face and when I pull him about it, he says, 'Here is Wilks, after 15 years of saving the planet, after leading four expeditions and after having helped to save an entire continent from mining, pitching his tent in the middle of a shit heap! It's so funny!'

After dinner we are inundated with callers. The record was 15 people inside the Apple hut and amongst them is Juan Laden, the guy I interviewed years back as a possible winter-over team member. But we're wiped out; dirty, grimy and grubby, wondering what this is all about. Then the Navy erect a hut right next to ours which houses two naval guys, one of whom is to film our every move, day or night. Another five days of this, by which time we'll be ready to drop from exhaustion or from some foul disease picked up from living in this surreal dump, run by Kafkaesque management personnel who have authority over regular, likeable and thoroughly personable ordinary men and women who like to hang out with us.

21 January 1992
Wake at 1400 – 13 hours of solid, dreamless sleep. A lovely, sunny, windless day greets me as I crawl out of my tent onto the dump in which I live while Swenson films me for posterity. Nothing much to report today except that we finally began broadcasting the FM radio station which, to judge by the comments from our visitors, people are picking up. I hope they like Martini's choice of music! Wojtek and I are left to handle the visitors as Sabine takes off to do some photography, Swenson to film and Andy to Scott Base.

22 January 1992
Swenson and Sabine are already pottering about and I wake Andy and Wojtek at 1130. Tea, breakfast and then Swenson, Sabine and I go to Cape Armitage to see the 'rogue' barrels Sabine discovered yesterday. On our return, we consider how the final scene in this somewhat farcical

production will unfold. The beakers (scientists) who dropped by earlier return at 1930 and interview me for the FM station and then I saunter down to Hut Point to call the ship on 68 VHF (must have line-of-sight for the connection) and have the usual but mandatory conversation with Dana before sorting things out with Ken for tomorrow.

Helos arrive with journalists from the ship and with Ian who will fix the broken repeater with Andy and we discuss the pull-out on Saturday. Then another Mactown employee, Chris, arrives to interview me on video and by now the hut is full to overflowing and snow is carpeting the grime of Mactown and our dump of a tent site. Twelve people crammed into the hut singing along to guitar, drinking wine and tea. It's all very pleasant but at 2345 we have to kick the itinerants out to plan for tomorrow. Swenson is insistent that he wants to tell the NSF to remove their surveillance hut next to ours – a useless thing to do as it will not impede our removal operations and will only serve to antagonise the authorities unnecessarily. I dread going to bed as the tent is so uncomfortable and I simply can't sleep. We are literally sleeping on piles of rubbish beneath the fly sheet.

23 January 1992

It snows very heavily during our Mactown walkabout, all very Antarctic except we're in the middle of a small and very scruffy town. I'm sure I lost a few pounds today carrying Richard's tripod all over Mactown. Off to Scott Base on my own at 1330 as agreed with the OIC after Swenson petulantly says he's decided not to go with me. He and Sabine have an almighty row and I walk off and leave them to it. Dave Geddes (OIC) and I walk around Scott Base (with Tim and Richard) and he is perfectly civil and clearly and rightly proud of the base they operate.

Back to Hut Point at 1730 and call for the helo to take Tim, Richard and Erling back to the ship. Back at the hut it's already crowded with the night shift of visitors and Ian cooks us up a half-decent meal. Swenson, Sabine and I then get involved in a very terse debate about when we should remove our facilities from Mactown. Swenson insists it has always been our intention to remove ourselves on Sunday and argues for staying until Saturday night and even until Sunday. Then Sabine gets uptight because she overheard me saying to Ken on the radio earlier that if the Sound was too heavily iced up and we couldn't bring the ship in, maybe we should forget the planned rally. I defend my views and we reach a stalemate, at which point I storm off for a solo walk down to the Point to gather my thoughts and to cool off.

The atmosphere is tense when I get back and to remove myself from the situation, I go with Wojtek and Andy for drinks at Scott Base as per the invitation this morning. On our return we sit around in virtual silence before turning in, Wojtek and I turning the mats in our tent to try to avoid the notorious hump in the floor.

24 January 1992

Walk to the Apple in a strong, biting wind, overcast skies and the threat of snow. No-one is keen to go outside except Sabine who seems impervious to the cold and who never stops working. The atmosphere is still tense and I know I'll have to have this out with Swenson sometime soon. Walt Simpson (one of the mates) calls at 1700 and gets us to pick up the reply to criticisms of our actions Dana has written to the NSF. Keith collects it from the helo at the Point and delivers it to the NSF. The copy he brings back to the hut is read avidly: we note wryly that it contains none of the controlled outrage we suggested and neither does it clearly address the points made in the complaint. As more late-nighters arrive at midnight, I make my excuses and head for the tent, the dump and the lump of metal which digs into my back all night.

25 January 1992

Everything is in order for the helos to arrive at 1330 to shuttle in 16 of the crew for the walkabout and rally. By 1430 all bar the deck crew, who will arrive at 1700, are ashore. We wander up to the Apple where I brief everyone about the plans – nothing special, just another photo opportunity and a chance for the crew to feel as though they've been engaged in a protest. The crew disperse for a walk about until 1700 and Wojtek and I keep the brew going in the hut. The helo with the deck crew arrives at 1700 and Ken immediately produces my last bottle of rum which I was saving for the trip home. By the time we get to the Apple, we've had a few tots and we meet the stragglers of the crew returning from their walkabouts. Beers and various bottles of hooch appear and we set off in merry mood, a pathetic band of protesters as we wend our way to the NSF Chalet, banner unfurled for the cameras. Dana sidles up to me and tells me she thinks I should make the speech, at which I tell her, 'You're supposed to be the campaigner.' This comment is captured on the sound tape Richard is using to accompany his film – very embarrassing – but I'm past caring, frankly.

The NSF are nowhere to be seen and we proceed with Dana's speech followed by mine to an audience of the crew and – happily – 50 Mactown residents who turn up for the rally. We wander back to the hut and while others are shuttled back to the ship, I lay into the remnants of my bottle of rum. Tony and Mick decide to stay over and people from Mactown turn up in their droves tonight. Quite a wild party ensues. At midnight we organise a wrecking party and take sledge-hammers to the green box which has seen five years of continual service for GP in Antarctica. Within ten minutes, it's matchwood. The last night in the dump. I won't be sorry to see the back of Mactown.

26 January 1992

It's minus 15, blowing 40 knots and visibility at Cape Evans is low. We begin packing up anyway and Ken tells us on the VHF that flights will commence at 1330. We only need five lifts in total and then we pull out us trampers and we're through. Still, Flat Point is crowded with Mactown employees waiting to wave us off. One guy in particular, Juan, has been a regular visitor and is now constantly by my side asking repeatedly if he can come with us and I feel bad when I have to tell him categorically that the answer is no. The helos finally set down at Hut Point and Dave walks up with me to check out the job in hand. I marshal Dave as Swenson hooks up the loads and after an hour it's finally our turn to get out of this stinking place for the last time. I clamber into Paula's helicopter with Swenson while Richard films from Dave's machine.

Paula's departure is spectacular. In front of the waving knot of people, she lifts off backwards and climbs thus to two hundred feet. She then puts the nose down and does a swooping roll to the left over their heads, putting us at 90 degrees to the ground as she climbs out over Mactown and towards home and the ship. Unpack, luxuriate in a steaming hot shower, cards and then bed at 0100.

27 January 1992

I had a phone call from Gaye this morning which left me depressed and hurt, all for no good reason, of course. I'm blinded by an irrational jealousy stemming from the news that, despite leaving Gaye careful instructions about how to communicate through the computer at home, she has been unable to get a message through to me in all the time I've been away and now 'Phil' is helping her to sort out the problem. For the rest of the day I'm moody and thoughtful and I can't function properly. Work on deck is mechanical and I resolve to speak to Gaye again when the satellite comes up at 2100. Of course, the phone on board is occupied at 2100 and by the time I get to use the phone, there's no answer, Gaye presumably having gone to work. I call Mum instead and say a few pleasantries for her birthday which occurred when I was in Mactown. I get to bed at 2330 still hurting, but realising that I'm being stupid and unfair to Gaye.

28 January 1992
Call Gaye the moment I wake up and make my apologies to her. I feel so much better after speaking to her and making my peace. I can't wait to see her again and to feel her love all around me. Work on deck all day and Ken tells me we'll be finished at the end of the week. The shore is looking empty now: the green building we erected six years ago has gone. I feel a loss inside, yet privileged to have been part of this long and successful effort. After work, Ken and I sit chatting and drinking beer. He opens up and we have a good discussion about love, life and families and the meaning of the universe which, after a few rums, all seems very clear and sensible and makes you wonder why you didn't see it all before. We call Bogart at midnight and chat to him for 30 minutes. Ken insists he comes to Auckland to meet what Ken calls 'this momentous expedition'.

29 January 1992
It's a glorious day – no wind, brilliant sunshine – a classic Antarctic summer's day. It proves, however, to be an exhausting one. Load after load of panels from the remaining structures ashore arrive and are dropped by the helicopters on the hangar top, to be craned quickly onto the main deck, moved aft, stacked and lashed. We're all wiped out by 1800 and after dinner the saloon is dotted with snoring deckies. Try to have an early night but the noise from the mess keeps me awake and disturbs my sleep. Even ear-plugs don't work and it's 0100 before I finally nod off.

30 January 1992
Wind is 30 knots, temperature minus 8, with a wicked windchill factor taking the perceived temperature to minus 40. No deck work and no flying today. Shower and then Gaye phones to tell me she loves me. A few beers

with Ken till 2300 then to bed, only to be kept awake by the chinking of cups and people conversing in the mess directly opposite my cabin.

31 January 1992

Wind has dropped a little and deck work resumes. A hard day tomming up, lashing, stowing before it starts to blow again; 35 knots of wind and the weather claggs in. Work ceases at 1530 and I sleep, listen to music and play chess. Very depressed tonight and I wish I was out of this time warp.

1 February 1992

Ken calls me to work and I go to my cabin to don pants, thermals, pile trousers, socks and walk the 2 yards to the mess for juice, tea and porridge. Back to the cabin to don windproof outers, balaclava, hat, boots and tuck gloves under my arm. Slightly immobilised thus, I walk towards the door to the deck before realising I need to use the loo. On deck, Wojtek and I lash and tom the ton or so of wooden panels from the base sections. It's an awkward, fiddly job requiring much balancing in awkward places, made worse by a biting wind from the south which freezes the condensation on whiskers and numbs fingers. Tea breaks and smokos are welcome and eagerly taken to get away from conditions which seem worse every day.

At the afternoon smoko I enter the lounge to see Erling and Richard lounging on the settees watching a video and I give them both a few caustic remarks at which they turn not a hair. Ken asks me to prepare a list of names for the helo flight lottery to the Wright Valley and then I become embroiled in a wobbly Dana throws because this 'task' has been taken away from her. I hand her the list and absolve myself from any further involvement.

The Scott Base guys arrive for dinner as planned, in deteriorating weather, and it seems as though they are destined to spend the night here. I go to Bas's cabin for a beer, chat and some music and as I rise from the edge of the bottom bunk, I crack my head a fearful wallop which immediately rises into an egg-proportioned lump. So far, we've sustained only minor cuts and bruises although while I was at Mactown, Ken jammed his arm between a barrel of fuel and the guard rail which almost resulted in a break. I take a quick stroll round the deck before turning in and see that the weather did indeed crap out earlier and that the ship is looking very picturesque under a six inch covering of snow.

2 February 1992

Very little to report today as I stayed in bed reading and listening to music until 1830 after Ken insisted on a day of complete rest for me last night. The evening passed amicably playing darts and chess. We have a vast store of surplus frozen food on board which we don't have room to store and which we will be forced to dump overboard before we reach NZ due to their importation restrictions. Ken suggests that we give it to the Soviets who will arrive at Mactown tomorrow, an admirable suggestion which is eagerly approved. The best way to do this is by going alongside their vessel when it is at anchor opposite Mactown tomorrow. Wojtek will speak to the Soviets tomorrow and invite them on board to discuss details. Apparently, Dana went to see Ken last night and admitted, in what was a very generous and difficult gesture, that her role of 'expedition leader' was superfluous to this effort and that even without her, the job would have been done just as efficiently and effectively. It must have taken a lot of courage for her to make such an admission and my attitude towards her has softened a good deal as a result.

3 February 1992

It's a fine day – no wind and brilliant sunshine – but stormy over by the coast so our planned recovery of the Marble Point depot is delayed until 1500. We finally arrive there at 1900 and soon the helos are bringing back all the gear we installed two years ago, returning for fresh loads with some crew who want to see another part of the Antarctic. By 2300 our Marble Point operation is finished and we look forward to Paula's birthday party which turns out to be a very noisy but enjoyable affair. Bed at midnight.

4 February 1992

At 0900, we have already contacted the Soviet ship, the *Professor Federov*, and are steaming down the Sound to meet her and to hopefully transfer the excess food. They ask us to wait a while as they are busy and we do so all day, waiting for news from them about arrangements for the transfer of the food. Ken speculates that the Americans have put the squeeze on them about dealing with us and I suggest to Dana that we move out of the ice-clogged Sound and wait opposite Cape Evans for the Soviets to meet us on their way out. Still she wants to wait, hoping our persistence and very presence will force a meeting. It's a vain hope as they will not in a million years want to be seen by the Americans to consort with us right in front of McMurdo.

We sit out the day in 10 tenths pack with the thin strips of water here and there visibly freezing. I phone Gaye just before 2000 and have the most wonderful, intimate and warm conversation with her. I'm elated for the rest of the evening and float to bed at 0100.

5 February 1992

Ken skilfully talks Dana out of waiting around here any longer and we sail at 1000 out of the Sound through heavy pack ice back to Cape Evans, the Soviets now an afterthought. Work on deck tightening the retaining chains and tomming in a bright, cold day. The satcom tower sections arrive after lunch and we crane them to the main deck and lash them in position. Stooge around sweeping the deck and generally tidying up and then call it a day.

6 February 1992

I'm up late and resign myself to getting on with the tramp team report today but I'm on deck for a while with Keith, lashing satcom tower sections, putting gear down the hold and generally tidying up until lunch. We sit off beautiful Cape Evans on a still and sunny day. I begin my report but then get seduced into a game of computer chess, a bizarre but addictive game which one is destined to lose or, at best, to force a stalemate. After dinner and galley duty, we trampers meet to discuss the report. From then on until 0200, I'm engaged in a series of pleasant but deep discussions with Ken, Bas, Erling and Dave about life and death before turning in. Are we all cracking up? It's time to get out of here, that's for sure, but not before I somehow find time to do my dobying and change my bedclothes.

7 February 1992

After lunch I crack on with the report while people are jollying at Cape Byrd, helicopters clattering above. By dinner, I'm halfway through the report and arrange a further tramp meeting at 1900 by which time we're en route back to Mactown to meet the Soviets who have finally agreed to a meeting. Despite my fears of heavy ice in the Sound, it's virtually ice free and Wojtek, Tim and Dana disappear on an inflatable to the Soviet ship, only to be seen again, at 2100, a little worse for the drink. They return with some Kiwis and Yanks in tow and I retire to my cabin to keep out of the way.

426

In previous years, this socialising would have been my responsibility and I relish the fact that I can just butt out of these meetings at which, invariably, a lot of polite politicking takes place. At 2230, I sneak a look into the saloon where a major party seems to be in full swing. Dana comes to my cabin telling me she needs to talk to me – now there's a first. It appears that the Soviets have been contracted by Adventure Network Industries (ANI) to deliver 400 barrels of fuel which they wanted left at Mactown. The authorities will not accept the fuel there as it 'encourages and co-operates with private expeditions which is contrary to US policy' so the Soviets are in a bind. ANI have therefore asked them to drop the fuel at Marble Point which they can't do as there's no fast ice to moor against and they have no helicopters or boats to use as transport.

They ask for our help (and accept the food and fuel offer which they wanted all along, but from which they were discouraged by their dependence on the Americans). Dana has refused to help them out of this dilemma and tells me that she feels a direct action is in order to prevent the fuel being discharged at Marble Point. It is clear that she's already had a disagreement with Ken over this point and I tell Dana what, presumably, Ken has told her – that she's trying to carve out any sort of action to justify this expedition in terms of a 'campaigning event', which it isn't, and that to attack the Soviets for trying to do something we did years ago is outrageous.

Ken then comes to me and gives me a hard time about not being more involved in these issues and for keeping a low profile. I tell him that my disinclination to get involved stems from the fact that I've never been invited to be an adviser on this trip so why should I do so now, especially when on the few occasions I have offered my advice, it has been promptly ignored? Ken tells me he understands and by way of endorsement tells me that at Cape Byrd, Dana told Keith not to enter the buildings to which Swenson gave her a two-word and very direct reply.

8 February 1992
I am determined to finish the Mactown report today and get up early in order to do so. I consult Sabine about a few things which have escaped my skimpy notes and by 1430 I am almost through. I copy the almost-completed draft and then work on deck, receiving the last of the contaminated soil from shoreside. People begin arriving back from Cape

Evans and dinner is a lively affair as people let off steam and talk is all about our departure tomorrow. Dana has still said no word about the Soviet barrels affair and I'm tempted to make some sort of intervention. Ken bemoans the fact that we're still completely unaware of what plans Dana has laid.

9 February 1992

It is 'visit the empty beach day' and at 1300, we begin shuttling people onto the beach for a final look around. In worsening weather we go off individually or in small groups and indulge our thoughts about this place, now bereft of any signs of our five-year presence. Ken organises the return flights earlier than expected due to snow squalls, rapidly reduced visibility and freshening winds. I manage to grab only 30 minutes or so ashore and wander the length of the beach on which so many dramas and episodes of our six year campaign have been acted out.

I sit down on a rock and survey the scene, lost in my memories of the first abortive year, the success and jubilation of the second, the smoothness of the operation in the third, the high drama of the fourth when we opposed the French airstrip and ran into the Japanese whaling fleet; my yearning to have been involved in the 1989-90 expedition, my advisory role in the sixth when Gaye and I used my role as a starting point for our Antipodean sojourn and now the seventh, in which despite my presence, I feel a little cheated of being able to finish the job in the role in which I started. Nonetheless, I am here, and I'm grateful to Dog for ensuring that I could see the campaign out. The beach is empty and only the memories of the winterers and of those in whose hearts this place will remain forever haunt the beach now.

Back on board, the weather is blowing up badly and we sit, talk and play darts and chess in subdued mood. The rumour goes around the ship that we'll stay another day to give ourselves a longer period of time ashore and I determine to ensure that Swenson takes me to a few of his favourite spots tomorrow.

Into the evening and the weather is marginal enough to allow Cornelius and Liz a special flight ashore after they plead their case to Arne. On their return, I notice that we're underway and Ken comes to my cabin waving a bottle of whisky at me. He tells me we're leaving and to 'come and get the last sight of Cape Evans.' I can't believe we're going now without enjoying another day at 'our' beach, but as it turns out, we're simply moving out into deeper water for some reason. Nonetheless, Ken and I go to the helideck and sit on the old sofa the helo guys use. We wrap ourselves in a blanket while we risk a slurp of whisky from frozen tumblers in a toast to ourselves and to the expedition. I go straight to bed afterwards, still lost in my thoughts and strangely isolated from what is going on on-board. Bas comes to my cabin three times in the next hour to tell me Tommy Cooper jokes.

10 February 1992

This is our last day in the vicinity of Cape Evans, now a few miles distant. Today we sail north, making our way at a crawl across the Southern Ocean, stopping here and there to soak up the Antarctic atmosphere and then to Auckland and from there, home. Ken calls me at 0800 to tell me we're going to risk everything to get the last Marble Point loads on board in a very strong wind of around 50 knots He tells me to put all my gear on as it's very cold and the windchill factor is high. It's a hairy few hours as the helicopters come in over the hangar, bucking wildly in the wind as we deckies rush around craning the loads to the main deck, stowing them hurriedly and lashing down cargo and bolting up the holds against the rigours of the seas.

Ken asks me to hook up the inflatable and I jump into it from the deck, timing my jump to the rise and fall of the boat bucketing on the waves. Ken asks Arne to create a lee as the wind is so strong and we finally get the boat inboard as Ken hoists away on the crane and dumps the boat on the deck as I scramble out. Then we lift it to the boat deck and lash it down. We're all set. As we steam away from the rapidly receding Cape Evans, so quickly reduced to a mere smudge on the horizon in the gathering gloom, we all gather on the aft deck and watch it disappear, lost in our own thoughts. Goodbye, Cape Evans. You've been good to us and I hope we've been good to you. You'll always be in my thoughts. So many human dramas are invested there.

Liz appears with a bottle of champagne and we gather in a huddle to toast absent friends and the end of a seven year history. There's many a damp eye among us – including mine – and we gradually drift off to our cabins and face the reality of watches beginning again. I prepare to go on watch with Arne as Ken has agreed he won't take watches until we finally start the long sea passage back to Auckland. Wojtek is allocated to the 8-12 also and we agree with Shuan that we'll go two on, one off, for the duration.

As I write, we're following the *Professor Zubov* into Terra Nova Bay and I discover that our hasty departure was caused by Dana's decision to persist with her 'direct action' plans to protest about the dropping off of the ANI barrels. The Soviet ship apparently went straight past us in the night, not bothering to stop to collect the food and water we had promised her. A crew meeting ensues at which Dana discusses our 'policy' towards the proposed Soviet action and asks if a vote is necessary. I despair. Bed early, couldn't sleep, the sea gently rolling us along from the stern.

11 February 1992
By 1000, we're closing Terra Nova on a sparkling, clear morning. No sign of the Soviets. The helo clatters into the sky at 1130 to look for them to the south, with no success. Sleep as soon as I come off watch and wake to find most people ashore inspecting the now-deserted Italian base (summer only). The Campbell Ice Tongue with Mt Melbourne as a backdrop proves irresistible for the cameras – it is a spectacular place.

13 February 1992
Watch at 0800 to see the same long, low southerly swell and driving snow showers. We lump along, closing Cape Hallet at noon, in zero visibility. Arne takes us into the pack ice and we crunch along for an hour to find relatively open water close to the Cape. Some are flown ashore despite my protest about disturbance to the penguins. I sleep, finish my book and then traipse to the helideck for the crew photo. I put the finishing touches to the Mactown report, eat dinner and then prepare for the crew meeting at which we will learn, hopefully, of our itinerary.

Incredibly, Dana calls for a secret ballot to decide if we should go to Leningradskaya or not, asking people to write '27' on pieces of paper she hands out if they vote for going straight back to Auckland, or '9' if they'd prefer to go to Leningradskaya.

I walk out in protest. Only an hour previously I had advised Dana yet again to give firm leadership by telling the crew the decision, but allow anyone with overriding opinions to influence the decision if they wish. The inevitable happens – it's a draw – and since I have refused to enter into the playacting, I have the deciding vote which I still refuse to cast. Ken berates me later for not participating and gives me a hard time about the chance of the crew deciding, for once, the fate of the trip. I tell him I think it's all nonsense and that there is a perfectly acceptable way of going about these things and giving the crew a chance to influence the ship's itinerary without degenerating into the farce of writing on bits of paper. We sit at Cape Hallet in beautiful weather and scenery which defies belief. Bed at 0200.

14 February 1992

My day off. I wander into the mess at 1700 as dinner is being served and as the rattle of the anchors announces our arrival at Cape Adare. It's a clear, bright afternoon with a strong wind and an average swell. All bar me and a few others are away to shore to see Borchgrevink's hut and the penguins. By 2200 all are back and we lift the hook and set course for Campbell Island, six days away. We take our final look at Antarctica proper and say our own silent farewells to this place which has affected so many lives, so many people and has, for a while at least, been afforded some protection.

15 February 1992

Sea state is good: 25 knots of wind, following sea. On watch the wind and swell came round and hit us from the starboard quarter, but still the motion beats pitching. During the afternoon, as I lie on my bunk reading, the ship begins to move more violently and we take some very big rolls. Dinner becomes a pantomime of flying cutlery and plates. On watch the weather is quite astonishing. We're in the tail of a depression, catching easterlies of 50 knots. The waves approaching from the starboard quarter are 30 feet high and we roll through them with a violent motion which has us hanging on to anything available to prevent us falling over.

18 February 1992

Make it to the bridge for 0800 to see a fine, bright day. Sunshine, big SE swell and light airs. Wash down the bridge on the lee-side and then my darling phones as planned, to tell me that Clem Shaw has pitched for a TV programme with Channel 4 about tourism with me as the presenter. Securing work without even being present is gratifying! Back on watch full of the joys and we pass 60 South at noon. Ken sends Dog a message berating him for his decision not to meet us in Auckland and then Dana comes to tell me that I've been asked to make myself available for interviews in Auckland. On watch at 2000 and prepare to dump our organic garbage as we're north of 60 South. Ken tells us that we can now go on one off, one on stand by and one look-out, so I go below and wait for the watch to end at 0000. Since videos are showing, much to Ken's uncontrollable disgust, we repair to my cabin for beers and a tot of rum. Bed at 0030.

19 February 1992

Huge seas attack the ship from the NW. They pick the ship up from the port bow and scream beneath the hull, giving the ship a corkscrew motion while rising and dropping through 20 feet at the same time. It really is quite a show and the porthole in the cabin, despite my efforts, is leaking badly. A fearsome sight greets me as I reach the bridge for watch duties. We cut across huge swells on our northerly course. The ship rolls almost onto her beam ends from time to time and the sound of crashing crockery can be heard clearly on the bridge.

Earlier, I was on galley duty and fell to the floor as the ship rolled. I simply slid back and forth across the floor with mop, bucket and a tide of hot soapy water, unable to stand up. At 2230, Ken and Arne confer and we alter course to 020 which makes life easier. Port quarter seas now and we fairly fly along. We'll miss Campbell Island on this course, but who cares? Party atmosphere after watch and Bas requests the Tommy Cooper video. Halfway through, video-junkie Erling has the cheek to come and complain about the noise and he is roundly told to 'go to hell' by all of us. Bed at 0030.

20 February 1992

On watch to see that we've altered course for Campbell again, despite worse seas than yesterday. It transpires that the Campbell Island guys have requested the use of the helicopter for bird counting and that Dana has decided to go there, despite the prospect of 12 hours flogging against the weather and against Ken's professional advice that we should clear the Southern Ocean as quickly as possible. Lumpy seas, vertical walls of water, re-tomming cargo – all very uncomfortable. And so we lump our way out of the Southern Ocean. I hand Dana a copy of the final Mactown report, but she says nothing. Anchor at Campbell at 1830. Crew meeting to vote on the length of stay and I find it all too galling for words. Bed at midnight, just wishing for this all to be over.

21 February 1992
Most people already ashore by the time I rise. Work on deck with Ken, declining to go ashore, and drink in the bouquet of the greenery wafting from the shore. Wild party ensues in the late evening.

22 February 1992
Woke nursing a hangover and a black eye sustained in the melee last night. Not on watch today so literally lazed around all day reading and listening to music. Underway at 1000 and at midnight we're at 51 South.

23 February 1992
Liz came to talk to me today to ask why there has been such poor communications from the campaign to the crew and if there's still time to concoct an official finale to the trip. I refer her to Dana as my hands are tied. Evening watch puts us at 46 South and we're planning a 28th February arrival. I'm too tired to ponder or worry further about what has gone right or wrong with this trip. The job's done. It could have been much better than just ok, but that's the summation: it has been ok when it could have been fantastic. Bed at 0030 in a down mood.

24 February 1992
Moderate swell and sunny skies. Sunbathe on the helideck, read, music and banter with Bas and Albert. Bemoan the lack of celebratory atmosphere on board and I feel annoyed that I didn't do something earlier to change a few things. But that would have led to conflict and it was probably better for me to have kept as silent as I did, except when I felt an overpowering need to say something. People are in good spirits, however, and looking forward to landfall. Should be off the Banks Peninsular tonight.

26 February 1992
Watch this morning was pleasant enough – gentle following sea, sunny and land in sight at last, Mahia Point off to the port. Gaye calls, is effusive with her love and suddenly everything is right with the world again! Fire off a message to Carol (Stewart), asking her to book me an earlier flight. Then Dog calls to discuss some filming he wants done on board, for a PBS contract he's negotiating. Dana comes and apologises to me for

being 'so lousy at communicating' and I have to doff my cap again to her courage and honesty. By 1930 we're anchoring at Waiheke Island. Dana asks me if I'll speak at the crew meeting. A lacklustre party ensues while some people get into a huddle to prepare a song to sing in response to the Mauri welcome we'll receive tomorrow. Bed at 0130 with my mind focussed on one thing – getting the hell out of here and home at the earliest opportunity.

28 February 1992

Finally lift the hook and get underway for Auckland at noon. It's blowing hard on a bright sunny day and then we're alongside and people on the quayside are waving and cheering. The Customs niceties are waived and before long people are clambering all over the ship and chaos ensues. Marc Defourneaux's first letter he pulls from his stack of mail is a tax demand. Welcome back to the real world!

As can be imagined, a party ensued on the ship and for me at least, as well as for Athel von Kurtlittz who happened to be in town on Greenpeace business and for Bas Beentjes, it was a party which went on all night. My earlier message to Carol Stewart in the Auckland office to ask her to book me an earlier flight home resulted in a flight the very day after arrival so the celebration of my last night on a Greenpeace ship would have to be memorable. It was.

Out on deck as the dawn lightened the sky, Bas played and sang 'Tangled Up In Blue' note-perfect, a fitting finale to my marine career. As the sun came up over Auckland Harbour, I wiped the tears from my eyes as I went to my cabin to ask Sekita, Rien Achteberg's daughter, to vacate my cabin where she had crashed, to allow me to pack, (the previous night I had embarrassingly forgotten a dinner date with her). I headed for the airport early in the morning, leaving others to discharge, store and dispose of the several tonnes of Antarctic base, rubbish, contaminated soil and equipment we had dutifully dragged back with us from the ends of the Earth. It was a rushed, perfunctory and unsatisfactory end to a highly successful and innovative seven year project. I had left behind a lot of good friends without saying appropriate farewells, but the truth was that I had had a bellyful of Greenpeace and simply wanted to get home and start a new life.

My dear Gaye was waiting for me at Heathrow. We fell into each other's arms and I realised how deeply I had missed her and, perhaps more importantly, that the Antarctic campaign was well and truly over and Greenpeace, so I thought at that point, would have no reason to venture again into the Southern Ocean. I had money in my pocket, and my beautiful Gaye on my arm and we grandly hailed a cab home to our Battersea flat overlooking the park.

I began working with my old friend and Greenpeace mentor, Reg Boorer, who had a small office in Regent Street and soon Gerry Matthews joined us to make a trio. A former head of Friends of the Earth, David Gee, was also around at the time and we all got together to form a company, WBMG Communications. On paper, it had a lot going for it: I still had a reasonably high media profile, Reg was well-connected in the public relations/communications business, Gerry was known to many in the higher echelons of business and David Gee had a wife who was in TV and he himself was well known in academic and university policy development circles.

We worked hard and took opportunities as they came, writing papers around election issues from an environmental position and getting our name in front of the right people to develop the business. It was, to be frank, an unholy alliance, however. I was not in the mood – never have been, I suppose – to pander to the vagaries and whims of the effete advertising/communications industry and unfortunately, that is precisely what we at WBMG were required to do. I wore shirts and ties grudgingly and when I did wear a shirt, it was, as Reg pointed out to me with fizzing annoyance, 'always two sizes too small for you.'

If we were kept waiting for an appointment, I would often suggest that we left. I was a little belligerent in the meetings we did manage to attend, I suppose, but I was still – had I known it – subconsciously wrestling with the aftermath of Greenpeace. I hadn't really settled at all, despite trying hard to give the impression that I was now resigned to a less active means of achieving environmental improvement.

After my return from Antarctica in 1989, Clem Shaw, an old film producer friend of mine, had cut together a wonderful film from the footage brought back from that memorable trip and I was appointed as the adviser to the production. I also did most of the voice-over commentary, using extensive passages from my diary. Janet Suzman did the main voice-over and the three months or so we spent with Simon Clayton, the editor, in the small cutting rooms off Berwick Street in London's Soho, were a pleasure. Paul Brown, environmental correspondent of the Guardian, a treasured friend and shipmate on the 1988-1989 voyage, wrote the first draft of the script and all-in-all, we were greatly pleased with the outcome which was screened under the banner Antarctic Warriors.

Greenpeace were only mildly happy: Tony Marriner, who at that time was still running the Film Division now known as Greenpeace Communications, saw the film and commented, 'The best I can say about it is that it didn't do Greenpeace any harm.' I figured he must have thought about that particular comment for a long time. But now Clem and I, having been turned down by Channel 4 on the 'Antarctic Tourism' idea, began submitting proposal after proposal to Channel 4 TV, to ITV and to the BBC. One was finally accepted: Channel 4 commissioned us to look critically at the track record of Greenpeace and to ask in a filmic manner if the Greenpeace era had come to a natural end. We began work on, Greenpeace: end of an era?

Again, Simon Clayton was the editor, Paul Brown the scriptwriter and I was the adviser and one of the interviewees. Janet Suzman again did the eventual voice-over. It proved to be one of the most galling experiences Clem, with twenty-five years in the film business, had ever experienced. Greenpeace moaned and groaned the entire way through the edit, claiming that the latest cut did not do justice to the fact that, as far as they were concerned, and using Melchett's own words, 'they were taking more risks today than ever before.'

His words were hardly supported by the pictures: the lead singer of the rock band U2 being carried ashore (so as not to get his boots wet, said Suzman's cutting commentary) at Sellafield for a 'protest' which was in fact merely a photo opportunity for the press, and pictures of my old shipmate, Grace O'Sullivan risking her life to put a nuclear flag on the anchor chain of a nuclear capable aircraft carrier. Even the latest anti-whaling pictures from the Antarctic actions in 1992 were re-runs, as they all were, of the seventies actions, or those we had carried out in the recent past.

Greenpeace went ballistic when they saw the final cut and their political commissar, Nick Gallie, whom I myself had employed as advertising/PR/ fundraiser, wrote a long letter to Clem arguing why things in the film did not reflect the truth. His treatise was eminently refutable and I gave Clem all the ammunition he needed to take to a meeting with Gallie at which the issues were to be sorted out. Clem was in a difficult position: he was negotiating with the organisation his film sought to examine in a direct but certainly not hostile manner and he needed Greenpeace to co-operate and agree to the international release of the film which originated largely from their archives and to which they had ownership rights.

Clem agreed to change the ending of the film to reflect the fact that 'direct actions' were still part of the Greenpeace philosophy and stuck in a few minutes of actions in an attempt to placate them. However, in my mind, the 'direct actions' being undertaken by Greenpeace had been diluted for the most part into 'demonstrations' because they no longer sought to prevent an act of environmental vandalism but merely to draw attention to it. The difference is hugely significant. Amending the film cost Clem several thousand pounds of his own money since Channel 4, who were happy with the first cut, would not agree to stump up more. After screening in 1992, Greenpeace refused to sign the release for international distribution, despite the fact that over 25 nations had requested purchasing rights. Clem was furious but hamstrung. The only course of action open to him was the legal route which he did not have the resources to pursue.

It was, in his words, 'the single most incredible act of censorship by a supposedly open and democratic non-governmental organisation' he had ever experienced or heard of. But Greenpeace got their way and despite appeals from myself and others they remained unmoved. The abiding image of Greenpeace sitting back and laughing up its sleeve at the likes of Clem and I, haunted me. I quietly fumed over the old shares issue which had still not been resolved to anything like my satisfaction. I mentally brought it forward on my agenda.

Meanwhile life went on and Gaye and I revelled in our flat and our relationship. The rocky patch we had encountered on my return from the Antarctic – which revolved around my own insecurities when I was away in the Antarctic and then whether or not we would start a family – seemed to have evened out and our evenings and weekends were filled with visits from good friends and a social life around Lavender Hill which was becoming familiar and comfortable.

My mother continued to live her somewhat isolated life in Kidbrooke and every time Gaye and I went to see her, which we tried to do at least once a week, we both felt sad at the sight of her face at the window as she saw us drive off on the motorbike. My brother and sister-in-law did her proud, however, and at every opportunity, they invited mother down to stay for a day or two and at Christmas, they never failed to have mother to stay for the duration of the holiday and involved her in a very active and concentrated party season. All-in-all, mother was with family for much of her time, but the knowledge that she lived alone was a burden for us all.

The Thermal Oxide Reprocessing Plant (Thorp) – a huge billion pound proposed development at Sellafield designed to reprocess the generation of spent nuclear fuel known as 'oxide fuel' – far hotter and more radioactive than the Magnox fuel which was the only type hitherto reprocessed by BNFL – was under review by the government. A second and definitive consultation process was announced by the government and while I held such 'evaluations' in a healthy contempt, there was a small chance that if sufficient evidence could be generated in favour of abandoning the commissioning of the plant, we might just be able to beat it. It was a long shot, but one, we agreed at WBMG, which was worth going for.

I wrote a proposal to Sir James Goldsmith via his brother, Teddy – a veteran green campaigner and founder of the Ecologist magazine – someone I had known since the early FoE days. I asked for £100,000 to finance the commissioning of three reports looking at the economics, the plutonium potential and the health impacts of the plant. The lion's share of the budget was to be dedicated to the purchase and operation of a huge hot-air balloon in the shape of a white elephant. The idea behind this (what now seems) extravagant purchase was that the balloon would represent a flying question mark about Sellafield – was it the 'eighth wonder of the world', as BNFL claimed, or was it simply a huge, lumbering white elephant? We argued that if we took the balloon to all the high profile events over the summer of 1993 – fetes, county shows, sporting events, etc. – and used the focus it would create as a platform from which to ask people to 'make their verdict' on Thorp, through the mechanism of an even-handed presentation of the facts, we could use the results in a nationwide 'poll' of public opinion to present to the government.

We got the money, commissioned the balloon purchase and began planning the tour. Penny Ephson, with whom I had worked on the Ideal 'Green' Home Exhibition, came to help us plan and promote the tour and we linked up with a Greenpeace splinter group, Phoenix, who provided the pilots and technical back-up. The entire episode proved to be as stimulating and as fun as it was exasperating. What we didn't appreciate, of course, was that hot air balloons can only fly safely in virtually no-wind conditions and those conditions are generally prevailing in the very early morning or around dusk. Thus I spent weeks driving my bike up and down the country at ungodly hours to meet the balloon crew (all of whom were enthusiasts and would have gone to hell and back for the joy of silent balloon flying), only to find that almost without exception, not even local press or media would even think of rolling out of bed at such an hour to report on the balloon's presence, never mind film it.

In the event, we managed a decent amount of local coverage and the Financial Times and the Guardian featured the balloon and the 'white elephant debate' as we dubbed it, but in the main, the project was a huge waste of time. The reports we commissioned from our old friend Peter Taylor gained us much-needed publicity and a good airing of the risks associated with separating plutonium – nuclear bomb material – from spent nuclear fuel at a plant on the edge of one of the most beautiful areas of the UK – the Lake District.

Sadly, Thorp went ahead as predicted, although we had, in truth, given it a good run for its money. Even the Greenpeace judicial review which challenged the legality of allowing Thorp to be commissioned was beaten in the courts. The international meeting we convened at which twenty experts signed a letter calling on the government to think carefully before allowing sufficient plutonium for 5000 warheads to be liberated from spent nuclear fuel fell on deaf ears.

The Ark Trust was coming on the agenda slowly but surely. I had supported the earlier incarnation of Ark in 1989 by working for it for free, as and when required. I had written an article in World magazine singing its praises and encouraging people to join it. I had met and discussed Ark activities with Peter Gold, its millionaire benefactor, and with Keith Hamp, my old friend from the 60s and Gold's accountant, who, through various twists of fate involving his brother-in-law, Albie Burkett, had ended up working for a company with which I was destined, by an equally peculiar set of circumstances, to cross paths.

Peter Gold ran a chemical products company and had attempted to use the Ark 'green' label product brands to boost his sales and it was this connection which brought Ark, and thus Reg and therefore me, into contact with them. Peter Gold bemoaned the fact that Ark had taken a nosedive in terms of its profile and hence its ability to shift his products over the years, and he spent a lot of time grilling me and Reg about our impressions of the causes behind it. It was clear to both Reg and I that Ark was not going anywhere. Peter, as chairman of the company, resolved to sort the problem out and to bring Reg – and me – into the frame. The idea excited me as many of the projects we were working on fitted nicely into the Ark 'lifestyle' template. At one notable meeting, Peter Gold asked me how much I would charge to take over the running of Ark campaigns. I told him, half in jest, that he couldn't afford me and that I would prefer it if he would use the WBMG consultancy to plug such gaps as were necessary. It was just one more gesture of corporate magnanimity which was to be thrown back in my face within a few months.

Meanwhile, the usual procession of former Greenpeace/Antarctic contacts trekked through our flat in Parkgate Road. One of the more colourful people to arrive regularly was Peter Malcolm, veteran of the Footsteps of Scott expedition in 1985/86 and subsequent shipmate with me on the 1987/88 Greenpeace trip. Over a few beers in the Crown Hotel on Lavender Hill, Peter outlined the situation in Antarctica which I had lost touch with. He suggested that a commercial opportunity existed for a shipping operation which would help governments to implement their own adjunct to the Antarctic no-mining agreement known as the Madrid Protocol.

This agreement, signed in 1991, required all Antarctic operatives to begin cleaning up the legacy of waste and environmental mismanagement that thirty years of scientific work had bequeathed to the area in the form of local squalor and industrial litter on a huge scale, such as we had witnessed at McMurdo. The idea immediately fired my imagination: it could be the solution to all the vague plans we had laid when lumping home from the Antarctic about bringing key people together in a post-Greenpeace venture – the Greenwave idea Ken and I had discussed on the ship – which would enable us to work profitably together in a way that gave us a non-Greenpeace income and did some environmental good into the bargain.

Polar Ventures was born and within a few weeks I had tracked down the ideal ship – a small, ice-strengthened cargo vessel with a long and distinguished Antarctic pedigree. The *Kista Dan* was built in 1952 and had plied Antarctic waters ever since. She was used by Sir Ranolph Fiennes in his Transglobe expedition between 1979 and 1982, after which she was laid up in Greece. A millionaire Greek had bought her and had half-converted her to a luxury dive-ship before abandoning his plans after gutting all the accommodation on the main and lower decks. She was then purchased by Nick Savage who ran Cardinal Holdings but who had also given up on conversion plans. She was now languishing in Syros in the Greek Islands and was available for £150,000.

Ken Ballard was over on a visit from the USA where he now lived just outside Chicago with his wife-to-be, Michelle. He was at a loss to know what to do with his life after the Antarctic trips had finished. (Ken is an Antarctica-phile of the first order and lives for the challenge of going places where only few have previously been). I outlined the plan to him on the telephone and he agreed to come with me to look at the ship in Syros. I called Athel von Koettlitz, our longstanding friend who had an equally long Greenpeace history, and asked him to give us an opinion on the mechanical aspects of the ship. He agreed.

In early May 1994 we met in Athens to make the connecting local flight to Syros. On arrival, the ship's resident seaman, a Greek guy called Notis, met us at the airstrip and drove us into the small town which was dominated by a large, blue ship moored stern-to at the small quay – the *Kista Dan*. We checked into a small hotel right on the quay and quickly walked the hundred metres or so to the ship. She was a beauty – flared bow, bridge and accommodation aft, and a long foredeck beneath which were cavernous holds. The bridge itself was tiny and sported none of the navigational aids we had become so used to on the *Gondwana*. In fact, the bridge was devoid of any furniture, bar a wheel and an engine room pitch-control console. The main deck accommodation was gone, leaving a large, cavernous and empty space. The same was found on the lower deck while the upper, or boat deck, did sport five original cabins decked out in beautifully worn oak. From the bridge, the teak deck stretched away forward to the bow. It was indeed a beautiful ship and its suitability to our needs was further confirmed when we learned that she used only three tonnes of fuel a day: we would be able to undercut any competitor by a huge margin!

We stayed in Syros for three days, poring over the ship and getting to know her as well as our limited stay would allow. We spent most of our time plotting and planning over bottles of Amstel beer in the local bars and eating refreshing Greek salads. On a whim, I decided to check with the telephone directory people to see if Nick Savage's number was listed since we had been informed that he lived in Mykonos, the 'party island' of Greece. I called Nick and we agreed to meet in a restaurant that evening. Unknown to him, I intended to ask him to give us the ship since I felt positive that no millionaire could possibly hold out for a measly £150,000 which stood in the way of such a creditable and worthy project. During the next two hours, Nick listened patiently to our story while he drank mineral water and flatly refused to reduce the price of the ship – I guess that's why he was a millionaire and we were broke.

Based on Ken's report of the deck work which needed to be carried out and on Athel's engine and machinery report, we estimated we'd need a total of £300,000 and I immediately set to work writing up a proposal outlining the project which was touted round to all the banks within a week. Not one of them listened, said yes or helped, contrary to all their loaded and seductive advertising hype. It was going to be a long haul and a saga which was to take us two and a half years to see resolved and which would soak up the slender cash reserves Ken and I had accumulated after spending three months of every year in Antarctica where you can't spend money no matter how hard you try. It also sucked up and spat out the investments of friends, relations and other individuals alike as each, in their turn, either through loyalty, stupidity or the sheer cheek of the idea, stumped up a thousand here, five hundred there. I kept a meticulous log of who had put up what amounts of money, determined, sooner or later, to repay them all.

As things stood in 1993, despite the fact that I was earning very little money, my horizons were broad. I was sitting on the TSB Environmental Investment Committee with John Burton and David Bellamy, amongst others; I was part of the Blue Planet Group and soon to be a director and share-holder; I was engaged in attempting to raise the funds for the purchase and refit of the *Kista Dan* under the banner of a newly established company, Polar Ventures Ltd; I was still the (hugely underemployed) London representative of the Programme for Belize; I was still being asked to give the odd lecture here and there and was also writing a book.

Ark was getting closer to becoming a reality as Reg negotiated control of the organisation away from the incumbent in a series of meetings with Peter Gold, and two other projects for which I had had the initial ideas for were underway. McTaggart made one of his periodic appearances in London and I met him at the airport, offering to run him into town on the back of the bike, an offer which he accepted, to my mild amazement. As we swept into London, he gripped my shoulders so hard that I had difficulty in steering and he later told me that he had spent the entire journey of 30 minutes or so working out the best way to roll so as to minimise damage to himself 'when we came off'. Such faith in my driving was comforting.

It just so happened that a few other guys were in town at the same time and it also just so happened that the *Greenpeace: end of an era?* Channel 4 programme, in which McTaggart featured, was about to be screened on TV that very evening.

The story of how I managed to get him on film is worth relating and is germane to what happened next. Months previously, I had called David to ask if he would be prepared to be interviewed for the film which was then only in the planning stages. He told me that since he felt he owed me a favour or two, he would grant me the request – in itself a unique event as he rarely gave interviews – and that subsequently, we would stand even in the brownie points stakes. Clem Shaw was delighted at the news and we arranged to take a film crew to Amsterdam for the shoot. I warned Clem that McTaggart was fickle and might decline the interview at the last moment so, in order to put the maximum pressure on him not to welch on the agreement, I insisted there should be no further contact until we were in Amsterdam. I refused to take two calls from McTaggart during that period of time for fear that he would tell me the deal was off.

We arrived in Amsterdam, checked into a hotel and called the elusive McTaggart. Sure enough, he was backing off at a rate of knots. I told him, 'David, we have a film crew here, plus a producer and a director. We have invested a lot of money in this trip and we're committed to the film. It will happen with or without you and under those terms it'll be better with you in it. At least you'll be able to put a few records straight.'

He replied, 'Yeah, but let's meet at the Central railway station, take a walk and discuss it. I'm still not too sure.'

I grabbed Clem and we hot-footed it to the station to meet him from the train. I figured that although he would not be pleased to see Clem, it would force him to commit: he would have a harder time declining the interview with Clem in his presence than if he only had me to deal with. As he stepped from the train, he smiled when he saw me but the smile faded quickly when he saw Clem. He grabbed me and said in a whisper, 'I thought I told you to come alone, asshole!' I smiled. I had learned something from him over the years.

By 1100 we were sitting in a bar eating omelettes and drinking beer. After a few cursory attempts to indicate his reluctance to go through with the interview, he said, 'Ok, let's do it.'

Even then, when he was sitting in front of the camera, he refused to allow the camera to turn over until he was ready and until I had loosened him up with a couple of rums and cokes. He refused to have me in the room during the shoot and so I wandered around for a couple of hours. When I returned, the crew, Clem and David were chatting away amicably as the equipment was being packed up and we parted with an agreement to have dinner that evening. McTaggart was in fine form over dinner, holding centre stage as he reminisced about the old days and trotted out some of the more fanciful stories which had, over the years, assumed mythical status.

Back in London a few months later, after I had driven McTaggart back to London from the airport, we enjoyed a quiet night over a couple of drinks and an Indian take-away meal when Gaye mentioned quite innocently that the film was on TV. David insisted that we watch it and fell ominously silent after ten minutes. When it had finished, he simply said, 'Well, that's me and you finished with Greenpeace forever, man. Holy shit.' Before we could get into yet another of our extremely heated disagreements, I went to bed.

The following weekend, at David's suggestion, we all trundled down to Lewes, booked into a hotel, and settled down to have a minor reunion. Ken, Martini, who was on a visit to his native homeland, Holland, and who had nipped across with his daughter to see us, Athel, Steve Morgan, our veteran Antarctic photographer, Carol Stewart who was on an extended stay in the UK, Gaye and myself were there. By midnight we were all in jovial mood and repaired to Gaye's and my room to continue the evenings' entertainment. I overheard David talking to Martini about the film and he was not holding back on the expletives while describing it.

I intervened. 'Hey, David, it's not that bad a film and it looks at an organisation which exists and survives in the public domain and at the behest of the public. It can stand scrutiny, can't it?'

He turned his steely gaze on me and said, 'Listen, man, I only agreed to that interview because I knew you needed the £4,000 fee you were in line for. I owed you and I delivered. I can say what I like about that film. You got your interview and your money.'

I was, well, gobsmacked is the only word for it really. I think my jaw actually hung open for a while. 'You asshole!' was my considered retort. 'You're telling me that you agreed to the interview just so that I could earn some money?'

'Yessir.'

I rummaged around in my jacket pocket and withdrew my cheque book. I wrote out a cheque for £4,000 and dropped it on the floor in front of him. 'There's your pound of flesh back, you no good sonofabitch. Stick the money up your ass as far as it will go. I don't need you or the money and I certainly don't need your charity.'

Unbelievably, he took the cheque and put it in his pocket! And since I had long since spent the money, the cheque would bounce anyway. But I turned away and pretended that I didn't give a damn. The evening degenerated from then on. We went over and over old ground until the small hours of the morning, alternately berating then praising each other, and ending up by agreeing to forget the whole damn thing, except that he still had my cheque and I was damned if I would ask him for it back. Later, he apparently burned the cheque but then kept me guessing by pretending it was a piece of scrap paper he had burned.

When people left our room, the floor was littered with crisps, empty packets of cigarettes and empty beer bottles. Steve Morgan kept opening our bedroom door, thinking that he lived there, only to be ushered away to find his own room whereupon he would turn up again five minutes later with a dazed and uncomprehending expression of his face. For weeks afterwards, I scanned my bank statements with trepidation but the cheque was never presented.

Strangely enough, McTaggart and I became closer than ever before after that weekend and he began coming to London on a regular basis, largely, it must be said, not to see me, but to negotiate deals for the sale of his organic olives which he was now growing in increasing volumes on his Italian farm where he had retired, five years previously. Retired is hardly the word to use actually, since he didn't know its meaning. But on his visits, he would quite happily hunker down on our settee or spend time with Gaye and I wandering around town and playing pool and snooker. It was good to be in his company and to see him relax for a while. It was a fresh side of David that I had rarely seen although he did deflate me a little by telling me that he loved coming to London because he could understand and speak the language – which was not the case in Italy. And did he exercise his larynx! He didn't stop talking from one minute to the next – to waiters, to perfect strangers, to the wildest-looking skinheads in the Crown Hotel pub – in fact to anyone who would listen, and he was never short of an audience.

Ken was now in regular touch from his home just outside Chicago as we planned and plotted the Polar Ventures project for which I worked tirelessly, trying to raise the money. Our first break came when David Iggulden, a long-serving Greenpeacer who had taken part as a mate on the ill-fated Southern Quest expedition in 1985, under the leadership of Robert Swan, suggested that his boss, millionaire Australian Michael Watt, might be interested in helping the project. A meeting was arranged after Watt had read the project summary. He is a self-made man and proud of his achievements, if a little brusque in his manner. He gave a strong indication that while he felt we would never make any money cleaning up the Antarctic, he found the project sufficiently interesting to catch his imagination. He wanted to see the ship for himself and we flew business class to Athens and then on to Syros via Geneva.

Subject to the engineering report on the vessel, Michael agreed to purchase her on our behalf. He negotiated directly with the owner, Savage, and called me once the ship was in his ownership. In a brief ceremony in Michael's office a few days later, I handed him a one pound coin and he signed over the ship's papers to me. I legally owned the *Benjamin Bowring*, née *Kista Dan*, one of the most famous Antarctic ships still afloat. I went out and bought the record Zorba the Greek and when I got home that night, Gaye and I danced around the living room to celebrate the fact that we were now shipowners.

Over the course of the next few months, Michael Watt waxed and waned about committing further money to the project and then indicated that he would put £600,000 in, subject to the securing of a large tax break

446

on the 'donation'. The problem was that it could not be passed off as donation since Polar Ventures was a limited company, not a charity and his promise of money would be viewed by the tax office as an investment on which he was entitled to no tax advantages at all.

Robert Swan, polar walker extraordinaire and long-term Antarctic acquaintance became interested in the Polar Ventures project and offered to help us find the money. He gave us an introduction to Hambros Bank through one of its directors, Eivind Rabben. At the same time, Paul Brown suggested over lunch one day that the World Wide Fund for Nature might be interested in the project. I sent the proposal to Robin Pellew, the newly appointed director. Robin called me about a week later and said, 'I've just read your Antarctic proposal. It's great and I would like to see you about it. Can you get to Beauchamp Place this afternoon?'

We met. He liked the project and wanted in. The very next day I was on a plane with Robin, en route for Gland in Switzerland where his international staff were waiting to hear about the project. As I waited for the appointed time for the meeting, I wandered up and down Gland's well-heeled, semi-rural streets, sweltering in my suit and tie as the summer sun beat down. I found a small cafe, ordered a beer and spent the hour I had to fill pondering the circumstances which had led me to be sitting here in Switzerland, in a suit, waiting to convince a bunch of strangers that they should cough up nearly a million pounds to allow me to get back to the place which still consumed me.

I had never, I concluded, been sufficiently distanced from my immediate activities long enough to make any rational decisions about where I was going or what I was doing. I had led an in-your-face life and had allowed – invited, even – events to dictate my course of action rather than the other way round. Of course, life itself is a series of coincidences and prevailing circumstances, but I had never really made concrete, hard decisions to which I had stuck, regardless of the consequences, preferring to allow myself to be pushed hither and thither by what I considered to be overwhelming imperatives. I realised then, as I sat staring into my beer, that I was a victim rather than a beneficiary of the 60s.

During my childhood and adolescence, my life was filled with sunshine, hope, good friends and a tight family life and I had railed against the conformity it offered with a vehemence which shook family and friends with its intensity. I publicly hated the very conformity and security it offered while I privately craved the normality I eschewed. Then, when I had that normality in my hand, I spat in its face and walked away. When I was in a relationship, I wanted to be out of a relationship and when I was on my own my first thought was to secure a relationship. When I was at sea, I wanted to be back on land and when I was back on land, I craved the romanticism of being at sea. When I worked for Greenpeace, I wanted out and now I was out, I wanted back. The new ship was a surrogate Greenpeace and I knew that it represented to me the ability to demonstrate that I could do things on my own, without having the safety net and the peer group support of an organisation I had helped build into what was, in effect, an extended family. I was out of the family and I would show them, as I had shown everyone else, that I didn't need them and that I could make it on my own – I hoped.

Only one thing really concerned me: for the first time I could remember, I had begun to worry about money and future security for Gaye and I. I was now 48 years of age. I had no trade, no profession as such, and although I was well-known in the green movement, my reputation was one of activist and mouthpiece rather than as a researcher or lobbyist and it appeared to me that the way the green movement was going required fewer of the former and more of the latter. I could only afford to dip into my meagre savings – in the bank only courtesy of one David Fraser McTaggart – sparingly. I had no pension, no insurance scheme and no income to speak of, my Montagne Jeunesse relationship having long ago ground to a halt. I pushed those unwelcome thoughts to one side, drained my beer glass and prepared to enter the lion's den.

The WWF board in Gland were far less enthusiastic about the Antarctic project than Robin Pellew. I was asked to carry out additional work in support of the project. Progress was infuriatingly slow.

Life intruded on my maritime ambitions. My Uncle Jim, my mum's sister Emmy's husband, larger than life and twice as loud, died of a sudden and fatal heart attack as he walked across the kitchen one morning. A docker all his life, he had attempted to school me in the art of football, but considered me tackle-shy and lacking in 'bottle'. It was rumoured that Jim had money which he jokingly promised to leave me but the most flamboyant bouquet at his funeral was from the betting office in the High Street.

Jim's death left Emmy alone in her flat in Selsey and after a period in which Mum helped Emmy cope with her grief, Mum decided to ask her if they should live together. Mum moved into Emmy's flat shortly after broaching the idea. This was a great relief for us all and gave Mum a new lease of life. Of the four daughters born to Nan, three – Mother, Emmy and Beattie – were widows. The fourth sibling, Ivy , is married to George Wood and they live in Orpington, Kent, where they have lived all their married lives. George Cremore, the only boy of the brood, married Doreen and they live in Swindon, Wiltshire. All the siblings and their surviving spouses began to meet up more regularly and to enjoy one another's company for weekends, more often than not lubricated by homemade wine. Mum had began to live her life again, although it is true to say that she never even glanced at another man after Dad died, despite the fact that she remained, to her dying day, an attractive woman. She never fully recovered from Dad's untimely and painful death.

As I continued to pursue the Antarctic ship project, Reg announced that an agreement had finally been struck between Roisin – the erstwhile 'leader' of the almost defunct Ark – and Peter Gold, who, through his company, sold Ark products and was therefore its only source of income. Ark would be handed over to Reg who had made it clear over the preceding months that I would be invited onto the board and that we could begin to 'kick Ark back into shape'. I was excited at the prospect. It would exercise my strategic campaigning mind again and would also offer me some form of modest income. I asked Reg to ensure that Bryn Jones, co-founder of Ark, would be accommodated in the agreement either by offering him a position or, should he decline, at least ensuring that we could count on Bryn's support rather than his vitriol. Reg deflected my counsel.

I privately determined to make such approaches as I saw necessary to Bryn. In the spirit of getting Ark off to a good start, I introduced not only Robin Pellew of WWF but also Robert Swan to a project Reg had been toying with, namely the Clean Air Campaign or, as Reg dubbed it, the 'Breathe Easy' campaign. This introduction was largely prompted by the fact that Robert Swan had told me how his asthmatic month-old baby, Barney, had nearly died while being forced to breathe highly polluted air in dense, unmoving traffic on Putney Bridge a few weeks earlier. Both Robert Swan and Robin Pellew, on behalf of WWF, pledged £2000 each to the Ark project and I was pleased to see that my introductions had a positive outcome.

After writing a draft project proposal, I began to feel that things were moving on without me. Suddenly, meetings were taking place to which I was not invited. Documents appeared to which I was not privy. The final slap in the face came when I noticed a box of business cards lying on a desk: 'Gerry Matthews: Director, Ark Campaigns.' When I asked Reg about it, he told me it was a 'temporary measure' to help Ark over the immediate hurdles of incorporation. Pretty soon, Reg dispensed with any pretence. At meetings to discuss Ark matters, he simply walked to the door of the meeting room and closed it in my face. He had appointed Gerry, it finally transpired, because Reg felt he was 'like-minded' and slotted into the public relations and advertising ambience Reg had constructed around Ark more appropriately than I did. There was some truth in that view, of course, but the way Reg was going about it was rude and insulting, in my opinion, and I let him know it.

I was both deeply hurt by what I saw as Reg's betrayal of me and seriously angry. I tried to rationalise events. I tried to see Reg's side of it. But even accepting the inevitable that Gerry was far more 'PR savvy' than I (although there was a discussion to be had around that, given my previous fifteen years in one of the most media-savvy organisations around), there was no way I could forgive Reg for the way in which he had treated me. I could not bring myself to face him and resorted to writing a withering attack on him in a letter. He had shown himself in his true colours and when I finally discussed events with Bryn Jones, now another of Reg's rebuffed former colleagues, Bryn showed no surprise and was quite matter of fact about the entire episode. But losing Reg's confidence and friendship was earth-shattering, as though a familiar part of my life's furniture had been removed.

Reg did his best to paper over the cracks of this split in the intervening years and sent me, on one notable occasion, a letter in which he claimed that we were close politically and not very far apart in most respects. He also added that his Parkinson's disease had worsened and that his 60th birthday was due and asked me if I could find it in my heart to bury the past. I refused, much to the disappointment of my wife who was beside herself at my obstinacy. Ivan Taylor, our mutual friend from the early days of Marshall Street, was likewise deeply affected by the break up and regularly sought to mediate.

Ivan was a difficult man to resist in that he was so avuncular, funny and completely without a shred of bile in his body (unless you were an authority figure). He would always be ready with a joke, would go to extraordinary lengths to bring you novel presents and would turn the ordinary into something special. We would ritually go to Ivan and Jean's on Cup Final day. We would watch the match and then the Eurovision Song Contest, justifying our viewing habits by ensuring that we were sufficiently merry by the time the song contest came on that we would spend the entire three hours ridiculing it and hooting royally at the antics of the singers and the presenters.

Ivan was a warm, generous person who could not stop joking or playing the fool. He, Reg and another guy with whom they worked in a small graphic design office in the early days of our friendship won a few pounds on the pools and issued a press release about the 'win' accompanied by a picture of the three winners with black oblongs covering their eyes to ensure anonymity. He went to endless lengths to entertain us on Cup Final day and always made great play of the fact that I was a Millwall supporter, even going to the lengths of inviting another mysterious and, as it turned out, entirely fictitious Millwall supporter to his house one year to see the Cup Final.

So it was a huge shock to me when, in 2007, Reg called me on my mobile to tell me that Ivan had died. He had been unwell with some ill-defined complaint for some time and confided once, when we were kicking a ball around, that he had had no sensation in his feet or lower limbs for some years. Ivan's death caused me to relent on the Reg issue and I hope that Ivan somehow knew that Reg and I did what he begged us to do for many a long year. We patched up our differences and are now friends again.

Chapter 32

A birth and my own re-birth

Ken Ballard was by now, in 1994, living permanently in the UK, having decided to throw in his lot with Polar Ventures and accept that his stormy relationship with his wife of only two months was breaking up beyond the point of reconciliation. I continued to work on the Polar Ventures project from the WBMG offices in Regent Street but the situation was becoming intolerable and the atmosphere was poisonous. Not only had I fallen out with Reg but David Gee and Gerry Matthews were on a war footing over the releasing of funds on a project about ecological tax reform which David had asked Gerry to mentor. An almighty row one day in the office had these two mild-mannered people on the point of squaring up to each other.

I found it hard to keep the smile off my face at this spectacle. WBMG had foregone any vestige of a pretext that it was a partnership. That particular claim lay in tatters on the floor of the office and only Gerry's energy in keeping the company alive for his own purposes allowed it to survive in some sort of hollow, meaningless guise. But presumably this suited Gerry and I was not in any sort of mood to do more than wave another attempt at making something work goodbye. It was not that I had no work – I had too much of it – but it was the converting of that work into income which I found difficult, a situation I have regularly found myself in throughout my working life. Despite the cool reception in Gland, the WWF board had committed money to the polar ship project, to the tune of £300,000. Through the offices of my old Antarctic friend, Robert Swan, a further £300,000 had been raised in debt servicing loans from Hambros Bank. After a round of tedious but important meetings at which WWF's financial advisers and trustees were variously wheeled in to pull the project apart, we were still in the running and technically we had all the necessary cash on the table. Hambros Bank called in their own ship surveyors and carried out yet another inspection on the ship – the third. The results were positive. We shook hands with Robin Pellew and Eivind Rabben, the Norwegian Hambros' director, and agreed to meet two weeks hence to finalise the deal.

I fully appreciated that Robin Pellew was skating on thin ice with respect to this deal. It was clear that, despite the promise of financial support, his board was not greatly enamoured of the project. Nothing, however, could have prepared me for the bombshell he dropped when he called a few days before what was to be the final meeting.

His opening gambit should have warned me. 'I hope you're sitting down, Pete.'

As the sorry story of failed fundraising projects, internal opposition and the collapse of a financial deal with prospective third parties unfolded, my world also began collapsing as I grunted into the phone at appropriate moments and tried to hide my crushing disappointment.

I mumbled 'Ok, Robin. See you at the next meeting', crashed down the phone into the cradle and lay my head on the table before me, closing my eyes.

To give Robin his due, he turned up to face the music at the next meeting held at Hambros. He reiterated his apologies and was suitably chastened about the whole sorry episode. Towards the end of the meeting, obviously feeling under enormous pressure, he attempted to brighten the mood by telling us that while the £300k was a non-starter, he could commit £100k. While this was very welcome news, it left us with a gaping financial hole and far from meeting to discuss the nature of the contract between us, we were now forced to slink away and lick our wounds, pondering how on earth we were going to find someone to stump up the lost £200k.

As we left the room I took Robin to one side and asked him point blank if that money was firm, to which he replied in the affirmative. I also asked him, in the earshot of other people in the meeting, if he would compensate Ken and I for all the expenditure we had incurred in getting this far on the project. We had a lawyer's fee of £2,500 to pay and we had each individually committed £5,000 to the venture so far. He promised he would review any claims from us with great attention and favour. It took us three months to force the money to pay the lawyer's fee and we never saw a penny in compensation for the investment Ken and I had put into the project. Letters, updates, alternative suggestions and direct appeals for Robin to contact me concerning the project and the on-going availability of the £100K all met with a resounding silence. We were back to square one and the polar ship project which had come so close to success receded into the file of programmes marked, 'Close, but no cigar.'

I vowed that the project would happen: it was simply too good an idea to allow a minor set-back to interrupt its progress.

Three months later, I read with a sinking heart and a sense of inevitability that Onyx, the big waste company whose logo was appearing all over London as its operatives swept the filthy streets, and the giant French water company, Vivendi, had merged to form Onyx Vivendi Environmental and had secured a £100 million contract with the Australian Antarctic Division to clean up and remove two of its redundant stations. But I was still the legal owner of a ship and was still in the process of raising money for her refit. We had most of the necessary parts in place: we had a ship, we had a skeleton crew and we had a contract negotiated with the Polish Antarctic Division on a memorable trip to Warsaw a few months earlier, thanks, largely to Wojtek Moskal. We didn't have the money with which to operate a programme but I was convinced this would change when the *Kista Dan* was brought back to London and we set about planning for a berth for her in the Pool of London, just upstream of Tower Bridge where the *Rainbow Warrior* had berthed all those years ago before setting off for Iceland.

Hearing of our intentions, Sir Ranulph Feinnes contacted me. In a very generous gesture, he put us in touch with his chief engineer who came to Syros and went through the ship and imparted all his knowledge to our own people. Sir Ranulph also sent me two beautiful prints of his Transglobe Expedition which today hang proudly on the wall of the corridor in our Suffolk cottage.

I trawled the agencies for experienced seamen to help with the project and slowly but surely built up a full crew for the ship. Shell agreed to pay for the bunkers and for lube oil. My flagging spirits in the face of the Onyx Vivendi development and Mike Watt's understandable hesitancy at WWF's pullout were raised slightly at the prospect of getting the vessel back to London, but the hurdles were still significant. We drew up a list of basic safety requirements for the ship – lifeboats, life vests, HF and VHF radios, fire fighting equipment – the list was endless and the bill was enormous. Still we felt we could raise the funds.

Then came a near-fatal blow. While routinely running the main engine, the chief engineer decided to test it under load and put the ship into 'slow ahead' while she was being restrained by the warps. As the engine laboured to move the vessel forward, the valve popped and a stream of what appeared to be milk exited the main engine in a hot jet which hit the bulkhead. This indicated that the main engine oil reservoir was contaminated with bilge water and the search began immediately to find where the ingress was occurring. After much crawling around in the bilges, much cursing and sweating, the engineers traced the point of ingress to a cracked pipe which was drawing dirty water into the oil reservoir from the bilges. It could be 'sleeved' quite easily and quickly – covering the bit of pipe in which the crack was found by a 'sleeve' of metal – but of course, since we were doing everything 'by the book' for the sake of keeping our Lloyds accreditation and certification (required by the type of clients we were hoping to attract), we had to inform the Lloyds inspector. To our huge consternation, he determined that in order to do things in the manner required by Lloyds, the ship would be required to go into the shipyard, the engine room would need to be made free of gas and the entire length of pipe renewed. Total cost? Circa £40,000.

Via the ever-helpful David Iggulden, I made a request for further funds from Michael Watt, only to be told that his largess was at its limits. His accountant, we were told, had submitted a report which predicted further and potentially limitless haemorrhaging of money from Michael's account. Apparently, Michael walked into his office one morning, shortly after having received the accountant's advice, and when Iggulden asked him what he was to tell us about the money, he reportedly said simply, 'Oh, the Antarctic project. Yeah, tell the guys I'm no longer interested.' With such casual words are entire worlds upended and spirits ground into the soil.

We were staring into the abyss. To save a few drachmas, we moved the ship to a less busy and less costly mooring, alongside a little-used quay, away from the main port of Syros. The local harbour operators organised the move as the crew had been stood down to save costs while I decided what we were to do. The warps on the ship were left looser than was sensible for the position in which she was left after the move from the main Syros berth. Consequently, she drifted off the quay a greater distance than she should have. A freak storm swept over Syros from a direction which is apparently unusual in the islands. The *Kista Dan* was blown many yards from the quayside by the storm winds and sprung back towards the quayside by the warps. She hit the quayside along her port side many times as the storm passed, pushing her off and allowing her to spring back time after time. She was a write-off. The port-side ribs had been bent and put out of line by the repeated battering and we could do no more than sell the vessel to a Turkish ship breaker. She was taken away and turned into a few million razor blades or whatever ship breakers do with battered and useless ships.

The Polar Ventures dream was over. Friends, family and enthusiastic supporters had contributed £10, £50 and, in some cases of close friends, several thousands of pounds to this project and despite doing so in the knowledge that it was a risk, the realisation of the project's failure was a bitter pill for us all. The idea of putting ships to better use than travelling the oceans in order to disrupt activities with which we disagreed remained a tantalising aspiration rather than a reality. But we came so close . . .

During the frenetic period between 1995 and 1997, while the Antarctic ship project died an untimely and lingering death, other projects were finding their way to me with metronomic regularity. But one project to which I can claim no original involvement or initiation came literally out of the blue and was, in fact, dubbed 'Blue Planet' by its originator, Bob Duffield. The project was based on the fact that every airline ticket is unique to the traveller to whom it is issued. Bob's simple idea, which he apparently had while flying back from New York a month or so previously and looking out on the blue of the atmosphere through which he was flying, was to use the airline ticket number as a lottery number. Every month, one lucky passenger would win a life-changing amount of money if his or her ticket number matched the number drawn from the pot via, for instance, the International Air Travel Association which might administer the project.

The activities which went along with the project were what attracted me more than the financial reward side of it. It was proposed that as part of the Blue Planet experience, passengers would be encouraged to get involved in in-flight games, quizzes and interactive pastimes to give them greater insight into the ecology, politics, geography and demographics of the countries over which they were travelling. The beneficiary charity to which the profits from the lottery would be dedicated would be subject to passenger preference.

The project's demise – for die a death it did – was preceded by two years of quite incredible intrigue, activity and jockeying for position which involved very large US 'not for profit' organisations such as the

Pew and Ford Foundations and investment levels that were eye-watering. It involved just about every contact we had collectively accumulated over the years, including my old mentor at Friends of the Earth, the late Richard Sandbrook, then heading up the International Institute for Education and Development (IIED). During the course of the project development, Richard was discussing projects with Kurt Hoffman at the Shell HQ in London, where Kurt ran the Shell Foundation, when he complained of feeling unwell. He was taken to hospital and diagnosed with cancer. He died very soon after his diagnosis, spending the time he had left writing his memoirs. The memorial service for Richard which took place months later was attended by literally hundreds of people and he was billed as one of the most influential 'development' campaigners of his time.

Blue Planet took us all on a roller-coaster ride of highs and lows worthy of the Polar Ventures experience but with the added disadvantage of witnessing friendships and alliances wither and die before our very eyes. It was all very disagreeable but it did plant the seed of an idea to remove myself from the London-based 'project factory' and repair to the relative sanity of the countryside when the time felt right, and, in truth, that time was fast approaching.

Gaye and I had to move from our lovely top floor flat overlooking Battersea Park as the owner was selling the property. We did think of trying to buy the flat as it was so conveniently situated and the times we had spent in it were memorable and dear to us both. We probably experienced our most hedonistic couple of years while living first on Lavender Hill and then in the flat on Parkgate Road, but the notice to quit sharpened our focus. Gaye had let me know in no uncertain terms that she wanted children, a step which I had more or less given up on at my time of life. I had just turned 49. Gaye is eighteen years my junior and, at 31, was keen to start a family. It suddenly occurred to me that becoming a parent, a life-changing event and something I had dismissed as having passed me by a long time ago, was now a reality. Gaye wanted my children. I could scarcely believe my luck!

We moved to Silverthorne Road, dumped our gear and went on a bike tour of Scotland. It was a memorable holiday – the weather was extraordinarily fine for the time of year. The Scottish roads are built for bike riding – smooth surfaces and long, lazy curves winding through beautiful scenery, often along the shores of lochs which stretch to the horizon. We took the ferry to Eigg, Rhum and Muck. We saw minkes whales and dolphins. But most incredibly, Gaye fell pregnant. I was going to be a dad after all. I could barely contain my excitement! The trip back, however, was far from exciting but once again, Gaye's fortitude in the face of howling winds and driving rain made me all the surer of this woman.

On our return to London, we decided that we would have to find a house to buy. In March 1996, we moved to number 48, Seely Road, a semi-detached property just off Amen Corner, down the road from Tooting Broadway. We paid £38,000 for it and put down a deposit of £12,000, thanks largely to the money I had hoarded from the benevolence of McTaggart a few years previously and our ability, somehow, to use this nest egg over the years as frugally as possible. We were happy at Seely Road, although the regular deposits of half-eaten pizzas outside the house, particularly on Saturday and Sunday mornings, were very dispiriting, as was the constant thump-thump of passing boy-racers whose cars sported massive sub-woofers, the more efficiently to annoy others with inane and tuneless music.

Nonetheless, we persevered and made the best of it and registered at St George's hospital to ensure that Gaye's pregnancy and the baby's growth were monitored adequately. By May the next year, the baby was a week or two overdue and the doctors decided that it was time to hasten the birth through induction. Gaye and I camped at the hospital and began the long vigil as we waited for baby to arrive. I remember that there was a test match on the TV and when Gaye experienced a contraction and was distracted for a while, I turned the TV over from the film she was watching – *Gone with the Wind* – just to check the score. It has since become a bit of family folklore that Dad watched the cricket while the baby was born.

The birth was complicated. The baby was reluctant to make an entrance and Gaye was in pain as she pushed and pushed in vain. When the baby finally decided to make an entrance, I was, apparently, shaking Gaye's leg the better to encourage the baby to appear. Eventually, at 20 minutes past 8 on the evening of the 25th May, 1996, she arrived – a girl! A beautiful baby girl! The nurses quickly whisked her away as she had had oxygen restricted during the birth. The umbilical cord was apparently wrapped around her neck and she could have suffered brain damage. But within minutes they brought our precious bundle back to us, giving her a clean bill of health, and I held my beautiful baby in my arms as tears streamed down my face (just as they are now as I recall the moment). The baby smiled at me. I swear to God, as Gaye is my witness, she smiled at me when she was only a few minutes old.

I phoned my mum, 'Mum! We've got a beautiful baby daughter! Yes, I'm a dad!'

I phoned Gaye's mum. I phoned everyone I could think of. I was a dad and everyone was going to know about it. A few days later, as we lay in bed with our daughter snuggled between us, we named her Emily May – Emily to acknowledge my side of the family (Mum's sister Emily had never been able to have children) and May to reflect Gaye's side of the family, after her own aunt's middle name. I could not quite come to terms with the fact that I had a child. I had to keep repeating to myself that I was a dad. Every morning, I took little Emily in my arms and gazed at her face and warmed in her smile and in her chuckles. I was truly in love, possibly for the first time ever. I loved my wife and I loved my daughter. After all the bounty that life had given me thus far, surely the gift of such a wonderful wife and daughter were more than I had a right to expect. Still, I wasn't complaining and I determined to grab whatever good fortune came my way with both hands.

As my projects waxed and waned in their fortunes, I ducked and dived, trying to keep the money coming in. Times were tough and the responsibility of keeping the mortgage paid and food on the table for three of us weighed heavily. I was still acting as a member of the Conservation Society's Green Investment Panel along with John Burton, my old Friends of the Earth colleague with whom I had never lost touch, and with Professor David Bellamy whose instantly recognisable face I had grown up with in the 70s.

I was invited to a reception one evening at the Royal Geographical Society, the building where the Conservation Foundation occupied a number of offices. It was to mark the 25th anniversary of the Conservation Foundation's establishment. The Prince of Wales was guest of honour. To my amazement, David Bellamy began his introductory speech by saying that two things were of particular note: that he and the Foundation were still here after 25 years and, secondly, that he never thought he would see the day when Pete Wilkinson would turn up to a meeting in a suit (I had taken Gaye's instructions to heart and put on my only suit for the occasion). That he would mention me in such august company was typical of the man and he and I spent many years working on issues together.

The much reduced activities of the Blue Planet project kept me going and allowed us to survive this lean spell. WBMG had long since accepted its fate and disbanded. I moved to a different office in the Regent Street offices at Linen Hall and continued to administer the project as it gradually ground to a halt.

During the evenings, Gaye and I would discuss the future and what we wanted for our Emily May. She was a gorgeous baby and it hurt me to take her to the shops or even outside the house at all, so filthy was the air, so dirty the streets and so noisy the environment. The forecourt of the police station on Tooting Broadway was filled to the brim with litter. I asked the police to send me details of the last prosecution for littering. The desk sergeant looked at me as though I was mad.

We began looking around for property out of town and each weekend, we would travel up from London and spend two days looking at a variety of properties around the Halesworth/Beccles area while Emily stayed with Gaye's mum and dad, Sylvie and Gerry. One property stood out from all the others – Meadow Cottage in Peasenhall. Set back from the road amid fields, it was a pretty and secluded detached cottage, but at £160,000, it was beyond our means. We had only £120,000 to spend after calculating that we could raise a small profit on Seely Road. We looked and looked and eventually settled on a cottage in Laxfield, but days before we exchanged contracts we were gazumped. In desperation, I suggested to Gaye that we revisit Meadow Cottage and make a silly offer. If that failed, we would give up the idea of moving for now and make the best of things in London.

Meadow Cottage was overpriced which was a factor in our favour. Through the estate agent, we offered our top price, £40,000 below the asking price – £120,000. To our incredulity and delight, we were told that it could be ours for £125,000. We accepted, and in April 1998 we moved into Meadow Cottage, Peasenhall.

Chapter 33

The world becomes a different place, a second child and two deaths.

I had somehow convinced the Blue Planet board that I could continue to run the project – such as its modest needs required – from the depths of Suffolk. The Blue Planet money was the only income coming into the Wilkinson household and was unreliable at that, promising to be terminated at any moment when time was finally called on the project. I remember thinking one morning that we had just enough in the bank to pay the mortgage and feed ourselves for a month, but nothing beyond that. The outlook was bleak, but a walk down a country footpath with Emily on my back in her carrier changed all that. Although I was, and remain, a sceptic about the way in which the countryside is managed, the delights of the bucolic lifestyle, compared to the areas of London which we could afford to live in, were overwhelming. Just to breathe in the relatively pure air and see the occasional butterfly was so invigorating. We had made the correct call, without a doubt, but it was now time to concentrate on increasing my earning power and re-establishing myself as a consultant.

I took the bull by the horns. I called Colin Duncan, Communications Director for British Nuclear Fuels Ltd (BNFL), and asked him if he had ever thought about getting together with the greens to discuss their differences of opinion and see if any common ground could be identified. He asked me to act as a broker for talks about talks, and I then went – with some trepidation – to Lord Melchett. The first question Melchett asked me after I had outlined the idea of dialogue with the 'enemy' was, 'What's in it for us?'

Despite mainstream green scepticism about the dialogue initiative, it worked. Over a six year period, brokered and facilitated by the redoubtable Steve Robinson of the Environment Council, the dialogue attracted, at its peak, over 150 representatives of NGOs, regulators, the industry, government, trades unions and local authorities. It was not an easy process and some still argue to this day that it did little to advance the green cause, but it broke down barriers and gave NGOs a much clearer insight into the nuclear industry, its management, its failures and its aspirations.

From my perspective, the greatest achievements of the dialogue were the agreement that Magnox spent nuclear fuel reprocessing – the source of huge contention, as well as a radioactive burden sent down the pipeline into the Irish Sea in the form of liquid radioactive waste – would end by 2012, and the work done by the plutonium working group which examined means by which plutonium could be dispositioned. Even in 2002 this work was considered seminal. Needless to say, the Nuclear Decommissioning Authority (NDA) ignored those cutting edge, collaborative deliberations when it was established in 2005 and has gone about doggedly and stubbornly reinventing the wheel.

While the nuclear dialogue was drawing to a close, David McTaggart's book, Shadow Warrior, was being ghostwritten by a close friend of his, Helen Slinger. At the same time, a film about McTaggart's life was being shot and Helen came to the UK to interview me on film for the documentary. We spent a few very enjoyable days revisiting my old haunts around Islington and even managed to gain access to the old Greenpeace office at Graham Street which had been taken over by Andersons, the wood merchant next door, but to which we were graciously granted access. It was a highly charged and emotional time for me as I wandered around the now empty offices where years ago we had experienced so much fun, laughter, depression and elation. It was difficult for me to keep the tears from my eyes as I talked to the camera and Helen about the old days and, in particular, McTaggart's overriding influence on them.

A few days later I was at home and the phone rang. It was Helen, now back in Canada. She sounded distraught and came straight to the point, 'Pete. David's dead. He was killed in a car crash in Italy earlier today.'

I burst into tears.

Helen said, 'I knew you would cry with me, Pete.'

I stood looking at the wall while the tears coursed down my face, listening to Helen sobbing down the line.

This guy, who had been in my thoughts either consciously or sub-consciously, for the last 25 years, had been taken from us. He had given me the breaks and had placed his faith and trust in me regularly and routinely, sure in the knowledge that I wouldn't let him down or that, if I did, it would be for good reasons and that I would eventually come good. He did that on the Antarctic campaigns and I will always be proud that I met and hopefully surpassed his highest expectations, although he would never have told me so and I would never have asked him to do so. His trips to the UK and the time he spent with us will always be treasured memories – scary and a bit fraught from time to time, but what is life without living close to the edge? He was a colossus in my life and in the lives of most people he met. His passing left a void which has been hard to fill. I later learned that he had probably had a heart attack while driving and had driven into an oncoming car, killing the driver. The accident occurred on the 23rd March 2001.

Thankfully, he did not live to see the Twin Towers attacks on the 11th September of the same year. I have no idea how he would have reacted. One thing is certain, however: he would not have been inactive. McTaggart was a creature created for the big events in life and there was nothing much bigger than the attacks on that day, nor the manufactured response of the Bush/Blair alliance which took us into a new and terrifying dimension of terrorism and Anglophobia from which we will not recover for a generation. I am convinced that McTaggart would have demanded that these earthshaking events catapult Greenpeace into doing justice to the 'peace' part of its name, something it has historically been reluctant to do with the exception of the McTaggart-inspired opposition to nuclear weapons testing.

In early summer, 1999, Gaye fell pregnant for the second time. While Emily was born a Londoner, our second child would be born in Suffolk. In February 2000, Gaye and I went to Ipswich hospital for the birth of our second child. We were told to go home again, as we were 'far too early'. As we walked down the stairs in the maternity wing Gaye suddenly stopped. 'The baby's coming.'

Back we went to the delivery ward where they quickly put Gaye into bed and within minutes the baby was born. This time, there were no hold ups or scares. Our second daughter, Amy Rose, was born with little fuss or bother at 7am on the 7th February 2000. Incredibly, we had another daughter and I felt blessed beyond belief.

There can be no greater joys in life than snuggling up in bed on a Sunday morning with your wife, a newborn baby and her four year-old sister. I distinctly recall the morning when, the day after Amy Rose was brought home, we told Emily that we were going to name her sister Amy to acknowledge one of my mum's middle names and Rose, a middle name of Gaye's mum.

Emily bore the awkward handle of Wilkinson-Jerrom which caused a few problems at school and Gaye and I talked of tying the knot to make things easier for the children in later life and also to cement what was clearly going to be a long-term relationship. We made plans to marry and on September the 23rd (my father's birthday) 2000, we were married at Peasenhall Church with our beautiful Emily and Gaye's niece, Katie, as bridesmaids.

It was a wonderfully crisp, early autumn day of sunshine and light and we were married with all our family and friends around us and to the evident delight of my mum, who had longed for the day that her 'rebel' son would declare himself settled and with a family to look after. Cindy Barnes, our next door neighbour with whom we had become good friends, sang a duet in the church with a friend. They sang In My Life by Lennon and McCartney, one of our favourite songs. It was a delightful day and I asked my old mate Bryn Jones to be best man. The afternoon and evening were pure heaven: Gaye's dad – one time steel guitarist for Slim Whitman – reunited as many of his old band as he could and played a mixture of country and rock long into the night, much to the delight of all present. Our wonderful neighbours, the Barnes, opened up their entire house and garden for the occasion and all the Wilkinson-Jerroms crawled all over their beautiful house all afternoon and evening, with many people sleeping there too. It was a memorable occasion and to this day I often hear people recall it with fondness.

Mum and Aunty Emmy came to ours for Christmas every year and we would also entertain Gaye's mum and dad on Christmas Eve before they went back to London for their own family party on Christmas day. Needless to say, Mum and Emmy doted on the kids and loved to visit the cottage for those few precious winter days, showering the kids with presents and love for the entire period they were with us. Mum was getting old: she was approaching her eighty-second birthday, had emphysema from her fag-smoking days and mentioned more and more frequently that she would not 'go on forever'. I, of course, laughed this off, telling her that she had years and years left in her yet. During the Christmas holidays

464

in 2003, Mum confided in Gaye that she did not think she would survive the next year and that this would be the last time she would be at Meadow Cottage. She didn't confide these things to me: she also told Gaye that, as much as she loved me and as much as she knew I loved her, she had never been able to get close to me. I was always 'distant', she claimed.

Mum and Emmy went home to their flat in Selsea just before New Year, 2004. A week later, Emmy called me to say that Mum was complaining of stomach pains and would be going to the doctor's. Later that day, mum was admitted to hospital. She had endometriosis and the diseased part of her stomach would have to be removed in a four hour operation.

At the hospital, Mum looked well enough, although she was using an oxygen mask. It was Friday and she was about to have the operation. The following few days were nightmarish and Mum died, unable, despite her miraculous revival just before I left her, to summon sufficient energy to recover from the operation.

At the funeral, I was too distraught to speak and Gaye stepped in for me. I had written the following eulogy to Mum, but I couldn't deliver it.

Mum's Eulogy

Looking around the faces here today, I'm sure I don't have to tell you what Minnie Amy Edith Wilkinson was like as a woman, as a friend, as a mother, a mother-in-law, as a sister, a grandmother or as a neighbour. She wore her heart on her sleeve; she embraced life and did not suffer fools easily. She spoke her mind – sometimes too freely – and she did not mince her words. To me, at least, she was life, the constant reassuring presence always there at the end of the phone, someone we'd see infrequently, someone we'd bring to our home with equal infrequency. But she was there – with her migraines and her giddiness, with her laboured breathing and her increasing frailty – she was there for us all.

When I look back on Mum's life, I realise I don't know a great deal about it. Childhood for me was a time of freedom and adventure, of bombed sites and car-free streets in Deptford, with Mum calling us as the sun went down to come home to the prefab, to Gyp the dog, to warmth, safety and to a loving family life. When we moved to the flats on Evelyn Street, it seemed that life changed so quickly:

Brian left to get married, I left to pursue, as Mum said to a nurse at St Richard's hospital not two weeks ago, my life as a rebel. Then Dad got ill and died and Mum was faced with a life alone and a life in a strange flat in Kidbrooke which she managed to deal with for a long time. Closing the front door of that flat on Mum as we'd say goodbye used to break my heart.

'Bye, love, see you at the window', she'd say. And there her face would be as she waved. Then she'd be alone with her thoughts and her memories for another painful lonely day.

When Uncle Jim died and she moved to Selsey with Emmy, it was like a rebirth for Mum and for the rest of us. To know that she was with her sister, that she was no longer alone in that flat was a massive relief. Mum thrived in Selsey and great credit goes to Aunt Emm for helping to make such a happy home for them both. Like any other couple living together under one roof, it wasn't always a bed of roses, I know. Sometimes, the acrimony could peel the wallpaper, but Mum's last ten years, I like to think, were some of her happiest. She had loved in her long life and she was loved, right up to the end. She lived a happy life, a varied life and I am proud to have been able to give Mum what I know she wanted most – both of her children settled and happy. It just took me a lot longer than it did Brian, but she knew that I'd found my true love in Gaye and that made her happy.

Of course we knew that Mum wouldn't go on forever although sometimes I wondered. And when I thought of her death, I felt I could deal with it in a detached way, a philosophical way: she would die one day and she would have had a good innings and that was that. How wrong I was. Nothing in the world could have prepared me for the emotions I experienced at the hospital over the weekend before she died. Although I knew in my heart it was hopeless, I wanted her to live more than anything else in the world. When I arrived on the Friday night, she was unaware I was there. I thought she would die any moment. Suddenly, this woman whom I had taken for granted all my life, was before me fighting for life. She was no longer that constant, distant, comforting presence but she was here, before me in all her human frailty: she filled my whole world, my every second. I breathed every breath she struggled to draw. I lavished love on her as I never had before.

I prayed to God either to take her quickly or to allow her to improve – not bad going for an agnostic. And improve she did. Over that weekend, she went from death's door to eating small amounts of food, smiling, winking and joking with the nurses. She came off the hateful oxygen mask so she could talk, interact and drink when she wanted. When I left her in the comfort of her grandsons on Sunday afternoon, I felt she had a chance – a slim one, but a chance. She squeezed my hand as I left and said, 'What will I do without you, boy?' I told her I'd be back later in the week, and kissed her. Then she went and died and I asked why. The answer wasn't hard to find.

Mum was making the sort of effort she was used to making, the sort of selfless act which had characterised her life. She made that Herculean recovery for her family, as a repayment for all their love and attention. And when they were gone, she could go too. She could allow her body to give up the effort of breathing and she could die in peace and dignity.

I realised for the first time in my life that weekend just how much I loved my mother. And in her wake, I can only comfort myself and hopefully others by telling myself that she had a full and happy life, that she loved and was loved, that in her final days she saw all those who meant so much to her, that she was able to say her goodbyes in the only way she knew how, that she did not suffer greatly and that her end was peaceful. God rest her soul.

I'd finally like to add a word of thanks to my brother Brian, sister-in-law Margaret and to my dear wife Gaye. Brian and Margaret were with Mum as she died and have been a constant source of strength and support over these difficult days. And I don't think I could have gotten through this time without the loving and tender support of Gaye.

Thank you all three, but most of all thank you Mum and safe journey, love.

Life had another cruel act to play out on us Wilkinsons, although it was, thankfully, five years after Mum died so she did not have to suffer this emotional trauma. My brother Brian was diagnosed with cancer of the stomach. He underwent a highly invasive and protracted operation which, the doctors told Margaret, his wife, had removed all the cancerous cells and he would recover. It would take a long time for his rearranged digestive system to repair itself, but there was nothing to stop this happening. He came home but was never really well. He suffered a thrombosis and then was diagnosed with malnutrition as he had been drip-fed for months.

He went back into the hospital for a further check up. The doctor told him that the cancer had spread through his body via his bloodstream and that he had less than a week to live. With fortitude which is unimaginable to me, he did not tell his wife or children this devastating news for the entire weekend. But on Monday, December 14th 2009, he told his wife the awful news. He was taken into a hospice and died on the 18th December, a week before Christmas.

He was always, always happy and laughing: his buoyancy and bubbliness of character were irrepressible, but I felt he needed a break. He gave up work when he was only 50 and thereafter, as far as I'm aware, did little more than look after Margaret, although that in itself was a selfless task. Of course, he revelled in his children and their growth, development and company and went on fishing trips with them which remain vivid and pleasurable memories for the kids, along with his antics and jocular character which seemed to rise above any and all the clouds in Brian's life. His children gave him a glowing and much-deserved 'end of life' report at the funeral and at the subsequent memorial service which they organised because so few people could attend the actual funeral held in January, 2010, during the awful icy weather that prevailed for most of that month and into February.

All his sons were at his side when he died and for that I was, and am, eternally grateful. But while they lost a much-loved dad and while Margaret lost a much-loved and loving husband, I also lost a brother. It occurred to me at the funeral that I had known Brian for the longest of all those present and yet not once was I asked to speak about my brother or his life. Margaret was remote from me at the funeral, an attitude I blamed on the shock of the experience she had just been through, but even in the years since his death, we have not been in touch more than once or twice, something which saddens me. I know instinctively that there is no malice in her attitude towards me and nor is there any hint of it in the fact that we see the boys only rarely. I think it is more a case of benign blindness to my own loss caused by the enormity of their own loss, losing their much-loved father so suddenly and at such a young age.

As I walked with Gaye from the funeral, I reflected that I was the last of my immediate family left. Dad, Mum and now Brian had all died. Even today, a few years after Brian's death, his passing causes me real and tangible pain. When I think of Brian, I catch my breath, finding it difficult to believe that he is dead and the pain is still raw and sharp, like an open wound. Dad's death has receded to a dull ache and time has done its job well: sometimes I have difficulty recalling his face and his presence and when I think of Mum, to whom I was the closest of the three, my heart leaps, my stomach sinks and the absence of her awkwardness and cussedness washes over me in a wave of nostalgia and melancholy, invariably causing a tear or two.

Chapter 34

Reprise

Motorbikes have played an important role in my life. Ever since I took the plunge and bought a Honda 550 from a guy at Greenpeace, whom I was convinced was a police plant, I've loved them. After the chain snapped on the Honda and wrapped itself around the back wheel, causing me to fight the bike for about 500 yards down Goswell Road, I decided to buy a shaft-driven bike and, being envious of Tony Marriner's BMW R100RS, I began looking out for one.

I found, hidden away at the back of a shop exclusively selling stylish Italian motorcycles, a beautiful, smoke red R100 RS, upright and staid by comparison with the sleek lines of the Italian bikes. I paid £2,000 for it and sold it, two years later for £1,800, to Dr John Large, a nuclear engineer and Greenpeace consultant. He had it for years. He broke both stands (side and centre) and used to park it by leaning it up against walls, a habit which caused the hitherto pristine fairing to become scratched, chipped and ugly. Years later, the clutch gave out and he sent me a jokingly indignant letter of complaint.

On my return from my Antarctic six year stint, I bought another BMW R100RS which Gaye and I used to travel all over Europe before I traded it in for a K range bike – the ever-reliable 'black bike'. I sold that to a colleague just before I got married in 2000, on the grounds that bike riding for a family man was not the most sensible or safe way of getting around and in any case, we needed the money. But two years ago, I bought a K100 RS Classic, 1984 which I'm planning to have restored and repainted so that, in my dotage and when the kids have left home, Gaye and I can once again take to the road in the carefree abandon which only comes with biking.

My campaigning instincts would not let me rest, no matter how much I tried to turn myself into a bona fide consultant. I fretted about Greenpeace still. I worried that Sellafield was still operating, still creating its waste streams for which there was no accepted management solution and still poisoning the Irish Sea with its poisonous waste. The BNFL national nuclear dialogue had been useful in that it demonstrated to the nuclear industry that anti-nuclear campaign groups were, in the main, reasonable, well-versed in the issues and, to some extent, collaborative. The stakeholders involved in the dialogue included government departments and the civil servants that ran them.

Soon after the dialogue ended, I was asked to help set up a national stakeholder dialogue to precede the arrival of the Liabilities Management Unit (LMU) which was the forerunner of the Nuclear Decommissioning Authority (NDA), responsible for the de-constructing of the old Magnox station around the country and managing the UK's stockpile of legacy waste. Fred Barker was an automatic choice as a partner for me in this venture and we worked together for a number of years acting as consultants for Defra, then the DTI and other offshoots of the nuclear industry. Fred told me that he had never earned so much money as he had while working with me: he must have been poorly paid beforehand, then, as we didn't earn fantastically well and the irony of his statement was not missed by me or Gaye. Years earlier, during the BNFL national dialogue, Fred had complained so bitterly that I was wearing a stakeholder hat during the meetings, but a consultant's one when setting them up, that I was forced to resign my consultancy with the Environment Council, a move which cost me around £10,000.

In late 2002 I was in the far north of Scotland having a meal in the famous Scrabster seafood restaurant after having visited the Dounreay plant as part of my DTI duties. I had previously applied to join a new government committee which was to examine all the options for the long-term management of the legacy radioactive waste created over the past 50 years by our love affair with nuclear power and its deadly daughter, nuclear weapons. My mobile phone rang: it was the chairperson-elect of the committee, offering me a position on the committee which I accepted. I was now in the employ of the government, although, curiously, I was not an employee when it came to sick leave, holidays or pension. Government committee appointees are in a strange never-never world of duality, neither an employee nor a consultant. Nonetheless, at £300 a day plus expenses, it was not to be sniffed at, as well as looking good on my CV. And in any case, I now had the opportunity to parade all my prejudices against disposal, a practice I had campaigned against for decades. In fact, the more I thought about it, the more prosaic the situation became.

Had it not been for the successful campaigns against radioactive waste disposal in the Atlantic all those years ago, a committee to examine radioactive waste management options would not have been necessary. Subsequent campaigns against the disposal of waste at Billingham, Elstow and other places dotted around the country and, more importantly, the stunning campaign Friends of the Earth ran in the 90s against the 'Rock Characterisation Facility' at Longlands Farm in Cumbria, had demonstrated that opposition was organised, well-informed and determined. Successive government plans to impose disposal on communities or in the international commons of the oceans had been defeated time after time. Now they had been finally forced to deal with the problem in a sensible and rational way – by seeking the advice of a properly constituted and expert panel of individuals. I considered myself just as expert on radioactive waste management as any other member of the panel of thirteen people who formed the first incarnation of the Committee on Radioactive Waste Management, despite my lack of diplomas and fancy titles.

Among those individuals were some friends: Professor Gordon McKerron was someone whom I knew from the past, as was Professor Linda Warren. Fred Barker was there as well, of course: my nemesis/partner never seemed to leave me. Professor Brian Clark was a new acquaintance, alongside most of the other appointees. Within weeks of the committee beginning its business, the chairperson, a woman of extraordinary presence and clearly a considerable asset to the committee, decided that a job she had been offered to join the Irish Water Board was a chance she could not afford to miss and she jumped ship. Gordon McKerron became our new chairperson. Within the first few months, Professors Bavistock and Ball had either resigned or been fired from the committee for what I can only describe as quite extraordinary behaviour. They seemed to think that the review we were charged with carrying out was exclusively a scientific exercise and were outraged to the point of rudeness when social sciences were mentioned. After their departure and the recruiting of a female Army colonel called Fiona Walthall – apparently she held the highest rank in the army you could aspire to – we were finally all set to begin work in earnest.

With a few months to go before the deadline set by government for the final report to be presented to ministers of the sponsoring departments, we were required to declare our individual positions on radioactive waste management options. This was basically a choice between disposal and storage, the 'exotic options' such as entombment in polar ice, firing off to the sun, etc. having been rightly condemned to the realms of fantasy. Unsurprisingly, I found that I was in a minority of one in my view that storage had the edge over disposal.

As the time drew near for the report to be presented, a draft was written by three of the committee members. They wrote through the night. The rest of us had perhaps three hours to review it but there was no time to examine, to ponder, to cogitate on what the words actually meant and what we had meant by them. Professor Andy Blowers, hugely influential in the debate and the architect of the recommendation contained in the report, calling for communities to volunteer their involvement, crafted the phrases which called for a recognition that disposal was the best option, but only 'in the current state of knowledge', and, in order to increase that state of knowledge, there should be an 'intensified programme of research and development' into the uncertainties around disposal. In my innocence, I supported these recommendations and signed up to the report, making its findings unanimously supported by all committee members.

I thought that I had signed up to a series of recommendations which would be undertaken in sequence: i.e. if the research programme increased our level of knowledge to the point where we could demonstrate that disposal was safe, and if we could then find a volunteer community to accept a repository, then we should initiate a disposal programme. In fact, I had signed up to a package of recommendations which most of my co-committee members as well as government officials and ministers saw first and foremost as a 'get-out-of-jail-free' card and secondly, as actions which could be carried out in parallel. The speed with which the report's findings were accepted and then published amid suitable trumpeting was unseemly and clear evidence that we had been used as a convenient fig leaf for the government's revived nuclear power aspirations. Even before we had finalised and submitted the report, the government announced its plans for an additional 10 gigawatt of nuclear generated electrical capacity.

In September 1976, Sir Brian Flowers, Chairman of the Royal Commission on Nuclear Power, released their sixth report called 'Nuclear Power and the Environment' in which he recommended that, 'There should be no commitment to a large programme of nuclear fission power until it has been demonstrated beyond reasonable doubt that a method exists to ensure the safe containment of long-lived, highly radioactive waste for the indefinite future.' It seemed quite clear to me, that CoRWM had been convened to definitively remove that hurdle which had dogged governments for 30 years.

I wrote to the sponsors, after we were disbanded, with my views about the process which I considered to have been flawed, and the way in which the government had interpreted the recommendations and findings of the report. I also wrote to show that in my opinion, most people interviewed during the CoRWM process had opted for storage. I applied for membership of the second incarnation of CoRWM, as did Andy Blowers. Neither of us was accepted although Andy was at least given the privilege of an interview, something denied to me.

I received an email suggesting that in 2005 there should be a reunion of *Rainbow Warrior* crew and Antarctic expeditionaries in New Zealand to commemorate the 20th anniversary of the sinking of the *Warrior* and Fernando's death, and to celebrate the winning of the campaign to protect the 'sixth continent' which had been afforded the legal force of the Antarctic Treaty to ensure that no mining took place there at least until 2041, 50 years after the historical agreement which the expeditions Greenpeace undertook in the 80s were pivotal in securing. It was a trip that Gaye and I could not resist and we set about making plans to travel with the kids half way round the world to see old friends and re-acquaint ourselves with the past. Paul Brown, my old mate from the Guardian, and his wife Maureen, were also invited as 'honorary Greenpeacers' and we made plans to fly together as a group.

Before we left, Gaye made me promise to book myself in for a hip replacement operation. Over the previous two years, I had developed a pronounced limp and the last x-ray taken at the hospital showed significant and extensive deterioration of the right hip joint. I was constantly in pain and doing anything at all which involved movement was painful. I knew if I didn't have it done, I'd end up in a wheelchair, but for now, I put such thoughts behind me and planned for the trip of a lifetime for me, Gaye and the kids.

Amy must have watched *The Incredibles* cartoon film at least six times but still insisted in watching the last few minutes of it yet again as we circled Auckland, waiting for clearance to land. She wasn't that interested in the fact that 10,000 feet below was the collection of islands, beaches and building in which I had left a small part of my heart thirteen years before. I never thought I would go back to New Zealand but here I was, about to go through the immigration rigmarole again, this time – my seventh – with my young wife and two daughters in tow. I was bursting with pride and couldn't wait to see old friends, especially my 8-12 watchmate, Ken Ballard, who had stayed in New Zealand after the final trip south, married a beautiful Maori woman, Tanya, and now had a child of his own.

In the intervening years, we had lost Mike Maloche, the carefree helicopter pilot who so skillfully flew us safely back to the *Gondwana* through one of the strongest winds I had ever experienced in the Antarctic. The first night at the reunion, I sat talking and drinking with Chris Robinson, the guy who drove the inflatable in which we confronted the seamen dumping radioactive waste into our Atlantic ocean in 1978, twenty-seven years previously. Chris died of liver cancer in 2008. There, too, was Henk Haazen, our logistics co-ordinator from the 'nervous centre' on the old *Black Pig* in 1986, Susi Newborn from the very early days of Greenpeace in London, Jim Cottier, Bob Graham, Pete 'Gloomy' Bouquet and many, many more. As we approached Waiheke Island where we were to hold the gathering of veteran Greenpeacers from those distant days, I was already dreading the parting scheduled for three days hence. With these people is stored a wealth of determination, dogged resilience and purposefulness. These people built Greenpeace from nothing. They shared situations of unutterable, jaw-dropping danger which they faced with stoicism beyond their years. In those people resides quiet, mutual respect. In every eye contact an entire history of experience and memories is exchanged. Every single one of them could be entrusted with your life or the lives of your wife and children. Many is the time I've had to rely on these people and I did so with absolute certainty that they would not let me down, nor I them.

The three days we spent on Waiheke Island will stay with me forever. We spent the second day reminiscing in twos, threes or as a group as one after another we told our stories of fun, joy, heartache and fear: stories which have since been enshrined in Greenpeace legend, stories which deserve telling but which will remain the precious and largely private memories of a group of cognoscenti, the better to bind them together. Some of those stories are contained in the previous chapters, but one deserves repeating here as it is illustrative of the lengths to which we were prepared to go in order to get our message out to the world.

We had film of Greenpeace swimmers forming a human picket line in the open ocean, directly in the path of the giant whale factory ship, the *Nissin Maru*. As we left for the Antarctic that year, 1989, it was our intention to disrupt the Japanese whaling season in the Southern Ocean as much as possible and the departure of the *Nissin Maru* from Australia was too good an opportunity to miss. We sped as fast as the MV *Greenpeace* would go to an area where we could intercept her and brave crew members volunteered to form the human barrier by forming a line of swimmers in what were undoubtedly shark-infested waters. Despite their presence, which the captain of the factory ship had been made aware of, the vessel ploughed through the picket line. As you can imagine, the film was dramatic and we needed to get it back to shore quickly, but we only had a helicopter with a range insufficient to make it back to the Australian mainland.

Ken Ballard called David Iggulden, a Greenpeace supporter and back-up person who had been active in the Antarctic with Robert Swan in previous years, and who was known to us as a highly reliable and very effective logistics person. 'Iggy' hired a fixed wing aircraft which was available at Lord Howe Island and agreed a mid-air rendezvous point with Ken. The plan was to transfer the can of film from the helicopter to the fixed wing 'on the wing'. But how? At the appointed time the helicopter took off from the ship and made the rendezvous. Ken had attached a long line to a weighted bag carrying the can of film and through radio communication and visual alignment the two aircraft closed on each other, the helicopter flying at a height which allowed the weighted bag to be played out on its line. The fixed wing had to fly close to stalling speed so as not to overshoot the helicopter and the pilot somehow maintained position as the can dropped lower and lower, foot by foot, closer and closer to the open door on the side of the fixed wing aircraft. By deft manoeuvering at the crucial time, the bag was drawn close enough to the plane for Iggy to grab it. He quickly removed the can, allowing the still weighted bag to be thrown clear of the plane for Ken to retrieve carefully and slowly back into the helicopter.

The film was screened that evening on Australian TV and franchised around the world. Japan's determination to fly in the face of international outrage at their continued whaling activities was announced to the world in the most dramatic way.

After the 'memory fest' we indulged in during that day on Waiheke, we visited the olive grove which had been planted in memory of David McTaggart. Fifty people duly wound their way up the steep-sided hill to pay our respects to the old boy. On the narrow plateau at the top, a Maori group led by the local elder greeted us with a traditional hukka. It was traditional for the male elders of each 'side' to greet each other first, and only after the intimidating 'hukka' of greeting had been performed by the Maori elders. As this was being performed by Maoris in full tribal costume, contorted faces, screams and all, Emily calmly marched to the front of the group and stood watching the proceedings. She was one of the first to receive the traditional Maori greeting of nose-to-nose intimacy. After our response, delivered by our own elder, Captain Jim Cottier, we exchanged songs although our offerings were a weak rendition of a Maori song which only four of us knew followed by a gutsy rendition of the highly appropriate What shall we do with the drunken sailor?

In fact, both Emily, just ten, and Amy, then only five, went 'native' quite quickly. We didn't see Amy for hours on end and then she would appear, in strange garb – headband, poncho – in the company of other kids to announce casually that she was 'off to the beach'. What a place for kids to be brought up.

We told our tales and relived our pasts in an atmosphere of overdue and genuine bonhomie. Each telling brought memories to technicolour life and the presence of the people with whom those experiences were shared served only to focus the poignancy and sharpen the pain – so relatively recently did we do these things but so finally were they gone, so utterly were they irretrievable and so long ago did it all seem.

I craved to learn what people had done after they turned their backs on Greenpeace and how they had carved an alternative living out of the shards of a life so brutally shattered and contorted by a fledgling organisation's demands. Many have remained with Greenpeace in one capacity or another. Others left in the aftermath of the bombing when the money came flooding in from a stunned world eager to empathise with a band of environmentalists at the loss of their ship and of their friend.

The bombing was a watershed in the development of Greenpeace. Some say it facilitated the organisation's growth into a global force.

Others feel that it vulgarised and sullied an organisation once driven by its heart not its head and made it complacent and flabby. One thing is certain, however: The veterans with whom I now stood and who created a global organisation through sheer determination and cussedness have no Greenpeace pension, no compensation for the years they worked for next-to-nothing while building a colossus to hand on to those who could choose Greenpeace or an equally adequately-paid position in the commercial sector.

Once Greenpeace divested itself of its undesirable elements and could afford decent wages, it was surprising how attractive it became to people who previously had given the organisation a wide berth. These veterans had, by and large, demonstrated in a post-Greenpeace life the sort of adaptability they demonstrated while building Greenpeace and without which it could not have survived. Photographer, ship charterer, ship builder, carpenter, policy adviser, restauranteur, tour organiser – each has taken what life has dealt them and moved on, scorning the temptation to cling to and suck from the teat of an organisation which could so easily have become a security blanket, a benevolent fund, a provider, rather than an awkward, demanding tool through which to change the world at considerable personal cost.

As we left Waiheke earlier than expected due to unavoidable logistics of travel and combining family holidays with meeting up with old friends, the goodbye we received was enough to turn the stoniest of hearts into soups of nostalgia and melancholy. Fifty people lined the veranda of Henk and Bunny's house as we drove our campervan out of the valley. They hooted us a farewell fit to cause me to pull over when we were out of sight and weep like a baby. In every one of those people, I saw heaving seas, ice-scapes to make you draw a sharp breath, perilous situations and a bonhomie which all the smuggled endangered species in the world couldn't buy. I saw Greenpeace on that veranda. It exists in the hearts and minds of those people and in those we have already left behind – McTaggart, Maloche, Shaw, Robinson, Cummins, John, Johnston, Periera and others.

As we left New Zealand on the ball-breaking flights home via Hong Kong, I tried to assess what this trip had meant to me personally, to my family and in the greater scheme of things. We had used our two and a half weeks well and had managed to cram in the whole nine yards – dolphins, glow-worm caves, hot springs, geysers, Maori dances, unbelievable

478

beaches and precious time with even more precious friends. But what of the organisation which had been the catalyst to bring us all together so long ago? How is it faring?

The reunion allowed us to wallow and luxuriate in the company of old friends and in our memories of the past, but also to question what those who had followed us in Greenpeace were doing with the legacy we had left them. Some of us were not impressed with the way in which things were going and I dug out the document I had drafted years ago with McTaggart and others at David's farm in Italy which called for restraint on pay, greater focus on campaign objectives and strategy and a less hierarchical structure in the offices. Offices which were now paying their senior staff a comparable wage to commercial corporate executives. This document, in its first draft known as the 'East Grinstead Declaration' (named after the place it was first concocted), was leaked to the Observer newspaper and Geoffrey Lean wrote it up under the banner of 'Founders turn on Greenpeace incumbents' (to paraphrase) and caused a great stir, especially as McTaggart, correctly, accused me of leaking the story. While he publicly expressed disgust at the leak, privately, he expected nothing less. This is the Observer story:

Greenpeace 'fatcats' leaders condemned by founders

Greenpeace's leaders are paid too much, have lost their focus and must become more democratic, say the founders of the environmental organisation.

In a devastating report, 16 founders, led by David McTaggart, for many years Greenpeace's guiding spirit, complain about falling membership and a loss of "inspirational initiative". They express "profound concern about what seems to be happening to the Greenpeace we helped to create."

Their report was sent to the pressure group's 25th anniversary celebrations last week in Vancouver, Canada. It was written after a meeting of the 16 at Mr McTaggart's farm in Italy last month. Those present included Nick Hill, the first captain of the Rainbow Warrior, Monika Griefahn, who became environment minister of Lower Saxony, Pete Wilkinson, one of the founders of the pressure group in Britain, and John Castle, a long-time skipper of Greenpeace boats who spearheaded the action against the Brent Spar.

They write that – together with others who could not attend – they "can legitimately claim to be the founders of the organisation which is now managed by those at whom this document is directed." They add that they "have a right to insist that the organisation which broke new ground in environmental campaigning continues in that tradition, continues to be at the cutting edge of environmental reform and does not simply become part of the institutionalised political landscape of the 21st century."

They say that the amounts paid to Greenpeace's leaders are alienating its supporters. Thilo Bode, its international executive director, is paid the equivalent of pounds 68,800 a year – roughly what a City international equity trader earns. Lord (Peter) Melchett, the executive director of Greenpeace in Britain, is paid slightly over pounds 40,000.

The report calls for a "ceiling on salaries" and "a levelling out of the hierarchical structure" and adds that "the current methods of attracting new people are not necessarily going to provide the organisation with committed environmentalists."

It says: "Many supporters – whose hearts and minds were touched by Greenpeace's simple, direct and straightforward approach – are disappointed by the salary levels reported in the media and are now withdrawing their support."

The number of paying supporters worldwide has fallen from 4.8 million in 1990 to just over 3 million today. The report describes the slump in membership as "a warning sign which demands careful review" and says that membership levels provide "one of the surest ways of measuring the effectiveness of campaigns, strategies and tactics."

It says that members – who have traditionally been used mainly as a source of funds – should be enfranchised and involved more. "There is a need to encourage the internal democratisation of the organisation, leading to the development of a different culture."

Peter Melchett said last week that he "welcomed" the report, which was circulated at the Vancouver meeting. It was "very interesting and very helpful" and "would certainly be taken into account."

He added that it "did not seem to be all that unexpected, given what some of the people who have left Greenpeace are saying. We are an organisation of passionate people with passionate views."

Back home and with the CoRWM experience out of the way, I looked around for new challenges, but first I had to get my hip replaced. In February 2006 I was admitted to Ipswich hospital and underwent what the admissions person charmingly reminded us inductees was 'major surgery'. I found myself in the company of old men and women as we listened to the advice being given in the 'pre-operation' class we were all advised to attend. At 59, I was one of the youngest patients there and felt like a spring chicken compared to others, but of course, I couldn't walk like a spring chicken and the operation was an absolute necessity. Within four days I was back home, walking with sticks, but on the road to recovery although it wasn't straightforward.

The untimely announcement regarding government intentions to build a new generation of nuclear reactors came while CoRWM (www.corwm. org.uk) was still in the throes of writing its final draft report. Thus the nuclear debate had gone from assessment (of the disposal option for nuclear waste in particular) into the aspiration to implement disposal and the CoRWM draft report which indicated its majority preference for disposal was clearly instrumental in giving the government the confidence vit needed to make the announcement. My value to the process was clearly over. They now needed implementers, not facilitators. They needed pronuclear apologists rather than genuine assessors. Nuclear new build was 'back on the agenda with a vengeance' as the odious Blair put it. My work just dried up almost overnight. I made a keynote speech for the Nuclear Industry Association at which I was the only anti-nuclear voice. I made them laugh, I was controversial and I was constructive while being pointed and, of course, unflinching, in the anti-nuclear message I gave. But it didn't change anything.

I was approached by Good Morning TV after the speech and invited to be interviewed with a hint that they were looking for a 'green' anchor person. Gaye will tell anyone that cares to listen that I blew a chance to have a regular spot on TV by being dismissive, long-winded and too technical for GMTV, apparently. I also gave the keynote speech to Golder Associates about stakeholder engagement and, to my relief, and largely thanks to the efforts of a senior Golder Associates consultant, Mark Hannan, I was asked if I would accept a job with Golder. Given that I was close to broke at the time I was asked, I was very surprised to find myself replying in the negative.

'No, thanks, I won't take a job. I haven't had a job since I was in my teens and I'm not going to break that habit in my 50s.' An awkward silence followed in which I reflected on what I had just said. I quickly added, as I imagined Gaye's face looming across the dining room table, 'But I'd be happy to accept a consultancy'.

And so, between the years of 2006 and 2010, I worked, part-time, as a stakeholder consultant to Golder Associates, a company which assisted mining companies all over the world. Their nuclear activities mainly involved de-watering, site characterisation and decommissioning work, but the company never seemed to fully appreciate how valuable and pivotal stakeholder engagement can be to a business, and despite a desire to make it work, my consultancy with Golders came to an abrupt end when the Department of Health-financed project I inherited from a Golder colleague had its funding withdrawn in the aftermath of the 2008 comprehensive spending review. A £250,000 a year project was terminated at a stroke and my consultancy with Golders followed suit within a matter of weeks.

The biggest cloud on the horizon just now is the revival of the nuclear industry and the prospect of building new, larger and equally dangerous nuclear plant at ten locations across the country, one location being Sizewell, about six miles from where we live. Perhaps the looming spectre behind even that unwelcome development is that the opposition we could count on in the 80s is no longer available: to all intents and purposes, there is no co-ordinated, organised or cohesive anti-nuclear movement in the UK today.

Was it all worthless? Will Greenpeace be reduced to a historical footnote, a curio for future generations to pore over, research and wonder at as we do today with the Luddites and the Levellers? What on earth was it all about? Was it a genuine attempt at fundamental change or just a conscience-salving distraction for middle-class, guilt-ridden intellectuals? Perhaps it was both. Are they working quietly, effectively and busily behind the razzamatazz of the headlines to change political policy to put 'green' at the heart of contemporary politics? I like to think so, but the evidence is to the contrary.

Chapter 35

The green 'movement': crusaders or careerists?

In the 70s and 80s, Greenpeace was an uncomfortable alignment of North American and European hotheads and malcontents, mostly with big egos and bigger mouths. I'm no exception. What held it together was the knowledge that in the process of undertaking its campaigns and direct actions, it was talking a common language, its objectives were clearly defined. Greenpeace was achieving success, slowly at first but with a gathering momentum, and it was laying the foundations for a larger, more organised successor organisation to turn the trickle of victories into an avalanche and, ultimately, to cause a green revolution.

Greenpeace routinely made the news because their actions were ground-breaking and because they were imaginative and novel. Their photos and film were guaranteed to be dramatic and newsworthy because of the novelty of the actions they recorded. Media attention creates pressure on the industry and politicians who are then more likely to capitulate in the face of public opinion. As a tabloid journalist told me in Iceland in those early whaling campaigns, 'Greenpeace are box office.' The question today is how can the organisation maintain that box office appeal and, moreover, what tactical philosophy should it adopt in order to best translate that appeal into campaign victories?

Between 1970 and 1990, non-violent direct action (NVDA) reached its pinnacle as a means of protest. It was a golden time for exponents of this form of demonstrating dissent. NVDA was planned and designed to prevent an 'abuse' taking place – hence the inflatables in front of the harpoon-equipped whale catchers, beneath tipping platforms of waste disposal ships and the attempted blocking of the Sellafield pipeline. The symbolism of the sacrificial 'green' forming the only barrier between the environmental vandal and the vulnerable environment was powerful and potent.

It is true, however, that, in later years, we occasionally indulged in demonstrations dressed up as direct actions: the hanging of the banner across Big Ben calling for a 'Time to Stop Nuclear Weapons Testing' is a case in point. Towards the end of the 90s, Greenpeace was carrying out more 'demonstrations' than direct actions as the opportunities for, the novelty of and, more importantly, the potential penalties incurred for interfering with legitimate and legal activities threatened the financial viability of the organisation and the freedom of its personnel. As Paul Brown remarked on many occasions, 'If you're a one-man-and-a-dog operation, you have little to risk.' Bob Dylan said the same. But conversely, when you have assets, ships, offices, pensions, wealth, good incomes and job security, the thought of risking those things is far less attractive. Even in the 90s, Greenpeace was finding it more and more difficult to justify tactics which risked its assets and, moreover, these tactics were becoming stale and increasingly unattractive to the media.

In 2011, I heard that Greenpeace was about to spend £14 million on a new, purpose-built ship when, at the last count, they already had three perfectly serviceable ships at their disposal. All Greenpeace's former vessels were second-hand and were bought as cheaply as possible: the *Rainbow Warrior* was a former marine research ship and purchased for around £30,000 and the *Cedarlea* cost a mere £5,000 in the 80s. The spending of such an enormous sum as £14 million on a ship seemed to me an act of wilful extravagance. It was not only, in my opinion, a frivolous use of a huge amount of supporters' money, but it would also further discourage the loss of the ship to legal action, collision or impounding and would therefore cramp campaign styles.

I wrote to the chairman of Greenpeace International to express my views. His reply was unconvincing. It was to be a 'state of the art' vessel, I was told, an investment in the future and an example of how all ocean-going vessels should be constructed. However, I also learned that the radio room was to be reinforced, the better to withstand an invading force of police or irate whalers, allowing the environmental message to continue to be transmitted even under siege conditions, indicating that old tactics were still planned and that, presumably, Greenpeace was prepared to risk a £14 million asset in direct action.

Two issues are thrown up by the decision to purchase such a costly vessel: what should Greenpeace plan for over the next ten years in terms of campaigning tactics and how should it spend its considerable wealth to further the aims of the organisation? Investing £14 million in a ship is a clear indication that Greenpeace intends to continue its marine-based operations. The reinforcing of the radio room equally clearly shows its intentions on campaign tactics. So are we simply to expect a richer version of the of organisation to take to the seas and are these deductions correct and, if so, do they represent the most effective way forward for the world's pre-eminent environmental organisation?

Greenpeace's recent history does not give cause for confidence in its ability to manage its considerable post-*Warrior*-sinking wealth. Before that outrage, a scant eight years after we set up in the UK in 1977, we scratched around for money and the growth of the organisation was staccato, growing after an action or after sustained exposure in the media but generally increasing at a relatively slow although somewhat erratic pace. Even so, when Greenpeace International was established in 1983, the contributions made to the central body from the national offices – set at 24% of gross income in order to retain the rights to the licence allowing the national office to use the name 'Greenpeace' – still amounted to hundreds of thousands of dollars with the largest contribution being made by Greenpeace USA from money raised largely through direct mail (a method we resisted strongly in the UK until the inevitable capitulation). But with the sinking of the *Rainbow Warrior* and the death of Fernando Pereira, everything changed. The French attempt to stop Greenpeace in its tracks backfired in a spectacular manner and was the turning point in Greenpeace's growth. Far from withering on the vine, Greenpeace grew and became rich within a very short space of time.

In a Sunday Times article published on the 22nd October 1995 under the headline, 'Greenpeace's millions hidden around the world', the accusation was made that, ten years after the atrocity in Auckland, a meeting to decide how to trim $3 million from its budget and to fire 50 people, attended by one hundred Greenpeace executives in Tunisia, ran up a £150,000 bill At the time the article was published, Greenpeace's income had more than quadrupled from its 1985 income of $45 million to a peak of $179 million in 1991. The interesting thing is not that Greenpeace 'hid' its wealth in a mixture of limited companies, trusts, foundations and charities around the world – every financially astute company does that and an organisation fighting for environmental improvement is doubly entitled to ensure it keeps as much of its cash as possible – but that it paid out over $400,000 to 'executives ousted in recent power struggles'. One beneficiary was allegedly paid over $100,000 in compensation and an American fundraiser allegedly trousered $130,000 and was required to sign a confidentiality agreement.

Such liberal greasing of palms is quite breathtaking. It knocks the $15,000 that McTaggart engineered for me for 10 years service into a cocked hat. What it does, more than that, of course, is to render the decades of collective sacrifice made by a core group of people who built Greenpeace in the early days, and who were lucky to go home with £30 at the end of the week, almost irrelevant and totally unrecognised. Men and women who ate rice for weeks and little else on the *Rainbow Warrior* as they confronted the Icelandic and Spanish whaling ships, not for the cameras but to prevent the killing, have gone largely unsung and certainly uncompensated. Many of these people are now struggling to make ends meet; ignored and even unknown by the incumbents who have little, if any, apparent interest in or knowledge of Greenpeace history. The irony of it all is, of course, that in 1984, the late David McTaggart, the architect of the Greenpeace method of in-your-face, direct action and strategy-led campaigning which characterised Greenpeace in those days and a key architect of the modern green movement we know today, said to a journalist, 'We're not building an empire here. We're just having a go. We want results.'

Greenpeace appears to me to be caught on the horns of a dilemma. It seems loath to abandon the tried and tested tactics of occupying equipment used in activities to which they object. At the same time, it must appreciate that such 'occupying' has become passé and that new and innovative – perhaps even collaborative – methods of achieving their goals must be explored. Traditional tactics have become jaded and less and less attractive to the media and the public. In fact, I believe they are so dated as to be a positive encumbrance to Greenpeace's development. Its dogged adherence to direct action appears to have the effect of stifling innovation, vision or arm-chancing. It brands the organisation as a 'one trick pony'. As such, and in the absence of innovation which keeps the authorities on their toes and enhances its appeal, it has become predictable and mundane. There was probably no greater example of this than the climbing of The Shard in London by Greenpeace activists who referred to the admittedly brave climb as a 'direct action', which it was certainly not, being neither an action in the original sense of the word, nor direct, in that it purported to draw attention to the potential despoliation of the Arctic – hundreds of miles to the north – by oil drilling.

From where I sit (which admittedly gives me only a Euro-centric, not to say a Suffolk-centric view of the Greenpeace world, and I fully acknowledge that this view is likely to be biased), there has been a reluctance to address the 'peace' part of the organisation's name or to indulge in any of the political, societal and equality issues which stem from conflicts of which there are an increasing number around the world. There has been a virtual absence of alignment and co-operation between the overtly environmental organisations with those which focus on humanitarian, peace, development and aid issues: they are, after all, two sides of the same coin.

Personally I have seen no evidence of a modernising, political attitude within Greenpeace. The organisation appears to be paralysed by a paucity of ideas, by an inability to rekindle the spirit of invention and the kind of brass balls for which it was known in the 70s and 80s. In the same way it became world-renowned during that time for its uncompromising, confrontational attitude, it has to all intents and purposes failed to use that innovative spirit to explore new avenues of campaigning activities, approaches and tactics to push forward the green agenda and to ensure that it is placed where we all hoped it would be after forty years of campaigning – at the centre of political and social agendas. It no longer has the capacity to make jaws drop. Cranking the 'direct action' handle stopped returning 70s and 80s levels of publicity a long time ago. Direct action is passé.

The challenge Greenpeace faces today is to mould a multicultural, international organisation into a vibrant, essential movement which can take the prevailing climate of opinion, embrace the political and societal landscapes and turn them to its advantage through innovation, vision, imagination and boldness of action. It has to use its wealth to change the world, not throw money at capital projects which are more about image and prestige than about its core agenda. No-one should underestimate the size of that challenge but that is what the organisation was set up to do and the incumbents must accept that ships rot and depreciate while ideas germinate, grow and appreciate.

If ever Greenpeace sought an appropriate opportunity to review its strategy, consider a departure from its traditional method of operation and develop a new dynamic, surely the time is now. Millions of people consider themselves 'green', millions are sick and tired of a world in which we seem capable of sinking to unprecedented depths of depravity with consummate ease; a world in which the very life-support systems which sustain us are being ravaged and dismantled and in which, year on year, there is less peace and less green. Against that backdrop, the largest, most important organisation in the world to which people automatically turn as the natural home for the realisation of their hopes and aspirations is not only ignoring the potential for further growth and influence, but it is betraying the efforts of its founders and the hopes of a generation.

The government announcement in 2005 that it was to revive the nuclear option came as a shock after its previous backing of renewables. The prospect of returning to the anti-nuclear fray was a prospect I didn't relish: firstly, I had no organisation around me as I had when running Greenpeace; secondly, the intervening 20 years had convinced me that a fundamental change in the attitude to environmental campaigning was required. I had collaborated with government and the industry itself in that time to what I considered good effect. No, it hadn't stopped nuclear being reconsidered, but neither had all the confrontational work we did in the 80s.

In my view, my time as a collaborative green during the BNFL national nuclear dialogue years, working with the DTI, Defra and the embryonic NDA helped to broach the idea of working with the opposition to find compromises. Colleagues, however, saw things differently. I was vilified by a few former colleagues. A lawyer, Jamie Woolley, who occasionally worked on green legal issues, snubbed me routinely. Stewart Kemp who at one time ran the Nuclear Free Local Authorities group, called me 'damaged goods', despite the fact that he then went on to take a job with the pro-nuclear Cumbria County Council and has since been directly involved in the partnership seeking a nuclear dump in Cumbria. I was cast as someone who had forsaken 'true green' principles by 'dissembling'.

At a rally outside Sizewell, at which I spoke, I was called a 'collaborator'. By accepting a position on the government's Committee on Radioactive Waste Management, I was seen by some as legitimating the process which, they argued, should be subject to a universal green boycott. I joined the Sizewell site stakeholder group as a co-opted member. This was taken by a minority of erstwhile colleagues as further evidence of my traitorous nature. After joining the Nuclear Consulting Group, and having written a chapter for its manifesto on radioactive waste management, I was summarily dropped from the membership for reasons which have never been made clear to me, despite many attempts to discover what lay behind it. Others snubbed me and assumed that, since I was now talking with the nuclear industry and their cohorts, I had abandoned my principles, when in fact I was simply attempting to apply my principles in a manner which I felt had half a chance of being successful.

I was attempting to balance two concerns which are of vital importance to me: the ability to make an income to support my family and remaining true to my environmental principles. Traditionally, I had achieved this – or at least a semblance of it in terms of income – by working for Greenpeace. But Greenpeace was not offering me work. Overtures I made to them about campaign ideas, working together or consultancy work were rejected. I applied for a position in New Zealand Greenpeace – head of campaigns – and, although I was, apparently, 'hugely respected in the organisation', that respect did not stretch to offering me the position. Some of my colleagues expected me to resist consultancy work offered by the regulators or by any of the agents of the industry I had spent a lifetime fighting, as though to do so would immediately corrupt me and force me to abandon principles I had held for forty years.

I was faced with the need to demonstrate my adherence to my beliefs and principles when acting as a stakeholder while acting in an even-handed and equivocal way when earning a crust acting as a facilitator. I achieved this feat with a far greater level of tolerance and trust from the regulators – particularly the Office of Nuclear Regulation – than that of many of my NGO colleagues. I was trusted to park my sympathies far more readily by the nuclear industry when I chaired meetings than I was by my peers, one of whom even issued a Freedom of Information request to the Office of Nuclear Regulation to ascertain my day rate, so suspicious and unaccepting was he of my ability to manage a dual role to the satisfaction of my employers and the NGO I represented.

The 'green movement', as it is referred to, is not a movement at all. It is a fractured, loose association of individual groups, often just a handful of people, often with their own agendas. They frequently compete against one another for ideas, for media attention and for credit. At campaign meetings, there is a reluctance to share strategy information for fear that others may adopt it or that the opposition may get wind of it through leaky communications. Any attempt to suggest a structure, a strategy or a plan of action is generally kicked into the long grass and ultimately forgotten. Those initiatives which do survive an initial mauling are frequently strangled at birth by green zealots who sacrifice the long-term viability of a programme for the short-term satisfaction of giving the opposition a public kicking. While this is all good rough and tumble, the reality is far more worrying in that government, industry and vested interest are able to deal with a fragmented green lobby with one hand tied behind its back, safe in the knowledge that the malcontents are disorganised and can be picked off easily. Yet any suggestion for unity among greens; any initiative to develop a strategy which brings together even those communities threatened with new nuclear power stations, let alone on the bigger economic and societal issues we face today, is rarely mentioned, least of all implemented.

Alliances have their problems, as I found out to my cost many years ago, but in today's world of unremitting environmental impoverishment and societal upheaval, coupled with unprecedented green technological innovation and advance, unless the left and the greens unite and stamp some sort of authority on the political map in a concerted and coherent way which is attractive and accessible to the electorate, we will pay a price from which it will be difficult to recover.

My post-CoRWM world looked this way from my perspective and nothing much has changed in the years since we reported to government. I moved from CoRWM to Golder Associates and found that I had more and more time on my hands when that contract was terminated. From the relative comfort of regular and well-paid work, Gaye and I agreed to splash out money on extending the cottage. The work – to add a good-sized and highly utilised kitchen (Gaye's idea) as opposed to what would have been a highly under-used conservatory (my idea) – along with other modifications throughout the cottage, cost far more than we had budgeted for.

Gaye was now carving out her own career as a teacher. She took an Open University degree course and achieved a BA with honours after three years of study. She then joined local schools as a trainee teacher and qualified, in 2010, as an English teacher. Gaye worked extremely hard during this period and her determination to finish an education which was denied her in earlier years was total. She achieved all her goals and deserves every credit for the tremendous application, fortitude and diligence. As money went out of our account to pay the bills for the building work, less and less came in as my work dried up and the more we relied on Gaye's teaching to keep us afloat.

Gaye's dad, Jerry West, used to be the steel guitarist for Slim Whitman, travelling the world with him in the 60s. Until fairly recently, Jerry still gigged and is remembered in Suffolk where American Air Force bases were situated long after the war and where Jerry regularly played. Gaye's mum, Sylvia, was a sometime singer with a variety of bands Jerry played with over the years. Jerry and Sylvia are the titular heads of a very large family of Eastenders and my relationship with Gaye, my engagement and eventual marriage to her in 2000, brought me into contact with a bewildering array of relations. At the Easter family day out which only ceased to be celebrated a few years ago, there were, on one occasion, eighty people from the Jerrom stable.

My relationship with Gaye's immediate family has been strained over the years, largely due to my own curmudgeonly attitude to life and to my bouts of grumpiness. Much of my aversion to the family get-togethers stems, I'm sure, from my experiences as a child at Aunt Lil's parties where performing was mandatory and where introversion of any description was frowned upon and taken as disapproval of the jollifications, as if being anything but ecstatic about being 'with the family' was unthinkable. I find it difficult to be happy to order and this has caused problems in Gaye's family environment in which getting together happens with metronomic regularity, where 'performing' in one guise or another is encouraged and where the assumed, inherent importance of 'family' is unquestioned, regardless of the tenuous nature of the links between individuals required to 'get on' regardless of what might be their polarised political views and lack of common interests.

Of course the person who suffers most from the awkwardness this creates is Gaye herself. She has routinely been put in invidious positions due to my reluctance to attend family parties and we have arrived at an uneasy truce whereby Gaye and the children will go to the parties without me. It is to her eternal credit that she has accepted this situation and agreed to bear this burden which is at times intolerable but one which she and I recognise as the least-worst solution to an intractable problem of which I am the chief architect.

There is, therefore, good evidence to demonstrate that I have been marked out as 'awkward'. The way I look at the world and the way my background and experiences have moulded my views shape how I respond to everything with which I interact and I am told by my wife that I am probably autistic in some minor way. I see things and react to things directly and sometimes without reference to the impact my reactions might possibly have on others. This outlook naturally colours and, some would say, warps my view of the world but not, in my opinion, to the extent where my antipathy towards modernity generally and celebrity in particular becomes distorted. I believe there is every reason to rail against the excesses of today's' modern and shallow world where technological innovation runs so far ahead of our intellectual capacity to assimilate it that we are in danger of losing our human points of reference and where we celebrate and reward vacuous celebrity and mediocrity over social worth to a quite obscene degree.

What more is there to say of the greens and the environmental issues to which I have dedicated my life? 'Green' has become the mantle that anyone professing concern about climate change can adopt. 'Carbon footprint' is the phrase which even those guilty of the most heinous environmental crimes can use by way of buffing up their eco-credentials. Even governments, local authorities, nuclear power advocates, those who have prosecuted and supported wars of questionable legality, resulting in the deaths of tens of thousands, can claim to be green if they play the carbon card.

The green agenda has been hijacked by the climate issue and has rendered that agenda narrow, weak and meaningless, devoid of the breadth and depth of the original and limited in terms of its reach. Carbon has become the short-cut to eco-credibility but in the process has left environmentalism diminished and impoverished. And while climate change is indeed an important concern, and one which has to be addressed, it should not be allowed to draw a veil over the raft of issues

– habitat loss, species extinction, human conflict, resource use, pollution, energy, transport, planning, welfare, education – which drove early green pioneers. Campaigning has likewise been impoverished by our modern concerns and distractions. It is now a common experience to be urged on a daily basis to support a variety of causes through the medium of the internet. One click of the mouse can wipe away the guilt of inactivity, the nagging acceptance that something ought to be done. Click! There, it is, done. Campaigning reduced to an electronic signal travelling through the ether to register discontent, although I would not deny that it has, in particular isolated instances, produced spectacular results.

In 2005, thirty-four years after the tactic was first utilised in the Pacific, and twenty-eight years after we had used it in the North Atlantic, Greenpeace returned to Icelandic waters to put inflatables between the catcher ships and their prey. The slaughter of Harp seal pups on the Newfoundland ice-floes is back to its bloody height of 250,000 animals clubbed to death in front of their lactating mothers. Discharges from Sellafield's reprocessing plants, Thorp and B205, continue to contaminate the slow-flushing, shallow Irish Sea with millions of gallons of radioactive liquid on a daily basis. One child dies every four seconds somewhere in the world. Eighty eight million children have died between 2000 and 2009. Three billion people live on less that $10 a day. 2.6 billion people lack basic sanitation. The world is in political, economic and environmental turmoil.

There have been victories over the years, of that there is no doubt, and the international community has acted decisively on some issues such as ozone layer depletion, acid rain and lead in petrol. And Greenpeace has had its victories too, perhaps the most telling being that of McTaggart's ultimately successful fight against French atmospheric nuclear weapons testing in the Pacific. But if these victories are to be more than pyrrhic, there must be a concerted effort to change hearts as well as minds. A new and vibrant movement must emerge from the mess of this early 21st century world. I can think of no better vehicle to effect that change than Greenpeace. If our job in the 70s was to catapult environmental issues onto the agenda through confrontational actions and uncompromising campaigning, it is the job of the incumbents to take that process forward, to be as uncompromising and as cussed and determined as we were and to make peoples' jaws drop with the imaginativeness and vision of the campaigns but do it in a way which brings people together rather than divides them.

Endispiece

Auckland has been mercilessly developed since I was last there, thirteen years ago. 'Downtown' is now a humming, modern metropolis whereas once it struggled to the status of a pale imitation. Gone is the plethora of bars sporting 'leaners' as opposed to tables in which Greenpeace activists, working class 'pakehas' and Maoris hungrily swilled as much ice cold beer before the mandatory closing time of 6pm. Buildings have risen to alter the skyline out of all recognition. Perhaps most disconcertingly and certainly most poignantly, the half-submerged raft in the fishing dock which acted as a convenient drying out stopover for cormorants has been removed. Too tacky by half for modern Auckland. And the Floating Restaurant where we would wander to chat up the barmaids and quaff late night beer and whisky has tragically been towed away to an unknown fate.

It's true that thirteen years ago Auckland was garish in its own America's Cup kind of way and that even then it had pretensions of adulthood, but today's Auckland is brutal in its full coming-of-age plumage. It was into the harbour waters of this older, less brassy Auckland that, 20 years ago, French secret agents slipped and quietly placed two limpet mines on the hull of Greenpeace's flagship, the *Rainbow Warrior*, and sank her. Fernando Periera, Greenpeace's Portuguese cameraman, taking his chance to retrieve his cameras from his cabin after the first and surely (we thought) the only blast, paid the ultimate price as the second bomb ripped a six foot hole in the *Warrior's* side. France detonated her 'force de frappe' on far-off Muroroa Atoll, without the attentions of the *Rainbow Warrior* although a replacement vessel did not allow their crimes to go unreported or unopposed.

For the seven years before my last stint in Auckland, between 1985 and 1992, I lived and worked in Auckland between September and December of every year, preparing for Antarctic expeditions, five of which I led, on one of which I acted as observer and the final one on which I led the 'temporary remote Antarctic monitoring programme' (Tramp) – Greenpeace shorthand for a bunch of busybodies nosing around the giant US base at McMurdo. Our turning of the spotlight onto Antarctic environmental abuse occurred too late to stop the Americans leaving

Scott's Winterquarters Bay lifeless through heavy metal contamination and the impact of thousands of tons of 'tide cracked' junk metal and discarded vehicles which were simply left on the winter sea ice to await the summer thaw. Thankfully, all bases now more closely observe the codes of practice and most return their waste as a matter of course. So changed is the attitude to casual, routine, industrial-scale littering of the pristine global park which is Antarctica that the British Antarctic Survey perversely and in a statement full of self-denial, claims that today there is no waste problem on the continent.

They are right, of course, if you ignore the abandoned bases which are now rapidly being marketed as 'heritage' sites; if you ignore the legacy pollution problems such as Winterquarters Bay and if you focus exclusively on the recent conversion to removing waste generated by re-supply activities, and the waste remediation measures some nations have belatedly instituted. Despite these welcome advances, the imprint of man's tenure on the ice is all too evident even today. Receding, climate-changed ice sheets are revealing long-forgotten, discarded waste, the origin of which has been lost due to the absence of adequate records.

Such international media attention as we Greenpeacers were able to direct on Antarctic environmental degradation over the years between 1985 and 1991 augmented and focused an intensive campaign to save the Antarctic from minerals exploitation. This campaign was masterminded by the late David McTaggart after American Antarctic aficionado and campaigner Jim Barnes had convinced him of its worth. The congruity of the campaigns to save Antarctica and to prevent the French from remorselessly turning a Pacific atoll, thousands of miles from Paris, into a radioactive cesspit was not lost on most of us. The ship on its way to protest the nuclear testing was sunk on orders from close to the top of French administrative power. The resolve of those on board the one on its way to protest the trashing of a continent doubled.

Margaret Thatcher, in a froth of crusading anti-Soviet and anti-terrorist vitriol, still could not bring herself to utter a solitary word of sympathy for Fernando or condemnation of the French for an indefensible act of terrorism – the first ever in New Zealand. The Greenpeace Antarctic ship en route for New Zealand was diverted via Muroroa where an exhausted and emotional crew did their best to vent the anger of the world on an impervious French military. Today, Antarctica is safe from minerals exploitation at least until 2041 and the French no longer explode nuclear weapons at Muroroa.

The old Greenpeace died with the *Rainbow Warrior* sinking. Its death was certified when McTaggart died in 2001. That may not be a bad thing, the Greenpeace McTaggart nurtured and crafted was built on confrontation and controversy. Times have demonstrably changed. But has the organisation changed as well? Sadly, in my opinion, it has not. It appears to be locked in the past. In my view it has not evolved. It has not demonstrated the intellectual flexibility or adaptability needed to occupy the vast untouched hinterland of campaigning opportunities offered by a world so fundamentally altered from the days of its birth. Nor has it released its true potential, employed its wealth wisely or encouraged its vast support base to democratise environmentalism which still remains ghettoised, and the preserve of the cognoscenti. Some of its claims are flimsy and hard to justify. It has failed to set any sort of radical, collaborative, broad-based agenda in which ordinary people, communities and society at large, can engage and with which it can identify. In my opinion, Greenpeace never crossed the Rubicon of turning jaw-dropping, innovative tactics from the negative to the positive. It can, should and must change, for in Greenpeace rest the hopes and aspirations of millions. It cannot betray that trust and faith.